PRICING
MAKING PROFITABLE DECISIONS

McGraw-Hill Series in Marketing

PRICING

MAKING PROFITABLE DECISIONS

SECOND EDITION

Kent B. Monroe

Professor of Marketing
Department of Business Administration
College of Business
Virginia Polytechnic Institute and State University

McGraw-Hill, Inc.
New York St. Louis San Francisco Auckland Bogotá
Caracas Lisbon London Madrid Mexico City Milan
Montreal New Delhi San Juan Singapore
Sydney Tokyo Toronto

This book was set in Times Roman by ComCom, Inc.
The editors were Bonnie K. Binkert and Elaine Rosenberg;
the production supervisor was Richard Ausburn.
The cover was designed by Rafael Hernandez.

PRICING

Making Profitable Decisions

3 4 5 6 7 8 9 10 11 12 13 14 BKMBKM 9 9 8 7 6

ISBN 0-07-042782-8

Library of Congress Cataloging-in-Publication Data

Monroe, Kent B.
    Pricing: making profitable decisions / Kent B. Monroe.—2nd ed.
        p.   cm.—(McGraw-Hill series in marketing)
    Includes bibliographical references.
    ISBN 0-07-042782-8
    1. Pricing.   I. Title.   II. Series.
HF5416.5.M66   1990
658.8'16—dc20   90-5565

ABOUT
THE AUTHOR

KENT B. MONROE (D.B.A., Illinois) is Robert O. Goodykoontz Professor of Marketing, Virginia Polytechnic Institute and State University, Blacksburg, Virginia. He has pioneered research on the information value of price and has chapters on pricing in the text *Modern Marketing Management* (Random House, 1980), in *Marketing Handbook, Vol.2: Marketing Management* (Dow-Jones-Irwin, 1985), and in *Handbook of Modern Marketing* (McGraw-Hill, 1986). Dr. Monroe has presented papers before various national associations, The Pricing Institute, The Conference Board, and the Professional Marketing Research Society (Toronto, Canada). His research has been published in the *Journal of Marketing Research, Journal of Marketing, Journal of Consumer Research, Management Science, Journal of the Academy of Marketing Science,* and the *Journal of Business Research.* He has served as a consultant on pricing, marketing strategy, and marketing research to business firms, governments, and the United Nations. He regularly conducts executive training programs for business firms, nonprofit organizations, and universities in the United States and Canada. He served as chairman of the American Marketing Association's Development of Marketing Thought Task Force, 1984–1988, and is currently a director of the Association for Consumer Research. He is editor-elect of the *Journal of Consumer Research.*

CONTENTS

PREFACE

This book is designed to provide the reader with an integrative framework for making pricing decisions. Economic and marketing principles are synthesized with accounting and financial information to form a basis for analyzing pricing alternatives within legal, corporate, and competitive constraints.

Pricing is a multidisciplinary and multifunctional subject. From a corporate viewpoint, it is a responsibility of top management that encompasses financial, marketing, and legal considerations. However, there are conceptual and operational conflicts in theory and practice between economists, accountants, financial managers, and marketing managers. Because of these conflicts and the many disciplines involved, pricing has seldom been taught as a unique course for business students. Indeed, the author's experience with executives involved with the pricing function indicates that they are often frustrated by the lack of a good, informative source on pricing principles. Further, executives lament the fact that MBA and undergraduate business students lack training in the area of pricing.

Fortunately, during the 1980s, academics as well as managers recognized the importance of pricing. A number of business schools developed courses on pricing, either at the undergraduate or MBA level, usually in the marketing area. Businesses began to establish separate administrative functions for their pricing analysis and decision making as they accepted an active role in price setting. In 1987, the Pricing Institute was formed in New York to offer conferences and executive training courses on pricing. In fall 1989, Frost & Sullivan published the *Journal of Pricing Management* to provide business managers with an information source on pricing. Also, businesses that were deregulated during the 1980s have recognized the need to move toward a market-oriented way of setting prices and have struggled to embrace this perspective. Finally, not-for-profit organizations have discovered the strategic importance of pricing for their long-run survival.

BACKGROUND

This book represents a substantial revision of the first edition, published in 1979. As with the original edition, the material has been carefully tested in the classroom as well as in executive seminars throughout this country, Canada, and Europe. In particular, much of the new material is the direct result of executive inquiry, conversations with managers, and the experience of consultants who specialize in pricing. Every technique presented and illustrated in the book is being used by some companies in relation to their pricing function.

THE PLAN OF THIS BOOK

The objectives of this book are to systematically present the factors to be considered when setting price and to show how pricing alternatives can be developed and analyzed. As observed in Chapter 1, many contemporary pricing practices are short-run reactions to environmental pressures, and although these short-run–oriented decisions may work for some companies for a specific problem or time period, rarely are they generalizable. Thus, the thesis of this book, as outlined initially in Chapter 1, is that pricing must be long run in nature and that managers must take a proactive approach. Further, the proactive approach to pricing requires a market orientation and specifically considers how customers develop value perceptions. The proactive approach is more difficult than simply adding a profit margin to cost estimates; nevertheless, the ability to make profitable pricing decisions is substantially enhanced by taking this analytical approach.

Building on the proactive theme of the book, Section 2, carefully analyzes the price–demand relationship. The demand variable, through the way customers form value judgments, becomes an upper limit on the pricing discretion of the firm. Further, to understand how customers develop value perceptions requires an examination of how customers perceive prices, price changes, and price differences. Thus, after a review of the economic principles useful for understanding the price–demand relationship in Chapter 2, the rapidly emerging evidence from behavioral price research is presented in Chapters 3 and 4. Since the mid-1960s an impressive body of research evidence has accrued on how people perceive prices. This evidence is reviewed and translated into implications for pricing managers.

Chapter 5 continues the behavioral orientation by presenting some analytical methods for determining the relationship between customers' value perceptions and prices. These techniques are used by some of the most progressively managed companies. Chapter 6 then reviews the many research approaches available to determine how customers perceive prices and to estimate the underlying price–volume relationship in different markets. These two chapters have been developed in response to the many requests of managers for material on how to do pricing research and value analysis.

Section 3 considers another major factor for developing profitable prices: cost. Some people may feel that too much space is given to developing proper cost information, but the reality is that business firms still are cost oriented and, because of this orientation, make some fundamental pricing mistakes. The traditional approaches to developing cost information for pricing and other decisions are, for many firms, obsolete. Therefore, a careful understanding of a better approach to costing is developed in Chapters 7 and 8. The approach is extended beyond production or manufacturing to marketing and distribution in Chapter 9. Understanding marketing and distribution costs is very important not only for the manufacturing firm but for retailing and merchandising companies as well as service providers. Finally, Chapter 10 reviews the full-costing and target-return approaches to pricing with the objective of demonstrating the illogical nature of these approaches.

Whereas Sections 2 and 3 develop the analyses and techniques for considering demand and cost in pricing, Sections 4 and 5 apply this material to specific pricing decisions and price administration. Because of the intricate relationship between price and customers' value judgments, the complexity of pricing decisions is a major point of the chapters in these sections. Chapter 11 discusses the experience curve and its application to pricing. The discussion of the experience curve is placed at the beginning of the sections on decisions and administration because it provides a way of forcing managers to think in terms of the important relationship among price, volume, and costs and, therefore, profits. While some people suggest that the experience curve is not used as much as it once was, the problem is it has frequently been misused as a pricing tool, primarily because managers simply did not understand the rationale of the experience phenomenon. Chapters 12 and 13 review the complexity of pricing products and services over their life cycles and the issues of developing prices for a firm selling many products and services. Illustrations are developed in these chapters to demonstrate the practical applications of the economic, behavioral, and costing material developed in Sections 2 and 3.

Section 5 reviews the important issues of administering prices to and through the distribution channels. Primarily, it is in the administration of the pricing function where both legal and competitive constraints must be recognized. Also, administering the pricing decisions ultimately determines the relative success of the pricing strategy. Until recently, most firms paid little attention to the importance of managing the pricing function; therefore, they often unknowingly (and sometimes intentionally) violated laws concerning pricing and misinterpreted buyers' or competitors' responses to pricing decisions.

Section 6 covers additional topics on pricing that represent either specialized pricing issues such as competitive bidding or important emerging issues such as the pricing of services and pricing for international markets. Although the pricing of services and the development of prices for international markets should follow the basic analyses and considerations discussed in Chapters 2–10, there are often additional nuances that need to be recognized. The material presented in Chapter 18 describes some of these nuances and considerations. Chapter 19 presents an overview of an important area of pricing research that has been quite active during the 1980s: developing pricing decision models. Chapter 19 highlights the key points and implications of these models without detailing their mathematical sophistication.

Finally, Section 7 reviews the material presented in the previous 19 chapters and offers some prescriptions for improving the overall pricing function of the firm.

The book concludes with a comprehensive glossary of pricing terms.

ACKNOWLEDGMENTS

Over the past few years, a number of individuals have encouraged and supported the development of this book. The students at Virginia Polytechnic Institute and State University helped in many ways, particularly by serving as "test subjects" for the material. Also, the many business managers who have helped by talking with me, serving as students in executive development seminars, and asking questions have been instrumental in the gestation of this book. The reviewers of the manuscript offered positive advice, and the book reflects many of their suggestions. Amiya K. Basu, Purdue University; Albert J. Della Bitta, University of Rhode Island; David Gardner, University of Illinois; Nessim Hanna, Northern Illinois University; Meir Karlinsky, Carnegie Mellon University; Fred Kniffin, University of Connecticut; Donald Lichtenstein, University of Colorado—Boulder; James Littlefield, Virginia Tech; Tridib Mazumdar, Syracuse University; Akshay Rao, University of Minnesota; Massoud Saghafi, San Diego State University; and Joe Urbany, University of South Carolina, all read parts of the manuscript and were very helpful. Special thanks to a friend and colleague, R. Krishnan, who gave his time and friendship throughout the development of the manuscript.

I also had some very special assistants who deserve thanks. Julie Bils typed the material from the first edition onto disks and was an enormous help as we began the revising and writing of this book. Noreen McElhone provided the technical assistance as we attempted to refine the word processing to be compatible with the McGraw-Hill system. She also developed the procedures for obtaining permissions from other publishers and authors to reproduce or adapt their works. Ruh Peretta implemented the system developed by Noreen and helped me proceed through many of the administrative aspects of preparing the manuscript. Karen Ridley did last-minute library research to ensure the text is as current as possible. Special gratitude goes to Scott Monroe, who spent the summer of 1989 in library research, developing the indexes, working on the price definitions, making all noneditorial changes in the manuscript on the computer, and putting the instructor's manual on disks. I also thank all my current and former doctoral and master students who have worked with me on pricing research over the years and have been a constant source of stimulation and encouragement.

As is always the case, members of my family have been supportive and have allowed me to escape to the study to work on the book. I am grateful to my companion and wife, Norma, for her help and encouragement, and to Karen and Scott for their understanding and support.

During the time this revision was being prepared, three McGraw-Hill editors provided help and encouragement. Sam Costanzo encouraged me to start the revision and Mike Asher patiently waited for the chapters to start coming in. Bonnie Binkert, the current editor, has been a help both in getting reviews for the book and in quietly but persistently persuading me to stick to deadlines without sacrificing quality. She certainly has been an important catalyst in bringing this book to fruition.

Kent B. Monroe

PRICING
MAKING PROFITABLE DECISIONS

INTRODUCTION

The purpose of Section 1 is to introduce the topic of pricing and to develop the strategic importance of the pricing variable. Chapter 1 defines price and illustrates several ways price can be changed. After some important environmental pressures on pricing decision makers are discussed, some of the approaches that have been used to cope with these pressures are presented. Chapter 1 concludes with a brief overview of the implications of these current pricing practices.

What for what?

"Hey!"
"Hey yourself."
"You wanna buy this?"
"Let's see it."
"Can't. You might drop it."
"Me?"
"Promise?"
"Well, no . . ."
"No assurance, no bird in the hand."
"I promise."
"Ok. Here it is."
"What is it?"
"Give it back to me."
"Why? I just got it."
"You don't appreciate it."
"I don't even know what it is."
"I can't tell you."
"I don't want it."
"I'll give you a hint."
"OK."
"It's late."
"Late? For what? Dinner?"
"Late. Old. Don'cha get it?"
"You mean late 18th or 19th Century?"
"Slow but right."
"Hmmmmm. It's heavy."
"Right again."
"And expensive?"
"Depending . . ."
"On what?"
"The value of it."
"To me?"
"To you."
"$2.98."
"Bandit. Give it back."
"Relax, I like it."
"So do I. $10 or nothing."
"Give me another hint."
"Geology."
"Geology? It's a disguised rock."
"You have no shame."
"But I have questions."

"It has value."
"$3.98."
"Out of the question!"
"I give up. What is it?"
"It's a . . . no, I can't."
"You really don't know."
"Does a lawyer know law?"
"*You* have no shame."
"But I have answers."
"Answer then."
"Ok. It's a rare Odonsplit."
"What's an Odonsplit?"
"That's it. In your hand."
"What's it for?"
"That's the wrong question."
"That's the only question."
"I have a suggestion."
"What?"
"Take it home and try it."
"Try it? How? What? Where?"
"That's up to you."
"I don't want it."
"Why not?"
"It's a mystery."
"Then it has value."
"Well, yes, but . . ."
"$8.98?"
"$4.98."
"$8.75?"
"$5.25."
"Forget it. I'll keep it."
"I can't forget it now."
"Then you'll take it?"
"On two conditions."
"Speak."
"If I can't use it, I return it."
"Agreed. The other?"
"If I like it, we trade."
"What for what?"
"This."
"What is it?"
"It's a very rare Tickfaw."

David Holmstrom

CHAPTER 1

EFFECTIVE
CONTEMPORARY PRICING
PRACTICES

Consider a potential car buyer from Chicago. His first choice, an Oldsmobile Cutlass Supreme, was just what he wanted—but its price, $14,100, was simply too high. He was about to settle for a smaller $12,000 Pontiac Grand Am when he noticed the prices of some used cars, like the $11,500 one-year-old Pontiac Grand Prix with only 5,000 miles on it and almost a full warranty. He could not overlook the nearly $3,000 difference between his first choice and the Grand Prix, which he purchased.[1] This example illustrates a theme that is repeated throughout this book: it is relative prices that are important to buyer choice.

Now consider the problem of the automobile maker. As price differences between new and used cars widened, used cars became more attractive to buyers. The typical response of the automobile firms was to increase the prices of their new models to improve the profit margin per car sold, leading to a wider price gap between used and new cars and making it more difficult to sell new cars. One reason why used car prices were not increasing as demand for new cars decreased is the increase in rental fleet sales, leading to an increase in one-year-old used cars for sale. Rental fleet sales plus leases accounted for 36 percent of new car sales in 1988, up from 25 percent in 1975. Selling new cars to rental companies at per unit reduced prices had led to an increase in competition from used car sales at the consumer level.

As this example illustrates, the pricing decisions for a modern organization are complex and important. Traditionally, these decisions have been made by following

---

[1]See "With Deals This Good, Why Settle for New?" *Business Week,* July 3, 1989, p. 81.

the pricing practices of another organization or by following pricing practices established in the past. In recent years, North American business firms have encountered foreign competitors who often set lower prices for comparable products or for better quality products. Firms have also been faced with uncertain economic conditions, raw material shortages, decreasing liquidity, increasing production costs, changing interest rates, uncertain monetary exchange rates, and inadequate cash reserves for replacing plant and equipment.

The economic and competitive pressures mentioned have led to new marketing approaches and strategies, particularly in the area of pricing. However, careful analysis and research for pricing decisions have not been the traditional policy of American businesses. Hence, many firms have not been prepared to change pricing strategies. Moreover, many of the popular pricing strategies discussed in contemporary general business periodicals are often simplistic reactions to complex forces and may produce unanticipated consequences. Indeed, as will be demonstrated in this book, many of these practices have led to serious pricing errors.

Pricing practice remains largely intuitive and routine, and the pricing literature has not produced sufficient new insights or approaches to stimulate most business people to change their methods of setting prices.[2] Of many reasons for this lack of creative development of new approaches to solving pricing problems, two are illustrative: (1) for a lengthy period of time the economists' traditional theory of price dominated despite the obvious lack of realism in the theoretical structure; and (2) until recent environmental changes in the markets for goods and services, the seller's problem was not price but rather demand stimulation using promotional activities. Thus, there was little "payoff" in studying how buyers respond to prices, price changes, and price differences, or how to determine a set of prices that would lead to an optimal position for the firm.

In recent years, a new attitute toward pricing has begun to emerge. In 1987, the Pricing Institute was founded to provide a mechanism for encouraging new thinking about pricing and for disseminating new ideas about pricing issues. The Institute offers training programs in pricing and sponsors annual pricing conferences in various cities in the United States and Canada. In 1989, an international company based in New York announced the establishment of a *Journal of Pricing Management,* to begin publication in the fall of 1989. Also, many marketing departments in universities have established courses focusing on pricing. Further, with deregulation and the enactment of free trade regulations between more countries, the importance of pricing has been widely recognized.

The purpose of this chapter is to define price and illustrate the complexities of pricing decisions. To amplify the importance of these decisions, some environmental pressures influencing management and pricing will be discussed. Then the chapter will review how businesses have attempted to cope with these environmental pressures, the implications of these current pricing strategies, and some major pricing errors that have resulted from these attempts.

[2]Thomas Nagle, "Pricing as Creative Marketing," *Business Horizons,* 26 (July–August 1983), 14–19.

ROLE OF PRICE

The basic purpose of an economic society is to allocate resources among the members of the society to maximize the welfare of the society as a whole. To achieve this welfare objective each resource should be used to perform the function that effects its most efficient contribution to society. But what is the mechanism that seeks to achieve this objective? In a planned economy, e.g., the Soviet Union or East Germany, the central planning agency develops plans for allocating resources. In a market economy, the price system allocates resources. That is, prices furnish the guideposts that indicate how resources should be used. Prices determine *what* products and services should be produced and in what amounts. Prices determine *how* these products and services should be produced. And prices determine *for whom* the products and services should be produced.

Thus, prices affect incomes *and* spending behavior. For the consumer with a given income level, prices influence what to buy and how much of each product to buy. For business firms, profits are determined by the difference between their revenues and their costs; their revenues are determined by multiplying price per unit sold by the number of units sold.

Price changes also play a major role in a market economy. When the quantity demanded for a product or service is greater than the supply available, buyers bid the price up, as has happened in the market for housing in many cities. If costs remain the same per unit sold, the higher price leads to greater profits and an incentive to invest in resources to produce even greater quantities of the product. Thus, the producers are able to bid more for raw material resources, thereby directing these resources into that industry. In addition, higher prices may stimulate a greater rate of innovation and the development of new technology. On the other hand, if available supply is greater than demand, there are pressures to decrease prices and reduce output. These pressures lead producers to convert their resources to alternative uses. Thus, rising prices direct resources to the bidder of greatest desire (stimulating supply), and rising prices curtail demands of the least urgent bidders (rationing supply). Declining prices have the opposite effects.

DEFINITION OF PRICE

Within this economic context, it is usual to think of price as the amount of money we must sacrifice to acquire something we desire. That is, we consider price as a formal ratio indicating the quantities of money (or goods and services) needed to acquire a given quantity of goods or services. Or

$$\text{Price} = \frac{\text{quantity of money or goods and services received by the seller}}{\text{quantity of goods and services received by the buyer}}$$

Thus, when the price of a box of cereal is quoted as \$2.89, the interpretation is the seller receives \$2.89 from the buyer and the buyer receives one box of cereal.

Similarly, the quotation of two shirts for $35 indicates the seller receives $35 and the buyer receives two shirts.

Now, suppose the seller wishes to change the price quotation. To illustrate the complexity of pricing, there are several ways to change the preceding ratio. Moreover, the following discussion illustrates a major error made by many organizations. That is, many organizations pay attention only to the numerator of the ratio (the amount of money to be received) and ignore the denominator. Also, by focusing their attention on the numerator, they encourage their customers to think of price only in monetary terms. However, firms that take a value orientation to pricing consider both sides of the ratio. For example, even though the 1986 average price for a certain grade of copper traded on the New York Commodity Exchange (COMEX) was less than 62 cents per pound, a large producer sold it for an average price more than 20 percent over the COMEX price. Similarly, the price of a first-class hotel room in a major southeastern city varied between $32 and $178 for one night, single occupancy. The airlines sell the same commodity, a coach seat between two cities on the same flight, at different prices. The different dollar prices reflect the differences in the value of the product or service as perceived by the buyer (the denominator in the ratio).[3]

Some time ago a shortage of cocoa beans resulted in a shortage of chocolate for candy manufacturers. This shortage of chocolate resulted in an increase in the price of chocolate. Prior to this shortage, a multipack of six candy bars was priced at 89 cents. One candy company changed price by increasing the quantity of money to be given up by the buyer and quoted its candy at $1.19 for six candy bars. Thus, one way to change price is to *change the quantity of money or goods and services to be paid by the buyer.*

However, another candy company changed the price of their multipack by decreasing the number of candy bars in a multipack to five and quoted their candy at 89 cents for five bars. Therefore, a second way to change price is to *change the quantity of goods and services provided by the seller.* A seller may change the quantity of goods and services by changing the number of items, or the quantity of goods and services may be changed by changing the weight (contents). For example, a box of cereal may be reduced from 16 to 14 ounces and sold for the same amount of money.

A third way a seller can change price is by *changing the quality of goods and services provided.* If the quantity ratio remains unchanged but the quality has been decreased, then the price has actually increased because the buyer receives less. If quality is raised without changing the quantity ratio, then the price has decreased. (In Chap. 4 it will be demonstrated that this particular method also changes the value of the exchange.)

Price can be changed by *changing the premiums or discounts to be applied for quantity variations.* Suppose a seller quotes a 5 percent discount for all quantity

---

[3]George F. Leaming, "Should You Price Your Unique Product or Service Like a Commodity? Or Your Commodity Like a Unique Product or Service?" Presented at the First Annual Pricing Conference, The Pricing Institute, New York, December 3–4, 1987.

purchases of 100 units or more. If each unit sells for $4.00, then anyone who purchases 1 to 99 units pays $4.00 per unit. However, if a customer buys 150 units, then the price is actually $3.80 per unit. Price can also be changed by offering premiums with purchases, such as trading stamps, toys, glasses, or frequent-purchase rewards. In each case, if the quantity ratio remains constant, a premium serves to reduce the actual price paid, because the buyer receives additional goods or services.

Changing the time and place of transfer of ownership is a fifth way to change price. A concept in the retailing of furniture provides for a complete inventory to be stored at the retail store, thereby allowing the buyer to take immediate possession instead of waiting several months for delivery. These furniture stores generally have three different price tags on the furniture. If the buyer wishes to pay cash and take the item home, he or she pays a lower price than the buyer who pays cash and has the store deliver the item. The buyer who prefers an installment purchase and delivery pays the highest price. These different price tags explicitly recognize the differences in selling costs and services, and the furniture store, in effect, transfers the delivery costs to the buyer. However, if a buyer can find a similar product at another store with the same lowest price tag and free delivery, then the actual price he or she pays would be even lower.

Often the actual price is changed if the *place and time of payment are changed.* Being able to purchase a product and having 90 days to pay without interest is an actual reduction in price over paying at the time of purchase. Many retail revolving charge accounts provide for no interest charges if the balance is paid within 30 days. Since money has a time value, permitting customers to have the merchandise for a time without paying for it is a reduction in price. In addition, many business firms give discounts for cash payments made at the time of purchase or within a short period of time after purchase. For example, if payment is received by the tenth of the month, a 2 percent discount may be allowed.

Changing the acceptable form of payment is a seventh way of changing price. Some stores do not accept checks, other stores operate on a cash-only basis, and other stores accept credit charges for regular customers. As indicated, being able to buy on credit without interest being charged can be a price reduction if the additional service does not increase the formal ratio.

Thus, *price is the amount of money and services (or goods) the buyer exchanges for an assortment of products and services provided by the seller.* The variety of ways to change price makes pricing a very important marketing decision. As mentioned previously, paying attention to both the numerator and denominator provides opportunities to make the offer more unusual, even if the product otherwise is considered to be a commodity. Further, as we will develop in Chaps. 3–5, changing the nature of the product or service that is provided, who pays for transporting the goods, or terms of transaction affect not only the apparent price but also the value of the transaction to the buyer and seller. The important point to understand now is that there is more to the determination of price than simply establishing the monetary amount to be exchanged for goods and services.

IMPORTANCE OF PRICE DECISIONS

Pricing a product or service is one of the most vital decisions made by management. Price is the only marketing strategy variable that directly generates income. All the other variables in the marketing mix generate costs: advertising, product development, sales promotion, distribution, packaging—all involve expenditures. Often firms determine prices by marking up cost figures supplied by the financial division and therefore are left with only their promotion and distribution decisions. But the pressures of adapting to today's economic environment are placing additional burdens on the profits of a firm.

Recently, three surveys were conducted (1982, 1984, 1986) to determine relative changes in pricing strategies.[4] The 1986 survey indicated that the number one objective of pricing was profits, as opposed to market share and growth. This emphasis on profits seemed to stem from increased threats to long-term survival due to pressures from competition, changes in buyers' buying power, and other environmental problems. Overall, pricing was viewed as a major pressure point for managerial decision making. Several of these environmental pressures are discussed next.

Faster Technological Progress

The revolution in industrial science has had several important impacts on pricing. First, accelerating technological progress has reduced the gap between invention and innovation, i.e., the time lag between invention and commercialization. Today, it is only a matter of a very few years before a new idea is translated into a commercial product. In fact, many of the inventions for space exploration have already been adapted for industrial and consumer use. Technological progress also has reduced the average life of products. Thus, a new product does not have much time to become profitable, and any pricing mistakes made during introduction will diminish potential profitability. Finally, in our affluent and technologically advanced society, people have been freed from many of the mundane activities associated with their basic needs. As a consequence, they are spending more time and money on skiing, weekend trips to resorts, travel, and other forms of recreation. One result of this intensified competition for the consumer's income is that demand for many goods and services is increasingly sensitive to relative prices and shifts in prices, as indicated in the automobile example at the beginning of this chapter.

Proliferation of New Products

Product innovation has also resulted in a "population explosion" of new products. One clear result is that product lines have been widened, and often the distinctiveness

---

[4]Barbara Coe, "Perceptions of the Role of Pricing in the 1980's Among Industrial Marketers," *Proceedings of the Summer Educators' Conference* (Chicago: American Marketing Association, 1983), pp. 235–240; Barbara Coe, "Shifts in Industrial Pricing Objectives," *Proceedings of the Summer Educators' Conference* (Chicago: American Marketing Association, 1988), pp. 9–14.

of products has been decreased. The widening of the range of choice has blurred market segments and made it possible for small price differentials to produce large shifts in demand. Thus, the process of determining prices for an entire product line has become more delicate, more complex, and more important.

Increased Demand for Services

During the 1960s the United States became a service-oriented economy, and the demand for services is still increasing. In virtually all instances this rapid increase in demand has led to rapid increases in prices, because pure services consist mainly of labor, and productivity gains have been low. Such price increases for services (many of which are now regarded as necessities) have led to public concern and to increased governmental activity (e.g., in health care). Many of these price increases have resulted from a naive approach to pricing without regard to underlying shifts in demand, the rate that supply can be expanded, prices of available substitutes, consideration of the price–volume relationship, or the availability of potential substitutes.

We have also witnessed an increase in demand for services built into products. These "product-attached" services basically provide additional conveniences for the user and reduce the effort and time needed to use the products. For example, new fabrics, self-cleaning ovens, and computer-assisted appliances all are designed to be easier to use than earlier products.

These product-attached services can help protect the product from competition by offering perceived value or benefits commensurate with the monetary price. Basically, these services must provide perceived economic advantage to the buyer as well as providing a source of income to the seller. And where there are varying sensitivities of demand for these attached services, there are the possibilities of differential prices for different market segments.

Increased Foreign Competition

During the 1980s we witnessed a substantial increase in the flow of foreign-made products into the United States and Canada, due to the liberalization of foreign trade and the reduction of trade barriers, the narrowing of superiority in productivity, and the emergence of new industrialized nations. However, in addition to these factors, the increase in foreign competition is due to some incorrect pricing policies and attitudes of American business.[5] For example, competition from firms in Europe and Asia has increased, usually—at least initially—with lower priced, high-quality goods. In fact, today all VCRs sold in the United States are produced in a foreign country. In the past, we believed that with our superior technology and product quality we had a shelter from foreign competition and therefore additional pricing

---

[5]See "It's Time for America to Wake Up," *Business Week,* November 16, 1987, pp. 158–177.

discretion. The proliferation of foreign-made products for sale in the United States has increased the amount of price competition faced by domestic producers. Today, it is clear that there are no shelters from foreign competition.

The Changing Legal Environment

Initially, many of the preceding environmental changes caused substantial amounts of public concern, resulting in legislation and new forms of regulation. Concern with the increased cost of medical services, automobile insurance, legal services, repair services, education, and foreign competition led to new and proposed legislation at the federal, state, and local levels. But, beginning in the late 1970s and continuing into the 1980s, many previously regulated industries were deregulated. Truck, plane, and bus transportation companies suddenly were making pricing decisions previously made by regulators, and new companies were entering the transportation field. Smaller companies removed the shackles of regulation and entered new markets, sometimes with lower prices and sometimes with differential services. Similarly, the financial services industry faced new competition from previously nonfinancial service companies such as Sears, and there was a surge in new types of financial products and services. These changes in the legal environment resulted in a turbulence never before experienced by these deregulated industries. As a result, pricing decisions have become more complex and more difficult, but they are increasingly more important than ever before.

Economic Uncertainty

During the mid-1970s our economy was beset with recurring and persistent inflation, coupled with periodic shortages of basic materials such as petroleum and paper. Both of these economic factors placed additional pressures on the costs of producing goods and services. In addition, material shortages often forced firms to reduce their product lines and to reevaluate their efforts to develop new products. Firms found that across-the-board price increases led to customer resistance and often exacerbated a tenuous demand relationship. As a result, many firms rediscovered the need for new approaches to developing pricing strategies.

Summary

The need for correct pricing decisions has become even more important as competition has become more intense.[6] Due to the increasing rate of technological progress, the time lag between invention and commercial innovation has shortened the average life of new products and has encouraged quicker competitive imitative responses. Technological progress has widened the alternative uses of buyers' money and time and has led to a greater density of substitute products and services. The demand for

---

[6]See "Can America Compete?" *Business Week,* April 20, 1987, pp. 45–69.

pure and product-attached services remains strong, resulting in increased pressure on pricing decisions. A major impact of these environmental pressures has been to make product and service pricing more delicate, more complex, more important. The following two quotes are as accurate now as they were originally, and perhaps they will be even more accurate in the future:

> More and more, today's pricing environment demands better, faster, and more frequent pricing decisions than ever before. It is also forcing companies to take a new look at pricing and its role in an increasingly complex marketing climate.[7]

> Above all, . . . an ability to adapt to the new pricing environment will characterize those companies that succeed in competing over the next decade.[8]

To cope with all these environmental changes and pressures, firms have tried to reduce their product lines, become more aware of the costs associated with producing their products, pressured government for laws to protect them from foreign competition, and generally attempted to follow traditional approaches to pricing. "Current Pricing Strategies," the next section, briefly reviews how some firms have attempted to cope with this new pricing environment. Implications of these pricing strategies will also be discussed.

CURRENT PRICING STRATEGIES

To cope with new environmental pressures, many sellers have placed relatively greater emphasis on costs and profits and less emphasis on building sales and satisfying customers. Essentially, the decision objectives seem to have been (1) to reduce the risk of low-margin products, (2) to avoid bottlenecks (i.e., capacity limits to production), and (3) to improve cash flows. The strategies evolving from these objectives can be categorized as either cost-based strategies or selling strategies. As will be seen, these strategies are primarily reactive to environmental pressures and do not reflect what will be described shortly as a proactive approach to pricing. A proactive pricing strategy is based on considering the effect of price on demand and on how customers form perceptions of value. On the other hand, a reactive strategy focuses primarily on the firm's internal costs, usual methods of selling, or following a competitor's pricing decision.

Cost-Based Strategies

Many of the current pricing strategies and the related product decisions have their origins in cost considerations and, in general, ignore demand factors. Among these strategies are

1 Dropping high-volume, low-margin products
2 Increasing the emphasis on cost-plus pricing

---

[7]"Pricing Strategy in an Inflation Economy," *Business Week,* April 6, 1974, p. 43.
[8]"Flexible Pricing, Industry's New Strategy to Hold Market Share Changes the Rules for Economic Decision-Making," *Business Week,* December 12, 1977, p. 78.

3 Delaying price quotations until after the order is completed

4 Increasing prices across the board on an average increase in costs throughout the firm

5 Minimizing new product additions and adopting skimming or high-price policies for new products

These strategies assume that buyers must buy the product or service from the seller; they fail to use the marketing concept. However, as has been illustrated, buyers do have many alternative uses of their income and alternative sellers to buy from.

Selling Strategies

Other strategy changes affect the role of price in selling activities. Among the changes are

1 Dropping marginal customers or sending them to distributors

2 Assigning more accounts to fewer salespeople and assigning salespeople to larger geographical territories

3 Pricing attendant services separately from the major product or pricing related products separately

4 Reducing or eliminating cash and quantity discounts

5 Denying salespeople the opportunity of quoting prices different from the price list, except by prior approval from a price administrator

6 Placing more emphasis on long-term contracts to reduce selling, production scheduling, and inventory costs

To understand the possible implications of these pricing decisions, both positive and negative, we will first consider a conceptual orientation to the setting of prices. Then we will be in a position to criticize these cost-based and selling-based reactive strategies.

CONCEPTUAL ORIENTATION TO PRICING

Five essential factors should be weighed when setting prices. As seen in Fig. 1-1, *demand* considerations establish a ceiling, or maximum price, that can be charged. The determination of this maximum price depends on the customers' perceptions of value in the seller's product or service offering. On the other hand, *costs* set a floor, or minimum possible price. For existing products, the relevant costs are the *direct costs* associated with the production, marketing, and distribution of these products. For a new product, the relevant costs are the *future direct costs* over that product's life cycle. The difference between what buyers are willing to pay (perceived value) and the minimum cost-based price represents an initial pricing discretion. However, this range of pricing discretion is narrowed by *competitive factors, corporate profit and market objectives,* and *regulatory constraints.*

Primarily, competitive factors act to reduce the price ceiling, whereas corporate objectives and regulation act to raise the minimum possible price. Principally, corpo-

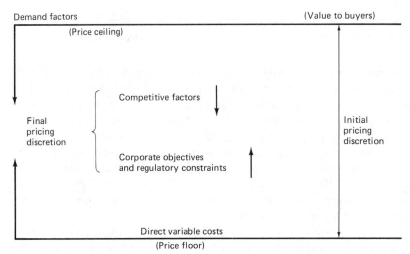

FIGURE 1-1
Conceptual orientation to pricing.

rate objectives translate into financial requirements that necessitate higher prices in order to cover fixed costs and overhead and meet profit goals. Therefore, simply covering direct variable costs normally results in an insufficient price level. Government regulations (e.g., pollution controls and safety standards) often force the costs of production up. Regulation of certain marketing practices (e.g., safe packaging) and legal regulation against predatory pricing as well as the need to protect a product from potential liability suits all have an upward effect on the pricing floor.

Normally, after considering all of these factors, there will be a much narrower range of pricing discretion. Depending on the type of product and characteristics of demand and competition, this pricing discretion could still be relatively large or it could be nonexistent. Regardless, as the conceptual figure shows, there are several very important factors to consider when setting prices. To focus only on costs obviously ignores many other important factors.

IMPLICATIONS OF CURRENT PRICING DECISIONS

As indicated in Fig. 1-1, before a new price policy or strategy is determined, a number of factors should receive careful thought. Management should analyze the effect of proposed prices on demand, costs, competition, and other elements of the marketing and distribution strategy.

Demand Implications

How the firm's customers respond to a change in price is a fundamental consideration, for the eventual effect on sales volume and revenue is determined by the degree to which buyers' demands are sensitive to price. However, price setters often misunderstand or overlook some basic factors. Four such factors are discussed next.

Market Versus Product Elasticity   Price elasticity of demand is a measure of the degree to which buyers are sensitive to price changes. In any market characterized by several functionally substitutable products there are actually two demand schedules: (1) demand for the general product *(primary demand)* and (2) demand for the firm's specific offering *(secondary demand)*. Generally, it would be expected that secondary demand would be more responsive to price changes, i.e., would be more price elastic. However, as developed in Chap. 2, price elasticity varies by brand, stage of the product's life cycle, and whether the price is increased or decreased. Hence, there is the danger that a seller may make an incorrect assumption about the price elasticity of a particular product.

The problems encountered by a Texas manufacturer of metal home improvement products illustrate this danger. Usually when new home construction is slow, the demand for home improvement products is high, and demand is relatively price inelastic. However, because of increased prices for steel and aluminum, this manufacturer raised prices of the home improvement products. Despite the fact that new housing starts remained low, the firm's sales fell quickly when prices were increased.[9] The difficulty was that there are other sellers of home improvement products, e.g., wood-based products, and when they did not raise their prices as did the manufacturer of metal home improvement products, the price elasticity was actually elastic. (In Chap. 2 we will make a distinction between "own-price elasticity" and "cross-price elasticity" and demonstrate how each of these indicators of sensitivity to price changes affects the product's price elasticity.)

Derived Demand for Buyers' Output   Many businesses sell their products and services to other businesses which perform additional value-added processing before selling their output to the final users. Thus, sellers involved in business marketing need to know the degree to which the market for their customers' products actually is price elastic. If price is elastic, a reduction in price in the customers' market would increase demand for the initial seller. Hence, manufacturers selling to such buyers— if their product represents a significant portion of these buyers' product costs—may curtail sales opportunities by eliminating discounts or low-margin products.

Likelihood of Competitive Entry   An emphasis on high-price strategies may encourage the entry of competitors when entry barriers are low and when demand is actually price elastic. Thus, buyers may quickly accept a new competitor's product because of the high prices. Moreover, continued high prices or rapidly increasing prices may force buyers to reconsider their needs and perhaps actively seek out competitive substitutes.

---

[9]Joseph P. Guiltinan, "Risk-Aversive Pricing Policies: Problems and Alternatives," *Journal of Marketing,* 40 (January 1976), 12.

Demand Consequences of a Product Line   Most firms sell a wide range of products requiring a variety of marketing strategies. Generally, the firm has several product lines, i.e., groups of products that are related because they are used or marketed together. Within a product line there are usually some products that are functional substitutes for one another and some products that are functionally complementary. For example, a photographic product line would include cameras, film, flashbulbs, projectors, screens, and other accessories. Because of the demand interrelationships and because there are usually several market targets, the product-line pricing problem is one of the major challenges facing a marketing executive.

To compound the pricing problem, complementarity may exist even if the products are functionally substitutable. For example, one researcher discovered that a substitute relation existed for the product-line brand versus competitors' brands but that a complementarity relationship existed between brands within the product line.[10] Thus, continuing with the camera line example, several models of cameras, although competing for a buyer's choice, may enhance overall demand for the camera line because of the brand name, the perception of a "full line," or a positive association from one model to another. Moreover, by adding new items or reducing certain prices, a firm may increase demand for already existing products.

Emphasis on weeding out low-volume and/or low-margin products may have unanticipated consequences, depending on the effect a full line has on demand. Even though a particular product's direct profit contribution is small, it may actually "build traffic" for higher margin products. As indicated earlier, there is evidence that functionally substitutable products within a product line actually complement each others' sales. Furthermore, prices at the low-price end (and often the lowest margin product) may positively affect buyers' perceptions of the entire product line. Thus, product-line decisions based only on cost considerations may result in a weakening of demand for the seller's product line. These issues are explored in greater detail in Chap. 13.

Cost Implications

It is important for the firm to be aware of the composition and behavior of product costs in order to know when to accelerate cost recovery, how to evaluate a change in selling price, how to profitably segment a market, when to add or delete products from the product line. Even so, as developed in Chaps. 7–10, *cost should play a limited part in pricing.* Costs indicate whether the product can be made and sold profitably at any price but not the amount of markup or markdown on cost buyers will accept. Accurate cost information guides management in selecting a profitable product mix and in determining how much expense can be incurred without sacrificing profit.

Many current pricing decisions are cost-oriented and simplistic, and they elevate

[10]Glen Urban, "A Mathematical Modeling Approach to Product Line Decisions," *Journal of Marketing Research,* 6 (February 1969), 40–47.

the role of costs in pricing decisions while diminishing the role of demand. This emphasis on costs and profit margin may lead to additional problems.

Cost-Plus Pricing   Adopting cost-plus pricing methods ignores the consideration of price–volume–cost relationships. The experience curve indicates that as cumulative production volume doubles, costs decline by a constant, predictable percentage. One way to build volume is to reduce price and place managerial pressure on forcing costs down. Thus, volume-oriented pricing may lead to additional reductions in cost and the maintenance or actual increase in profit margins. However, many firms incorrectly use a volume-oriented pricing strategy because they incorrectly assume the benefits of the experience curve without understanding the very specific conditions under which a volume-oriented strategy can be profitable. Chapters 8 and 11 will explore these issues in detail.

To illustrate the error of assuming the benefits of the experience curve, consider a large manufacturer of small electric motors who decided to reduce prices by a substantial amount. It was expected that volume would increase by a greater amount, and that this increase in volume would reduce unit production costs by an amount greater than the price reduction. Thus, the manufacturer expected to sell more units at a larger contribution margin than previously. Additional sales volume did result; however, unit costs did not decline and the firm actually lost money because of the decision. What management had not realized was that the experience curve effect, if it does occur, will occur early in the product's life cycle. The small electric motors were a 20-year-old product line!

Maximizing Margins   Elimination of low-margin products should be considered in terms of its incremental effect on costs. Many of the costs associated with a product or service are joint or common costs, which will persist when the product or service is deleted. Hence, the only costs relevant for the deletion decision are those costs that are directly traceable to the product or service that may be deleted. Unless the deletion decision permits increased production of other products, the net change in profit contribution may be negative.

Pricing with Scarce Resources   When a critical production resource is in short supply, the firm must allocate the resource across its various products. Paying strict attention to profit margins may lead to a less profitable position, because high-margin items may require disproportionate amounts of the critical resource, and production capacity will be underutilized. In such circumstances, pricing should encourage sales of those products that *maximize the contribution per resource unit* used. Often, low-margin products can achieve this objective better than high-margin products. This point will be developed in greater detail in Chap. 8.

One multiple-product company decided to push sales of a new product that was expected to be the strength of the firm in the future. The sales force successfully responded by doubling the new product's sales in the next year. However, the firm could not meet the production requirements of this increase in sales and maintain production on its other products. Consequently, orders for some of the older products could not be accepted, with the net result that the firm incurred a net operating loss for the year. The problem was that the older products actually took less production time (scarce resource) and therefore contributed more dollars per hour of production than the new product. By refusing orders on these older products to favor the new product, the firm actually was accepting less contribution to profit per production hour than before the decision was made to emphasize the new product. Further, despite producing at full capacity and turning orders away, the managers believed that they could not raise the price on any products.

Marketing and Distribution Strategy Implications

Rarely does the pricing decision occur in isolation. Generally, price interacts with other elements of the marketing strategy, and therefore several additional implications are important.

The Product Life Cycle   As products go through the product life cycle—introduction, growth, maturity, and decline—the role of price and promotion varies to meet buyer, competitive, and technological changes. As the product enters the maturity stage, and competitive price differences become more important to buyers, a seller's discount and service policies become important marketing strategies. Routine elimination or cutting back of discounts or services without regard to the product's life-cycle stage could be detrimental to the seller. Further, eliminating discounts could produce negative distributor reactions and cost the manufacturer a portion of the reseller's support. Issues of pricing over the product life cycle are covered in Chap. 12, and pricing issues relative to distribution are discussed in Chaps. 14 and 15.

Sales Force Management   Centralizing pricing authority and eliminating a salesperson's ability to quote prices consistent with local competition reduces the flexibility of the sales force. Further, as prices are increased and discounts and services curtailed, the salesperson must smooth over adverse reactions while explaining product shortages and order backlogs. In effect, the sales job is significantly altered, which can lead to increased sales force dissatisfaction and personnel turnover.

PROACTIVE PRICING

Pricing is one of the most important marketing decision variables. It is also a very complex and difficult decision. Traditionally, business firms and educators have paid relatively little attention to developing new approaches to making price decisions. Although many of the environmental pressures noted in this chapter have been discussed for several decades, few people have paid much attention to the issues these pressures create. In the 1970s the full effect of these environmental pressures became apparent and firms were ill-prepared to develop new pricing strategies.

However, business leaders and educators have begun to search for new approaches to solving pricing problems. Some firms have been quite successful in developing new strategies and in organizing for the price decision. Unfortunately, other firms have imitated these successful strategies and often have discovered that the overall situation is not similar; thus, some undesired consequences occurred.

Firms that have been successful in making profitable pricing decisions have taken what may be called a *proactive pricing* approach.[11] By consciously attempting to consider the effects of a pricing decision on how buyers perceive prices and how buyers develop perceptions of value, these firms have managed to leave less money on the table in competitive bid situations and have been able to successfully raise or reduce prices without competitive retaliation. Through deliberate acquisition and careful analysis of pertinent information, they have become aggressive pricing strategists and tacticians.

There are two essential prerequisites for becoming a successful proactive pricer. First, it is necessary to understand how pricing works. Because of the complexities of pricing in terms of its impact on suppliers, salespeople, distributors, competitors, and customers, the simple prescriptions of traditional microeconomic theory simply do not fit the realities of a modern market system. Indeed, as indicated by this list of those whom pricing impacts, companies that focus primarily on their internal costs often make serious pricing errors.

Second, it is essential for any pricer to understand how customers perceive prices and price changes. As will be developed in Chaps. 3 and 4, most buyers do not have complete information about alternative choices and most buyers are not capable of perfectly processing the available information to arrive at their "best" choice. Price frequently is used not only as an indicator of how much money the buyer must give up, but also as an indicator of product quality. Moreover, differences between the prices of alternative choices also affect buyers' perceptions. Thus, it is imperative that the price setter know who makes the purchase decision for the products or services being priced and how this buyer perceives price information. As will be documented in Chap. 3, failure to follow this basic prescription leads to some major pricing errors.

SUMMARY

This chapter reviewed several of the contemporary environmental pressures and current pricing practices that have been tried to cope with these pressures. It was suggested that many of the current pricing practices need to be based on additional analyses, particularly in the development of cost and demand information. Moreover, there are a number of other important factors that need to be considered when setting prices. For successful pricing one must know how pricing works and how customers perceive prices.

The prescriptions for successful pricing articulated in this book emphasize the acquisition of correct and timely information about customers, competitors, costs, and the firm's objectives. However, this information must also be carefully analyzed prior to the determination of pricing strategies and tactics. Sections 2 and 3 present

---

[11]Elliot B. Ross, "Making Money with Proactive Pricing," *Harvard Business Review,* 62 (November–December 1984), 145–155.

techniques for acquiring and analyzing the relevant information for pricing decisions.

Section 4 explores how to use these analytical techniques for developing prices over product life cycles and for pricing multiple products or services. Section 5 discusses ways to increase pricing flexibility by developing a price structure. In Section 6, techniques for deciding what price to bid in an auction or in a competitive bidding situation are discussed. Also in Section 6, specific issues of pricing services for both profit and not-for-profit companies are presented. Pricing for export marketing will also be explored. Finally, Section 7 summarizes the pricing issues covered in the book and offers a set of guidelines for developing and implementing a proactive approach to pricing.

DISCUSSION QUESTIONS

1 The chapter cites two reasons for the scarcity of new approaches to pricing. Can you think of any additional reasons why pricing has been a neglected marketing decision variable?
2 The chapter provides the example of two candy companies changing the price of the multipack of candy bars. Assume that the strategy used by the first company resulted in a 50 percent decrease in volume during the first year after the price change, but that during the second year volume was down only 30 percent from predecision levels. Assume further that late in the second year chocolate is again scarce and expensive. If you were the price administrator for this company, what pricing alternatives would you consider?
3 Assume, for the situation described in Question 2, that you are the price administrator for the second company. During the first two years after the price change described in the chapter, your multipack candy volume remained at predecision levels. Now you are faced with the same scarcity of chocolate. What pricing alternatives would you consider? Are any of these alternatives different from those listed in Question 2? Why or why not?
4 Before making a final decision for either of the two candy companies described in Questions 2 and 3, what additional information would you want? If the information was available, how would you use it?
5 What do you think should be the role of a pricing manager or price administrator? What type of education or training should a price administrator have?
6 In Question 5, would your answer be different if you assumed the price administrator worked for a retail store? Why or why not?

SUGGESTED READINGS

Bailey, Earl L. (ed.): *Pricing Practices and Strategies* (New York: The Conference Board, 1978).

"Flexible Pricing," *Business Week,* December 12, 1977, pp. 78–88.

Guiltinan, Joseph P.: "Risk-Aversive Pricing Policies: Problems and Alternatives," *Journal of Marketing,* 40 (January 1976), 10–15.

Guiltinan, Joseph P., and Kent B. Monroe: "Making Sound Pricing Decisions in the Current Economic Environment," *Executive Scene,* 3 (Fall 1974), 11–16.

Nagle, Thomas: "Pricing as Creative Marketing," *Business Horizons,* 26 (July–August 1983), 14–19.

Ross, Elliot B.: "Making Money with Proactive Pricing," *Harvard Business Review,* 62 (November–December 1984), 145–155.

PRICES AND DEMAND

One of the most important cornerstones of price determination is a product's demand, i.e., the volume of a product that buyers are willing to buy at a specific price. To be able to analyze alternative pricing decisions, the price setter must estimate the amount that will be demanded at each alternative price. These volume estimates can then be used to provide both a revenue estimate and a cost estimate for each price alternative and hence the profitability of each price.

The discipline of economics provides the basic theory of how prices should be set. However, despite the analytical pricing solutions provided by economic theory, the theory has limited practicality. Most of the limitations of economic theory arise because of the many necessary simplifying assumptions it makes in developing theories. Indeed, theoretical models seldom approximate the real world. Nevertheless, economic theory does provide some important analytical concepts for practical pricing decisions.

There are five chapters in this section. Chapter 2 briefly describes the traditional economic theory of price determination. A number of concepts introduced in the chapter are used throughout the book: revenue, elasticity, marginal revenue, and marginal costs. These concepts are important in any discussion of price. Some recent important advances in economic theory are introduced. Sparked by essays by Scitovszky and Stigler, conceptual issues related to price–quality relationships, economics of information and price search behavior, price signaling, and price bundling have been introduced to the pricing field. This emergence of nontraditional economic thinking on pricing represents an important recent development.

One of the most important factors in the price–demand relationship is how buyers use price in their purchase decision processes. As Chaps. 3 and 4 demonstrate, the behavioral dimension of price is complex and different than assumed in the traditional economic theory of price determination. Applications of recent findings from price perception research developed in Chaps. 3 and 4 are used extensively in Sections 4–7.

One of the prerequisites for using the proactive pricing approach developed in this book is an understanding of how customers perceive prices. The behavioral theories on price perception and important empirical findings and implications are presented in Chaps. 3 and 4. An important extension of the material in Chap. 4 concerns how customers form value judgments given their price perceptions. Chapter 5 argues that it is these value judgments that determine the willingness of customers to pay particular prices for the products and services they desire. As pointed out in Chap. 1, profitable pricing revolves around successful adaptation to the external factors affecting prices and profitability. A key aspect of this adaptation is the development of a value-oriented pricing strategy. Chapter 5 develops the concept of value analysis and techniques for transforming information on customers' value judgments into pricing strategies.

Finally, Chap. 6 reviews traditional and newer techniques for estimating price–volume relationships. Perhaps the most frequently asked question is: "What will happen to unit sales if prices change by X percent?" There are a number of ways to estimate either the historical or the prospective price–volume relationship, and these methods are described in Chap. 6.

CHAPTER 2

ECONOMICS OF PRICE DETERMINATION

There is a large body of literature describing how business organizations should determine their selling prices. This literature has a rich tradition and, although theoretical in nature, provides some important analytical concepts for practical pricing decisions. This chapter has three purposes: (1) to summarize the traditional economic theory of price determination, (2) to delineate useful concepts for actual pricing decisions, and (3) to review some recent developments in economics relative to pricing.

PRICE DETERMINATION IN THEORY

In our economy, pricing decisions are made by a complex of private and public institutions. Many of these decisions are made within large, multifaceted, and complex profit-oriented as well as not-for-profit organizations. The way these pricing decisions are made is considerably different from the decision process described by traditional economic theory. The essentials of the economic theory of the firm tell us how a firm will decide which production technique (or method) to use and what the particular input proportions will be to produce the desired product. Given its production method and its decision as to what to produce, the firm seeks to minimize its input costs. The firm then decides the quantities of each product it plans to sell and the price per unit at which it hopes to sell each product. The input purchase plans and the sales plans the firm chooses depend on

1 The objectives of the firm
2 The time span of the plans

Economic analysis uses three time periods: (1) market period, which is so short that managerial plans cannot be changed; (2) short run, where there is sufficient time to vary some input plans; and (3) long run, where all input plans are capable of being changed. The objective of the firm is assumed to be profit maximization.

It is important to note that this economic theory to be briefly described is not intended to indicate how firms actually do or should make pricing decisions, or how buyers do or should respond to these pricing decisions. Economic theory is more concerned with the behavior of aggregates or markets, and particularly how persistent and widespread behavior leads to stable results, called equilibrium. One important aspect of the economic perspective is the view of the firm as a price taker rather than a price maker. That is, the managerial decision is to determine the quantity to produce, and the market through the forces of supply and demand sets price. (This is in contrast to a marketing perspective where price is viewed as a decision variable, rather than as a given.) As noted, the major decisions made by the firm in this economic theory is what to produce and how much to produce. The price that results is given by the market as the forces of demand and supply interact to produce a market-clearing price. Hence, we should not uncritically adopt economic concepts, methods, or assumptions for the development of marketing-oriented pricing principles.[1] However, the criticisms of the traditional economic approach to pricing that are a part of Chaps. 2, 3, and 4 are intended not to evaluate the theory per se but to draw attention to the limitations of the theory for an uncritical application to pricing decisions.

The Profit-Maximizing Firm

Figure 2-1 illustrates how a firm interested in maximizing profits determines how much to produce in the short run when price is constant, i.e., price cannot be changed. Since price is constant the total-revenue curve must go through the origin (if zero units are sold, total revenue will be zero), but in the short run some costs are fixed, so the total-cost curve does not go through the origin. Since the firm is assumed to know its costs for each possible output level, determining how much to produce is not a difficult task. As long as revenue received from the sale of an additional unit of output (marginal revenue) is greater than the additional costs of producing and selling that unit (marginal cost), the firm will expand output. Since price is constant, marginal revenue equals price, and the firm will produce at the quantity level where marginal revenue (price) equals marginal cost. (In economic analysis marginal is defined as the change resulting from a unit increase in effort.) Thus, in Fig. 2-1 profits are at a maximum where total revenue minus total cost is the greatest, or where the slope of the total-revenue curve equals the slope of the total-cost curve. [In quantitative analysis slope measures the amount of change in the dependent variable (revenue or costs) produced by a unit increase in the indepen-

---

[1]John R. Hauser, "Pricing Theory and the Role of Marketing Science," *Journal of Business,* 57 (January 1984), S65–S71; Thomas Nagle, "Economic Foundations for Pricing," *Journal of Business,* 57 (January 1984), S3–S26.

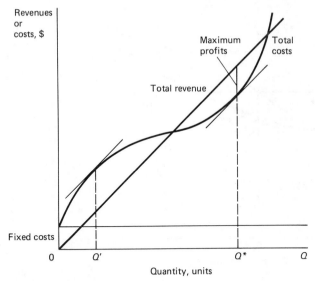

FIGURE 2-1
Output determination for a profit-maximizing firm—short run
(constant prices).

dent variable (quantity).] Note that for profits to be at a maximum, the total-cost curve must lie below the total-revenue curve. Thus, maximum profits can be obtained when the quantity produced is Q^* units, whereas losses are at a maximum at Q' units. Should the firm produce more units than Q^*, its total-cost curve is increasing faster than the total-revenue curve, implying that marginal costs are now greater than marginal revenues. Figure 2-2 simply plots the marginal cost and average cost curves against quantity. (Since price is assumed to be constant, marginal revenue equals price.) Since the slope of the total-cost curve is the increase in total cost per unit increase in quantity, the slope is marginal cost. Figures 2-1 and 2-2 summarize the key information about cost curves. As shown in Fig. 2-2, marginal cost is equal to average cost once, slicing up through the average-cost curve at its minimum point. Thus, with marginal cost rising, the firm will have a finite solution if it produces at the level where marginal cost equals marginal revenue.

As shown in Fig. 2-3, the same conditions hold in the long run, but now the total-cost curve goes through the origin, as does the total-revenue curve. Maximum profits are still where marginal revenue equals marginal cost.

Figure 2-4 shows the situation when prices vary. Now the firm determines its output on the basis of where marginal revenue equals marginal cost, but the price it receives for its output is determined by the demand curve and varies according to how much is produced. Thus, as quantity produced increases, the price per unit the firm receives for its output decreases. That is, price is set at the level where the firm can sell its entire output. The long-run solution, as seen in Fig. 2-5, is similar to the constant-price situation; however, when prices can vary, the total revenue curve is not linear.

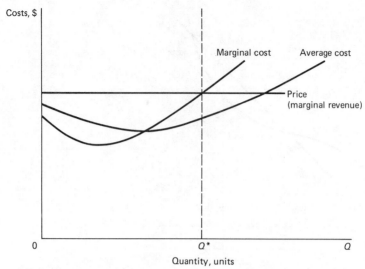

FIGURE 2-2
Output determination for a profit-maximizing firm—short run (constant prices).

A firm having complete knowledge about its costs and revenues and managed by a rational expert would always maximize profits. However, complete information usually is not available and managers are fallible human beings. Thus, actual firms depart more or less from the maximum-output or least-cost solutions. These departures may be errors or conscious decisions not to be operating at the short-run production level that maximizes profits. Essentially, the short run means that the firm faces more constraints than it faces in the long run. If managers believe that the change in output (moving away from the optimum output) is not permanent— e.g., there is an increase in demand—then they would not want to add to the firm's permanent capacity to produce the product. Moreover, if the increase in demand is permanent, the firm might want to adjust to the increase slowly, to have a better idea of what the final demand will be before adding permanent capacity to meet that demand. Thus, firms spend relatively long periods of time on their short-run cost curves. This point will become more important when the cost considerations underlying profitable pricing are discussed in Chaps. 7–10.

Challenges to the Profit-Maximization Objective

The assumption of profit maximization has been challenged for two basic reasons.[2] First, profits do not appear to be the only objective of managers of the firm. And

[2]Richard M. Cyert and James G. March, *A Behavioral Theory of the Firm* (Englewood Cliffs, N.J.: Prentice-Hall, 1963), p. 8.

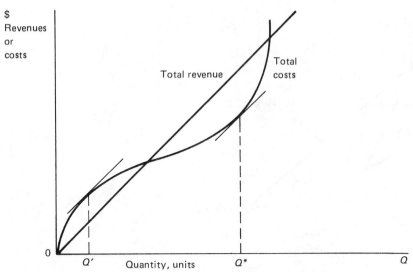

FIGURE 2-3
Output determination for a profit-maximizing firm—long run
(constant prices).

second, managers who are concerned about profits may not appear to be attempting to maximize.

It has been argued that a business firm is a complex organization comprised of individuals with a set of individual motives. That is, some people are working solely for the money they earn, others are also concerned with the social relationships that evolve, and some are interested in shouldering responsibility or wielding authority. In addition, the participants within the organization are probably very much concerned with long-run survival and hence would be interested in maintaining a given level of security for the organization (i.e., the chances the organization will still exist in the indefinite future). Generally, the key to long-run survival is the ability of the organization to adapt to environmental pressures and constraints. Hence, the actual objectives of the business organization (or any organization) are determined through an interaction of a wide range of personal objectives and pressures and constraints from the organization's external environment.

A second challenge to the profit-maximization assumption accepts the importance of profits but questions whether managers really attempt to maximize profits. It suggests instead that their goal is to attain *satisfactory* profits. Satisfactory profits represent a level of aspiration that managers use to assess alternative strategies. In essence, if a strategy is predicted to generate an acceptable level of profits, then the strategy is good enough and is implemented.

The simple rule of the profit-maximizing firm is to continue to expand output

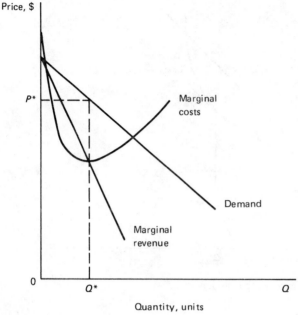

FIGURE 2-4
Output determination for a profit-maximizing firm—short run (varying prices).

FIGURE 2-5
Output determination for a profit-maximizing firm—long run (varying prices).

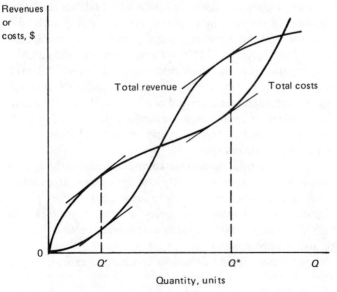

until the marginal cost of the last unit produced equals the marginal revenue obtained from the sale of that unit. It is important to understand that marginal cost is not the same as average cost (total costs divided by total output). As will be developed in Chaps. 7–10, marginal cost serves neither as a guide to how much to produce in traditional economic theory nor as a guide to the appropriate price to charge in price determination. The inappropriate use of average cost in pricing leads to attempts to maximize the profit margin rather than total profits. It will be shown in Chap. 8 that making pricing decisions on the basis of profit margins may lead to inappropriate pricing decisions. Although firms may not attain profit maximization exactly, profits seem to be a primary reason for people to hold stocks in business firms and a primary justification for recent acquisition and takeover activity. It would seem that departures from apparent attempts to maximize profits reflect imperfect information about costs and demand, instead of a willingness to accept less rather than more profits.

ECONOMIC THEORY OF BUYER BEHAVIOR

We now turn to discussing how price is believed to affect demand. We begin with the economic theory of buyer behavior, which provides the framework for most of the social criticisms of pricing practices by manufacturers and retailers. (In Chap. 3 we will enlarge this theory by introducing the results of recent behavioral research on the influence of price on buyer behavior.) Finally, we will discuss various measures of demand sensitivity to price.

Essentially, the buyer has two decisions to make: (1) what products should be purchased and (2) how much should be purchased of each product. The quantity of each product to buy depends on (1) the price of that product, (2) the prices of all other products, (3) the income of the buyer, and (4) the buyer's tastes and preferences. Given the prices of all products, and given their income, buyers make their purchases according to their own tastes and preferences. The consumer is assumed to be rational and to choose among alternative products so as to maximize satisfaction (utility).

Assumptions

As indicated, utility means want-satisfying power, resides in the mind of the buyer, and is common to all products and services. Utility is subjective, not objective, and it is assumed that a choice of product A over product B means the buyer perceives product A as having more utility than product B. (In subsequent chapters we will prefer to use the term value rather than utility, but the meaning will remain the same.) The theory of buyer behavior based on the assumption of rational behavior and utility maximization involves several additional assumptions about the buyer:

1 The buyer calculates deliberately and chooses consistently.

2 Deliberate choice rules out habit or impulse buying.

3 Consistent choice rules out vacillating and erratic behavior; the buyer acts predictably.

4 If the buyer prefers product A to product B, and prefers product B to product C, then consistency requires that he or she prefers A to C.

5 Within these conditions of behavior, buyers choose as if they are maximizing utility.

6 To maximize utility the buyer knows all alternatives and is not ignorant about any aspect of his or her purchase.

7 Because of this perfect knowledge, there is never a gap between the satisfaction the buyer expects from a purchase and the actual fulfillment realized from the purchase.

8 Want and subjective utilities are not influenced by prices, i.e., higher priced products do not provide additional utility or value simply because of their higher prices.

9 Finally, it is assumed that total utility increases at a diminishing rate as more of a product or service is acquired.

Solution

The solution to the question of how much of a product a buyer will purchase requires the assumption of diminishing marginal returns to utility as quantity purchased increases. (As we saw in discussing the profit-maximizing firm, diminishing marginal returns implies the utility or value curve is concave.) The quantity purchased (assuming a fixed income constraint) is determined by the point at which total utility is maximized.

Since prices are given to buyers (i.e., buyers do not negotiate prices with sellers) and each buyer has a fixed income, how do buyers determine the total assortment they will purchase from the wide array of alternatives available to them? Since it is assumed that prices serve only to indicate the amount of money buyers must give up to acquire a product, the amount of a particular product to be acquired depends on the relation between the marginal utility of acquiring an additional unit and the price of that additional unit. Further, the assumption of diminishing marginal utility implies that buyers are capable of ranking all alternatives in terms of increasing preference, and that they purchase first the most preferred product. Buyers will continue to buy additional units of the preferred product until the marginal utility of acquiring an additional unit becomes equal to or less than the marginal utility realized from purchasing a unit of the second most preferred product. This decision process continues until the amount allocated for the shopping trip has been exhausted. The result of this decision process indicates that the marginal utility obtained from the last penny spent on product A must equal the marginal utility obtained from the last penny spent on product B and so on for all products purchased.

To summarize, in economic theory, price is assumed to influence buyer choice because price serves as an indicator of how much the buyer must give up (sacrifice). Assuming the buyer has perfect information concerning prices and want satisfaction of comparable product alternatives, he or she can determine a product mix that maximizes satisfaction within a given budget constraint. Further, if the buyer does not act to maximize want satisfaction, he or she is acting irrationally. The implication is that buyers should choose the low-price alternative if there is a choice between at least two differentially priced, similar products.

However, buyers really do not have complete and accurate information about the utility received from a set of products or the prices of these products. Somehow buyers do acquire sufficient information about products and about the satisfaction received from these products to decide which products to purchase with a given budget. Lacking complete information about the utility associated with the product, the buyer assesses the product on the basis of known information. Generally, one piece of information available to the buyer is the product's price. Other pieces of information about anticipated purchases are not always known, or are known less frequently than price, and the buyer cannot be sure how reliable and how complete this information is. And lack of information may introduce uncertainty about the buyer's ability to predict correctly the want satisfaction available through purchasing the product. *Hence, buyers may use price as an indicator of product cost or sacrifice as well as an indicator of product quality (want satisfaction attributes).* This attractiveness attribute of a product's price will be amplified in Chaps. 3 and 4. We now turn to discussing some concepts useful when analyzing price alternatives.

SOME USEFUL CONCEPTS FROM PRICE THEORY

The overview of the theory of the firm and the theory of the buyer so far has been primarily qualitative. That is, we have postulated that the lower the price of an

FIGURE 2-6
Concept of price elasticity. (*Note:* The reader will note that traditional economic texts place price on the vertical axis and quantity on the horizontal axis. However, assuming that quantity demanded depends on price, then the correct procedure is to place price on the horizontal axis and quantity on the vertical axis.)

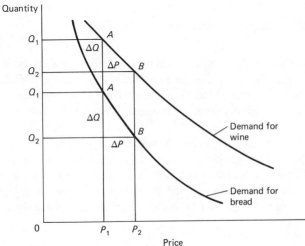

item, the more a buyer is likely to buy. However, it has not been possible to say how much more the buyer is likely to buy. Moreover, as seen in Fig. 2-6, we can say that for a particular price, P_1, there is a greater demand for wine than for bread, and that if price increases to P_2, there will be a greater decrease in demand for bread than for wine. It is also possible to say that the demand for wine is less sensitive to changes in price, but that the demand for wine is greater than the demand for bread at any similar price. But these qualitative statements do not tell us the extent to which price and demand are related for each product, nor can we easily compare loaves per dollar to bottles per dollar. The concept of *elasticity* provides a unit-free measure of the sensitivity of one variable to another, and it provides a quantitative way of making comparisons across entities. The first set of concepts from economic theory that are useful for pricing, different types of elasticities, is introduced next.

Demand Elasticity

In Chap. 1 and in this chapter we have occasionally referred to the concept of demand sensitivity. That is, we have been concerned with the responsiveness of demand to price changes. *Price elasticity of demand* measures the responsiveness of the quantity demanded for a product or service to a change in the price of the product or service. Specifically, price elasticity of demand is defined as the rate of percentage change in quantity demanded relative to the percentage change in price:

$$E_d = \frac{(Q_1 - Q_2)/Q_1}{(P_1 - P_2)/P_1} = \frac{\Delta Q/Q_1}{\Delta P/P_1} = \frac{\Delta Q}{\Delta P} \times \frac{P_1}{Q_1} \qquad (2\text{-}1)$$

where E_d = price elasticity of demand
ΔQ = quantity change in demand
ΔP = change in price
Q_1, P_1 = original quantity demanded and price, respectively

If it is assumed that quantity demanded falls as price increases, then $E_d < 0$; if there is a positive relation between demand and price change, then $E_d > 0$, i.e., demand increases as price is increased. For the generally assumed case of a downward-sloping demand curve, Fig. 2-6 graphically depicts the concept of price elasticity for both bread and wine.

To illustrate the concept of price elasticity, assume that price of a camcorder was $1,200, and annual sales at this price totaled 5,000 units. In January 1989, the price was dropped to $1,050 and annual sales reached 5,500 units. In January 1990, the price was dropped to $990 and annual sales reached 10,000 units. Using Eq. (2-1) we can compute the price elasticity for each of these price changes. For these price changes, we have

$$E_d = \frac{(5,000 - 5,500)/5,000}{(\$1,200 - \$1,050)/\$1,200}$$

$$= \frac{-500/5,000}{\$150/\$1,200} = \frac{-500}{\$150} \times \frac{\$1,200}{5,000} = -0.80$$

and

$$E_d = \frac{(5,500 - 10,000)/5,500}{(\$1,050 - \$990)/\$1,050}$$

$$= \frac{-4,500/5,500}{\$60/\$1,050} = \frac{-4,500}{\$60} \times \frac{\$1,050}{5,500} = -14.3$$

With the exception of the special kinds of demand curves seen in Fig. 2-7, the price elasticity of demand is not the same at all prices, nor is the elasticity of demand in any particular range of prices the same as the slope of the demand curve for it over that range of prices. In Fig. 2-6 the slope of the demand curve between points A and B is $\Delta Q/\Delta P$, which is not the formula for the elasticity given in Eq. (2-1). The higher the price the product is sold at, the smaller will be the quantity demanded and the greater will be the value of E_d; i.e., E_d approaches zero in value. Furthermore, if the value of the price elasticity of demand is less than -1, that is, $-\infty < E_d < -1$, then demand is elastic and sellers' revenues will rise if there is a small reduction in price. Table 2-1 summarizes the elasticity measures and their relationships to total revenue.

FIGURE 2-7
Demand curves for special cases.

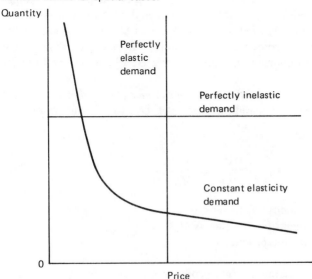

TABLE 2-1
RELATIONSHIP OF PRICE ELASTICITY OF DEMAND TO TOTAL REVENUES

Value of E_d	Description	Effect on Total Revenues of	
		Small Price Rise	Small Price Reduction
0	Perfectly inelastic	Increase	Decrease
$-1 < E_d < 0$	Inelastic	Increase	Decrease
-1	Unitary elastic	No change	No change
$-\infty < E_d < -1$	Elastic	Decrease	Increase
$-\infty$	Perfectly elastic	Decrease	Increase

Often other measures of demand sensitivity are used to explore the implications of change. *Income elasticity of demand* is the responsiveness of the quantity demanded of a product or service to a change in personal income.

$$E_I = \frac{(\Delta Q)}{\Delta I} \times \frac{(I)}{Q} \qquad (2\text{-}2)$$

where E_I = income elasticity of demand
ΔQ = quantity change in demand
ΔI = change in personal income

If E_I is negative, this implies that the product is an inferior good. That is, as income goes up, fewer units are demanded. For example, as income goes up, some households will switch some of their meat purchases from hamburger to steak and consume less hamburger. If E_I is positive, then demand increases as income increases, but there are two different possibilities. If $0 < E_I < 1$, then the product becomes less important in the households' consumption plans even though total expenditures increase, e.g., necessities such as food and clothing tend to comprise less of the family's total expenditures as income increases. Finally, if E_I is greater than 1, then the product becomes more important as income increases, e.g., leisure and recreational activities.

A third measure of demand sensitivity is *cross-price elasticity of demand,* which measures the responsiveness of demand for a product, Q_A, to a change in price of another product, Q_B.

$$E_c = \frac{\Delta Q_A}{\Delta P_B} \times \frac{P_B}{Q_A} \qquad (2\text{-}3)$$

where E_c = cross-price elasticity of demand
ΔQ_A = change in demand for product A
ΔP_B = change in price for product B

If E_c is negative, then in general the two products are *complementary;* if E_c is positive, then in general the two products are *substitutes.* For example, razor blades are complements to razors, but different brands of razors are substitute products. Cross-price elasticity is often used as a measure of the effects of competitive price changes.

For example, assume the price of a Kodak 35-millimeter camera is $145.00 and a comparable Minolta is $149.00. Further assume the quantity demanded for the Kodak camera is 50,000 units and the quantity demanded for the Minolta is 100,000 units. Suppose Kodak reduces the price of its camera to $142.00. The quantity demanded for the Kodak camera increases to 60,000 units, and the quantity demanded for the Minolta decreases to 95,000. (Because of overall increases in market demand for 35-millimeter cameras, the demand increase experienced by Kodak is not all at the expense of demand for the Minolta camera.)

The cross-price elasticity of demand for the Minolta camera can be computed using Eq. (2-3):

$$E_c = \frac{-5,000}{-\$3} \times \frac{\$145}{100,000} = 2.42$$

Relationships Among the Elasticities of Demand

For the moment, if the theory of consumer demand concerns the decision to buy either of two products, A and B, and the quantities to purchase of each, we can illustrate the relations among these three elasticities. Each of these products has a price, P_A and P_B; the consumer must decide how much to purchase of each, Q_A and Q_B; and the consumer has a budget or income available to spend, Y. The consumer will have six elasticities of demand with respect to the three things that will influence the purchase decision: two *own-price elasticities*, E_A and E_B, two *cross-price elasticities*, $E_{A\,B}$ and $E_{B\,A}$, and two *income elasticities*, $E_{A\,I}$ and $E_{B\,I}$ (note the subscripts of these elasticities). These six elasticities describe how buyers behave relative to changes in price of either product or changes in income.

To demonstrate the relations among the elasticities, let's trace what might happen if the price of A is reduced while everything else remains unchanged. We would expect under normal circumstances that Q_A, the demand for A, would increase. There are two basic reasons to expect this increase. First, some buyers noting the lower price of A would switch some of their purchases from B to A. The extent of this crossover would depend on the $E_{B\,A}$, the degree that demand for product B is sensitive to changes in the price of A. This crossover is called the *substitution effect*. Second, after the quantities usually purchased of products A and B, the buyers will have some money left over. Since the marginal utility of acquiring more units of A is now greater than P_A, buyers will increase the units purchased of A to restore the equilibrium between the marginal utility of an extra unit of A and its new, lower price, the *income effect,* expressed as $E_{A\,I}$. Thus, the ordinary price elasticity is composed of a substitution effect (cross-price elasticity) and an income effect (income elasticity). The income effect normally adds to the elasticity, making it a more negative number. In Chap. 3 we will provide some evidence about these relative effects on price elasticity.

Revenue Concepts

As mentioned in our discussion of price elasticity of demand, there is a relationship between sellers' revenues and the elasticity of demand for their products. To establish this relationship we need to define the concepts of total revenue, average revenue, and marginal revenue. *Total revenue* is the total amount spent by buyers for the product or service.

$$\text{TR} = PQ \qquad (2\text{-}4)$$

where TR = total revenue
P = price of the product
Q = quantity demanded at price P

Average revenue is the total outlay by buyers divided by the number of units sold, or the price of the product.

$$\text{AR} = \frac{\text{TR}}{Q} = P \qquad (2\text{-}5)$$

where AR is average revenue. The average revenue curve and the demand curve are the same. *Marginal revenue* refers to the total change in total revenue resulting from a change in sales volume.

$$\text{MR} = \frac{\Delta \text{TR}}{\Delta Q} \qquad (2\text{-}6)$$

Price and Marginal Revenue   The normal, downward-sloping demand curve reveals that to sell an additional unit of output, price must fall. The change in total revenue—marginal revenue—is the result of two forces: (1) the revenue derived from the additional unit sold, which is equal to the new price; and (2) the loss in revenue that results from marking down all prior salable units to the new price. If force (1) is greater than force (2), total revenue will increase, and total revenue will increase only if marginal revenue is positive. This relationship between total revenue and marginal revenue can be illustrated using Fig. 2-8. As shown in Fig. 2-8, $\Delta Q = Q_2 - Q_1$ and $\Delta P = P_1 - P_2$ where P_1 is the initial price, P_2 is the new (lower) price, Q_1 is the (smaller) sales quantity at P_1, Q_2 is the (larger) sales quantity at price P_2, ΔQ is the unit increase in sales as price falls from P_1 to P_2, and ΔP is the decrease in price necessary to increase sales by ΔQ. It can be shown that marginal revenue is

$$\text{MR} = P_2 - \frac{Q_1 \, \Delta P}{\Delta Q} \qquad (2\text{-}7)$$

If $\Delta Q = 1$, we see that MR is positive only when the revenue generated from the new price is greater than the loss in revenue resulting from marking down all previously salable items.

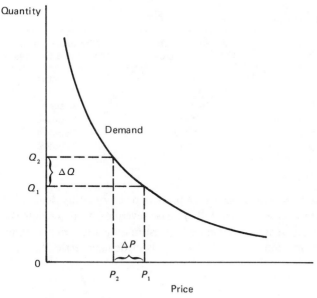

FIGURE 2-8
Price–quantity demanded relationship.

Price Elasticity and Marginal Revenue   It can also be shown that the relation between marginal revenue and price elasticity of demand is given by

$$\text{MR} = P_1 (1 + \frac{1}{E_d}) = P_1 \frac{(E_d + 1)}{E_d} \tag{2-8}$$

This relation between marginal revenue and price elasticity of demand has been used by the United States Postal Service to justify its postage rates. When applied to rate setting, this relation has been called the *inverse elasticity rule.* Historically, first-class mail has been the most price inelastic class of mail, with estimates ranging from -0.1 to -0.3. Since all classes of mail have been price inelastic, price increases will result in increases in total revenue (positive marginal revenue) as shown in Table 2-2. Because first-class mail is the most inelastic, a 3-cent price increase per ounce will produce most of the needed new mail revenues. As a result, the postage rates for other classes of mail generally have not had as large a percentage increase as first-class mail.

Thus, marginal revenue varies with price and with the price elasticity of demand. Table 2-2 shows the relationship between revenues and price elasticity for both the negative price–demand relationship and the implied positive price–demand relationship from the price–quality studies discussed in Chap. 3.

As Table 2-2 indicates for the generally assumed negative price–quantity demanded relationship, revenues will increase if price is increased and demand is price inelastic; further, revenues will fall if price is increased and demand is price elastic. But if buyers infer quality to the product or service on the basis of price and thereby

TABLE 2-2
RELATIONSHIP BETWEEN REVENUES AND PRICE ELASTICITY

Price–Demand Relationship	Value of E_d	Marginal Revenue When Price Increases	Marginal Revenue When Price Decreases
Negative	$-1 < E_d < 0$	Positive	Negative
Negative	$E_d = -1$	Zero	Zero
Negative	$-\infty < E_d < -1$	Negative	Positive
Positive	$0 < E_d < 1$	Positive	Negative
Positive	$E_d = 1$	Positive	Negative
Positive	$1 < E_d < \infty$	Positive	Negative

perceive a higher priced item as more attractive, a positive price–quantity demanded relationship ensues and an increase in price will increase revenues. To determine the effects of changing price on demand, a method of estimating the price–volume relationship is required. Some commonly used methods of demand estimation are discussed in Chap. 6.

Consumers' Surplus

As can be seen in Fig. 2-8, there are usually some consumers willing to pay more than any particular price in order to acquire a given product. This means that the price charged for the product is lower than those buyers' *perceived value* for the product. The difference between the maximum amount consumers are willing to pay for a product and the amount they actually pay is called *consumers' surplus:* the money value of the willingness of consumers to pay in excess of what the price requires them to pay. This difference represents what the consumers gain from the trade. The difference is the money amounts of *value-in-use* minus *value-in-exchange;* for voluntary exchanges this is always positive. Value-in-use always exceeds value-in-exchange simply because the most consumers would pay must be greater than what they actually pay, otherwise they would not enter into the trade.

Figure 2-9 illustrates the concept of consumer surplus. In the figure, for price P_1, the amount demanded is Q_1. The area under the demand curve above the line P_1A represents the consumers' gain from acquiring Q_1 units at price P_1. Note that the total area under the entire demand curve represents the *total willingness to pay* across all consumers (value-in-use). The total willingness to pay at price P_1 is the total area under the demand curve to the left of the vertical line AQ_1. The value-in-exchange is the area of the rectangle Q_1AP_10, while consumers' surplus is the cross-hatched area above this rectangle. Consumers' surplus, then, is the consumers' net gain from trade.

Sellers, like consumers, will engage in trade only if they can realize a net gain from the transaction. Since any price above the seller's long-run marginal costs represents a profit surplus, the extent that the trade is profitable to the seller is given by P_1ABP_2, the area in Fig. 2-9 above the quantity sold at the price that equals marginal cost, P_2. This area represents the seller's gain from the transactions and is called *sellers' surplus.*

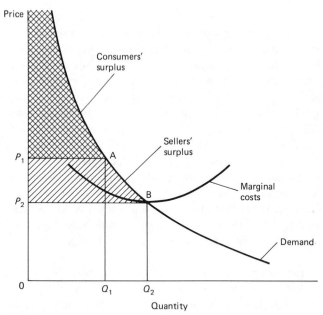

FIGURE 2-9
Consumers' and sellers' surplus.

We will return to the concept of consumers' surplus in Chap. 5. The important point to grasp now is that the price at which exchange takes place is not the equivalent of value, as is often assumed. Total willingness to pay (value-in-use) is comprised of value-in-exchange and consumers' surplus. It is this latter concept that becomes an important consideration in the determination of prices. Rather than concentrating on the cost considerations when setting price, the pricing problem becomes one of determining potential customers' perceived value-in-use and pricing accordingly. Indeed, this relationship between price and perceived value represents an important area of consumer research.

SOME IMPORTANT EXTENSIONS FROM ECONOMIC THEORY

Economics of Information

In 1944, observing the purchase behavior of "friends and their wives," Scitovszky concluded that "more often than not people judge quality by price."[3] He also argued that judging quality on the basis of price was rational behavior since it merely represented a belief that price was determined by the interplay of the forces of competitive supply and demand. That is, the forces of supply and demand would lead to a natural ordering of competing products on a price scale, such that there would be a strong positive relationship between price and product quality.

---

[3]Tibor Scitovszky, "Some Consequences of the Habit of Judging Quality by Price," *Review of Economic Studies,* 12 (1944–45), 100.

Although buyers were assumed not to possess perfect knowledge about the capability of alternative products to satisfy their wants, they were assumed to be perfect information processors. Furthermore, buyers could objectively use price cues to infer product quality, assess the amount of want satisfaction derived from a given quality level, and proceed to optimize choice. Optimal choice was still determined by the tradeoff of the marginal utility gained from a product choice relative to the utility sacrificed by paying the price. Further, it was implicitly assumed that buyers would gain perfect information about actual quality and would continue purchasing only if the marginal utility gained was greater than or equal to utility sacrificed. Thus, it was natural for price to be an appropriate signal of product quality.

Attempts to test this simple model have proceeded along three research streams. Initially, products were tested to determine whether there was a positive correlation between "objective" or measurable product quality and market price.[4] Since then a number of studies have reported that the relationship between price and quality is inconsistent across products and generally not as strong as would be expected given Scitovszky's reasoning.[5]

In 1961, Stigler noted that economists traditionally had ignored the issue of differential information available to sellers and buyers.[6] That is, the seller may know the quality of the product, but buyers do not know the quality until after purchase and use. Hence, in the interest of obtaining higher profits, a firm could set a high price that did not reflect the actual level of quality built into the product. However, such a strategy could succeed only if buyers are unable to evaluate the product's attributes (and quality) prior to purchase or not completely evaluate the product after a single purchase (or several purchases). Thus, there is a situation in which the information about a product's quality is known by the seller but not known by buyers, a condition of asymmetric information. Since Stigler's article, a second stream of theoretical research has developed to investigate the question of when it is in the interest of the firm to let the marketplace know the quality of its product using price, advertising, warranties, or other signals.

The essence of Stigler's argument is that buyers inform themselves about products in the marketplace only when the marginal return from gathering more information equals or exceeds the marginal costs of doing the search. Because different buyers perceive different costs of and benefits from such a search, some buyers will be better informed than others. The existence of less informed buyers allows sellers to charge higher prices, leading to a spread or dispersion of prices for similar products in the market.

The issue of concern is how external information cues can be utilized by the seller

---

[4]Alfred R. Oxenfeldt, "Consumer Knowledge: Its Measurement and Extent," *Review of Economics and Statistics,* 32 (1950), 300–314.

[5]Eitan Gerstner, "Do Higher Prices Signal Higher Quality?" *Journal of Marketing Research,* 22 (May 1985), 209–215; Gerard J. Tellis and Birger Wernerfelt, "Competitive Price and Quality under Asymmetric Information," *Marketing Science,* 6 (Summer 1987), 240–253; David J. Curry and Peter C. Riesz, "Prices and Price/Quality Relationships: A Longitudinal Analysis," *Journal of Marketing,* 52 (January 1988), 36–51.

[6]George Stigler, "The Economics of Information," *Journal of Political Economy,* 69 (June 1961), 213–225.

to convey information about the product to the market. Specifically, a *signal* is a piece of information that can be revealed to the market at some cost to the provider. (Note that this research is not concerned with whether the external cue is perceived by buyers as intended by the seller. We will return to this point in Chap. 3.) A signal is an observable, alterable (by the seller) characteristic that may affect buyers' assessments of product quality. For this external cue to serve as a signal:

1 There must be observable differences in a product characteristic or attribute across sellers.

2 There must be differences to the sellers in the cost of providing the cue.

3 The quality of products in the market must be perceived to vary directly with the characteristic or attribute.

The third requirement is critical, because if buyers know the quality does not vary as the signal varies, then the signal cannot be used to convey differences in quality across competing products.[7]

This research has enhanced our information on the relationship between price and quality. However, by concentrating on the seller and on issues of market equilibrium, the research misses an important issue: When and under what conditions do buyers assume a positive relationship between product quality and various external cues? The third research stream, examining whether buyers do infer product quality on the basis of price, addresses this issue and will be summarized in Chap. 3.

Price Bundling

Bundling is the practice of marketing two or more products and/or services at a special price.[8] Although this is not a new practice—consider season sports or symphony tickets sold at lower prices, differential prices for à la carte meals and complete dinners, and special "getaway weekends" with transportation, hotel, and rental car at a "package" price—it has been analyzed thus far primarily from an economic perspective. Because this practice is widespread in marketing, we will explore it fully in Chap. 13, as part of our discussion of product-line pricing.

Other Applications of Economic Analyses

During the past decade, economic analysis has been conducted on a number of pricing problems. Attempts have been made to analyze issues of price segmentation, timing of discount offers, development of pricing strategies over the product life cycle, pricing superstars, pricing used products, and pricing in two parts (fixed fees plus variable usage charges like a bank credit card). Although the analysis often

---

[7]Akshay R. Rao and Kent B. Monroe, "The Impact of Product Familiarity on the Price–Perceived Quality Relationship," *Journal of Consumer Research*, 15 (September 1988), 253–264.

[8]Joseph P. Guiltinan, "The Price Bundling of Services: A Normative Framework," *Journal of Marketing*, 51 (April 1987), 74–85.

suffers from the strict assumptions made about the behavior of the buyers and sellers, much has been learned about pricing from these analyses. In particular, these analyses have produced some interesting and potentially useful ideas for developing pricing strategies. Because many of them have strategic implications, we will introduce them at different points in the text.

SUMMARY

This chapter briefly reviewed the economic theory of price determination and discussed some economic concepts useful for analyzing pricing alternatives. The reader should remember that these concepts, in and of themselves, have limited usefulness for price determination. However, when these concepts are extracted from their theoretical domain and applied within the constraints of reality, they are powerful analytical tools. The concepts of elasticity and marginal revenue are very important, but they must be applied to decisions affecting the future, where uncertainty prevails. Hence, it is critical to provide the price setter with useful analytical techniques, techniques that permit executive judgment and experience to systematically become a part of the decision-making process. Later chapters will clarify and apply this point.

DISCUSSION QUESTIONS

1 If the business firm does not seek to maximize profits, what are some alternative objectives?
2 For each profit objective listed in your answer to Question 1, what do you think is the role of price? For each of these objectives, what might be the behavioral objectives of the managers of the firm?
3 Assume a firm makes three products, A, B, and C. Assume the profit equation for this firm is given by

$$\text{Profits} = (P_1 - c_1)Q_1 + (P_2 - c_2)Q_2 + (P_3 - c_3)Q_3 - f$$

where P_i is price, c_i is variable cost, Q_i is volume sold at price P_i, and f is fixed costs ($i = 1,2,3$). If the firm wishes to increase profits, what things in the equation can it attempt to change? List as many changes as possible.
4 A manufacturer of videocassette recorders sold 500,000 units in year 1 at a price of $500 each. In year 2, the price was reduced to $390, and 700,000 units were sold. In year 3, the price was reduced to $250 and 1,200,000 units were sold. Calculate the historical price elasticity of demand for each price change.
5 What do you think happened to the cost of producing a unit of the videocassette recorder of Question 4 when annual production increased from 500,000 units in year 1 to 1,200,000 in year 3? Explain your reasoning.
6 Can you think of some products for which demand would be (a) income elastic and (b) income inelastic?
7 In Question 6, what would the role of price be for a product that is income elastic?
8 Distinguish between the concepts of value-in-use and value-in-exchange.

SUGGESTED READINGS

Bell, Carolyn Shaw: "On the Elasticity of Demand at Retail," *American Journal of Economics and Sociology,* 20 (October 1960), 63–72.

Cyert, Richard, and Charles Hedrick: "Theory of the Firm: Past, Present, and Future; An Interpretation," *Journal of Economic Literature,* 10 (June 1972), 398–412.

Devinney, Timothy M. (ed.): *Issues in Pricing: Theory and Research* (Lexington, Mass.: D.C. Heath, 1988).

Nagle, Thomas: "Economic Foundations for Pricing," *Journal of Business,* 57, part 2 (January 1984), S3–S26.

Ratchford, Brian T.: "The New Economic Theory of Consumer Behavior: An Interpretative Essay," *Journal of Consumer Research,* 2 (September 1975), 65–75.

Tellis, Gerard J.: "Beyond the Many Faces of Price: An Integration of Pricing Strategies," *Journal of Marketing,* 50 (October 1986), 146–160.

Urbany, Joel E.: "An Experimental Examination of the Economics of Information," *Journal of Consumer Research,* 13 (September 1986), 257–271.

CHAPTER 3

USEFUL FINDINGS FROM PRICE PERCEPTION RESEARCH

PERCEPTION THEORY

Do we know how price influences individual buyers in their purchase decisions? As discussed in Chap. 2, it has generally been assumed that the behavior underlying the decisions of what to buy and how much to buy was embodied in the downward-sloping demand curve. That is, as the price of a product increased, fewer buyers would decide to purchase the product, and those buyers who still purchased the product would be disposed to purchase fewer units than before. Hence, it has been assumed that price serves only as a measure of purchase cost (sacrifice) to the buyer. However, research evidence indicates that the role of price is more complex than that of a simple indicator of purchase cost to buyers. In this chapter, the traditionally assumed role of price as a determinant of buyer behavior is contrasted with the emerging evidence of the complexity of price as an influence on purchase decisions.

As suggested in Chap. 1, a successful proactive pricer sets price to be consistent with customers' perceived value. To understand how customers form value perceptions, it is important to recognize the relative role of price in this process. However, as a first step, it is important to understand how people form perceptions and how the perceptual process influences their perceptions of product or service quality and value. We will first see how people form perceptions and then consider a conceptual model of the relationship among price, perceived quality, and perceived value. In Chap. 4, the discussion of this model will be expanded to consider how people evaluate products or services as well as offers such as sales promotions.

Perception

Perception basically involves the process of *categorization*. That is, we tend to place new experiences into existing classifications of familiar experiences. Thus, when buyers are confronted by a price different from what they believe they previously paid, they must decide whether the difference between the old and new prices is significant to them. If the price difference is perceived to be insignificant, they may classify the two prices as similar and act as they have in the past. Moreover, if the prices of two alternative products are perceived as comparable, even though they are not identical, some buyers may perceive the prices as equivalent and choose on bases other than price. On the other hand, if the price differences are perceived as significant, buyers may classify the products as different and make their choices on the basis of price. As will be developed in this chapter, this price-based choice may favor the higher priced alternative, again, not usually thought likely in the traditional model described later.

During this process of perceptual categorization buyers make heavy use of information cues, or clues. Some of these cues are price cues, which influence buyers' judgments of whether price differences are significant. For example, buyers may utilize the actual prices of products or services as an informational stimulus that implies product quality. This review of some of the findings from behavioral research about how buyers perceive prices will raise questions that we still cannot answer. However, despite these unanswered questions, marketing managers must be concerned with identifying the cues used by buyers, so as to obtain accurate buyers' perceptions of the products or services offered.

Traditional Model

The traditional model of buyer behavior leading to the downward-sloping demand curve assumes that the decisions of what to buy and how much to buy depend on (1) the prices of all goods, (2) the level of income or amount of purchasing power, and (3) the tastes and preferences of the buyer. Assuming perfect information about prices, a fixed level of income (budget), and knowledge about tastes and preferences, the buyer maximizes satisfaction by minimizing the price paid for each good.

Criticism of the Model

The assumption of "rational behavior" implies

1 Perfect information about prices
2 A buyer who is capable of perfectly processing information
3 Prices that do not affect subjective wants or satisfactions
4 Perfect information about tastes and preferences

As noted in Chap. 1, assumptions 1, 2, and 4 are clearly not present. Further, it would be expected that buyers' preferences or choices would depend on how they evaluate the quality or benefits to be received from a product relative to the cost or sacrifice inherent in the price. Thus, it can be argued that buyers' perceptions of value represent a tradeoff between the quality or benefits they perceive in the product relative to the sacrifice they perceive by paying the price:

$$\text{Perceived value} = \frac{\text{perceived benefits}}{\text{perceived sacrifice}} \qquad (3\text{-}1)$$

where perceived benefits are a function of perceived quality, perceived quality is positively related to price, and perceived sacrifice is positively related to price.

In Eq. (3-1), price may have both attracting and repelling attributes. For example, a new mustard was packaged in a crockery jar. Significant sales did not develop until

FIGURE 3-1
Conceptual relationship of price, perceived value, and willingness to buy.

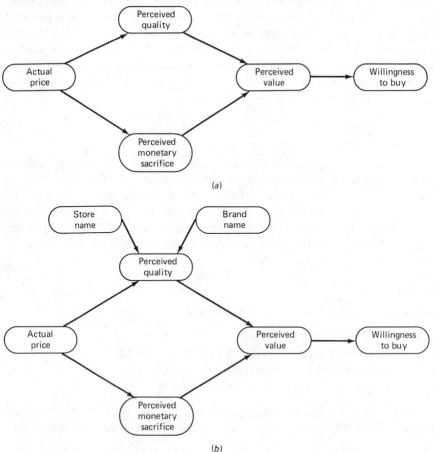

the price was increased from 49 cents to $1.00 a jar. Moreover, available research indicates that buyers generally are not able to assess perfectly a product's quality (the ability of the product to provide satisfaction). Rather, *perceived quality* is the relevant variable, and under appropriate conditions, the perceived quality in a product is positively related to price. It is expected that perceptions of value are directly related to buyers' preferences or choices; i.e., the larger a buyer's perception of value, the more likely the buyer would be to express a willingness to buy or preference for the product.

The model in Fig. 3-1*a* illustrates the role of price on buyers' perceptions of product quality, sacrifice, value, and willingness to buy. The model suggests that buyers use price as an index of perceived product quality as well as an index of the perceived sacrifice that is made when purchasing a product or service. Perceived value represents a tradeoff between buyers' perceptions of quality and sacrifice and is positive when perceptions of quality are greater than perceptions of sacrifice. The model posits a positive relationship between price and perceived quality and price and perceived sacrifice. Willingness to buy is positively related to perceived value. Figure 3-1*b* indicates that buyers may also use brand name and store name as indicators of product quality.

MULTIDIMENSIONAL ROLE OF PRICE ON BUYERS' PERCEPTIONS

The dual, conflicting nature of price complicates the question of how price affects purchase decisions. It has been common to refer to the "irrational" effects of price on behavior as *psychological price* phenomena. The concepts of customary prices, odd prices, and price lines are among these effects. Theoretically, a consumer subject to psychological price factors would be perceptually sensitive to certain prices, and a slight departure from these prices in either direction would result in a decrease in demand.

Despite the apparent acceptance of these "psychological" phenomena, there is little evidence to support this "magical" or "illusory" nature of prices. As the brief review in the next section indicates, these pricing practices have their origins in traditional ways of retailing and of restraining the sales clerk from pocketing money from the sales transaction. Moreover, buyers are accustomed to these pricing practices and might be uncomfortable if products were not priced this way. It is important to reiterate that these traditional "psychological" pricing practices have little or no real research evidence to support them, despite their popularity. Later in this chapter we will consider stronger documentation about the behavioral research on how buyers perceive prices and the subsequent managerial errors that are made by not applying such research evidence.

Traditional Psychological Pricing

Customary pricing is the method of pricing where all price alternatives are excluded except a single price. The historical example is the 5-cent candy bar or package of gum. With customary prices, sellers adapt to changes in costs and market conditions by adjusting the product size or quality, assuming the buyer would consider paying only one price. Moreover, common experience suggests that some sellers do use certain prices more frequently than others. Today, it is very unlikely that this practice has much acceptance or use.

Odd price is a term that refers to a price ending in an odd number (e.g., 1, 3, 5, 7, 9) or to a price just under a round number (e.g., 99, 98). Research justifying the use of this pricing practice has largely been of an anecdotal nature. Ginzberg[1] imposed experimental patterns of odd and even prices on selected items in a large mail-order catalog and could not discover any generalizable result of the study. Later, Gabor and Granger[2] concluded that the dominance of pricing below the round figure in some markets may be largely an artifact. That is, if sellers use odd pricing regularly, then some buyers will consider the odd price as the real or usual price and the round figure price as incorrect and respond in a negative way. A study of pricing in the food industry revealed that retail food prices indicated that prices ending in 9 were most popular and those ending in 5 were second most popular. More than 80 percent of the retail prices ended in 9 or 5.[3]

Marketing people who use these prices apparently assume a jagged demand curve, as seen in Fig. 3-2. Such an assumption implies that buyers will buy less as prices are lowered until a *critical price* is reached. In the vicinity of this critical point, buyers would purchase greater quantities. The demand curve in Fig. 3-2 assumes an inverse relationship overall between price and quantity sold. For example, demand is greater at 99 cents than at $1.39. Yet, between prices of $1.04 and $1.09, demand increases slightly, perhaps due to the "psychological" impact of the $1.05 and then the $1.09. It should be pointed out that this is an implied assumption of the practice of setting prices at odd values, particularly those ending in either a 5 or a 9. There is no known research evidence indicating that this assumption is correct. In fact, the available evidence tends not to support the "magical numbers" belief.

Research by Schindler and Wiman[4] raises questions about the correctness of this hypothesis. In essence, they determined that consumers had greater difficulty remembering odd prices than even prices and had a tendency to underestimate actual odd prices. The fact that buyers have more difficulty remembering odd prices than even prices implies that the odd prices are not as noticeable. And if they are not as noticeable, it is less likely that they have an additional positive influence on demand. A consultant to the restaurant industry was asked about the use of odd pricing for restaurant menus. He replied that he had learned about odd pricing in his first marketing course, but that since he had been consulting to the restaurant industry,

[1]Eli Ginzberg, "Customary Prices," *American Economic Review,* 26 (June 1936), 296.
[2]Andre Gabor and Clive Granger, "Price Sensitivity of the Consumer," *Journal of Advertising Research,* 4 (December 1964), 40–44.
[3]Lawrence Friedman, "Psychological Pricing in the Food Industry," in Almarin Phillips and Oliver E. Williamson (eds.), *Prices: Issues in Theory, Practice, and Public Policy* (Philadelphia: University of Pennsylvania Press, 1967), pp. 187–201.
[4]Robert M. Schindler and Alan R. Wiman, "Consumer Recall of Odd and Even Prices," Working Paper 83-10, College of Business Administration, Northeastern University, Boston, 1983.

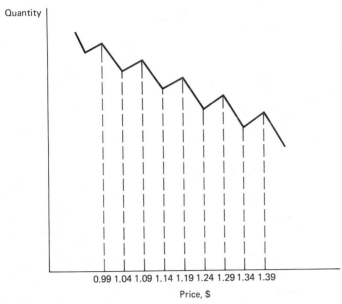

FIGURE 3-2
Assumed demand curve for odd pricing.

he did not believe that odd pricing had any real impact on the food sales of restaurants.

Moreover, additional research indicates that odd pricing seemingly communicates a low-price image *and a low-quality image.*[5] As will be developed in this chapter, this finding indicates that perceived price has *meaning,* or connotation, that is distinct from its objective meaning in terms of perceived monetary sacrifice. While a seller may wish to communicate a low-price image to the market, using an odd-pricing strategy may communicate that the products and services are also of low quality. Indeed, some department stores attempt to differentiate themselves from discount stores by pricing their merchandise with even numbers only, such as $1.50, $5.00, or $25.00. As depicted in Fig. 3-1, use of an odd-pricing approach may lead to a lower overall perception of value if customers infer a lower quality to products and services in stores that use odd prices.

Price lining controls the price of an entire inventory of a particular item. Merchandise is offered at a number of specific but limited prices, usually three. Once the lines are set, prices may be held constant over a period of time, and changes in market conditions are adapted to by adjusting the quality of the merchandise in each line. For example, a clothier may traditionally offer three lines of sportscoats priced at $150, $125, and $90.

---

[5]Robert M. Schindler and Thomas Kibarian, "Image Effects of Odd Pricing," Working Paper, Graduate School of Business, University of Chicago, Chicago, 1987.

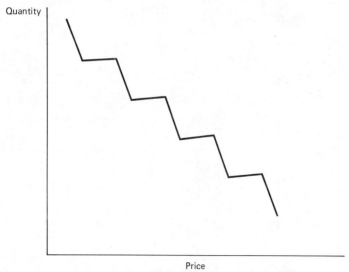

FIGURE 3-3
Assumed demand curve for price lining.

Such a retailer apparently assumes most people will pay between $150 and $90 for a sportscoat. Further, this price policy assumes that most people perceive prices for sportscoats between $90 and $125 as roughly equivalent. Hence, price cuts within this range would not increase the overall quantity sold. Figure 3-3 illustrates the demand curve assumed by the policy of price lining. The horizontal areas of the curve indicate the price ranges that are perceived by buyers as equivalent. (Such a perceptual phenomenon has been referred to by psychologists as stimuli being not noticeably different.)

Traditional pricing practices relying on critical prices or magical numbers have not been supported by the limited research available. However, retailers have found some pricing practices work better than others, thereby suggesting there are some buyer-perceptual phenomena underlying observed response patterns. However, as illustrated by recent research on odd–even pricing, the opportunity for making strategic pricing errors apparently is enhanced when the different roles that price plays in influencing buyers' perceptions and behavior are not recognized by the price setter.

Price Awareness and Price Consciousness

Do buyers search for the lowest priced alternatives and do they know the prices they pay? According to economic theory, the buyer is assumed to have perfect information concerning prices and to want satisfaction of comparable product alternatives. For example, buyers are assumed to know the prices they pay. Furthermore, it is assumed that buyers are price sensitive in that they will search for lower priced choices. The term *price awareness* refers to the ability of the buyer to remember prices, whereas *price consciousness* denotes the buyer's sensitivity toward price differentials.

A buyer is characterized as price conscious to the degree he or she is unwilling to pay a high price for a product and willing to refrain from buying a product whose price is unacceptably high. Moreover, the price-conscious shopper will not be willing to pay for distinguishing features of a product if the price difference for these features is too large. Conversely, a shopper who is relatively less price conscious may be willing to pay more for a product in a fashionable store or for a product whose features are appealing.

Until recently, very little evidence was available on the extent of buyers' price awareness. In general, price awareness has been assumed to be negatively correlated with income and other income-related factors like social status, household size, and marital status.[6] That is, shoppers with low incomes are more likely to be price conscious and, as a result, more price aware than shoppers with high incomes. However, only two studies have found a negative relationship between buyers' income and memory of prices paid.[7] Other research has not found a relationship between buyers' income, household size, marital status, or education and buyers' memory of prices paid.[8]

Although economic explanations of price consciousness and price awareness generally have not been successful, another study found that placing a price on each item (as opposed to using a shelf label) resulted in better exact price recall and that a structured list of unit prices helped shoppers estimate the relative expensiveness of brands within a product category.[9] The difficulty with these studies is that they do not consider how and why shoppers pay attention to price or how price information is stored in memory. Recently, several researchers have explored buyers' information processing to develop causal explanations of buyers' use of and memory for price information.[10] Their findings indicate that shoppers who attempt to process price information because of their concern about prices, their involvement with the

[6]Andre Gabor and Clive Granger, "On the Price Consciousness of Consumers," *Applied Statistics,* 10 (November 1961), 170–188; Peter R. Dickson and Alan G. Sawyer, "Point-of-Purchase Behavior and Price Perceptions of Supermarket Shoppers," Working Paper, Report No. 86-102, Marketing Science Institute, Cambridge, Mass., June 1986.

[7]F. E. Brown, "Who Perceives Supermarket Prices Most Validly?" *Journal of Marketing Research,* 8 (February 1971), 110–113; *Progressive Grocer,* "What Shoppers Know—and Don't Know About Prices," November 1974, pp. 39–41.

[8]Gabor and Granger, "On the Price Consciousness of Consumers," op. cit.; Valarie Zeithaml, "Consumer Response to In-Store Price Information Environments," *Journal of Consumer Research,* 8 (March 1982), 357–369; Dickson and Sawyer, op. cit.

[9]Zeithaml, ibid.

[10]Valarie A. Zeithaml, "Encoding of Price Information by Consumers: An Empirical Test of the Levels of Processing Framework," in K. Bernhardt, I. Dolich, M. Etzel, W. Kehoe, T. Kinnear, W. Perreault, Jr., and K. Roering, eds., *The Changing Marketing Environment: New Theories and Application* (Chicago: American Marketing Association, 1981), pp. 189–192; Christine P. Powell, "An Experimental Investigation of Recognition as a Measure of Price Awareness," Unpublished M.S. thesis, Department of Marketing, Virginia Polytechnic Institute and State University, Blacksburg, 1985; Tridib Mazumdar, "The Effects of Learning Intentions and Choice Task Orientations on Buyers' Knowledge of Price: An Experimental Investigation," Unpublished doctoral dissertation, Department of Marketing, Virginia Polytechnic Institute and State University, Blacksburg, 1987; James G. Helgeson and Sharon E. Beatty, "Price Expectation and Price Recall Error: An Empirical Study," *Journal of Consumer Research,* 14 (December 1987), 379–386.

product, or the amount of attention they give to the selection are more likely to remember the prices paid. However, many buyers do not make explicit attempts to remember prices of items purchased. Thus, the role of price information in influencing buyers' purchase decisions is considerably more complex than generally assumed in traditional thinking.

The Price–Perceived Quality Relationship

Based on the research evidence concerning buyers' price awareness and price consciousness, it is clear that buyers do not use price solely as a measure of cost (sacrifice). Buyers also use price as an indicator of product quality. Beginning with Leavitt's study,[11] a third area of research, mentioned in Chap. 2, has attempted to verify that buyers do perceive a positive price–quality relationship.

The early studies that investigated the price–perceived quality relationship considered situations in which the only differential information available to respondents was price. These studies found that perception of product quality was a function of price. Moreover, they found that buyers tend to prefer higher priced products when price is the only information available, when there is a belief that the quality of available brands differs significantly, and when the price differences between choices are large.[12]

A frequent criticism of these studies is that when price is the only information available, people naturally will relate product quality to price. Hence, later price–quality studies experimentally varied other cues in addition to price. The individual findings of multicue studies have been mixed, in that some studies observed positive price–perceived quality relationships whereas other studies did not find this relationship to be significant.[13] Although the statistical significance of the various efforts has been inconsistent, two comprehensive reviews of this research stream clearly indicate a positive price–perceived quality relationship exists. However, a number of limitations and issues of this research need to be addressed.[14]

Spurred in part by business concern with product and service quality as well as a recognition of the limitations of previous price–perceived quality research and conceptualizations, there has been a renewed interest in the price–perceived quality

---

[11]Harold J. Leavitt, "A Note on Some Experimental Findings About the Meaning of Price," *Journal of Business,* 27 (July 1954), 205–210.

[12]Kent B. Monroe, "Buyers' Subjective Perceptions of Price," *Journal of Marketing Research,* 10 (February 1973), 70–80.

[13]Ibid.

[14]Kent B. Monroe and William B. Dodds, "A Research Program for Establishing the Validity of the Price–Quality Relationship," *Journal of the Academy of Marketing Science,* 16 (Spring 1988), 151–168; Kent B. Monroe and R. Krishnan, "The Effect of Price on Subjective Product Evaluations," in Jacob Jacoby and Jerry Olson (eds.), *Perceived Quality: How Consumers View Stores and Merchandise* (Lexington, Mass.: Lexington Books, 1985), pp. 209–232; Akshay R. Rao and Kent B. Monroe, "The Effect of Price, Brand Name, and Store Name on Buyers' Perceptions of Product Quality: An Integrative Review," *Journal of Marketing Research,* 26 (August 1989), 351–357; Valarie A. Zeithaml, "Consumer Perceptions of Price, Quality, and Value: A Means–End Model and Synthesis of Evidence," *Journal of Marketing,* 52 (July 1988), 2–22.

relationship. Indeed, major business publications indicate that superior product and service quality can represent potent competitive advantages.[15] Moreover, it is recognized that customers' perceptions of quality, benefits, and value comprise the reality faced by business and service organizations.

Some recent conceptual developments relating price and perceived quality include addition of the external cues of store and brand name and two important moderating variables: perceived product and price *differences* and buyers' *familiarity* with the product or service.[16] Krishnan found that only when the perceived differences between prices or product attributes (intrinsic cues) were relatively large would significant differences in buyers' perceptions of quality occur.

Rao and Monroe showed that as buyers become familiar with a product they are more likely to use intrinsic cues rather than price or other external cues as indicators of product quality. However, highly familiar buyers (experts) use either price or intrinsic cues as indicators of quality, depending on whether their knowledge includes information about the reliability of price as a quality indicator. That is, if buyers know that there is a positive price–quality relationship in the product market, they will probably use price as a quality indicator. It has been argued further that if buyers know there is a weak price–quality relationship in the product market, they will be more likely to use intrinsic product cues to assess product quality. Thus, the strength of the use of price or other external cues, such as brand or store name, as indicators of product quality depends on the relative perceived differences between different cues and on the degree to which buyers know about the product and actual price–quality relationships.

Figure 3-4 shows these extensions to the initial model of Fig. 3-1. The reader will note that the basic notion of Fig. 3-1 that perceptions of quality are compared or traded off with perceived monetary sacrifice to form perceptions of value remains in the extended model. However, actual price has been replaced by perceived monetary price because evidence seems to indicate that buyers may translate the actual price into different perceptions of the price.[17] The variable, product familiarity, as discussed earlier, moderates buyers' use of price to infer product quality. The brand name and store name are represented as other extrinsic cues, i.e., cues or information that is not a part of the product or service per se. The bracketed variables related to the intrinsic cues of the reference product and the perception of monetary price will be clarified in the next section. At this point, what is being reflected in this part of the figure is that price judgments are compar-

[15]See "Top Management Takes Up the Challenge," *Business Week*, November 1, 1982, pp. 68–69.

[16]William B. Dodds, "An Experimental Investigation of the Effects of Price, Brand, and Store Information on the Subjective Evaluation of Products," Unpublished doctoral dissertation, Department of Marketing, Virginia Polytechnic Institute and State University, Blacksburg, 1985; R. Krishnan, "An Investigation of the Price–Perceived Quality Relationship," Unpublished doctoral dissertation, Department of Marketing, Virginia Polytechnic Institute and State University, Blacksburg, 1984; Akshay R. Rao and Kent B. Monroe, "The Moderating Effect of Prior Knowledge on Cue Utilization in Product Evaluations," *Journal of Consumer Research*, 15 (September 1988), 253–264.

[17]Jacob Jacoby and Jerry Olson, "Consumer Response to Price: Attitudinal, Information Processing Perspective," in Yoram Wind and Marshall Greenberg (eds.), *Moving Ahead with Attitude Research* (Chicago: American Marketing Association, 1977), pp. 73–86.

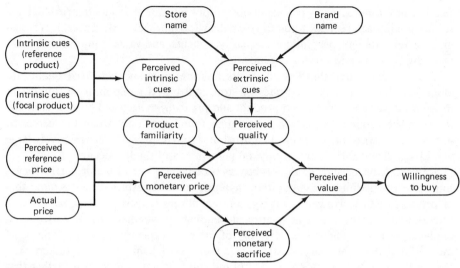

FIGURE 3-4
Second model: price, perceived quality, perceived value, and willingness to buy.

ative in nature. That is, a price is judged as acceptable or not in reference to another price, whether that price is in the buyer's memory or externally available in an advertisement or is the price of another product or brand. In Chap. 4 we will return to this discussion when the relationship between price and perceived value is developed more fully. However, we need to consider some additional concepts from price behavioral research that have important implications for price management and for amplifying the idea of how prices influence customers' perceptions of value. In the next section, we will discuss some major pricing errors that are made when decision makers ignore buyers' perceptions that do not relate directly to monetary price.

Summary

In the formulation of Eq. (3-1) and Figs. 3-1 and 3-4, it is indicated that price has both attracting and repelling attributes. When price is used as an indicator of cost or sacrifice, increasing price has the effect of reducing demand for the product or service. However, if price is used as an indicator of quality or benefits, increasing price has the effect of increasing demand. Moreover, available research evidence indicates that buyers generally are not able to assess perfectly product or service quality (the ability of the product to provide satisfaction). Rather, *perceived quality* is the relevant variable. Perceptions of value are directly related to buyers' preferences or choices. Perceived value represents a tradeoff between buyers' perceptions of quality and sacrifice and is positive when perceptions of quality are greater than the perceptions of sacrifice.

MAJOR PRICING ERRORS

In this section, we continue to develop important information about how people perceive prices and price differences. We highlight the second prescription for becoming a proactive pricer: *it is essential to understand how customers perceive prices, price changes, and price differences.* Initially, the concepts of price thresholds will be developed and two major pricing errors will be illustrated. Then the concept of reference price will be presented and a third major pricing error will be illustrated. Underlying the entire discussion is the key pricing principle: *prices should be set to reflect customers' perceptions of value.* This section will also present behavioral research evidence that provides information on how to overcome these errors.

Absolute Versus Relative Price

A recent experience of a major snack food producer illustrates the *error of not recognizing the difference between absolute price and relative price.* Several years ago, the price of a specific size of this brand's potato chips was $1.39 while a comparable size of the local brand was $1.09, a difference of 30 cents. Over a period of time, the price of the national brand increased several times until it was being retailed at $1.69. In like manner, the local brand's price increased to $1.39. However, while the local brand was maintaining a 30-cent price differential, the national brand obtained a significant gain in market share. The problem was buyers perceived a 30-cent price difference relative to $1.69 as less than a 30-cent price difference relative to $1.39. This example illustrates the notion of *differential price thresholds,* or the degree to which buyers are sensitive to relative price differences. After briefly reviewing two other common pricing errors, we will discuss the effect of price thresholds on perceptions of price and the implications these perceptions have for pricing management.

Perceived Value Versus Price

Michael P. Redington, marketing group manager, Frito-Lay Inc., tells of a local tortilla chip producer in the Phoenix market that did not understand the relationship between price and perceived value.[18] The local tortilla chip enjoyed a competitive advantage until Frito-Lay upgraded its Tostitos chip. Instead of raising its monetary price to continue to reflect a perceived quality–value relationship similar to Tostitos, the local producer reduced its quality and maintained the original monetary price. Customers soon recognized that the local chip was now an inferior product, and they shifted their purchases to Frito-Lay. The local producer did not understand that there are limits or absolute thresholds to the relationship between price and perceived quality and perceived value. The local company further failed to recognize the important link between perceptions of quality and perceptions of value.

---

[18]"Panelists Offer Pricing Strategy Advice for Consumer and Industrial Products," *Marketing News,* February 1, 1985, pp. 1, 10–11.

Pricing Strategy Versus Pricing Tactics

In the past few years, evidence has emerged confirming the existence of a reference price serving as an anchor for price judgments. It has been suggested that price does not serve as an indicator of product or service quality unless there is a perceptible difference in price from the buyer's reference price. In judging prices buyers may use as a reference point the range of prices last paid, the current or perceived average market price, a perceived fair price, or an expected price.

The concept of reference prices confirms the important point that buyers judge or evaluate prices comparatively. That is, to judge whether a price is acceptable, too high, or too low, a buyer compares it to another price, the buyer's *reference price* for that particular judgment. Not recognizing this key point has led to a third pricing error: *not distinguishing between pricing strategies and pricing tactics.*

When considering how buyers perceive prices, bear in mind that perception is relative. That is, a specific price is compared to another price or to a reference price. Firm X, for example, was introducing a new product with a low introductory price of $1.49, although the product was targeted to sell at a price of about $1.75. Later, when it was time to remove the introductory price, the regular price was set at $2.00 to cover increased manufacturing costs. The product failed to sustain sufficient sales volume to warrant its continued existence. The error in this situation was the pricing tactic of a too-low introductory price, which established a *baseline or reference price* of $1.49 rather than $1.75. Hence, the $2.00 price, when compared to $1.49, was perceived to be too expensive and buyers stopped buying.

When sellers advertise both the offered price and a (higher) comparative regular price, they are attempting to impose a reference price for consumers' comparisons. To convince consumers to accept the higher price as a reference price, the sellers may include such words as "formerly," "regularly," or "usually" to describe the higher price. Words can be used in a variety of ways to enhance consumers' perceptions that a sale is taking place and that the offer represents a savings to consumers. Since prices are evaluated comparatively, the judgment of acceptability depends not only on consumers' price expectations, but also on information provided in promotions or advertisements.

When we return to the issue of the relationship between price and perceived value in Chap. 4, some important evidence on the strategic use of reference prices will be presented. We now turn to behavioral research evidence on price thresholds and then on reference prices.

Price Thresholds

The first two errors discussed indicated that there are absolute limits or thresholds to how buyers perceive prices. Further, it was suggested that it is perceived relative differences between prices that influence buyers' sensitivity to prices, price changes, and price differences. In this section, the psychological basis for these points will be summarized and evidence from price research will be offered. We focus on determining why these major errors in pricing seem to exist.

It has been established that humans have upper and lower limits of responsiveness to physical stimuli such as sound and light. For example, those of us who have taken hearing tests are aware that some sounds are either too low or too high for us to hear. The low and high sounds that we can just barely hear are called our lower and upper *absolute* hearing *thresholds*. Much of the interest in thresholds originates in Weber's law, which suggests that small, equally perceptible changes in a response correspond to proportional changes in the stimulus.

$$\frac{\Delta S}{S} = K \qquad (3\text{-}2)$$

where S = magnitude of the stimulus
$\quad \Delta S$ = change in S corresponding to a defined change in response
$\quad K$ = constant

Weber's law applies to the perception of changes in a stimulus, i.e., *to perceived differences between two intensities of a stimulus*. For example, Weber's law suggests that if a product's price being raised from $10 to $12 is sufficient to deter us from buying the product, then another product originally priced at $20 would have to be repriced at $24 before we would become similarly uninterested. That is,

$$\frac{\$2}{\$10} = \frac{\$4}{\$20} = 0.20 = K \qquad (3\text{-}3)$$

(This example assumes that noticing a price increase is sufficient to change purchasing behavior. As pointed out later, in our discussion on price elasticity, this connection between perceived price change and willingness to buy is more complex than the simple assumption made here to illustrate the concept.)

Later, Fechner reformulated Weber's law and derived what is now known as the Weber–Fechner law.

$$R = k \log S + a \qquad (3\text{-}4)$$

where R = magnitude of response
$\quad S$ = magnitude of stimulus
$\quad k, a$ = constants

These two laws provide the basis for discussing the behavioral issues underlying two errors: (1) not recognizing the relationship between perceived value and price, and (2) not distinguishing between absolute price and relative price.

Absolute Price Thresholds   The importance of the Weber–Fechner law to pricing is that it provides an expression relating a price (stimulus) and a response. In particular, the Weber–Fechner law advances the notion that a buyer has a lower and upper price threshold, which implies that a buyer has a *range of acceptable prices* for a purchase. Furthermore, the existence of a lower price threshold implies that there are positive prices greater than $0 which are unacceptable because they are considered to be too low, perhaps because buyers are suspicious of the product's quality. Practically, this concept means that buyers have upper and lower price limits for their considered purchases. Rather than one acceptable price for a product or service, there is some range of acceptable prices.

Research conducted in Europe and the United States using a variety of methods has consistently confirmed the existence of a range of prices buyers are willing to pay.[19] As expected, the research has also determined that the acceptable price range for a product shifts downward as buyers' income declines. Moreover, as income falls, the upper price threshold drops less than the lower price threshold, implying that a low price is a more powerful deterrent to higher income groups than is a high price to lower income groups. It should also be recognized that these price limits are not constant but shift as buyers obtain more information about the actual price range in the market or about the range of prices in a specific product line.[20]

Thus, people apparently refrain from purchasing a product not only when the price is considered to be too high, but also when the price is considered to be too low. It may be that people suspect the quality of a product if its price is too much below what they consider to be an acceptable price. This phenomenon of refusing to buy if the price is too low is not considered in the economic theory of consumer behavior we reviewed in Chap. 2.

Also, at a given time there can be an unexplained psychological barrier to price changes—an apparent reluctance to pay more than a certain amount. The candy bar example in Chap. 1 illustrates this point. People initially were not willing to pay more than $1.00 for a multiple pack of candy bars. However, they eventually adapted to paying more than $1.00, and prices now reflect this acceptance. During the mid-1980s, cereral manufacturers found consumer resistance to paying more than $2.00 for a box of dry cereal. As with the candy example, consumers adapted, and we now find dry cereal priced for more than $2.00 a box. When IBM introduced its PC-jr personal computer, it was priced at about $1,200. In the first nine months, approximately 70,000 units were sold. Price was then reduced to under $900 and 200,000 units were sold in the next three months, primarily to the household market. At that time, there was an apparent reluctance of consumers to pay more than $1,000 for a home personal computer.

The acceptable price range concept is useful in understanding why buyers perceive that price is an indicator of quality. Particularly, when buyers perceive that prices are relatively lower than they expect, they may become suspicious of the

---

[19]Kent B. Monroe and Susan M. Petroshius, "Buyers' Subjective Perceptions of Price: An Update of the Evidence," in Harold H. Kassarjian and Thomas S. Robertson (eds.), *Perspectives in Consumer Behavior,* 3rd ed. (Glenview, Ill.: Scott, Foresman, 1981), pp. 43–55.

[20]Anthony D. Cox, "New Evidence Concerning Consumer Price Limits," in Richard J. Lutz (ed.), *Advances in Consumer Research,* Vol. 13 (Provo, Utah: Association for Consumer Research, 1986), pp. 268–271.

product's quality. At such low prices, this low perceived quality may be posited to provide less satisfaction than the perceived sacrifice of the low price. Hence, the mental tradeoff illustrated in Fig. 3-1 may lead to a negative perceived value. Further, similar to the findings about using odd pricing, an unacceptable low price may actually reduce perceived value for the buyer. At the other extreme, a perceived high price may lead to a perception of sacrifice that is greater than the perceived quality, also leading to a reduction in buyers' perceptions of value. Thus, it is important for price setters not only to consider the relationships among price, perceived quality, and perceived value, but to recognize that there are limits to these relationships.

Differential Price Thresholds   Usually a buyer has alternative choices available for a contemplated purchase and selects from among these choices. The prices of these alternative choices may provide cues (or information) that facilitate the decision process. However, even if the numerical prices are different, it cannot be assumed that the prices are *perceived* to be different. Hence, the problem becomes one of determining the effect of *perceived price differences* on buyer choice.

Weber's law has often been cited as the basis for inferences concerning perceived price differences. As Weber's law would indicate, it has been suggested that the perception of a price change depends on the magnitude of the change. It has also been discovered that people are more sensitive to price increases than to decreases.[21] Moreover, the value of K in Eq. (3-2) varies for different products.[22] The immediate implication is that buyers will be more sensitive to price changes for some products, i.e., have lower differential price thresholds. In other words, for some products, a price change may not be perceived, thereby suggesting that these products have a relatively high K value.

As the tortilla chips example illustrates, relative price is a more important concept than absolute price. As developed in Chap. 2, the concept of price elasticity (either own-price or cross-price elasticity) indicates how buyers perceive a price relative to another price, whether that price be the previous price paid, the price of the leading competitive offering, the highest or lowest price in the product line, or the expected price to pay. In particular, price elasticity of demand, E_d, indicates the sensitivity of buyers to a price change for a particular product. Thus, if buyers *perceive* that the product's price is different from the last time they purchased it, then the issue is whether this perceived price difference makes a difference in their purchasing behavior. For example, a price reduction from $1.30 to $1.25 may not be sufficient to induce buyers to buy more of the product, whereas a price reduction to $1.15 might lead to an increase in demand. It should also be understood that buyers must be able to remember the previous price before they can perceive a price change;

[21]Joseph U. Uhl, "Consumer Perception of Retail Food Price Changes," paper presented at Association for Consumer Research Conference, Amherst, Mass., August 1970.

[22]Peter Cooper, "Subjective Economics: Factors in Psychology of Spending" and "The Begrudging Index and the Subjective Value of Money," in Bernard Taylor and Gordon Wills (eds.), *Pricing Strategy* (Princeton, N.J.: Brandon/Systems, 1970), pp. 112–131.

research reported earlier in this chapter suggests that they do not always remember prices of the products purchased.

From behavioral price research, several important points about price elasticity have emerged. First, buyers, in general, are more sensitive to perceived price increases than to perceived price decreases. Not only is this result consistent with some recent behavioral research on how people perceive gains and losses, but it is also consistent with earlier research on how buyers adapt to price changes. In practical terms, this difference in relative price elasticity between price increases and price decreases means it is easier to lose sales by increasing price than it is to gain sales by reducing price. (Later, when we introduce costs into the analysis in Chap. 8, this relative difference in elasticities becomes important in terms of determining the profitability of price changes.)

Research also confirms that price elasticity of demand varies over brands within the same product category. In one product category, elasticity varied from -0.84 to a -4.56.[23] Price elasticity also varies over market segments but seems to be independent of market share.[24] However, price elasticity is not independent of the relative price level. The further a brand's price is from the product category's average price, in either direction, the lower will be its price elasticity. Figure 3-5 illustrates this point for ice cream. What is illustrated in Fig. 3-5 is that although ice cream might be considered a commodity, in actuality there are several price–market segments, that is, there are groups of buyers (market segments) willing to pay very different prices for ice cream. Further, these brands of ice cream can be distinguished on the basis of perceived quality as well as price (cents per 4-ounce serving). Also, each price–market segment can be described by a distribution of unit sales against price, which resembles a normal frequency distribution.

Consider the high-price–excellent-quality market segment. The high-price brands Häagen-Dazs and Frusen Glädjé are at the high end of this price segment while Howard Johnson's is at the lower end, but closer to the prices of Breyers and Sealtest. The demand for Häagen-Dazs and Frusen Glädjé, despite their being high-priced brands, is relatively inelastic. Indeed, "it's the quality and the name. People don't care what it costs."[25] These two brands are at the high extreme end of the price distribution for ice cream, and if either brand decided to compete by reducing price, it would find that its demand would become more price elastic as the price moved toward the average price in the high-price category. Moreover, when brands like Häagen-Dazs and Frusen Glädjé entered the market priced above the then high-priced ice cream, Baskin Robbins, they in effect moved Baskin Robbins toward the overall category average price, making demand for Baskin Robbins more price sensitive, and took command of the high-price segment.

Earlier, Kraft Inc. had successfully positioned Breyers as a higher priced brand than its other brand, Sealtest, and, as demonstrated in Fig. 3-5, separated them in

[23]William T. Moran, "Insights from Pricing Research," in Earl L. Bailey (ed.), *Pricing Practices and Strategies* (New York: The Conference Board, 1978), pp. 7–13.
[24]Ibid.
[25]See "Pricey Ice Cream Is Scooping the Market," *Business Week,* June 30, 1986, pp. 60–61.

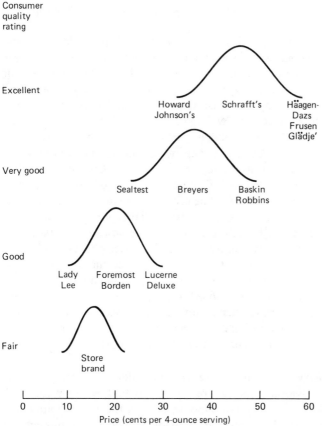

FIGURE 3-5
Price–market segments—ice cream. (Adapted and reprinted by
permission from *Harvard Business Review.* An exhibit from Elliott
B. Ross, "Making Money with Proactive Pricing," *Harvard Business
Review,* 62 (November–December 1984), 149; copyright © 1984
by the President and Fellows of Harvard College; all rights
reserved.)

terms of price as well as appeal.[26] Thus, if a brand's price is already at the extreme
end of the market's price range, then a more substantial price change will be needed
to produce a perceived price change. And extreme prices, high or low, will become
more price elastic as the prices are changed toward the market average or as
competitors' pricing moves the brand's price toward the market average. Finally, as
these points illustrate, the substitution effect described in Chap. 2 is generally a more
important determinant of a brand's price elasticity than is the income effect. Hence,

[26]Samuel R. Gardner, "Successful Market Positioning—One Company Example," in Earl L. Bailey
(ed.), *Product-Line Strategies* (New York: The Conference Board, 1982), pp. 40–43.

the perceived price difference between perceived similar offerings is a key aspect of a brand's price positioning.

Besides these important characteristics affecting a product's price elasticity, several other points should be considered. Sometimes a product may provide a *unique benefit* or have a *unique attribute* that buyers value. These unique benefits or attributes serve to make the product less price sensitive. *How the product is used and the context in which it is used* may influence its price sensitivity. In one research study, it was determined that buyers were willing to pay significantly more for a pair of pants to be worn to a symphony or cocktail party than if the pants were to be worn at a football game or rock concert.[27] The *relative dollar magnitude of the purchase* may influence buyers' sensitivity to price differences. Consumers tend to be more price sensitive on their "big-ticket" purchases than on routine grocery purchases. Similarly, industrial firms may not be very sensitive to the price of routine supplies but may be highly sensitive to a raw material that represents a significant portion of their production costs. Finally, the *frequency of past price changes* can influence buyers' sensitivity to price changes. If prices have been changing relatively frequently, buyers may not have adjusted to the previous price change when a new change occurs. This phenomenon is most likely to occur when inflationary pressures lead to frequent price increases. As is developed in the next section, if buyers have not adjusted to the last price increase, then another price increase will be perceived as a larger increase than it actually is, making them more sensitive to the increase. This point raises the concept of reference prices, discussed next.

Adaptation-Level Theory   Various researchers have suggested that price perception and therefore behavioral response are relative to the present price level, actual or perceived. This price perception hypothesis has a theoretical foundation in *adaptation-level theory,* which suggests an individual's behavior represents an adaptation to three classes of stimuli or cues: focal, contextual, and organic.[28] In price perception, immediate interest falls on the focal and contextual cues. *Focal cues* are the stimuli the individual is directly responding to. *Contextual,* or *background, cues* are all other behaviorally based stimuli. *Organic cues* refer to the inner physiological and psychological processes affecting behavior. In this perspective, comparative purchase offers, including price, are the focal stimuli; available resources, purpose of purchase, and store environment are the contextual stimuli. In a pricing context, adaptation-level theory suggests that price perception depends on the actual price and the individual's reference price or adaptation level (AL).

The concept of adaptation level or reference price supports the important point that buyers judge or evaluate prices comparatively. That is, the acceptability of a price is judged by comparison to another price. The comparative price is the buyer's reference price for that particular judgment. Failure to recognize this key point has

---

[27]Kent B. Monroe, Albert J. Della Bitta, and Susan L. Downey, "Contextual Influences on Subjective Price Perceptions," *Journal of Business Research,* 5 (December 1977), 277–291.

[28]Harry Helson, *Adaptation-Level Theory* (New York: Harper & Row, 1964).

led to the third pricing error introduced earlier: not distinguishing between pricing strategies and pricing tactics. Some specific examples of these errors will be discussed shortly.

In the past few years, evidence has emerged confirming the existence of a reference price serving as an AL for price judgments.[29] It has been suggested that price will not serve as an indicator of product quality unless there is a perceptible difference in price from the buyer's reference price. For example, in the mustard example at the beginning of this chapter, the original price, 49 cents, was not perceptually different from the price of other brands.

Some important implications of adaptation-level theory on price perception are[30]

1 Price perceptions are relative to other prices and to the product's use.

2 There is a reference price for each discernible quality level for each product category and this price influences judgments of other prices.

3 There is a region of indifference about a reference price such that changes in price within this region produce no change in perception.

4 The reference price may be some average of the range of prices for similar products and need not correspond to any actual price or the price of the leading brand.

5 Buyers do not judge each price singly; rather, each price is compared with the reference price and the other prices in the price range.

Assimilation-Contrast Effects   Several pricing studies have suggested that the prevailing range of prices for a product category affects the buyer's reference price for that category.[31] Since the magnitude of the price range is affected by the lowest and highest price (end prices) in the range, we would expect that these two end prices also affect price judgments. That is, we have isolated three different price cues as affecting price judgment: the reference price, the lowest price, and the highest price. Prices used by individuals to make perceptual judgments about other prices (AL, end prices) are called *anchoring stimuli*. By *price judgment* we mean the individual's assessment of whether a price is too low, just right (acceptable), or too high. And, as indicated previously, buyers compare each price to the reference (anchor) prices and to the other prices in the range. Hence, the research and managerial question is: What happens when these reference or anchor prices change?

When a new price is introduced at or near the end (high or low) of a current series of acceptable prices (price range), the buyer's judgment is displaced (moves) toward this new price and a new reference price is *assimilated* into the price range; the buyer will then consider the new product as a reasonable substitute for the present product.

[29]Monroe, op. cit.

[30]Fred E. Emory, "Some Psychological Aspects of Price," in Bernard Taylor and Gordon Wills (eds.), *Pricing Strategy* (Princeton, N.J.: Brandon/Systems, 1970), pp. 98–111.

[31]Kent B. Monroe, "Objective and Subjective Contextual Influences on Price Perceptions," in P. D. Bennett, J. N. Sheth, and A. G. Woodside (eds.), *Consumer and Industrial Buying Behavior* (New York: Elsevier–North Holland, 1977), pp. 287–296.

However, when this new price is too remote (outside) from the current price range, the price may be perceived as belonging to another product-price category—the *contrast effect.*

In Chap. 4, we will develop the application of reference prices to comparative price promotions. At this point, the concepts of adaptation-level or reference price and assimilation-contrast effects will be discussed and applied in more detail. We now consider some managerial implications of the multidimensional nature of price perceptions.

IMPLICATIONS FOR PRICING STRATEGIES AND TACTICS

Although the theoretical concepts and research findings reviewed generally apply to consumer marketing, the experiences of some industrial marketing firms affirm that industrial buyers frequently perceive prices similarly. For example, a purchaser of water pipes for a community in Iowa considered the highest priced pipes as the best pipes—"the Cadillac of the industry." But beyond the applicability of these findings and concepts to different markets, there are some important implications for distinguishing between pricing strategies and tactics (the third error described earlier in this chapter).

Product-Line Pricing

In product-line pricing, the evidence suggests that the lowest and highest prices in the product line are more noticeable than those between and hence *anchor* buyers' judgments. These end prices, along with the reference price, may accentuate the perceived value for a given product (a bargain) or may diminish the perceived value (too expensive), depending on where the product's price lies in the product line. These same phenomena may occur when a single product is compared with a number of competitive products. Further, if either or both end prices are outside the acceptable price range, a contrast effect may develop, and the products would be evaluated within a different context. The implications of this phenomenon are discussed in more detail in Chap. 13.

The perception of a sale price may depend on the position of the price in the price range. If the sale price is below other offerings, buyers may perceive a bargain (assimilation effect), or buyers may not believe that the sale price is a reduction from the advertised original price (contrasting effect). For example, buyers might react more favorably if a $600 television set were on sale for $450 than if this set were advertised as being on sale at $299. We explore the implications of this situation in Chaps. 4 and 14.

If the price range is narrowed by shifting the end prices toward the middle of the range, or if there is little variation in prices, price becomes less dominant in purchase decisions. One reason for this result is that buyers will have greater difficulty discriminating among alternative choices leading to assimilation effects (no perceived price differences). Where there are few price differences, buyers tend to base their choices on other factors, such as brand names.[32]

Order of Presenting Prices

The order in which buyers are exposed to alternative prices affects their perceptions. Buyers who are exposed initially to high prices will perceive subsequent lower prices as less expensive than they would if they were initially exposed to low prices.[33] Figure 3-6 illustrates the results from research testing the effect of the order of price presentation on buyers' judgments of the relative expensiveness of alternative prices. In the *descending price series,* people were asked to evaluate the prices for a product beginning with $23 and going successively to lower prices (i.e., $22, $21, . . . , $11, $10). In the *ascending price series,* people were asked to evaluate the prices for the same product beginning with $7 and going successively to higher prices (i.e., $8, $9, . . . , $19, $20).

The common prices ($10–$20) were judged to be significantly more expensive by the people evaluating them in the increasing order of magnitude, i.e., the ascending price series, than by the people judging these same prices in the decreasing order of

---

[32]Kent B. Monroe, "The Influence of Price Differences and Brand Familiarity on Brand Preferences," *Journal of Consumer Research,* 3 (June 1976), 42–49.
[33]Albert J. Della Bitta and Kent B. Monroe, "The Influence of Adaptation Levels on Subjective Price Perceptions," in S. Ward and P. Wright (eds.), *Advances in Consumer Research* Vol. 1 (Boston: Association for Consumer Research, 1974), pp. 359–369.

FIGURE 3-6
Effect of order of presentation on price perceptions.

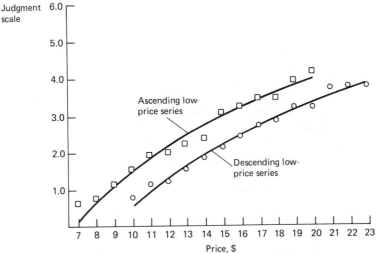

magnitude, i.e., the descending series. When a reference or adaptation-level price is higher than the price being judged, the perceptual phenomenon of contrast makes the lower price appear less than it is. Similarly, when the reference price is lower than the price being judged, this contrast effect makes the price being judged appear to be more than it is. This perceptual effect helps explain why people are generally more sensitive to price increases than to price decreases. However, there is more to the explanation of why behavioral research helps explain this relative difference in buyers' sensitivities to price changes. We will develop this explanation in Chap. 4.

New-Product Pricing Strategy

It has been common for sellers to introduce new products with short-term introductory low-price promotions. One of the objectives of this pricing tactic is to induce people to try the product to facilitate market penetration. However, evidence indicates that this tactic of introducing a new product to the market using a short-term introductory low sale price produces lower long-run sales volume than if the product is introduced at its regular price.[34] Figure 3-7 and Table 3-1 illustrate this research result. In this research, a new brand was introduced at a low introductory price in

[34]Anthony Doob, J. Merrill Carlsmith, Jonathan L. Freedman, Thomas K. Landauer, and Tom Soleng, "Effect of Initial Selling Price on Subsequent Sales," *Journal of Personality and Social Psychology,* 11 (1969), 345–350.

FIGURE 3-7
Sales effect of an introductory low price.

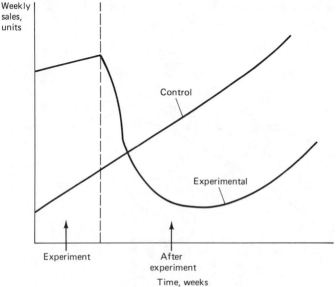

one set of stores and at the normal selling price in a matched set of stores. After a short period of time the low introductory price was raised to the normal selling price and sales were monitored in both sets of stores during the entire period.

The results of these experiments are summarized in Table 3-1. In all five experiments the results are similar. The introductory low price produced more sales than in the control condition, but after the low price was raised to the normal selling price, sales were greater in the control condition. Although one might hastily conclude that the sales results in the experimental condition simply reflect a downward-sloping demand curve, the time-series pattern of sales in the study belies this simple explanation. Whereas the control sales curve exhibits a steady growth in sales, the experimental sales curve drops and remains below the control sales curve after the prices are changed.

The implication is that the tactic of using an introductory low price to generate short-term sales actually may hinder the development of a favorable long-term sales pattern. "When mouthwash is put on sale at $.25 customers . . . may tend to think of the product in terms of $.25. . . . When, in subsequent weeks, the price increases to $.39, these customers will tend to see it as overpriced, and are not inclined to buy it at this much higher price."[35] That is, the introductory low price serves as a reference price for evaluating a perceived price increase when the price is raised to

[35]Ibid.

TABLE 3-1
EFFECT OF INITIAL SELLING PRICE ON SUBSEQUENT SALES

Product	Experimental Condition	Price, $	Length of Treatment, Weeks	Average Weekly Sales, Units*	
				During Experimental Price	After Experimental Price
Mouthwash	Experimental	0.25	1½	300	365
	Control	0.39	5	270	375
Toothpaste	Experimental	0.41	3	1,280	1,010
	Control	0.49	8	860	1,050
Aluminum foil	Experimental	0.59	3	4,110	3,275
	Control	0.64	8	2,950	3,395
Light bulbs	Experimental	0.26	1	7,350	5,270
	Control	0.32	4	5,100	5,285
Cookies	Experimental	0.24	2	21,925	22,590
	Control	0.29	6	21,725	23,225

*Not reported directly but estimated from graphical presentation of the data in Anthony Doob, J. Merrill Carlsmith, Jonathan L. Freedman, Thomas K. Landauer, and Tom Soleng, "Effect of Initial Selling Price on Subsequent Sales," *Journal of Personality and Social Psychology,* 11 (1969), 345–350.

its normal price. And the contrast effect accentuates the price increase and makes it appear even greater than it is. Moreover, as mentioned earlier, people are more sensitive to perceived price increases. In another area, magazines find it particularly difficult to trade subscribers up to regular subscription rates if the first subscription term is bought at a discount price. Clearly, buyers' reactions to reduced prices are more favorable than to increased prices. In Chap. 4, we will introduce ways to communicate an introductory low-price price strategy so as to minimize these negative effects that result from price perception. What is important to understand now is that buyers perceive and evaluate prices in very complex ways. Further, pricing decisions based on recognition of these price perceptions often are quite different from those that rely on traditional economic theory.

SUMMARY

Perception basically involves the process of categorization. That is, we tend to place new experiences into existing classifications of familiar experiences. Thus, when buyers are confronted by a price different from what they believe they had previously paid, they must decide whether the difference between the new and old prices is significant to them. If the price difference is insignificant, they may classify the two prices as similar and act as they have in the past. However, if the price difference is perceived as significant, they may classify the new price in a new price product category and change their purchase behavior.

During this process of categorization buyers make heavy use of cues or clues. Some of these cues are price cues, which influence buyers' judgments of whether the price differences are significant. The review of some of the behavioral phenomena underlying this perceptual process has perhaps raised more questions than we currently can answer. However, as buyers we can become more sensitive to the way price can influence our judgments about products that we are considering buying. At the same time, *the price setter must be concerned with identifying the cues used by buyers, so that he or she can act to secure accurate perceptions of the offering.* As we saw in this chapter, ignoring the way buyers perceive prices can lead to major pricing errors. Further, placing primary emphasis on the cost aspects of setting prices likely will enhance the kind of errors illustrated in this chapter.

Finally, the predominant use and misuse of large discounts by retailers may have several undesirable results. Buyers may learn that the "true" or "usual" price is not the advertised regular price but the sale price, and they then may develop their price perceptions and value judgments using the lower sale price. Another problem arises when retailers use fictitious "regular" prices to enhance buyers' value perceptions and thereby deceive buyers. Such practices inevitably will lead to public policy regulating these deceptive practices. These issues are discussed in Chaps. 4 and 14.

DISCUSSION QUESTIONS

1 a Listed below are two sets of prices. Without calculating the differences, which pair of prices, set A or set B, *appears* to be further apart?

A		B	
$83	$67	$87	$71

b In the next set of prices, which pair of prices, set A or set B, *appears* to be most different?

A		B	
$79	$93	$75	$89

c If you followed the directions and did not calculate the differences, what strategies or rules did you use?

2 a Listed below are three sets of prices. Without performing any calculations, which set of prices *appears* to have the highest average?

A				B				C			
$87	$81	$75	$69	$89	$79	$73	$71	$84	$81	$75	$72

b Which set of prices *appears* to have the lowest average?

c What strategies or rules did you use to make your judgments?

3 In Chap. 1, the pricing problem of two candy companies was considered. Assume you are the price administrator for the second company. As you consider how to change the price of your multipack candy from five for 89 cents, are there any behavioral implications of your alternative strategies? (Refer to your answer to Discussion Question 3 of Chap. 1.) In what way do you think the concept of a reference price (AL) applies to this decision problem?

4 a Assume you are interested in purchasing a pair of slacks to wear to a football game or a rock concert. In a store, you find five different pairs that are acceptable in terms of style, fit, fabric, and color. The prices of these pants are $7, $9, $15, $21, and $29. Which price do you find most acceptable? Why? Are any prices unacceptable? Why?

b Suppose the prices were $17, $19, $25, $31, and $39. Which price do you find most acceptable? Why? Are any prices unacceptable? Why?

c Assume the purpose of your purchase is to buy a pair of pants to wear to church, a cocktail party, or a symphony. Would your answer to part a change? Why? Would your answer to part b change? Why?

SUGGESTED READINGS

Doob, Anthony, J. Merrill Carlsmith, Jonathan L. Freedman, Thomas K. Landauer, and Tom Soleng: "Effects of Initial Selling Price on Subsequent Sales," *Journal of Personality and Social Psychology,* 11 (1969), 345–350.

Jacoby, Jacob, and Jerry Olson: "Consumer Response to Price: Attitudinal, Information Processing Perspective," in Yoram Wind and Marshall Greenberg (eds.), *Moving Ahead with Attitude Research* (Chicago: American Marketing Association, 1977), pp. 73–86.

Monroe, Kent B., and R. Krishnan: "The Effect of Price on Subjective Product Evaluations," in Jacob Jacoby and Jerry Olson (eds.), *Perceived Quality: How Consumers View Stores and Merchandise* (Lexington, Mass.: Lexington Books, 1985), pp. 209–232.

Monroe, Kent B., and Susan M. Petroshius: "Buyers' Subjective Perceptions of Price: An Update of the Evidence," in Harold H. Kassarjian and Thomas S. Robertson (eds.), *Perspectives in Consumer Behavior,* 3rd ed. (Glenview, Ill.: Scott, Foresman, 1981), pp. 43–55.

Moran, William T.: "Insights from Pricing Research," in Earl L. Bailey (ed.), *Pricing Practices and Strategies* (New York: The Conference Board, 1978), pp. 7–13.

Olson, Jerry: "Price as an Informational Cue: Effects on Product Evaluations," in A. G. Woodside, J. N. Sheth, and P. D. Bennett (eds.), *Consumer and Industrial Buying Behavior* (New York: Elsevier–North Holland, 1977), pp. 267–286.

Rao, Akshay R., and Kent B. Monroe: "The Moderating Effect of Prior Knowledge on Cue Utilization in Product Evaluations," *Journal of Consumer Research,* 15 (September 1988), 253–264.

Zeithaml, Valarie A.: "Consumers Perceptions of Price, Quality, and Value: A Means–End Model and Synthesis of Evidence," *Journal of Marketing,* 52 (July 1988), 2–22.

CHAPTER 4

PRICE AND CUSTOMERS' PERCEPTIONS OF VALUE

As indicated in Chap. 3, recent behavioral research has yielded additional explanations of how people form value judgments and make decisions when they do not have perfect information about alternatives. These new developments further our understanding of why buyers are more sensitive to price increases than to price decreases and how they respond to comparative price advertisements (e.g., regular price $65, sale price $49), coupons, rebates, and other special price promotions. The common element in these explanations is that buyers judge prices comparatively, i.e., a reference price anchors their judgments. A reference price may be an external price in an advertisement or the shelf price of another product; it may also be an internal price the buyer remembers from the last time a similar purchase was made, an expected price, or some belief about the price of a product in the same market area. As the argument is developed in this chapter, it is important to understand that eventually the external reference prices must be internalized in some way if they are going to affect the buyer's decision.

Underlying the development of the points in this chapter is the recognition that people seldom are good information processors and that they often take shortcuts. These shortcuts may lead to errors in judgment and choice, but they may also facilitate the choice process. For example, as we discovered in Chap. 3, buyers who know that price and quality are positively related in a particular product category may correctly use price as an indicator of product quality. In other instances, however, the shortcuts may lead to errors of judgment. These developments are consistent with our criticisms of the economic model of buyer behavior discussed in Chap. 3.

EFFECTS OF REFERENCE PRICES ON PERCEIVED VALUE

Several decision variables can help us understand how price influences perceptions of value and eventual product choice. First, the *context* of the purchase decision, including the way the offer is presented, *frames* the buyer's evaluation and choice. For example, the way a sale is advertised will influence buyers' judgments about the value of the offer. As a further example, consider the following scenario.[1] You have been lying on the beach with a friend for most of a hot summer day. Deciding that it is time for a beer, you announce your intentions of buying one to your friend. If the only place that you can buy a beer is a half mile away at a fancy resort hotel, what do you expect you would have to pay for the beer? On the other hand, if the beer is sold in a small, run-down grocery store, what do you expect you would have to pay? Research indicates that most people expect to have to pay much more for the beer in the resort hotel than in the grocery store. The context of the place of purchase affects a buyer's internal reference price.

A second important variable is the *availability* of information. People tend to put more weight on information that is most readily available, even if it is contradictory. That is, information that is more easily recalled from memory either because of its recency or its impact will have a stronger effect on the purchase decision.

Another important issue that has direct impact on pricing is the *anchoring* effect introduced in Chap. 3. The order of price presentation anchors buyers' judgments as do the low or high prices in a product line. Also, people tend to adapt to prices that are presented as the original prices. For example, antique dealers often overprice their items, in anticipation that buyers will want to negotiate over the price. But the initial high price serves as an anchor, and generally the negotiated price is higher than it would have been without this initial high anchor price.

Finally, people often choose an alternative they *associate* with some past success, or they refuse to choose an alternative they associate with a previous failure. Price setters often fail to recognize when market conditions are favorable for a price increase, because a previous attempt to raise prices led to a sharp decline in sales. That is, people generalize from single instances of success or failure to perceived similar choice situations even when there are important differences in the choice environment.

Price and Perceived Value

The models in Figs. 3-1 and 3-4 illustrate the role of price on buyers' perceptions of product quality, sacrifice, value, and willingness to buy. These models suggest that buyers use price not only as a measure of sacrifice, but also as an indicator of product or service quality. As indicated by Eq. (3-1), perceived value represents a tradeoff between buyers' perceptions of quality and sacrifice. We have also seen that buyers' knowledge of the product and of actual price–quality relationships in the market

---

[1]This scenario is adapted from Richard Thaler, "Mental Accounting and Consumer Choice," *Marketing Science,* 4 (Summer 1985), 199–214.

moderates the extent to which price is used to infer product quality. Hence, the degree to which buyers believe that there is a price–quality relationship influences their value perceptions and willingness to buy. One other important concept that has been developed is that it is relative price rather than actual price that is the significant price factor. Moreover, in comparing prices, buyers' judgments are influenced by the relative or perceived differences between the actual or offer price and the reference price. Using these key ideas in price perception, we now complete the development of how perceived price influences buyers' judgments of value.

Consumers' perceptions of a price derive from their interpretations of the price differences (real or implied) *and* from their interpretations of focal and contextual cues in the offer. Consumers make their purchase decisions in a two-step process. First they *judge* the value of an offer; then they *decide* whether to make the purchase. It is also possible that they will postpone the purchase decision until they have more information about the offer and/or about other offers in the marketplace. Of concern here is (1) how buyers use price information and other cues to judge the value of the offer and (2) the influence this evaluation has on their purchase decisions.

Buyers evaluate prices by comparing them either to other prices available for comparison or to reference prices that are stored in memory. For example, when sellers advertise both the offered price and a (higher) comparative (regular) price, they are attempting to impose an external reference price instead of the consumers' internal reference price to be used for comparisons. To convince consumers to accept the higher price as a reference price, sellers include such words as "formerly," "regularly," and "usually" to describe the higher price. Words can be used in a variety of ways to enhance consumers' perceptions that a sale is taking place and that the offer represents a savings to consumers.

Consumers usually have a set of prices that are acceptable for them to pay for products they purchase. If an offered price is not acceptable, consumers are likely to refrain from purchasing the product and will either search for an acceptable offer or forgo any purchase. Since prices are evaluated comparatively, the judgment of acceptability depends not only on consumers' price expectations but also on information provided in promotions or advertisements. The perception of savings conveyed by price advertising leads to positive or favorable behavioral responses.

The available evidence on how consumers perceive price advertisements is based on theoretical explanations and on empirical research. The theoretical explanations offer predictions about how consumers are likely to form value perceptions and the impact these perceptions have on their purchase or information search decisions. The empirical research documents the correspondence between the theoretical explanations and consumers' behaviors.

Perceived Product Value

It has been argued that consumers first *judge* the value of an offer and then *decide* whether to purchase the item. One aspect of this purchase decision is whether the buyer believes that information about the offer is sufficient to support a choice. The total perceived value of a product being considered for purchase is comprised of (1) *acquisition value* (the expected benefit to be gained from acquiring the product less the net displeasure of paying for it) and (2) *transaction value* (the perceived merits of the offer or deal).

Acquisition Value As suggested earlier, buyers' perceptions of acquisition value represent a cognitive tradeoff between the benefits they perceive in the product and the sacrifice they perceive to be required by paying the monetary price of the product:

$$\text{Perceived acquisition value} = \frac{\text{perceived benefits}}{\text{perceived sacrifice}} \qquad (4\text{-}1)$$

[Note: Equation (4-1) should not be read as an exact mathematical formula but rather as a comparison of perceived benefits to perceived sacrifice.]

In part, the perceived benefits of a product are related to the buyers' judgments about the product's quality. Lacking perfect information about the inherent quality of the product, many consumers tend to believe that there is a positive relationship between a product's price and its quality ("You get what you pay for"). Thus, other things remaining the same, a higher priced product would be perceived to provide more benefits because of its higher perceived quality. However, at the same time, a higher price increases buyers' perceptions of their sacrifice. Thus, within some range of prices, the perceived benefits in the product will be larger than the perceived sacrifice, and buyers will perceive that there is positive acquisition value in the product. Other things remaining the same, the greater the perceived acquisition value, the greater is the likelihood that a consumer would be willing to purchase the product. However, in addition to evaluating the product's value, buyers also evaluate the offer itself.

Transaction Value By drawing on the recent findings in behavioral decision theory summarized previously, a more complete model of consumer choice can now be developed.[2] Replacing the utility function of economics with a value function the model uses three key propositions:

1. The value function is based on *perceived* gains and losses relative to a reference point. (The premise that people respond to relative differences rather than absolute levels has been discussed previously.)

2. As seen in Fig. 4-1, the value function is assumed to be concave for gains and convex for losses, relative to the reference point.

3. People are more sensitive to the prospect of a loss than to the prospect of a gain.

[2]Daniel Kahneman and Amos Tversky, "Prospect Theory: An Analysis of Decision Under Risk," *Econometrica,* 47 (March 1979), 263–291; Thaler, ibid.

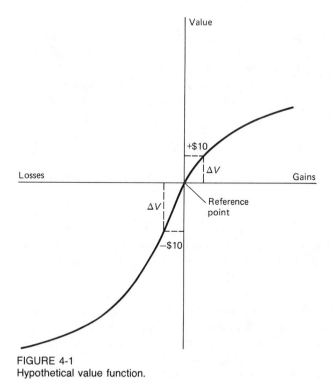

FIGURE 4-1
Hypothetical value function.

In Fig. 4-1, the gain of $10 is contrasted to a loss of $10. To provide a reference point, the current position is represented by the origin. Note that the concavity of the gain portion of the value function indicates that the function increases at a slower rate as gains become larger. However, the convexity of the loss portion of the value function at the smaller loss amounts indicates that the function increases at a faster rate initially and then behaves like the gain function. In the figure, a $10 gain is plotted against a $10 loss. It is apparent that the decrease in perceived value for the $10 loss is greater than the increase in perceived value for the $10 gain. This difference in perception between losses and gains helps explain the different degrees of price sensitivity between price increases and price decreases mentioned in Chap. 2. This point will be explained more completely shortly.

Of concern in our conceptualization is how buyers evaluate a purchase situation in which the buyer gains a product but loses the money paid for the product. Similar to the model seen in Fig. 3-1, buyers first *judge* the value of the offer and then *decide* whether to make a purchase. To explain the role of price in this process, three price concepts are used. The *perceived benefit* of the product is equivalent to the utility inherent in the *maximum price* the buyer would be willing to pay for the product. The *acquisition value* of the product is the perceived benefits of the product at this maximum price compared to the actual selling price, i.e., $p_{max} - p_{actual}$, which is equivalent to the perceived value concept. The *transaction value,* or the merit of paying the actual price, is determined by comparing the buyer's reference price to the actual price: $p_{ref} - p_{actual}$. Transaction value is positive if the actual price is less than the buyer's reference price, zero if they are equal, and negative otherwise. Thus, perceived value (PV) is the weighted sum of acquisition value (AV) and transaction value (TV):

$$PV = v_1(AV) + v_2 (TV) \qquad (4\text{-}2)$$

or

$$PV = v_1 (p_{max} - p) + v_2 (p_{ref} - p) \qquad (4\text{-}3)$$

where the v_1 and v_2 represent different subjective weights placed by buyers on these two relationships. Figure 4-2*a* shows these extensions to the original model of Fig. 3-1.

Enhancing Transaction Value   As indicated previously, the reference price may be internal to the buyer (e.g., an expected price, a believed fair or "just" price, or a remembered price) or it may be an external price in the purchase situation. The use of comparative price advertising or price tags to communicate the usual or regular price and a lower actual price is an attempt to provide buyers with a price frame of reference and to capitalize on transaction value by augmenting buyers' perceptions of value. Coupons or rebates are also used to enhance transaction value, but the efforts expended to redeem coupons or qualify for rebates may increase perceived sacrifice.[3] Figure 4-2*b* shows this extension to the original model.

Including an external reference price in a purchase offer allows the seller to frame the buyers' choices. Comparative-price advertising or point-of-purchase tags giving the usual or regular price and the lower asking price (sale price) provide buyers with a price frame of reference. In the context of the theoretical development sketched here, a price frame of reference enhances perceived value by enhancing both perceived acquisition value (perceptions of quality associated with the higher external reference price) and perceived transaction value (reduction in sacrifice associated with the lower sale price).

The presence of a reference price compared to the sale price suggests a "deal" or "bargain" and strengthens positive transaction value, or the perceived reduction of a sacrifice or loss (the price normally paid for the product). Since people value a reduction in a loss more than a gain of the same magnitude, by emphasizing the reduction in sacrifice (the amount paid for the product, or loss), the comparative price advertisement enhances transaction value more than a sale price-only presenta-

[3]Kent B. Monroe and Joseph D. Chapman, "Framing Effects on Buyers' Subjective Product Evaluations," in Melanie Wallendorf and Paul Anderson (eds.), *Advances in Consumer Research,* Vol. 14 (Provo, Utah: Association for Consumer Research, (1988), pp. 193–197.

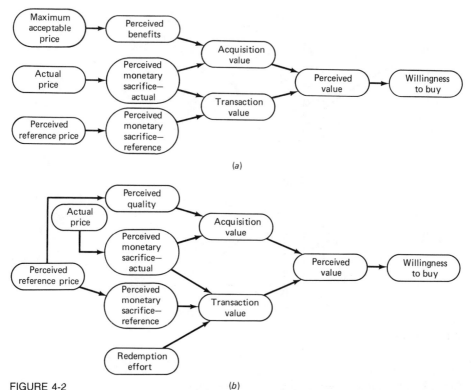

FIGURE 4-2   (b)
Price, perceived quality, acquisition value, transaction value, and perceived value.

tion would. The reduction in sacrifice is perceived as an *increase* in value (i.e., an increase in transaction value).

Transaction value can have a positive or negative effect on overall perceived value. Positive transaction value is the perceived reduction of a loss by a small gain (i.e., the original or reference price minus the savings perceived by a lower price or the amount of a rebate). When the components of the offer are framed in terms of a gain and a loss, the perceived value of the offer is enhanced because positive transaction value combines with acquisition value. Similarly, if a buyer perceives that a price has increased, this increase is perceived as a loss. The value function of Fig. 4-1 can be redrawn as a demand curve, with the buyers' reference price shown as P_{ref} (Fig. 4-3). A price increase viewed as a loss would be perceived to be larger than the same proportionate price decrease viewed as a gain. The observation we made earlier in this chapter about demand being more sensitive to price increases than to price decreases has a theoretical as well as an empirical foundation.

In Fig. 4-3, a $10 price increase is perceived as a loss in that the buyer has to pay more than previously. Hence, the loss in perceived value at price P_2 is greater than the perceived gain from a $10 price reduction, P_1.

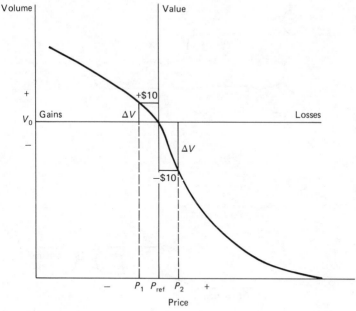

FIGURE 4-3
Value function.

Summary of the Price–Perceived Value Relationship

Throughout Chaps. 3 and 4 we have been developing a behavioral explanation of how buyers perceive price and how these perceptions influence their perceptions of value. Adaptation-level theory indicates not only that there is a reference price but that it changes. Reference price is affected by contextual effects such as frequency of previous price changes, buyers' expectations about future prices, the order that price information is presented to buyers, the advertisement of prices, and the intensity of price promotion.[4]

Assimilation-contrast theory indicates that there is a latitude of acceptance of prices. This theory also suggests that the acceptable price range may be affected by the amount of price variation for a product category as perceived by buyers. Another implication derived from assimilation-contrast theory is that there is likely to be a range of prices around the reference price within which little change in demand is likely in response to a price change, i.e., the price resulting from the price change may not be perceived as very different (see the theoretical discussion on Weber's law in Chap. 3).

[4]K. Gurumurthy and John D. C. Little, "A Pricing Model Based on Perception Theories and Its Testing on Scanner Panel Data," Working Paper, Sloan School of Management, M.I.T., Cambridge, Mass., July 1987; Christopher P. Puto, "The Framing of Buying Decisions," *Journal of Consumer Research,* 14 (December 1987), 301–315; Russell S. Winer, "A Reference Price Model of Brand Choice for Frequently Purchased Products," *Journal of Consumer Research,* 13 (September 1986), 250–257.

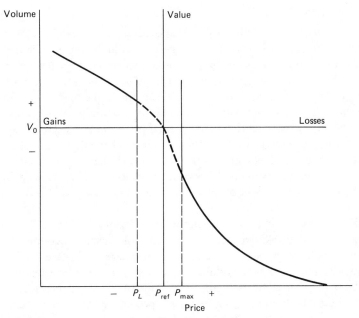

FIGURE 4-4
Value function. (Adapted from K. Gurumurthy and John D. C. Little, "A
Pricing Model Based on Perception Theories and Its Testing on Scanner
Panel Data," working paper, Sloan School of Management, M.I.T.,
Cambridge, Mass., July 1987, p. 17.)

Finally, the psychological argument recognizes that people respond differently to perceived gains and perceived losses and suggests that buyers are more sensitive to price increases (perceived loss) than to price decreases (perceived gain). Figure 4-4 illustrates the implication of combining these behavioral theories on the demand curve for a product. The dashed portion of the demand curve within the range of acceptable prices (defined between the lowest acceptable price, P_L, and the highest acceptable price, P_{max}) indicates that there is likely to be less change in demand in response to a perceived small price change (difference) relative to the buyer's reference price. However, once the price difference (i.e., $p_{ref} - p$) is perceived to be important by the buyer, there is likely to be a more noticeable change in demand. These price differences can occur because of a price increase or decrease, or because of comparative-price advertising in which the seller provides an external reference price for comparison. Thus, it is clear that small price differences, whether due to a price change or to differences between perceived similar offerings, are less likely to produce significant demand responses.

One important issue connected with comparative-price advertising is the plausibility of externally supplied reference prices. Do buyers perceive them as believable? If not, does the behavioral explanation provided here change? The next section discusses this issue.

Effects of Plausible Reference Prices

In a comparative-price advertisement, the buyer is exposed to two prices: the higher usual or regular price and the lower sale price. To be able to judge the acquisition value inherent in the advertised offer the buyer must be able to determine which price to use to help assess the product's relative quality or benefits. If the advertisement suggests that the product is usually or regularly sold at the higher price, and if consumers believe that the quoted higher price indeed is representative of the product's market value, then it is likely that the higher regular price will be used to assess the product's quality and benefits. But if consumers do not believe that the higher price is plausible, then they will likely substitute a price lower than the advertised regular price to make their assessments of product benefits. That is, they will substitute another price to use as a point of reference to make assessments of quality and benefits.

One of the possible ways that buyers judge whether the advertised reference price (usual or regular price) is plausible depends on their idea of a usual price for the product in question in the marketplace (i.e., they have an internal reference price). Perhaps they frequently purchase the product or recently saw price information about similar products in other advertisements. Their price knowledge then forms the basis of their expectations about usual prices for the product in the marketplace. We will refer to this price expectation as an *internal reference price*. If buyers have an internal reference price for a product, they will probably compare this internal reference price to the advertised reference price to determine the plausibility of the advertised reference price. If the advertised reference price is judged as plausible or believable, then they are likely to use that price to assess the product's benefits and quality. But if the advertised reference price is judged as implausible or not believable, buyers will either use their internal reference prices to judge product quality and benefits or they will search for more price information before judging the product.

Effects of Implausible Reference Prices

Do advertised reference prices affect buyers internal reference prices? As suggested previously, buyers' internal reference prices are not static but continuously move in the direction of new price information. That is, buyers adapt their notion of expected market price when they receive new price information. Thus, if their internal reference price is below the advertiser's reference price, and if they judge the advertiser's reference price as implausible, their internal reference price is still likely to move toward the perceived implausible advertised reference price. This higher internal reference price will now be used to judge the product's quality and benefits. The net affect of an advertised reference price is to provide a higher comparison price for buyers to judge a product's acquisition value rather than using the lower sale price.

However, if buyers have no prior expectations about the usual price for the product being advertised, then the plausibility of the advertised reference price will probably be determined by the perceived difference between the advertised reference price and the advertised sale price. Other things remaining the same, the larger the perceived price difference, the more likely the advertised reference price will be judged as implausible. However, the semantic cues (words used to convey that a price has been reduced, such as regular, suggested list price, sale price) may be used by buyers to infer that the regular price is higher than the sale price. Thus, the buyers are more likely to form an internal reference price above the sale price but below the advertised reference price. As in the first situation, buyers will develop an internal reference price based on the available price information, including the perceived implausible advertised reference price. The perceived implausible price will serve as an anchor for their judgment, and the resultant new internal reference price will be affected by the magnitude of this implausible price. Again, buyers' internal reference prices for the advertised product will be displaced toward the advertised reference price.

In summary, when a product is featured in a comparative-price format, the higher advertised reference or regular price will be used either to directly assess the product's quality and benefits or to form a new internal reference price. If a new internal reference price is formed because the advertised reference price is judged as implausible, it will be used by the buyers to judge the product's quality and benefits. This judgment will be contrasted to the perceived sacrifice of the sale price to determine the perceived acquisition value of the product.

Plausible Versus Implausible Reference Prices

The preceding argument about the effect of an advertiser presenting a comparative reference price (usual or regular price) on buyers' internal reference prices is applicable also when discussing transaction value. That is, the effect of a plausible or implausible reference price is to move the buyers' internal reference price in the direction of the advertised reference price. To the extent that the buyers' internal reference price has increased, the perception of a "deal" or "bargain" is enhanced. Moreover, highlighting the reduction in the sacrifice required increases buyers' perceptions of transaction value. As in the case of acquisition value, the net effect of an advertiser's reference price is to move buyers' reference prices in the direction of the advertised reference price. Since the advertised reference price is higher than the sale price (actual selling price), there would be positive perceived transaction value, and the overall perceived value will increase. As perceived value increases, there is a greater likelihood the search for a "better offer" will decrease and buyers will be more willing to purchase the product at the advertiser's place of business. As discussed in Chap. 14, there are issues about whether such price promotion activity is deceptive.

Available Empirical Evidence

The evidence reviewed here pertains only to consumer perceptions of retail price advertisements and promotions. Advertised offers showing both a regular and a sale price are perceived as more believable and as providing more value for the money than are advertisements giving just actual price.[5] Other research indicates that advertisements featuring a product's regular price and the lower sale price received more positive responses in terms of acceptability and willingness to buy than did advertisements providing only the lower sale price and the percentage that the price had been reduced, even though the offers were financially equivalent. Also, respondents evaluating offers in advertisements with a discount from a regular price judged the offers to be more acceptable than offers with only a sale price (i.e., to provide more savings), and they expressed a greater willingness to buy. As the size of the discount increased, there was a positive relationship between acceptance of price as the lowest in the market area and the magnitude of the discount.[6] The implication is that the greater the amount of discount from a regular price, the more likely are consumers to accept the sale price as the lowest in the market area. This acceptance would lead to the inference that they would be less likely to search for a lower price because of the belief that the advertised sale price is the lowest.

Another study also indicated that an advertised reference price raised consumer estimates of the advertiser's regular price in comparison to an advertisement that did not contain a reference price. Moreover, the respondents were willing to attribute a 10–12 percent savings to any advertised price with unstated savings; they consistently perceived that reference price claims were about 25 percent above the true comparison prices.[7]

These findings suggest that the acceptance of an advertised regular (reference) price depends on the size of the sales discount and whether or not a regular price is quoted. Also, there seems to be a greater acceptance of any regular price provided in an advertisement—regardless of the ad's veracity. And as the perception of value increases with the increase in the price discounts, the intent to search for alternatives is likely to decrease. Further, the perception of value was greater for the sale price–regular price format (i.e., the comparative-price situation) than for the sale price–only format.

A recent study found that advertisements listing a high plausible reference price consistently enhanced perceptions of offer value in comparison to advertisements with no reference price. In one experiment, the presence of a reference price increased estimates of both the average market price and the advertiser's normal price,

[5]James G. Barnes, "Factors Influencing Consumer Reaction to Retail Newspaper 'Sale' Advertising," *Proceedings,* Fall Educators' Conference (Chicago: American Marketing Association, 1975), pp. 471–477; Edward A. Blair and E. Laird Landon, Jr., "The Effects of Reference Prices in Retail Advertisements," *Journal of Marketing,* 45 (Spring 1981), 61–69; Stephen E. Keiser and James R. Krum, "Consumer Perceptions of Retail Advertising with Overstated Savings," *Journal of Retailing,* 52 (Fall 1976), 27–37.

[6]Eric N. Berkowitz and John R. Walton, "Contextual Influences on Consumer Price Responses: An Experimental Analysis," *Journal of Marketing Research,* 17 (August 1980), 349–358; Albert J. Della Bitta, Kent B. Monroe, and John M. McGinnis, "Consumer Perceptions of Comparative Price Advertisements," *Journal of Marketing Research,* 18 (November 1981), 416–427; Joseph N. Fry and Gordon H. McDougall, "Consumer Appraisal of Retail Price Advertisements," *Journal of Marketing,* 38 (July 1974), 64–67.

[7]Blair and Landon, op. cit.

as well as increasing the perceptions of offer value. The strength of these effects increased with the size of the discount. Moreover, these effects held even when the advertised discount was well above normal expectations. In a second experiment, these same effects occurred, and the exaggerated reference price reduced the perceived benefits of search.[8]

Essentially, even if an exaggerated reference price is perceived as implausible by consumers, the extreme value can still influence offer value perceptions because buyers will have higher internal reference prices based on the exaggerated advertised reference prices. The effect of enhancing perceived offer value through the use of advertised discounts also reduced perceived benefits of search. And, as expected, the decreased perceived benefits from search increased the likelihood of acquiring the product from the advertiser. In the absence of knowledge about market prices (as might be the case for infrequently purchased products or for buyers who do not normally remember prices paid), a reference price that is perceived as implausible may still influence market price estimates and perceptions of offer value. Thus, retailers may be tempted to exaggerate advertised regular prices.

Recently, a study examining the effects of a comparative-price offering determined that the regular price–sale price presentation led to a significant increase in perceived value as the size of the discount increased. This increase in perceived value occurred primarily because perceived transaction value increased significantly *and* perceived acquisition value also increased significantly.[9] These particular results also suggest that acquisition value can be enhanced as the size of discount increases. Since acquisition value was defined earlier as $P_{max} - P$, as the sale price decreases relative to the maximum price buyers would be willing to pay, acquisition value is also enhanced, as these results indicate.

Finally, another study found support for the asymmetric price response to losses and gains as predicted. There was also support for the notion of a price-insensitive region around the reference price, as suggested by the acceptable price range concept. Indeed, when the price change was greater than about 16–17 percent, consumers seemed to respond to the price increase or decrease. Finally, frequent price promotions seemed to erode the effectiveness of the promotions.[10] This result suggests that frequent price promotions might lead to a reduction in buyers' reference price for the product, negating the perceived price difference in the offer.

---

[8]Joel E. Urbany, William O. Bearden, and Dan C. Weilbaker, "Advertised Comparative Price Effects on Buyer Perceptions and Behavior: A Model and Empirical Test," in Michael Houston (ed.), *Advances in Consumer Research,* Vol. 15 (Provo, Utah: Association for Consumer Research, 1988), pp. 334–340; Joel E. Urbany, William O. Bearden, and Dan C. Weilbaker, "The Effect of Plausible and Exaggerated Reference Prices on Consumer Perceptions and Price Search," *Journal of Consumer Research,* 15 (June 1988), 95–110. See also Donald R. Lichtenstein and William O. Bearden, "Contextual Influences on Perceptions of Merchant-Supplied Reference Prices," *Journal of Consumer Research,* 16 (June 1989), 55–66.

[9]Joseph D. Chapman, "The Impact of Discounts on Subjective Product Evaluations," Unpublished doctoral dissertation, Department of Marketing, Virginia Polytechnic Institute and State University, Blacksburg, 1987.

[10]Gurumurthy and Little, op. cit.

SUMMARY

Perception basically involves the process of categorization. That is, we tend to place new experiences into existing classifications of familiar experiences. Thus, when buyers are confronted by a price different from what they believe they previously paid, they must decide whether the difference between the new and old prices is significant to them. If the price difference is insignificant, they may classify the two prices as similar and act as they have in the past. However, if the price difference is perceived as significant, they may classify the new price in a new price/product category and change their purchase behavior.

During this process of categorization buyers make heavy use of cues or clues. Some of these cues are price cues, which influence buyers' judgments of whether the price differences are significant. Finally, the frequent and predominant use and misuse of deep discounting by retailers may have several undesirable results. Buyers may learn that the true or usual price is not the advertised regular price but the sale price; they may then develop their price perceptions and value judgments using the lower sale price. Another problem arises when retailers use fictitious "regular" prices to enhance buyers' value perceptions and thereby deceive buyers. These practices inevitably will lead to public policy regulating such deception. Perhaps, more than anything else, Chaps. 3 and 4 have demonstrated that buyers frequently do not use price in ways commonly assumed.

Buyers may also use price as an indicator of quality and value. Proactive pricers must learn how their customers perceive price and how these perceptions influence their perceptions of value. Ultimately, it is the relationship between price and customers' perceptions of value that determines purchase decisions.

DISCUSSION QUESTION

1 Carefully study the newspaper advertising for the retail stores in your area. What is the relative frequency of use of a regular price–sale price format? What words (semantic cues) are used to convey the notion of a sale? To what extent do these advertisements directly or indirectly attempt to enhance the consumers' perceptions of value? Are there any disclaimers in the advertisements? What impact, if any, do you think these disclaimers have on consumers' perceptions and value judgments?

SUGGESTED READINGS

Della Bitta, Albert J., Kent B. Monroe, and John M. McGinnis: "Consumer Perceptions of Comparative Price Advertisements," *Journal of Marketing Research,* 18 (November 1981), 416–427.

Lichtenstein, Donald R., and William O. Bearden: "Contextual Influences on Perceptions of Merchant-Supplied Reference Prices," *Journal of Consumer Research,* 16 (June 1989), 55–66.

Mobley, Mary F., William O. Bearden, and Jesse E. Teel: "An Investigation of Individual Responses to Tensile Price Claims," *Journal of Consumer Research,* 15 (September 1988), 273–279.

Monroe, Kent B., and Joseph D. Chapman: "Framing Effects on Buyers' Subjective Product Evaluations," in Melanie Wallendorf and Paul Anderson (eds.), *Advances in Consumer Research,* Vol. 14 (Provo, Utah: Association for Consumer Research, 1988), pp. 193–197.

Thaler, Richard: "Mental Accounting and Consumer Choice," *Marketing Science,* 4 (Summer 1985), 199–214.

Urbany, Joel E., William O. Bearden, and Dan C. Weilbaker: "The Effect of Plausible and Exaggerated Reference Prices on Consumer Perceptions and Price Search," *Journal of Consumer Research,* 15 (June 1988), 95–110.

CHAPTER 5

VALUE ANALYSIS

A cynic is a man who knows the price of everything, and the value of nothing.

—Oscar Wilde

What we obtain too cheaply we esteem too lightly; it is dearness only that gives everything its value.

—John Jakes, *The Rebel*

VALUE ANALYSIS THEORY

We have seen ample evidence that both industrial buyers and consumers tend to use price as an indicator of quality and value.[1] Moreover, it has been demonstrated that buyers generally do not use price merely as an indicator of the product's cost (i.e., amount of money to be sacrificed to acquire the product). Indeed, the low-price supplier seldom achieves a dominant market position. As developed in Chap. 1, price can be conceptualized as representing a relationship that indicates the quantities of money needed to acquire a given quantity of goods or services. Thus, we demonstrated in Chap. 1 that it is a mistake for sellers to think of pricing as only affixing

---

[1]Kent B. Monroe and R. Krishnan, "The Effect of Price on Subjective Product Evaluations," in Jacob Jacoby and Jerry C. Olson (eds.), *Perceived Quality: How Consumers View Stores and Merchandise* (Lexington, Mass.: Lexington Books, 1985) pp. 209–232.

a monetary amount to products or services; this is based on the erroneous assumption that buyers seek solely to minimize the price paid.

Successful proactive pricers focus on the concept of *value*, not *current price*. Indeed, these two terms are often confused in current discussions on price; some writers even suggest that price is synonymous with value. However, as demonstrated in Chaps. 3 and 4, buyers perceive value as a trade off between perceived quality and benefits in the product or service on the one hand and perceived cost of acquiring and using the product or service on the other. Price is a component of the perceived cost, but price also plays a role in buyers' perceptions of product or service quality. Hence, price is not the same thing as value.

This chapter continues to focus on value orientation as the proper approach to setting prices. The concept of value is defined in terms of the discussion in Chaps. 3 and 4, and methods for operationalizing the concept of value in price determination are offered. Value-oriented pricing is more difficult than cost-oriented pricing, but the potential for having a market-oriented pricing strategy that works is far greater than with any other pricing approach.

Value Versus Price

As demonstrated in Chaps. 1 and 2, price has a relatively clear meaning in economics and plays an important role in the working of markets. "It is, however, quite possible for price to be distorted in the short term by immediate concerns, which do not accurately reflect true worth over time. . . . Thus, a perfectly ripe tomato has a price today that in no way reflects its true value a month from now. . . . Value, on the other hand, conveys a more stable sense of worth within a broader temporal and conceptual context than price alone."[2]

Further, as demonstrated in Chap. 3, there is a clear relationship between perceived quality and perceived value and successful firms recognize this relationship. In the words of Ludwig Huck, formerly president of Curtis Mathes: "I felt strongly that customers would be responsive to a company that treated them with respect and care and had a principle of maintaining a high quality standard of products, coupled with salespeople who would serve and cater to the customers' needs."[3]

Included among the few companies that have learned that product quality and value are related and that emphasis on maintaining and improving quality is profitable are Boeing, Kodak, 3M, Caterpillar, Coca-Cola, John Deere, Procter & Gamble, and Whirlpool. Whirlpool has consistently positioned itself as a quality leader by designing and engineering into its appliances features that consumers value, such as automatic ice makers and energy-savers. Also, Whirlpool seeks to produce and sell appliances that have long lives with minimal repairs. The company strives to improve its products consistently, and it has a willingness to signal quality with

[2]David Rockefeller, "Value Versus Price," *Bell Atlantic Quarterly,* 3 (Spring 1986), 43.
[3]"Top Quality Battling Low Prices for Market Share," *Marketing News,* 20 (September 26, 1986), 12.

strong warranties. For example, the company recently offered a free replacement including delivery and installation for anyone not satisfied with the quality or performance of a new Whirlpool appliance within one year of date of purchase.[4] The essential point from these examples and quotes is that these companies and individuals have discovered that the key to success is the offering of products or services that deliver value to customers. And as developed in Chaps. 3 and 4, the relationship between benefits received and the total cost of acquiring the product or service is important:

$$\text{Perceived value} = \frac{\text{perceived benefits}}{\text{perceived price}} \qquad (5\text{-}1)$$

where perceived price = perceived total cost to the buyer: purchase price + start-up costs (acquisition costs, transportation, installation, order handling) + postpurchase costs (repairs and maintenance, risk of failure or poor performance)

perceived benefits = some combination of physical attributes, service attributes, and technical support available in relation to the particular use of the product, as well as the purchase price, and other indicators of perceived quality

Value Analysis and Value Engineering

Research needed to determine the buyers' perceived value of an offering includes value analysis and value engineering. Value analysis attempts to determine the relative value (utility) buyers place on the total product or service offering, i.e., the perceived benefits. It focuses on the process that customers use to determine the relative value to them of alternative product or service options. The focus of value analysis is on the customer and how customers determine the value of the product or service to them.

The following incident illustrates the need to focus on customers and how they develop perceptions of value. At a conference on marketing strategy, a representative of a telephone company was discussing how his company had taken a value-oriented approach to the marketing of its products. As he listed the new "value-added" features that had been engineered into the company's telephone system, an exasperated person in the audience yelled out "Who needs it?" This question ably pointed out that some of the features, although fine from an engineering point of view, were neither desired nor needed by most of the firm's customers.

Value engineering is an organized effort to analyze the ability of products or services to perform desired functions, satisfy needs, or provide pleasure or satisfaction in the most profitable manner.[5] Value engineering focuses on determining

4"AMA Cites Vertical Quality Integration," *Marketing News,* 22 (March 14, 1988), 26–27.
5Jerry J. Kaufman and Ron F. Becker, *Value Engineering: An Executive Overview* (Houston: Cooper Industries, 1981).

essential product functions and characteristics and the cost of providing these functions and characteristics. The cost is determined by evaluating alternative concepts,
designs, engineering procedures or processes, and raw materials.

It is also important to consider the customers' cost of ownership over the normal
life of the product. "The disciplines of marketing, engineering and manufacturing,
as well as other supporting disciplines, working together maintain a focus on the
requirements, design and cost, as seen from the customers' sense of value."[6] Whirlpool is an excellent example of value engineering leading to value enhancement.[7]

FOUR COMPONENTS OF PERCEIVED VALUE

To use value analysis and value engineering in pricing, it is useful to distinguish four
ways that customers may evaluate a product and service to assess its perceived
acquisition value:

1. Cost—the sum of all costs required to acquire and use the product or service.
2. Exchange—the perceived value of the brand, company, or store where the
product is sold.
3. Aesthetics—the value that customers place on the properties or attractiveness
of the product.
4. Relative use—the way a product is used.

These four components are briefly discussed next.

Cost

That price or purchase cost is the only cost of relevance is a fallacy which marketers
are beginning to realize. There are numerous components to the cost of a product.
Traditionally, costs include search, risk of nonperformance, service, maintenance,
and any other life-cycle costs involved in the purchase and use of the product. For
consumers, purchase costs include the price of the product or service as well as time
and psychological costs involved in the shopping or searching for the acquisition.[8]
"Sticker price" is only one component of cost that purchasers consider in the buying
decision. As indicated in Eq. (5-1), start-up costs and postpurchase costs are also
important. One objective of value engineering is to achieve the desired performance
level of the product or service at the lowest cost of ownership. If the product or
service can be delivered to the customer only at a total cost more than the customer
is willing to pay, then the product will be of little value to the customer.

Exchange

This component refers to a number of market-related factors that influence perceptions of value. One important aspect of the exchange component is the notion of

[6]Ibid., p. 2.
[7]See also "Smart Design: Quality Is the New Style," *Business Week,* April 11, 1988, pp. 102–117.
[8]Wesley Bender, "Consumer Purchase Costs," *Journal of Retailing,* 40 (Spring 1964), 1–8, 52.

brand equity. That is, firms over time have developed an image of excellence for their products, brands, or service. The reputation of the firm or brand for quality products, additional efforts to provide prompt and reliable parts and/or service to customers (e.g., Caterpillar's promise to deliver parts anywhere in the world within 24 hours), and trustworthy salespeople and customer service personnel all enhance perceptions of value by improving perceptions of quality or benefits provided. This image of excellence for companies like DuPont, Sony, and American Airlines fosters buyers' willingness to pay some premium to acquire the products or services of these firms. Since buyers are usually not able to evaluate the product or service prior to purchase and use, they rely on the firm's or brand's reputation as a signal of quality and, therefore, value.

Aesthetics

Henry Ford was once quoted as saying that customers could have a car of any color as long as it was black. However, in contemporary marketing, it is clear that color, style, design, and interior furnishings all contribute to customers' perceptions of value of automobiles. In recent years, too, consumers generally have been willing to pay higher prices for color-toned appliances than for the traditional white appliances. Similarly, product attributes such as hardness of a drill bit, softness of a fabric, or taste of a cola drink enhance the attractiveness of a product to prospective buyers and increase its perceived value. Although technical innovation remains the key value element of consumer electronics, style, design, and color are playing an increasingly important role in their sales. At the Consumer Electronics Show in June 1987, Sharp introduced television sets in six colors. The large portable radios and cassette players—"boom boxes"—were in strong pastel colors, with rounded corners and edges and fewer knobs.[9]

Relative Use

How a product is used along with its ability to reduce costs or improve gains through its use enhance its perceived value. For example, a machine's value will increase with its life span or its reduced fuel consumption. A new machine that leads to labor or raw material savings or to increased output per hour over alternative machines also will be perceived as delivering more value. As indicated in Chaps. 3 and 4, perceived value may also change relative to the way the product is used or its intended use.

THE CONCEPT OF BENEFITS

In any purchase decision, the buyer is seeking to acquire benefits. To provide benefits a product or service must be able to (1) perform certain tasks or functions, (2) solve identified problems, or (3) provide specific pleasures. Thus, a product is not bought

---

[9]"Smart Design: Quality Is the New Style," op. cit.

for its particular components, materials, or expertise but rather for what the product or service does. For example, people do not buy quarter-inch drill bits. They buy the ability to make quarter-inch holes. The drill bit has no extrinsic value except for the benefit of making the hole. This point is vital and is more than mere semantics.[10]

Figure 5-1 illustrates the conceptual framework for benefit analysis. The figure shows the important triad of firms, products, and services, and customers contribute to the nature of the benefits delivered. As shown by the right side of the figure, benefits delivered must be consistent with benefits desired by customers. The benefits wanted by customers or users provide a key element to firms and the products or services they offer. Value is created when the benefits delivered by the products or services match the benefits wanted by the customers or users. Customers or users have different behavioral characteristics that affect and determine the benefits they want as well as how the products or services satisfy their wants. As mentioned in Chap. 3, research has demonstrated that the willingness of people to pay different prices for products that perform similar tasks or functions varies according to the projected use or purchase situation. Also, as mentioned, the critical variable may be the particular characteristics or attributes of a product, such as hardness of a drill bit. Buyers knowledgeable about these "intrinsic cues" may use these cues to evaluate the relative benefits and value of the product. Thus, product characteristics or

[10]Martin Christopher, "Value-In-Use-Pricing," *European Journal of Marketing*, 16, No. 5 (1982), 35–46.

FIGURE 5-1
Conceptual framework for benefit analysis. (Adapted and reprinted with permission from James H. Myers and Edward Tauber, *Market Structure Analysis* [Chicago: American Marketing Association, 1977], p. 153.)

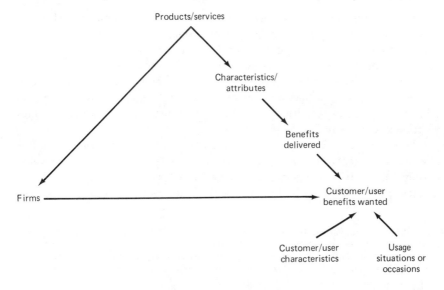

attributes are perceived to be important insofar as they deliver certain benefits to customers.

The benefit concept has certain implications for providers of goods and services. First, it is necessary to identify the benefits that the customers will perceive the product or service to offer. Second, it is necessary to determine the relative importance of those benefits that the customers place on the product or service. The key point is that it is the customers' perceptions that are important. If customers perceive that an organization offers a better product, better technical advice, or service, then that organization has a differential advantage.[11]

Current research suggests that buyers' willingness to pay a particular price for a given offering depends on their perception of total relative value.[12] In any specific pricing situation, it is essential to determine those attributes of the offering that are most important to the buyer. Then, to determine the relative value of different attribute combinations, either tradeoff analysis or conjoint measurement is used. (These techniques are discussed in Chap. 6.) Finally, the research needs to determine the perceived performance of competing products on these key attributes.

The key to value analysis is to remember that customers want something done and someone pleased. Buyers want something enclosed, held, moved, separated, cleaned, heated, cooled, or whatever, under certain conditions, in certain situations, and within certain limits. Also, buyers want a shape, color, aroma, texture, sound, feel, taste, a "precious" material, something to bring pleasure to themselves or to others they wish to please. That is, a product or service is purchased because of its ability to perform a certain task or function, solve a particular problem, or provide specific pleasures. It is what the product or service does and how well it does it that provides value.

VALUE-ORIENTED PRICING

The key point of this discussion is that current and prospective buyers will make purchase decisions on the basis of perceived value. Since perceived value is a tradeoff between perceived quality and perceived benefits with the perceived monetary sacrifice, buyers do not determine a product's value solely on the basis of minimizing the price paid. Customers must be educated about the use and value of products and services. Moreover, the price set must be consistent with customers' value perceptions. That is, a product perceived to be of higher value than competitive offerings will be granted the privilege of a premium price.

As discussed in Chap. 3, price is perceived differently by all types of buyers. For example, current clients or loyal buyers will perceive price and the price–value relationship differently from a periodic customer, and a prospective buyer will likely have another perception. Table 5-1 illustrates these different possible perceptions of

[11]Benson P. Shapiro and Barbara B. Jackson, "Industrial Pricing to Meet Customer Needs," *Harvard Business Review,* 56 (November–December 1978), 119–127.

[12]Irwin Gross, "Insights from Pricing Research," in Earl L. Bailey (ed.), *Pricing Practices and Strategies* (New York: The Conference Board, 1978), pp. 34–39.

TABLE 5-1
PRICE–VALUE PERCEPTIONS

Type of Buyer	Definition	Price Perceptions
Prospect	A potential buyer of a firm's offerings	Price too high Competitor's price is lower Price–value relationship is unfavorable Price too low
Customer	A regular or periodic buyer of a firm's offerings	Price is acceptable Price is competitive Price–value relationship is acceptable Price is similar to competitor's price
Client	A buyer with whom the firm has an ongoing mutually beneficial relationship	Price–value relationship is excellent Price is very acceptable Price is not critical Price is fair

Source: Adapted and reprinted with permission from Howard Berrian, "Marketing Value Versus Marketing Products/Services," in Edwin E. Bobrow and Mark David Bobrow (eds.), *Marketing Handbook, Volume 1: Marketing Principles* (Homewood, Ill.: Dow Jones–Irwin, 1985), p. 22.

price. For clients, it is apparent that the value received is perceived to be more than the price of the product or service. Indeed, it is likely that because of the perceived value received these buyers are not highly concerned with the price, at least within limits. Mercedes-Benz, Tiffany's, Disneyland have successfully premium priced their products because of the higher perceived quality or benefits (premium value) of their offerings. The objective of value-oriented pricing is not simply pricing as high as feasible but rather pricing in relation to the in-use benefits that buyers perceive they will gain from purchasing the product or service.

For example, IBM has routinely priced its products above competition. The price premium is not simply dependent on superior machine performance or size. Rather, IBM offers customers something of value to induce them to pay a price premium. Their nonhardware services such as after-sales service have been perceived to be superior, their products have been perceived to be more reliable, and they have offered more assistance in developing applications. Their ability to provide a benefit package led to customers' acceptance of a premium price for IBM products.

IMPROVING PERCEIVED VALUE

Essentially, perceived value can be improved by increasing the ability of the product or service to perform a function or task, solve a problem, or provide pleasure. Perceived value can also be improved by reducing the total costs associated with acquiring and using the product. Figure 5-2 illustrates the various combinations that can be used to influence perceived value, some of which are favorable and some unfavorable. The most desirable combination is to provide more perceived benefits

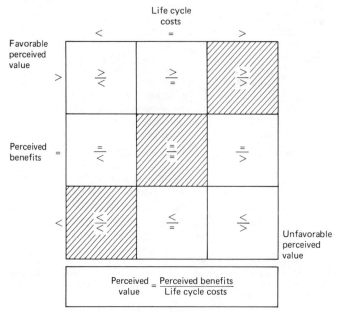

FIGURE 5-2
Improving perceived value.

at less perceived cost (upper left box). The cost in this relationship includes the selling price and all subsequent costs to the customer of acquiring, installing, maintaining, and using the product over its useful life (concept of life-cycle cost). Other favorable combinations include increasing perceived benefits while holding customer costs constant (upper middle box), or holding perceived benefits constant while reducing customer costs (middle left box). The lined boxes represent equivalent tradeoffs between perceived benefits and customer costs and result in no net change in perceived value. The lower right boxes represent unfavorable combinations that should be avoided. What this figure is intended to demonstrate is that efforts to improve perceived value cannot concentrate only on the costs of providing the product to customers.

In the early 1980s, frozen TV dinners became more sophisticated, including such offerings as lobster Newburg and beef tips in burgundy sauce. The sophistication of these offerings was heavily promoted and prices per dinner ranged from $4 to over $5. However, retail sales had peaked by 1985 and had fallen 20 percent early in 1988. "After a trial period, most consumers realized that the price–value equation wasn't balanced," said the general manager at General Foods.[13] To overcome this difficulty, the producers began to concentrate on improving the quality of the dinners by adding cheese to the fettucini and cutting fat from the turkey. They also provided

[13]"Why Fancy Frozen Foods Need a New Recipe," *Business Week,* April 25, 1988, p. 89.

a means to prevent overcooking and lowered the price of the dinners. That is, a simultaneous strategy of providing better quality and reducing the purchase price led to an improvement in perceived value.

Firms that become enmeshed in cost competition fail to see that strategic advantage can be gained through offering customers better perceived benefits—i.e., value—even at a higher price. Firms like 3M and Hewlett-Packard have shown that a value-based strategy can be an effective way to gain a competitive edge.

DETERMINING CUSTOMERS' RELATIVE ECONOMIC VALUE

Value analysis can be used for pricing by considering the *perceived relative economic value* of the product from the perspective of the customer. This approach recognizes that the maximum price that can be set is that at which the customer disregards the difference between the product and the next best economic alternative (maximum acceptable price, or reservation price).[14] As established in Chap. 2 and Fig. 2-9, the difference between the maximum amount customers are willing to pay for a product and the amount they actually pay is called *consumers' surplus* (perceived acquisition value). This difference represents the customers' gain from making the purchase and is the sum of the money amounts of *value-in-use* minus *value-in-exchange*. Consumers' surplus represents the consumers' net gain from trade. This concept as developed in Chap. 2 assumes customers are fully informed about the product and about competitive alternatives. However, as demonstrated in Chap. 3, buyers are seldom fully informed about products or prices; hence, perceived value is the sum of acquisition value plus transaction value. As we develop the concept of relative economic value in this section, it is important to remember this vital point.

To use the concept of relative economic value for pricing a product requires the determination of customers' *reference product,* customers' *life-cycle costs* using the reference product, and the *improvement value* of the product relative to the reference product.

Reference Product

The reference product should ideally be the customers' next best alternative for meeting the same need as the current or proposed new product. This reference product may be the existing model about to be replaced or it may be the competing product being used by customers. The key point here is that the reference product must be the same reference product customers will use to make their comparisons.

Life-Cycle Costs

Life-cycle costs represent all costs that a customer will incur over the product's useful life. These costs include the actual purchase price, start-up costs, and postpur-

---

[14]John L. Forbes and Nitin T. Mehta, "Value-Based Strategies for Industrial Products," *Business Horizons,* 21 (October 1978), 25–31.

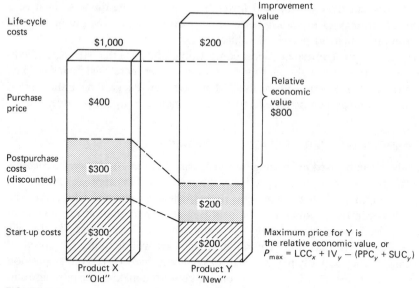

FIGURE 5-3
Determining maximum acceptable price to buyers.

chase costs (Fig. 5-3). Postpurchase costs include all costs incurred by the customer once the product has been installed and is in use. For example, fuel, service contract, and other costs that will be incurred to keep the product functional are postpurchase costs. These costs, because they represent outlays over time, should be discounted back to the present time using an interest rate that reflects the customer's desired return on investment. Similarly, start-up costs include installation, training, and related costs that will be incurred before the product is fully operational. For consumer energy-related products, the concept of life-cycle cost could lead to substantial increases in perceived value if sellers attempted to help consumers understand this concept. This type of information was mandated to be disclosed in the 1975 Energy Policy and Conservation Act.[15]

Improvement Value

The improvement value of the product represents the potential incremental satisfaction or profits the customer can expect from this product over those of the reference product. This enhancement of customers' satisfaction or profit potential may occur because of attributes of the new product that improve productivity (reduce costs or increase output per unit of time), increase the value of the customers' output and, potentially, the output's price, or simply provide more pleasure.

[15]R. Bruce Hutton and William L. Wilkie, "Life Cycle Cost: A New Form of Consumer Information," *Journal of Consumer Research,* 6 (March 1980), 349–360.

Maximum Acceptable Price

The maximum price that could be set is the price that makes the customer ignore the economic difference between the "new" product and the reference product (Fig. 5-3). In equation form this maximum price is

$$P_{\max_y} = \text{LCC}_x + \text{IV}_y - (\text{PPC}_y + \text{SUC}_y) \qquad (5\text{-}2)$$

where $P_{\max_y}$ = maximum acceptable price of product y
LCC_x = life-cycle costs of the reference product
IV_y = improvement value for the "new" product
PPC_y = discounted postpurchase costs for the new product
SUC_y = start-up costs for the "new" product

To illustrate this concept, assume that the old reference product has a current purchase price of $400, that its postpurchase costs (discounted) are $300, and that its start-up costs are $300. Therefore,

$$\text{LCC}_x = P_x + \text{PPC}_x + \text{SUC}_x \qquad (5\text{-}3)$$

or

$$\text{LCC}_x = \$400 + \$300 + \$300 = \$1,000 \qquad (5\text{-}4)$$

Now assume the "new" product, because of its efficiency in reducing material costs per unit of output and its ability to increase the number of units produced per hour, has an improvement value of $200. Further assume that the discounted postpurchase costs are $200 and the new product's start-up costs are $200. Therefore, the maximum acceptable price is

$$P_{\max} = \$1,000 + \$200 - (\$200 + \$200) \qquad (5\text{-}5)$$

or

$$P_{\max} = \$800 \text{ (relative economic value)} \qquad (5\text{-}6)$$

DETERMINING SELLER'S PRICE

Seller's Pricing Discretion

The maximum price of $800 in Eq. (5-6) may not be the price that "sells" to potential customers. If the price represents an economic indifference point, then some additional inducement may be necessary to convert customers to the "new" product. Further, it is important that the seller consider internal pricing factors such as costs and objectives. As was suggested in Chap. 1, the seller's pricing discretion represents

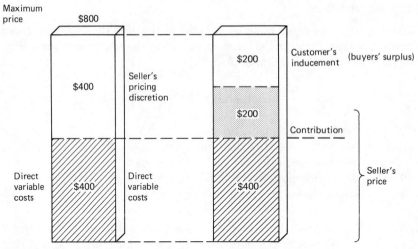

FIGURE 5-4
Determining seller's price.

the difference between the maximum acceptable price in the marketplace and the direct variable costs associated with producing and selling the product. That is,

$$\text{SPD} = P_{\text{max}} - \text{DVC} \tag{5-7}$$

where SPD = seller's pricing discretion
P_{max} = maximum acceptable price
DVC = direct variable costs of producing and selling the product

For our illustration, assume the direct variable costs for producing and selling this "new" product initially total $400. Therefore,

$$\text{SPD} = \$800 - \$400 = \$400 \tag{5-8}$$

That is, the seller has a leeway of $400 for setting the actual price for the "new" product (Fig. 5-4). The problem now is to determine how much of an inducement customers will need to switch to the product.

Customers' Inducement

As we have discussed, the maximum acceptable price represents an economic indifference point to customers. At this price some customers will be willing to switch but others will have some degree of inertia. Therefore, to obtain the volume necessary to make the product a feasible alternative, a price lower than $800 must be considered. Other subjective considerations that influence the outcome will include possible competitive reactions (e.g., price reductions on the reference product) and market entry with an imitative product. Also, the firm may need to consider the wisdom of generating a large sales volume quickly to reduce per unit direct variable costs (this "experience curve" effect is discussed in Chap. 11). In any event, a price less than the maximum acceptable price represents the customers' inducement (consumers' surplus).

To complete the illustration, assume the new product's price is set at $600. This price will give the seller a $200 contribution per unit to fixed costs and profit while providing a $200 inducement to customers. Once this decision has been made, the final step is to develop a communication and sales strategy that reaches and convinces customers of the product's value to them.

ESTIMATING IMPROVEMENT VALUE

One of the major difficulties of applying the relative economic value concept is estimating the relative improvement value of the product or service *as perceived by current and prospective buyers.* Sometimes the product offering is so new that it is difficult to accurately estimate its relative value to customers. Moreover, the improvement value may vary over time and over customers. In particular, the value of the product may be contingent upon the nature of the buyer, how the buyer uses the product, or variations in perceived benefits of the product by different buyers. For example, one industrial firm developed new and relatively sophisticated testing equipment for use in hospital laboratories. The firm calculated that labor savings alone would allow hospitals to recover the cost of the equipment in 12–18 months, depending on the size of the hospital. However, deterred by the hidden cost of recalculating fees and obtaining approvals for the new fees, and not fully understanding the economics of the new equipment, hospitals were reluctant to purchase. In this section, two examples will show how estimates of the relative improvement value of new products can be developed.

Weighting Incremental Benefits

Sometimes because of time pressures it is not feasible for a company to do a complete customer analysis to determine the relative economic advantage of a new product. However, it is still feasible to examine the new product and with experienced product managers and salespeople estimate the incremental perceived value of the product. The Sudbury Corporation faced such a situation and the disguised example that follows illustrates the approach developed to solve the problem.

The Sudbury Corporation manufactured equipment for the application of adhesive materials in its customers' production and packaging operations. The company was the leading producer of such equipment with a nearly 40 percent market share. However, in recent years, it had lost considerable competitive edge, and although its products and services were still perceived to be superior, it no longer had the ability to set premium prices much above competitor prices. The company embarked on a strategy of developing and introducing a series of new products to regain its competitive edge and improve its profitability. It believed it could develop new products that would be perceived to offer greater value to its customers than current products. As the first new product was ready to be introduced to the market, the company was concerned with estimating the premium price to charge for the new product relative to the current product's price. Because of time pressures it was felt to be too late to do any form of market research.

The company brought together representatives of its research and development staff, product managers, and sales managers to discuss the problem. The research and development people outlined the five major advantages of the new equipment relative to the existing equipment. These advantages, labeled incremental benefits, are listed in Table 5-2. On average, it was estimated that users of the new equipment would realize a 35 percent material savings from the efficiencies of the machine, the number of adhesive applications per hour would increase about 10 percent, the increased ease of adapting the equipment to different types of adhesive applications would be about 5 percent, quality of applications would be improved, and since the machine would require less routine maintenance, it also represented an improvement over the old machine. The product managers and salespeople had difficulty correlating the relative importance of these incremental benefits as estimated by the research and development people to potential purchasers, so it was decided to give each benefit an equal relative weight of 0.2. (It should be noted that this weighting procedure is necessary only if there is more than one relative incremental benefit. Also, the sum of the benefit weights should be 1.0.) Each improvement factor then was multiplied by its benefit weight and the products of the multiplication were summed to get an overall estimate of the product's relative improvement value. As shown in Table 5-2 this estimate was 14 percent, implying that a price premium of 14 percent over the existing equipment might be feasible.

At this point considerable discussion took place. The marketing people questioned whether all potential buyers would perceive the new product as envisioned by the research and development staff. It was also suggested that a 14 percent price premium would not lead to a recovery of the development costs in the planned time. It was agreed that only heavy users of equipment similar to the new product would be likely to consider the required investment feasible. Thus, the analysis illustrated

TABLE 5-2
INITIAL FRAMEWORK FOR VALUE ANALYSIS

(1) Incremental Benefit	(2) Improvement Factor, %	(3) Benefit Weight	(4) Weighted Factor, % (2) × (3)
Material savings	35	0.2	7.0
Output/hour	10	0.2	2.0
Adaptability	5	0.2	1.0
Quality of applications	10	0.2	2.0
Less maintenance	10	0.2	2.0
		1.0	14.0

TABLE 5-3
FRAMEWORK FOR VALUE ANALYSIS: HEAVY USERS

(1) Incremental Benefit	(2) Improvement Factor, %	(3) Benefit Weight	(4) Weighted Factor, % (2) × (3)
Material savings	50	0.5	25.0
Output/hour	10	0.1	1.0
Adaptability	5	0.1	0.5
Quality of applications	10	0.2	2.0
Less maintenance	10	0.1	1.0
		1.0	29.5

in Table 5-2 was repeated by considering only the heavy-user segment of prospective buyers.

As seen in Table 5-3, the dramatic increase in the material savings for the heavy users led to a substantial increase in the overall improvement value estimate. Further, because of the dollar savings a heavy user would realize by using less adhesive material, the relative importance of this benefit was believed to be much higher. After this repeat of the analysis, it was decided to concentrate marketing efforts on the heavy user segment with a price premium over the existing "old" product of 22 percent.

The relative importance of this analytical exercise is that for the first time, this firm attempted to price its new product in terms of the market segment's expected perceptions of value, and not solely on the company's internal profit needs. Indeed, the initial financial arguments suggested a price premium of 50 percent should be set. However, it was clear that even without doing the necessary market research to obtain a better idea of potential buyers' value perceptions, a 50 percent price premium was simply too much to charge.

Contingency Pricing

Sometimes, particularly when the "new" product is comprised primarily of delivered services (e.g., an engineering consulting project), the value of the service probably cannot be calculated before its delivery. Even though the provider of the service is sure that the service will be of value to the client, it would be difficult to determine what its economic value is. One way to develop a pricing solution for this problem is for the seller to share some of the risks of delivering this value to the buyer through a contingency pricing arrangement. There are several well-known forms of contingency pricing: money-back guarantees, real estate agents' commissions based on a percentage of the selling price, lawyers' or professional sports agents' fees based on a percentage of the damage award or contract negotiated. In the following example, the price is comprised of a fixed fee with a guarantee geared to the amount of the economic benefits realized by the customer.

The EMS Company was an engineering services firm that suggested means of controlling and reducing energy use in large buildings.[16] EMS was one of three companies submitting a bid to a school district that wanted to reduce its expenditures for energy (heating oil, gas, and electricity). In the most recent year of operation, the school district had spent nearly $775,000 on energy, and the proposed budget for the coming year was $810,000. The school board was interested in a long-term solution to its energy use problem, particularly committing less of the budget to energy and more to direct education expenses. EMS developed a proposal providing for a computer-controlled system that monitored energy use and operated on–off valves for all energy-using systems. The proposal specified a five-year contract with a fixed price of $254,500 per year, with a guarantee that the school district would save at least that amount of money each year or EMS would refund the difference. Included in the proposal was a carefully devised plan to take into account energy prices, hours the buildings were in use, and degree days as a basis for calculating the actual savings. After five years the school district would own the system and have the option of purchasing a continuing monitoring service by EMS for an annual fee of $50,000.

Although two other firms submitted multiyear bids of $190,000 and $215,000 annually for three and five years respectively, neither bid provided any guarantee for energy savings. Despite some questions about accepting the highest bid, the school board accepted the EMS proposal, because at worst the cost of the service was zero. During the first year, actual calculated savings exceeded $300,000. Interestingly, had the firm submitted a cost-plus bid, the bid would have been about $130,000 per year. The use of contingency pricing by EMS removed the risk from the school board's decision and added $600,000 in profit contribution to EMS.

SUMMARY

As the two examples illustrate, value-oriented pricing can help prevent the error of setting a price too high relative to perceived or delivered value as well as that of setting a price too low relative to the value provided to and desired by customers. In the first case, the Sudbury Company probably would have set a price considerably higher than even the heavy-user segment would be willing to pay. Pricing from the viewpoint of satisfying internal profit needs only would have ruined their attempts to regain a competitive edge and to set prices above average market prices for their products. In the second case, the EMS Company developed a procedure for signaling the uncertain economic value to be delivered with a guarantee and successfully charged a premium price well above the cost-plus profit margin price. (See Chap. 2 for a discussion of signaling.)

As this chapter demonstrates, buyers seek to maximize the value received from purchasing products and services. Typically, they are interested not in what it costs the seller to provide the products or services but rather in the price–value relation-

---

[16]This example is adapted from Peter J. LaPlaca, "Pricing That Is Contingent on Value Delivered," presented at the First Annual Pricing Conference, The Pricing Institute, New York, December 3, 4, 1987.

ship. Buyers are seeking benefits in the form of having certain functions performed, problems solved, or pleasures received. Value is created when the benefits delivered by the products or services match the benefits wanted by customers/users/clients at a price consistent with this value. It is customers' perceptions that are important when developing a value-oriented pricing strategy. A product or service perceived to be of higher value than competitive offerings will be granted the privilege of obtaining a premium price by the market.

DISCUSSION QUESTIONS

1 In Chap. 1 several examples indicated that even sellers of "commodity" products or services can set above-market average prices. What are some reasons why these sellers are able to set prices above market? List some products or services for which sellers set prices above market and some reasons why each of these products or services is higher priced.

2 Review the suggested relationship among price, perceived quality, and perceived value developed in Chap. 3. List some ways a firm can strategically increase its customers' perceptions of the value of its offerings. Do any of these ways have the potential of creating misperceptions and therefore deceiving customers? If so, how would you avoid such a situation?

3 In recent years, many retailers have chosen to become aggressive price promoters featuring on a routine basis 40, 50, 60 percent off sales. Others, like Dayton Hudson, Macy's, and The Limited, have been able to succeed without such extensive promotions. Why?

4 A company has developed an innovative product that has an incremental value of $200 over competitive products. The competitive products have, in general, a purchase price of $500, start-up costs of $100, and postpurchase costs of $300. The new product would have start-up costs of $50 and postpurchase costs of $250. What is the economic value of the new product to customers? If the company wanted to set purchase price $25 below the competition, what would be the value of the customer inducements?

5 Recently a public social service agency that provides family counseling services decided to shift away from fee schedules based on clients' ability to pay. Instead, the agency asked clients who had completed the counseling program to pay what they thought the program was worth to them. (Payment schedules were arranged to fit the clients' income levels.) What do you think happened when they tried this approach? Why?

SUGGESTED READINGS

Christopher, Martin: "Value-In-Use-Pricing," *European Journal of Marketing,* 16, No. 5 (1982), 35–46.

Forbes, John L., and Nitin T. Mehta: "Value-Based Strategies for Industrial Products," *Business Horizons,* 21 (October 1978), 25–31.

Rockefeller, David: "Value Versus Price," *Bell Atlantic Quarterly,* 3 (Spring 1986), 42–49.

Shapiro, Benson P., and Barbara B. Jackson: "Industrial Pricing to Meet Customer Needs," *Harvard Business Review,* 56 (November–December 1978), 119–127.

CHAPTER 6

METHODS OF ESTIMATING
THE PRICE–VOLUME
RELATIONSHIP

The past four chapters have stressed the importance of demand in determining the price of a product or service. There has been an implicit assumption that there are ways to determine the responsiveness of demand to alternative prices. As indicated in Chap. 2, the measure of the responsiveness of demand to price differences is the price elasticity measure. If the concern is how volume sold for a product will change relative to a price change for that product, then the measure is price elasticity of demand. But if the concern is how volume sold for product A will change relative to a change in the price of product B, then the concern is the cross-price elasticity of demand. Numerical estimates of the degree of sensitivity of demand for a product to price differences can improve the ability of managers to set prices correctly. However, as the methods of estimating the price–volume relationship are reviewed in this chapter, it should be apparent that reliable estimates of price sensitivity require careful thought and planning. There are many ways to get quantitative estimates of the relationship; each method has advantages and limitations.

PRICING STRATEGY AND PRICING RESEARCH

Traditionally, business firms have not routinely used market research as a basis for pricing strategies. They rarely develop or maintain information systems that are up to date on market and competitive responses to price changes, short-term deals or promotions, or product introductions and deletions. Yet pricing has a major impact on the profitability of an enterprise (or on the ability of a not-for-profit organization to break even), and without information on the results of past pricing decisions or on likely responses to contemplated pricing decisions, a firm is ill-equipped to make informed pricing decisions.

The usefulness of pricing research depends on the firm's pricing objectives and the pricing strategy chosen. If the firm follows a cost-plus approach to pricing, then pricing research on the nature of customer response or competitive response will not be very helpful except to forecast the likely results from a chosen price or price change. Similarly, if the firm primarily follows the pricing practices of competition, pricing research again will have little impact on the chosen prices, but rather may be used to forecast the likely impact of the decisions. However, as discussed in Chaps. 2–5, a well-developed pricing strategy begins with an understanding of how customers and competitors react to prices and their degree of sensitivity to specific prices or price levels and to price changes or price differences.

Some Fundamental Questions

To be able to estimate customers' and competitors' reactions to pricing decisions, there are a number of basic questions that need to be answered. These questions include the following:

- Does the product or service perform a particular function, solve a problem, or provide pleasure for customers? Can these particular functions, problems, or pleasures be identified?
- To what degree do customers tend to associate product or service quality with price?
- How easy or difficult is it for buyers to determine the relative quality of the product or service before purchase? Do buyers tend to search for alternatives before purchase?
- What are the benefits that the product or service provides to different types of buyers?
- What is the size of the market for this product or service?
- What is the maximum amount that customers are willing to pay?
- What is the minimum amount that customers are willing to pay?
- What is the most acceptable set of prices for these customers?
- How much would these customers buy at these different prices?
- To what degree is the demand for the product or service sensitive to price differences?
- Are there different groups of customers with different levels of price sensitivity?
- How do customers purchase the product?
- Are customers aware of prices for this product category?
- Do customers perceive that substitute products or services are available?
- How are competitors likely to react to a particular price change, relative price difference, or pricing tactic?
- To what extent have competitors' pricing strategies and tactics affected the firm's sales volume in the past?

- To what extent have competitors' sales been responsive to their price changes? To the firm's price changes?
- Have competitors' past pricing moves been a surprise?
- Whom do customers perceive to be the firm's major competitors?

Several of these questions can be answered by maintaining an information system that tracks customer and competitor responses to economic conditions and to pricing changes. Other questions can be answered by doing secondary research. However, many of the questions need to be addressed by specific primary research.

Three Basic Pricing Research Issues

A multitude of techniques can be used to conduct a specific pricing research activity. However, three important issues about the conduct of the research must be settled regardless of the technique.

First, will price sensitivity be tested for a single product or brand by itself or in the context of competing products? If there is no readily available reference product for customers, then initially testing the relative willingness to buy for the product in isolation is not too dissimilar from actual market conditions. However, when viable alternatives exist for customers, testing the effect of the price alternative in isolation implicitly assumes there will be no competitor reaction and buyers will be relatively unlikely to shift to a competitive offering.

Second, will customers' responses to the price be tested directly or indirectly? Often, a direct approach (e.g., asking customers if they would be willing to pay a specific price for a product) increases buyers' concern for the price and, as a result, they may respond in a way they think is "rational" rather than according to their perceptions or beliefs. However, an indirect approach (e.g., asking respondents pricing questions within the context of questions about brand name or advertising) requires the researcher to assume that the underlying beliefs and perceptions have been measured, without strong evidence that this is so.

Finally, will each person be asked to respond to one price or to several prices? Obtaining people's responses to a single pricing situation makes it less likely that they will guess the underlying research question and try to provide "rational" responses. However, a single-price scenario makes it more difficult to determine each buyer's relative price sensitivity, and only aggregate measures can be obtained.

As we review the different pricing research approaches, these issues will be developed further.

GENERAL PRICING RESEARCH APPROACHES

Surveys

Perhaps the most frequently used method of estimating price sensitivity is the survey of brand preferences and purchase intentions. A questionnaire is administered through personal interviews, telephone interviews, or the mail. Its basic objective is to elicit facts and opinions from respondents relating either to a prediction of the quantity they would be willing to buy at various prices or to their intent to buy in the near future. In one brand preference study housewives were asked to indicate the amounts they would be willing to buy at selected prices.[1] It was concluded from the responses that baking powder was price inelastic and that higher prices could be charged. Analyzing a set of consumer questionnaires, another company determined that their product was being purchased primarily by high-income households, implying that sales could be increased at lower prices (demand was elastic).[2] This conclusion was verified when prices were lowered.

A different approach is used by the Survey Research Center at the University of Michigan. The Center periodically asks a representative sample of consumers about their attitudes toward spending, saving, credit, prices, and other economic matters. This information is used to construct an index of consumer sentiment toward the economy in general and a measure of intentions to buy certain types of consumer durables. Although there is some controversy about the predictive accuracy of the intentions approach, the intentions survey does provide a general estimate of demand for automobiles and other durables several months ahead of the demand. It does provide information useful in predicting consumers' reactions to changes in the price level, but it does not provide information on specific price elasticities for specific products.

Survey research to determine buyers' sensitivities to prices appears to be relatively easy to conduct and is one of the least costly research methods; nevertheless, it is possible to elicit unreliable responses unless care is taken to develop the questions. One problem is that people tend to anticipate the answers the interviewer or surveyer desires or to offer a socially desirable answer. Thus, when facing a direct question as to which of a set of prices would be preferred or acceptable, buyers often may indicate the lowest price option, since this would be a "rational" answer. Usually such direct questions overestimate the degree to which buyers are sensitive to price and lead to pricing decisions that are not reflective of what buyers are really willing to pay. A second problem is that the survey typically elicits responses from people at a time when they are not very interested in making a purchase of that type of product. Thus, they may not give much thought to their answer, and the answer may be considerably different than if they were seriously considering purchasing the product. There are ways to overcome these limitations; several approaches will be discussed later.

As an example of a direct survey that did not work well consider the approach used by a major hotel chain. Business guests were asked to complete a questionnaire distributed by the front desk clerks. The questionnaire was long and covered all aspects of the hotel's operations. To determine the relative price levels these business guests would be willing to pay at such a hotel, one of the questions asked for a price that the guest would consider to be too high, as well as the highest acceptable price. For some time this questionnaire indicated that the chain's prices in various cities

[1]Edward R. Hawkins, "Methods of Estimating Demand," *Journal of Marketing,* 21 (April 1957), 428–438.
[2]Ibid., p. 430.

always seemed to be about as high as business guests would pay. Eventually, management realized that respondents also were asked to indicate the price they were currently paying and that they were unwilling to indicate that they would have paid more than the current rate. By biasing the responses to the current room rate, this direct survey did not provide information on what prices the business guests might actually have been willing to pay at this hotel.

Experimentation

Much of the research reported in the last three chapters on buyers' perceptions of prices resulted from controlled manipulation of prices. Indeed, many of the commercial techniques currently in use stem from the adaptation of the experimental techniques used to measure buyers' price perceptions. The advantage of the experimental approach is the opportunity it provides to isolate and control various market factors that may affect market demand and then to observe buyers' reactions to changes in one or more of these factors. However, in laboratory experimentation, the disadvantage is that the laboratory is not a natural shopping environment. Whether the findings from a laboratory study could be replicated in a natural environment is an important issue.

An alternative to laboratory experiments is to measure demand responsiveness to price and price changes in the marketplace by manipulating store prices in specific market areas and observing the effect on sales. Although such field experimentation is done in a natural shopping environment, the lack of control over other factors that affect sales—advertising, competition, weather—makes it difficult to know whether the changes in responses are the result of the price manipulations. Also, the passive observation of buyer behavior does not provide information about whether buyers actually perceived differences in prices, either from a previous shopping opportunity or from differences in alternative choices. If aggregate sales volume changes, the exact reason for the change is not known.

Perhaps the most serious problems associated with field experimentation are the time and expense required to change prices and monitor sales for the particular items. The availability of optical scanning equipment greatly increases both the speed and accuracy of obtaining sales volume data, but it still remains difficult to obtain estimates for more than a few products at a time. Careful application of experimental research designs, sampling methods, and statistical tests to evaluate the results will help control and measure the effects of extraneous factors.

Statistical Methods and Models

A number of approaches rely on regression or econometric analyses of price–sales volume data to estimate price elasticity. An econometric approach develops a mathematical equation or equations relating demand for a product to several variables, such as price, income, store location, and consumer density. Data are then collected on the dependent variable, sales volume, and the independent variable simultaneously. Statistical techniques are then used to estimate the parameters of the equation(s) so as to derive an equation relating the independent variables to the dependent variable.

Often, however, some of the independent variables are also affected by demand, and to overcome this particular problem, a multiple-equation model is developed. For either single-equation or multiple-equation models, once the parameters are estimated from the empirical data, the equations may be used to predict the effect on demand of a change in price or any other independent variable.

To get an understanding for this type of approach, consider a study designed to determine the effect of price-off coupons on sales of bathroom tissue. One of the underlying problems with couponing and other short-term price deals is that buyers frequently accelerate their purchases to take advantage of price promotions. In the current example, if buyers simply accelerate their purchases of the brand of tissue being couponed, then an apparent increase in sales due to the promotion would actually not be an increase at all. That is, the coupon promotion would be stealing sales from a future period, and really generating no net increase in sales. To consider this issue, the researchers included an independent variable called *interpurchase time,* the amount of time that elapses between purchases of the product. Further, it was reasoned that the quantity previously purchased would affect both the household's interpurchase time and the amount it would buy in the current period, because a household that purchased a larger quantity than usual as a result of the promotion would be able to delay future purchases because it would have a higher inventory of tissue on hand than usual. Thus, the effect of a promotion is to cause people to purchase more than usual in a given time by accelerating their purchases. Using consumer scanner panel data, over 7,000 purchase records were examined to develop and test the following model:

$$Q_t = bQ_{t-1} + cE_t + dP \qquad (6\text{-}1)$$
$$E_t = gQ_{t-1} + hP \qquad (6\text{-}2)$$

where Q_t = current quantity purchased
Q_{t-1} = quantity purchased on the previous occasion
E_t = elapsed time between current and previous purchases
P = average coupon effect averaged across brands
b,c,d,g,h = empirically derived regression coefficients

The results of the analysis produced estimates of the coefficients in quantity units (rolls of bathroom tissue) and time (days):

$$b = -0.042 \text{ rolls}$$
$$c = 0.013 \text{ rolls}$$
$$d = 0.806 \text{ rolls}$$
$$g = 1.154 \text{ days}$$
$$h = 0.049 \text{ days}$$

These values represent the average effects over the entire data set and have the following interpretation: (1) an increase in purchase quantity of one roll leads to the next purchase being reduced on average by 0.042 rolls; (2) increasing the interpurchase time by one day leads to an increase on average by 0.013 rolls on the next purchase occasion; (3) a coupon purchase involves on average 0.806 more rolls than noncoupon purchases; (4) increasing purchase quantity by one roll leads to an increase in interpurchase time by 1.154 days; and (5) a coupon purchase leads to an increase in interpurchase time of 0.049 days.[3]

Panels

The preceding example, besides illustrating the nature of econometric modeling, showed the use of data generated from a consumer panel. In a consumer panel, the few thousand households that comprise the panel record their purchases by brand and price in a daily diary. The data are then aggregated across the panel on a weekly or biweekly basis.

The advantage of these data is that observations accumulate quickly to establish an adequate data base to develop and test models. Also, it is possible to identify purchases made with the use of coupons or at a special lower price. The major disadvantage is that the panel is not likely to be representative of the general population and the ability to generalize is limited. Another disadvantage is the possibility of errors because the respondent either forgets to record a purchase or makes an incorrect entry. Today, a number of research companies are using scanner panel data whereby the purchases of the panel are recorded automatically at the time of store checkout. Panel members must identify themselves at the point of checkout for this procedure to work.

Panel data are limited to a small percentage of consumer packaged products, because of the difficulty of getting people to record all their purchases. There is still some question about the reliability of the estimates based on panel data, but they do offer a way to obtain observations over a short period of time, making the estimates closer to the reality of the market than are the results of other survey approaches.

SOME SPECIFIC PRICE RESEARCH TECHNIQUES

We now consider different ways of estimating how buyers' respond to prices, price changes, or price differences. The set of fundamental questions posed at the beginning of this chapter reflect the behavioral points discussed in Chaps. 2–5. That is, to estimate the maximum amount buyers are willing to pay one must determine their highest acceptable price, or reservation price, referred to as the upper price thresh-

---

[3]This example is drawn from Scott A. Neslin, John Quelch, and Caroline Henderson, "Consumer Promotions and the Acceleration of Product Purchases," in Katherine E. Jocz (ed.), *Research on Sales Promotion: Collected Papers* (Cambridge, Mass.: Marketing Science Institute, 1984), Report No. 84-104, pp. 22–46.

old. Questions about whether buyers infer product quality on the basis of price relate to buyers' unwillingness to pay low prices because of suspicions about quality. Thus, the lowest acceptable price or lower price threshold needs to be estimated.

An important issue in pricing products or services is determining what benefits buyers obtain from purchasing or acquiring the product. Part of the research issue here is determining what attributes or features of the product are valued by buyers and estimating the relative perceived value of these attributes. It is also important to determine whether buyers are aware of prices they pay and how sensitive they are to differences in prices occurring because of a price change or differential pricing by competitors.

The discussion in Chap. 4 on reference prices and framing is very important in developing and interpreting techniques for obtaining buyers' responses to prices. As pointed out in Chaps. 3 and 4, price judgments are comparative in nature. Thus, simply asking people to respond to a hypothetical price without carefully providing a frame of reference forces the respondent to use his or her own reference point. That this error can lead to incorrect inferences about a firm's prices is illustrated by the following example.

A restaurant in a university conference center was experiencing some difficulty in generating sufficient revenues to break even. Explanations offered for this situation included prices that were too high and an image that the restaurant catered to conference attendees and did not offer a full-service menu. To determine how people in the local area perceived the restaurant, a consulting firm was hired to conduct a market survey. On the pricing issue, respondents were asked to agree or disagree with this statement: "Prices at the Top Hat restaurant are about right." As would be expected, a proportion of the respondents agreed with the statement and almost as many disagreed with it. Interviews were conducted with a sample of the respondents to determine why they had answered this question in the manner they had. Some respondents disagreed with the statement because they compared the restaurant to a fast-food operation and judged the prices were too high; others disagreed with the statement because they compared the restaurant to a fancy restaurant and judged prices to be low. Respondents who agreed with the statement tended to compare the restaurant to another moderately priced restaurant in the area. Failure to provide respondents with a consistent frame of reference for answering the question could have led to a serious pricing error, because the management had interpreted the majority of disagreements to mean the restaurant should reduce its prices, when in fact the prices were not perceived to be too high by a majority of respondents. Thus, an important pricing research principle is to provide respondents a frame of reference that is consistent with the research question and is consistent across respondents, unless the research is explicitly studying the effect of varying the frame of reference on responses.

Estimating Price-Level Sensitivity (Absolute Price Thresholds)

The objective of determining buyers' upper and lower price thresholds is to determine the range of prices that are acceptable to pay for the product or service. As suggested in Chap. 3, most buyers do not consider buying a product at only one specific price but instead are willing to buy within a range of prices.

Direct Question Approach   One approach to determining upper and lower price thresholds, originally developed in France in the 1950s, simply asks respondents two questions:[4]

1. What is the *minimum price* you would be willing to pay for [product and/or brand specified]? (That is, below what price would you seriously doubt its quality?)
2. What is the *maximum price* you would be willing to pay for [product and/or brand specified]? (That is, beyond what price would you feel it would not be worth paying more?)

This procedure is simple and easy to implement, but it has the potential problem of being too direct. That is, it may put the idea into respondents' minds that there should be either a price that is too low or a price that is too high.

The analysis is also relatively easy. Excluding "don't know" answers, the proportions for each price are collected, beginning with the lowest price for those who would not buy because it is too low and ending with those who would not buy

[4]Jean Stoetzel, "Psychological/Sociological Aspects of Price," in Bernard Taylor and Gordon Wills (eds.), *Pricing Strategy* (Princeton, N.J.: Brandon/Systems, 1970), pp. 70–74.

FIGURE 6-1
Determining price limits: direct question approach.

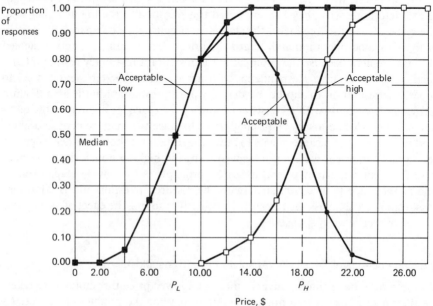

because it is too high. The cumulative proportion of those who find a price to be unacceptable because it is too low is labeled $L(P)$; the cumulative proportion of those who find a price to be unacceptable because it is too high is labeled $H(P)$. Subtracting $H(P)$ from $[1 - L(P)]$ at each price gives the proportion that would be willing to buy at each price, $[B(P)]$. An example set of data is shown in Table 6-1 and plotted in Fig. 6-1. To determine the lower and upper price limits for the product, usually the median percentage for each distribution (50 percent in the cumulative distribution) is used. As illustrated in Fig. 6-1, the low price limit is $8.00 and the high price limit is $18.00. And as indicated in Table 6-1, 90 percent of the respondents believed that prices of $12.00 and $14.00 were acceptable, with 75 percent of the respondents accepting a price of $16.00. Thus, it would appear that a price around $14.00 would have the highest acceptance in the market.

As is readily seen, this approach is convenient but does not provide sufficient information to understand whether the price that maximizes the percentage between the minimum and maximum acceptable price curves is the price that buyers find most acceptable. Moreover, each respondent provides only two prices, the lowest and highest acceptable prices. An easy extension is to give the respondents a price scale covering all the feasible market prices that might be charged for the product and ask respondents to indicate all the prices they would find acceptable. To determine whether the prices that have not been checked as acceptable are truly unacceptable, the respondents can be given a second scale and asked to indicate all unacceptable prices. Each respondent then can be asked to indicate the price that would be most acceptable to pay for the product. Figure 6-2 illustrates how these questions may be posed to respondents.

TABLE 6-1
DETERMINING PRICE LIMITS USING THE DIRECT QUESTION APPROACH

Price, $	Low Frequency, %	Low Unacceptable Cumulative $L(P)$	Low Acceptable Cumulative $[1 - L(P)]$	High Frequency, %	High Unacceptable Cumulative $H(P)$	Buy Price $B(P) = [1 - L(P)] - H(P)$
0.00	0.00	1.00	0.00	0.00	0.00	0.00
2.00	0.05	1.00	0.00	0.00	0.00	0.00
4.00	0.20	0.95	0.05	0.00	0.00	0.05
6.00	0.25	0.75	0.25	0.00	0.00	0.25
8.00	0.30	0.50	0.50	0.00	0.00	0.50
10.00	0.15	0.20	0.80	0.00	0.00	0.80
12.00	0.05	0.05	0.95	0.05	0.05	0.90
14.00	0.00	0.00	1.00	0.05	0.10	0.90
16.00	0.00	0.00	1.00	0.15	0.25	0.75
18.00	0.00	0.00	1.00	0.25	0.50	0.50
20.00	0.00	0.00	1.00	0.30	0.80	0.20
22.00	0.00	0.00	1.00	0.15	0.95	0.05
24.00	0.00	0.00	1.00	0.05	1.00	0.00
26.00	0.00	0.00	1.00	0.00	1.00	0.00
28.00	0.00	0.00	1.00	0.00	1.00	0.00

Product: Man's T-shirt (package of three, white)

Place X marks above the prices acceptable to you
(you would consider paying).

Place check (√) marks above the prices unacceptable
to you (you would not consider paying).

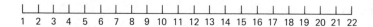

Please indicate the price that would be most acceptable
to pay: $ _____

FIGURE 6-2
Scales for determining acceptable prices.

The analysis of the data is similar to the analysis sketched earlier for the direct question approach. Cumulative percentages of each price that is judged to be too low, too high, and most acceptable are developed and graphed. As before, the median price that is too low is labeled the low price limit, the median price that is too high is labeled the high price limit, and the median most acceptable price is labeled the most acceptable price. The principal advantage of this approach is that individuals' evaluations of each price are obtained with little additional effort on their part. Also, it is likely that the curve depicting the distribution of acceptable prices is not a smooth, bell-shaped (normal) curve but rather is skewed, indicating that the subjective price scale is logarithmic in character.[5] (Recall that the Weber–Fechner law discussed in Chap. 3 suggests this logarithmic relationship.)

Price Sensitivity Meter   The disadvantage of the direct question approach is it forces a person to judge each price as acceptable or not. The price sensitivity meter (PSM) approach takes the direct question technique further. Instead of two questions, four questions are asked:

1. At what price would you consider this [product and/or brand] to be so inexpensive that you would have doubts about its quality?

[5] For evidence of this phenomenon see Andre Gabor and Clive Granger, "Price as an Indicator of Quality: Report on an Enquiry," *Economica,* 46 (February 1966), 43–70; Kent B. Monroe, "The Information Content of Price: A Preliminary Model for Estimating Buyer Response," *Management Science,* 17 (April 1971), B519–532; Kent B. Monroe, "Buyers' Subjective Perceptions of Price," *Journal of Marketing Research,* 10 (February 1973), 70–80.

2. At what price would you still feel this product was inexpensive yet have no doubts as to its quality?

3. At what price would you begin to feel this product is expensive but still worth buying because of its quality?

4. At what price would you feel that the product is so expensive that regardless of its quality it is not worth buying?

These four questions can be asked in an interview or as a part of a survey questionnaire. When used in a printed questionnaire, inclusion of a price scale like that in Fig. 6-2 gives respondents a better opportunity to recognize feasible prices for the product. Attempting to recall prices that might be feasible for a product without some retrieval cues makes the task quite difficult and probably introduces variation in responses across individuals.

The initial analysis is identical to that for the direct question approach. The cumulative frequency distributions for prices that are too low and too high are developed, and estimates of the lower and upper price limits are obtained using the median from each distribution (Table 6-2 and Fig. 6-3). As shown by the calculation of the buy response percentages, $B(P)$, the point of lowest buyer resistance is where $B(P)$ is the largest value, at about \$10. This point of lowest resistance is also where the unacceptable-high and unacceptable-low curves intersect. Note that at this price

TABLE 6-2
DETERMINING PRICE LIMITS USING THE PSM APPROACH

Price, $	Low			High			Buy Price $B(P) = [1 - L(P)] - H(P)$
	Frequency, %	Unacceptable Cumulative $L(P)$	Acceptable Cumulative $[1 - L(P)]$	Frequency, %	Unacceptable Cumulative $H(P)$	Acceptable Cumulative $[1 - H(P)]$	
1.00	0.00	1.00	0.00	0.00	0.00	1.00	0.00
2.00	0.05	1.00	0.00	0.00	0.00	1.00	0.00
3.00	0.05	0.95	0.05	0.00	0.00	1.00	0.05
4.00	0.05	0.90	0.10	0.00	0.00	1.00	0.10
5.00	0.10	0.85	0.15	0.00	0.00	1.00	0.15
6.00	0.10	0.75	0.25	0.00	0.00	1.00	0.25
7.00	0.10	0.65	0.35	0.00	0.00	1.00	0.35
8.00	0.20	0.55	0.45	0.00	0.00	1.00	0.45
9.00	0.20	0.35	0.65	0.05	0.05	0.95	0.60
10.00	0.05	0.15	0.85	0.05	0.10	0.90	0.75
11.00	0.05	0.10	0.90	0.10	0.20	0.80	0.70
12.00	0.05	0.05	0.95	0.20	0.40	0.60	0.55
13.00	0.00	0.00	1.00	0.25	0.65	0.35	0.35
14.00	0.00	0.00	1.00	0.15	0.80	0.20	0.20
15.00	0.00	0.00	1.00	0.05	0.85	0.15	0.15
16.00	0.00	0.00	1.00	0.05	0.90	0.10	0.10
17.00	0.00	0.00	1.00	0.05	0.95	0.05	0.05
18.00	0.00	0.00	1.00	0.05	1.00	0.00	0.00
19.00	0.00	0.00	1.00	0.00	1.00	0.00	0.00
20.00	0.00	0.00	1.00	0.00	1.00	0.00	0.00
21.00	0.00	0.00	1.00	0.00	1.00	0.00	0.00

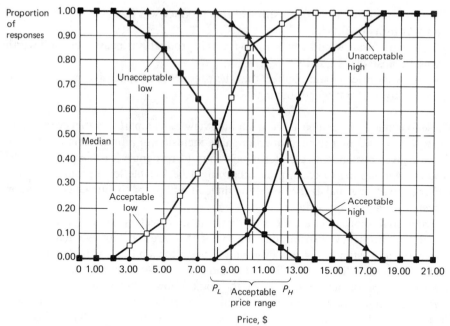

FIGURE 6-3
Determining price limits: PSM approach.

the two acceptable cumulative curves also intersect, indicating, as would be expected, the price of highest receptivity. The point where the unacceptable-low and acceptable-low curves intersect is the point at which 50 percent of the respondents are indifferent to the price because of quality concerns. Where the unacceptable-high and acceptable-high curves intersect is the price where 50 percent of the respondents are indifferent because of concerns of relative expensiveness. Between these low- and high-price limits is the acceptable price range. The buy response curve covering the acceptable price range for this data set is illustrated in Fig. 6-4. It should be noted that usually there will be some overlap between prices that are unacceptable or acceptable at both the high and low limits, providing for a small band of indifferent prices at the limits. Generally, most buyers are willing to go a little bit higher or a little bit lower before they completely refrain from a willingness to purchase. For this reason, it is useful to ask respondents to indicate those prices that are acceptable to pay as well as those prices that are unacceptable to pay.

It would be useful to add a fifth question to this approach:

5. What price would be the *most acceptable* price to pay?

Because it is likely that the buy response curve covering the range of acceptable prices will be skewed, obtaining buyers' most acceptable price adds useful information about their perceptions of prices for the product category. In addition, questions

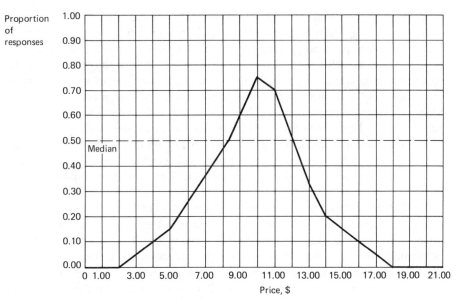

FIGURE 6-4
Buy–response curve.

about their relative knowledge of the alternative products or services available, their recent purchase and use history of the product, their estimate of the last price paid, and their belief about the relative spread of prices for the product category in their market area will help to determine whether there are segments of buyers with different acceptable price ranges and the reasons for these differences.

It has generally been the case that buyers who are frequent purchasers of a product have narrower and more distinct acceptable price ranges. Also, the more buyers believe that there are small differences in prices across suppliers, the narrower will be their acceptable price range.[6] In any case, when doing pricing research, it is imperative to obtain information about buyers' perceptions and knowledge of prices as well as their purchase and use experience with the product category. Without this information, it will not be easy to interpret their responses to the price questions.

To illustrate this last point, consider the situation one research company faced after conducting a price-sensitivity study. The overall empirically derived demand curve seemed to have the expected inverse relationship between price and predicted sales volume, yet in the middle of the price range the demand curve appeared to be flat. Fortunately, the company had collected additional information about the re- spondents' perceptions and beliefs about the product category. A careful analysis of

[6]Rustan Kosenko and Don Rahtz, "Buyer Market Price Knowledge Influence on Acceptable Price Range and Price Limits," in Michael J. Houston (ed.), *Advances in Consumer Research,* Vol. 15 (Provo, Utah: Association for Consumer Research, 1988), pp. 328–333.

this information revealed a segment of buyers had a strong belief that there was a positive price–quality relationship, and this belief strongly influenced their responses in the middle of the price range. That is, consistent with the tradeoff model discussed in Chaps. 3 and 4, within their acceptable price range, their willingness to buy the product increased as the price increased, particularly around the price that was most acceptable to pay. The effect of this price–quality belief by a segment of the buyers made the aggregate demand curve flatten out as they were willing to increase their purchases while the other segment of buyers were reducing their willingness to buy as the price increased. Recognizing that there were two distinct market segments based on the strength of the belief in the price–quality association led the company to introduce a second brand with additional quality at a price premium.

Price Categorization   As indicated at the beginning of Chap. 3, people perceive and classify objects according to categories. That is, whenever we notice a price, we compare it to the price that we use as a reference or standard. Another approach to determining buyers' acceptable prices and price thresholds is to ask buyers to sort a set of prices for a product into smaller groups or categories according to how they perceive these prices to be similar or dissimilar to each other. This technique can be done by personal interviews, mail surveys, or experiments.

When respondents are interviewed in a setting that allows them to have some working space, the instructions given in Fig. 6-5 (opposite) are used. If the research is being conducted by a mail survey, a response sheet similar to Fig. 6-6 is used. After the respondents sort the prices into categories, they should be asked to label any groups of prices that are unacceptable. If possible, they should be asked to indicate why the prices in these groups are unacceptable. For the groups of prices that are acceptable, they should be asked to label the set of prices that is most acceptable to them. Generally, a wide range of prices, perhaps as many as fifty, should be used. Experience has indicated that people will be able to group this many prices into five to seven categories.

The analysis proceeds as described for the direct question approach for each of the price categories identified: unacceptable-low, acceptable-low, most acceptable, acceptable-high, and unacceptable-high. If respondents are able to indicate the reasons for the unacceptable prices (e.g., too cheap or too expensive), then these labeled categories form the two additional categories. Respondents who can provide labels for the unacceptable price categories provide information on why they labeled the prices unacceptable. Figure 6-7 illustrates how the cumulative proportion curves might look for a particular research effort. As before, using the median response, when 50 percent of the respondents indicate that a particular price might belong in a particular price category or the price category adjacent to it, then that price forms a category limit. Thus, the category limits are defined as the prices where the probability of a price being included in a designated category equals the probability of its being included in the immediately adjacent category. A vertical line drawn from the price axis to the cumulative proportion curve for any category at the median response point represents the width of each price category in dollars. These procedures provide a quantitative record of the respondents' definitions of each

FIGURE 6-5
Instructions for price categorization.

1. Developing Categories

In a general way, you have just been told what you are going to be doing in the next few minutes. Now let us explain the complete procedure. If, after reading the procedure, you have any questions, please raise your hand and the research assistant will come to you and answer your questions.

Imagine that you are in a store to buy a pair of semicasual shoes and that each slip of paper that you have in the envelope (handed to you) is a price tag on the shoes. Assume you can buy the color, size, style, etc., of your choice. Since price is the only basis for your decision, you carefully sort through the price tags.

Now take out the price tags in the envelope and sort them into any number of piles you choose. To help you start we are providing you with two category designations for your piles: (1) Too Cheap to Buy, and (2) Too Expensive to Buy. If you find any prices that you think are too cheap to buy, pile those tags on the left and mark this pile with the Category Identification Slip marked "Too Cheap to Buy." Similarly, if you find any prices that are way too high for you—that are simply prohibitive in price—pile them on your right and mark this pile "Too Expensive to Buy." *Remember these two categories for your piles are provided as a starting point. You need not use these two categories if you do not find any prices (slips) that belong in these two categories.*

Decide on the piles on the basis of which prices (slips) seem to belong together. Do not be concerned about how many are in the piles or how many piles you create. If you change your mind, please feel free to rearrange things.

After you are finished placing prices in as many or as few piles as you like, raise your hand to indicate that you have completed this task. The research assistant will come to you and explain further procedures.

Are these instruction clear? If so, please proceed. If not, raise your hand and the research assistant will come and help you.

2. Labeling the Price Categories

Now you are provided with labels for naming the piles as categories. Use as many labels as you need. For naming the categories, follow these instructions:

1. On the one pile with the prices that are *most acceptable to you,* place the label "MOST ACCEPTABLE."
2. Place the "ACCEPTABLE" labels on any other pile or piles that are also acceptable. (Do not be concerned about how many piles you label "acceptable.")
3. Place the label "UNACCEPTABLE" on any pile or piles that are unacceptable to you.
4. On the piles labeled "UNACCEPTABLE" indicate, if you wish, any reason for their unacceptability.

Please return any unused labels to the research assistant. Please raise your hand to indicate that you have completed this part of the research study.
Thank you for your cooperation.

FIGURE 6-6
Price categorization response sheet: mail survey.

PRODUCT:	Semicasual shoes
DIRECTIONS:	For this product, we have listed a series of prices below. First look at all the prices. Then place each price *anywhere* you feel is appropriate, in the column marked "price," to indicate your rating of that particular price for this product. You can indicate any number of prices at any spot.
ASSUME:	Your choices of style, color, and size are available.

PRICES:

$ 5	$ 6	$ 7	$ 8	$ 9	$10	$11	$12	$13
$14	$15	$16	$17	$18	$19	$20	$21	$22
$23	$24	$25	$26	$27	$28	$29	$30	$31
$32	$33	$34	$35	$36	$37	$38	$39	$40
$41	$42	$43	$44	$45	$46	$47	$48	$49

UNACCEPTABLE—TOO EXPENSIVE:

UNACCEPTABLE—EXPENSIVE:

ACCEPTABLE—HIGH:

MOST ACCEPTABLE:

ACCEPTABLE—LOW:

UNACCEPTABLE—INEXPENSIVE:

UNACCEPTABLE—TOO CHEAP:

category. In particular, the width of the acceptable price range in Fig. 6-7 is categories 3 to 5. The dotted line (at about $15) indicates the center of the respondents' price scale. The scale center is the limit between the two middle categories if the individual respondent used an even number of categories or the midpoint of the middle category if the individual used an odd number. Again, the median scale center across all respondents is used as the scale center for the sample.

The advantage of the categorization approach is it does not implicitly assume that there is only one definable set of acceptable prices in the market. In both the direct question and PSM approaches, an attempt is made to force the data onto one buy response curve or distribution. In the categorization approach, using a wide range of prices and explicit evaluations of prices enables the researcher to determine whether there are actually several acceptable price ranges corresponding to buyers who are more interested in relatively lower prices, buyers who will accept medium-level prices, and buyers who accept relatively higher prices. Also, asking buyers to indicate those prices that are most acceptable provides a means of determining whether there might be one price that clearly emerges as the best price for the product or service. Moreover, in the two earlier approaches a judgment that a specific price is acceptable or unacceptable reflects a subjective evaluation by an individual and is based on that person's set of purchase-influencing variables, an evaluative set of categories already established from past behavior.

The categorization approach is designed to establish a measurement scale when

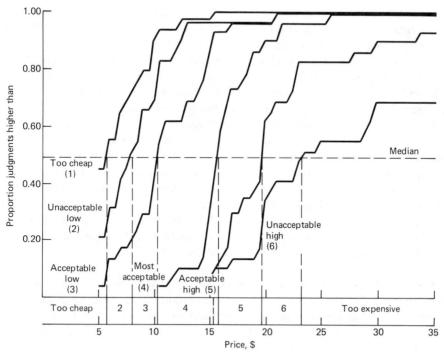

FIGURE 6-7
Using price categorization to determine respondents' price scale.

the underlying judgments are subjective in nature. In addition, this technique allows the respondent to react to a wider set of prices and removes the problem that the respondent knows the specific value of the price. This approach permits individuals to establish their own categories, both in number and width. Thus, the resulting scale is more likely to reflect their true subjective perceptions, without the researcher's perceptions being reflected in the scale.[7]

Magnitude Scaling   The approaches just outlined directly or indirectly ask respondents to express their judgments by choosing among a limited set of categories labeled with such cues as acceptable–unacceptable. As noted, when the researcher limits the number of response categories, responses are constrained to this limited number of categories. In particular, attempting to categorize prices into either an acceptable or unacceptable category may overly constrain the respondents who are providing the relative price judgments. Moreover, no information is obtained concerning the intensity of people's feelings about the acceptability of the prices, which

[7]For a more detailed discussion of this approach, see Kent B. Monroe, "Measuring Price Thresholds by Psychophysics and Latitudes of Acceptance," *Journal of Marketing Research,* 8 (November 1971), 460–464.

also limits the value of these approaches. Although inferences can be made as to why some prices might be considered too low to be acceptable (e.g., buyers are suspicious of quality), no specific evaluations of a product's perceived quality or relative value are obtained. In magnitude scaling, it is possible to elicit information about the intensity of respondents' judgments and how they make price–quality or price–value judgments. Underlying the approach is the fundamental belief that people can provide meaningful information about the magnitude of their sensory experiences.

This approach asks respondents to judge a product, service, and/or price relative to a reference product, service, and/or price. It can effectively be applied in face-to-face interviews, telephone interviews, or mail surveys. The most widely used form of magnitude scaling is *numeric estimation,* where respondents are instructed to assign numbers to the stimulus product or price relative to a standard number for the reference product or price. This approach is similar to the technique used to judge gymnasts or divers in competition, where the judging is on a 1 to 10 scale.

When attempting to measure the price–value relationship for a particular product or service, the following procedure might be used:

1 Respondents are asked to describe the current product or service that they are using. In particular, they should be encouraged to indicate the attributes and features of the product that are most important to them and the benefits that they receive from these attributes or features. Then they are asked to assign the current or reference product an index value of 100.

2 The product or service to be evaluated is described in terms of its attributes, features, and benefits delivered. Respondents are asked to judge the relative quality of the "new" product by assigning it a number above or below 100. That is, they are asked to compare the "new" product to the "old" or "current" product. They are instructed to give the "new" product a number greater than 100 if they believe it is of better quality than the "current" product or a number less than 100 if it is perceived to be inferior. For this step, the instructions on how to assign the number are very important. For example, "If you think that the 'new' product is about 10 percent better in quality, then assign it a 110; if you think it is two times better, give it a number of 200. But if you think the product has about 10 percent less quality, give it a number of 90; if you think it is half as good, give it a number of 50. Choose a number that reflects how you rate the new product relative to the 100 you assigned to the product you currently use."

3 For their price judgments, respondents next are instructed to give the price they currently are paying a number of 100. (As discussed in Chap. 3, it is possible that a significant number of respondents may not be able to remember the price they paid for the reference product. However, this is not a serious problem, since the issue is how much more or less the person is willing to pay for the new product relative to the old one.)

4 Then, the same instructions given in step 2 are used to ask the respondents to indicate the price that would be acceptable for the new product, i.e., how much more or less they would be willing to pay for the product. It should be noted that the respondents do not have to remember the correct price for the current product, only that they evaluate the new product relative to an index of 100 for the old product.

5. If several product–price combinations are being evaluated, the procedure is repeated by asking the respondent to evaluate the next "new" product against the original reference product.

This approach provides proportionate judgments about a product's perceived value relative to the natural price scale. By using several product–price combinations, a scale can be developed that reflects the proportional perceived differences between price and different product attributes. The data can readily be analyzed using regression analysis. Usually, taking the logarithms of the numerical responses before doing the regression analysis provides for an estimated linear relationship between price and the different attributes used in the study.[8]

Estimating Sensitivity to Price Differences

The research techniques described thus far are concerned with determining the relative willingness of buyers to pay particular prices for a product or service. The primary objective of such research is to determine buyers' upper and lower acceptable price limits and the likelihood that there are several price-market segments for the product. Also, if the respondents in the sample represent the actual potential population of buyers, estimates of the relative size of these different price/market segments can be obtained. This type of information is of strategic importance when developing a price strategy for a new product that may be relatively novel to the market.

For established products, or when introducing a new model into an established product line, a second issue of price sensitivity concerns the degree that demand may be sensitive to price differences (differential price thresholds). As discussed in Chap. 3, sensitivity to price differences is important when deciding whether to change price for a product (demand price elasticity) or when attempting to establish a price differential for a product relative to comparable alternatives (cross-price elasticity). Strategically, it is an important issue when positioning products within a line or relative to competition. In this section, several techniques for estimating sensitivity to price differences will be presented.

Sequential Preferences: Two Brands   When the objective is to determine sensitivity to price differences for comparable brands, one approach is to ask respondents to indicate their brand preference as the price of a brand is changed. This approach can be used in a mail survey or in either telephone or personal interviews. When comparing two brands, A and B (actual brand names would be used), it is important

---

[8]For additional technical information as well as marketing applications of this technique, see Milton Lodge, *Magnitude Scaling: Quantitative Measurement of Opinions* (Beverly Hills, Calif.: Sage Publications, 1981); Paul J. Hensel and Noel M. Lavenka, "On the Extension of Psychophysical Scaling and Cross-Modality Triangulation to the Measurement of Product Quality," *Proceedings,* Summer Educators' Conference (Chicago: American Marketing Association, 1984), pp. 411–415; Bruno Neibecker, "The Validity of Computer-Controlled Magnitude Scaling to Measure Emotional Impact of Stimuli," *Journal of Marketing Research,* 21 (August 1984), 325–331; and Paul A. Scipione, "Perceived Value Gauged by Indexing Purchaser Response," *Marketing News,* 20 (April 11, 1986), 15.

first to establish each respondent's preference when prices are equal. Then, while holding the price constant for one of the brands, the price of the other brand is systematically changed by constant amounts, both increases and decreases from the original equal price point.

Respondents' reactions to these price differences can be obtained by asking them to indicate which brand they would prefer, A or B. This simple response method permits estimating the price difference necessary to induce a switch from the preferred brand, but it does not indicate the relative intensity of respondents' preferences. The rating sheet illustrated in Fig. 6-8 permits a recording not only of their preferences, but also whether these preferences are relatively strong or weak. These additional data may provide sufficient information to determine the relative size of a loyal segment vs. a brand-switching segment. Moreover, allowing respondents to indicate an indifferent or no-preference response provides important information about the size of a price difference necessary before a switch might occur. In effect, a no-preference response when there are price differences indicates the differential price premium that one of the brands might successfully use in the market. To avoid

FIGURE 6-8
Response sheet for sequential preferences: two brands.

DIRECTIONS: Below are some pairs of brands of spray cologne mist. For each pair please indicate your brand preference by circling the number that corresponds most closely with the description of your brand preference. Assume that you are interested in purchasing this product for yourself or a friend and that the pair represents the only choice available.

	Brand A				Brand B			
Price	Prefer A to B Strongly	Prefer A to B Moderately	Prefer A to B Slightly	No Preference	Prefer B to A Slightly	Prefer B to A Moderately	Prefer B to A Strongly	Price
$14.00	1	2	3	4	5	6	7	$ 14.00
14.00	1	2	3	4	5	6	7	14.25
14.00	1	2	3	4	5	6	7	14.50
14.00	1	2	3	4	5	6	7	14.75
14.00	1	2	3	4	5	6	7	15.00
14.00	1	2	3	4	5	6	7	15.25
14.00	1	2	3	4	5	6	7	15.50
14.00	1	2	3	4	5	6	7	15.75
14.00	1	2	3	4	5	6	7	16.00
14.00	1	2	3	4	5	6	7	16.25
14.00	1	2	3	4	5	6	7	16.50
14.00	1	2	3	4	5	6	7	13.75
14.00	1	2	3	4	5	6	7	13.50
14.00	1	2	3	4	5	6	7	13.25
14.00	1	2	3	4	5	6	7	13.00
14.00	1	2	3	4	5	6	7	12.75
14.00	1	2	3	4	5	6	7	12.50
14.00	1	2	3	4	5	6	7	12.25
14.00	1	2	3	4	5	6	7	12.00
14.00	1	2	3	4	5	6	7	11.75

potential order of presentation effects, the order of the brands, the order of the price manipulations, and the reference brand should be randomly varied over respondents. Standard statistical significance tests can be used to determine whether there are significant differences in preferences across the price difference conditions and at what specific price differences these results are significant.

The mean preferences for the various price differences can also be graphed as seen in Fig. 6-9. Negative price differences indicate a price advantage for the test brand, and hence low mean judgments indicate preferences for the test brand. The opposite situation exists for positive price differences (a scale value of 4.0 represents a neutral or indifferent preference). In Fig. 6-9, brand A exhibits a clear preference strength over brand B at all price differences. Note that until brand A has a 9-cent price premium over brand B, it enjoys a stronger brand preference. However, while brand A has some preference strength relative to brand C, it is not as strong because at a price premium of 3 to 6 cents respondents are essentially indifferent in their preferences between brands A and C.

Sequential Preferences: Multiple Brands   In an extension of the two-brand preference test, respondents are presented with several brands with identical prices and are asked to indicate a preference for one brand. The price of one of the brands is then systematically varied up or down over a sufficient range of prices to determine preference changes relative to the price structures. The brand whose price is changed

FIGURE 6-9
Sensitivity to price differences: sequential preferences approach.

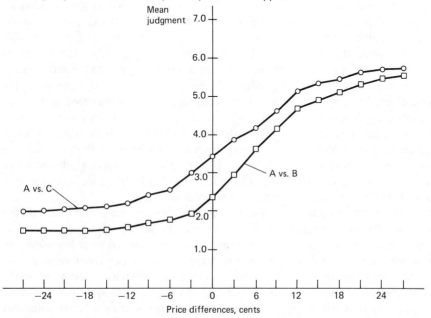

is varied over respondents, and the order of presentations is randomly varied as described above; this provides additional information about the relative price positions of the various brands being tested. The analysis is similar to that for two brands. In addition, it is possible to graph (1) the proportion of times a brand was chosen at different price scenarios (brand share) and (2) the proportion of times a brand was chosen at various prices or price differences with other brands.

Experimental Demand Curve   In an approach similar to the sequential multiple-brand preference task, only the price of the test brand is varied over conditions. The purpose is to estimate the demand curve of the test brand relative to the prices of competing brands. The sample should be divided into a minimum of five different prices for the test brand. (Depending on resources, using up to eight different prices would provide better information.) Each respondent is given one array of brands including the test brand and the price of each brand is clearly marked. For each brand, the respondent is asked to use a rating scale to indicate the likelihood of buying. The only variation across the five to eight treatments is the price of the test brand.

Using analysis of variance and multiple comparison tests, those prices for the test brand that produced significant differences in respondents' perceptions can be determined. Trend analysis can be used to determine the relative price–volume relationship for the test brand. The actual shape of this relationship can be found using regression analysis. In addition to obtaining respondents' ratings of their intentions to buy, it would also be relatively easy to get them to rate their perceptions of product quality and relative product value.

Tradeoff Analysis   As developed in Chaps. 3 and 4, buyers generally make tradeoffs when evaluating alternative product offers. Indeed, the notion of acquisition value explicitly suggests that buyers compare the actual price of the item with the highest price that they would be willing to pay, P_{max}. Also, the notion of transaction value suggests that buyers compare a reference price to the actual price. When we recognize that most product or service choices, for consumers or for organizational buyers, requires not only comparing prices, as indicated earlier, but also comparing different attributes at varying levels, it is clear that some form of conscious or unconscious tradeoff must occur. The need to make tradeoffs while simultaneously evaluating multiple alternatives with multiple attributes occurs because no one alternative is likely to be perceived as superior on all evaluative dimensions. For example, buyers may have to trade off a higher price against higher perceived quality or a higher price against faster delivery.

As pointed out in Chaps. 3 and 4, it is buyers' perceptions of the total relative value of an offering that may result in a willingness to pay a premium price for that offering. These perceptions are acquired through experience and prior knowledge as well as communications from sellers. The buyers' relative perceived value of one alternative versus another can be conceived as the price differential that would make them indifferent to the choice of alternatives. Strategically, it would be useful to know not only that one alternative is perceived as representing a better value but also what aspects of the offering contribute to its perceived value. Tradeoff analysis is designed to determine the relative value buyers place on different factors or attributes of alternative offerings.

In a general sense, tradeoff analysis uses either what may be called a *limited-profile approach* or a *full-profile approach.* In a limited-profile approach, attributes which comprise a subset that buyers perceive to be important are varied in alternative scenarios, usually in a limited number of levels. In a full-profile approach, called *conjoint analysis,* all of the important attributes are varied over as many levels as is reasonable for the respondents. We begin with an example of limited-profile tradeoff analysis and follow that with a discussion of conjoint analysis.

The management at DuPont was interested in determining the relative values placed on six of the important attributes of a specialty industrial product. A survey of decision makers in the market was conducted by an outside market research firm under the direction of the corporate market research division.[9] Two levels of performance for each of six attributes were defined and respondents were asked to consider an offering with all the attributes at the high level. They were then told to assume that the selling company was faced with increasing costs and was considering sacrificing performance on one attribute by reducing it to the lower level rather than raising price (see Table 6-3). Each respondent was then given a pair of attributes (e.g., quality and retraining) and asked to indicate which attribute should be kept at the high level and the strength of this preference. Next, the respondent indicated the dollar values to the price difference that would be acceptable to retain the higher level of performance on each attribute. (A number of other paired comparisons were provided for a similar ranking and dollar assignment.) Finally, the respondents were asked to rate DuPont and its major competitor on their perceptions of how these two firms performed relative to the six attributes.

Based on the data and statistical analysis, a scale of relative dollar value for each attribute was constructed for each respondent. Figure 6-10 shows the average scale

---

[9]This example is adapted from Irwin Gross, "Insights from Pricing Research," in Earl L. Bailey (ed.), *Pricing Practices and Strategies* (New York: The Conference Board, 1978), pp. 34–39.

TABLE 6-3
LIMITED PROFILE TRADEOFFS

Attribute	High Level	Low Level
Quality	Impurities less than one part per million	Impurities less than 10 parts per million
Delivery	Within one week	Within two weeks
System	Supply total system	Supply chemical only
Innovation	High level of R&D support	Little R&D support
Retraining	Retrain on request	Train on initial purchase
Service	Available locally	Available from home office

Source: Adapted and reprinted with permission from Irwin Gross, "Insights from Pricing Research," in Earl L. Bailey (ed.), *Pricing Practices and Strategies* (New York: The Conference Board, 1978), p. 37.

results. To determine the maximum premium that a buyer would pay for the DuPont offering relative to its competitor, the relative dollar values for each attribute were weighted by the perceived performance differences between DuPont and the competitor using this equation with all six attributes:

$$RPV = Q[PPQ_d - PPQ_c]$$
$$+ I[+PPI_d - PPI_c] + \cdots + R[PPR_d - PPR_c] \qquad (6\text{-}3)$$

where RPV = relative perceived value, or price premium for indifference
Q = quality
PPQ_d = perceived performance quality, DuPont
PPQ_c = perceived performance quality, competitor
I = innovation
PPI_d = perceived performance innovation, DuPont
PPI_c = perceived performance innovation, competitor
R = retraining
PPR_d = perceived retraining level, DuPont
PPR_c = perceived retraining level, competitor

Table 6-4 lists the calculated average contribution of each attribute to DuPont's price premium relative to its nearest competitor. Note that even though quality was

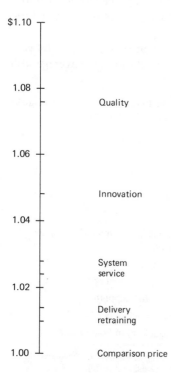

FIGURE 6-10
Relative attribute values. (Adapted and reprinted with permission from Irwin Gross, "Insights from Pricing Research," in *Pricing Practices and Strategies,* Earl L. Bailey [ed.], [New York: The Conference Board, Inc., 1978], p. 38.)

TABLE 6-4
RELATIVE ATTRIBUTE
CONTRIBUTION TO PRICE
PREMIUM

Attribute	Premium
Quality	$1.70
Innovation	2.00
System	0.80
Service	0.25
Delivery	0.15
Retraining	0.40
Total	$5.30

Source: Adapted and reprinted with permission from Irwin Gross, "Insights from Pricing Research," in Earl L. Bailey (ed.), *Pricing Practices and Strategies* (New York: The Conference Board, 1978), p. 39.

the most important attribute to the buyers, because there were few perceived performance differences between DuPont and its competitor, it does not contribute as much to the price premium as does innovation. Thus, not only did DuPont determine its relative price premium over a competitor, but it also was able to determine the relative contribution each attribute made to this premium. This additional information about relative perceived performance and customers' perceived importance of these attributes provides a basis for developing not only a pricing strategy, but also an integrated marketing strategy.

Conjoint Analysis   Perhaps marketing management's most perplexing pricing problem is determining the volume effect of a change in price. To evaluate the effect requires estimating buyers' sensitivity to the price change, likely competitive reaction to the price change, and the impact of competitors' pricing actions on sales volume. Moreover, the price change must be coordinated with other product and promotion decisions to provide an effective marketing program. As observed previously, buyers seldom are able to find a purchase alternative that is ideal on all dimensions. Thus, they trade off perceived negatives of one offer against perceived positives of that offer and compare the relative attractiveness of the offer to other offers. An individual's decision to purchase is a function of many individual personal variables and many subtle buying influences that are a part of the perceived benefits of the product or service, the purchase situation, the use occasion, the buyer's reference group, and associated perceptions and values. Conjoint analysis has been designed to provide a flexible diagnostic method of exploring these buying complexities to determine the relative perceived value in different product attributes including price.

To understand how conjoint analysis works, it would be helpful to present three

TABLE 6-5
HOTEL FACTOR DESCRIPTION AND LEVELS

Factor	Level	Factor	Level
Associated services		Lounge/entertainment	
Message service	2	Type of lounge	3
Limo to airport	2	Atmosphere	2
Laundry/valet	3		
Atmosphere/facilities		Security/safety	
Hotel size	2	Sprinkler system	3
Corridor/view	2	Smoke detector	2
Pool location	2	Security guard	3
Room		Price range	
Quality of decor	4	Very low price	5
Size	3	Low price	5
Bathroom amenities	3	Medium price	5
In-room TV/entertainment	3	High price	5
Recreation			
Game room	2		
Tennis courts	2		
Whirlpool/Jacuzzi	2		
Sauna	2		

terms commonly used when discussing conjoint analysis: factors, levels, and utility. *Factors* are the product or service attributes that provide the relative benefits buyers derive from acquiring and using the product. Table 6-5 lists such factors for a hotel. *Level* refers to the number of different options available for a particular factor. In Table 6-5, note that two levels of hotel size are being considered, but five levels of price, characterized as price ranges, will be studied. *Utility* refers to the quantified degree of preference a person has for a particular factor.

The underlying assumption of this approach is that buyers can be modeled as perceiving a product option as a combination or bundle of features; each feature has a separate utility that can be exchanged with any other feature that has the same utility value. Purchase decisions are made on the basis of these utilities. However, buyers are unaware of the utilities that they attach to different features. All that buyers can do is indicate their preferences for different combinations of features. Conjoint analysis is a quantitative technique for breaking down buyers' overall preferences into utilities for each product or service feature.

To see how conjoint analysis works, assume a buyer is presented with a choice of two types of hotel and that the buyer has the utilities for the different features listed in Table 6-6. Hotel A is a small hotel with small rooms, an outdoor pool, and color TV with HBO; it is priced at $55 per night. Hotel B is a large hotel with standard-size rooms, indoor pool, whirlpool and sauna, and color TV with HBO; it is priced at $95 per night. For this buyer, Hotel A has a total utility of 4.7 (1.0

TABLE 6-6
FEATURES AND UTILITIES FOR A HOTEL

Feature	Utility
Facilities (two levels)	
Small, two-story hotel, 100 rooms	1.0
Large, multistory hotel, 500+ rooms	0.8
Room (three levels)	
Standard-size room	0.6
Large room	0.8
Small room	0.2
Recreation/entertainment (four levels)	
Indoor pool	1.0
Outdoor pool	0.4
Color TV, HBO	1.2
Whirlpool, sauna	0.8
Price (single room) (three levels)	
$55	1.9
75	1.7
95	1.5

+ 0.2 + 0.4 + 1.2 + 1.9); Hotel B has a total utility of 5.9 (0.8 + 0.6 + 1.0 + 0.8 + 1.2 + 1.5). Given this choice, the buyer would select Hotel B. For Hotel A to be successful with this buyer, it would have to increase the total utility by at least 1.2. One way to do that would be to enclose the pool and add a whirlpool and sauna, leading to an increase in utility of 1.4.

How are these utilities obtained? To determine the buyers' utilities, a researcher in consultation with the hotel manager decides on the particular combinations that are of interest to the buyers and develops presentation packages. Different "hotel packages," usually summarized on cards, are given to the buyers, who are asked to indicate their relative preference for each package. Possible hotel packages include the following:

small hotel, small room, outdoor pool, color TV with HBO, $55;
small hotel, small room, indoor pool, color TV with HBO; $75;
small hotel, medium room, outdoor pool, color TV with HBO; $75;
large hotel, small room, outdoor pool, color TV with HBO; $75;
large hotel, medium room, indoor pool, whirlpool, color TV with HBO, $95.

In the example in Table 6-6, there are 96 possible combinations (2 × 3 × 4 × 3). In the larger illustration in Table 6-5, there are over 16 billion combinations. A computer can estimate a utility for each feature for each respondent. Figure 6-11 illustrates some possible utility results.

Conjoint analysis has been widely used in commercial market research and price

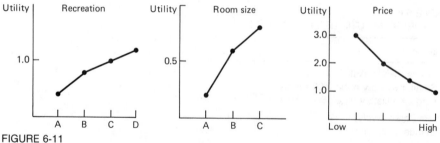

FIGURE 6-11
Different utility curves for hotels.

has been the focus of application approximately 40 percent of the time.[10] Yet there are some issues that need to be understood when considering its application. First, the underlying model of buyer behavior may not be appropriate. Instead of adding up each feature utility individually, buyers may prefer a particular bundle of features more than the simple sum of their parts. For example, some people may perceive that certain amenities of a hotel should come as a package rather than individual add-ons.[11] Second, the same feature may have different utilities in different products. A security guard may have a higher utility for a city hotel than for a hotel in a suburban or rural location. Conjoint analysis assumes that a feature has the same utility across similar products.

A third problem occurs when different people interpret a particular attribute differently. For example, large-size room might be interpreted as a 20- by 20-foot room by one person and a 14- by 14-foot room by another. It is likely, therefore, that utilities for the same descriptive feature may vary due to the respondents' interpretations as well as to reactions to a "large-size room." A fourth problem occurs when no attempt is made during analysis to determine whether there are distinct market segments for the product or service. As suggested earlier in the chapter, a price–quality segment and a price-conscious segment could lead to average utilities for price that are incorrect. Finally, there may be so many combinations that not all are tested. One way to overcome part of this problem is to ask some additional questions about features not in the combinations used.

Despite these issues, conjoint analysis has been widely used in pricing research. Careful use of the technique is necessary to reap its potential advantages.[12]

[10]Dick R. Wittink and Philippe Cattin, "Commercial Use of Conjoint Analysis: An Update," *Journal of Marketing,* 53 (July 1989), 91–96.

[11]Stephen M. Goldberg, Paul E. Green, and Yoram Wind, "Conjoint Analysis of Price Premiums for Hotel Amenities," *Journal of Business,* 57 (January 1984, part 2), S111–132.

[12]Some additional sources to consult for applications of conjoint analysis are Paul E. Green and Yoram Wind, "New Way to Measure Consumers' Judgments," *Harvard Business Review,* 53 (July–August 1975), 107–117; Earnestine Hargrove, "Conjoint Study Lends Support to Financial Decisions," *Marketing News,* 20 (August 29, 1988), 28; Patrick J. Robinson, "Applications of Conjoint Analysis to Pricing Problems," in David B. Montgomery and Dick R. Wittink (eds.), *Market Measurement and Analysis* (Cambridge, Mass.: Marketing Science Institute, 1980), pp. 183–205.

Simulated Shopping Experiments One criticism often raised about the foregoing methods is that, in one way or another, each is a variation of paper and pencil tests; none measures how buyers would actually behave in a real purchase situation. That is, buyers are not making actual product choices but are only indicating preferences or perceptions. To overcome this criticism, some researchers have devised a purchase simulation wherein buyers are asked to assume they are actually shopping and to make choices as normally as possible. The respondents are shown pictures, given descriptions, or given product samples and are asked to make actual selections. Prices are varied in different versions (treatments) to enable the researcher to estimate the buyers' sensitivity to price differences. When product samples are available, respondents are often allowed to keep their choices. The locations used for these simulations can be the individuals' homes, an area in a shopping center or mall, a laboratory designed to represent a store, or a mobile trailer in a parking lot. The advantage of the simulated-purchase experiment is that buyers have no way of identifying the test brand and should make a choice based on their thought processes.

In one simulated experiment adult women shoppers in three suburban shopping centers near Boston were asked to choose from four brands of maple syrup. Within this research, the researchers varied three levels of product grade (Fancy, Grade A, Grade B), two levels of content information (present and not present), and five prices for the test brand, Vermont pure maple syrup ($1.50, $1.75, $2.00, $2.25, $2.50).[13] A price of $0.75 (the prevailing retail price at the time and place of the study) was placed on a card in front of the three commercial brands (Aunt Jemima, Log Cabin, and Vermont Maid) while the price of the pure maple syrup was varied according to the specific price treatments. The subjects first rated each of the four brand choices on five dimensions including perceived quality, and then were given the following instructions:

> Now you may select and take home a bottle of syrup of your own choosing. Here is $2.75. We would like you to purchase one of these 12-ounce bottles of syrup, using this money. Select a bottle from the table, priced as marked. Any change remaining after you have made your purchase is yours to keep, along with the bottle of syrup. Let me remind you again that all four bottles contain 12 ounces of syrup. Which one would you like to purchase?[14]

Results of this study indicated that demand for pure maple syrup was inversely related to price. However, a complete contribution-to-profit analysis (see Chap. 8) revealed that the most profitable prices were $2.25 and $2.50. Three years after this experiment, the price of the pure syrup was $2.40, and the commercial brands were priced at $0.85. The large price increases in pure maple syrup after the study did

[13]Alan G. Sawyer, Parker M. Worthing, and Paul E. Sendak, "The Role of Laboratory Experiments to Test Marketing Strategies," *Journal of Marketing,* 43 (Summer 1979), 60–67.
[14]Ibid., p. 61.

not lead to a decrease in sales; in fact, demand was so strong that promotion budgets were decreased.[15]

Multiple-Choice Simulated Experiments   One problem with the single-choice simulation is that it is unclear whether inferences can be made about buyers' relative sensitivity to price differences across choices. That is, some respondents may be more predisposed to exhibit a degree of price sensitivity regardless of the product category, i.e., there may be a price-conscious segment of people. One way to study whether there are respondents who are prone to be price conscious and whether they have an unrealistic effect on the test results is to have the respondents make multiple choices. An example of one such simulation is described next.

The research department of a large national advertising agency conducted two experiments in the Chicago area to measure buyers' sensitivity to price differences.[16] The first experiment involved one product, packaged cake mix; the second experiment involved several product categories and prices. In the second experiment, 900 women participated in two shopping centers and at a downtown Chicago location in mobile research trailers. Subjects were shown a sequence of colored slides. Each slide showed a picture of a grocery shelf containing the products with prices. Each subject saw each product category once with only one set of prices. Subjects were instructed to assume they were doing their regular shopping and that the prices were typical of the prices in the Chicago area. After looking at each slide, the respondents indicated the brand they would prefer to buy. The experimental design for the second experiment is shown in Table 6-7.

One of the important results of this multiple-choice experiment was that responses to price changes were different for price increases as opposed to price decreases, as pointed out in Chaps. 3 and 4. Further, response patterns toward the brand that changed price differed and response patterns for the other brands in the tests differed depending on whether price for the test brand was increased or decreased. A second important observation was that preferences tended to gravitate toward the "middle-priced" brands. In particular, there was a tendency to not prefer the test brand at either the high or low price treatments. Further, preferences for non–test brands also were greatest when they were the middle-priced alternatives. These results clearly indicated the concept of the absolute price threshold and the resultant implication that buyers do have ranges of acceptable prices that are bounded by relatively low and high prices, even for name brands.

[15]Other reports about shopping experiments can be found in Gerald J. Eskin and Penny H. Baron, "Effects of Price and Advertising in Test Market Experiments," *Journal of Marketing Research,* 14 (November 1977), 499–508; Andre Gabor, Clive W. J. Granger, and Anthony Sowther, "Real and Hypothetical Shop Situations in Market Research," *Journal of Marketing Research,* 7 (August 1970), 355–359; William M. Motes, Stephen B. Castleberry, and Susan G. Motes, "A Longitudinal Test of Price Effects on Brand Choice Behavior," *Journal of Business Research,* 12 (December 1984), 493–503; John R. Nevin, "Laboratory Experiments for Estimating Consumer Demand: A Validation Study," *Journal of Marketing Research,* 11 (August 1974), 261–268.

[16]Kent B. Monroe and David M. Gardner, "An Experimental Inquiry into the Effect of Price on Brand Preference," *Proceedings,* Fall Conference (Chicago: American Marketing Association, 1976), pp. 552–556.

TABLE 6-7
RESEARCH DESIGN: MULTIPLE-CHOICE EXPERIMENT

Product	Brand	Price Treatment			
		1	2	3	4†
Cake mix	A	39	39	39	39
	B	39	39	39	39
	C	13	13	13	13
	D	35	43	33	39
	(test)				
Canned vegetables	A	25	25	25	25
	B	26	28	25	25
	(test)				
	C	25	25	25	25
	D	21	21	19	21
	E	25	25	25	25
Canned beans*	A	25	25	25	25
	B_1	24	24	24	24
	B_2	17	17	17	17
	C_1	25	24	24	24
	C_2	15	20	13	17
	(test)				
	D	17	17	17	17
Frozen dinners*	A	29	33	35	39
	(test)				
	B	33	39	45	39
	C	33	39	49	39
	D_1	59	69	59	59
	D_2	65	69	65	65

*Brands indicated by a subscript were represented by two varieties of the product category.
†Control treatment.
Note: All prices in cents.
Source: Kent B. Monroe and David M. Gardner, "An Experimental Inquiry into the Effect of Price on Brand Preference," *Proceedings,* Fall Conference (Chicago: American Marketing Association, 1976), pp. 552–556.

SUMMARY

As noted in Chap. 1, the prerequisites for taking a proactive approach to pricing include (1) knowing how prices work, and (2) understanding how customers perceive prices. As detailed in Chaps. 2–5, the assumption that prices work exactly as prescribed in traditional economic theory, and that buyers simply use price as an indicator of their sacrifice or cost, leads to naive and often unprofitable pricing strategies and tactics. It should be clear that the role of price in buyers' decision making is complex and dynamic. Recognizing these complexities means that pricing decision makers must consciously develop and maintain an information system that continuously provides information about markets, competitors, and current clients or customers as well as prospective buyers. The complexity of buyer behavior relative to price means that such an information system must be augmented with carefully designed and executed pricing research. Pricing research implemented without a working knowledge of how buyers behave relative to price may lead to irrelevant research results.

To illustrate this last point, recently a major airline decided to determine the degree of price sensitivity of a one-way ticket between two cities. The price of a coach fare between the two cities had been $149 and was the price initially set by the discount-oriented competitor. The major airline set an experimental price for the one-way fare at $199 and quickly found out that a $50 price differential shifted traffic to the discount carrier. When asked how they had decided on a $50 price differential, the response was "we pulled a nice round figure out of the air." Surprisingly, an important aspect of pricing, determining the relative price premium to charge, was pulled out of the air! A more careful research effort would have developed a systematic approach by slowly raising the price of the fare, perhaps initially up to $155, to determine when travelers would believe that the tradeoff between the perceived better airline service and the higher price made them indifferent between the two airlines. Several of the techniques described in this chapter could have been used to determine this price differential before executing the actual market experiment. As it was, the results of the $199 trial simply scared the airline from doing additional and more carefully developed price-sensitivity research.

In a more successful effort, a hospital introduced a program to establish overnight accommodations for their patients' families. After a careful internal analysis of costs and rates charged by nearby full-service hotels, a nightly rate of $55 was set. However, after four months, the program had an average monthly use of only 2–8 guests instead of the projected 21 guests per night. Market research indicated that the hotels and motels within a mile of the hospital charged, on average, $38 per night, with a range of $27–$54 per night, single occupancy. Respondents to a survey indicated that the maximum acceptable room rate for a majority of them was $35. After the price was reduced to $36, the use rate increased from 114 nights in August 1987 to 243 nights in January 1988, with no additional marketing activity. What the hospital concluded was that "pricing a hospital product should be based on the market value instead of product cost."[17] Indeed, despite a price reduction of $19 per night, there was a net monthly revenue gain of $2,478.

These examples and the material presented in the last five chapters indicate three important principles about price and the need to develop a careful research program to facilitate pricing decisions. First, it is abundantly clear that price is an important part of the marketing mix. To make pricing decisions primarily on the basis of internal financial considerations ignores this important principle. Customers make their purchase decisions on the basis of perceived value, not what it costs the seller to produce and have available for sale. Thus, the second principle is that a buyer's perception of value is the important consideration in purchase decisions. Similarly, the third principle is that it is relative price, not absolute price, that is the key to

---

[17]Donna A. Newman and Terrance M. Tucker, "Research Shows Hospital Best Pricing Strategy," *Marketing News,* 22 (August 29, 1988), 16.

understanding how pricing works in the marketplace. Buyers' determinations of perceived value are contingent on their perceptions of relative price differences, not absolute price level. A successful pricing research program must consider these fundamental principles of how price influences buyer behavior.

DISCUSSION QUESTIONS

1 When doing research concerning buyers' responses to price, what are some specific differences about the price variable that make it difficult to ask people directly about their reactions?
2 Compare and contrast the different techniques for determining the maximum amount that buyers are willing to pay.
3 What are some specific conceptual differences between determining buyers' sensitivities to price levels and their sensitivities to price differences? What are the different types of pricing decisions relevant to each type of research issue?
4 As a project, develop an approach for determining the degree to which buyers can remember the prices they have paid for different products and services.
5 For a particular product that would be of interest to your fellow students, develop a questionnaire to determine the degree they tend to associate product quality with price.
6 As an alternative project for the product considered in Question 5, develop either a tradeoff or conjoint analysis research project.
7 Discuss the relative importance of developing a pricing information system for pricing decisions. What would be the role of specific pricing marketing research projects in this information system?
8 Discuss this statement: "Anyone can set price; all you have to do is add up your costs, add the profit margin you want, and your price is the result."

SUGGESTED READINGS

Eskin, Gerald J., and Penny H. Baron: "Effects of Price and Advertising in Test Market Experiments," *Journal of Marketing Research,* 14 (November 1977), 400–508.

Green, Paul E., and Yoram Wind: "New Way to Measure Consumers' Judgments," *Harvard Business Review,* 53 (July–August 1975), 107–117.

Gross, Irwin: "Insights from Pricing Research," in Earl L. Bailey (ed.), *Pricing Practices and Strategies* (New York: The Conference Board, 1978), pp. 34–39.

Hensel, Paul J., and Noel M. Lavenka: "On the Extension of Psychophysical Scaling and Cross-Modality Triangulation to the Measurement of Product Quality," *Proceedings,* Summer Educators' Conference (Chicago: American Marketing Association, 1984), pp. 411–415.

Monroe, Kent B.: "Measuring Price Thresholds by Psychophysics and Latitudes of Acceptance," *Journal of Marketing Research,* 8 (November 1971), 460–464.

Nevin, John R.: "Laboratory Experiments for Estimating Consumer Demand: A Validation Study," *Journal of Marketing Research,* 11 (August 1974), 261–268.

Sawyer, Alan G., Parker M. Worthing, and Paul E. Sendak: "The Role of Laboratory Experiments to Test Marketing Strategies," *Journal of Marketing,* 43 (Summer 1979), 60–67.

Wittink, Dick R., and Philippe Cattin: "Commercial Use of Conjoint Analysis: An Update," *Journal of Marketing,* 53 (July 1989), 91–96.

DETERMINING RELEVANT
COSTS FOR PRICING

Perhaps the one aspect of the pricing function that most concerns business executives is the development of valid and useful cost information. Chapters 7 to 10 present methods of developing valid cost information for the pricing function. The material focuses on the decisions to be made, not on cost accounting theory.

Chapter 7 discusses cost concepts and classifications, the ways these different types of costs behave, and the ways to identify patterns of cost behavior. One important issue in price planning is to estimate future costs rather than concentrating on current or past costs. Thus, the chapter concludes by reviewing ways to forecast prices, not only for the development of prices, but also for the estimation of the costs of future acquisitions of materials and supplies.

Chapter 8 develops the key cost analysis methods and explores ways of using the data for analyzing pricing alternatives; it also discusses the effect of changing the underlying cost structure and shows how break-even analysis can be used in a dynamic price–volume–profit situation. An important problem when analyzing pricing alternatives is to estimate the effect on demand (volume) when prices are changed. Since the price setter cannot know prospective price elasticity of demand, the chapter develops a way to compute implied price elasticities for a given profit objective.

One of the least developed areas of costing is the analysis of the marketing effort and the determination of profit contribution by product line, customer account, order, sales territory, and salesperson. However, proper costs for pricing must include all costs that may change when activities are changed or redirected. Chapter 9 explores additional costing approaches to obtain data for analyzing the marketing effort.

Chapters 7, 8, and 9 present methods for determining relative contributions to covering fixed costs and profits by various profit segments. However, there are also nondirect costs, such as factory overhead and general selling expenses, which are not directly traceable to profit segments. Over time various formulas have been used to allocate these costs to products and other profit segments of the business. Unfortunately, the fixed costs allocated by these formulas, although quick and easy to calculate, are illogical. Chapter 10 explores the disadvantages of these methods of assigning overhead and presents a method of assigning the cost burdens to those segments of the business that are responsible for incurring the particular burden. A clear advantage of the more systematic approach is its utility for justifying price differences, a topic explored initially in Chap. 9 and discussed from a legal perspective in Chap. 16.

CHAPTER 7

THE ROLE OF COSTS IN PRICING DECISIONS

COST FUNDAMENTALS

As is well known, profits are the difference between revenues and costs. Price directly affects the quantity that can be sold in the marketplace, hence Chaps. 2–6 analyzed the effect of price on demand. Given the selling objectives of a firm, the demand variable provides an upper limit on the pricing discretion of the firm; this limit is the willingness of buyers to purchase at a stated price. The other variable directly affecting profits—costs—sets a floor to a firm's pricing discretion. If prices are too low in comparison with costs, volume may be high but profitless.

Objective cost data are essential for deciding what price to set. Only by determining the difference between costs and the price under consideration and then balancing that margin against the capacity necessary to produce the estimated volume can the seller determine the value of the product in terms of its contribution to recovering the seller's initial investment.

To get maximum practical use from costs in pricing, three questions must be answered: (1) Whose costs? (2) Which costs? and (3) What is the role of costs? As to whose costs, three classes of costs are important: (1) those of prospective buyers, (2) those of existing and potential competitors, and (3) those of the seller. Cost should play a different role for each of the three, and the pertinent concept of cost that is relevant will differ accordingly.

Buyers' Costs

The costs to prospective customers can be determined by applying the techniques of value analysis to prices and performance of alternative products to find the price that will make the product or service attractive to buyers (see Chap. 5).

Competitors' Costs

Competitors' costs are usually the crucial estimate in appraisal of competitors' capabilities. For products already in the marketplace, the objectives are to estimate (1) their staying power and (2) the floor of retaliation pricing. For the first objective, the pertinent cost concept is the competitors' long-run incremental costs. For the second, their short-run incremental costs are relevant.

Forecasts of competitors' costs for competing products that could affect a product's future can help assess the capability of competitors. These forecasts also provide an estimate of the effectiveness of a product pricing strategy to discourage entry. For this situation, the cost behavior to forecast is the relationship between unit direct costs and cumulative experience as the seller's and rivals' products move through their life cycles (see Chaps. 8 and 11). These cost forecasts should consider technological progress and should reflect the potential head-start cost advantages that might have been attained by one of the sellers.

Sellers' Costs

The sellers' costs play several roles in pricing a product or service. First, a new product must be prepriced provisionally early in the R&D stage and then again periodically as it progresses toward market. Forecasts of production and marketing costs will influence the decision to continue product development and ultimately to commercialize. The concept of cost relevant for this analysis is a prediction of direct costs at a series of prospective volumes and corresponding technologies.

Second, the sellers' cost is important in establishing a price floor that is also the threshold for maximizing return on the product investment over the long run. For both jobs, the relevant concept is future costs, forecast over a range of volume, production technologies, and promotional outlays in the marketing plan. The production, marketing, and distribution costs that matter are the future costs over the long run that will be incurred by producing and selling this product.

Importance of Costs in Pricing

In Chap. 2, it was pointed out that in traditional economic theory, prices are set by the interplay of the forces of demand and supply. Hence, for the individual firm, costs play a role in deciding what to produce and how much to produce, given the market price. In Chaps. 3–5, considerable attention was given to the relative importance of buyers' perceptions of relative value as the key to price determination. Essentially, buyers trade off the perceived value of the product or service against the perceived total cost of acquiring and using the product or service.

Within this perspective, customers seldom are concerned with what it cost the seller to be able to offer the product or service for sale. Thus, it can be argued that to determine a "price that will sell" the seller's costs have relatively little importance. Indeed, cost is probably the least important factor to consider when setting product or service prices.[1] Note that this statement implies a relative ranking and in no way suggests that costs can be or should be ignored when establishing prices. Moreover, the common practice of adding a percentage (usually of some aspect of production costs) to cover selling, marketing, distribution, and general administrative costs is an inadequate recognition of this point. Indeed, marketing and distribution costs are of the same importance as are production and material costs.

Despite this point, which will be developed throughout this section of the book, the most commonly used method to set prices is the cost-plus or full-cost method of pricing.[2] Probably the two strongest reasons for the prevalence of this pricing approach is that traditionally it has been associated with the notion of the "just price" and that "objective" cost data are easier to obtain from pricing research than are "subjective" price–volume estimates. The origin of the just price can be traced back to medieval times when a merchant was expected to earn a livelihood and a fair return, but no more. Prices were expected to be set at a just level, defined as the value of labor added to the value of raw materials.[3]

As will be seen in Chap. 10, the full-cost approach, although seemingly objective, is neither objective nor logical. When considering the cost aspect of a pricing decision, the crucial question is what costs are relevant to the decision. When cost-plus methods of pricing are used, and the cost portion of the formula is arbitrarily determined, the resultant price may be incorrect because the pricing formula does not allow for demand or for competition. Further, depending on the nature of the market and the type of pricing decision to be made, the relevant costs will differ.[4]

It is important for the seller to know the determinants and behavior of product and service costs in order to know when to accelerate cost recovery, how to evaluate a change in selling price, how to profitably segment a market, and when to add or eliminate products from the product line. Even so, costs play a less important role in determining the selling price than does information about demand for the product or service. Cost information indicates whether the product can be made and sold profitably at any price, but it does not indicate the amount of markup or markdown on cost buyers will accept. Proper cost determination guides management in the selection of a profitable product–service mix and the determination of how much cost can be incurred without sacrificing profit.

Costs for pricing must deal with the future. Current or past information probably will provide an adequate basis for profit projections only if the future is a perfect mirror of the past. Product costs must be based on expected purchase costs of raw materials, labor wage rates, planned marketing expenditures, and other expenses to

[1]Herbert F. Taggart, "Distribution Costs," in Sidney Davidson and Roman L. Weil (eds.), *Handbook of Modern Accounting,* 2nd ed. (New York: McGraw-Hill, 1977), pp. 43-1–43-36.

[2]V. Govindarajan and Robert N. Anthony, "How Firms Use Cost Data in Price Decisions," *Management Accounting,* 65 (July 1983), 30–36.

[3]Barbara W. Tuchman, *A Distant Mirror: The Calamitous 14th Century* (New York: Ballantine Books, 1978).

[4]Rein Abel, "The Role of Costs and Cost Accounting in Price Determination," *Management Accounting,* 60 (April 1978), 29–32; Alfred R. Oxenfeldt, "The Computation of Costs for Price Decisions," *Industrial Marketing Management,* 6 (1977), 83–90.

be incurred. In addition, information about research and market development and expected administration costs is needed. Information on product and service costs should be regularly developed to determine whether changes have occurred that will affect the relative profitability of the organization. It is planned costs that are important, not past costs, since profit planning necessarily deals with the future.

The purpose of this chapter is to discuss different concepts of costs and ways of classifying costs. As has been observed, it is important for the seller to know the determinants or causes of product and service costs as well as their behavior. This chapter also discusses ways of identifying patterns of cost behavior and ways to forecast the prices of future cost components such as materials, equipment, and supplies.

COST CONCEPTS AND CLASSIFICATIONS

To determine profit at any volume, price level, product mix, or time, proper cost classification is required. Some costs vary directly with the rate of activity; others do not. When these different costs are mixed together in a total unit cost, it is not possible to relate sales volume to costs or to determine what costs will change due to pricing decisions. As a result, the pricing decision is likely to be reduced to a formula that can lead to serious errors. However, if the cost data are properly classified into their fixed and variable components and properly attributed to the activity causing the cost, the effect of volume becomes apparent and sources of profit are revealed.

It is important to emphasize the concept of *activity*. Commonly, costs that vary with production rate, such as labor or materials, have been classified as variable costs, and all other costs, including marketing and distribution costs, have been classified as fixed. However, it will be stressed in Chaps. 7–9 that such a classification scheme is inappropriate for proper cost classification. For example, the travel costs of supporting a salesperson vary directly with number of miles traveled. Also, when a salesperson is paid on commission, selling costs vary with sales. As shown in Chap. 9, and again in Chap. 16, order processing costs vary with the complexity of the order. Therefore, it is important to recognize that the cost concepts defined in the next section apply to marketing and distribution activities as well as production.

Cost Concepts

Direct Costs   Direct costs (also called *traceable* or *attributable* costs) are those costs incurred by and solely for a particular product, department, program, sales territory, or customer account. These costs may be fixed or variable. Material and labor costs can be traced to a unit of product. The administrative salaries, rent, and other office expenses can be traced to the district sales office and therefore are direct costs of the sales territory.

Indirect Traceable Costs   Indirect traceable costs can be objectively traced to a product, department, program, sales territory, or customer account if the costs can be identified with that unit. These costs, although not incurred solely for a product, may be objectively identified with the product. They may be fixed or variable. Materials used in the production of several products can be objectively traced to or identified by the rate of usage for the production of each product. Classic examples include maintenance and repairs, heating, power, and lighting of plant and offices. When organizations use a full-costing approach, often very difficult cost allocation problems occur.

When cost allocations are used for pricing purposes, the sales volumes are usually estimates or forecasts, implying that several average unit cost figures need to be developed, depending on the relative range of forecasted sales. When there are parallel or joint production or sales methods, the cost allocation process can become very complex and arbitrary, resulting in "subjective" cost estimates rather than the assumed "objective" estimates. Thus, only when there is a reasonably objective means of tracing an indirect cost to the appropriate business segment for which it is incurred should the cost be assigned. Otherwise, it should be handled as a common cost.

Common Costs   Common or general costs support a number of activities or profit segments. These costs cannot be objectively traced to a product or segment based on a direct physical relationship to that product or segment. The administration cost of a sales district is common to all units of product sold in that district. A common or general cost does not change when one of the activities it supports is discontinued. Hence, discontinuing a product in the line will not affect the administration costs of the district or of other general expenses such as market research or research and development.

Opportunity Costs   An opportunity cost is the marginal income forgone by choosing one alternative over another. Essentially, opportunity costs reflect the "cost" of not choosing the best alternative or opportunity. As will be developed in Chap. 8, these costs are relevant when operating at or near full capacity or when resources are in scarce supply. If a decision is made not to produce a product with the largest contribution per resource unit consumed, then the difference between the income earned and the larger income that could have been earned is income forgone (opportunity cost). In a similar manner, when the organization is operating well below capacity, then sales volume becomes the limiting or scarce factor, and instead of maximizing contributions per scarce resource unit, the relevant decision criterion would be maximization of contribution per sales dollar. In these two situations, opportunity costs are relevant to price setting and need to be included in the development of relevant costs for the decision.

Cash and Noncash Costs   Costs can lead to cash (or out-of-pocket) outlays or bookkeeping (depreciation or amortization) entries. The noncash costs essentially have an impact on the cash flows but do not reflect actual dollar outlays in a particular accounting period. As shown in Eq. (7-1), cash flow comprises net income (after all accounting expenses have been deducted) plus noncash accounting charges.

$$\text{Cash flow} = \text{net income} + \text{depreciation} + \text{depletion} + \text{amortization} \qquad (7\text{-}1)$$

Consider, for example, depreciation expenses. There are very good reasons for charging depreciation, but the amount calculated is by some arbitrary formula and does not necessarily have to be set aside when the entry is made in the accounts. Depreciation as an allowable expense serves to reduce the organization's tax obligations, thereby enhancing the cash flow of the organization. However, it is not an actual cash or out-of-pocket expense and is not a legitimate cost in setting prices. When analyzing the implications of particular price–expected volume combinations on profitability or financial status, these noncash costs become relevant. But they are not relevant for the determination of actual selling prices.

Cost Behavior

In addition to classifying costs according to ability to attribute a cost to a product or profit segment, it is also important to classify costs according to variation with

FIGURE 7-1
Cost behavior patterns. *(a)* Variable cost, *(b)* semivariable cost, *(c)* fixed cost.

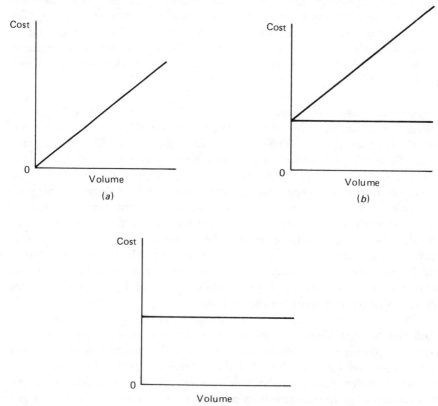

the rate of activity. As noted previously, unless costs can be segmented into fixed and variable costs, it is not possible to trace the effects of changes in price, volume, or product selling mix on costs.

Direct Variable Costs   Costs that vary directly with an activity level are called direct variable costs. As production is increased in a given time period a proportionately higher amount of labor and materials is used. Assuming no changes in scale economies as the volume is increased, these direct variable costs will be constant per additional unit produced. However, there usually is a point where unit direct variable costs change due either to economies of quantity raw material purchases or to increased labor unit costs resulting from overtime or a second shift. Figure 7-1a illustrates direct variable costs.

In pricing, direct variable costs are also known as *out-of-pocket costs,* since these costs are incremental to the decision to make and sell and therefore require an outlay of immediate cash. One test of a unit variable cost is whether it is readily discontinued or whether it would not exist if a product were not made. Direct variable costs include those costs which the product incurs unit by unit and includes such costs as productive labor, energy required at production centers, raw material required, sales commissions, royalties, and shipping costs. The major criterion of a direct variable cost is that it be traceably and tangibly generated by, and identified with, the making and selling of a specific product.

Semivariable Costs   Some costs vary with activity rates but are not zero at a zero activity rate. Plant supplies are needed in some minimum amount to get activities started, and then additional quantities are required as the level of activity increases. Hence, these semivariable costs consist of a base amount that is constant in relation to activity and a variable amount that varies directly with changes in the activity level. Figure 7-1b illustrates these costs.

Period Fixed Costs   Generally, fixed costs occur because of a legal, contractual, or moral obligation. Some of these costs, although fixed for the planning period, are assigned to specific projects by management to fulfill company objectives. These *specific programmed costs* refer to costs used to generate additional revenues; they include opening a new sales district office or warehouse or a special advertising program for a specific product line. These direct fixed costs are separable because they can be charged to the product line or activity that is the recipient of the incurred cost.

Other costs are also fixed for the planning period, but they are incurred for the entire company and are common to the various products or activities. Examples of these *general programmed costs* are general and administrative salaries, research and development, and general marketing expenses. Other costs are neither separable nor inescapable during the planning period. These *constant costs are common* and are incurred as long as the firm is in business. Common costs support a number of activities or profit segments. These costs cannot be objectively traced to a particular type of service or product based on a direct physical relationship to that service or product. The administrative cost of a service facility is common to all units of service provided in that facility. A common or general cost does not change when one of the activities it supports is discontinued. Hence, discontinuing a product or type of service will not affect the administration costs of the facility or the general expenses such as market research or research and development. Included in these costs are depreciation, real estate taxes, rent, and interest payments on mortgages. In pricing, all the period fixed costs are referred to simply as fixed costs as long as the costs will be incurred in the planning period. These fixed costs are illustrated in Fig. 7-1c.

Table 7-1 summarizes the cost concepts and behavior discussed in this section. As the table indicates, some directly attributable costs vary directly with the activity level, and some costs, although fixed, are directly attributable to the activity level. For example, advertising expenses incurred for a specific product, even though fixed

TABLE 7-1
COST CLASSIFICATIONS

Classified According to Variation with Activity Rate	Cost Component	Classified According to Ability to Trace or Attribute the Cost to a Product or Segment
Costs vary linearly with activity rate	Raw materials Utilities Shipping Royalties Sales commissions	Directly traceable or attributable
Costs vary with activity rate, but are not zero at zero activity level	Operating labor Direct supervision Maintenance Plant supplies	
	Rent Insurance Taxes Depreciation	Directly traceable or attributable, but independent of activity level
Costs do not vary with activity level	Payroll General plant overhead Storage facilities Medical and safety expenses	Indirectly traceable or attributable to a product or segment
	General administration Sales administration Market research Research and development	Common or general costs not easily traceable or attributable to a product or segment

Source: Adapted and reprinted with permission from Donald R. Woods, *Financial Decision Making in the Process Industry* (Englewood Cliffs, N.J.: Prentice-Hall, 1975), p. 212.

by contract for a period of time, are directly attributable to that product. Hence, it is important to clarify specifically what is meant by the terms *direct* and *indirect. The directly traceable or attributable costs are those that we can readily determine as contributing to the product cost. However, whether a direct cost is variable, fixed, or semivariable depends on properly determining the source of that cost.*

Determinants of Cost Behavior

As Table 7-1 indicates, no cost is inherently fixed or variable. Further, whether a cost is fixed or variable depends on whether that cost varies as the organization's activity level changes. Traditionally, it has been customary to consider variable costs as those costs that vary with production volume, usually measured in terms of product units. For example, material cost is usually considered a variable cost because it varies directly with changes in production activity.

However, when analyzing costs for the purpose of setting prices, or for justifying price differences, it is important to recognize that there are other sets of activities in addition to production that are cost incurring. For example, a salesperson's travel expenses vary directly with the distance traveled (e.g., $0.25 per mile). Or a salaried salesperson's expenses in serving an account vary directly with the amount of time spent serving a customer account. Or the shipping department's cost of preparing an invoice may vary directly with the number of items on an invoice. For the U.S. Postal Service, the cost of providing a particular class of service varies with the number of pieces mailed, the weight, and the distance these pieces are mailed. In general, a cost is a variable cost if the cost changes because of a change in the activity causing that cost. The question is whether the cost changes as the relative level of activity changes per unit of activity, not whether the total cost of that activity changes on an annual basis irrespective of the total volume of the activity.

On the other hand, fixed costs are affected by long-range planning decisions. Some of these fixed costs are long-term lease commitments and depreciation costs, which remain constant over periods of time. These general programmed costs originate in capacity decisions, whereas specific programmed costs result from decisions on how to use that capacity. These specific programmed costs are planned expenditures to generate a sales volume or to handle a specified level of administrative work. Thus, managers can increase the specific programmed costs whenever they decide to do so.

Different decisions may produce different levels of fixed costs. For example, shut-down fixed costs are usually lower than operating fixed costs of a plant. Required power levels are lower and security and maintenance personnel are fewer when a plant is shut down than when it is running.

Fixed costs may also differ with the extent to which a fixed cost is traceable to a specific time period. Administrative salaries, lease payments, and taxes are direct costs of the time period in which they are paid. However, other fixed costs reflect a lump-sum payment that is apportioned over a series of future time periods. Depreciation, amortization, and depletion expenses are common costs apportioned over specific time periods; they vary according to the computational procedure employed.

Because depreciation costs are subjective and reflect prior decisions, they are irrelevant for pricing and other planning decisions. Unfortunately, they are often lumped in with other fixed costs, "unitized" according to some estimate of projected volume, and become a part of the cost that price is expected to recover. *Depreciation, amortization, and depletion costs should be separated from other period expenses for the purpose of pricing.*

Although costs are not inherently fixed or variable, it is essential that an organization identify the behavior pattern that they follow. It is vitally important to know which costs vary with changes in activity levels and which costs remain constant.

Recovery of Costs

One frequently offered reason for a full-cost pricing approach is that each product or activity should carry its "fair share of the burden." That is, the objective is to recover the costs incurred while performing the activities of the organization. On the other hand, pricing based on direct variable costs is criticized because the organization may end up "giving the product away." That is, the costs of performing the organization's activities will not be recovered. There is no disagreement that those costs incurred solely for and because of a particular business segment—i.e., direct variable and direct period costs—should be recovered. The question arises over the recovery of indirect and common period costs.

Direct period costs normally should be recovered in the period in which they are incurred and are relevant for pricing purposes. The recovery of indirect period costs, such as an investment in a production plant, generally depends on an arbitrary decision on how long the facility will last or be useful to the organization. Therefore, for pricing purposes, the amount to be recovered per period must be flexible and reflect the nature of the product-market fluctuations. The ultimate concern is whether the dollars invested in the facility or activity earn the desired rate of return over the useful life of the facility or activity. Thus, the appropriate concern is not whether the product recovers a fixed amount of the indirect period cost in a particular year or period but whether, over a reasonable number of periods, it makes a sufficient contribution to justify its continuance.

The determination of the contribution each product or service should make to the recovery of indirect period costs and common period costs is a managerial decision and should not be determined by an inflexible and arbitrary allocation rule. Depending on the level of analysis, the following hierarchy of cost recovery can serve as a starting point:[5]

1 Direct product, customer, or sales territory costs

2 Direct product, customer, or sales territory costs plus desired contribution to the costs of product group, customer group, or sales region

---

[5]Walter Georges and Robert W. McGee, *Analytical Contribution Accounting: The Interface of Cost Accounting and Pricing Policy* (New York: Quorum Books, 1987).

3 Direct costs as in (1) and (2) plus desired contribution to division, cost center, or total organization

The determination of these desired contributions must consider relative external factors such as competition, stage of the product's life cycle, demand, and general economic conditions. Although this approach is considerably more difficult than a cost-plus formula, the price setter is forced to actively consider the realities of the marketplace when determining prices. This is clearly an advantage, since the important sources of profitability are external to the organization, and considering only the internal need to recover costs often leads to poor pricing decisions.

Cost Behavior Analysis

Essentially, there are two broad approaches to determining how a cost behaves. One approach focuses on the decision maker, the other on accounting records. Generally, the decision maker is asked to discuss the behavior of each cost within the department. For example, department managers will know that more labor and materials are used as production increases; they may also be able to identify causal factors of cost in addition to production. Table 7-2 is a typical cost behavior identification worksheet that may be used during these interviews.

This personal judgment approach is the most widely used method to estimate cost behavior. Experienced managers and engineers over time have stored in their memories a considerable amount of information that can be useful when developing cost behavior estimates. However, judgments cannot be documented and the assumptions that each individual uses to develop the estimates usually are unknown.

Correlation and regression analyses are commonly used to identify cost behavior patterns from accounting data.[6] Such an approach, because it relies on historical data, assumes that the past reflects the future. Further, the approach assumes that

[6]See George J. Benston, "Multiple Regression Analysis of Cost Behavior," *Accounting Review,* 41 (October 1969), 657–672.

TABLE 7-2
COST BEHAVIOR IDENTIFICATION FORM
Department: _____

Cost	Variable Varies with	Semivariable Varies with	Fixed
Direct labor	Production		
Direct materials	Production		
Supervision			(X)
Supplies		Production	
Power	Machine time		
Maintenance		Machine time	

the data properly describe the dynamic events producing the costs. For example, analysis of yearly U.S. Postal Service data suggested that as first-class mail volume increased, the cost of stamps remained constant. However, what the data failed to show was the increasing reliance on postage meters by business customers of the U.S. Postal Service.

Regression procedures normally attempt to measure changes in costs in relation to changes in activity. Changes in materials cost are measured in relation to changes in output to determine the behavior pattern of materials cost. With the availability of high-speed computers and software programs, regression analysis is easy to carry out and inexpensive.

Moreover, by using computers, companies are able to monitor costs continuously across product lines, sales territories, or customer accounts. Today, virtually all moderate-size companies use the computer to monitor costs.[7] United States Elevator uses the computer to monitor daily and monthly cost fluctuations. The cost of every raw material component is reviewed daily by the president.[8] The International Telephone and Telegraph controller reviews monthly cost-monitoring reports for each operating division.[9] The Jewelry Division of Zale Corporation gets a daily computer printout showing the current relationship between cost and margin on all Zale inventory.[10]

When historical data are out of date or not reliable, or when production volume is not the main independent variable, then observation and experimental techniques may be used. The two most popular observational techniques are time studies and work sampling. Time studies are used in manufacturing to determine labor and machine time costs. They are also used in clerical operations, e.g., to determine how long an order taker requires to record standard information such as name, address, customer number, and shipping and billing instructions. Time studies or sales call reports may be used to determine the costs of a sales call on an established customer relative to a prospective customer. In work sampling, the analyst makes a series of observations across various functions and employees. The amount of time for a particular function is determined by multiplying the total time on all functions by the relative percentage for a particular function obtained from the sample.

Experimentation is most likely to be used when the organization can change an aspect of its operation and observe the resultant effect on the cost of the operation. Experimentation is not used often because it may hamper the efficiency of the operations.

Another approach is to develop a trend of the relative costs from period to period. Particularly when using the experience curve to develop pricing strategy, it is necessary to track relative costs over time so as to be able to forecast costs into the future.

[7]"Flexibile Pricing," *Business Week,* December 12, 1977, p. 88.
[8]Ibid.
[9]Ibid.
[10]"Pricing Strategy in an Inflation Economy," *Business Week,* April 6, 1974, p. 43.

The experience curve can also be used to forecast competitors' cost over time. Chapter 10 will discuss the use of the experience curve in pricing.

FORECASTING COSTS AND PRICES

In 1988, the computer companies were facing a continuing shortage of dynamic random-access memory chips (DRAMs) that was threatening growth prospects and profit margins. With demand for the chips exceeding the ability and willingness of Japanese producers to expand production, computer makers were rethinking their product and pricing strategies. The spot market price for 256-kilobyte DRAMs rose from $1.75 to $11.50 by early 1988. With memory chip costs ranging from 5 percent of the cost of a mainframe computer to 25 percent of the cost of an engineering workstation, the need to forecast both spot market prices and contract prices was apparent as computer firms wrestled with whether to let their computer prices continue to decline, hold at 1988 levels, or increase for 1989. Further, besides developing prices for new computers, these manufacturers also had to develop prices for memory expansion boards. Given the prescription that the relevant costs for pricing are future costs, the need to develop accurate forecasts of 1989 chip prices was of strategic importance in developing prices for new computers and expansion boards in a dynamic, competitive market. Moreover, the effect of new chip production capacity expected by mid-1989 also needed to be analyzed.[11]

In many pricing decision contexts where competitive prices tightly constrain a firm's pricing discretion, it is crucial to forecast the trend in market prices for a product. Price forecasts are used in decisions about marketing strategy, new investments, budgeting, and estimating costs of materials purchasing.[12] However, such forecasts are based primarily on management's intuition despite emerging theory and techniques of price forecasting. Moreover, even though profitability depends on prices, costs, and sales volume, more effort has been expended on forecasting costs and sales volume than on forecasting prices.

The purpose of this section is to review the methods of price and cost forecasting. Some approaches, such as the price exclusion charts, are more appropriate for forecasting prices of commodities for a seller of the commodity. Other approaches, such as experience curves, are useful not only for forecasting prices of inputs to the production process but also for forecasting cost trends of the company, competition, or industry. From an economic perspective, if we know the appropriate demand and supply schedules for a product, service, or commodity, it should not be difficult to forecast price. Unfortunately, it is not possible to have precise demand and supply information for a product at a particular time. Nevertheless, some useful tools for forecasting prices and costs help reduce the uncertainty of business planning.

Essentially, there are three approaches to price and cost forecasting: statistical

---

[11]"When the Chips Are Down," *Business Week,* June 27, 1988, pp. 28–29.

[12]George B. Hegeman, "The Art of Price Forecasting," in Robert Ferber (ed.), *Handbook of Marketing Research* (New York: McGraw-Hill, 1974), pp. 4-286–4-294.

trend analysis, judgmental methods, and simulation models. Often, however, a particular forecast uses a combination of these approaches.

Statistical Trend Analysis

Statistical trend analyses rely on historical data to extrapolate from the past into the future. Among these techniques are price exclusion charts, experience or learning curves, and regression and correlation analysis. Two major cautions must be observed when using these techniques:

1 They rely on historical data that may not portray current and future trends.
2 The apparent mathematical sophistication underlying them may lull the decision maker into ignoring other relevant judgmental factors affecting future prices.[13]

If these precautions are observed, these techniques provide a useful starting point and often are sufficiently accurate for most planning purposes.

Price Exclusion Charts[14]   Price exclusion charts provide a way of determining the range of infeasible prices for a product. Exclusion charts are totally empirical and require information on a large number of products competing in the market.

As seen in Fig. 7-2, a price exclusion chart is constructed by plotting price versus production for each end use (market). A semilogarithmic scale is used with production volume being plotted on a logarithmic scale and price on an arithmetic scale. The purpose of the chart is to show the various price–volume combinations that competing products have experienced in the past. By then drawing a line so that nearly every price–volume point falls below and to the left, an exclusion area is determined showing what prices are infeasible.

The U.S. Tariff Commission provides such data annually for synthetic organic chemicals. Price–volume exclusion charts using these data have been successful in medicinals, flavor and perfume materials, plasticizers, surface-active agents, and pesticides. But exclusion charts have not been successfully applied to product groups like dyes and organic pigments.[15] Clearly, a price exclusion chart will not forecast a specific price, but it seems to indicate some price–volume limits for a particular market.

Experience Curves   It has been shown that costs decline by some characteristic amount each time accumulated production is doubled.[16] Accordingly, because of the competitive nature of most products, prices tend to decline along a similar pattern as long as competitive relationships are stable. Given these long-term predictable

[13]See Theodore D. Frey, "Forecasting Prices for Industrial Commodity Markets," *Journal of Marketing,* 34 (April 1970), 28–32.
[14]This section is based on Hegeman, op. cit.
[15]See D. J. Massey and J. H. Black, "Predicting Chemical Prices," *Chemical and Engineering News,* October 20, 1969.
[16]*Perspectives on Experience* (Boston: Boston Consulting Group, 1970).

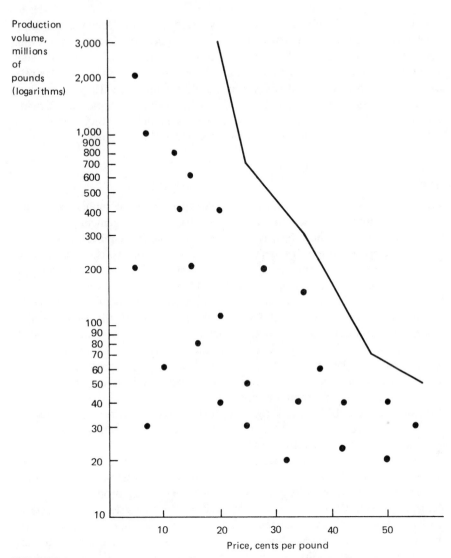

FIGURE 7-2
Price exclusion chart.

cost and price behavior patterns, it becomes relatively easy to forecast costs and prices. Recently, a number of applications and approaches have been reported that make this technique a useful and practical tool for forecasting prices.

Regression and Correlation Analysis It has been established that prices for some products follow long-term trends marked by periodic cyclical or seasonal factors. Time-series analysis can be used to establish the existence of these trends and to identify the cyclical or seasonal factors affecting prices. Once the trends are established and the cyclical or seasonal patterns identified, the firm is in a position to plan both materials and finished-goods inventories by forecasting prices for such items. Furthermore, time-series analysis permits the establishment of lead–lag relationships for forecasting price changes. It can also be combined with regression and correlation analysis to isolate possible causal relationships for price movements. Finally, these techniques permit the use of computer models for forecasting prices. For example, Weyerhauser has reported success using these models.[17]

Judgmental Methods

As indicated, the statistical methods, because of their apparent sophistication and precision, often lull management into ignoring the value of management's experience and intuitive judgment. The proper use of judgment typically requires management to divide the forecast period into a short-range segment—one to three years—and a long-range forecast that anticipates basic changes in the industry. Generally, it takes two to three years for capital investment to become productive capacity.

In the short range, specific attention must be paid to competitors and the demand–supply balance in the market. Of particular importance is the need to project any new productive capacity becoming available during the short-range period. If the demand–supply balance is loose, what are the prospects that some competitors or suppliers will set their prices to cover their variable costs or make extra efforts to find export customers in other markets? Will some competitors stockpile inventories and wait for a better demand–supply situation?

If the demand–supply balance is tight, what are the costs of starting up marginal capacity? How long will it take? As prices rise during a tight market, when will buyers begin shifting to substitute products?

In December 1976, the synthetic fiber industry had negative earnings for the second straight year. Most synthetic plants were running below the break-even points. The industry helped create this situation by expanding production capacity 30 percent between 1973 and 1976. This additional capacity led to an excess of supply capability relative to actual demand, forcing a decrease in prices of 10 percent on the average. Yet at the same time, polyester staple fiber production was running at 90 percent of capacity, and a price increase was forecast for this segment of the industry. Thus, the industry productive capacity relative to the expected demand for the output has an important bearing on how prices will behave. For companies that use fibers to make cloth and clothing, the relative differences in the price behavior of these different types of fiber will have an important impact on their planning activities, including pricing.[18]

The long-range forecast is initially a forecast of capacity changes due to invest-

---

[17]Massey and Black, op. cit.

[18]See "The Losses Pile Up in Synthetic Fibers," *Business Week,* December 6, 1976, pp. 46–50; Paul C. Christopherson, "Product Pricing in the Chemical Industry," *Financial Analysts Journal,* 33 (November–December 1977), 54–62.

ment in plant and new technologies. Therefore, the forecaster must examine the investment policies and criteria of competitors. What competitors have inherently lower investment costs per unit of output? Do some competitors have specific tax savings or investment credits? Do some competitors have location advantages over others? What is the return on investment rate for the industry leaders?

The investment criteria and expansion economics of the industry leaders provide the basis for predicting new increments of capacity. What price would induce the leaders to expand capacity given their return criteria? What other firms would be likely to be influenced by the leaders?

Given some estimates of available capacity over the next three or more years, the forecaster must also check whether this new capacity is consistent with the market's growth. Clearly, if new-capacity growth is greater than market growth, excess supply will force prices down.

Many of these judgments can be combined with statistical or other analytical models to provide a sophisticated forecasting system. In one case, linear programming models were used to forecast the cost and availability of naphtha and the value of commercial aircraft.[19] In another, Bayesian decision analysis was used to combine judgment and statistical analysis for forecasting the price of the petrochemical butadiene.[20]

Simulation Models

Some firms have developed complex computer models that simulate the economy and competitors, incorporating production costs, inventory control, market share, and investment planning. Essentially, these models are an upgrading of the judgment techniques discussed earlier, but they allow for a number of "what if" questions to be answered assuming different levels of capacity expansion, market growth, and general economic activity. A major abrasives company currently uses a large simulation model to enable it to forecast market prices for its products as well as material input costs. Moreover, by including up-to-date market and company information in the model, the company also has a basis for comparing actual performance against its forecasts.

SUMMARY

Costs set a floor to a firm's pricing discretion. But when considering the cost aspect of a pricing decision, the crucial problem is to determine what costs are relevant to the decision. Moreover, it is also important to know the determinants and behavior of these costs in order to analyze the full impact of the pricing decision.

The purpose of this chapter has been to discuss cost concepts and classifications, how these types of costs behave, and how to identify patterns of cost behavior. We

[19]Hegeman, op. cit.

[20]Donald G. Frederick, "An Industrial Pricing Decision Using Bayesian Multivariate Analysis," *Journal of Marketing Research,* 8 (May 1971), 199–203.

currently have sufficient knowledge about generating and analyzing cost data. With the aid of high-speed computers and statistical programs, the decision maker is able to know the relevant costs for pricing purposes. Perhaps more than anything else, managers need to exert the will to develop detailed cost studies of their operations. The next three chapters illustrate the types of analyses that can be performed if proper cost data are available.

DISCUSSION QUESTIONS

1 a Develop a comprehensive list of the different types of costs that are incurred in the manufacturing process.
  b Assuming a general situation, classify these costs as
   (1) Direct, indirect, or common costs.
   (2) Variable, semivariable, or fixed costs.
  c What was your rationale in making these classifications?
2 a Develop a comprehensive list of the different types of costs that are incurred by a manufacturer in the marketing and distribution of its products.
  b Assuming a general situation, classify these costs as
   (1) Direct, indirect, or common costs.
   (2) Variable, semivariable, or fixed costs.
  c What was your rationale in making these classifications?
3 a Develop a comprehensive list of the different types of costs that are incurred by a retailer.
  b Assuming a general situation, classify these costs as
   (1) Direct, indirect, or common costs.
   (2) Variable, semivariable, or fixed costs.
  c What was your rationale in making these classifications?
4 a Develop a comprehensive list of the different types of costs that are incurred by a service organization, such as a bank, hospital, or tax consulting service.
  b Assuming a general situation, classify these costs as
   (1) Direct, indirect, or common costs.
   (2) Variable, semivariable, or fixed costs.
  c What was your rationale in making these classifications?
5 Review the different types and classes of costs identified in the four questions above. Are there any differences in the nature and behavior of the costs across these different types of organizations? What implications, if any, do these differences have for developing pricing strategies?

SUGGESTED READINGS

Abel, Rein: "The Role of Costs and Cost Accounting in Price Determination," *Management Accounting,* 60 (April 1978), 29–32.

Corr, Arthur V.: "The Role of Cost in Pricing," *Management Accounting,* 56 (November 1974), 15–18.

"Costing," *Management Decision,* 25, No. 5 (1987), 42–47.

Georges, Walter, and Robert W. McGee: *Analytical Contribution Accounting: The Interface of Cost Accounting and Pricing Policy* (New York: Quorum Books, 1987).

Govindarajan, V., and Robert N. Anthony: "How Firms Use Cost Data in Price Decisions," *Management Accounting,* 65 (July 1983), 30–36.

Oxenfeldt, Alfred R.: "The Computation of Costs for Price Decisions," *Industrial Marketing Management,* 6 (1977), 83–90.

Weathers, Henry T.: "Managerial Profitability," *Management Accounting,* 56 (July 1974), 25–27, 34.

CHAPTER 8

PROFITABILITY ANALYSIS
FOR PRICING DECISIONS

In the 1930s, the president of a company asked his controller why, with a sales increase of $100,000, profits had fallen $20,000. The controller, Jonathan Harris, devised a cost accounting system that showed profits as a function of sales. Today, his system of accounting is known as *direct costing.* [1]

As defined in Chap. 7, a direct cost is a cost that is traceable to an object, activity, sales territory, product line, or customer account. It was also pointed out that direct costs are independent of cost behavior in that they may be fixed costs or variable costs. A direct costing system attributes only those costs that can be objectively traced to an activity. Thus, no arbitrary cost allocations of common costs are assessed to that activity.

From a decision perspective, a direct cost system shows cost changes in production as output increases or decreases. Marketing plans can be improved when direct cost information documents the effect on contribution to profits of changes in prices, promotion expenses, product mix, or other marketing activities designed to influence demand and revenues. However, the impact of production and marketing changes on profits can be determined only when both the cost and revenue changes resulting from a change in activity are determined. A direct cost approach facilitates such a determination. Contribution analysis focuses on the change in profits resulting from changes in activity levels and derives from a direct costing approach.

---

[1]Jonathan N. Harris, "What Did We Earn Last Month?" *NAA Bulletin,* January 1936, p. 501.

This chapter develops the key aspects of contribution analysis and shows ways in which valid cost information is used for product management. The chapter first introduces traditional break-even analysis, which is then extended to a more dynamic method called *profit analysis*. After offering some useful guidelines for break-even analysis, the chapter shows in detail how profit analysis may be used to evaluate alternative price choices.

Figure 8-1 provides a view of the material we will be developing in this chapter and what is to follow in Chaps. 9 and 10. Figure 8-1 shows the building blocks—direct, indirect, variable, and fixed—explained in the preceding chapter. The concept of out-of-pocket or cash costs was also explained in Chap. 7. In this chapter, we develop the concept of contribution and apply this concept while discussing direct labor and direct material costs. Indirect manufacturing costs refer to other manufacturing expenses, such as supplies, which are not incurred solely for a particular production activity but can be objectively traced to the activity. Marketing and distribution costs are discussed in Chap. 9. Note also the distinction between conversion costs and manufacturing costs. Conversion costs refer only to the actual value-

FIGURE 8-1
The elements of price. (Adapted and reprinted with permission from Phillip F. Ostwald, *Cost Estimating,* 2nd ed. [Englewood Cliffs, N.J.: Prentice-Hall, Inc., 1984], p. 315.)

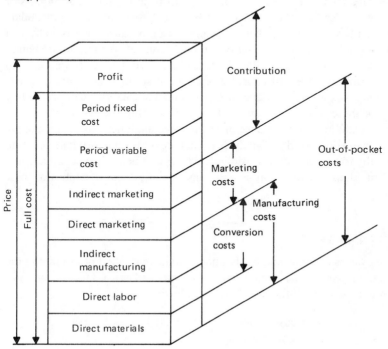

adding part of manufacturing, i.e., direct labor and indirect manufacturing. For the discussion in this chapter, all period costs will be considered to be fixed costs. The distinction between period variable and period fixed costs will be made in Chaps. 9 and 10.

ELEMENTS OF PROFITABILITY

There are four basic elements that affect the profitability of any multiproduct or multiservice organization:

1 Price per unit of each product or service offering, P_i
2 Costs: variable costs per unit of each offering, VC_i, and fixed costs per period,
3 Volume produced and sold of each offering, Q_i
4 Dollar sales mix of the offerings sold

In profitability analysis, profit measures include contribution margin per unit, total contributions per period, profit–volume ratio, contribution per resource unit, net operating profit, net income (profit after taxes), and earnings per share. Each of these profit measurements will be introduced and defined in this chapter. The analytical approach developed in this chapter will be essentially the same regardless of the type of measurement used. However, preferences among indicators of profit will be distinguished.

The actual data for the analysis may be in the form of (1) units and dollars or (2) dollars only. Preferably, the data should be in the form of units and dollars (i.e., price per unit, variable costs per unit, unit sales), because then the effect of each of these four elements of profitability can be calculated. A more limited analysis can be performed if the data are in dollars only (i.e., dollars of revenues, total variable costs). Initially, we will consider only the first three elements of price, costs, and volume, i.e., a single-product organization. The analyses will proceed by assuming two of these three elements constant and isolating the effect of the third element on profits. When we have developed the basic analytical approach using a single product, we will expand the analysis to include a multiple-product situation and introduce the fourth element, the dollar sales mix. When the experience curve is introduced in Chap. 11, the analysis will consider additional dynamics of these elements.

BREAK-EVEN ANALYSIS

Break-even analysis is a simple and easily understandable method of examining the relationship among fixed costs, variable costs, volume, and price. Detailed analysis of break-even data will show the effect of the following:

1 Decisions that convert costs from variable to fixed or vice versa
2 Decisions that reduce or increase costs

3 Decisions that increase sales volume and revenue
4 Decisions to change selling prices

To illustrate the concept of break-even analysis and its application to pricing decisions consider a specialty retailer who buys T-shirts from a supplier at $8 each and sells them for $10 each. Assume that the fixed costs are $10,000 per year and that estimated sales volume is 10,000 shirts per year. The data in Table 8-1 summarize this situation. The data in the "One shirt" column suggest that the retailer earns $1 of profit per shirt sold. However, one difficulty with this conclusion is that profit per shirt is $1 *only if* 10,000 shirts are sold during the year. If fewer shirts are sold, average unit profit is less; if more shirts are sold, average unit profit is more. A second problem with the one-shirt presentation in Table 8-1 is that fixed costs are portrayed as though they vary with the number of units bought and sold. In this illustration, rent is fixed at a lump amount of $10,000, and it is illogical to develop an average fixed cost per unit. Indeed, *fixed costs should not be unitized.* The contribution approach provides a mechanism for us to determine the effect of different sales volume on profits and to determine a break-even point.

Each time a shirt is sold, a contribution to fixed costs and profit of $2 is generated. The number of shirts that must be sold before the retailer breaks even is $10,000/$2.00 = 5,000 shirts. This figure is the retailer's break-even point: the level of sales volume which produces total contributions equal to the period fixed expenses. Only when shirt 5,001 is sold will the retailer realize any profit for the year. The unit profit of $1 indicated above obviously is incorrect since no profits are realized until sales exceed 5,000 shirts.

The break-even *point* occurs when sales revenue exactly covers all costs, i.e., the level of sales revenue when profits are zero. Or, as illustrated, the break-even point is the amount of sales revenue that generates contributions equal to the period fixed costs.

Using the shirt example, the break-even formula is

$$BEQ = \frac{FC}{P - VC} \tag{8-1}$$

TABLE 8-1
PLANNING DATA FOR RETAIL SHIRT STORE

	One Shirt	10,000 Shirts Per Year
Sales	$10.00	$100,000
Out-of-pocket costs	$ 8.00	$ 80,000
Fixed costs	1.00	10,000
Total costs	$ 9.00	$ 90,000
Profits	$ 1.00	$ 10,000

where BEQ = break-even sales quantity (units)
    FC = period fixed costs
    P = selling price per unit
    VC = direct variable costs per unit

Applying the shirt data we obtain

$$\text{BEQ} = \frac{\$10,000}{\$10 - \$8} = 5,000 \text{ shirts}$$

Alternatively, the break-even formula can be expressed in terms of sales revenue:

$$\text{BES} = \frac{\text{FC}}{\text{PV}} \qquad (8\text{-}2)$$

where BES is the break-even sales revenue and PV is the profit–volume, or PV, ratio, which indicates the proportion of sales dollars available to cover fixed costs after deducting variable costs:

FIGURE 8-2
Break-even chart for the retail shirt store.

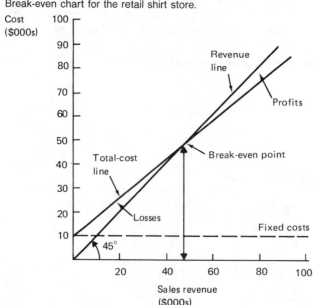

$$PV = \frac{P - VC}{P} \tag{8-3}$$

Using the shirt data we obtain

$$PV = \frac{\$10 - \$8}{\$10} = 0.20$$

and therefore

$$BES = \frac{\$10,000}{0.20} = \$50,000$$

Often it is desirable to picture the economic character of a business firm by showing the break-even analysis on a break-even chart. Essentially, there are three rows on a break-even chart. One row shows the fixed expenses over the volume range, another shows the total costs, and the third is the revenue line. The break-even point is the intersection of the revenue line and the total-cost line.

We normally plot the sales revenue on the x (horizontal) axis and costs are plotted on the y (vertical) axis. Both are expressed in identical dollars on an identical scale. Thus, the 45-degree revenue line will indicate the same value whether referred to from either the cost or revenue scale. The point where the total-cost line intersects the revenue line is the sales volume where total costs equal total sales revenue. Figure 8-2 shows the break-even chart for the retail shirt store. How to extend break-even analysis to include an analysis of the impact on profits follows.

PROFIT ANALYSIS

Virtually every planned action or decision in an organization affects costs and therefore profits. Profit analysis attempts to determine the effect of costs, prices, and volume on profits in order to determine the best course of action to follow. Accurate and objective data about the contributions made by each product gives management a sound basis for determining how to allocate advertising and selling efforts to individual products or product lines.

Perhaps the most important piece of data resulting from a profit analysis is the *marginal income ratio,* or the *contribution ratio,* which is usually referred to as the *profit–volume ratio* (PV). As indicated earlier, the PV ratio is the proportion of sales available to cover fixed costs and profits after deducting variable costs. Equation (8-3) gives the computational formula for PV on a unit basis. In the following data the contribution ratio or PV is the contribution of $3,500 ($10,000 − $6,500), divided by sales, or 35 percent. [That is, PV can also be calculated using (total contribution dollars/total dollar sales).] Thus, 35 cents out of each sales dollar contributes toward paying fixed costs and providing a profit.

Sales	$10,000
Variable costs	6,500
Fixed costs	2,500
Profit	$ 1,000

Once the PV has been calculated it is possible to determine the effects on profits of additional sales volume. If $1,000 of additional sales were generated, the additional profits would be $1,000 × 0.35, or $350. Since the fixed costs of $2,500 have already been covered by the original $10,000 of sales, additional volume contributes 35 cents of every sales dollar to profits. Thus, a 10 percent increase in sales produces a 35 percent increase in profits. A second increase in sales of 10 percent will produce a 28.5 percent increase in profits [($1,100 × 0.35)/($1,000 + $350)]. It is important to note that this analysis is possible only when all direct costs have been separated into their fixed and variable components.

In multiproduct firms it is important to place emphasis on achieving the maximum amount of contribution revenue instead of attempting to maximize sales revenues. Each product faces different competition, has a different demand elasticity, and perhaps depends for its sales, at least in part, on the sales of the other products in

TABLE 8-2
DETERMINING CONTRIBUTIONS AND PROFITS FOR A PRODUCT LINE

Item	Product A	Product B	Product C	Product D	Total
Unit variable cost	$ 9.00	$ 10.00	$ 11.00	$ 12.00	
			Before		
Unit selling price	$ 15.00	$ 16.00	$ 17.00	$ 18.00	
Unit contribution	$ 6.00	$ 6.00	$ 6.00	$ 6.00	
Units sold (000s)	50	60	40	30	180
Total revenue	$750,000	$960,000	$680,000	$540,000	$2,930,000
Total contribution	$300,000	$360,000	$240,000	$180,000	$1,080,000
Less: Fixed costs					$1,000,000
Net profit					$ 80,000
			After		
Unit selling price	$ 14.00	$ 19.00	$ 18.00	$ 20.00	
Unit contribution	$ 5.00	$ 9.00	$ 7.00	$ 8.00	
Units sold (000s)	70	40	40	25	170
Total revenue	$980,000	$760,000	$720,000	$500,000	$2,960,000
Total contribution	$350,000	$360,000	$280,000	$200,000	$1,190,000
Less: Fixed costs					$1,000,000
Net profit					$ 190,000

the line. Table 8-2 shows the effect of changing product prices of a product line.[2] In the "Before" situation, the firm subjectively set its prices at a uniform contribution level and ignored competition, demand elasticity, and product-line interdependence. However, after examining pricing decisions, management discovered that product A was price elastic, implying that a price reduction would lead to a greater percentage increase in sales volume. Product B was being priced below competition and increasing its price to competitive levels would leave the total contribution unchanged, although revenues would decrease. Products C and D were found to be demand inelastic; therefore, prices could be increased, leading to increases in revenues. As Table 8-2 indicates, the firm was able to earn twice the profit with less unit sales and about the same revenue.

Extension of Break-Even Analysis

As we have seen, the break-even chart assumes that each dollar of revenue will have the same cost, the same profit–volume ratio, and eventually the same profit. However, in the real world of business, operations are not uniform. In fact, over time, we would expect changes in out-of-pocket (variable) costs, fixed expenses, and prices, with resultant changes in profits.

In terms of the break-even chart, a decrease in variable costs with no corresponding change in fixed expenses decreases the slope of the total-cost line, resulting in a lower break-even point. An increase in variable costs increases the slope of the total-cost line, leading to a higher break-even point.

If prices are increased and the volume remains the same, contributions are increased. This occurs because each sales dollar has less out-of-pocket content. Thus, the effect is to lower the slope of the total-cost line, producing a lower break-even point.

If only fixed costs are increased, the result is an increase in the break-even point, causing profits to start later, but at the same PV rate. Therefore, any changes in the price, volume, or cost variables can be shown on the break-even chart.

To illustrate some of the dynamics of the analysis assume the data are as shown in Table 8-3. Now assume the firm wants to consider adding new equipment. It is believed this new equipment will reduce labor costs by $200,000 per period for the same volume level. However, acquisition of the machinery will lead to an increase in fixed expenses of $100,000. As Table 8-4 and Fig. 8-3 show, the break-even points are identical for the original and the proposed situations. However, the new situation would contribute 40 cents of profit per sales dollar above the break-even point, as compared to the original situation, which contributed only 20 cents of profit per sales dollar above the break-even point. This illustration provides an indication of the dynamics of break-even analysis. The guidelines that follow illustrate these dynamics.

[2]This example is borrowed from Spencer A. Tucker, *Pricing for Higher Profit* (New York: McGraw-Hill, 1966), pp. 86–87.

TABLE 8-3

1. Sales revenue (price = $10/unit)		$1,000,000
2. Direct material cost	$400,000	
3. Direct labor cost	400,000	
4. Total direct variable cost (2 + 3)	$800,000	
5. Fixed costs	100,000	
6. Total costs (4 + 5)		900,000
7. Contribution (1 − 4)		$ 200,000
8. Profit–volume ratio (7 ÷ 1)		0.20
9. Break-even sales (5 ÷ 8)		$ 500,000
10. Unit sales ($1,000,000÷$10)		100,000
11. Unit contribution (7 ÷ 10)		$ 2.00
12. Break-even quantity (5 ÷ 11)		50,000

TABLE 8-4

1. Sales revenue	$1,000,000
2. Variable costs	$ 600,000
3. Fixed costs	$ 200,000
4. Total costs (2 + 3)	$ 800,000
5. Contribution (1 − 2)	$ 400,000
6. Profit–volume ratio (5 ÷ 1)	0.40
7. Break-even sales (3 ÷ 6)	$ 500,000

Some Useful Guidelines for Break-Even Analysis

Let us return to the specialty retailer who buys shirts from a supplier at $8 each and sells them for $10 each. Fixed costs are $10,000 per year and estimated sales volume is 10,000 shirts per year. Recall that for this situation the break-even point is 5,000 shirts, or $50,000.

Now if fixed costs are increased to $15,000 per year, the break-even point becomes

$$BES = \frac{\$15,000}{0.20} = \$75,000$$

If price is raised to $11, the PV becomes 0.273 (i.e., $3/$11), and

$$BES = \frac{\$15,000}{0.273} = \$55,000$$

If fixed costs remain at $15,000 but the shirts are purchased for $7, the PV becomes 0.30 (i.e., $3/$10), and the break-even point is

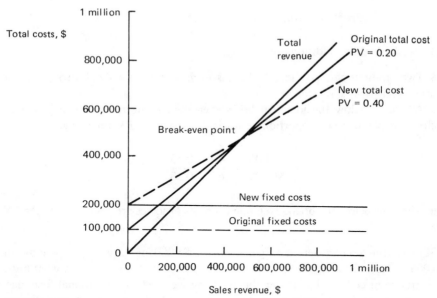

FIGURE 8-3
Effect of changing the cost structure.

$$\text{BES} = \frac{\$15{,}000}{0.30} = \$50{,}000$$

These three examples provide useful guidelines.

1 A change in fixed costs affects only the break-even point.

2 A change in the price and/or variable costs affects both the break-even point and the PV.

3 An increase in prices and/or a decrease in variable costs can offset an increase in fixed expenses (assuming volume remains unaffected).

We have seen that with fixed costs at $15,000, price at $10, and variable costs at $7, the break-even point is the same as in the original example. However, are profits the same? To answer this question we need an additional formula.

$$\text{Profit} = (\text{sales revenue} \times \text{PV}) - \text{fixed costs} \qquad (8\text{-}4)$$

Applying this formula to the original situation for a sales level of $70,000 we get

$$\text{Profit} = (\$70{,}000 \times 0.20) - \$10{,}000 = \$4{,}000$$

And for the new situation

$$\text{Profit} = (\$70,000 \times 0.30) - \$15,000 = \$6,000$$

Thus, we have three additional guidelines:

4 Two products can have identical break-even points but will still earn profits or losses at their own PV rate.
5 Above or below the identical break-even points, the ratio of two products' profits or losses will be proportionate to the rate of their PV rates, e.g.,

$$\frac{\$4,000}{\$6,000} = \frac{4}{6} = \frac{0.20}{0.30}$$

6 Above or below the break-even point, profits or losses are generated by the PV rate.

Suppose the retailer sets a target profit of $5,000 on target sales volume of $80,000. If variable costs are $8.50 per shirt and fixed costs are $15,000, what must the shirts be priced at? To answer this question we need two additional formulas. (Note that a profit objective is treated as a "fixed" expense in the analysis; we elaborate on this point later in the chapter.)

$$PV = \frac{\text{target profit} + \text{fixed expenses}}{\text{sales revenue}} \qquad (8\text{-}5)$$

$$= \frac{(\$5,000 + \$15,000)}{\$80,000} = 0.25$$

$$\text{Price} = \frac{\text{variable costs}}{1 - PV} \qquad (8\text{-}6)$$

$$= \frac{\$8.50}{(1 - 0.25)} = \$11.33$$

This example provides another guideline:

7 When the objective is to determine a price for a target PV, divide the appropriate variable costs by the complement of the target PV.

These seven guidelines provide a basis for examining the effect of changes in the product's or firm's underlying cost structure. Profit analysis is an extension of break-even analysis in that it is possible to use the methodology of break-even analysis to examine the effects on profits of changes in costs or prices. The concept that allows us to perform such analyses is the PV ratio. As will be demonstrated in this and subsequent chapters, the PV ratio is an important analytical concept. The key to its application is the ability to classify relevant costs according to their behavior—fixed or variable—and according to their traceability to the business segment being analyzed.

Limitations of Break-Even Analysis

As the guidelines suggest, break-even analysis is useful for studying the relations among prices, costs, and volume. It is helpful for analyzing pricing alternatives, developing cost control programs, or making decisions about expanding productive capacity. However, an inherent weakness of the technique is the assumption that variable costs remain proportional to volume at all output levels. Further, it is assumed that price is constant over the relevant volume levels. The assumption of variable costs remaining proportional to volume will be relaxed in Chap. 11 when we discuss the experience curve phenomenon. One way to overcome the constant-price assumption is to build different price–volume–cost scenarios into the analysis; this adaptation will be developed in Chap. 12 when discussing new-product pricing.

Another important limitation is that the costs used in the analysis may be relevant only over a limited range of volume. That is, if volume is below or above certain capacity levels, the underlying variable and fixed costs may differ. For example, going to overtime or a second shift will raise the labor costs per hour and will increase the per unit labor costs. Similarly, an additional quantity discount given for added materials purchases may reduce material costs per unit. Also, qualitative changes in the product or service may change the underlying cost structure and lead to different break-even points.

Used appropriately and with an understanding of its limitations, break-even analysis can be valuable for a number of important business decisions. It can be used to analyze the profitability implications of alternative prices for a new product. It can be used to analyze the implications of changing the cost structure, e.g., shifting from a relatively high variable-cost to a relatively high fixed-cost structure. The key element in these decisions is the influence of volume changes on profitability when organizations have different relationships between fixed and variable costs. To understand these relationships we now turn to the concept of leverage.

USING LEVERAGE FOR DEVELOPING PRICING STRATEGIES

In the physical sciences, leverage is the application of a small amount of force to one end of a rigid mechanism balanced on a fulcrum to raise a heavy object at the other end. Similarly, when a relatively small change in sales volume leads to a larger change in operating profits (earnings before interest and taxes), leverage is at work. There are two types of leverage: operating leverage and financial leverage. Whenever a firm incurs a fixed operating cost (regardless of the level of its activities), it is using *operating leverage* to amplify the effect of sales volume on operating profits (i.e., profits before interest and taxes). *Financial leverage* is created by employing interest-bearing debt for capital formation (irrespective of its operating profit), which amplifies the effect of a change in operating profit on earnings per share.

In today's business environment it is essential to understand the concept of leverage, how it occurs, and how to use it to manage the firm's pricing function. Leverage of a firm is an important factor in the shareholders' evaluations of a firm's risk. However, a firm's leverage has additional implications for its operating managers: it is through leverage that fluctuations in demand for the firm's products and services are amplified into its financial results (e.g., changes in operating profits or earnings per share). Since leverage is at the interface of the marketing and financial management of the firm, operating managers should consider it as a mechanism for translating marketing decisions into desired financial results.

The financial health of a firm depends on marketing strategies because (1) marketing strategies directly influence profitability and because (2) financial issues serve to constrain marketing strategy options.[3] It is clear that price influences the firm's financial position through its direct impact on revenues. Moreover, the impact of price on sales volume influences costs and the development of marketing strategies. The purpose of this section is to integrate the concepts of leverage and marketing-oriented pricing strategies. It will be shown that firms with different degrees of operating and financial leverage that compete in the same product markets will have different abilities to use price as a strategic variable.[4]

Operating Leverage

Operating leverage occurs when an organization has fixed operating costs that must be met regardless of sales volume. The operating leverage of a firm is related to the ratio of total fixed costs to total variable costs. Firms with a higher proportion of total costs represented by fixed costs will have a higher operating leverage for a specific sales volume. The airlines are a dramatic example of firms with relatively high fixed costs. Once the break-even point in terms of passenger miles is reached, the revenues earned from each additional passenger contribute almost entirely to profits. To measure the effect of a change in sales volume on profits, we calculate

$$\text{Degree of operating leverage} = \frac{\text{percentage change in operating profits}}{\text{percentage change in sales volume}}$$

or

$$\text{DOL} = \frac{\Delta \text{OP}}{\text{OP}} \div \frac{\Delta Q}{Q} \qquad (8\text{-}7)$$

where DOL = degree of operating leverage

ΔOP = change in operating profits

OP = operating profits in the previous period (before interest and taxes)

ΔQ = change in sales volume (units)

Q = sales volume in the previous period

[3] Paul F. Anderson, "The Marketing Management/Finance Interface," in Neil Beckwith, Michael Houston, Robert Mittelstaedt, Kent Monroe, and Scott Ward (eds.), *Proceedings,* Summer Educators' Conference (Chicago: American Marketing Association, 1979), pp. 321–329.

[4] Portions of this section are drawn from Tridib Mazumdar and Kent B. Monroe, "Using Leverage for Developing Pricing Strategies," *Proceedings,* Summer Educators' Conference (Chicago: American Marketing Association, 1986), pp. 303–308.

Note that Eq. (8-7) is essentially of the same form as the price elasticity definition given in Chap. 2. Indeed, operating leverage is a measure of the degree to which operating profits are sensitive to changes in sales volume. Thus, if demand is sensitive to small price changes, i.e., elastic, then increases in sales volume due to small price changes may lead to greater changes in operating profits if the DOL is greater than one.

For example, assume a firm had sales of 100,000 units last period with an operating profit of $50,000. In the current period, sales increased 20 percent to 120,000 units and operating profits increased 40 percent to $70,000. Thus DOL = 40 percent/20 percent = 2.0. Therefore, from the base sales level of 100,000 units, for every 1 percent change in sales, there will be a 2 percent change in operating profits *in the same direction as the sales change*. This magnification of changes in sales volume on profits occurs for either increases or decreases in sales so long as the cost structure (i.e., variable costs per unit and fixed costs) and price remain unchanged.

It is also possible to compute DOL for any level of sales using

$$DOL = \frac{\text{dollar contributions at sales volume } Q}{\text{dollar operating profits at sales volume } Q} \qquad (8\text{-}8)$$

Consider the data in Table 8-5 for three competing firms. The firms have identical prices and unit sales, and firms A and B have identical total costs and operating profits. Because of the employment of different mixes of fixed and variable costs, firm A has a DOL of 1.5, while firms B and C have DOLs of 3.0 and 1.2 respectively. If sales for each firm increase 10 percent, then operating profits will increase 15 percent for A, 30 percent for B, and 12 percent for C. Also, the increase in dollar profits is given by the PV ratio multiplied by the percentage sales increase: $30 for A, $60 for B, $60 for C. However, the operating leverage and PV ratio cut both ways, in that a 10 percent decrease in sales will reduce operating profits of firms B and C by $60, and A's operating profits will decline by $30. Thus, both the operating leverage and PV ratio indicate the responsiveness of a firm's operating profits to a change in sales volume.

Relationship Between Operating Leverage and the PV Ratio

There is an important difference between the operating leverage and PV ratio concepts. For a given cost structure, the PV ratio of a firm is constant at all levels of sales. But the degree of operating leverage changes as the firm's sales level changes, being undefined at break-even volume and then continuously decreasing as sales volume increases above break-even. The value of DOL approaches the value of one as sales volume increases for a given cost structure.

Despite this difference, both profit–volume analysis using the PV ratio and operating leverage are important tools for strategy development. With a given cost

TABLE 8-5
DETERMINING OPERATING AND FINANCIAL LEVERAGE

			Firm	
		A	B	C
A.	**Operating data**			
	1. Price per unit	$10	$10	$10
	2. Direct variable cost/unit	7	4	4
	3. Contribution/unit (1 − 2)	3	6	6
	4. PV ratio (3 ÷ 1)	0.3	0.6	0.6
	5. Total fixed costs	$100	$400	$100
B.	**Financial structure**			
	6. Debt	$300	$700	$700
	7. Equity	700	300	300
	8. Number of shares	70	30	30
C.	**Profitability measures**			
	9. Sales volume (units)	100	100	100
	10. Revenues (1 × 9)	$1,000	$1,000	$1,000
	11. Total variable costs (2 × 9)	700	400	400
	12. Total contribution (10 − 11)	300	600	600
	13. Operating profits (12 − 5)	200	200	500
	14. Interest (12% × 6)	36	84	84
	15. Profits before tax (13 − 14)	164	116	416
	16. Taxes (50% × 15)	82	58	208
	17. Profits after tax (15 − 16)	82	58	208
	18. Earnings per share (17 ÷ 8)	$1.17	$1.93	$6.93
D.	**Leverage**			
	19. Operating leverage (12 ÷ 13)	1.50	3.00	1.20
	20. Financial leverage (13 ÷ 15)	1.22	1.72	1.20
	21. Combined leverage (19 × 20)	1.83	5.16	1.44

structure and a given price of a product, a firm can use profit–volume analysis to determine its level of unit sales to achieve certain profit objectives. Using operating leverage analysis, a firm can determine the impact of a change in sales volume on its operating profit vis-à-vis competitors. This impact will depend on the respective levels of current sales volume and leverage positions of the firms. Also, through leverage analysis, the effects of a price change on the operating profits of competing firms with different leverages and output levels can be readily examined. To see the implications of these points let's consider the evaluation of different pricing alternatives for an established product for a firm.

TABLE 8-6

	Decision Alternative		
	No Price Change	Decrease Price 6.2%	Increase Price 7%
Unit selling price	$ 10.00	$ 9.38	$ 10.70
Unit variable costs	7.50	7.50	7.50
Unit contribution	$ 2.50	$ 1.88	$ 3.20
PV	0.25	0.20	0.30
Fixed costs	$ 1,000,000	$ 1,000,000	$ 1,000,000
Desired profit	$ 5,000,000	$ 5,000,000	$ 5,000,000
Required sales revenue*	$24,000,000	$30,000,000	$20,000,000
Required unit volume†	2,400,000	3,200,000	1,870,000

*Required sales revenue = (desired profit + fixed costs)/PV.
†Required unit volume = required sales revenue/price.

Testing Pricing Alternatives

Whenever management considers changing prices it should consider the reactions of the market to the proposed changes. Moreover, the effect of any price change on volume, contributions, and operating profits must be explicitly evaluated. The data in Table 8-6 show the result of evaluating three pricing alternatives: (1) keep price

FIGURE 8-4
PV break-even chart: alternative pricing decisions.

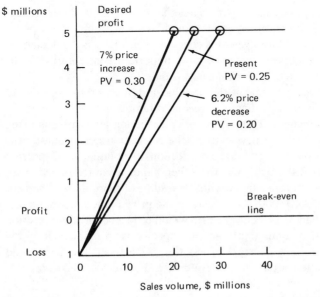

TABLE 8-7
PERMISSIBLE VOLUME DECREASE TO OFFSET PRICE INCREASE

Price Increase, %	Percentage Maximum Volume Decrease Permissible						
	PV Ratio						
	0.10	0.15	0.20	0.25	0.30	0.35	0.40
1	9.09	6.25	4.76	3.85	3.23	2.77	2.44
2	16.67	11.76	9.09	7.41	6.25	5.41	4.76
3	23.08	16.67	13.04	10.71	9.09	7.89	6.98
4	28.57	21.05	16.67	13.79	11.76	10.26	9.09
5	33.33	25.00	20.00	16.67	14.29	12.50	11.11
6	37.50	28.57	23.08	19.35	16.67	14.63	13.04
7	41.18	31.82	25.93	21.88	18.92	16.67	14.89
8	44.44	34.78	28.57	24.24	21.05	18.60	16.67
9	47.34	37.50	31.03	26.47	23.08	20.45	18.37
10	50.00	40.00	33.33	28.57	25.00	22.22	20.00
15	60.00	50.00	42.86	37.50	33.33	30.00	27.27
20	66.67	57.14	50.00	44.44	40.00	36.36	33.33
25	71.43	62.50	55.56	50.00	45.45	41.67	38.46
30	75.00	66.67	60.00	54.55	50.00	46.15	42.86
35			63.64	58.33	53.85	50.00	46.67
40			66.67	61.54	57.14	53.33	50.00
45				64.29	60.00	56.25	52.94
50				66.67	62.50	58.82	55.56

at $10.00 per unit; (2) decrease price 6.2 percent to $9.38 per unit; (3) increase price 7 percent to $10.70 per unit.

The concept of demand price elasticity indicates that if demand is elastic, reducing prices will lead to increased revenues, and if demand is inelastic, increasing prices will lead to increased revenues. However, this concept of elasticity is insufficient to decide which alternative to choose, since the more important consideration is the effect of a price change on the contributions and profits.

The data in Table 8-6 indicate that if the firm has a desired profit objective of $5,000,000, changing price means different levels of volume and sales revenue are required because the PV changes. Thus, if the price reduction alternative is being considered in order to penetrate a new market, the relevant research question is whether the price reduction can generate an addition to volume of 33 percent [(3,200,000 − 2,400,000)/2,400,000]. On the other hand, a contemplated price increase of 7 percent must not result in a decline in volume of more than 22 percent [(1,870,000 − 2,400,000)/2,400,000]. Obviously, if the price reduction results in a volume increase of more than 33 percent, the firm would be in a better profit position after the price reduction, assuming production capacity is available. Or if the price increase leads to a volume decrease of less than 22 percent, the firm would be in a better profit position after the price increase. Figure 8-4 illustrates this situation.

Figure 8-4 is constructed by noting that for each price alternative, the maximum

TABLE 8-7 *(Continued)*

Price Increase, %	Percentage Maximum Volume Decrease Permissible							
	PV Ratio							
	0.45	0.50	0.55	0.60	0.65	0.70	0.75	0.80
1	2.17	1.96	1.79	1.64	1.52	1.41	1.32	1.23
2	4.26	3.85	3.51	3.23	2.99	2.78	2.60	2.44
3	6.25	5.66	5.17	4.76	4.41	4.11	3.85	3.61
4	8.16	7.41	6.78	6.25	5.80	5.41	5.06	4.76
5	10.00	9.09	8.33	7.69	7.14	6.67	6.25	5.88
6	11.76	10.71	9.84	9.09	8.45	7.89	7.41	6.98
7	13.46	12.28	11.29	10.45	9.72	9.09	8.54	8.05
8	15.09	13.79	12.70	11.76	10.96	10.26	9.64	9.09
9	16.67	15.25	14.06	13.04	12.16	11.39	10.71	10.11
10	18.18	16.67	15.38	14.29	13.33	12.50	11.76	11.11
15	25.00	23.08	21.43	20.00	18.75	17.65	16.67	15.79
20	30.77	28.57	26.67	25.00	23.53	22.22	21.05	20.00
25	35.71	33.33	31.25	29.41	27.78	26.32	25.00	23.81
30	40.00	37.50	35.29	33.33	31.58	30.00	28.57	27.27
35	43.75	41.18	38.89	36.84	35.00	33.33	31.82	30.43
40	47.06	44.44	42.11	40.00	38.10	36.36	34.78	33.33
45	50.00	47.37	45.00	42.86	40.91	39.13	37.50	36.00
50	52.63	50.00	47.62	45.45	43.48	41.67	40.00	38.46

loss occurs when zero units are sold. This maximum loss equals fixed costs, or $1,000,000. The data of Table 8-6 indicate that the desired profit of $5,000,000 requires a sales revenue of $24,000,000 if price is $10.00, $30,000,000 if price is $9.38, and $20,000,000 if price is $10.70. Connecting these three points on the desired profit line with the maximum loss point at zero sales volume produces the PV break-even chart of Fig. 8-4.

Computing Necessary Volume Changes

It is possible to determine the necessary volume changes to maintain a level of profitability for any given PV value. Tables 8-7 and 8-8 give the percentage volume changes necessary to offset different percentage price changes. Figures 8-5 and 8-6 (p. 180) give an alternative way of making these calculations.

For example, suppose that a firm is considering raising price 9 percent and its current PV ratio is 0.30. Table 8-7 and Fig. 8-5 both indicate that as long as volume does not decline more than 23 percent, the firm's profitability will be enhanced. Similarly, if the firm was considering a 9 percent price decrease, then Table 8-8 and Fig. 8-6 both indicate that volume must increase at least 43 percent to maintain the same level of profitability as before the price change.

In general, for a price decrease, the necessary volume increase before profitability is enhanced is given by

$$\text{Volume increase } (\%) = \left(\frac{x}{PV - x}\right) 100 \qquad (8\text{-}9)$$

where x is the percentage price decrease expressed as a decimal.

Similarly, for a price increase, the permissible volume decrease before profitability is harmed is given by

$$\text{Volume decrease } (\%) = \left(\frac{x}{PV + x}\right) 100 \qquad (8\text{-}10)$$

where x is the percentage increase expressed as a decimal.

To illustrate these two formulas consider the volume changes necessary for, a 9 percent price decrease and then for a 9 percent price increase. Further, assume the current PV ratio is 0.30. From Eq. (8-9) the percentage volume increase is

$$\text{Volume increase } (\%) = \left(\frac{0.09}{0.30 - 0.09}\right) 100 = \left(\frac{0.09}{0.21}\right) 100 = 42.86\%$$

From Eq. (8-10) the percentage volume decrease is

TABLE 8-8
MINIMUM VOLUME INCREASE REQUIRED FOR PRICE DECREASE

Price Decrease, %	Percentage Minimum Volume Increase Required						
	PV Ratio						
	0.10	0.15	0.20	0.25	0.30	0.35	0.40
1	11.11	7.14	5.26	4.17	3.45	2.94	2.56
2	25.00	15.38	11.11	8.70	7.14	6.06	5.26
3	42.90	25.00	17.65	13.60	11.11	9.38	8.11
4	66.67	36.36	25.00	19.05	15.38	12.90	11.11
5	100.00	50.00	33.33	25.00	20.00	16.67	14.29
6	150.00	66.67	42.86	31.58	25.00	20.69	17.65
7	233.33	87.50	53.85	38.89	30.43	25.00	21.21
8	400.00	114.29	66.67	47.06	36.36	29.63	25.00
9	900.00	150.00	81.82	56.25	42.86	34.62	29.03
10	∞	200.00	100.00	66.67	50.00	40.00	33.33
15		∞	300.00	150.00	100.00	75.00	60.00
20			∞	400.00	200.00	133.33	100.00
25				∞	500.00	250.00	166.67
30					∞	600.00	300.00
35						∞	700.00
40							∞

$$\text{Volume decrease } (\%) = \left(\frac{0.09}{0.30 + 0.09}\right) 100 = \left(\frac{0.09}{0.39}\right) 100 = 23.08\%$$

Computing Required Price Elasticities

Once an alternative price proposal has been evaluated according to the volume changes necessary to enhance profitability, implied price elasticities can be computed. Recall that price elasticity of demand is defined as the percentage change in volume relative to a percentage change in price. From the example of Table 8-6, we have demonstrated that a proposed price decrease of 6.2 percent required a minimum volume increase of 33 percent before profits could be increased, if the current PV ratio is 0.25. This condition gives us the following required price elasticity of demand:

$$E_d = \frac{33\%}{-6.2\%} = -5.32$$

A price elasticity of demand of -5.32 indicates that demand must be quite elastic before the price reduction can be profitable. If management does not believe that demand is sufficiently price elastic, then the alternative of reducing price by 6.2 percent is not economically justified.

TABLE 8-8 *(Continued)*

Price Decrease, %	Percentage Minimum Volume Increase Required							
	PV Ratio							
	0.45	0.50	0.55	0.60	0.65	0.70	0.75	0.80
1	2.27	2.04	1.85	1.69	1.56	1.45	1.35	1.27
2	4.65	4.17	3.77	3.45	3.17	2.94	2.74	2.56
3	7.14	6.38	5.77	5.26	4.84	4.48	4.17	3.90
4	9.76	8.70	7.84	7.14	6.56	6.06	5.63	5.26
5	12.50	11.11	10.00	9.09	8.33	7.69	7.14	6.67
6	15.38	13.64	12.24	11.11	10.17	9.38	8.70	8.11
7	18.42	16.28	14.58	13.21	12.07	11.11	10.29	9.59
8	21.62	19.05	17.02	15.38	14.04	12.90	11.94	11.11
9	25.00	21.95	19.57	17.65	16.07	14.75	13.64	12.68
10	28.57	25.00	22.22	20.00	18.18	16.67	15.38	12.50
15	50.00	42.86	37.50	33.33	30.00	27.27	25.00	23.08
20	80.00	66.67	57.14	50.00	44.44	40.00	36.36	33.33
25	125.00	100.00	83.33	71.43	62.50	55.56	50.00	45.45
30	200.00	150.00	120.00	100.00	85.71	75.00	66.67	60.00
35	350.00	233.33	175.00	140.00	116.67	100.00	87.50	77.77
40	800.00	400.00	266.67	200.00	160.00	133.33	114.29	100.00

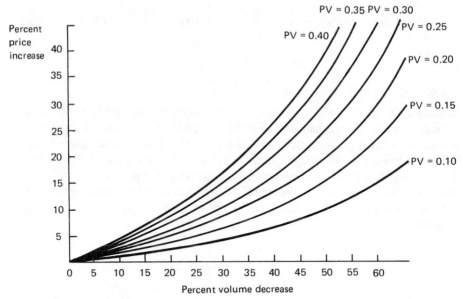

FIGURE 8-5
Permissible volume decrease to offset price increase.

FIGURE 8-6
Minimum volume increase required for price decrease.

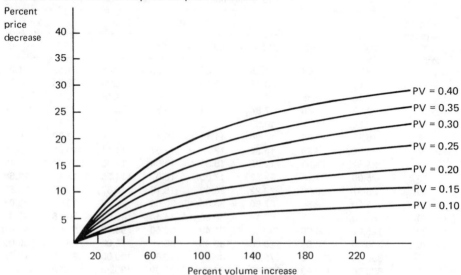

Similarly, the alternative of increasing price 7 percent produces a required price elasticity of

$$E_d = \frac{-22\%}{7\%} = -3.14$$

When evaluating a price increase, it is important to remember that the estimated volume decrease is the maximum permissible if profits are to be enhanced. Hence, the actual price elasticity must be less elastic than the computed -3.14. For example, if management believes that price elasticity of demand is around -2, then the price increase of 7 percent will be profitable, but a price decrease of 6.2 percent will harm profits. Conversely, if management believes that price elasticity of demand is around -6, then the price decrease of 6.2 percent will enhance profits.

Financial Leverage

As defined previously, financial leverage refers to the use of debt in financing a firm. Interest on debt that is sold to obtain financing normally is a fixed financial charge that must be paid regardless of the level of the firm's earnings. The greater the use of debt, the greater the financial leverage and the more that fixed financial costs are added to fixed operating costs to enhance the impact of changes in sales volume. The degree of financial leverage (DFL) is defined as the ratio of the change in operating profits before interest and taxes relative to the change in operating profits before taxes:

$$DFL = \frac{\% \text{ change in operating profits before interest and tax}}{\% \text{ change in operating profits before tax}}$$

or

$$DFL = \frac{\Delta OP}{OP} \div \frac{\Delta OPBT}{OPBT} \tag{8-11}$$

where ΔOP = change in operating profits before interest and taxes
OP = operating profits in the previous period (before interest and taxes)
$\Delta OPBT$ = change in operating profits before taxes (after interest)
$OPBT$ = operating profits before taxes (after interest) in the previous period

As with operating leverage, it is also possible to compute DFL for any level of operating profits using

$$DFL = \frac{OP}{OP - iD} \tag{8-12}$$

where i = the interest rate on the debt
$\quad\quad D$ = the amount of debt

Referring back to Table 8-5, we see firm A has financial leverage of 1.22 while B and C have financial leverage of 1.72 and 1.20 respectively. Firm B, employing more debt as a proportion of its financing than either A or C, has greater financial leverage. Now, if all firms experience a 10 percent increase in operating profits, the impact on earnings per share (EPS) is greater for firm B than either A or C. It can be shown that

$$\% \text{ change in EPS} = DFL \times \% \text{ change in operating profits} \quad\quad (8\text{-}13)$$

Thus, EPS will increase 17.2 percent for B, 12.2 percent for A, and 12 percent for C. As before, DFL cuts both ways; a 10 percent decrease in operating profits would affect firm B more severely than either A or C.

Combined Leverage

When financial leverage is combined with operating leverage, the effect of a change in sales volume on earnings per share is magnified. Combining Eqs. (8-8) and (8-12) produces an expression for the degree of combined leverage DCL:

$$DCL = DOL \times DFL$$

or

$$DCL = \frac{(P - VC)Q}{OP} \times \frac{OP}{OP - iD}$$

giving

$$DCL = \frac{(P - VC)Q}{OP - iD} \quad\quad (8\text{-}14)$$

It can also be shown that DCL is equal to the ratio of the percentage change in operating profits before interest and taxes to the percentage change in sales volume. As we would expect, the data in Table 8-5 indicate that the combined leverage for firm B is considerably higher than for either A or C. Now considering both operating and financial leverage in combination, a 10 percent increase (or decrease) in sales volume would result in an 18.3 percent increase (decrease) in operating profits, return on equity, or earnings per share for A. For B, this same 10 percent increase (or decrease) in sales volume would lead to a 51.6 percent increase (decrease) in operating profits, return on equity, or earnings per share. Clearly, firm B is more highly leveraged than either A or C. Depending on the nature of demand for the firms' products, firm B may have a competitive advantage when initiating price changes to affect sales volume.

Requirements for Successful Price Reduction Strategies

For a given cost structure and financial structure, reducing price to increase volume and profits may be quite difficult. Indeed, as shown in Table 8-8, a low-contribution margin product (low PV ratio) must be capable of generating large increases in volume for even small price reductions. Thus, there are two minimum requirements for a price reduction strategy to be profitable: (1) the product must have a relatively large contribution margin prior to the price reduction, and (2) the product market must be in a growth situation. Essentially, this second requirement means that demand for the product or service must be price elastic to obtain proportionally larger increases in sales volume due to the price reduction and that the product should be in the growth stage of the product life cycle. For a price reduction strategy to be both profitable and competitively advantageous, a third requirement is that its combined leverage should be greater than its competitors'. Pricing decisions provide maximum leverage when they capitalize on existing competitive advantages.[5]

[5]See William E. Johnson, "Trade-offs in Pricing Strategy," in Earl L. Bailey (ed.), *Pricing Practices and Strategies* (New York: The Conference Board, 1978), pp. 44–53.

FIGURE 8-7
PV break-even chart for the retail shirt store.

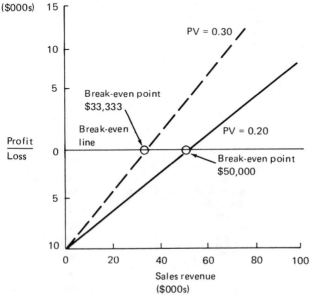

THE EFFECT OF THE DOLLAR SALES MIX

In a multiple-product business, different products produce different profit volumes. Even the shirt store example at the beginning of this chapter could have a product mix. The retailer could sell ties with a PV of 0.10, shirts with a PV of 0.20, sweaters with a PV 0.40, and pants with a PV of 0.30. With a PV of 0.10 for ties, the retailer would have to sell twice as many ties as shirts to gross the same contribution as shirts alone, but only half as many sweaters as shirts would have to be sold to generate the original contribution. Therefore, depending on the relative product sales mix, it would be possible to generate greater profits on fewer sales or smaller profits on more sales.

Within a multiproduct firm, each product generates a different amount of volume, a different cost structure, including variable and fixed costs, different unit prices, and, of course, different revenues. These important factors not only are different, but they are changing. And as developed earlier in this chapter, the conventional break-even chart is not dynamic and assumes a single-product situation.

However, multiple lines, each corresponding to a product or decision alternative, can be drawn on a PV chart. It is then possible to show variations in profit with volume and the effect of changes in prices on PV and profit. Figure 8-7 presents a PV break-even chart for the retail shirt store. On this chart we can contrast the profit at any volume for shirts with a PV of 0.20 to pants with a PV of 0.30. At this point, the chart is drawn as though the retailer faces the alternative of either selling shirts or selling pants. Now we will show how to combine the products in the analysis.

TABLE 8-9

Product	PV	Percentage of Total Dollar Volume
A	0.40	40
B	0.20	30
C	0.10	30

Annual common fixed costs: $500,000

TABLE 8-10

(1) Product	(2) PV	(3) Proportion of Total Dollar Volume	(4) Weighted PV (2) × (3)
A	0.40	0.40	0.16
B	0.20	0.30	0.06
C	0.10	0.30	0.03
Composite PV			0.25

The PV break-even chart can be used to analyze the relative profit contributions of each product in a product line. The analysis as developed thus far must now be modified to consider relative differences in cost structure, volume generated, and profit contribution by each product in the line. To illustrate how we can adapt the PV analysis to the multiproduct firm, consider the data given in Table 8-9.

As the data show, each product has a different PV value and different planned volumes as a percentage of the firm's total dollar volume. The problem now is to integrate these PVs and planned volumes to determine the appropriate PV for the analysis. In multiple-product problems the PV is determined by weighting the PV of each product by the percentage of the total dollar volume for all products. The appropriate calculations for this example are seen in Table 8-10.

The composite PV is used to determine the break-even point.

$$\text{BES} = \frac{\text{fixed costs}}{\text{PV}} = \frac{\$500,000}{0.25} = \$2,000,000$$

For a total sales volume of $4,000,000, operating profits are

$$\text{Profit} = (\text{sales} \times \text{PV}) - \text{fixed costs}$$
$$= (\$4,000,000 \times 0.25) - \$500,000 = \$500,000$$

FIGURE 8-8
Composite PV break-even chart.

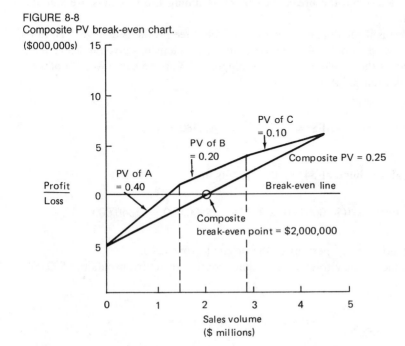

TABLE 8-11

Product	PV	Percentage of Total Dollar Volume
A	0.40	20
B	0.20	50
C	0.10	30

TABLE 8-12

(1) Product	(2) PV	(3) Proportion of Total Dollar Volume	(4) Weighted PV (2) × (3)
A	0.40	0.20	0.08
B	0.20	0.50	0.10
C	0.10	0.30	0.03
Composite PV			0.21

Figure 8-8 illustrates this example. Note that because there are common fixed costs, we cannot determine the unique break-even point for each product. Rather, we can only determine the break-even point assuming the products are simultaneously sold.

What happens if the dollar volume mix of the three products changes? To illustrate, assume the data of Table 8-9 change to the relationships given in Table 8-11. Table 8-12 shows the development of the composite PV. For a composite PV of 0.21, the new break-even point is

$$\text{BES} = \frac{\$500,000}{0.21} = \$2,380,950$$

For a total sales volume of $4,000,000, profits are

$$\text{Profit} = (\$4,000,000 \times 0.21) - \$500,000 = \$340,000$$

Thus, profits now are 68 percent of the original profit level.

To determine the new total sales volume required to return profits to $500,000, we compute

$$\text{Sales} = \frac{\text{desired profit} + \text{fixed costs}}{\text{PV}}$$

$$= \frac{\$500,000 + \$500,000}{0.21} = \$4,761,905$$

Or total sales must increase by 19 percent to regain the original profit level if the dollar sales volume mix shifts as indicated in Table 8-11.

When a shift in dollar sales mix results in a poorer PV, management frequently attempts to recover the profit level by an across-the-board increase in prices. Although the effect of this increase in prices helps to restore the original PV, this pricing reaction could lead to a further decline in profits. This deterioration of profits may occur because management has attempted to force the external factors of competition and demand to support the internal need for profit. When an across-the-board increase in prices leads to a substantial decrease in sales volume, it is quite possible that the remedy has aggravated the problem.

When there are differences in the PVs among products in a line, a revision in the product selling mix (i.e., dollar sales mix) may be more effective than an increase in prices. That is, a firm, by shifting emphasis to those products with relatively

FIGURE 8-9
Effect of changing the product mix.

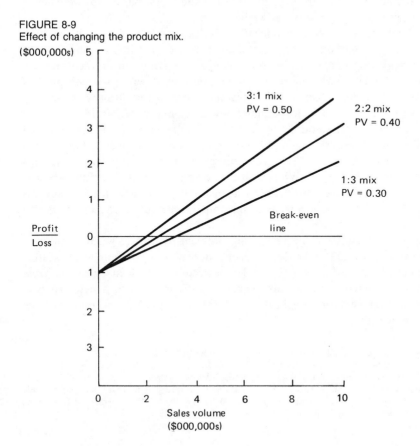

higher PVs, has a good opportunity to recover some or all of its profit position. For example, assume that a firm with common fixed costs of $100,000 sells two products: A with a PV of 0.60 and B with a PV of 0.20. Figure 8-9 illustrates the effects of changing the proportion of the product selling mix. It should be clear that the slope of the PV line depends on the relative proportion of the product selling mix. Hence, profit at any sales level is a function of prices, volume, costs, and the dollar sales mix.

PRICING WITH SCARCE RESOURCES

In recent years, business people and economists have faced unexpected economic problems: shortages of critical materials, uncontrollable inflation even during a recession, and a lack of sufficient amounts of new capital to overcome material shortages. During 1973 and 1974 the world demand for materials overtook supply, with sudden shortages of metals, wood products, and agricultural products.[6] "Typical of the problems faced by industry were those of Del Monte where the company faced shortages of fruits and vegetables, glass for jars, tinplate for cans, fibreboard for boxes, and labels for the jars and cans."[7] In the late 1980s many firms were facing shortages of productive capacity and skilled labor.

To cope with these shortages and with other economic problems, it has been suggested that the marketing manager assume new responsibilities and develop alternative marketing strategies.[8] As often happens when an unexpected problem occurs, many different marketing strategies have been tried, with varying degrees of success. As suggested in Chap. 1, it has become apparent that firms must develop a positive response to cope with the many new economic uncertainties.

The problem of scarce resources has led some companies to prune their product lines by eliminating slow-moving and low-margin products. However, the elimination of products on the basis of the size of margin is primarily a defensive strategy that ignores the role of price. When a firm is operating at or near full capacity, or when key resources are scarce, the firm must determine how scarce resources can be allocated to its products so as to maximize contribution to fixed costs and profits.

This section discusses the special pricing problem that arises when a multiple-product firm is operating at or near capacity or when key resources are scarce. The purposes of the section are (1) to demonstrate the inadequacy of the gross margin criterion when resources are scarce and (2) to develop a new criterion using contribution analysis. Applications of this new decision criterion will be developed in Section 4.

[6]"The 1970's: A Second Look," *Business Week,* September 14, 1974, pop. 50–162.
[7]"The Two-Way Squeeze on New Products," *Business Week,* August 10, 1974, pp. 130–132.
[8]Philip Kotler, "Marketing During Periods of Shortage," *Journal of Marketing,* 38 (July 1974), 20–29; Nessim Hanna, A. H. Kizinbash, and Albert Smart, "Marketing Strategy under Conditions of Economic Scarcity," *Journal of Marketing,* 39 (July 1975), 63–67; Avraham Shama, "Management & Consumers in an Era of Stagflation," *Journal of Marketing,* 42 (July 1978), 43–52.

The Problem of Common Resources[9]

The multiproduct firm typically manufactures various product lines using joint or common resources—the same plant and equipment, for instance, as well as research and development facilities. The same selling, administrative, and warehousing facilities may be used in the production and sale of the various products. Moreover, a critical or scarce resource may be used in production.

Because product prices must reflect the competitive situation and the reactions of buyers as well as costs and corporate objectives, not all products make the same use of resources per dollar of revenue or per dollar of out-of-pocket costs. However, when determining prices, it is important to consider the degree to which products (or special orders) use available facilities (capacity) and consume available resources. Otherwise, the firm may be short of the necessary resources to obtain the desired level of contribution.

Indeed, pricing special orders or composing the product line strictly on contribution (gross margin) may result in the exhaustion of available resources without obtaining the target contribution. In Table 8-13A, the basic price and cost data for

[9]Much of the material in this section is adopted from Kent B. Monroe and Andris A. Zoltners, "Pricing the Product Line During Periods of Scarcity," *Journal of Marketing,* 43 (Summer 1979), 49–59.

TABLE 8-13
PRODUCT-LINE CONTRIBUTION ANALYSIS

	Product			Total
	A	B	C	
	A. Unit Data			
1. Price	$ 2.20	$ 3.00	$ 4.00	
Variable costs:				
2. Direct labor	$ 1.20	$ 0.70	$ 0.60	
3. Direct materials	0.41	1.54	2.40	
4. Total	$ 1.61	$ 2.24	$ 3.00	
5. Contribution (1 − 4)	$ 0.59	$ 0.76	$ 1.00	
	B. Data for planning period			
6. Demand (units)	6,200	8,100	5,000	
7. Revenue (1 × 6)	$13,640	$24,300	$20,000	$57,940
8. Direct labor (2 × 6)	$ 7,440	$ 5,670	$ 3,000	$16,110
9. Direct materials (3 × 6)	$ 2,542	$12,474	$12,000	$27,016
10. Contribution (5 × 6)	$ 3,658	$ 6,156	$ 5,000	$14,814
11. Tons of material required	500	2,500	2,400	5,400
12. Units per ton (6 ÷ 11)	12.4	3.24	2.083	
13. Tons per unit (11 ÷ 6)	0.081	0.309	0.480	

a product line are provided. Table 8-13B provides the demand forecasts, cost estimates, and required supply of a common resource material to meet the demand
forecast.

As shown in Table 8-13A, product C contributes $1.00 per unit sold to cover fixed
expenses and profits. This unit contribution by product C is $0.24 larger than B's
unit contribution and $0.41 larger than A's unit contribution. However, in Table
8-13B it can be seen that because of total expected demand, the total dollar contribution is larger for product B, with product C ranked second, and product A ranked
third.

In this illustration, two common resources—labor and material—are required to
produce the three products. However, the mix of labor and material required to
produce a unit of each product is quite different. Indeed, product A is a relatively
labor-intensive product since 74.5 percent of its direct variable costs derive from
labor. However, products B and C owe only 32.3 and 20 percent, respectively, of
their direct costs to labor. Hence, products B and C require much more material
input.

Now suppose that this common material resource currently is scarce and the firm
has been advised that it can acquire no more than 3,000 tons during the planning
period. Furthermore, the supply of this material is expected to be below demand for
at least several years. The firm must now consider the alternatives of reducing the
production of each product, eliminating a product and reducing the production of
the other products, or some reasonable combination of these two choices. Clearly,
the firm has a problem of allocating the scarce resource to its products in the product
line.

Resource Allocation Criteria

A number of criteria have been used to make this decision. Some firms allocate the
scarce resource according to the *unit contributions* (gross margin) of each product.
Since product C has the largest unit contribution, the first 2,400 tons would be
allocated to C and the remaining 600 tons to B. As Table 8-14 shows, the total
contribution for the planning period would be $6,477, or $8,337 less than total
contributions with no scarce resource.

Other firms make their allocations on the basis of *total contributions.* Since
product B has the largest total contribution, product B would be allocated 2,500
tons. Product C would be allocated 500 tons because its total contribution is second
in amount for the planning period. The total period contribution under this plan
improves to $7,197 but still is $7,617 less than period contributions with no scarce
resource. If the firm adopted either of these two plans, it would be necessary to
eliminate product A from the line.

A third alternative would be to allocate the scarce material *proportionately on the
basis of resource requirements.* Since product A requires 500/5,400, or 9 percent of
the scarce resource if no constraints are present, it would be allocated 9 percent, or
270 tons of material. The material would be allocated to B and C in similar fashion
and total period contribution improves to $8,197.

TABLE 8-14
ALTERNATIVE RESOURCE ALLOCATIONS

Criterion	Resource Units	Units Produced	Total Contribution
Contribution per unit:			
A	0	0	$ –0–
B	600	1,944	$1,477
C	2,400	5,000	5,000
			$6,477
Total contribution:			
A	0	0	$ –0–
B	2,500	8,100	6,156
C	500	1,041	1,041
			$7,197
Proportion of resources required:			
A	270	3,348	$1,975
B	1,410	4,568	3,472
C	1,320	2,750	2,750
			$8,197

As is apparent from Table 8-14, the contribution or margin criteria are inferior to the third allocation criterion. Moreover, contribution to overhead and profits is greater under the third alternative and it is not necessary to eliminate a product from the line.

As demonstrated, pricing a product line strictly on gross contribution or margin may result in the exhaustion of available resources without the largest possible contribution to profits being obtained. Essentially, the margin approach does not consider how much of the scarce resource is consumed per unit of output.

The data in Table 8-13 demonstrate that a ton of the resource material is necessary to produce 12.4 units of A, 3.24 units of B, and 2.083 units of C. As shown in Table 8-14, a resource allocation method that allocates less resources to C and B and more to A improves contribution. Hence, what is necessary is to develop a criterion that utilizes the information on how products consume scarce resources.

TABLE 8-15
CONTRIBUTION PER RESOURCE UNIT (CPRU)

	Product		
	A	B	C
1. Contribution	$3,658	$6,156	$5,000
2. Resource units	500	2,500	2,400
3. CPRU (1 ÷ 2)	$ 7.28	$ 2.46	$ 2.08

Contribution Per Resource Unit Criterion

As the data in Table 8-13B indicate, 0.081 ton of the scarce resource is required to produce a unit of product A, 0.309 ton to produce a unit of product B, and 0.48 ton to produce a unit of product C. At current prices (Table 8-13A), each unit of A produces $0.59 contribution. Thus, 0.081 ton of scarce material helps produce a $0.59 contribution. Therefore, a ton of the material produces $0.59/0.081, or $7.28 contribution per ton. Similarly, for product B, the contribution per ton is $0.76/0.309, or $2.46. And for product C, the contribution per ton is $1.00/0.48, or $2.08. These calculations, which can also be made using the period planning data from Table 8-13B, are shown in Table 8-15.

What the data of Table 8-15 indicate is that the first 500 tons of the scarce material should be allocated to product A since each ton used in product A contributes more to profits and to covering fixed costs. This allocation procedure is followed because product A has the highest *contribution per resource unit* (ton). And when the resource is in limited supply, the decision criterion is to allocate resources to the profit segments with the highest contribution per resource unit (CPRU). Following this decision criterion, Table 8-16 shows that product C, the highest priced, largest unit margin product, is a candidate for elimination.

This illustration suggests a fundamental principle: *When the volume of products that could be sold is greater than the resource capacity to produce them, the largest contribution (and profit) results from providing those products, services, and orders that generate the greatest contribution per resource unit used.* The factors that cause the bottleneck could be machines, equipment, time, skilled labor, materials, or cash.

Pricing the Product Line Using CPRU

If the firm wishes to maintain the prices shown in Table 8-13, then the best decision is to use the CPRU criterion and suspend production of product C. However, from a marketing viewpoint it may be desirable to keep product C in the line. For example, demand for product C may be expected to grow in the near future, or the product may be necessary to complete the product line.

The firm should then consider repricing products C and B to increase their relative CPRUs. Initially, the analytical question is "What should the prices of C

TABLE 8-16
RESOURCE ALLOCATION USING CPRU

Product	Resource Units	Units Produced	Total Contribution
A	500	6,200	$3,658
B	2,500	8,100	6,156
C	0	0	–0–
			$9,814

TABLE 8-17
PRICING TO EQUALIZE CPRU

	Product	
	B	C
1. Desired CPRU	$ 7.28	$ 7.28
2. Total resources required	2,500	2,400
3. Desired contribution (1 × 2)	$18,200	$17,472
4. Variable costs	$18,144	$15,000
5. Total revenue required (3 + 4)	$36,344	$32,472
6. Original demand forecast	8,100	5,000
7. New selling price (5 ÷ 6)	$ 4.49	$ 6.49

and B be so as to equalize contribution?" Table 8-17 shows that the price of C must be $6.49 and the price of B must be $4.49. However, it is unlikely that the original demand forecast will be valid at these prices. Hence, a lower production volume would be required, which would reduce some of the firm's demand for the scarce material. What is needed is a solution technique that incorporates price–volume relationships as well as cost–volume relationships. We will now consider such a solution technique.

If the firm desires to reprice some or all of the products in the line, then, assuming a constant price of the scarce material, higher prices will improve the contribution per resource unit consumed. But raising the prices of some or all of the products in the line can naturally be expected to reduce demand, and the pricing decision may be used to allocate demand. (Some executives have confided to the author that they followed such a pricing policy during the oil crisis of the mid-1970s.) Also, the reduction of product-line demand due to price increases leads to lower production requirements, which reduces the firm's demand for the scarce material.

It should be apparent that, to do further pricing analysis, one must know the demand curve for each product in the line. One of the approaches described in Chap. 6 can be used to develop estimates of the price–volume relationships. Given the ability to obtain reasonable price–volume estimates for each product, the pricing problem becomes amenable to solution using a computerized technique.[10]

To illustrate, assume the price–volume relationship is linear for each product, as seen in Fig. 8-10. The prices that will enable the firm to achieve maximum total contribution subject to the scarce resource constraint are given in Table 8-18. Given the demand relationship depicted in Fig. 8-10, the prices given in Table 8-18 enable the firm to maximize contributions.

However, management may feel that such relatively large price increases are not desirable because of potential loss of customer goodwill, relative competitive prices, and potential government intervention. Further, such large price increases may dampen long-run demand, particularly if one or more of the products is in the

---

[10]The mathematical programming solution technique is described in Monroe and Zoltners, ibid.

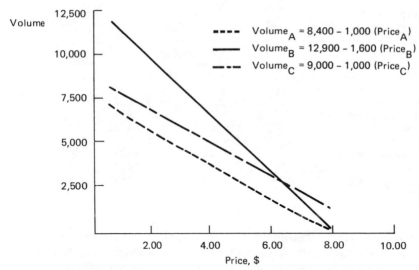

FIGURE 8-10
Linear price–volume relationship.

growth stage of its life cycle. The firm may also wish to have wider price differentials to maintain perceptual differences in the product line (see Chaps. 3 and 12). Hence, the solution technique should be used to find the optimum solution; the firm can then estimate the profit implications of moving to another solution because of realistic, but unquantifiable, marketing considerations.

The effect of adjusting the optimal prices may be assessed using the CPRU criterion with a different set of prices. For example, a firm may believe that the prices should be no higher than $5, $5, and $6 respectively; the product manager may feel that these prices are realistic and suitable for both the long-run objectives and environmental considerations of the firm. Total demand at these prices will exceed the firm's production capacity. The solution seen in Table 8-19 is the best product mix using the CPRU criterion relative to the prices stated. Table 8-19 shows that the price constraint causes the total contribution to profit to decline by $1,347.04. In general, the CPRU criterion provides the best solution when there are resource constraints and price ceilings.

SUMMARY

One of the most important lessons of this chapter is that the four elements of profitability—price, costs, volume, and dollar sales mix—are strategically interdependent. Moreover, the analytical techniques developed in this chapter make it clear that there are strategic tradeoffs among these four elements. It should also be understood that pricing decisions are not easy to make and that simplistic formulas, such as cost-plus approaches, make unavoidable assumptions about markets, costs, technology, and relative competitive position that may be incorrect.

TABLE 8-18
OPTIMAL SOLUTION, LINEAR PRICE–VOLUME FUNCTION, AND RESOURCE
CONSTRAINTS

	Product		
	A	B	C
Price	$ 5.03	$ 5.27	$ 6.18
Volume	3,370	4,468	2,820
Contribution	$11,525.40	$13,538.04	$8,967.60
Resources required (tons)	271.77	1,379.01	1,353.82

Total contribution: $34,031.04
Total resources required: 3,004.6 tons*

*Excess due to rounding the prices.

TABLE 8-19
OPTIMUM PRICE SOLUTION: RESOURCE AND PRICE CONSTRAINTS

	Product		
	A	B	C
1. Price	$ 5.00	$ 5.00	$ 6.00
2. Variable cost	1.61	2.24	3.00
3. Contribution (1 − 2)	$ 3.39	$ 2.76	$ 3.00
4. Demand (units)	3,340	4,900	3,000
5. Units produced	3,400	4,900	2,528
6. Resources required (tons)	274.19	1,512.34	1,213.47
7. Contribution (3 × 5)	$11,526	$ 13,524	$ 7,584
8. CPRU (7 ÷ 6)	$ 42.04	$ 8.94	$ 6.25

Total contribution: $32,634
Total resources required: 3,000 tons

One of the most common tradeoffs made is price for volume, i.e., trading a price reduction for increasing volume or market share. However, both the profitability analysis using the PV ratio and the impact of leverage on profitability suggest that management should attempt to determine the relative worth of added market share in terms of what added market share requires with regard to forgoing short-term profits.

To analyze the tradeoff between price and volume, operating leverage is an important concept. For example, Table 8-8 indicates that a firm with a PV ratio (contribution margin) of 0.20 requires a minimum volume increase of 33 percent to offset a 5 percent decrease in price. Another firm with a PV ratio of 0.60 would require only a 9 percent increase in volume to offset a 5 percent decrease in price. Clearly, the second firm gets greater leverage from volume gains than does the first firm.

A similar assessment should be applied to different products within a product line and across product lines. Different products and different product lines inherently have different cost structures and therefore different possibilities to leverage volume.

As noted, price–volume relationships vary over time. In periods of tight capacity or resource bottlenecks, maximum profit leverage can be attained by emphasizing those products with the highest contribution per *resource unit.* Conversely, when there is excess capacity, maximum profit leverage can be attained by emphasizing those products with the highest contribution margin per *sales dollar.* Thus, pricing and marketing strategies and tactics should be developed to shift product dollar sales mix to preserve profitability in periods of slack capacity and to obtain maximum profit leverage in periods of tight capacity.

The concept of financial leverage indicates that competitive reaction to price reductions to gain volume and market share may differ due to the relative mix of debt to equity financing between competitors. Moreover, combining financial leverage with operating leverage suggests that differences in size, degrees of vertical integration, methods of distribution, and financing will make some competitors more sensitive than others to the price–volume tradeoff. Indeed, companies in Japan and Europe traditionally have maintained substantially higher debt to equity ratios than their North American competitors. This stronger leverage position has provided a competitive advantage in pricing that has made a low-price strategy profitable, particularly for products with strong market growth. Clearly, the frequently implied principle that more market share (volume) is better is a pricing myth that needs to be recognized. As suggested in this chapter, there are specific conditions that must be met before a price-reduction strategy becomes profitable. This chapter has developed the key cost analysis method useful for evaluating pricing alternatives. A contribution approach has the advantage of forcing an analysis of costs in terms of causal factors. Those factors that are directly related to the costs incurred in the production and sale of a product are included as relevant to the cost analysis.

Break-even analysis was introduced and expanded to consider cost, demand, and profit implications of alternative prices. In addition, the analysis permits an examination of alternative cost structures and their implications for establishing the cost bases of prices.

Expanding break-even analysis to include the profit implications of alternative price decisions provides some dynamics to an otherwise static analytical method. This chapter demonstrates how use of the PV ratio can help determine necessary or permissible volume changes for considered price changes. Moreover, since it is difficult to estimate future or prospective price elasticities of demand, the chapter also shows how to compute implied price elasticities for necessary or permissible volume changes. Once management knows the conditions that must prevail before a price alternative will enhance profitability, it is in a position to make the best decision relative to the objectives of the firm and competitive factors.

Perhaps the main advantage of direct cost and contribution analysis is that it permits the calculation of those costs which are affected by the particular decision being analyzed. These costs and, more important, the cost changes can be traced to the decision, and the decision maker has an objective basis for selection among alternative choices. Closely related, direct costing provides a way of calculating the

TABLE 8-20
ADVANTAGES OF CONTRIBUTION DATA FOR PRICING DECISIONS

The use of contribution information facilitates
1. The determination of correct prices for individual products and/or orders
2. Selecting target prices for desired PV to classes of buyers or markets
3. Identifying the most profitable products, customers, markets
4. Identifying which products need management's attention
5. Selecting and improving the product mix
6. Determining the pricing floor
7. Evaluating proposals to increase profits by increasing prices and/or increasing volume
8. Clarifying the understanding of costs by company personnel responsible for pricing
9. Getting all departments to speak a common language in talking about prices and profits
10. Estimating profits from alternative future proposals
11. Establishing a better reward-for-performance basis of compensating the selling effort

---

Source: Adapted and reprinted with permission from Spencer A. Tucker, *Pricing for Higher Profit* (New York: McGraw-Hill, 1966), pp. 93–94.

profit contribution on various products, product lines, markets, accounts, or salespersons. Contribution data, as summarized in Table 8-20, have many additional advantages. Finally, through direct costing and the development of contribution data, management is given the opportunity to avoid arbitrary formulas to allocate common costs when establishing prices.

After noting that during times of scarcity the firm is faced with problems of determining the optimum product mix and a set of profit-maximizing prices, this chapter has developed a criterion for these decisions. It has been shown that the largest contribution per resource unit (CPRU) criterion should be used. Further, as many firms have recognized, price may be used effectively to shift demand to the products with the largest CPRUs. However, when prices are changed, the quantity demanded changes and a new optimum product mix results.

The structure of this decision problem is amenable to analysis using computer programming procedures. Taking a specific product-line example, the chapter briefly illustrated the use of the CPRU principle. Any price–volume relationship that can be readily estimated by a product manager can be used in the analysis. If a linear relationship is used, the manager needs to provide only two price–volume estimates for each product in the product line. If other types of demand functions are used, the manager must provide several price–volume relationships. In any event, a firm's periodic planning efforts typically provide and utilize such price–volume estimates.

Additional reasons for focusing on maximizing contribution are to minimize data requirements for the solution technique and to observe the dynamic price–volume–cost relationships as the product mix changes. As long as fixed or period costs do not change when the product or sales mix is altered, maximizing contribution will provide the optimum strategy. The accounting data required are the direct product cost and the amount of scarce resource needed to produce an order or product. Such data can be obtained from a firm's cost accounting system.

The contribution per resource unit criterion is best used when productive capacity is constrained by a bottleneck. Factors that may cause the bottleneck are machines, equipment, time, skilled labor, materials, or cash. Any industry or product line that depends heavily on a single resource would be particularly suited to the use of the CPRU criterion and the analysis outlined in this chapter. For example, product lines heavily dependent on petrochemicals, the paper industry, drugs, and fertilizers all are dependent on critical materials. Several years ago the candy industry could obtain sugar but, because of high prices, did not have the cash resource to acquire the necessary sugar tonnage to meet demand. At one time, the high price of cocoa beans produced a chocolate constraint on the candy industry.[11]

This chapter has demonstrated the inadequacy of the gross margin criterion for product-mix and pricing decisions when the firm is operating at capacity due to resource constraints. It has been shown that the contribution per resource unit is a superior criterion and that pricing and production decisions may be enhanced using this criterion.

DISCUSSION QUESTIONS

1 Assume the specialty retailer discussed in this chapter determines that fixed costs have increased to $21,000 per year. Further assume that the shirts can now be acquired for $9 and that the retailer raises the retail price of shirts to $12.
   a Compute contribution dollars per shirt.
   b Compute PV ratio.
   c Compute break-even quantity.
   d Compute break-even sales (dollars).
   e Draw a break-even graph.
2 For the specialty retailer in Question 1, assume fixed costs decrease to $18,000 per year. Repeat parts a to e of Question 1. Describe the changes that have taken place.
3 For the specialty retailer in Question 1, assume the supplier raises the price of the shirts to $10. What price must the retailer charge for the shirts to obtain the same break-even point in sales dollars at this new price?
4 For the specialty retailer in Question 1, assume yearly shirt sales have been 20,000 shirts.
   a Calculate the profits earned before taxes.
   b Assume the situation depicted in Question 3. For the new price you calculated in Question 3, determine the maximum volume decrease permissible, if profits are to remain at the amount determined in part a of Question 4.
   c Calculate the implied price elasticity of demand for your answer in part b.
   d Describe the results of your calculations in parts b and c.
   e Prepare a PV break-even chart for part b.
5 An electronic equipment manufacturer has been producing 15,000 units of a special electronic component for one of its most important customers for the past three years of a five-year contract. The contract calls for delivery of these parts at $15 each. Direct labor and material costs are $10.50 per unit. Direct fixed costs are $20,000. At the beginning of the fourth year, a new customer requests a one-year contract to purchase 10,000 units of this part at a price of $11 per unit. The manufacturer's controller estimates that production costs at 25,000 units would be about $10.25 per unit and that total fixed costs

---

[11]See "Inflation Bites Chocolate Again," *Business Week,* August 29, 1977, p. 28.

would increase to $30,000. Analyze this situation. Be sure to consider all implications of the situation. What action would you recommend?

6 The Justso Manufacturing Company produces and sells five models of an electric drill. The following data are for 19X1:

	Model				
	A	B	C	D	E
Price per unit	$ 20.00	$ 22.50	$ 25.00	$ 30.00	$ 35.00
Variable costs per unit	$ 14.00	$ 15.00	$ 16.00	$ 18.00	$ 20.00
Sales (units)	15,000	20,000	40,000	30,000	20,000

Common fixed costs were $100,000.

a Calculate the composite PV for the electric drill product line. Explain the meaning of the composite PV.

b Assume that prices and variable costs remain the same, but sales for 19X2 are A, 20,000 units; B, 40,000 units; C, 30,000 units; D, 20,000 units; and E, 15,000 units. Compute a new composite PV ratio.

c Compare the composite PV ratio for 19X1 to the composite PV ratio for 19X2. What is the reason for the change? What might be some underlying causes for the situation at the end of 19X2?

d The marketing research director has submitted a report to the vice-president of marketing that competitive prices for similar electric drill product lines range from $25 to $75. The report also indicates that customers perceive the Justso product line as lower quality when compared to competitive drills. The vice-president is perplexed because he knows that engineering and performance tests indicate that the Justso line is more durable and performs as well as competitive drills. Can you offer an explanation for the customers' perception?

e Design a new pricing schedule for the electric drill product line. What factors influenced your solution? If the product-selling mix returns to the 19X1 relationship, what would be the composite PV for the product line? Explain the reasoning you used to set the price differentials between models in the line.

7 When a firm is faced with scarce resources or is operating at productive capacity, what are some of the pricing problems that may result?

8 What problems are created by simply raising prices when the demand for a firm's output is greater than the firm can supply?

9 Why is the CPRU criterion superior to other criteria when a firm is operating with scarce resources?

10 a When a common resource is used to produce multiple products, what problems result when a firm tries to reprice its product line?

b Would these problems be similar if the firm added a new product to the line that was produced using a resource common to the product line?

c Would your answer to part b differ if the common resource was not in scarce supply?

11 What information is necessary when repricing a product line under conditions of scarce common resources?

SUGGESTED READINGS

Anderson, Lane K.: "Expanded Breakeven Analysis for a Multi-Product Company," *Management Accounting,* 57 (July 1975), 30–32.

Anderson, Paul F.: "The Marketing Management/Finance Interface," in Neil Beckwith, Michael Houston, Robert Mittelstaedt, Kent Monroe, and Scott Ward (eds.), *Proceedings, Summer Educators' Conference* (Chicago: American Marketing Association, 1979), pp. 321–329.

Böer, Germain B.: *Direct Cost and Contribution Accounting* (New York: Wiley, 1974).

Grinnell, D. Jacque: "Product Mix Decisions: Direct Costing Vs. Absorption Costing," *Management Accounting,* 58 (August 1976), 36–42, 53.

Johnson, William E.: "Trade-offs in Pricing Strategy," in Earl L. Bailey (ed.), *Pricing Practices and Strategies* (New York: The Conference Board, 1978), pp. 44–53.

Klein, Donald J.: "Direct Costing Is Alive and Well, and Doing Nicely, Thank You!" *Cost and Management,* May–June 1982, pp. 46–51.

"Learning to Live with Leverage," *Business Week,* November 7, 1988, pp. 138–156.

Martin, James R.: "Multiproduct Profit Analysis: Contribution Margin Vs. Gross Profit," *Cost and Management,* September–October 1982, pp. 22–27.

Mazumdar, Tridib, and Kent B. Monroe: "Using Leverage for Developing Pricing Strategies," *Proceedings, Summer Educators' Conference* (Chicago: American Marketing Association, 1986), pp. 303–308.

Monroe, Kent B., and Andris A. Zoltners: "Pricing the Product Line During Periods of Scarcity," *Journal of Marketing,* 43 (Summer 1979), 49–59.

Sizer, John: "Accounting Information for Marketing Management: Needs of Multi-Product Companies," *The Accountant,* January 16, 1975, pp. 67–75.

CHAPTER 9

MARKETING AND DISTRIBUTION COST ANALYSIS

One of the least developed areas in costing is the analysis of marketing efforts and distribution methods and their effects on profit contributions by product line, customer account, order, sales territory, or salesperson. When we reflect on the size of advertising and sales promotion budgets of most companies, we might assume that management has information on the relative profitability of marketing expenditures. Also, since distribution costs may approach 25 percent of the cost of doing business for manufacturers, we might expect that the costs of marketing and distribution are known to managers. Typically, this is not the case, and the marketing effort includes spending inefficiencies that are considered "unavoidable costs of marketing."[1] However, proper costs for pricing must include all costs that may change when activities are changed or redirected. This chapter expands cost analysis to include additional approaches for obtaining data when activities are changed or redirected.

As the cost components of Fig. 8-1 indicate, marketing costs are classified as direct or indirect. And, as defined in Chap. 7, direct marketing and distribution costs are variable or fixed. Similarly, indirect marketing and distribution costs are variable or fixed. This chapter expands the contribution analysis of Chap. 8 to include marketing costs. Since marketing and distribution cost accounting is not a well-developed technique, emphasis is placed on the need for and the benefits of marketing cost data for marketing decision making. The chapter also demonstrates how data can be obtained for analyzing the marketing and distribution functions of the firm.

---

[1]Richard A. Feder, "How to Measure Marketing Performance," *Harvard Business Review,* 43 May–June 1965, pp. 132–142.

NEED FOR MARKETING AND DISTRIBUTION COST DATA

It has been estimated that anywhere from 5 to 15 percent of marketing expenditures are at a loss. Indeed, in most businesses a small proportion of customers, products, territories, or orders is responsible for most of the firms' profits.[2] There are many reasons for such misdirected efforts.

Attempts to achieve too high a market share.

Failure to adjust marketing efforts to variations in demand.

Failure to adjust national and international marketing strategies for product or market dissimilarities.

Available data not reported in sufficient detail to permit profitability analysis by product, market, or other meaningful profit segment.

Data not presented on a comparative basis or incomplete.

Product and distribution cost data that are averages or outdated standards, not reflecting current and future costs in serving a market or customer group.

Marketing managers who make little effort to define their information needs.

Poor communication between marketing, accounting, and systems personnel.

Responsibilities of Marketing and Distribution Management

Clearly, the major responsibility for obtaining better marketing and distribution cost information lies within the realm of marketing management. Among these responsibilities is the need to define the types of decisions requiring better cost information. Management must also determine the value expected from better information. For example, one company determined that a theoretical sales effort allocation plan suggested annual savings of $500,000 over the current practice. A limited test of the new plan revealed that it would cost $50,000 to install the necessary information system, but that the annual savings would approximate $400,000. Other companies have reviewed their costly errors to determine how better information might have prevented them. Moreover, since the deregulation of transportation services, the cost savings opportunities in transportation and warehousing as well as the opportunities to improve customer service make it mandatory to obtain better marketing and distribution cost information.[3]

Benefits of Marketing and Distribution Cost Data

Today, the typical business firm, manufacturer, wholesaler, or retailer sells a relatively large number of products. Each of these products is in a different market and faces different degrees of competition. Consequently, to compete effectively, each product requires its own marketing mix. Moreover, these firms sell to different types and sizes of customers in different geographical locations. Essentially, then, marketing management is concerned with identifying and selecting alternative courses of

[2]Donald W. Jackson, Jr., and Lonnie L. Ostrom, "Grouping Segments for Profitability Analyses," *MSU Business Topics,* 28 (Spring 1980), 38–44.

[3]Gene R. Tyndall and John Busher, "Improving the Management of Distribution with Cost and Financial Information," *Journal of Business Logistics,* 6, No. 2 (1985), 1–18.

action that lead to more profitable sales volumes. To identify profit opportunities, management needs to know how profit changes in response to sales volume shifts that occur when marketing expenditures change.

It is necessary to have cost information

- By product
- By market (sales territory, shipping area, advertising area)
- By channel of distribution
- By class of customer [type of retailer, type of wholesaler for consumer marketing, SIC (Standard Industrial Classification) code for industrial marketing]
- By size of customer
- By key accounts
- By average order size
- By type of marketing expenditure (sales calls, discounts, advertising and promotional costs)
- By transportation mode
- By physical facility (manufacturing plant, warehouse or distribution center, retail outlet)

When analyzing alternative decisions, the proper information is the marginal or incremental profit contribution that covers fixed costs and profits after subtracting all direct and indirect traceable costs. By placing the accent on incremental profit opportunity and having relevant marketing and distribution cost data, the organization can

pinpoint the market segments with highest profit opportunities,
determine the level of selling effort to achieve profit objectives,
decide when to accept new orders or introduce new products,
determine the costs of different distribution patterns,
determine realistic prices,
establish a basis for cost justification defenses against price discrimination complaints,
design sales incentive plans,
establish sales call patterns, and
set minimum order quantities.[4]

NATURE OF MARKETING AND DISTRIBUTION COST ANALYSIS

Marketing and distribution cost analysis involves a study of the organization's entire marketing function. The purpose of the analysis is to identify and measure marketing

[4]Examples of market segment accounting are given in Leland L. Beik and Stephen L. Buzby, "Profitability Analysis by Market Segment," *Journal of Marketing,* 37 (July 1973), 48–54; Frank H. Mossman, Paul M. Fischer, and W. J. E. Crissy, "New Approaches to Analyzing Marketing Profitability," *Journal of Marketing,* 38 (April 1974), 43–48; V. H. Kirpalani and Stanley S. Shapiro, "Financial Dimensions of Marketing Management," *Journal of Marketing,* 37 (July 1973), 40–47; Patrick M. Dunne and Harry I. Wolk, "Marketing Cost Analysis: A Modularized Contribution Approach," *Journal of Marketing,* 41 (July 1977), 83–94; Jackson and Ostrom, op. cit.; and Frank H. Mossman, W. J. E. Crissy, and Paul M. Fischer, *Financial Dimensions of Marketing Management* (New York: Wiley, 1978).

and distribution cost elements to determine the profitability of different market/sales segments, such as products, customers, territories, and sales order sizes, and to eliminate or reduce losses resulting from misdirected marketing efforts.

In its simplest form, this analysis can be made from five sets of data: (1) names and location of customers, (2) types of businesses of customers, (3) number of each customer's orders in a given period, (4) total sales to each customer in the same period, and (5) total sales and gross profits on each product in the line.[5] Additional data frequently available include (6) number of shelf-stock and full-case orders, (7) number of deliveries, (8) method of delivery, (9) type of merchandise ordered, (10) method of payment, and (11) amount of returns. These data can be collected from customer records using a basic document such as an invoice or bill of lading.[6]

Most firms' records will permit an extensive approach to analyzing marketing costs. Regardless of the sophistication of the firm's records, several common errors should be avoided. First, marketing costs should not be allocated to products, customers, or other profit segments on the basis of sales volume, since most marketing costs are not caused by sales. (Sales *result* from these activities and expenditures but do not cause the costs. An exception to this statement is a sales compensation plan formulated in part on commissions based on sales generated.) Second, general and administrative costs should not be arbitrarily allocated to profit segments. And, third, legitimate marketing costs should not be "lumped" into general cost categories such as manufacturing or general and administrative costs. As observed in Chap. 7 and reiterated in Chap. 10, this lumping of marketing and distribution costs into general overhead not only is illogical but also precludes management from making informed pricing decisions.

Alternative Approaches to Marketing Cost Analysis

Marketing cost analysis may be traced back to a book published in 1908 by a cost accountant, A. Hamilton Church.[7] Church recommended that "office and selling" expenses be apportioned among products using a method that any competent person could rationally justify. During the next 20 to 30 years, this method of arbitrarily allocating selling costs to products became known as the *traditional approach.* Primarily, the developers of this allocation approach argued that marketing costs were not like production costs and therefore were not readily traced to individual products or product lines.

In the early 1930s, one of the foremost marketing scholars, Wroe Alderson, developed the basis of what today we call *marketing cost analysis.*[8] Alderson's

---

[5]Charles H. Sevin, *Analyzing Your Cost of Marketing,* Small Business Administration Management Aids No. 85, reprinted April 1971.

[6]Frank H. Mossman, Paul M. Fischer, and W. J. E. Crissy, "New Approaches to Analyzing Marketing Profitability," *Journal of Marketing,* 38 (April 1974), 44.

[7]A. Hamilton Church, *The Proper Distribution of Expense Burden* (New York: The Engineering Magazine, 1908).

[8]An excellent history of marketing cost analysis is contained in Paul F. Anderson, "Distribution Cost Analysis Methodologies, 1908–1941," *The Accounting Historians Journal,* 6 (Fall 1979), 39–51; and Joseph A. Hopkins, "Distribution Cost Analysis—Development during 1940–1976," Virginia Polytechnic Institute and State University, 1977. Unpublished paper.

method was further developed by Charles Sevin and is referred to today as the *net profit approach.*

In recent years, increasing emphasis has been placed on the *direct cost contribution approach.* As developed in Chap. 8, the contribution approach emphasizes the contribution in excess of direct variable costs and direct fixed costs made to cover fixed costs by different marketing profit segments. We will now define marketing cost classifications and then develop both the contribution and net profit approaches to marketing and distribution cost analysis.

Marketing Cost Classifications

Common fixed marketing costs are costs incurred in common for different profit segments and do not vary with the volume of sales or activities in any profit segment. For example, costs of institutional advertising of a company's name would not be allocated to individual segments.

Direct variable marketing costs vary with an activity and can be allocated to profit segments. Sales commissions, transportation costs, and some aspects of ordering and billing costs vary directly with sales volume, customer accounts, transportation rate or mode mix, and method of storing.

Separable fixed marketing costs are costs that can be allocated to specific profit/sales segments. Field supervision expenses and period warehousing costs are examples of fixed marketing costs that can be identified with specific segments.

CONTRIBUTION APPROACH

The contribution approach essentially extends the contribution method of cost analysis developed in Chap. 8. To illustrate the approach assume that a firm produces three types of lawn mower: X, a gasoline-powered mower; Y, an electric-powered mower; and Z, a gasoline-powered tractor mower. Assume further that the company has three sales territories: A, B, and C. Production variable costs for each product are given in Table 9-1 and include materials and labor. Product X is sold at a price of $100; Y is priced at $150; and Z is priced at $450.

Tables 9-1 and 9-2 illustrate three types of direct variable marketing costs: commissions, transportation, and order processing costs. In Table 9-1 these variable marketing costs are directly assignable to the territories because there is a direct relationship to the sales effort activity within each territory. In Table 9-2 these same variable costs are assigned to the three products again on the basis of a sales effort activity. It is also important to note that in Table 9-2 territory direct fixed costs are not allocated to the three products since there is no objective way to allocate these common marketing costs to each product.

The main distinction between the contribution approach and the net profit approach (described later) is that the contribution method avoids arbitrary allocation of common, fixed marketing costs. As noted in Chap. 8, once the contribution of each product or profit segment is determined, a PV ratio can be computed and alternative prices for each product can be analyzed exactly. For example, the PV ratio for product X in territory A is $57,500/$300,000, or 0.19. If the firm is

TABLE 9-1
MARKETING COST ANALYSIS—CONTRIBUTION BY TERRITORIES

	Territory			Total
	A	B	C	
Sales revenues				
Product X	$300,000	$150,000	$120,000	$570,000
Product Y	110,000	80,000	70,000	260,000
Product Z	90,000	120,000	110,000	320,000
	$500,000	$350,000	$300,000	$1,150,000
Variable costs				
Production	$350,000	$270,000	$180,000	$800,000
Marketing—commission	35,000	23,000	20,000	78,000
Marketing—transportation	9,000	7,000	6,000	22,000
Marketing—ordering	6,000	5,000	4,000	15,000
	400,000	305,000	210,000	915,000
Contribution	$100,000	$45,000	$90,000	$235,000
Direct fixed costs				
Rent	$ 2,000	$ 1,500	$ 2,500	$ 6,000
Salaries	11,000	8,500	9,500	29,000
Promotion	6,000	5,000	3,000	14,000
	19,000	15,000	15,000	49,000
Territory contribution	$ 81,000	$ 30,000	$ 75,000	$ 186,000
Common fixed costs				25,000
Total contribution				$ 161,000

TABLE 9-2
MARKETING COST ANALYSIS—CONTRIBUTION BY PRODUCTS
Territory A

	Product			
	X	Y	Z	Total
Sales revenue	$300,000	$110,000	$90,000	$500,000
Variable costs				
Production	$210,000	$ 80,000	$60,000	$350,000
Marketing—commissions	25,000	6,000	4,000	35,000
Marketing—transportation	4,000	3,000	2,000	9,000
Marketing—ordering	3,500	1,500	1,000	6,000
Total variable costs	$242,500	$ 90,500	$67,000	$400,000
Product contribution	$ 57,500	$ 19,500	$23,000	$100,000
Territory direct fixed costs				
Rent				$ 2,000
Salaries				11,000
Promotion				6,000
				$ 19,000
Territory contribution				$ 81,000

considering raising the price of gasoline-powered lawn mowers in territory A to $110—a 10 percent price increase—then using the formula from Eq. (8-10), volume in territory A can fall no more than 34.5 percent if the territory's profit contribution from product X is to be enhanced.

$$\text{Volume decrease } (\%) = \left(\frac{0.10}{0.19 + 0.10} \right) 100 = 34.5\%$$

NET PROFIT APPROACH

This approach, primarily of use to manufacturers and wholesalers, is adaptable for use by retailers as well. In general, reference will be to profit segments and it should be understood that these segments may be individual products, product lines, customer types, specific customer accounts, sales territories, or alternative channels of distribution.

The net profit approach attempts to allocate all indirect costs among the profit segments. Essentially, this approach is similar to the full-costing method (described in Chap. 10) and has the same disadvantages. Indeed, the contribution method avoids arbitrary allocation of common, fixed marketing costs. However, the Federal Trade Commission requires a full-cost allocation approach for justifying cost differences under the Robinson–Patman Act (see pp. 213–217). But, perhaps more appropriately, short-run decisions would be concerned more with the profit contribution

TABLE 9-3
FUNCTIONAL-COST GROUPS AND BASES OF ALLOCATION

Functional-Cost Group	To Products	To Customers	To Sales Territories
1. Selling—direct costs: personal calls by salespeople and supervisors on accounts and prospects; sales salaries, incentive compensation, travel, and other expenses	Selling time devoted to each product, as shown by sales-call reports or other studies	Number of sales calls times average time per call, as shown by sales-call reports or other studies	Direct
2. Selling—indirect costs: field supervision, field sales-administration expense, sales-personnel training, sales management; market research, new-product development, sales statistics, tabulating services, sales accounting	In proportion to direct selling time or time records by projects	In proportion to direct selling time or time records by projects	Equal charge for each salesperson
3. Advertising: media costs such as TV, radio, billboards, newspapers, magazines; advertising production costs; advertising department salaries	Direct, or analysis of space and time by media; other costs in proportion to media costs	Equal charge to each account; or number of ultimate consumers and prospects in each account's trading area	Direct analysis of media circulation records
4. Sales promotion: consumer promotions such as coupons, premiums; trade promotions such as price allowances, point-of-purchase displays, cooperative advertising	Direct, or analysis of source records	Direct, or analysis of source records	Direct, or analysis of source records
5. Transportation: railroad, truck, barge; payments to carriers for delivery on finished goods from plants to warehouses and from warehouses to customers; traffic department costs	Applicable rates times tonnages	Analysis of sampling of bills of lading	Applicable rates times tonnages

TABLE 9-3 *(Continued)*

	Functional-Cost Group	To Products	To Customers	To Sales Territories
6.	Storage and shipping: storage of finished-goods inventories in warehouses; rent (or equivalent costs), public warehouse charges, fire insurance and taxes on finished-goods inventories; physical handling, assembling, and loading out of rail cars, trucks, barges for shipping finished products from warehouses and mills to customers; labor, equipment, space, and material costs	Warehouse space occupied by average inventory; number of shipping units	Number of shipping units	Number of shipping units
7.	Order processing: checking and processing of orders from customers to mills for prices, weights, and carload accumulation, shipping dates, coordination with production planning; pricing department; preparation of customer invoices; freight accounting; credit and collection; handling cash receipts; provision for bad debts; salary, supplies, space, and equipment costs	Number of order lines	Number of order lines	Number of order lines

Source: Charles H. Sevin, *Marketing Productivity Analysis* (New York: McGraw-Hill, 1965), pp. 13–15.

made by specific segments. Thus, either the contribution approach or the net profit approach may be appropriate, depending on the purpose of the analysis.

There are two analytical steps in the net profit approach.

1 Marketing expenditures of a business are reclassified from a *natural-expense* basis into *functional-cost* groups. The functional-cost groups comprise all the costs associated with each marketing activity (function) performed by the business.

2 Functional-cost groups are assigned to profit segments on the basis of *measurable factors* that exhibit causal relationships to the functional costs.

A natural-expense item refers to the usual way expenses of a business are classified for accounting purposes; e.g., rent, wages. However, a natural expense such as wages may *functionally* be related to direct selling, selling supervision, order assembly, order billing, and credit. Each of these activities is a part of a separate marketing function and the natural-expense item, such as sales people's salaries, must be apportioned among several functional-cost groups. This concept of functionality follows directly from the idea of classifying costs as variable or fixed, according to activity as developed at the beginning of Chap. 7.

To classify marketing and distribution costs according to functions requires a study of the marketing activities performed by the business. The assignment of natural-expense items to functional-cost groups often is accomplished by means of work-measurement studies, space measurements, managerial estimates, and statistical techniques (see Chap. 7). As suggested in Chap. 7, it is important to establish a cause–effect relationship between various marketing costs and the corresponding functional-cost grouping. The discussion of cost classifications and cost behaviors of Chap. 7 is equally appropriate here. Table 9-3 gives examples of functional-cost groups and bases of allocation.

As Table 9-3 indicates, certain types of data are required before marketing costs can be assigned to products. Essentially, the data needed are

1 The average inventory value of finished goods
2 The amount of storage space required for these finished goods
3 The frequency with which the product is ordered (number of invoice lines)
4 The number of "packs" of the product sold (gross, cases, dozen)
5 The weight or number of units shipped
6 The proportion of selling time spent selling the product
7 Direct advertising costs

The data required for assigning marketing costs to customers are

1 The total number of invoice lines for the period
2 The total weight or number of units shipped
3 The number of sales calls
4 Any direct advertising or promotion costs
5 The number of orders placed by the customer
6 The average amount of accounts receivable

7 The number of invoices posted to accounts receivable

8 The amount of returns

The analysis of marketing costs by territory generally is simpler than the analysis either by products or by customers. When a firm's marketing activities are organized along well-defined geographical boundaries, a large proportion of marketing expenses is directly traceable to the territories. Hence, assigning indirect marketing expenses to territories is less burdensome than it is for products or customer accounts. Once functional expenses have been assigned to the marketing profit segments, a profit and loss statement is prepared for each segment.

To illustrate some of the problems with the application of the net profit approach, assume that the lawn mower manufacturer wishes to assign the rent, salaries, and promotion expenses of territory A to products X, Y, and Z. As indicated, the first step is to reclassify these natural-expense items into functional marketing cost groups. The relevant marketing cost groups for territory A are selling, advertising and promotion, order processing, and storage and shipping. The reclassification of the natural indirect expenses into functional costs is shown in Table 9-4. Table 9-5 shows the basis for allocating the functional expenses to each product, which is the second step in the net profit approach.

In Table 9-4, the rent is divided evenly by the order processing, storage, and shipping activities because salespeople work away from the territory office and an advertising agency handles the advertising and promotion activity. The district sales supervisor, who also sells and coordinates the territory's advertising and promotion activities, spends about 57 percent of the time in selling. Therefore, the supervisor's salary is divided proportionately between (1) selling and (2) advertising and promotion. The remaining $4,000 of salaries is divided between (1) order processing and (2) storage and shipping.

Once the natural expenses have been classified into functional expenses, the task is to assign each functional expense to the three products. Table 9-5 shows the allocation formulas and the data necessary to complete this task. From sales reports filed by the supervisor, it is determined that 50 percent of the selling time is devoted to product X, the gasoline-powered lawn mower. Hence, 50 percent of the $4,000 fixed selling expense is assigned to product X, as seen in Table 9-6. Advertising and

TABLE 9-4
CLASSIFYING NATURAL EXPENSES INTO FUNCTIONAL EXPENSES

	Natural Accounts	Selling	Advertising and Promotion	Order Processing	Storage and Shipping
Rent	$ 2,000	$ –0–	$ –0–	$1,000	$1,000
Salaries	11,000	4,000	3,000	2,000	2,000
Promotion	6,000	–0–	6,000	–0–	–0–
	$19,000	$4,000	$9,000	$3,000	$3,000

TABLE 9-5
BASES FOR ALLOCATING FUNCTIONAL EXPENSES TO PRODUCTS

Product	Selling: Proportion of Selling Time	Advertising and Promotion: Number of Advertisements	Order Processing: Number of Orders	Storage and Shipping: Number of Units Shipped
X	0.50	40	300	1,000
Y	0.30	40	75	733
Z	0.20	20	50	200
Totals	1.00	100	425	1,933
Functional expenses	$4,000	$9,000	$3,000	$3,000
Allocation formula	Direct proportion of selling time	Cost per advertisement: $\dfrac{\$9,000}{100} = \$90$	Cost per order $\dfrac{\$3,000}{425} = \$7.06$	Cost per unit $\dfrac{\$3,000}{1,933} = \$1.55$

TABLE 9-6
TERRITORY A: PROFIT AND LOSS BY PRODUCT

	Product			
	X	Y	Z	Territory
Sales revenue	$300,000	$110,000	$90,000	$500,000
Variable costs	242,500	90,500	67,000	400,000
Product contribution	$ 57,500	$ 19,500	$23,000	$100,000
Fixed costs				
Selling	$ 2,000	$ 1,200	$ 800	$ 4,000
Advertising and promotion	3,600	3,600	1,800	9,000
Order processing	2,118	529	353	3,000
Storage and shipping	1,550	1,140	310	3,000
Total expenses	$ 9,268	$ 6,469	$ 3,263	$ 19,000
Net profit	$ 48,232	$ 13,031	$19,737	$ 81,000

promotion expenses are assigned on the basis of the number of advertisements and the average cost per advertisement. Since product X was featured in 40 local advertisements, $3,600 ($90 × 40) is assigned to product X. Similarly, the remaining marketing costs are assigned to the three products on the basis of average cost per order processed and average shipping cost per unit shipped.

As shown in Table 9-6, the last step is to calculate the net profit for each product. Thus, an accounting profit or loss can be computed for the profit segments, which in this example are products. Note that the computation of marketing costs using the net profit approach has a distinct element of arbitrariness. When one arbitrary formula replaces another, the relative profitability of a profit segment can shift quite radically. Hence, as argued in Chap. 7, for pricing decisions the contribution approach facilitates the analysis of the profit impact of alternative prices.

AN EXAMPLE OF A COST-JUSTIFICATION STUDY

A detailed marketing and distribution cost analysis can be used to justify price differentials charged to different customers. Opportunities for differential pricing arise particularly when an organization uses a quantity discount policy. Differential pricing policy can lead to litigation based on the Robinson–Patman Act. A careful reading of the history of litigation under the Robinson–Patman Act reveals a woeful lack of attention to the pricing function by many firms. Most defenses to price discrimination charges have relied on hastily developed studies that, when subjected to cross-examination, have failed to justify the price differentials. (The Robinson–Patman Act and permissible defenses for price discrimination charges will be discussed in Chap. 16.)

Despite its relative lack of use, the cost justification defense remains one of the most viable defenses available. However, it is necessary for firms to develop cost accounting techniques for analyzing marketing expenditures and to refrain from lumping marketing and distribution costs into a general overhead category such as selling, general, and administrative overhead. The basic approach to marketing and distribution cost accounting was outlined previously. We will now see how one company studied its volume discount schedule and determined that the discount schedule lacked cost justification.[9]

The Company

The company in question produced and sold a product in a very competitive market. There were a number of variations of the product, which resulted from selling a basic unit plus a number of different modifying assemblies at the time of dealer installation. The product was sold to distributors through manufacturers' agents. The distributors sold to retailers, who sold the product to the final customers. The manufacturers' agents were paid sales commissions after the distributors' discounts were deducted.

Original Discount Structure

The distributors had been categorized into three classes depending on minimum order size. A Class I distributor was required to order a minimum of one item and received no discount. Typically, a Class I distributor ordered three items per order. A Class II distributor was required to order a minimum of six items and typically did order six items each time. A Class III distributor's minimum and usual order

[9]This example is adapted from James C. Cohrs, "A Cost Justification Study," *Management Controls,* 12 (November 1965), 230–235.

TABLE 9-7
SAMPLE PRICE LIST

Item	Distributor Class		
	I	II	III
Basic unit	$100.00	$ 97.00	$ 94.00
Modifying assembly A	75.00	72.75	70.50
Modifying assembly B	50.00	48.50	47.00
Modifying assembly C	25.00	24.25	23.50
Minimum order size (units)	1	6	18

All prices f.o.b. manufacturer's factory.

size was 18 items. The price quoted to Class III distributors was 6 percent less than the Class I price. Table 9-7 is a typical price list.

Identifying Relevant Costs

As Table 9-7 indicates, all prices were quoted f.o.b. manufacturer's factory. Further, all products were made for inventory. Consequently, differences in freight and manufacturing costs could not be used to justify price differences. It was determined that only those costs incurred in the ordering and billing, traffic (bills of lading), accounts receivable, credit and collection, and shipping departments could be used to justify price differences.

Preliminary Analysis

Initially, the treasurer and sales manager were asked to estimate the average cost of processing and filling minimum orders for each distributor class. After considerable discussion and some analysis of departmental records it was estimated that the order costs per order were I, $10.00; II, $12.50; III, $15.00. It was also determined that sales commissions paid to the manufacturer's agents were (on sales after discounts) I, 7 percent; II, 5 percent; III, 4 percent.

By using the foregoing estimates, order processing costs were calculated for a sale of 18 units of modifying assembly A to each distributor class as shown in Table 9-8. The order processing costs were based on the usual order size for each distributor class. Hence, for Class I, 18 items would require six orders at three items per order, or $10.00 per order × 6 orders = $60.00.

Table 9-9 summarizes the price and cost differences. Based on the preliminary analysis, the excess of a price difference over cost differences of $3.28 represented an apparent lack of cost justification. However, it was believed that a detailed study of the actual order processing and filling costs would lead to a discount schedule that could be cost justified.

TABLE 9-8
PRICE DIFFERENCES AND ASSUMED COST DIFFERENCES—MODIFYING ASSEMBLY A

Item	Distributor Class		
	I	II	III
Sales value of assembly A (unit)	$ 75.00	$ 72.75	$ 70.50
Sales value of assembly A (18 units)	1,350.00	1,309.50	1,269.00
Price differences			
Versus Class I		40.50	81.00
Versus Class II			40.50
Differential costs for 18 items			
Order filling and processing	$ 60.00	$ 37.50	$ 15.00
Sales commissions	94.50	65.48	50.76
Total	$ 154.50	$ 102.98	$ 65.76
Assumed cost differences			
Versus Class I		$ 51.52	$ 88.74
Versus Class II			37.22

TABLE 9-9
SUMMARY OF PRICE AND COST DIFFERENCES

Distributor Class	Price Difference	Cost Difference	Excess of Cost Difference Over Price Difference
I vs. III	$81.00	$88.74	$ 7.74
I vs. II	40.50	51.52	11.02
II vs. III	40.50	37.22	(3.28)

The Cost Study

A detailed cost study was undertaken to determine the activities involved in order processing and shipping as well as who performed these activities and the time spent performing them. The study program and results are outlined next.

Data Collection

1 Analyzed the company's organization to determine the departments involved in order filling and processing.

2 Determined the personnel and time spent in order filling and processing.

3 Obtained data on orders, back orders, and items processed.

4 Accumulated direct and overhead costs for each department involved in order filling and processing.

5 Determined typical times required to ship orders of various sizes.

6 Developed hourly cost rates for the shipping department (direct and overhead) for different annual volumes of shipments.

7 Determined sales and marketing activities that were transaction identifiable.

8 Allocated corporate overhead expenses to the order processing and filling function.

9 Computed the costs of filling various sized orders.

10 Determined whether distributors were ordering in specified quantities.

Results

1 About 70 percent of all shipments to each distributor class were for fewer than five components. Therefore, cost justification of the price list differences would not justify *actual* pricing practices.

2 The fixed cost of processing an order was $6.00.

3 Some order processing activities and shipping room time did not increase proportionately with order size. Therefore, these activities provided a source of differential costs.

4 Concluded that there was substantial lack of cost justification of list prices.

5 Estimated actual cost (Table 9-10).

6 Determined price and cost differences (Table 9-11).

Recommendations

Because the distributors were not ordering according to the minimum-order requirements and because not all price differences were cost-justified, it was recommended that another discount policy be adopted. The new pricing policy was recommended

TABLE 9-10
ORDER PROCESSING AND FILLING COSTS

Fixed Costs Per Order	
Order department	$3.64
Accounts receivable	0.35
Credits and collection	0.30
Traffic	1.71
	$6.00

Variable Costs Per Order		
Number of Units	Shipping	Order Department
1	$1.84	$0.05
3	1.95	0.07
6	2.27	0.08
18	3.25	0.22

TABLE 9-11
PRICE DIFFERENCES AND ESTIMATED COST DIFFERENCES
Assembly A

Item	Distributor Class		
	I	II	III
Sales value (18 units)	$1,350.00	$1,309.50	$1,269.00
Price differences			
Versus Class I		40.50	81.00
Versus Class II			40.50
Differential costs (18 units)			
Order processing—fixed	$ 36.00	$ 18.00	$ 6.00
Order processing—variable	0.42	0.24	0.22
Shipping	11.70	6.81	3.25
Sales commissions (7%, 5%, 4%)	94.50	65.48	50.76
Total	$ 142.62	$ 90.53	$ 60.23
Cost differences			
Versus Class I		$ 52.09	$ 82.39
Versus Class II			30.30
Excess of cost differences over price differences			
Versus Class I		11.59	1.39
Versus Class II			(10.20)

to provide for cost-justified price differences and to encourage customers to increase their average order size. It was also recommended that the discount schedule be based on dollar value of shipments rather than number of items shipped.

Table 9-12 is the discount schedule adopted. The sales commission of 6 percent was added to encourage the manufacturer's agents to make regular sales calls to smaller distributors averaging around $500 per order. Table 9-13 shows the cost justification for the new discount schedule.

IMPROVING DISTRIBUTION MANAGEMENT WITH COST
INFORMATION

Since the deregulation of transportation services, companies have begun to realize that distribution management can be a source not only of costs but, if managed well, of revenues. Indeed, many of the companies described in earlier chapters which are able to charge premium prices do so because they deliver better value through distribution service. Moreover, with distribution costs potentially, if not actually, representing a major portion of total costs, competitive advantage can be obtained through better management of the distribution function. Beginning in 1982, the National Council of Physical Distribution Management (NCPDM) and the National Association of Accountants (NAA) have been developing guidelines for establishing costing methods for distribution. In their reports on transportation and

TABLE 9-12
QUANTITY DISCOUNT AND SALES COMMISSION SCHEDULE

Sales Value at List Per Order	Quantity Discount as Percentage of List	Sales Commission, %
Less than $450	None	7
$450–$675	2	6
$675–$1,125	3	5
Over $1,125	4	4

TABLE 9-13
PRICE AND COST DIFFERENCES: NEW DISCOUNT SCHEDULE

Item	Quantity Discount Class			
	None	2%	3%	4%
Sales at list	$225.00	$450.00	$675.00	$1,125.00
Quantity discount		9.00	20.25	45.00
Net sales	$225.00	$441.00	$654.75	$1,080.00
Differential costs				
Order processing—fixed	$ 6.00	$ 6.00	$ 6.00	$ 6.00
Order processing—variable	0.07	0.08	0.11	0.17
Order filling	1.95	2.27	2.52	3.02
Sales commissions (7%, 6%, 5%, 4%)	15.75	26.46	32.74	43.20
Total	$ 23.77	$ 34.81	$ 41.37	$ 52.39
Differential costs (% of sales at list)	10.6	7.7	6.1	4.7
Versus no discount		2.9	4.5	5.9
Versus 2% discount			1.6	3.0
Versus 3% discount				1.4
Excess of cost differences over price differences (% of sales at list)				
Versus no discount		0.9	1.5	1.9
Versus 2% discount			0.6	1.0
Versus 3% discount				0.4

warehousing, it is clear that, as argued previously, the costs of these functions can be identified, classified by their behavior, and attributed to specific activities or business segments.[10]

By separating the costs of transportation, warehousing, ordering, billing, and invoicing into their fixed and variable cost components, it is possible to determine the effects on costs and profits of changes in volumes, rates, transportation mode

[10]*Transportation Accounting and Control: Guidelines for Distribution and Financial Management,* National Council of Physical Distribution Management and National Association of Accountants, 1983; *Warehouse Accounting and Control: Guidelines for Distribution and Financial Managers,* National Council of Physical Distribution Management and National Association of Accountants, 1985.

mix, and distribution center origin or destination. Moreover, such cost information can be used to plan for warehousing needs and locations and for use of public or privately owned facilities. With detailed distribution cost data it is possible to conduct sensitivity analyses by marketing region, territory, or product line. The result is to improve customer service while realizing overall cost savings. It has been shown that where efforts have been made to improve the cost and financial information of the distribution function, service performance has been improved while cost effectiveness of distribution has been enhanced.[11]

IMPROVING RETAIL MANAGEMENT WITH BETTER COST INFORMATION

Just like manufacturers, retailers traditionally have lumped a large proportion of their operating costs into overhead categories and then allocated these costs using arbitrary formulas. Historically, the yardstick for measuring profits was sales. That is, as long as sales were increasing, profits should be increasing. In the 1960s retailers recognized that a valuable asset was the amount of store space devoted to displaying and selling merchandise. (In the late 1980s, supermarkets began charging fees for shelf space allotted to national brands!)[12] Hence, measures of profitability were developed using sales per square foot as the criterion. Refinements of these profitability concepts continued into the 1980s, leading to other indicators of profitability such as gross margin, gross margin per square foot, and eventually gross margin return on investment.

As discussed in earlier chapters and detailed again in Chap. 10, these gross measures do not provide accurate information about the relative profitability of each and every product sold in the store. By lumping such costs as the salaries of buyers, inventory, shipping, and marking into an overhead category, it is not possible to determine the profit contribution of individual selling items. These nonmerchandise costs become uncontrollable by operating managers, and items that appear to be profitable may not be generating the return desired or required by the store.

For example, suppose the store's buyer of intimate apparel contracts to buy 144 black lace camisoles at $12 each with an expected retail price of $25. This contract seems to provide for a gross margin of $13, or 52 percent. However, shipping costs $150 and the unmarked items will require 10 hours of labor to receive, check, mark, and distribute to the floor at a direct cost of $80. If all 144 camisoles are sold at $25 and there are no other direct costs, the profit margin is now 45.6 percent. However, suppose that after three weeks, 50 camisoles remain unsold and the store reduces the price by 20 percent and advertises the sale in local media as well with point-of-purchase signs and a special display. The costs of the advertising, promotion activities, and display are $500. If the remaining 50 are sold during the sale, the actual profit contribution realized will be less than half of the original gross margin projected by the buyer.

[11]Gene R. Tyndall and John R. Busher, "Improving the Management of Distribution with Cost and Financial Information," *Journal of Business Logistics,* 6, No. 2 (1985), 1–18.
[12]See "Want Shelf Space at the Supermarket? Ante Up," *Business Week,* August 7, 1989, pp. 60–61.

As this simple example demonstrates, lumping nonmerchandise costs into selling and general and administrative overhead precludes a proper identification of the relative attributable costs and profit contribution made by merchandise lines. Further, operating managers have no way of understanding the impact of their decisions on the eventual profits earned.[13]

The types of costs that can be identified and classified according to their behavior and attributability are distribution costs, selling costs, and inventory costs. Distribution costs include all costs incurred in bringing the merchandise to the selling floor: shipping, receiving, checking, marking, and setting up on shelves or displays. Selling costs include commissions, base salaries of salespeople, packaging (bags, boxes, wrapping paper), and credit costs. Inventory carrying costs vary according to how long it takes to turn the merchandise and the costs of financing inventory. Depending on these two variables, inventory carrying costs can be a significant proportion of the merchandise costs. The benefits of doing a detailed marketing and distribution analysis for a retail organization are that the firm will be in a position to make better buying decisions, pricing and promotion decisions, and operating decisions related to store size and layout, department space allocations, and inventory management.

Is such a detailed analysis for a store with thousands of items worthwhile? Neiman-Marcus has implemented a profit contribution plan even though it has over 200 departments. Management has been able to develop standard costs for identified variable costs and is in a better position to make decisions to improve performance. Neiman-Marcus has over 9 million transactions per year; with an improvement of just 20 cents per transaction, the bottom line improves by $2 million per year.[14] For firms at any level of distribution, the potential for detailed marketing and distribution analyses is staggering.

STARTING A PROFITABILITY ANALYSIS PROGRAM

Perhaps the most frequently heard comment by managers when the details of a marketing and distribution cost analysis program are detailed is: "We have so many products; how can we even begin such an effort?" The way to begin is to work with the major selling products in the firm's offerings. Often a relatively small number of products or product lines contribute a substantial amount of both sales and profits to the organization. By concentrating initially on these products, the details of the program can be developed and the incremental performance improvements maximized.

A second recommendation is to group profitability segments together to simplify the analysis and reduce the costs of developing and implementing the program. For example, Neiman-Marcus determined that items within departments exhibited similar cost patterns. That is, individual departments seemed to emphasize common merchandise sources and marked merchandise in similar ways, and the inventory

---

[13]These points are amplified in Alan L. Gilman, "The Benefits of Looking Below Gross Margin," *Retailing Issues Letter,* 1 (November 1988), 1–4.

[14]Ibid., p. 4.

turns of merchandise within a department fell within a narrow time frame.[15] A cosmetics firm might develop product groupings according to lipsticks, nail polish, facial creams and distribution groupings such as drug stores, department stores, supermarkets.[16]

When establishing groups for profitability analysis, several important points should be observed:

1 The groups should provide management with relevant information on sales, costs, and profits, not with arbitrarily allocated information.

2 Within a group, sales, costs, and profits should behave in a similar manner (i.e., the items within a group should be homogeneous).

3 Data should be provided in an accurate and timely manner.

4 Revenues and costs should be separated out. Cost data should be separated into variable and fixed categories.

5 Groups should be mutually exclusive and collectively exhaustive.

6 Large-volume products or product lines or other large-volume segments should be analyzed separately and not grouped with low-volume categories.

Regardless of the level of aggregation, it is readily observable that performance can be enhanced when firms retreat from the illogical lumping of nonproduction costs (for manufacturers) or nonmerchandise costs (for retailers) into general overhead categories. Performance enhancement occurs because these organizations learn how costs behave and why they are incurred. Further, this information provides insights into the development of more profitable pricing strategies and tactics. For example, learning which products, customers, and channels are not profitable may lead to pricing decisions about when to impose service charges on low-volume orders, establishing volume discount price breaks, when to increase prices, negotiating with distributors about terms of trade, or managing the selling effort of salespeople.

Regardless of the changes that are implemented, improving the productivity of the marketing and distribution function for many organizations is the last frontier for establishing or maintaining a competitive advantage. Moreover, by emphasizing the profit contributions of these activities, the firm will be able to develop a decision support system that increases the effectiveness of its managers' decisions because they will understand what is under their control.

SUMMARY

As discussed in Chap. 8, the role of costs for pricing decisions, although limited, is very important. However, there is a great tendency to lump marketing and distribution costs into a general cost category, often called administrative, selling, and general overhead. Such a classification of costs is a gross error. Marketing and distribution costs, like production costs, can be classified into direct traceable,

---

[15]Ibid., p. 3.
[16]Jackson and Ostrom, op. cit.

indirect traceable, and common fixed costs. By so classifying these costs, management is in a position to know the effects of price changes on volume and on production, marketing, and distribution costs. Thus, given a precise measure of marketing and distribution costs, all relevant costs for pricing will be known.

Further, the firm would be in a position to estimate the profitability of various sales/profit segments at past prices and at alternative future prices. And by knowing which products, territories, or customer accounts are not profitable, price changes can be analyzed to discourage growth of unprofitable segments and to encourage growth of profitable ones. Control of marketing and distribution costs is enhanced and a method of reallocating marketing efforts to more profitable segments becomes a reality. Finally, as illustrated in this chapter, marketing and distribution cost analysis provides a means of justifying price differentials.

DISCUSSION QUESTIONS

1 A wholesaler of office supplies conducted a marketing cost study. At the conclusion of the study, the main results were summarized for the manager as seen in the accompanying table.

| | Account Classification | | | | |
	A	B	C	D	E
Number of accounts	500	400	300	200	100
Average order	$ 100	$ 300	$ 500	$ 900	$ 1,200
Annual sales	$500,000	$1,500,000	$2,250,000	$2,000,000	$1,800,000
Contribution	$150,000	$ 450,000	$ 675,000	$ 600,000	$ 540,000
Selling expense	$ 60,000	$ 50,000	$ 45,000	$ 25,000	$ 20,000
Delivery expense	50,000	50,000	45,000	30,000	20,000
Credit and collection expense	40,000	20,000	15,000	10,000	5,000
Order processing expense	30,000	30,000	25,000	20,000	15,000
Total expenses	$180,000	$ 150,000	$ 130,000	$ 85,000	$ 60,000
Profit (loss)	$ (30,000)	$ 300,000	$ 545,000	$ 515,000	$ 480,000

a Identify the marketing cost approach probably used by the company.
b What are some of the possible causes of class A accounts being unprofitable?
c Refer back to the "Definition of Price" discussion in Chap. 1. What are some ways that price can be used to enhance the profitability of serving class A accounts?
d Can you think of any other alternative solutions to enhance the profitability of serving class A accounts?

e On what bases do you think the wholesaler allocated the four types of expenses to the account classes? Can you think of other ways to allocate these expenses?

f Consider your answers to parts c and d above. If the wholesaler implemented your solutions, what changes might occur in the expense accounting? What assumptions did you make to arrive at these changes in the expense accounting?

2 A small electric appliance company made two products: a food blender and a food mixer. The company sold in two territories, A and B. The cost and revenue figures for 19XX appear in the accompanying table.

	Blender	Mixer
Selling price per unit	$40.00	$ 20.00
Sales volume in units		
Territory A	6,000	8,000
Territory B	4,000	13,000
Direct variable manufacturing costs per unit	$20.00	$ 9.00
Variable selling costs per unit	$ 2.00	$ 1.50
Variable distribution costs per unit	$ 4.00	$ 0.50
Promotion expenses per year	$2,500	$ 2,000

Fixed costs for territory A were $5,000 and for territory B were $5,400. Other fixed expenses for the firm amounted to $12,000.

a Perform a contribution analysis by products.

b Perform a contribution analysis by territories.

c The firm is considering an across-the-board price increase of 10 percent. What is the maximum permissible volume decrease before profitability is harmed?

d What additional information would you want before deciding to raise prices? Why?

SUGGESTED READINGS

Beik, Leland L., and Stephen L. Buzby: "Profitability Analysis by Market Segments," *Journal of Marketing,* 37 (July 1973), 48–53.

Boër, Germain B.: "Market Reporting Systems," in *Direct Cost and Contribution Accounting* (New York: Wiley, 1974), pp. 91–108.

Buzby, Stephen L., and Lester Heitger: "Profit Contribution by Market Segment," *Management Accounting,* 58 (November 1976), 42–46.

Corr, Arthur V.: "A Cost-Effectiveness Approach to Marketing Outlays," *Management Accounting,* 58 (January 1976), 33–36.

Dunne, Patrick M., and Harry I. Wolk: "Marketing Cost Analysis: A Modularized Contribution Approach," *Journal of Marketing,* 41 (July 1977), 83–94.

Jackson, Donald W., Jr., and Lonnie L. Ostrom: "Grouping Segments for Profitability Analyses," *MSU Business Topics,* 28 (Spring 1980), 39–44.

Kirpalani, V. H., and Stanley S. Shapiro: "Financial Dimensions of Marketing Management," *Journal of Marketing,* 37 (July 1973), 40–47.

Mossman, Frank H., W. J. E. Crissy, and Paul M. Fischer: *Financial Dimensions of Marketing Management* (New York: Wiley, 1978).

Mossman, Frank H., Paul M. Fischer, and W. J. E. Crissy: "New Approaches to Analyzing Marketing Profitability," *Journal of Marketing,* 38 (April 1974), 43–48.

Tyndall, Gene R., and John Busher: "Improving the Management of Distribution with Cost and Financial Information," *Journal of Business Logistics,* 6, No. 2 (1985), 1–18.

CHAPTER 10

DEVELOPING FULL-COST
ESTIMATES

The preceding three chapters presented methods for determining various profit segments' relative contributions to covering fixed costs and profits. However, indirect costs such as factory overhead and general administrative expenses are incurred and are not always traceable to profit segments. Over time, various formulas have been used to allocate these overhead costs to products and other profit segments of business. Unfortunately, the fixed costs allocated by these formulas, although quick and easy to determine, are illogical. Indeed, the exact way and the rate at which overhead is applied to profit segments differ from one company to the next—and frequently differ within a company.

This chapter explores the disadvantages of these methods of assigning overhead and presents a functional or activity-based method for assigning cost burdens to the segments of the business responsible for incurring the particular burden. As illustrated in Chap. 9, one clear advantage of the functional or activity approach is its utility for justifying price differentials.

The primary need for developing "full costs" is to enable the decision maker to know what costs the contribution covers. Those who favor traditional full costing for pricing purposes maintain that a knowledge of direct costs and contribution may provide an excuse for price cutting. That is, since the contribution amount is usually larger than the gross profit figure, the decision maker might be tempted to reduce prices. Hence, the full-cost advocates claim that fixed or period costs must be allocated so that each product or segment "carries its proper share," "pulls its own weight," or "is charged fairly." Over time, various methods of full-cost pricing have evolved, and, as shown in this chapter, each method leads to a different price.

Price should not be conceived as the residual of the costing process. Buyers generally are not concerned that the sellers have covered all their costs but rather with the perceived value of the product in relation to its price. Essentially, price must be acceptable to the market and above direct variable costs.

Developing a full-cost estimate provides the price setter with a range of acceptable prices from the cost floor (the out-of-pocket cost level) to the market-determined ceiling. As the building blocks of Fig. 8-1 illustrate, a direct costing approach can provide both the direct costs and the full costs, thereby enabling the price setter to know whether the contribution covers full costs. Such information should help prevent the occurrence of unwise price reductions.

On the other hand, direct costing helps prevent the use of formulas, magic numbers, factors, percentages, or other illogical techniques for determining price. Short-cut formulas victimize the decision process and the firm rides the roller coaster of profits and losses as the formulas approach or depart from actual costs. The formula approach is like spreading period costs with a bulldozer, filling in holes and leveling peaks.[1]

Today, there is increasing concern that current management accounting techniques are obsolete, and not very useful for managerial decision making.[2] To understand this argument, we will briefly review the history of management accounting and isolate the current arguments against contemporary management accounting. The full-cost method of pricing then will be developed, and the sensitivity of selling price to the way in which overhead is allocated to the product will be illustrated. Next we will develop the concept of overhead and illustrate how different methods may be used to assign overhead or common costs to profit segments. Each method of overhead application will be presented and discussed. The discussion will point out that many overhead costs can be classified as fixed and variable and that a functional approach can be used to assign these costs to products. The functional or activity approach is an adaptation of the net profit approach of assigning marketing costs discussed in Chap. 9. One widely used variant of full-cost pricing is target-return pricing, and this approach will be developed and illustrated at the end of the chapter.

MANAGEMENT ACCOUNTING: A HISTORICAL PERSPECTIVE

In recent years, problems of North American manufacturing have dominated debate in industrial and governmental arenas. Competition from higher quality, lower priced goods produced in Western Europe and Japan has caused great concern. Increasingly, there are admonitions that senior managers need to shift their focus from short-term measures of financial performance to indicators of longer run competitiveness and profitability. We continuously hear of firms reorganizing their activities and structures to better meet competition, but little has happened in the development of cost systems for managerial decisions, despite these organizational and activity changes. To understand today's costing practices, it is important to reflect on how these cost systems evolved over the past hundred years.

[1]Spencer A. Tucker, *Pricing for Higher Profits* (New York: McGraw-Hill, 1966), p. 32.
[2]See "The Productivity Paradox," *Business Week,* June 6, 1988, pp. 100–114.

The beginnings of modern cost accounting techniques apparently began in the 1850s to support the need for internal planning and control by textile mills and railroads.[3] Both textile mills and railroads needed some form of internal procedures to provide performance information on multiple processes and activities. The textile mills converted raw materials into a variety of finished goods and they needed to devise ways of efficiently managing the common resource, cotton. Railroads had an enormous number of cash transactions and needed a system for generating summary financial statements and evaluating the performance of various subunits and classes of service. Essentially, each of these industries had multiple products or services using a common resource.

During the 1880s, mass distribution and mass production firms emerged and adopted the internal accounting systems devised by the railroads. The Carnegie Steel Company developed a system that provided elaborate and detailed cost information on processes and products. For pricing, the company developed detailed cost estimates before submitting a bid to provide steel to a customer. Despite the elaborate nature of these cost systems, they focused only on the direct costs such as labor and materials, giving little attention to overhead or capital. Fixed costs were not allocated to products or periods. It was not until the "scientific management" movement of the early 1900s that firms began to measure and allocate overhead costs to products. A. Hamilton Church, an early developer of cost accounting techniques, argued against allocating overhead costs on the basis of direct labor and instead argued, as pointed out in Chap. 9, for direct measurement and accounting of these costs.[4] J. Maurice Clark in the 1920s advocated the use of statistical techniques for measuring costs and argued for the need to separate the cost accounting system from the financial accounting system.[5]

The development of managerial control systems apparently began with DuPont in the early 1900s and was extended and refined by one of the company's financial officers, Donaldson Brown. Later, when DuPont helped a financially troubled General Motors, Donaldson Brown worked with Alfred Sloan to develop the target return on investment approach for operational management. Based on this management control system, Donaldson Brown devised the target-return pricing formula that is still in use today. (We will develop and illustrate this approach later in the chapter.) It is important to note that GM did not use the formula blindly but, adjusted its prices according to economic and competitive conditions. Also, it was during this period of development that depreciation first became an element of fixed costs (perhaps coinciding with the beginnings of the U.S. federal income tax). Few developments other than the emergence of capital budgeting in the 1950s have been of note in the practice of managerial cost accounting.

As mentioned earlier, current managerial accounting practices have become obsolete. As this brief review of the early development of management accounting

---

[3]Robert S. Kaplan, "The Evolution of Management Accounting," *The Accounting Review,* 59 (July 1984), 390–418.

[4]A. Hamilton Church, *The Proper Distribution of Expense Burden* (New York: The Engineering Magazine, 1908).

[5]J. Maurice Clark, *Studies in the Economics of Overhead Cost* (Chicago: University of Chicago Press, 1923).

indicates, current practice differs in several important ways from initial developments, and current practice lags behind the realities of current manufacturing,
marketing, and distribution practice.[6] Although undoubtedly there are many reasons
for this state of affairs, one important reason is that today's accounting practices are
dominated by the conventions developed for external reporting. It is clear from
earlier chapters that there is a need to develop internal reports that are sensitive to
and supportive of management's information needs. Hence, like many European
companies, American firms need to develop a costing system that is useful for
internal operations, thereby requiring two sets of accounting reports. Indeed, many
managers, on being rebuffed by their accounting information systems, have resorted
to "guerrilla accounting" with separate internal information generated outside the
controller's office. Because accounting information often is not useful for managerial
decisions, managers sometimes reclassify cost information as suggested in Chaps. 7
and 8. Then, they perform the types of analyses developed in Chap. 8 before making
pricing and other marketing decisions. The "guerrilla" tactics occur because they
are unable to obtain cost information relevant to their needs from the accounting
department. In the remainder of this chapter, the illogical full-cost and target-return
pricing approaches are illustrated to clarify the inability of these approaches to help
managers become proactive pricers. Some prescriptions are offered for taking a more
functional approach to "full costing" in order to improve the limited role of costs
for pricing decisions.

FULL-COST METHOD OF PRICING

The full-cost method is popular because it is easy to explain and justify to buyers
and to the government. However, the main premise of the method is that all products
must bear their full share of costs. Thus, the method assumes that if all the assigned
costs are covered by the selling price, then all costs will be recovered.

Using the full-cost (or cost-plus) method of pricing, a percentage of variable costs
is added to the average variable costs to determine selling price. Presumably, this
percentage or margin covers overhead costs and profit. In equation form this decision rule is

$$\text{Price} = (1 + m) \text{ (variable costs)} \qquad (10\text{-}1)$$

where m is markup. As the equation indicates, the pricing decision actually reduces
to determining the size of m.

Sellers commonly resort to this pricing method because:[7]

---

[6]These indictments are well documented in Robert S. Kaplan, "Yesterday's Accounting Undermines
Production," *Harvard Business Review*, 62 (July–August 1984), 95–101; Robert S. Kaplan, "Accounting
Lag: The Obsolescence of Cost Accounting Systems," *California Management Review*, 28 (Winter 1986),
174–199; and Robert S. Kaplan, "Measuring Manufacturing Performance: A New Challenge for Managerial Accounting Research," *The Accounting Review*, 58 (October 1983), 686–705.

[7]R. L. Hall and C. J. Hitch, "Price Theory and Business Behavior," *Oxford Economics Papers*, No.
2, May 1939.

1 They do not know consumer preferences and therefore are unable to determine product demand and revenue schedules.

2 They do not know how rival sellers will react to price changes, but competitors are expected to follow price reductions and not follow price increases.

3 They do not know the degree to which demand is sensitive to price changes and therefore do not know the effects on revenues if prices are changed.

4 There is a traditional belief that prices ought to equal full cost, that full-cost pricing produces the "right" or "fair" price.

As these reasons suggest, the full-cost method of pricing provides for some price stability, and prices change only when average variable costs change. Presumably, since labor and material cost changes would similarly affect competing sellers, competitive reaction to price changes produced by cost changes would be predictable and in the same direction. Thus, pricing decisions based on markup rules are not thought to be responsive to demand or shifts in demand.

Perhaps the greatest weakness of this pricing method is that in practice full costs refer to fully allocated costs. Fully allocated costs refer to costs assigned to products using common facilities by the firm. Multiproduct firms may produce different products using essentially the same kind of inputs and equipment. Moreover, these products may benefit from the use of common administrative, selling, and distribution facilities. Usually these common costs are allocated to the products on an expected-volume basis using arbitrary allocation rules.

To appreciate how these arbitrary allocation rules affect selling price, consider the following four formulas:

I Assign production overhead as 150 percent of direct labor and to the total of labor, material, and production overhead, add 10 percent for administrative, selling, and distribution overhead (A, S, D overhead).

II Assign all overhead as 100 percent of direct material cost.

III Assign all overhead as 200 percent of direct labor cost.

IV Assign production overhead as 100 percent of direct material costs and all other overhead as 50 percent of direct labor cost.

Any of these formulas applied to labor and/or material costs will recover overhead *annually*. However, when applied to determine unit selling price, the results are quite different, as Table 10-1 shows. Table 10-2 summarizes these very different results. Note that product A's price could range between $23.10 and $36.30, depending on the overhead allocation formula. Even more dramatically, product C's price could range between $33.00 and $71.50. The executive may wonder why the concern, if everyone in the industry sets price in a similar way. The answer is that it is not possible to determine the relationship between price, volume, and costs to analyze different alternative approaches to maintaining or improving profitability. Hence, when inflation is a way of life, some resources are scarce, and customers are unhappy with frequent across-the-board price increases, the firm has inadequate cost data to make relevant pricing and product line decisions.

This example also illustrates a major reason why current cost accounting is

TABLE 10-1
EXAMPLE OF FULL-COST PRICING METHOD

Price Computations	Product A	Product B	Product C
Costs			
1. Direct labor	$ 2.00	$ 5.00	$20.00
2. Direct material	15.00	10.00	5.00
Formula I			
3. Production overhead (150% of 1)	$ 3.00	$ 7.50	$30.00
4. Subtotal (1 + 2 + 3)	$20.00	$22.50	$55.00
5. A, S, D overhead (10% of 4)	2.00	2.25	5.50
6. Total cost (4 + 5)	$22.00	$24.75	$60.50
7. 10% markup (m)	2.20	2.48	6.05
8. Selling price (6 + 7)	$24.20	$27.23	$66.55
Formula II			
9. Overhead (100% of 2)	$15.00	$10.00	$ 5.00
10. Total cost (1 + 2 + 9)	$32.00	$25.00	$30.00
11. 10% markup (m)	3.20	2.50	3.00
12. Selling price (10 + 11)	$35.20	$27.50	$33.00
Formula III			
13. Overhead (200% of 1)	$ 4.00	$10.00	$40.00
14. Total cost (1 + 2 + 13)	$21.00	$25.00	$65.00
15. 10% markup (m)	2.10	2.50	6.50
16. Selling price (14 + 15)	$23.10	$27.50	$71.50
Formula IV			
17. Production overhead (100% of 2)	$15.00	$10.00	$ 5.00
18. A, S, D overhead (50% of 1)	1.00	2.50	10.00
19. Total cost (1 + 2 + 17 + 18)	$33.00	$27.50	$40.00
20. 10% markup (m)	3.30	2.75	4.00
21. Selling price (19 + 20)	$36.30	$30.25	$44.00

considered obsolete. In many contemporary manufacturing firms, labor costs as a proportion of total manufacturing costs have declined as automation and computer-aided production processes became widespread. Thus, to attempt to allocate overhead costs by marking up labor costs simply further retreats from any semblance of logic. The solution, as outlined later in this chapter, is to go to activity or functional accounting. One company adopting this activity approach, which works by figuring out the costs of every operation, including overhead, deter-

TABLE 10-2
SELLING PRICES FROM FORMULAS I TO IV

Product	Formula			
	I	II	III	IV
A	$24.20	$35.20	$23.10	$36.30
B	27.23	27.50	27.50	30.25
C	66.55	33.00	71.50	44.00

mined that previous calculations for production costs were off by as much as 60 percent.[8]

A final point is that the foregoing full-costing decision rules do not consider the different ways in which assets are combined to produce the product. For example, in Table 10-1, product A is materials intensive, whereas product C is labor intensive. Does product A require more fixed capital in the way of processing machinery than does product C? If so, the burden that product A places on the firm is substantially different from that of product C. Yet none of the illustrated pricing formulas is able to reflect the different ways in which these products incur costs. (It should be noted that each of these formulas is used by industrial firms.)

THE NATURE OF OVERHEAD

The key to full-cost estimating is the method of charging period or time costs to individual products or orders. Direct product costs are generated with the product or service and exist only when the product is made or the service is offered. The period portion of variable costs does not vary directly with the product or service, but instead varies with overall output. For example, if sales increase 30 percent during the period, additional clerical help might be hired to handle the ordering and billing. There are also fixed period costs, e.g., real estate taxes, which are not identifiable with any specific product or service. These expenses occur at the same amount regardless of volume.

Overhead is that portion of period costs that cannot be objectively traced to particular operations, products, or other profit segments. To determine a full cost, this overhead must be allocated to the profit segments on some basis. *Overhead distribution* involves assigning overhead costs to individual units within a profit segment, e.g., products, customer accounts.

Overhead Distribution

Overhead costs are distributed to profit segments (1) as a percentage of direct labor cost or time; (2) as a percentage of direct labor and direct material costs; (3) as a

[8]"The Productivity Paradox," *Business Week,* June 6, 1988, pp. 100–114.

percentage of conversion costs; (4) as a percentage of direct material costs; (5) on the unit-of-product basis; (6) on a percentage of sales volume; (7) on a machine-hour rate method; or (8) on a functional basis. Each of these methods will result in differing applications of overhead costs for the same product and therefore are suspect as a means for determining price. Some of these methods may be actual rates, e.g.,

$$\text{Rate} = \frac{\text{actual overhead}}{\text{actual direct labor hours or direct labor costs}}$$

An actual overhead rate has the advantage of distributing the actual, incurred overhead cost. However, such a rate is not available until the end of the accounting period, it is a historic rate, and it is subject to seasonal and cyclical fluctuations as actual overhead costs and activity levels change. Normally, overhead rates are based on an operating plan or budget derived from recent and expected cost experiences.

Overhead Application

We now will review some currently popular methods used to determine full-cost estimates. As has been suggested, applying overhead to products or other business segments following arbitrary allocation rules often fails to accurately identify the actual costs that a product or product line is responsible for. Hence, the attempt to have each product carry its "fair share" of the burden may in fact be very unfair and, importantly, inaccurate. This lack of accuracy may have some very important implications for pricing the company's products and services. As each approach is presented, a brief commentary on the method will be made.

Direct Labor Cost   The assignment of overhead as a percentage of direct labor cost is one of the oldest and most popular methods.

$$\text{Rate} = \frac{\text{overhead charge}}{\text{direct labor cost}} \tag{10-2}$$

For example, if total overhead to be assigned is \$711,750 and total budgeted direct labor cost is \$474,500, then

$$\text{Rate} = \frac{\$711,500}{\$474,500} = 1.5 = 150\%$$

To illustrate the direct labor cost method and the other methods to be discussed, two products will be used for comparative purposes. Product A is made on older equipment and requires more labor than product B, which is produced on modern, relatively expensive equipment.[9] Table 10-3 lists the basic data for these two products and illustrates the application of the direct labor cost method.

[9]These examples are adapted from Spencer A. Tucker, *Pricing for Higher Profits* (New York: McGraw-Hill, 1966), pp. 32–40.

TABLE 10-3
OVERHEAD COSTS APPLIED ON THE BASIS OF DIRECT LABOR COST

Cost Element	Product A	Product B
Direct material	$ 6.00	$ 6.00
Direct labor	8.00	3.00
Overhead (150% of direct labor)	12.00	4.50
Total cost	$26.00	$13.50

This method assumes there is a direct relationship between overhead costs and direct labor and ignores the possibility that low-labor items, such as product B, require large overhead support. One result is that labor-intensive products may be overcosted, whereas low-labor products using expensive facilities may be undercosted. Hence, the expensive facilities are likely to be kept busy, perhaps even in excess of normal capacity. Consequently, this costing method may lead to unprofitable volume if price reductions are used to build volume of product B.

Direct Labor Plus Direct Material Costs   This method is applied using

$$\text{Rate} = \frac{\text{overhead charge}}{\text{direct labor cost} + \text{direct material cost}} \qquad (10\text{-}3)$$

Hence, if the overhead charge is $711,750 and total direct labor and material costs are $1,423,500, then

$$\text{Rate} = \frac{\$711,750}{\$1,423,500} = 0.50 = 50\%$$

This method assumes a direct relationship between the sum of direct material and direct labor costs and overhead costs. Hence, a relatively high-material-content product produced on inexpensive facilities will be overburdened because of the nature of its content. Thus, overhead may be assigned on the basis of two direct costs,

TABLE 10-4
OVERHEAD COSTS APPLIED ON THE BASIS OF DIRECT
LABOR PLUS DIRECT MATERIAL COSTS

Cost Element	Product A	Product B
Direct material	$ 6.00	$ 6.00
Direct labor	8.00	3.00
Total	$14.00	$ 9.00
Overhead (50% of total)	7.00	4.50
Total cost	$21.00	$13.50

both of which may vary without directly affecting actual overhead costs. As a result, products with the lowest combinations of materials and labor are assigned the least overhead burden, despite what the actual load on the firm may be. For example, if the low-material- and labor-content product is frequently ordered in small shipping amounts, the ordering, billing, and shipping burden may not be reflected in its actual overhead charges and the product will be undercosted. Table 10-4 illustrates this method.

Direct Material Costs   Now the rate is determined using

$$\text{Rate} = \frac{\text{overhead charge}}{\text{direct material cost}} \qquad (10\text{-}4)$$

If overhead charges are $711,750 and total direct material costs are $949,000 then

$$\text{Rate} = \frac{\$711,750}{\$949,000} = 0.75 = 75\%$$

As illustrated in Table 10-5, only one cost factor, materials, is used as the allocation base. Even though each product probably makes different use of the facilities, each has the same overhead burden. For industries that have uniform bulk materials, such as forgings, cement, sugar, or paint, this method is easy and equitable. But if products use facilities differing considerably in capital cost, it is a faulty cost allocation method.

Unit-of-Product Basis   The unit-of-product charge is determined by

$$\text{Overhead per unit} = \frac{\text{overhead charge}}{\text{expected total volume}} \qquad (10\text{-}5)$$

If overhead costs are $711,750 and the expected volume of products A and B is 52,350 and 90,000 units respectively, then the overhead charge per unit is

TABLE 10-5
OVERHEAD COSTS APPLIED ON THE BASIS OF DIRECT MATERIAL
COSTS

Cost Element	Product A	Product B
Direct material	$ 6.00	$ 6.00
Direct labor	8.00	3.00
Overhead (75% of direct material)	4.50	4.50
Total cost	$18.50	$13.50

$$\text{Overhead per unit} = \frac{\$711,750}{52,350 + 90,000} = \$5$$

Table 10-6 illustrates this method. Again we observe that products using the facilities differently have the same overhead charge, which is illogical. This method is frequently found in process production systems where a few products are made and where the products have common factors such as weight or volume.

Conversion Costs Using this method, the overhead rate is given by

$$\text{Rate} = \frac{\text{overhead charge}}{\text{direct labor cost} + \text{indirect manufacturing cost}} \tag{10-6}$$

If the overhead charge is $711,750, total direct labor cost is $474,500, and indirect manufacturing cost is $237,250, the overhead rate is

$$\text{Rate} = \frac{\$711,750}{\$474,500 + \$237,250} = 1.0 = 100\%$$

As Table 10-7 shows, this method is similar to the direct labor method in that it assumes that overhead costs vary with direct conversion costs. However, there is

TABLE 10-6
OVERHEAD COSTS APPLIED ON THE
UNIT-OF-PRODUCT BASIS

Cost Element	Product A	Product B
Direct material	$ 6.00	$ 6.00
Direct labor	8.00	3.00
Unit overhead	5.00	5.00
Total cost	$19.00	$14.00

TABLE 10-7
OVERHEAD COSTS APPLIED ON THE BASIS OF CONVERSION COSTS

Cost Element	Product A	Product B
Direct material	$ 6.00	$ 6.00
Conversion costs		
Direct labor	8.00	3.00
Indirect manufacturing	1.00	2.00
Period overhead (100% of conversion costs)	9.00	5.00
Total cost	$24.00	$16.00

a refinement in that some indirect manufacturing costs are charged directly to the products. Also, the method does not use material as a basis for allocating overhead costs. Both of these refinements are steps in the right direction.

Machine-Hour Rate   This method has the formula

$$\text{Rate per machine-hour} = \frac{\text{overhead charge}}{\text{machine-hours}} \tag{10-7}$$

As the formula indicates, a machine-hour rate is the cost of operating a profit segment for one hour in the processing of orders or products. The machine-hour rate is a rate of conversion cost. Overhead is applied to a product by multiplying the rate by the number of hours involved in specific operations. The machine-hour rate is expensive and is not universally applicable. It is best used when machinery operations comprise a significant portion of the product's total cost.

For example, if the total overhead is $711,750 and the total estimated machine-hours for the planning period is 71,175, then

$$\text{Machine-hour rate} = \frac{\$711,750}{71,175} = \$10 \text{ per hour}$$

Therefore, if product A requires 30 minutes of machine time and product B requires 2 hours, then the overhead charges are $10(0.5) = $5 and $10(2) = $20 respectively, as shown in Table 10-8.

The machine-hour rate represents a further refinement in allocating overhead, because it is based on the different ways in which the products use the facilities. However, even this method does not consider the different ways in which a product incurs overhead. All administrative and marketing expenses are lumped together with indirect manufacturing expenses. Hence, this method assumes a cause–effect relationship between total overhead and machine time.

Functional Costs   As discussed in Chap. 7, costs can be classified as either variable or fixed with respect to changes in activity levels. Materials and direct labor

TABLE 10-8
OVERHEAD COSTS APPLIED BY THE MACHINE-HOUR
RATE

Cost Element	Product A	Product B
Direct material	$ 6.00	$ 6.00
Conversion costs		
Direct labor	8.00	3.00
Total overhead	5.00	20.00
Total cost	$19.00	$29.00

generally are classified as variable costs. As Table 7-1 indicates, other costs may also be classified as variable. Hence, it would seem sensible to classify traditional overhead accounts also as variable or fixed. Indeed, as developed in Chap. 9, many marketing costs are variable and, even if fixed for the period, are directly or indirectly traceable to products, territories, or customer accounts.

To be able to classify overhead as either fixed or variable requires a careful study of how the particular costs are incurred. The following classification is a sample of how period costs (overhead) might be classified into variable or fixed:

Period Variable Cost	Period Fixed Cost
Plant supplies	Rent
Maintenance	Insurance
Power and light	Property taxes
Indirect labor	Depreciation
Order processing costs	General administration
Storage and shipping costs	Research and development

As the preceding list indicates, many costs are incurred during the period and are fixed in the sense that management has contractually agreed to incur these costs. These costs often can be shown to vary with activity levels, at least after some minimal level of activity has occurred. For example, salaried clerks are hired to take orders, but each order requires a specific amount of work, such as recording the customer's name and address, checking the customer's credit reference, and obtaining the customer's account number. However, the cost of processing an order for a specific quantity of a single item is lower than the cost of processing a multi-item order in terms of clerical time both in processing the necessary paperwork and in physically preparing the order for shipping. As discussed in Chap. 9, when the objective is to assign "full costs" to specific products, customers, or territories, then a careful analysis of how costs are incurred will permit a more logical determination of "full costs."

By applying the hour-rate method just described to classify manufacturing overhead into variable and fixed components and by using the net profit approach on marketing and distribution costs, there will be a much smaller pool of common or general costs that are not easily attributable to a product or profit segment (see Fig. 8-1).

In the illustration in Table 10-9, indirect manufacturing costs would be applied on the basis of the machine-hour rate. Direct and indirect marketing costs would be applied on the basis of the net profit method discussed in Chap. 9. Hence, for product A, objectively traceable costs are $20.00, or 89 percent of the "full costs"; for product B, the objectively traceable costs are $20.00, or 85 percent of the "full costs." Further, the direct costs for product A are $17.00 and for product B, $14.00.

For this firm, then, the minimum acceptable prices are $17.00 for A and $14.00

TABLE 10-9
OVERHEAD COSTS APPLIED TO PRODUCTS ON A
FUNCTIONAL BASIS

Cost Element	Product A	Product B
Direct material	$ 6.00	$ 6.00
Conversion costs		
Direct labor	8.00	3.00
Indirect manufacturing	1.00	2.00
Direct marketing	3.00	5.00
Indirect marketing	2.00	4.00
Period variable costs	1.20	1.80
Period fixed costs	1.30	1.70
Total cost	$22.50	$23.50

for B. If the market will accept a full-cost price and the desired profit margin over full cost is 20 percent, then prices could be set at $27.00 for A and $28.20 for B.

On the other hand, if the market is not ready to accept a full-cost price because of buyer reactions and competitive prices, management must consider less than full-cost prices. The direct costs provide the floor on prices. Finally, it is also possible that prevailing market prices for products A and B are higher, say $29 for A and $35 for B. Again, management would seriously want to consider departing from a "full-cost plus standard profit margin" price.

Summary

Full-cost, or cost-plus, pricing is a widespread practice, mainly because it is considered fair to both buyer and seller. Seemingly, the buyer is protected against overcharging and the seller is protected against a loss. However, full-cost pricing is useful only to give management a general indication of prices necessary to achieve specific profit objectives.

It is necessary for the seller to attribute the various types of costs to the products or facilities from which they derive. Direct costs that are identifiable with, and traceable to, a specific profit segment present no real difficulty. But the allocation of fixed or period costs requires some basis for applying these costs to the different profit segments. Despite the inherent logic in some of the methods for applying overhead, they are still arbitrary. It is indefensible to believe there is one right allocation method. As shown in Table 10-10, the full-cost estimate can vary significantly, depending on the method used to allocate period or overhead costs. Such differences result primarily from manufacturing methods. Generally, a product that is relatively labor intensive has a greater chance of being assigned a relatively larger overhead burden despite the burden it places on the manufacturing and marketing processes.

TABLE 10-10
SUMMARY OF DIFFERENT FULL-COST METHODS

	Full Cost	
Basis of Applying Overhead	Product A	Product B
Direct labor	$26.00	$13.00
Direct labor and materials	21.00	13.50
Direct material	18.50	13.50
Unit of product	19.00	14.00
Conversion costs	24.00	16.00
Machine-hour rate	19.00	29.00
Functional basis	22.50	23.50

PRICING FOR RETURN ON PRODUCT INVESTMENT

According to the formula for pricing developed by Donaldson Brown, prices are based on an average sales estimate, or "standard volume." The overall pricing objective was to determine a standard volume large enough to cover fixed costs and variable production costs at a price customers were willing to pay, while still permitting the firm to earn a target return on investment. It was Brown's contention that the pricing objective was to obtain the highest rate of return on capital consistent with attainable volume.[10] A popular pricing method, commonly called target-return pricing, has been developed from this initial pricing concept. In a classic study of pricing practice, "target return on investment was probably the most commonly stressed of company pricing goals."[11]

The purpose of this section is to review the traditional approach to determining a target-return price, namely, the calculation of the profit per unit sold at which the target return will be achieved if actual demand equals forecasted demand. However, it will be shown that such an approach ignores the differences in capital investment required to produce various products. Some investment, e.g., in materials, is time sensitive and requires a specific rate of return formula. To handle this problem of different types of capital, contribution analysis will be extended to include considerations of return on investment. The technique developed in this chapter is being used by a major chemical company.

Target-Return Pricing

Target-return pricing is the development of a set of product prices designed to provide a predetermined return on capital employed in the production and distribution of those products.[12] In this pricing method, both costs and profit goals are based

---

[10]See "Detroit's Dilemma on Prices," *Business Week,* January 20, 1975, p. 82.

[11]A. D. H. Kaplan, Joel B. Dirlam, and Robert F. Lanzillotti, *Pricing in Big Business* (Washington, D.C.: Brookings Institution, 1958), p. 130.

[12]Robert Lanzillotti, "Pricing Objectives in Large Companies," *American Economic Review,* 48 (December 1958), 921–940.

on standard volume. *Standard volume* is the volume or quantity expected to be produced in the following year or an average volume expected to be produced over a number of future years. For an expected volume, the firm determines what its unit labor and materials costs must be and allocates its fixed costs over the expected volume to obtain a fixed cost per unit figure. To these standard costs is added a percentage of capital employed per unit volume to arrive at selling price. In equation form, the pricing rule is

$$P_r = \text{DVC} + \frac{F}{X} + \frac{rK}{X} \qquad (10\text{-}8)$$

where P_r = selling price determined when the target return is used
DVC = direct unit variable costs
F = fixed costs
X = standard unit volume
r = profit rate desired
K = capital (total operating assets) employed

Target-return pricing helps prevent cyclical or seasonal changes in volume from affecting prices unduly. That is, the firm expects that averaging the changes in cost and demand over seasons or business cycles will enable the firm to realize a desired rate of return on investment. However, as in full-cost pricing, pricing decisions based on target returns are not thought to be responsive to demand or shifts in demand. Target-return pricing provides some stability in making pricing decisions, since standard volume and standard costs are usually based on expected volume over a planning period. However, it makes little allowance for price competition. Perhaps the major reason for using this pricing approach is management's increasing concern with allocating scarce capital resources over many alternative uses.

To illustrate the application of this method, assume the data given in Table 10-11A. From these data, the selling price of each product can be obtained using Eq. (10-8):

$$P_A = \$8.00 + \frac{\$400,000}{200,000} + \frac{0.15(\$1,000,000)}{200,000} = \$10.75$$

$$P_B = \$6.00 + \frac{\$800,000}{400,000} + \frac{0.15(\$2,400,000)}{400,000} = \$8.90$$

Table 10-11B summarizes the data for each product for comparison purposes. If the company makes only these two products, and the expected volume of the product mix is realized, the target return is achieved. However, this approach ignores a number of factors, which may result in one or both products failing to achieve the desired return.

Disadvantages of the Target-Return Approach   First, this approach assumes the product sales mix will remain in a 2:1 proportion, ignoring market reaction to the

TABLE 10-11
TARGET-RETURN PRICING

	Product A	Product B
A. Planning data		
1. Direct variable cost per unit	$ 8.00	$ 6.00
2. Total fixed cost	$ 400,000	$ 800,000
3. Expected volume (units)	200,000	400,000
4. Desired rate of return	15%	15%
5. Total capital employed	$1,000,000	$2,400,000
B. Summary data		
6. Selling price	$ 10.75	$ 8.90
1. Direct variable cost	8.00	6.00
7. Contribution (6 − 1)	$ 2.75	$ 2.90
8. Return on sales (7 ÷ 6)	25.6%	32.6%
9. Markup on cost (7 ÷ 1)	34.4%	48.3%
10. Return on capital {[(7 × 3) − 2] ÷ 5}	15%	15%

formularized prices. As will be discussed in Chap. 13, acceptance of a product line's prices depends on price differentials within the line as well as price differentials with competitive offerings. Thus, the prices as formularized may not lead to the desired rates of return. For example, if actual sales volume at these prices is 180,000 units for A and 400,000 units for B, then the return on capital for A is only 9.5 percent, and overall the firm will have a rate of return of 13.38 percent.

A second difficulty is that markup is based on fully allocated costs. As noted in this chapter, a full-cost approach distorts the effects from a shift in activities of demand. Indeed, no out-of-pocket costs were developed, and it is not possible to analyze the effect on contributions of setting lower prices.

Third, this approach assumes that each product in the product line carries capital investments in the same proportions. That is, no distinction is made in production costs between materials cost and conversion cost. Presumably a materials-intensive product will require relatively more capital investment than a product for which the major proportion of costs is for conversion (see Fig. 8-1). As indicated later, the materials aspect of the capital assets structure develops the firm's rate of return differently than a piece of fixed equipment.

The Pricing Dilemma of the Auto Industry The target-return approach to pricing produces a startling paradox in pricing theory. When demand slackens and expected volume fails to materialize, a firm that is intent on maintaining a desired rate of return must raise its prices. Notice that in Eq. (10-8) both fixed costs and desired dollar return on capital are divided by X, the standard unit volume. If, however, actual demand is less than X, then the expressions F/X and fK/X increase in value, leading to a higher price, P_r. To illustrate, assume that demand for product A is only 180,000 units. Applying this value to the formula (10-8) produces

$$P_A = \$8.00 + \frac{\$400,000}{180,000} + \frac{0.15(\$1,000,000)}{180,000} = \$11.06$$

During the recession of 1974–1975, the automobile industry faced such a dilemma. Auto prices rose an average of $1,000 while sales fell by 25 percent.[13] Yet the automobile industry could not reduce prices, partly because of the industry's belief that demand for automobiles is either price inelastic or barely price elastic. And, as shown in Chap. 12, when pricing a mature product, demand must be sufficiently elastic for a price reduction to increase revenues more than the increase in variable costs due to increased demand. (See also the economic argument of this point in Chap. 2.)

However, the automobile industry also faced this pricing dilemma because of its inflexible, formularized method of pricing. Indeed, there had been some shift in demand to smaller, less profitable cars, but the automobile industry was unable to analyze either the significance of the shift in the product mix or the effect on contributions of a change in prices. "The next step in the industry's long and sometimes lacerating evaluation may be a more flexible pricing formula. This would require a whole new line of industry thinking, however. The problem is that change comes slowly in Detroit—as slowly, in fact, as a price cut."[14]

Elements of Capital

As noted earlier, pricing for return on investment utilizes the concept of capital as a means of determining the proper markup for pricing decisions. But we have not defined what constitutes capital. First, it is important to recognize that *total capital* is composed of current assets and fixed assets. *Current assets,* or *variable capital,* include cash, accounts receivable, and inventories. The amount of variable capital employed in producing and marketing a product varies according to changes in output and sales. *Fixed capital* represents the current value of fixed facilities, equipment, land, and machinery used to produce and market a product. The amount of fixed capital employed does not vary with output and sales. The value of fixed capital changes over time due to depreciation and investment in new capital.

The relationship of these elements of capital to sales and the concept of return on investment is illustrated in Fig. 10-1. As the figure shows, total capital employed is $7,000,000, of which $3,000,000 is in current assets. The figure also shows that a return on capital can be improved if the turnover can be improved, either by increasing sales with the same capital base or maintaining sales with a smaller capital base. In the short run, the firm can obtain a smaller capital base by reducing the average investment in current assets.

For example, in the figure, the sales to inventory ratio is 16.67. In other words,

[13]See "Detroit's Dilemma on Prices," *Business Week,* January 20, 1975, pp. 82–83.
[14]Ibid., p. 83. For more recent discussion about the automobile industry, see "GM's Price Hikes: Foresight or Folly?" *Business Week,* April 14, 1986, p. 36; "Why GM Is Risking Higher Prices," *Business Week,* September 16, 1985, p. 33; "Detroit Tries to Rev Up," *Business Week,* June 12, 1989, pp. 78–83.

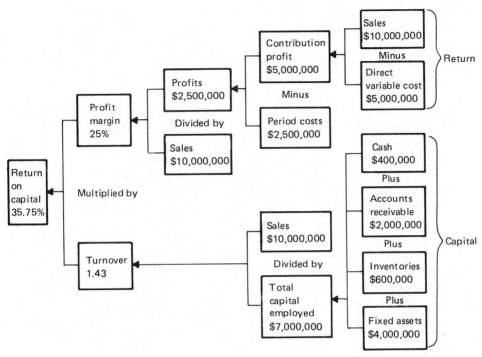

FIGURE 10-1
Return on capital. (Adapted and reprinted with permission from Sam R. Goodman, *Techniques of Profitability Analysis* [New York: Wiley, 1970], p. 117.)

inventory turns on the average 16.67 times during the planning period. If the average inventory could be reduced to $250,000, the sales–inventory ratio would be 40, and the overall return on capital would become 37.6 percent. If, through better management of cash, credit, and inventory, the current assets could be reduced by a million dollars, the capital turnover would become 1.67 and the overall return on capital would become 41.7 percent.

However, different products make different uses of the various elements of capital, and, as noted, variable capital varies with output and sales. We will discuss in Chap. 14 the role of the price structure in influencing the cash flow and level of accounts receivable. Now, we will develop the principle of pricing for product investment: *In the development of a product's price, the various elements of capital used to produce and market the product should be taken into account.*

Pricing for Contribution and Return

The goal of target-return pricing is to establish a target price to provide a contribution that will enable a firm to obtain a desired return on capital invested. From an analytical perspective, the objective is to establish a pricing method that facilitates the achievement of this pricing goal while incorporating the pricing principle established earlier in this chapter. Caution must be exercised in that, as with the automobile industry, a price that allows for a desired rate of return may not be acceptable to buyers or competitive in the marketplace. The method we will now develop is only the beginning of the pricing decision process.

In the production and sale of manufactured products two types of capital are used—variable and fixed capital. The variable capital includes cash, accounts receivable, and inventories. The amount of cash available is normally determined by cash management policy. For example, the controller may strive to maintain a cash balance equal to 15 days of expected cash disbursements. The amount of capital invested in accounts receivable is influenced by cash discount and credit policy. Inventory levels are generally planned to cover a predetermined number of production days for in-process and raw materials as well as a normal number of "selling days" for finished products. For example, the automobile industry tries to maintain new-car inventories between 40 and 60 days, assuming a normal rate of demand.

Generally, a manufactured product uses materials, labor, and equipment in the production process. From a cost perspective these inputs are segregated into material costs and conversion costs (see Fig. 8-1). Material costs usually constitute a variable investment in that they are more liquid, can be turned over faster, and can be adjusted as output demand varies. On the other hand, a significant portion of conversion costs relates to fixed operating facilities, representing a longer term investment that turns over at a slower rate.

For example, in Fig. 10-1, the amount of capital invested in cash is $400,000. Assume that this amount of cash represents a 20-day period of cash expenditures. Assume also that the firm wishes to earn a return of 25 percent on its capital. Therefore, $400,000 \times 20/360 \times 0.25 = \$5,555.56$ is the amount the firm must earn from this cash amount. As a percentage of the cash balance, the amount earned is 1.39 percent ($5,555.56/$400,000). Therefore, every 20 days, a cash balance of $400,000 must generate (earn) the amount of $5,555.56 if the firm is to receive a 25 percent return on its cash investment on an annual basis.

On the other hand, the fixed assets of $4 million are held throughout the operating year and must earn $1,000,000 if the 25 percent return is to be achieved. Hence, it is necessary to develop a means of pricing the variable assets in a product differently than the fixed assets. The key component of such a method is to segregate capital turnover into its fixed and variable elements rather than having one turnover ratio for all capital (see Fig. 10-1). The specific cost elements that comprise the direct variable costs should therefore be marked up individually to reflect their investment differences.

Developing the Markups[15]   Product A and product B in Table 10-12 can be used to illustrate this method of target-return pricing. Since both products have the same direct variable costs, they will make the same contribution if they are priced the

[15]This section is adapted from Spencer A. Tucker, *Pricing for Higher Profit* (New York: McGraw-Hill, 1966), pp. 159–178.

TABLE 10-12
BASIC DATA FOR TARGET-RETURN PRICING

Variable- Cost Elements	Product A	Product B
Materials	$15	$ 5
Conversion costs	3	13
Total variable costs	$18	$18

same. However, product A is materials intensive and requires relatively little labor and machine time; product B requires more labor and machine time. In most industries, product B would require considerably more investment in fixed capital than product A because it requires more than four times the amount of conversion effort needed for product A.

If products A and B are priced equally, then, ignoring market and competitive factors, at least one of the prices is incorrect from a target-return pricing perspective. Unless a distinction is made for differences in capital requirements, materials-intensive products are likely to be overpriced and fixed-capital-intensive products underpriced.

To develop separate markups for the different types of capital employed in

TABLE 10-13
ANNUAL PROFIT PLAN

A. Statement of Capital and Desired Return		
1. Total capital employed	$ 4,000,000	
2. Desired return (pretax)	20%	
3. Target earnings (1 × 2)	$ 800,000	
4. Period expenses	$ 1,500,000	
5. Target contribution (3 + 4)	$ 2,300,000	

B. Forecasts		
	Product A	Product B
6. Estimated sales (units)	500,000	800,000
7. Estimated materials cost	$7,500,000	$ 4,000,000
8. Estimated conversion costs	1,500,000	10,400,000
9. Total direct variable costs	$9,000,000	$14,400,000

C. Operating plan		
9. Total direct variable costs	$23,400,000	
5. Target contribution	2,300,000	
10. Required sales revenue (5 + 9)	$25,700,000	

producing a product, the first step is to develop an annual profit plan. As shown in Table 10-13, this annual plan consists of a statement of capital and desired rate of return, a forecast of unit sales, and an operating plan. It should be noted that, under this approach, the required sales revenue is derived from the plan, given the target profit objective, period expenses, and estimated sales volume. Clearly, the prices that result are derived from the sales revenue constraint developed in the annual profit plan.

Materials Cost Markup   The desired markup on materials cost is found by dividing the target return by the number of times the materials will turn over during the year. If, for example, the turnover is four times a year, then the markup on material investment is $^{20}\!/_{4}$, or 5 percent. Thus, each turn of material will provide a 5 percent return, and for the year a 20 percent return will be obtained. As seen in Table 10-14, the materials invested in each product will be marked up 5 percent.

Conversion Cost Markup   On an annual basis, the selling price of materials is $1.05 \times$ ($7,500,000 + $4,000,000), or $12,075,000. Since required revenues are $25,700,000, the markup on conversion costs must cover these costs plus target contribution, so that $13,625,000 is generated ($25,700,000 − $12,075,000). To avoid the distortion of marking up period costs, only the direct conversion costs are marked up. To determine this markup, the required revenues are divided by the total conversion costs:

$$\frac{\$13,625,000}{\$1,500,000 + \$10,400,000} = 1.145$$

As shown in Table 10-14, conversion costs will be marked up 14.5 percent to provide a return on fixed capital invested in manufacturing.

TABLE 10-14
PRICING FOR TARGET RETURN

Cost Element	Cost	×	Markup	=	Price
		Product A			
Materials cost	$15		1.05		$15.75
Conversion cost	3		1.145		3.44
Price to provide 20% return on capital					$19.19
		Product B			
Materials cost	$ 5		1.05		$ 5.25
Conversion cost	13		1.145		14.89
Price to provide 20% return on capital					$20.14

TABLE 10-15
CONTRIBUTION SUMMARY

	Product A	Product B
Target price	$19.19	$20.14
Direct variable costs	18.00	18.00
Contribution	$ 1.19	$ 2.14
PV	0.062	0.106

Applying the Separate Markups Table 10-14 shows the application of these separate markups in determining target selling prices. Although both products have the same direct variable costs, the target prices differ because of the different types of capital investment necessary to produce each product. As Table 10-15 shows, each product has a different contribution and PV ratio. If actual sales volume equals the sales estimate, then the target return is achieved. But, regardless of the different PV ratios, each product will earn the same return on total capital employed.

SUMMARY

The attempt to unitize period costs distorts prices and can actually lead to profitless prices and volume despite the relative "security" of believing the prices cover full costs. Full costing distorts the information needed to analyze the product mix and the marketing mix. Full-cost pricing fails to recognize that in multiproduct companies, the products are in different stages of their life cycles and will not be equally profitable. Finally, full-cost pricing does not recognize the benefits of low-price-induced volume, which may lead to lower per unit costs as volume increases. In the next chapter, the phenomenon of the experience curve is discussed and its impact on cost estimation is illustrated.

In this chapter, the problems of target-return pricing were discussed and a variation of the target-return method was illustrated. The primary advantage of the new method is that it recognizes variations in the type and amount of capital employed to produce different products. As a result of these variations, some products require larger markups to produce the same percentage return on capital. Use of this method will lead to a set of target prices that reflect the different types of investment needed for different products.

However, if final selling prices are set without consideration of market and competitive factors, this revised approach to target-return pricing will have the same disadvantages as the traditional approach. Moreover, the method relies on a unit-sales forecast that is developed without knowing the final selling price. Thus, this method should be used primarily to analyze the profit implications of alternative price/quantity estimates. As Table 10-15 indicates, neither dollar contributions nor PV ratios have to be equal for products to earn the same return on capital employed.

Firms must also consider the different ways capital is employed to produce different products.

DISCUSSION QUESTIONS

1 Discuss the role of cost in price decisions. How does the role of cost differ from that of demand?
2 Discuss the role of competition in price decisions.
3 Distinguish between full costing and direct costing for the purpose of pricing.
4 Direct costing as applied to pricing has sometimes been called marginal pricing or incremental pricing. Opponents of marginal pricing contend that this method of pricing may lead the price setter to accidentally or intentionally ignore costs that do not vary with volume. If this contention is correct, or at least possible, what safeguards would you propose to make sure the firm does not price its products unprofitably?
5 Most governmental regulatory agencies require a full-cost approach to rate setting. Why do you think they stress the full-cost approach? What are some arguments against the full-cost approach for regulating price? Can you think of a way to reconcile these differences in approach?
6 The Federal Trade Commission requires the use of full costs by any firm accused of illegally discriminating on the basis of price that wishes to use a cost-justification defense. What do you think is the rationale for this policy?
7 You are given the following information:

Item	Estimated Cost	Estimated Hours	Machine-hour Rate
Materials, per unit	$10.00		
Direct labor, per unit	2.00		
Machining, per unit		5	$7.50
Finishing, per unit		10	6.00
Bench work, per unit		20	6.50
Direct marketing	2,000		
Indirect marketing	500		
Variable overhead	1,400		
Fixed overhead	2,500		

a The forecasted sales volume is 1,000 units. If the firm uses the full-cost method of pricing and applies a markup, m, of 30 percent, what price should be set? (Note: The machine-labor rate includes manufacturing overhead.)
b Assume that just before the firm introduces this product to the market a competitor introduces a similar product priced at $250. What do you advise the firm to do? What is the logic of your recommendation?
c Assume that the competitor described in part b introduced the similar product priced at $350. What would your advice be? Why?
8 a Briefly describe the traditional approach to target-return pricing.
b What are the advantages and disadvantages of this approach?

9 a What is the pricing paradox that results when using the target-return approach to pricing?

b Illustrate this paradox by describing the problem of pricing automobiles.

10 Define the following:

a Variable capital.

b Fixed capital.

c Turnover.

d Return on capital.

11 a What is the principle of pricing for product investment?

b What cautions must be exercised when using a rate-of-return pricing approach?

12 Describe how markups for variable capital differ from markups for fixed capital.

13 The Delmarva Manufacturing Company is developing its operating plans for 19X1. The vice-president of finance recommends that the firm plan for a pretax return on capital of 25 percent. His report indicates that the firm currently has total assets of $10,000,000. The director of marketing research indicates that forecasts predict unit sales for product A of about 800,000 units and for product B of about 1,200,000 units. The vice-president of production estimates that these sales forecasts mean that production costs will be, per unit, as follows:

	A	B
Materials cost	$10	$ 5
Conversion costs	5	15

Fixed costs are estimated to be $2,500,000 for 19X1.

a Develop a profit plan for Delmarva.

b Develop a target price for products A and B. Assume materials turn over five times a year.

c What prices would you recommend? Why?

SUGGESTED READINGS

Anderson, Paul F.: "Theoretical and Implementational Problems of ROI Pricing," *Proceedings,* Special Conference on Marketing Theory (Chicago: American Marketing Association, 1980).

Deakin, Michael D.: "Pricing for Return on Investment," *Management Accounting,* 57 (December 1975), 43–44, 50.

"Detroit's Dilemma on Prices," *Business Week,* January 20, 1975, pp. 82–83.

Finerty, James J.: "Product Pricing and Investment Analysis," *Management Accounting,* 53 (December 1971), 15–18.

Kaplan, Robert S.: "Accounting Lag: The Obsolescence of Cost Accounting Systems," *California Management Review,* 28 (Winter 1986), 174–199.

Kaplan, Robert S.: "The Evolution of Management Accounting," *The Accounting Review,* 59 (July 1984), 390–418.

Lanzillotti, Robert: "Pricing Objectives in Large Companies," *American Economic Review,* 48 (December 1958), 921–940.

"The Productivity Paradox," *Business Week,* June 6, 1988, pp. 100–114.

Weston, J. Fred: "Pricing Behavior of Large Firms," *Western Economic Journal,* 10 (March 1972), 1–18.

Williams, Bruce R.: "Measuring Costs: Full Absorption Cost or Direct Cost?" *Management Accounting,* 58 (January 1976), 23–24, 36.

DEVELOPING PRICING STRATEGIES

Chapters 11 to 13 use the concepts and analyses presented in Chaps. 2 to 10 to discuss positive approaches to determining prices. The integration of both demand analysis and cost analysis for each decision is stressed.

In many pricing decisions it is crucial to forecast trends in market prices, particularly because competitive prices tightly constrain a firm's pricing discretion. Drawing on industrial examples, Chap. 11 extends the review of price forecasting methods presented in Chap. 7. Since price forecasting is also important in pricing products over their life cycles, Chap. 11 provides a transition from the demand and cost analysis given in Chaps. 2 to 10 to the determination of pricing decisions. Currently, the strategy of dominant market share is believed to be a basis of sales and profit growth. The experience curve phenomenon is often used to justify such a marketing strategy. Chapter 11 illustrates how the experience curve is used in pricing. Further, since many companies have attempted to develop pricing strategies using the experience curve as a strategy rather than an analytical technique, this chapter develops the conditions and requirements for an experience curve pricing strategy to be successful.

Chapter 12 focuses on the different pricing problems and solution approaches as the product matures through the life cycle. The chapter stresses analysis and planning pricing strategy. Behavioral and market implications are discussed, and costing and price forecasting techniques are applied. A major emphasis of Chap. 12 is the pricing of new products and services.

Most firms produce and sell many products that are demand related and sometimes also cost related. From a market perspective, such firms have discovered that there are specific price market segments for their products and that determining prices that differentiate these products is a complex process. Whether to add a midpriced product or reduce or increase the number of price offerings depends not only on the potential number of price market segments but also on clearly differentiating the products in the minds of buyers. Chapter 13 develops a behavioral approach to determining ways to position products in a line according to price. The chapter will also apply costing principles developed in earlier chapters to analyze the sales–volume mix and will suggest ways that pricing can be used to profitably change the sales–volume mix. This chapter will also explore the strategy of price bundling, a practice that has been widely used in recent years.

CHAPTER 11

EXPERIENCE CURVE PRICING

In many pricing decisions where competitive prices tightly constrain a firm's pricing discretion, it is common practice to forecast prices. Price forecasts are used in decisions about marketing strategy, new investments, budgeting, and purchase of materials.[1] However, such forecasts are based primarily on management's intuition, despite emerging theory and techniques of price forecasting. Moreover, even though profitability depends on prices, costs, and sales volume, much effort has been expended on forecasting costs and sales volume but little on forecasting prices. Indeed, many corporate plans forecast period sales volume, estimate the costs to reach the forecasted sales volume, and deduce the price "necessary" to achieve the profit objective.

This chapter provides a basis for moving from the problem of developing cost estimates covered in the preceding four chapters to the problem of setting prices. From an economic perspective, if we know the appropriate demand and supply schedules for a product, service, or commodity, it should not be difficult to forecast price. Unfortunately, it is not possible to have precise demand and supply information for a product at a particular time. Nevertheless, some useful tools for forecasting prices help reduce the uncertainty of business planning.

This chapter develops the specific technique of forecasting using the experience curve. The strategy of increasing market share has become a focal topic in the business literature. Price is often cited as a positive way to increase market share, i.e., decreasing prices faster than competition may lead to greater market share. The

---

[1]George B. Hegeman, "The Art of Price Forecasting," in Robert Ferber (ed.), *Handbook of Marketing Research* (New York: McGraw-Hill, 1974), pp. 4-286–4-294.

experience curve phenomenon is often cited as an explanation for this price–volume–market share relationship. Thus, for firms utilizing the experience curve there is a positive basis for developing a product's price over its life cycle.

Currently, there is some controversy of whether experience curve pricing is appropriate or possibly an obsolete approach. Critics of the approach cite examples of companies apparently using the experience curve as a basis of their marketing and pricing strategy and getting into difficulty. Yet there are examples of Japanese and United States companies that have successfully used the experience curve as a *tool* for developing pricing strategies. The Japanese used their ability to plan with the experience curve to achieve dominance in the motorcycle industry. Further, the Nippon Electric Company (NEC) has successfully used the experience curve to compete against AT&T and IBM in telecommunications and computers. Bausch & Lomb has used the experience curve to consolidate its position in the soft lens market.

What separates the winners from the losers in the use of the experience curve is an understanding of the experience curve, how it can be used to gain competitive advantage, and how to monitor the company's and competitors' progress down the experience curve. The experience curve is a tool to be used in developing pricing strategies; it is not a strategy per se. Correct use of this tool can be beneficial to a firm developing its pricing strategy. However, incorrect use of the experience curve—or simply assuming its existence—can lead to disastrous results.

THE PHENOMENON OF THE EXPERIENCE CURVE

It has been shown that costs decline by some characteristic amount each time accumulated volume is doubled.[2] Accordingly, because of the competitive nature of most products, prices tend to decline along a similar pattern as long as competitive relationships are stable. Given these long-term, predictable cost and price behavior patterns, it should become relatively easy to forecast costs and prices. Recently, a number of applications and approaches have been reported that make this technique a useful and practical tool for developing price strategies. Indeed, many companies have developed successful marketing and production strategies utilizing this relationship among costs, prices, and accumulated experience.

From a planning viewpoint, given the experience relationship, it is clear that a firm's costs can be projected. It is also clear that competitors' costs can be estimated given some basic market information. However, this cost–price relationship to accumulated experience does not occur by accident, and there are disadvantages in a strict utilization of this phenomenon.[3]

It is important to distinguish two approaches to this volume growth–cost reduction relationship. The *learning curve* (sometimes called the startup function or progress function) shows that *manufacturing costs* (primarily labor) fall as volume

[2]*Perspectives on Experience* (Boston: Boston Consulting Group, 1970).

[3]William J. Abernathy and Kenneth Wayne, "Limits of the Learning Curve," *Harvard Business Review*, 52 (September–October 1974), 109–119.

increases. Typical examples include air frames, industrial chemicals, and cameras. The *experience curve* shows that total unit costs of a product line decline over time as volume increases. Hence, the experience curve considers a broader range of costs, including material, marketing, and distribution costs. Gas ranges, facial tissues, motorcycles, and television receivers are typical examples.

Figure 11-1 shows the price–cost pattern for industrial chemicals.[4] Empirical data show that prices and costs tend to decline when reported on a *constant-dollar* basis. Hence, reductions in total costs for industrial chemicals should be predictable over time. The slope of the experience curve in Fig. 11-1 is 89 percent, which means that costs should decline about 11 percent during each period when *cumulative volume* doubles.

It is important to stress that this experience phenomenon is not automatic—it does not just happen. Rather, management effort is needed to ensure that it occurs, and its use as a technique in developing pricing strategies requires careful consideration. Management must know its direct and indirect product costs, must understand the sources of cost savings attributed to experience, and must estimate the actual experience curve that applies to its operation. Further, management must understand the particular circumstances when the experience curve can be used to its advantage. One industrial company had been manufacturing small electric motors for nearly 20 years when it decided to reduce its prices, increase sales volume, and

[4]S. A. Billon and William D. Robinson, "Price–Cost Relationships: Industrial Chemicals," in American Marketing Association, *Broadening the Concept of Marketing* (Chicago: American Marketing Association, 1970), p. 42.

FIGURE 11-1
Price–cost pattern, industrial chemicals (89 percent experience).

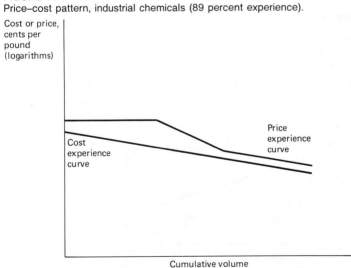

utilize the cost savings from sliding down its experience curve to improve profits. However, the firm lost substantial amounts of money because the experience effects were not available for a very mature product like small motors. Like many other firms, this company assumed the experience curve automatically operated at any time sales volume increased. The Sudbury Corporation, mentioned in Chapter 5, developed its annual operating plan by simply assuming it was further down the experience curve than its competitors. However, it had no idea what experience curve it was operating on, or even if it actually was realizing experience effects.

Costs and Experience

As noted, data show that costs tend to decline by a predictable amount each time accumulated experience is doubled. This phenomenon makes it possible to forecast not only one's own costs but also competitors' costs and industry average costs and prices. Generally this decline in costs ranges between 10 and 30 percent, with a usual decline of between 20 and 30 percent each time accumulated volume is doubled. In *constant dollars* this decline continues as long as demand for a product is growing. If demand is no longer growing, then the rate of cost decline slows down and approaches zero. Figure 11-2 is an example of a cost–price experience on a linear scale.

When accumulated volume of a product is increasing at a constant percentage rate, each year of product experience produces about the same percentage effect on cost. When plotted on log-log paper, percentage change is shown as a constant distance between two points (Fig. 11-3). A straight line means that a percentage change in one factor (accumulated volume) results in a predictable corresponding

FIGURE 11-2
Cost/price experience relationship.

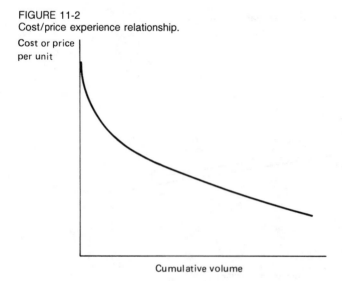

Cost or price per unit

Cumulative volume

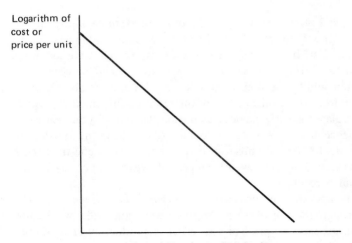

Logarithm of cost or price per unit

Logarithm of cumulative volume

FIGURE 11-3
Cost/price experience relationship.

change in the other factor (costs, price). The slope of the line reveals the nature of the relationship and can be read directly from the graph.

Three key points must be understood about the cost–price experience phenomenon. First, note that we are talking about *accumulated experience* (volume) over time and not about a doubling of the production or sales rate between two points in time. Table 11-1 illustrates this point. Assuming a constant market growth of 10

TABLE 11-1
ACCUMULATED EXPERIENCE

Year	Yearly Growth (10.0%)	Accumulated Experience	Periods of Doubling Experience, %
1	1.00	1.00	110.0
2	1.10	2.10	
3	1.21	3.31	121.0
4	1.33	4.64	
5	1.46	6.10	104.3
6	1.61	7.71	
7	1.77	9.48	
8	1.95	11.43	125.6
9	2.14	13.57	
10	2.36	15.93	
11	2.60	18.53	
12	2.86	21.39	

percent per year, column 2 shows the yearly sales index. For example, if sales in year 1 were 100,000 units, then sales in year 2 would be 110,000 units, and in year 3 sales would be 121,000 units. For the experience curve analysis, we are interested in the total production and sales from the beginning. Thus, at the end of year 2, accumulated experience would be the sum of sales of years 1 and 2, or 210,000 units. Analytically, we are interested in the amount of time that accumulated experience doubles. Thus, accumulated experience doubles during the second year relative to the first year's experience of 100,000 units. It doubles again during the fourth year, going from 200,000 units to 400,000 units, during the seventh year, and the twelfth year. Thus, during the second, fourth, seventh, and twelfth years, unit costs will have declined by a constant percentage.

The second point is that costs are measured in *constant dollars*. Hence, cost data must be deflated through the use of an appropriate economic deflator. Because inflation primarily masks the true price or cost effect of production or marketing improvements, price and cost data should always be developed on a constant-dollar basis to enable management to determine actual cost or price effects due to volume changes. Whenever inflation is a significant factor, as it was in the early and mid-1970s, a test of the sensitivity of the analysis to the inflation corrective factor should also be made.

Third, as noted in Chaps. 7–10, management must be careful about what costs are included in the analysis. As much as possible, costs that vary with activity levels should be considered, since any arbitrary cost allocations will tend to hide the real changes in costs. Hence, the emphasis should be on the controllable costs associated with value-added activities. That is, the relevant costs, as articulated in the previous four chapters, are the out-of-pocket or cash costs. In addition, variations in accounting practices between companies, or in the same company over time, will distort the cost–price trend line because of the distortions in reported costs.

Prices and Experience

Available data show that prices, in constant dollars, generally tend to decline by some given amount each time accumulated experience is doubled. In very competitive, rapid-growth, technological industries prices tend to parallel costs over time, as seen in Fig. 11-4. If prices do not parallel costs in early periods, then a kink in the price pattern may result, as seen in Fig. 11-5. During the introductory period, price may be set below cost to gain a foothold in the market (phase A) and in anticipation of lower costs in the future. (As shown in Chap. 12, some research demonstrates that in some circumstances, the best introductory pricing strategy is to price substantially below initial product costs.) In phase B, the initial seller and any entering sellers hold a price close to its initial level to recover operating losses incurred in the introductory period and to provide funds for rapid growth in capacity, working capital, research and development, and market development. Such a pricing strategy also encourages high-cost producers to enter the market. Eventually growth slows, late entrants cut prices to gain a foothold in the market, and the

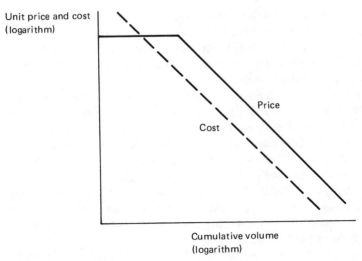

FIGURE 11-4
A stable cost/price experience relationship.

FIGURE 11-5
An unstable cost/price experience relationship.

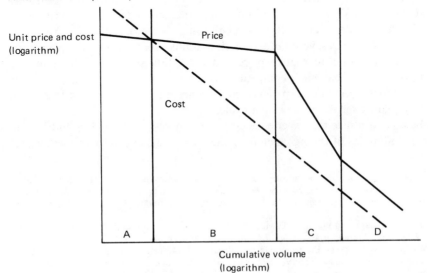

market leader reduces price to stem the erosion of market share. Thus, phase C, the shakeout period, prevails, and severe price competition forces prices to decline faster than costs.[5] Finally, in phase D, stability emerges as the price–cost relationship stabilizes. In phase D, the effect of experience on actual costs and prices becomes less noticeable and may actually disappear.

In a study of 82 petrochemical companies, it was found that the experience factor was the single most important variable explaining price declines.[6] Over intervals of five to seven years, the number of competitors, product standardization, and static scale economies were also significant explanatory variables of price declines.

In December 1975, video TV games were selling for $120–$130. In December 1976, these same games were selling in the $69–$79 range. By December 1977, these video games were selling for $19–$29. The primary reason for such a rapid decrease in price was that the electronic circuits for the games were mass produced in such volume that the labor, materials, and marketing costs per video game were a fraction of what they had been in the fall of 1975.[7]

At the end of April 1977, Texas Instruments (TI) reduced the price of one of its most popular digital watch models to $10, down from $20. In just over five years the price of a digital watch had fallen from $2,000 to $10! William B. Heye, Jr., manager of TI's Time Products Division, explained that lower prices were possible because production costs had dropped as volume grew. He indicated that initial production costs had been reduced 60 percent as volume increased.[8]

The reason for these greatly reduced prices lies in the incredible economies of scale realized in the manufacture of the computer chip. Every time cumulative volume doubled, the chips declined in cost about 30 percent. (That is, the cost experience curve for the computer chip was a 70 percent curve.) This basic decline in cost led to substantial declines in prices, and these in turn stimulated increased sales, which led to further reductions in costs. In 1971, a Sharp Electronics pocket calculator sold for $395; in 1978, a more sophisticated model sold for $10.95.[9]

The implications of such price–cost relationships are profound. The experience curve relates costs, prices, volume, and profit margins over time, providing a powerful tool for evaluating alternative price and marketing strategies. The ability to predict prices better than one's competition is a major strategic advantage over the long term. Finally, the price experience curve concept suggests the need to develop marketing plans over the product life cycle.

To be able to utilize the experience curve, it is necessary to understand how to obtain the estimates of the parameters of the curve. The appendix to this chapter

---

[5]Apparently the semiconductor industry has experienced such instability. See "The Semiconductor Becomes a New Marketing Force," *Business Week,* August 24, 1974, pp. 34–42. See also George S. Day and David B. Montgomery, "Diagnosing the Experience Curve," *Journal of Marketing,* 47 (Spring 1983), 44–58.

[6]Robert B. Stobough and Phillip L. Townsend, "Price Forecasting and Strategic Planning: The Case of Petrochemicals," *Journal of Marketing Research,* 12 (February 1975), 19–29.

[7]"TV's Hot New Star: The Electronic Game," *Business Week,* December 29, 1975; Peter Weaver, "Video Games Price Plummets," *Springfield* (Mass.) *Morning Union,* March 17, 1977, p. 25.

[8]"The Great Digital Watch Shake-Out," *Business Week,* May 2, 1977, pp. 78–80.

[9]"The Age of Miracle Chips," *Time,* February 20, 1978, pp. 44–58.

outlines an estimating procedure. We now turn to some of the caveats and principles of using the experience curve as a technique for developing pricing strategies.

MANAGING THE EXPERIENCE EFFECT

Although there is considerable empirical evidence supporting the experience curve phenomenon, its value can be realized only by careful management. There usually is not one but several experience curves for a product category for a firm, one occurring at every stage of the value-added process. That is, experience effects may be observed in research and development, procurement, fabrication and assembly, marketing, and distribution.

There are three major sources of the experience effect in each of these value-added stages. *Learning* occurs whenever people develop skills that allow them to be more efficient. These skills result from repetitive practice, the use of ingenuity, and increased dexterity. Discovering better ways to do the work, improving the work process, and dividing the tasks to permit specialization and standardization of the tasks may lead to increased productivity per worker. Learning may occur at all levels—production, marketing, and distribution.

Technological improvements are a second source of the experience effect. As volume increases, there are opportunities to improve the product and the production, marketing, and distribution processes. Changing from a labor-dominated production process to an automated one, substituting materials in the production process, and better management of the product–sales mix all result from increasing volume. Also, layout changes, improved ways of handling and storing materials and finished products, better maintenance procedures, and better distribution methods all provide the opportunity for reducing costs. However, these changes and activities, too, must be management directed; they do not just occur.

Economies of scale resulting from increased efficiencies due to size also contribute to the experience effect. Economies of scale can affect most value-adding functions and many factors combine to produce a downward trend in the cost curve as cumulative volume increases. The dominant factors influencing scale economies include improved technology for production, long production runs, integrating several manufacturing processes, the sharing of corporate resources across products, access to volume discounts in purchases, and shipping in full carload or truckload lots.

Types of Experience Curves

There are three important experience curves for strategic planning. The *firm's cost experience curve* relates changes in the firm's costs to changes in cumulative volume. This curve generally is the easiest to estimate, for it relies on internal cost and volume data. However, it is important to have appropriate data on direct and indirect traceable costs, including marketing and distribution. Further, these costs must be deflated costs reflecting only those costs representing a direct cash outlay. Thus, depreciation charges and general overhead are inappropriate for the analysis.

Competitor cost experience curves show the current costs of all direct competitors relative to their cumulative volume experience. These curves are more difficult to estimate because it is unlikely that competitors' costs can be known precisely. However, it is important not to assume that all competitors have essentially the same cost curve, or to assume that the first entrant or firm leading in market share has the cost advantage because of greater experience. Indeed, firms entering later may be able to operate on a steeper cost curve than the initial entering firm. Moreover, it is likely that they will be able to enter at a lower per unit cost than the first entrant, because of technology transfer and because suppliers have learned by serving the initial entrant. They may be able to enter with more current technology, a larger scale of operations, or distribution already in place. Further, over time, cost differentials tend to narrow between competitors.

Industry cost and price experience curves relate industry average costs and prices to cumulative volume. These curves are the hardest to establish, because it is difficult to determine average industry cost figures and actual selling prices. List prices are highly inaccurate because of discounts, rebates, and transportation allowances. Moreover, where there are several models with disparate features and accessories, and where different firms have different product and marketing mixes, the list prices will not be comparable. Further, as pointed out in Chap. 5, customers buy because they perceive value in use. And this perceived value can be changed by changing perceived benefits and services provided without directly changing the monetary price (see Fig. 5-2).

The Insatiable Appetite of Market Growth

As we saw in Chap. 8, price reduction strategies may be profitable when contribution margins or market growth is relatively high. Firms often develop price reduction strategies to "take advantage of the experience curve" because dramatic cost and price reductions have been reported for other products or industries. Tables 11-2 and 11-3 illustrate that this phenomenon not only requires growth but actually feeds on growth. Table 11-2 provides a per unit cost index for three experience curves—90, 80, and 70 percent—and for four levels of constant market growth—5, 10, 15, and 20 percent. It is apparent from Table 11-2 that differences for a particular experience curve are few whether the market is growing at a constant 5 or 20 percent. For a 90 percent experience curve, the per unit costs at the end of year 5 will range from 77 to 74 percent of the costs at the end of year 1. For an 80 percent experience curve, the costs at the end of year 5 will range from 58 to 52 percent of the year 1 costs, while for a 70 percent experience curve this range will be from 41 to 36 percent of the year 1 costs. Thus, although there is some interaction between the experience phenomenon and market growth, there are few differences across market growth rates if they are constant over time.

Table 11-3 illustrates the experience curve effect for a market that obtains an increasing rate of growth until year 5 and a decreasing rate of growth thereafter (similar to the concept of the product life cycle). Note that despite this growth pattern, there is little difference at the end of year 5, in terms of the cost indices,

TABLE 11-2
INDEXED COST REDUCTIONS: CONSTANT MARKET GROWTH

End of Year	Annual Market Growth			
	5%	10%	15%	20%
A. 90% Experience Curve				
1	1.00	1.00	1.00	1.00
2	0.90	0.89	0.89	0.89
3	0.84	0.83	0.83	0.82
4	0.80	0.79	0.78	0.77
5	0.77	0.76	0.75	0.74
6	0.75	0.73	0.72	0.71
7	0.73	0.71	0.69	0.68
8	0.71	0.69	0.67	0.65
9	0.69	0.67	0.65	0.63
10	0.68	0.66	0.63	0.61
B. 80% Experience curve				
1	1.00	1.00	1.00	1.00
2	0.79	0.79	0.78	0.78
3	0.69	0.68	0.67	0.66
4	0.62	0.61	0.60	0.58
5	0.58	0.56	0.54	0.52
6	0.54	0.52	0.50	0.48
7	0.51	0.48	0.46	0.44
8	0.48	0.46	0.43	0.41
9	0.46	0.43	0.40	0.38
10	0.44	0.41	0.38	0.35
C. 70% Experience curve				
1	1.00	1.00	1.00	1.00
2	0.69	0.68	0.67	0.67
3	0.55	0.54	0.53	0.51
4	0.47	0.45	0.44	0.42
5	0.41	0.39	0.37	0.36
6	0.37	0.35	0.33	0.31
7	0.34	0.31	0.29	0.27
8	0.31	0.29	0.26	0.24
9	0.29	0.26	0.23	0.21
10	0.27	0.24	0.21	0.19

for the three experience curves and the constant-growth results in Table 11-2. Indeed, the cost declines will be the same as if there had been a constant 10 percent market growth. The lesson of these two tables is clear: the use of price reductions to increase profits requires not only market growth but accelerating and large increments of growth. Although using price to build market share is a popular

TABLE 11-3
INDEXED COST REDUCTIONS: VARIABLE MARKET GROWTH

End of Year	Annual Market Growth, %	Experience Curve Slope		
		90%	80%	70%
1		1.00	1.00	1.00
2	5	0.90	0.79	0.69
3	10	0.84	0.69	0.55
4	15	0.79	0.61	0.46
5	20	0.76	0.56	0.39
6	15	0.73	0.51	0.34
7	10	0.70	0.48	0.31
8	5	0.68	0.45	0.28
9	3	0.67	0.42	0.25
10	2	0.65	0.41	0.24

strategy, it is clear that the firm must view this strategy as an investment and that the product must be expected to be sold in the marketplace for a lengthy period of time.

SUMMARY

This chapter reviewed methods of price forecasting with special emphasis on applying the experience curve to cost estimating. As explained in Chaps. 7–10, even though costs play a limited role in price decisions, they are an important determinant of prices and profits.

The key point of this chapter is that costs, prices, volume, and profit margins are related. And if these four concepts can be objectively related to one another, a powerful tool exists for evaluating alternative pricing strategies. Moreover, the capacity to predict prices over time is a strategic advantage for purchasing, production planning, demand estimation, and capital planning.

The cost–price experience curve provides a method for objectively relating costs, prices, volume, and profit margins. However, simply knowing how to use this tool will not in itself allow a firm to realize its benefits. Underlying the successful application of experience curves is a management philosophy that seeks every possible way to reduce costs while recognizing that a truly profitable product is one that satisfies customers' needs. Hence, management must remain market oriented.

Finally, cost, price, and volume analysis is a powerful conceptual and analytical tool. As shown in previous chapters, analytical techniques are not panaceas, nor do they simplify decision making. They do, however, provide a means for understanding the factors that cause certain predictable patterns to exist. Moreover, careful attention to trends and their underlying causes may help eliminate unsound pricing practices. The experience curve promises to be a useful analytical tool for forecasting costs and prices. In particular, using the experience curve to forecast the cost of a new product over its estimated life cycle can be helpful in planning the product's price during different life-cycle stages.

DISCUSSION QUESTIONS

1 Distinguish between a learning curve and an experience curve.
2 What is the role of cost estimating in developing a product's price?
3 Explain what is meant by the following concepts within the context of the experience curve:
  a Accumulated experience.
  b Constant dollars.
  c Cash flows.
4 Complete Table 11-1. In what year will accumulated experience double again?
5 The experience curve is often construed to reflect economies of scale due to mass production. Can you provide examples of economies of scale resulting from marketing?

APPENDIX: APPLYING THE EXPERIENCE CURVE

Opportunities to apply the experience curve are to be found in procurement, production, marketing, and finance. In purchasing, the experience curve may be used to negotiate a price or to analyze the make-or-buy decision. In cost estimation, decisions related to bidding, pricing, and capital investments may be based on the experience curve. Often contract negotiations are reopened after the experience of time and cost are known for the prototype unit. Indeed, aerospace firms follow this practice with the U.S. Air Force.

The experience curve can be defined if the total direct costs required to complete the first unit are established and if the improvement rate due to experience is specified. Alternatively, the experience curve can be defined if direct costs for a later unit and the experience curve rate are estimated.

The concept of constant reduction of cost (or time) between doubled accumulated volumes can be expressed as

$$TC_x = KX^{1-b} \tag{11-1}$$

where TC_x = cumulative total direct cost
  X = number of units
  K = cost estimate for the first unit
  b = slope parameter or a function of the experience (improvement) rate, $0 < b < 1$

The cumulative average cost, AC_x, is

$$AC_x = KX^{-b} \tag{11-2}$$

The experience curve is usually plotted on double logarithmic paper. The plot of Eq. (11-2) will result in a straight line on log-log paper. Thus, the function can be plotted knowing either two points or one point and the slope, e.g., cost of the first unit and the percentage improvement (experience rate, e.g., 20 percent cost reduction every time cumulative volume doubles).

Relationship Between *b* and the Experience Rate

To facilitate the estimation, the relationship between a, the experience rate, and b is given by

TABLE 11-4
RELATIONSHIP BETWEEN *A* (PERCENT EXPERIENCE) AND *B*

a	b	a	b
50	1.000	75	0.415
51	0.971	76	0.396
52	0.943	77	0.377
53	0.916	78	0.358
54	0.889	79	0.340
55	0.863	80	0.322
56	0.837	81	0.304
57	0.811	82	0.286
58	0.786	83	0.269
59	0.761	84	0.252
60	0.737	85	0.234
61	0.713	86	0.218
62	0.690	87	0.201
63	0.667	88	0.184
64	0.644	89	0.168
65	0.621	90	0.152
66	0.599	91	0.136
67	0.578	92	0.120
68	0.556	93	0.105
69	0.535	94	0.089
70	0.515	95	0.074
71	0.494	96	0.056
72	0.474	97	0.044
73	0.454	98	0.029
74	0.434	99	0.015
		100	0.000

Source: Adapted with permission from C. Carl Pegels, "Start Up or Learning Curves—Some New Approaches," *Decision Sciences,* 7 (October 1976), 711.

$$b = \frac{\log 100 - \log a}{\log 2} \tag{11-3}$$

Table 11-4 shows this relationship for a values ranging from 50 to 100.

Cost Estimation with Cost of First Unit Known

When both the cost of the first unit, AC, and the experience rate, a, are known, the cost of X units can be calculated directly. If cost of the first unit is \$1,800 and the experience rate is 80 percent, the total costs for eight units are

$$TC_8 = \$1,800(8)^{1-0.322} = \$1,800(8)^{0.678} = \$1,800\,(4.095)$$
$$= \$7,371.70$$

and the average cost for the eight units is

$$AC_8 = \frac{\$7,371.70}{8} = \$921.46$$

Alternatively, the average cost for the eight units could be calculated using

$$AC_8 = \$1,800(8)^{-0.322} = \frac{\$1,800}{(8)^{0.322}} = \frac{\$1,800}{1.953} = \$921.66$$

where the differences are due to rounding.

Finding the Experience Curve from Two Points

Suppose a company audited the twentieth and fortieth production units and found that the production costs were \$700 and \$635, respectively. The firm now wants to estimate the costs of producing the eightieth unit.

From Eq. (11-2), the average costs are

$$AC_{20} = K(20)^{-b} = \$700$$
$$AC_{40} = K(40)^{-b} = \$635$$

Taking logarithms,

$$\log 700 = \log K - b \log 20 \tag{A}$$
$$\log 635 = \log K - b \log 40 \tag{B}$$

Subtracting (B) from (A):

$$\log 700 - 635 = b(\log 40 - \log 20)$$
$$b = \frac{\log 700 - \log 635}{\log 40 - \log 20}$$
$$= \frac{2.8451 - 2.8028}{1.6021 - 1.3010} = \frac{0.0423}{0.3011} = 0.140$$

Looking at Table 11-4, we note that a b of 0.140 lies between $a = 91$ percent and $a = 90$ percent. Interpolating, we obtain an estimated value for a of 90.8 percent.

Using the data for the twentieth unit,

$$\log 700 = \log K - 0.14 \log 20$$
$$\log K = \log \$700 + 0.14 \log 20$$
$$= 2.8451 + 0.14\,(1.3010) = 3.02724$$
$$K = \$1.065$$

Therefore, the experience curve is

$$AC_x = \$1,065(X)^{-0.14}$$

Finally, for the eightieth unit, average costs are

$$AC_{80} = \$1,065\,(80)^{-0.14} = \frac{\$1,065}{(80)^{0.14}} = \frac{\$1,065}{1.845} = \$577$$

TABLE 11-5
ALTERNATIVE EXPERIENCE–COST SCHEDULES

Number of Units	Cumulative Average Cost When a Is		
	70%	80%	90%
1	$1,800	$1,800	$1,800
2	1,259	1,440	1,620
4	882	1,154	1,459
8	617	922	1,312
16	432	738	1,181
32	302	590	1,063
64	211	471	956
128	148	377	861
256	104	302	775
512	72	241	697

Developing Cost Estimates with *a* Unknown

Even if a firm can determine the cost of the prototype unit, it may be uncertain what experience rate will prevail. In such a situation, the firm may wish to determine alternative cost–experience patterns, using different values of *a*. In this way, the decision maker would be able to develop alternative cost schedules to assist in developing the new product's price.

Consider the situation where the cost of the first unit, AC, is $1,800, but the firm does not have a reasonable estimate of *a*. Assume that with previous new products the experience rate ranged between 70 and 90 percent. Table 11-5 shows the alternative experience–cost schedules for a values of 70, 80, and 90 percent. These cost schedules reveal the dramatic differences in feasible prices, depending on the actual experience curve that prevails. Indeed, if the 70 percent experience rate is attained, price is likely to be set lower, other things remaining the same. Figure 11-6 illustrates the same three experience curves.

FIGURE 11-6
Alternative experience–cost schedules.
PRICE FORECASTING

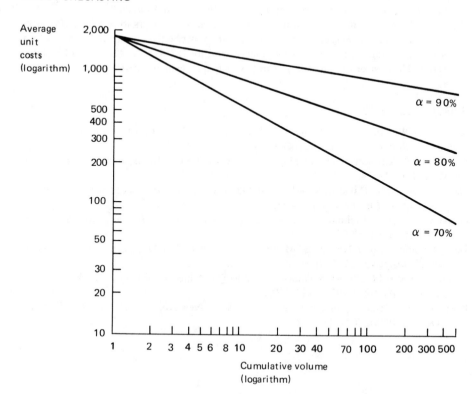

Discussion Questions

1 If costs of the first unit are $1,200 and the experience rate is 90 percent, find
  a The total costs for 10 units.
  b The average costs for 10 units.
  c The average costs for 100 units.
2 A company audited its fiftieth and hundredth production units and determined that the production costs were $900 and $800, respectively.
  a Determine the experience curve for this firm.
  b Estimate the average costs for the two hundredth production unit.
3 a Develop an experience–cost schedule for the situation where the average cost for the first unit is $1,800 and the assumed experience rate is 85 percent. Develop the schedule for the first 131,072 units.
  b What conclusions do you draw about the appropriate cost to use when determining price?
4 The Springer Manufacturing Corporation is considering producing and delivering 40 units of an industrial plating machine to a new customer. The customer has indicated that the maximum feasible price for each plating machine is $5,000. The average cost of building the first unit is estimated by research and development to be $8,000. In the past, the company has usually operated along an experience rate of 85 percent.
  a Several executives believe the potential price of $5,000 is too low. Prepare an analysis that addresses their concern. In your analysis show
    (1) The average and total costs for the following units: 1, 2, 4, 8, 16, 32, 40.
    (2) The total revenues received for 1, 2, 4, 8, 16, 32, and 40 units.
  b After the first 40 units have been delivered, the customer offers to purchase 100 additional units at $2,000 each. Prepare another analysis exactly like the one in part a, but show the average and total costs and total revenue for 1, 2, 4, 8, 16, 32, 64, and 100 units. (Hint: The cost of the fortieth unit in part a is the beginning cost for this problem.)

SUGGESTED READINGS

Abernathy, William J., and Kenneth Wayne: "Limits of the Learning Curve," *Harvard Business Review,* 52 (September–October 1974), 109–119.

Bump, Edwin A.: "Effects of Learning on Cost Projections," *Management Accounting,* 56 (May 1974), 19–24.

Day, George S., and David B. Montgomery: "Diagnosing the Experience Curve," *Journal of Marketing,* 47 (Spring 1983), 44–58.

Ghemawat, Panky: "Building Strategy on the Experience Curve," *Harvard Business Review,* 63 (March–April 1985), 143–149.

Hax, Arnoldo C., and Nicolas S. Majluf: "Competitive Cost Dynamics: The Experience Curve," *Interfaces,* 12 (October 1982), 50–61.

McIntyre, Edward B.: "Cost–Volume–Profit Analysis Adjusted for Learning," *Management Science,* 24 (October 1977), 149–160.

Pegels, C. Carl: "Start Up or Learning Curves—Some New Approaches," *Decision Sciences,* 7 (October 1976), 705–713.

CHAPTER 12

PRICING OVER THE PRODUCT LIFE CYCLE

Of all the marketing variables that influence demand, price is the one that has received the least attention from marketing professionals. Essentially, pricing practice remains largely intuitive and routine. Further, the pricing literature has produced few new approaches that would stimulate the practitioner to change the way prices are set. Despite its obvious lack of validity, the economist's theory of price has dominated the conceptual framework. And until recently, the seller was concerned primarily with stimulating demand.

However, as noted in Chap. 1, recent environmental changes in the market for goods and services have stimulated new interest in pricing. Yet many of the changes in pricing practices lack a clear-cut conceptual framework and often provoke unanticipated consequences. The previous chapters outlined cost and demand approaches to obtaining relevant information for pricing decisions. The next two chapters explore two important pricing decisions that must be made and offer ways to utilize the analytical framework developed in the previous chapters.

It is the thesis of this book that the management of a multiproduct firm should be concerned with managing products over their products' life cycles. Management, therefore, must develop plans that consider the life cycles of sales, total contribution, separable fixed costs, and separable assets employed with the different products. Moreover, management must control production and marketing costs as well as the level of common costs and common assets employed. Indeed, the experience curve evidence suggests that, as product sales grow, costs and prices decline, although this is not automatic. There is also a tendency for the level of common costs and common assets employed to increase with growth in product sales. Hence, common costs, if uncontrolled, can seriously erode direct-cost reductions due to accumulated experience.

The purposes of this chapter are to review the conceptual product life-cycle model and to present methods for developing pricing strategies during different stages of the product life cycle.

PRODUCT LIFE CYCLES—THE CONCEPTUAL MODEL

Although the product life cycle is most frequently pictured in terms of a sales trend, there are several relevant life cycles, as indicated in Fig. 12-1. Further, as Fig. 12-2 shows, the cash flow life cycle has direct relevance to payback and profitability. Indeed, Fig. 12-2 indicates that an earlier life-cycle stage—development—has relevance to the pricing decision.

Development Stage

In the development stage, the product concept is engineered from the idea to the actual design. During this stage no revenues, only costs represented by direct cash outflows, are generated (Fig. 12-2). Once the product idea is engineered, market tests are conducted to determine market acceptance and preparations are made for producing the product. Thus, the accumulated cash investment grows to a substantial

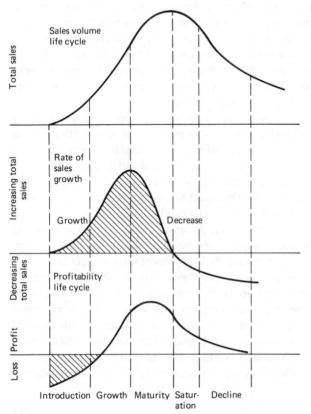

FIGURE 12-1
Product life cycles (sales, rate of sales growth, profitability).

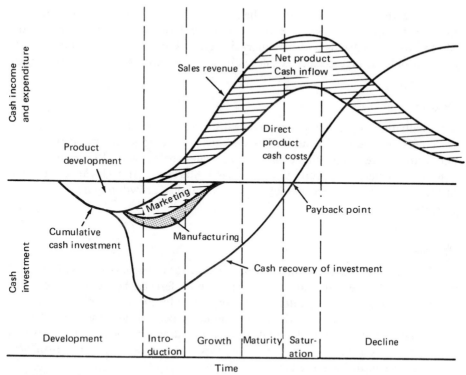

FIGURE 12-2

Investment life cycle. (Adapted and reprinted with permission from John Sizer, "Accountants, Product Managers and Selling Price Decisions in Multi-Consumer Product Firms," *Journal of Business Finance,* 4 [Spring 1972], 76.)

amount before the product is introduced for sale. Indeed, it is reported that IBM invested over $10 billion in the 1980s to develop a new series of high-speed computers.

Introduction

When a new product is introduced, initial market awareness is minimal and market acceptance is slow. If the firm is the only seller of the product, even though there may be functional substitutes, competition will be minimal. The firm's marketing efforts are geared to stimulating *primary demand* (demand for the product itself) and there may be some difficulty in gaining widespread distribution. The introduction stage is the period of initial success or failure for new products.

Growth

The product begins to make rapid sales gains as the rate of market acceptance accelerates. It becomes easier to obtain distributors, and competition increases as imitators introduce their versions of the product. Competitors' marketing strategies focus on stimulating *secondary demand* with emphasis on product differentiation. Market volume expands and new market segments are opened up. Unit costs (in constant dollars) may decline as sales volume grows, promoting still lower prices.

Maturity

Eventually the rate of market acceptance decreases as the number of new potential customers diminishes. Pressures of excess capacity lead to some price competition, and further price competition comes from private-label versions. Replacement sales constitute an increasing proportion of demand. Marketing strategies are designed to create customer preference and loyalty, and continued growth requires an increase in market share.

Saturation

At this stage, products and production methods have become standardized, and buyers generally are well aware of similarities and differences between products. The market is crowded by competitors, and competition for market share is very tough. The need for replacement is the major source of demand and there is extensive private labeling. Brand switching takes place, encouraged by pricing strategies that offer specials, better credit terms, more services, and increased discounts. Inefficient producers begin to leave the market.

Shakeout

The later stages of the maturity phase blend into the saturation stage at the shakeout phase. At this point prices tend to decline faster than do costs. As noted in our discussion of the experience curve phenomenon in Chap. 11, this shakeout phase is marked by competitive turbulence, and the high-cost sellers tend to be forced out of the market. Figure 12-3 illustrates this relationship between the experience curve and the product life-cycle at the industry level.

Decline

Sales begin to diminish as customers turn to new or better products. Private labels take an increasing share of the market and profits tend to be minimal. However, through product improvements and isolation of small but profitable market segments, some firms are able to maintain a continuing and profitable product offering.

Price Elasticity over the Product Life Cycle

This brief description of the stages of the product life cycle has alluded to possible differences in the degree to which buyers are sensitive to prices, price changes, or price differences over the life cycle. Indeed, this issue of whether differences in price

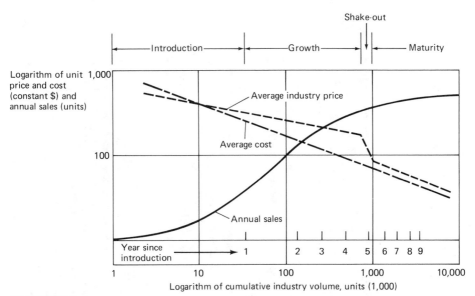

FIGURE 12-3
Product life cycle stages and industry price experience curve. (Reprinted with permission from George S. Day and David B. Montgomery, "Diagnosing the Experience Curve," *Journal of Marketing,* 47 [Spring 1983], 51.)

elasticity exist for the various stages in the product life cycle has led to speculation and empirical research. Initially, price elasticity was thought to increase (i.e., became more negative in value) as the product moved from its introductory stage through growth and into maturity. However, in the decline stage, price elasticity was expected to decrease, perhaps because the number of competitive offerings declined and the market segments that remained for the product became narrower. Later researchers either assumed or empirically determined that price elasticity decreased over the life cycle. Two empirical studies to estimate price elasticity over the product life cycle indicated that it either remained stable over time or declined as the products matured. Table 12-1 summarizes these reports on the dynamic behavior of price elasticity over the product life cycle.

What can we conclude from this limited evidence? As will be discussed later in this chapter, there are two broad strategies for pricing new products: skimming, i.e., setting relatively high prices, and penetration, i.e., setting relatively low prices. The decision to set initial prices high or low is based on special circumstances. But if the initial price is set high because some buyers are not price sensitive (i.e., have a relatively high reservation or maximum acceptable price), and if experience factors combine with product quality improvements and increasing competitive pressure from entering firms to lead to a declining price trend, then we would expect to see increases in price elasticity. However, if the initial price is set low to penetrate the market quickly because buyers are sensitive to prices, and if there is the possibility

TABLE 12-1
PRICE ELASTICITY OVER THE PRODUCT LIFE CYCLE

Reference	Product	Stage of Product Life Cycle						
		Introduction	→	Growth	→	Maturity	→	Decline
Mickwitz*		Increase	↑	Increase	↑	Increase	↑	Decrease
Parsons†		Decrease		Decrease		Decrease		
Wildt‡	Consumer products			(Promotion elasticity decreases over time)				
Simon§	Pharmaceuticals, detergents		Decrease Decrease		Decrease Decrease		Stable Increase	
Liu and Hanssens ‖	Inexpensive gift items				(Increases over time)			
Lilien and Yoon	Industrial chemicals		Stable		Decrease/ stable		Stable/ decrease	

*G. Mickwitz, Marketing and Competition (Helsingfors, Finland: Centratryckerick, 1959).
†L. Parsons, "The Product Life Cycle and Time-Varying Advertising Elasticities," Journal of Marketing Research, 12 (November 1975), 476–480.
‡A. Wildt, "The Empirical Investigation of Time Dependent Parameter Variations in Marketing Models," Proceedings of the Fall Educators' Conference (Chicago: American Marketing Association, 1976).
§H. Simon, "Dynamics of Price Elasticity and Brand Life Cycles: An Empirical Study," Journal of Marketing Research, 16 (November 1979), 439–452.
‖ L. Liu and D. Hanssens, "A Bayesian Approach to Time-Varying Cross-Sectional Regression Models," Journal of Econometrics, 15 (1981), 341–356.
Source: Gary L. Lilien and Eunsang Yoon, "An Exploratory Analysis of the Dynamic Behavior of Price Elasticity over the Product Life Cycles: An Empirical Analysis of Industrial Chemical Products," in Timothy M. Devinney (ed.), Issues in Pricing: Theory and Research, Lexington, Mass.: Lexington Books, 1988), p. 275.

of early competitive entries, then the price trend is likely to be increasing over time. If the product provides benefits and value to buyers, then even as the prices edge upward, we are not likely to see evidence of increased price sensitivity, at least until maturity.

Thus, it is difficult to make unequivocal statements about how price elasticity may change over the stages of the product life cycle. It depends on how the product is initially priced (which should reflect buyers' initial sensitivity to price), whether the product's price follows a decreasing or increasing trend over time (which is partly a reflection of the introductory pricing strategy), the degree to which sellers make quality improvements over time, and the degree to which buyers perceive real benefits and therefore value-in-use in the product. The lesson here is that each product will have its own unique pricing history, and the dynamics of price elasticity over the product's life cycle have to be monitored for each product.

Strategy Implications

The intuitive appeal of the product life cycle, its theoretical foundation in the adoption process, and empirical tests suggest the model has strategic implications.[1] Yet there is no fixed time length for a cycle or for the various stages within the cycle. If anything, advances in technology have led to a shortening of the typical life cycle.[2] And as seen in Figs. 12-1 and 12-2, the profitability life cycle is even shorter. Thus, it is important to recognize the following:

1 Products have a limited life.

2 Accelerating technological growth is likely to decrease a product's life span.

3 There is some correspondence between the industry experience curve and the product life cycle.

4 Sales and profits tend to follow a predictable trend.

5 Products require different marketing strategies at each stage of the life cycle.

6 Pricing strategy is vital at each stage of the life cycle, but particularly at the introduction stage.

BASIC PRICING DECISIONS

The pricing decisions for a modern business organization are complex and important. Established business firms today are encountering newer competitors who have

[1]See, for example, William E. Cox, Jr., "Product Life Cycles as Marketing Models," *Journal of Business,* 40 (October 1967), 375–384; Rolando Polli and Victor J. Cook, "Validity of the Product Life Cycle," *Journal of Business,* 42 (October 1969), 385–400; George Day, "The Product Life Cycle: Analysis and Applications Issues," *Journal of Marketing,* 45 (Fall 1981), 60–67; David M. Gardner, "The Product Life Cycle: A Critical Look at the Literature," in Michael Houston (ed.), *Review of Marketing* (Chicago: American Marketing Association, 1987), pp. 22–59; George S. Day, *Analysis for Strategic Market Decisions* (St. Paul: West Publishing Co., 1986).

[2]"New Products: The Push Is on Marketing," *Business Week,* March 4, 1972, pp. 72–77; William Qualls, Richard W. Olshavsky, and Ronald E. Michaels, "Shortening of the PLC—An Empirical Test," *Journal of Marketing,* 45 (Fall 1981), 76–80.

more efficient methods of production and generally lower labor costs. Foreign firms are able to set prices that are lower than comparable prices set by American businesses. As a result, more and more firms are rediscovering price as a crucial determinant of demand and are actively making pricing decisions.

As seen in Table 12-2, there are many kinds of pricing decisions that a firm must make. There is the decision on what specific price to charge for each product or service marketed. But the specific price depends on the type of customer to whom the product or service is sold. If different customers purchase in varying quantities, should the seller offer volume discounts? If the firm markets through a mixed distribution channel, what prices should be charged to wholesalers who in turn distribute the products to their retail customers, and what prices should be charged to retailers who buy direct from the manufacturer?

The firm must also decide whether to offer discounts for early payment. If the firm decides on a cash discount policy, it must then determine when a customer is eligible for a cash discount and how much to allow for early payment. Should the firm attempt to suggest retail prices or should it price to the immediate customer only?

Most firms sell many products, and the pricing questions just posed must be answered for each product. Additionally, the need to determine the number of price offerings per product and the price relationships between the products offered make the pricing problem more complex. For example, should a camera manufacturer produce and sell only one camera model or should several models be sold? Usually, the decision to sell several models of a product means the seller is attempting to appeal to several market segments. Once it is decided to offer a number of differently priced models, the seller must decide on the price of the least expensive model and on price differentials between each alternative offering.

Today's difficult pricing decisions require careful managerial planning. Since the traditional practice of pricing has been imitation of the pricing practices of others, it is likely that many managers will seek to follow the pricing prescriptions found

TABLE 12-2
BASIC PRICING DECISIONS

---

1. What to charge for the different products and services produced by the firm
2. What to charge different types of customers
3. Whether to charge different types of distributors the same price
4. Whether to give discounts for cash and how quickly payment should be required to earn them
5. Whether to suggest resale prices or only set the price charged one's own customers
6. Whether to price all items in the product line as if they were separate or to price them as a "team"
7. How many different price offerings to have of each item
8. Whether to base prices on the geographical location of buyers (i.e., whether to charge for transportation)

---

in the contemporary literature. However, each firm should carefully analyze its markets, competitors, and costs before developing a pricing strategy.

NEW-PRODUCT PRICING

One of the most challenging decision problems is determining the price of a new product. New-product pricing decisions are usually made with very little information on demand, costs, competition, and other variables that affect the chances of success. Given the rate of new-product introductions and the rate of failures, the importance of the new-product price decision is apparent.

Many new products fail because they do not possess the features desired by buyers or they are not available at the right time and place. Others fail because they have been wrongly priced, and the error can as easily be in pricing the product too low as in pricing it too high. One reason for new-product pricing errors is the lack of knowledge of how pricing decisions should be made. The decision maker often relies on intuition, and experience does not appear to measurably improve chances of success.

When the first home permanent kit was marketed in the 1940s, it was priced to sell slightly below $1.00. However, many women were suspicious of a product priced so low when permanents in beauty parlors were priced between $10 and $15. When the manufacturer of the home permanent kit discovered that the new product was priced too low, the price was raised a dollar to slightly under $2.00. Today, home permanent kits are accepted and well established in the market.

The difficulty in pricing a new product depends on the relative "newness" of the product. Some products are new in the sense that a product which already exists in the market is offered by a company that is new to the market. For example, the introduction of Cycle brand canned dog food in the mid-1970s signaled General Foods' entry into the canned dog food market, although the company had been in the dry dog food market earlier. Thus, this product that was new to General Foods was not new to the market. Generally, the price of functionally identical products is influenced by existing prices of competing products. The new product's price is likely to be similar to existing products' prices.

Some products are new both to the company and to the market, but they are functionally competitive with established products. For example, Maxim competed directly with regular and instant coffees, although it was the first freeze-dried coffee on the market. Pricing functionally competitive new products is more difficult, but the prices of similar products influence the decision. Perhaps the critical question is how much buyers will be willing to pay for perceived differences in function, utility, or appearance.

The most difficult new-product pricing problem occurs when the product is unique, i.e., functionally dissimilar to any other product. If the product is a major innovation in the market, there is much uncertainty surrounding the pricing decision. Essentially, the market is undefined, i.e., demand is unknown, and not all potential uses of the product are known. There are no comparable market experiences, e.g., channels of distribution, markups, or production and marketing costs. Potential customers will be uncertain about the product's function, reliability, or durability. They may be concerned about whether improvements will be made and the effects of these improvements on the product. Customers may also wonder whether prices will be reduced when more sellers are distributing the product and when mass production techniques lower production costs. Pricing decisions usually have to be made with little knowledge and with wide margins of error in the forecasts of demand, cost, and competitors' capabilities. The first black-and-white television set and the trash compactor are good examples of this type of new product.

Factors to Consider When Pricing New Products

As developed in Chap. 1, there are five essential factors to consider when setting price. Demand considerations provide a ceiling or maximum price that can be charged. The determination of this maximum price depends on the customers' perceptions of value in the seller's product/service offering. On the other hand, costs provide a floor, or minimum possible price. For a new product, the relevant costs are the future expected direct costs over the product's life cycle.

Loading irrelevant costs onto a new product's burden may simply push the price floor beyond the price ceiling, leading to a decision to set the product's price too high. Recently, a medical equipment producer, a supplies manufacturer, and an industrial machinery producer all experienced new-product failures when they set their introductory prices too high. Their pricing error occurred because of the felt need to recover their investment in product development too quickly. As mentioned in Chap. 11, to attract buyers, new products often need to be priced initially below total unit costs. When the experience factor leads to lower total unit costs, prices then lead to positive profit margins (see Fig. 12-3). The difference between what buyers are willing to pay and the minimum cost-based price represents an initial pricing discretion. However, this range of pricing discretion is narrowed by competitive factors, corporate profit and market objectives, and regulatory constraints. Primarily, competitive factors act to reduce the price ceiling, whereas corporate objectives and regulation act to raise the minimum possible price.

A product that is new to the world passes through distinctive competitive stages in its life cycle. The appropriate pricing policy is likely to be different for each stage. As new competitors enter the field and innovations narrow the gap of distinctiveness between the product and its substitutes, pricing discretion narrows. The distinctive "specialty" product becomes a "commodity" that is little differentiated from other rival products.

Throughout the cycle, continual changes in promotional and price elasticity and in costs of production and distribution require adjustments in price policy. Appropriate pricing over the cycle depends on the development of three different aspects of maturity that move in approximately parallel time paths: (1) technical maturity, indicated by declining rate of product development, increasing uniformity of competing brands, and increasing stability of manufacturing processes and knowledge about them; (2) market maturity, indicated by consumer acceptance of the basic service idea, by widespread belief that the products of most manufacturers will perform satisfactorily, and by enough familiarity and sophistication to permit consumers to compare brands competently; and (3) competitive maturity, indicated by increasing stability of market shares and price structures.

The core of new-product pricing takes into account the price sensitivity of demand and the incremental promotional and production costs of the seller. What the product is worth to the buyer, not what it costs the seller, is the controlling consideration. What is important when developing a new product's price is the relationship between the buyers' perceived benefits in the new product and the total acquisition cost. One approach for assessing buyers' perceived value is to conduct a value analysis as developed in Chap. 5.

Value Analysis

One of the most common errors associated with new-product pricing is the belief that the buyer acts solely to minimize the price paid. However, as shown in Chaps. 3–5, there is ample evidence that both industrial buyers and consumers tend to use price as an indicator of value. Indeed, the low-price supplier seldom achieves a dominant market position. For example, in the agrichemical industry, in the product category of fertilizers, the lowest priced product had, over time, maintained a market share of 2–4 percent with no recent sales growth. However, the company decided to raise the product's price to be consistent with competitive offerings, with the result that sales began to grow steadily. By pricing the fertilizer closer to the average price of fertilizers, the company enhanced its perceived value. (See Chaps. 3–5 for the development of behavioral principles related to price elasticity.) The ratio between benefits received (value) and the total cost of acquiring the product or service, as developed in Chap. 5, is important:

$$\text{Perceived value} = \frac{\text{perceived benefits}}{\text{price}}$$

where   price = total cost to the buyer: purchase price + acquisition costs + transportation + installation + order handling + risk of failure

perceived benefits = some combination of physical attributes, service attributes, and technical support available in relation to the particular use of the product

Research needed to determine the buyers' perceived value of an offering includes value analysis and value engineering. Value analysis attempts to determine the relative value (utility) buyers place on the total product/service offering, i.e., the perceived benefits. Value engineering attempts to determine methods of reducing the total cost without diminishing the delivered value.

Essentially, value analysis concentrates on increasing perceived value by increasing performance relative to customer needs and willingness to pay for that performance. Value engineering, on the other hand, concentrates on increasing value by decreasing costs while maintaining performance. Generally, the importance of value engineering increases as the product moves through its life cycle. Particularly, as maturity is reached, efforts must be made to identify unnecessary costs and arrange for their removal while maintaining performance levels.

Rate-of-Return Pricing

An extension of value analysis for pricing is rate-of-return pricing of new capital equipment. Industrial goods are sold to businesses in their capacity as profit makers. The technique is different for a producer's good (e.g., a truck) than it is for a consumer's good (e.g., a sports car), because an essential benefit purchased for a producer's good is the opportunity of increasing profits. Since a product represents an investment by the business customer, the test of whether this investment is desirable should be its profitability to that customer.

Rate-of-return pricing looks at a price through the investment eyes of the customer. It recognizes that the upper limit is the price that will produce the minimum acceptable rate of return on the customer's investment. The added profits obtainable from the use of equipment differ among customers and among applications for the same customer. Cutoff criteria of required return also differ, so prospective customers differ in the rate of return that will induce them to invest in a given product. Thus, rate-of-return analysis consists of inquiry into (1) the expected costs to buyers from displaceable alternative ways to do the job; (2) the expected cost-saving and profit-producing capability of equipment in different applications and for different market segments; and (3) the capital budgeting policies of customers, with particular emphasis on their cost of capital and their minimum rate-of-return requirements.

One approach assumes a competitor's product as the benchmark in measuring the rate of return that a given product will produce for specific market segments. The product's profitability is measured in terms of its superiority over the best alternative new equipment offered by rivals rather than by its superiority over the customer's old equipment. Rate-of-return pricing translates this competitive superiority into dollars of added profit for the customer and relates this added profit to the added investment. For each market segment, rate-of-return analysis reveals a price for a given product that makes it an irresistibly good investment to customers in view of their alternatives and at the same time extracts from the customers all that can safely be demanded.

Systematic Approach to New-Product Pricing

There are several approaches to determining a new product's price: intuitive, systematic, or simulation. In the intuitive approach the decision maker subjectively assesses the information available and, more by instinct than design, sets a price. Crude as this seems, it is probably the most frequently used approach. It is not at all uncommon in a marketing research project for a new product to be designed with price

TABLE 12-3
APPROACHES TO NEW-PRODUCT PRICING

Step	Dean*	Oxenfeldt†	Welsh‡
1	Estimate demand	Select market target	Estimate demand
2	Select market target	Choose brand image	Determine marketing requirements over product's life cycle
3	Design promotional strategy	Compose marketing mix	Plot product's expected life cycle
4	Choose distribution channels	Select a pricing policy	Estimate costs over life cycle
5		Determine a pricing strategy	Estimate competitor's entry capabilities
6		Select a specific price	Estimate competitor's probable entry dates
7			Select a specific price

*Joel Dean, "Pricing Policies for New Products," *Harvard Business Review,* 28 (November–December 1950), 28–36; "Pricing a New Product," *The Controller,* April 1955, pp. 163–165.
†Alfred R. Oxenfeldt, "Multi-Stage Approach to Pricing," *Harvard Business Review,* 38 (July–August 1960), 125–133.
‡Stephen J. Welsh, "A Planned Approach to New Product Pricing," *Pricing: The Critical Decision,* AMA Management Report No. 66 (New York: American Management Association, 1961), pp. 45–57.

already determined. The purpose of such a research project might be to investigate how to effectively design a communication campaign for the new product. Several authors have suggested pursuing a more systematic approach to new-product pricing. As Table 12-3 indicates, these approaches vary. Welsh's approach specifically takes a long-range view in that the three major determinants of price—demand, cost, and competition—are specifically estimated over the product's estimated life cycle. Both Dean's and Oxenfeldt's approaches, although subtler, also suggest a long-range view in that they emphasize the development of a marketing plan.

Thus, these three systematic approaches stress the development of a "true" marketing plan. Instead of viewing pricing as an isolated problem, the systematic planning approach considers price as only one of the variables that interact to determine product success. The pricing decision, therefore, is only one of several interrelated decisions to be made.

Some managers use mathematical models to help them determine the new product's price. Such an approach considers price and the other marketing mix variables concurrently in a computer simulation. By programming this model on a computer and inputting the necessary information, it is possible to experiment with values for different decision variables under several environmental assumptions over a simulated time period. The value of such an approach is that the decision maker can assess the relative implications of different assumptions and decision alternatives prior to making specific assumptions. Table 12-4 shows a combined systematic approach to new-product pricing. We will now discuss the first three steps: estimate demand, costs, and the profit-volume relationship. Steps 4–8, although a necessary

TABLE 12-4
SYSTEMATIC APPROACH TO NEW-PRODUCT PRICING

Step	Activity
1	Estimate demand at different prices over expected life cycle.
2	Estimate costs over expected life cycle.
3	Estimate price–volume–profit relationship.
4	Determine likely competitors.
5	Determine competitors' entry capabilities.
6	Estimate competitors' likely entry dates.
7	Determine a marketing strategy.
8	Estimate marketing requirements over product's life cycle.
9	Select a specific price.

part of pricing a new product, will not be discussed further. For step nine, select a price, we will discuss some issues related to selecting a relatively high price, a skimming price, or a relatively low price, a penetration price.

Estimate Demand for a New Product   The first step in new-product pricing is to estimate demand in the selected market targets. But how can demand for new products be estimated? How can the range of prices that people will consider acceptable for a new product be estimated?

The demand estimation problem can be separated into a series of research problems:

1 Will the product fill a need or want and therefore sell if the price is right?

2 At what range of prices will the product be economically acceptable to potential buyers?

3 What is the expected sales volume at feasible price points in the acceptable price range?

4 What is the extent of potential competitive reaction?

The research methods presented in Chap. 6 for estimating buyers' ranges of acceptable prices can be used to estimate the acceptable price range for a new product. Two basic kinds of information must be generated from potential users of the product: (1) the highest and lowest prices they would consider paying for the product and (2) the price last paid for the nearest comparable product or service. The first piece of information provides estimates of the acceptable price range and can be translated into a frequency distribution called a *buy response curve* (see Fig. 6-4). The midpoint price of the buy response curve provides an estimate of the price likely to be judged most acceptable by potential buyers, as well as an estimate of the proportion of buyers likely to consider buying the product at that price.

For industrial products, an easy way to find this acceptable range is to ask distributors, prime contractors, and consulting engineers, as well as purchasing analysts and engineers of prospect companies—all professionals experienced in looking at comparative product performance in terms of buyers' costs and requirements.

For consumers' goods, another approach is used. In estimating the price range of new products the concept of *barter equivalent* is useful. For example, a manufacturer of paper specialties tested a new product by purchasing a wide variety of consumer products totally unlike the new product, spreading them out on a big table, and asking consumers to select the products they would swap for the new product. Buyers have thus indicated a reference point they may use when contemplating the purchase of the new product.

A comparison of the midpoint of the buy response curve with the midpoint of the price-last-paid curve will indicate the degree of discretion available in pricing the new product. For example, if the midpoint of the buy response curve is at a higher price than the midpoint of the price-last-paid curve, then a price higher than the price last paid may have a degree of buyer acceptance. A limitation to this research approach occurs if the product is such a major innovation that buyers have no concept either of the product or of comparable alternatives.

Select Probable Prices   Once an acceptable price range for the new product has been estimated, specific alternative prices need to be selected for the analysis required in step three. To select these alternative prices, the buyers' viewpoint should predominate in pricing. For every new product there are alternatives. Buyers' best alternatives are usually products already tested in the marketplace. The new product will presumably be superior at meeting some buyers' needs, but the degree of superiority of any new product over its competition may differ widely among buyers.

Consider Buyers' Alternatives   When selecting probable prices, it is important to remember that buyers do not have to purchase the new product. Indeed, the prospective buyer of any new product does have alternatives, indirectly competitive products that provide a reference for appraising the price–performance package of a new product and for determining its relative attractiveness to potential buyers. An analysis of relative demand can be made in the following steps:

1 Determine the major uses for the new product. For each application, determine the product's performance characteristics.

2 For each major use, specify the products that are the buyers' best alternatives to the new product. Determine the performance characteristics and requirements which buyers view as crucial in determining their product selection.

3 For each major use, determine how well the product's performance characteristics meet the requirements of customers compared with the performance of these buyers' alternative products.

4 Forecast the prices of alternative products in terms of transaction prices, adjusted for the impact of the new product and translated into units of use. Estimate from the prices of these reference substitutes the alternative costs to the buyer per unit of the new product. Real transaction prices (after all discounts), rather than list prices, should be used to reflect marketplace realities. After the introduction of the new product, predicted price should reflect probable competitive adaptation to the new product. Where eventual displacement of existing alternatives appears likely, short-run incremental cost can forecast rivals' pricing retaliation.

5 Estimate the superiority premium; i.e., price the performance differential in terms of the value buyers place on the superior solution supplied by the new product.

6 Determine a "parity price" for the product relative to the buyer's best alternative product in each use. Do this for all major categories of customers. Parity is a price that encompasses the premium a customer would be willing to pay for comparative superiority in performance characteristics.

Price the Superiority Differential   Determining the price premium that the new product's superiority will most profitably warrant is the most intricate and challenging problem of new-product pricing. The value to the customer of the superiority of the new product is riddled with uncertainties: Will the product work? Will it attain its designed superiorities? How reliable and durable will it be? and How soon will it, in turn, become obsolete? These uncertainties influence the price customers would pay and the promotional outlay that would be required to persuade them to buy. Thus, customers' uncertainties will cost the seller something, either in price or in promotion.

In essence, the superiority premium requires translation of differential performance characteristics into dollars, based on value analysis from the buyer's viewpoint. The premium will differ among uses, among alternative products, and among categories of customers.

What matters is superiority as buyers value it, not superiority as calibrated by technicians' measurements or by sellers' costs. The optimizing premium—i.e., the price that would maximize profits in any specified time period—will depend on future costs as well as the hazy and dynamic demand schedule.

Estimate Costs   Perhaps the most common error management makes in pricing new products is to attempt to recover its investment in a new product as quickly as possible. A reasonable price for a new product is one that will attract both resellers and ultimate users. A high price requiring substantial selling effort to overcome buyer resistance will not receive enthusiastic support from distributors.

Further, a high price with an introductory discount designed to stimulate initial trial may, as suggested in Chap. 3, lead to a lower reference price level. Later, when the product is marketed at its "regular" price, the perception of an increase in price may forever dwarf the sales growth of the product. In addition, an introductory discount might be considered a deceptive pricing practice according to Federal Trade Commission guidelines.

A second common error made in pricing new products is to base initial prices on the wrong cost data. Including development costs and high initial unit production costs in the new product's costs is likely to result in a price that will repel both distributors and final customers and effectively kill the product. Development costs must be considered as an investment to be recovered over the life of the product.

The appropriate unit direct costs are those costs expected when the product reaches its growth stage or when steady production and sales rates are achieved. The value of the experience curve discussed in Chap. 11 becomes apparent for forecasting these relevant direct costs.

As outlined in Chap. 7, to get maximum practical use from costs in new product pricing, three questions must be answered: Whose cost? Which cost? and What role? As to whose cost, three classes of costs are important: (1) those of prospective buyers, (2) those of existing and potential competitors, and (3) those of the producer of the new product. Cost should play a different role for each of the three, and the pertinent concept of cost will differ accordingly.

Buyers' Costs The costs of prospective customers can be determined by applying value analysis techniques (discussed in Chap. 5) to prices and performance of alternative products to find the superiority premium that will make the new product attractive to buyers.

Competitors' Costs Competitors' costs are usually the crucial estimate in appraisal of competitors' capabilities. For products already in the marketplace, the objectives are to estimate (1) their staying power and (2) the floor of retaliation pricing. For the first objective, the pertinent cost concept is the competitor's long-run incremental cost. For the second, the short-run incremental cost is relevant.

Forecasts of competitors' costs for unborn competing products that could blight a new product's future or eventually displace it can help a firm assess the capability of prospective competitors. They also provide estimates of the effectiveness of a new-product pricing strategy to discourage entry. For this situation, the cost behavior to forecast is the relationship between unit direct costs and cumulative experience as the new producer and rivals move from pilot plant to large-scale mass production. These cost forecasts should consider technological progress and should reflect the potential head-start cost advantages that could be attained.

Also, when defining one's competitors, it is necessary to think globally. That is, future competitors may come from international companies in other parts of the world. With the development of free trade between the United States and Canada, the unified European economy in 1992, and the burgeoning of the Pacific Rim economies, competition is now worldwide.

Seller's Costs The producer's costs play several roles in pricing a new product. First, a new product must be prepriced provisionally early in the R&D stage and then again periodically as it progresses toward market. Forecasts of production and marketing costs will influence the decision to continue product development and ultimately to commercialize. The concept of cost relevant for this analysis is a prediction of direct costs at a series of prospective volumes and corresponding technologies. This includes imputed cost of capital on intangible as well as tangible investment.

A second role of the seller's costs is to establish a price floor (see Fig. 1.1). This price floor is also the threshold for selecting from candidate prices the one that maximizes return on a new product investment over the long run. The relevant concept here is future costs, forecast over a range of volume, production technologies, and promotional outlays in the marketing plan.

The production and distribution costs that matter are the future costs over the long run that will be added by making this product. The added investment necessary to manufacture and distribute the new product should be estimated; it should include intangibles such as R&D, promotion, and launching outlays as well as increased working capital. Then the added costs of manufacturing, promoting, and selling the product at various sales volumes should be estimated. It is important to calculate total costs with and without the new product. The difference can then be assigned to the new product. Present overhead that will be the same whether or not the product is added to the line should be ignored. Future additions to overhead that can be ascribed to the new product are alone relevant in pricing it. Two sets of cost and investment figures must be built up—one showing the situation without the new product and the other showing the situation with the new product added to the line, and both must show figures for several possible volumes. High costs of pilot-plant production and of early small-scale production plants should be viewed as intangible capital investment rather than current operating costs. The losses of a break-in period are a part of the investment on which a satisfactory return should be made.

Estimate the Price–Volume–Profit Relationship   The effect of the new product's price on its sales volume is the most important and most difficult estimate in pricing. The best way to predict the effect of price on sales volume for a new product is by controlled experiments: offering it at several different prices in comparable test markets under realistic sales conditions. When test marketing is not feasible, another method is to broaden the study of the cost of buyers' alternatives and include forecasts of their sales volume. Ideally, the analysis and planning for pricing a new product begins at the start of the product development stage. The investment analysis requires estimates of revenues and expenditures over time for each alternative under consideration. The analysis must project estimated cash flows over the entire investment life cycle. Therefore, it is necessary at the outset to have some preliminary price–volume estimates for the different stages of the product life cycle.

Much of the analysis relevant to the pricing of a new product involves contribution analyses similar to those developed in Chap. 8. For alternative feasible prices and expected reasonable costs, a profit–volume break-even chart like Fig. 12-4 can be constructed. The data are shown in Table 12-5. While the break-even chart of Fig. 12-4 reveals different break-even points for prices P_1 through P_6, it provides no information on price, demand, cost, and profit relationships. It simply confirms that for a given cost structure, a lower price results in a higher break-even point. What is needed is a way to incorporate demand into the chart, but price–volume estimates for the alternative prices must be developed first.

At this point in the analysis, it would be more realistic to develop several demand (volume) estimates rather than price–volume estimates for each alternative price. To simplify the presentation, assume only the most likely volume estimate for each price. Then, for each price–volume estimate, direct production and marketing costs must be estimated. It is again important to emphasize the need to consider realistic costs (i.e., costs that are comparable to costs to be incurred during the product's growth stage). It is also important to avoid the temptation to apportion common

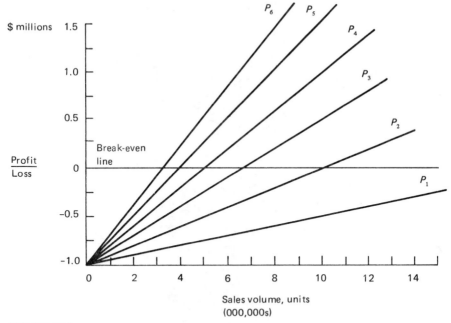

FIGURE 12-4
PV break-even chart: price–volume combinations for life-cycle pricing.

costs to the product since, as discussed in Chap. 8, any apportionment is essentially arbitrary. Full-cost estimates would be inappropriate because:

1 Full costs include past costs, which are not relevant to the pricing decision.
2 Overhead absorption rates are poor measures of the opportunity costs of using scarce resources.
3 Full costs may lead to cost-plus pricing, which does not consider demand or competition.

Table 12-5 shows the type of data that need to be generated. Note that the highest price, \$9.00 (P_6), is not necessarily the most profitable choice. Figure 12-5 is a plot of the profit and volume data of Table 12-5 on the PV break-even chart for each price. CC_1 is the contribution curve for the new product. The contribution curve shows the relationship between demand (D_1 to D_6), direct product profit, total contribution, and break-even points for alternative prices. Thus, the analysis has considered the estimated demand function and the relevant costs for the pricing decision.[3]

As the data in Table 12-5 and Fig. 12-5 show, the most profitable price is \$8.50 with a most likely volume estimate of 1,000,000 units. During the introductory stage,

[3]This analysis has been adapted from John Sizer, "Accountants, Product Managers and Selling Price Decisions in Multi-Consumer Product Firms," *Journal of Business Finance*, 4 (Spring 1972), 70–84.

TABLE 12-5
PRICE–VOLUME DATA FOR LIFE-CYCLE PRICING
Introductory Stage

Unit selling price	$ 6.50	$ 7.00	$ 7.50	$ 8.00	$ 8.50	$ 9.00
Unit variable cost	6.00	6.00	6.00	6.00	6.00	6.00
Unit contribution	$ 0.50	$ 1.00	$ 1.50	$ 2.00	$ 2.50	$ 3.00
PV	0.077	0.143	0.200	0.250	0.294	0.333
Volume (units)	1,500,000	1,400,000	1,300,000	1,225,000	1,000,000	800,000
Revenue	$9,750,000	$9,800,000	$9,750,000	$9,800,000	$8,500,000	$7,200,000
Fixed expenses	$1,000,000	$1,000,000	$1,000,000	$1,000,000	$1,000,000	$1,000,000
Variable costs	$9,000,000	$8,400,000	$7,800,000	$7,350,000	$6,000,000	$4,800,000
Profit (Loss)	$ (250,000)	$ 400,000	$ 950,000	$1,450,000	$1,500,000	$1,400,000

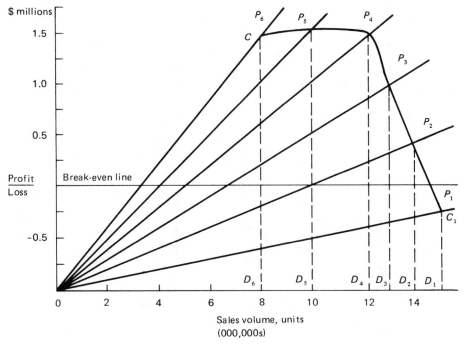

FIGURE 12-5
PV break-even chart: price–volume combinations for life-cycle pricing.

the firm seldom has full production capacity, since it frequently prefers to wait until the product has been successfully introduced before making additional investments in productive capacity. Indeed, assume during the introductory period the firm has productive capacity for only 900,000 units. As the data in Table 12-5 show, not until price is above $8.50 does estimated volume go below a million units. Therefore, the firm may wish to set the initial price around $9.00. Price may be reduced when (1) additional productive capacity becomes available, (2) competitors begin to enter the market, or (3) price elasticity increases. Figure 12-6 shows the break-even chart with the capacity constraint.

The advantage of the product profit–volume analysis is that it allows the manager to trace the implications of different introductory pricing strategies. For example, if the product is easily imitated by competitors, the firm may wish to pursue a low price policy (penetration pricing) to build early high volume and maintain a relatively higher market share in a growing market. In the example seen in Table 12-5, a price of $7.00 yields a short-term profit of $1,000,000 less than the maximum price of $9.00. This money represents a short-term opportunity cost that should be balanced by expected gains due to a higher market share during the growth stage of the product.

Another factor that might influence a low price policy would be the rate at which

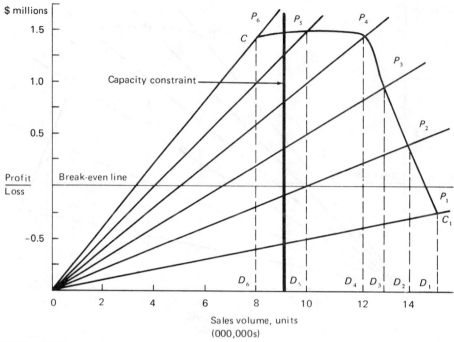

FIGURE 12-6
PV break-even chart: price–volume combinations for life-cycle pricing.

the experience factor reduces direct production and marketing costs per unit. For example, if experience could reduce the variable costs to $5.00 per unit for production of 1,400,000 units or more, then estimated profits for prices $7.00 and $6.50 would be $1,800,000 and $1,250,000 respectively.

Select a Price: Alternative Strategies

It has been generally assumed that there are two alternatives in pricing a new product: skimming pricing, calling for a relatively high price, and penetration pricing, calling for a relatively low price. There are intermediate positions, but the issues are made clearer by comparing the two extremes.

Skimming Pricing   Some products drastically improve accepted ways of performing a service or filling a demand. For these products a strategy of initial high prices (to be lowered at later stages) combined with large promotional expenditure during market development has frequently proved successful. A skimming-price strategy is appropriate for new products when:

1 Sales of the product are likely to be less sensitive to price in the early stages than when the product is "full-grown" and competitive imitations have appeared.

2 Launching a new product with a high price is an efficient device for breaking the market into segments that differ in price elasticity of demand. The initial high price serves to skim the cream of the market, which is relatively insensitive to price.

3 A skimming policy is safer during the exploration stage when elasticity of demand is unknown, since a high initial price serves as a "refusal" price. The extent to which costs can be reduced as the market expands and as value engineering improves production efficiency is difficult to predict.

4 High prices may produce greater dollar sales volume during market development than are produced by low initial prices. If so, skimming pricing will provide funds to finance expansion into the larger volume sectors of a market.

5 A capacity constraint exists.

6 There is realistic value (perceived) in the product/service.

Products that have been introduced recently following a skimming approach include most consumer electronic goods like VCRs, personal computers, and camcorders. When the Cabbage Patch Kids were introduced, they were priced low relative to the demand that developed for them. As a result, production constraints led to excess demand relative to the supply of the dolls, and a black market developed for the dolls.

Penetration Pricing   Despite its many advantages, a skimming-price policy is not appropriate for all new products. Using low prices as a wedge to get into mass markets early is appropriate when:

1 Sales volume of the product is very sensitive to price, even in the early stages of introduction.

2 It is possible to achieve substantial economies in unit cost of manufacturing and distributing the product by operating at large volume.

3 A product faces threats of strong potential competition very soon after introduction.

4 There is no class of buyers willing to pay a higher price to obtain the product.

Most new packaged foods that are relatively easy to imitate are priced following penetration strategy. The strategic objective is to build market share quickly, before rival sellers can enter the market.

A penetration pricing policy can be adopted at any stage in the product's life cycle, but this strategy should always be examined before a new product is marketed at all. Its possibility should be explored again as soon as the product has established an elite market. Sometimes a product can be rescued from premature death by adoption of a penetration price after the cream of the market has been skimmed.

One important consideration in the choice between skimming and penetration pricing at the time a new product is introduced is the ease and speed with which competitors can bring out substitute products. If the initial price is set low enough, large competitors may not feel it worthwhile to make a big investment for slim profit margins. The speed with which a new product loses its uniqueness and sinks from its sheltered status to the level of just another competitive product depends on several factors:

1 Its total sales potential. A big potential market entices competitive imitation.
2 The investment required for rivals to manufacture and distribute the product. A big investment barrier deters invasion.
3 The strength of patent and know-how protection.
4 The alertness and power of competitors.

Caution is suggested in the selection of a skimming or penetration pricing strategy. Generally there may be at least one current product that will serve as a frame of reference for potential buyers, and they are likely to use this product to form their opinions of the value and price of the new product. Where such a reference product exists, the price setter must determine the price differential (higher or lower price than the reference product) and fit the new product into the established population of existing products.

The factors mentioned earlier may suggest an overall pricing strategy for a new product. However, *these two alternative strategies should not be viewed as either/or alternatives.* They merely reflect two opposite strategy extremes. Considerable latitude therefore exists in choosing the specific price level for a new product. Attention is now turned to the problem of selecting the actual price level.

Ideally, the analysis and planning for pricing a product over its life cycle begin at the start of the development stage. One of the primary considerations for accepting a new-product proposal and initiating the developmental investment is the rate of return on investment expected during the product's life. But the investment analysis requires an estimate of revenues and expenditures over time for each alternative under consideration. And, as demonstrated in previous chapters, there is an explicit price–volume–cost relationship that influences both revenues and expenditures. As Fig. 12-2 indicates, the analysis must project estimated cash flows over the entire investment life cycle. Therefore, it is necessary at the outset to have some preliminary price–volume estimates for the different stages of the product life cycle.[4]

Summary

Pricing new products is an art. The important determinants in pricing product innovations are complex, interrelated, and hard to forecast. Experienced judgment is required in pricing and repricing the product to fit its changing competitive environment. This judgment may be improved by these guidelines:

1 Corporate goals must be clearly defined.
2 Pricing a new product should begin during its development stage.
3 Pricing a new product should be a continuing process of successive approximations. Rough estimates of the relevant concepts are preferable to precise knowledge of historical irrelevancies.

---

[4]See also James J. Finerty, "Product Pricing and Investment Analysis," *Management Accounting,* 53 (December 1971), 15–18.

4 Costs can supply useful guidance in new-product pricing, but not by cost-plus pricing. Three categories of costs are pertinent: those of the buyer, those of the seller, and those of the seller's rivals.

5 Cost establishes a reference base for picking the most profitable price. The only costs that are pertinent to pricing a new product are incremental costs—the added costs of going ahead at different plant scales. Costs of R&D and market testing are sunk and hence irrelevant.

6 The pricing implications of the changing economic status and competitive environment of a product must be recognized as it passes through its life cycle.

7 The product should be seen through the eyes of the customer and priced just low enough to make it an irresistible investment in view of available alternatives.

8 Customers' rate of return should be the main consideration in pricing novel capital goods. Buyers' cost savings (and other earnings) expressed as a return on their investment in the new product is the key to predicting the price sensitivity of demand and to pricing profitably.

9 The strategic choice between skimming and penetration pricing should be based on objective analysis.

PRICING DURING GROWTH

If the new product survives the introductory period, as demand grows both the *position* and *shape* of the contribution curve change. Usually, a number of competitors are producing and selling a similar product, and a market price emerges. There is a relatively wide range of market prices early in the growth stage, but this range narrows as the product approaches maturity.

Table 12-6 and Fig. 12-7 provide illustrative data for pricing during the growth stage. Three essential points should be noted: (1) the range of feasible prices has narrowed since the introductory stage; (2) unit variable costs have decreased due to the experience factor; and (3) fixed expenses have increased because of increased capitalization and period marketing costs. The pricing decision during the growth stage is to select a price that, subject to competitive conditions, will help generate a sales volume that enables the firm to realize its target contribution.

TABLE 12-6
PRICE–VOLUME DATA FOR LIFE-CYCLE PRICING
Growth Stage

Unit selling price	$ 6.00	$ 6.50	$ 7.00	$ 7.50
Unit variable cost	5.00	5.00	5.00	5.00
Unit contribution	$ 1.00	$ 1.50	$ 2.00	$ 2.50
PV	0.167	0.231	0.286	0.333
Volume (units)	2,800,000	2,500,000	2,000,000	1,400,000
Revenue	$16,800,000	$16,250,000	$14,000,000	$10,500,000
Fixed expenses	$ 2,500,000	$ 2,500,000	$ 2,500,000	$ 2,500,000
Variable costs	$14,000,000	$12,500,000	$10,000,000	$ 7,000,000
Profit	$ 300,000	$ 1,250,000	$ 1,500,000	$ 1,000,000

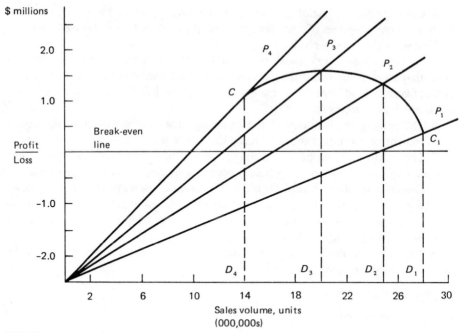

FIGURE 12-7
PV break-even chart: price–volume combinations, growth stage.

PRICING DURING MATURITY

As a product moves into the maturity and saturation stages, it is necessary to review past pricing decisions and determine the desirability of a price change. As the description of the product life cycle indicated, replacement sales constitute the major demand, and manufacturers also incur competition from private-labeled products. Market conditions do not appear to warrant a price increase; hence, the pricing decision usually is to reduce price or stand pat.

To price appropriately for late stages in the life cycle, it is important to know when a product is approaching maturity. When the new product is about to slip into the commodity category, it is sometimes desirable to reduce real prices as soon as symptoms of deterioration appear. Some of the symptoms of degeneration of competitive status toward the commodity level are:

1 Weakening of brand preference, evidenced by a higher cross-price elasticity of demand among leading products, with the leading brand unable to command its initial large price premium without losing position.

2 Narrowing physical variation among products as the best designs are developed and standardized. This has been dramatically demonstrated in automobiles and is still in process in personal computers.

3 The entry in force of private-label competitors.

4 Market saturation. The ratio of replacement sales to new-equipment sales indicates the competitive degeneration of durable goods.

5 The stabilization of production methods, indicated by slow rate of technological advance, high average age of equipment, and great uniformity among competitors' introduction technology.

When is a price reduction profitable? We know that when demand is price elastic reduced prices are profitable if costs do not rise above the increase in revenues. But since it can be expected that any price decrease will be followed by competitive price decreases, it is also necessary that the *market demand* curve be elastic within the range of the price reduction. Moreover, as demonstrated in Chaps. 8 and 11, the requirements for a profitable price reduction strategy include beginning with a relatively high contribution margin, opportunity for accelerating growth, a favorable combined leverage position (see Chap. 8), as well as a price-elastic demand. When a product has reached the maturity stage of its life cycle, it is most likely that these conditions will not exist.

For a product with many close substitutes, a firm's demand curve will probably be elastic. But if all sellers match the price reduction, the firm's market share will remain relatively constant, and any increase in the firm's demand will result from an increase in market demand. Therefore, to reduce price for a mature product, market demand must be elastic, the firm's demand must be elastic, and the marginal revenues associated with the increased volume must be greater than the marginal costs of producing and selling the additional volume.

To demonstrate these points, assume that a firm is selling 3,000,000 units at $6.00 per unit.[5] Further assume that both the market and the firm's demand are price elastic with an elasticity value of -1.43. Assume also that a price reduction by the firm is exactly matched by competitors, so that relative market shares remain constant. This means that a market-wide price reduction will increase market demand, but that each firm's demand increases only in direct proportion to its market share. The firm is considering reducing its price to $5.75, or 4.2 percent. Because demand price elasticity is -1.43, a 4.2 percent price reduction will increase demand by 6 percent ($-4.2\% \times -1.43 = +6\%$). The comparative effect of the price reduction on the firm's revenues is shown in Table 12-7A. With a price of $5.75 revenues will increase $285,000.

However, although revenues have increased, it is possible that profits have not increased. To determine the effect of the price decrease on profits, assume that variable costs per unit are $4.80 and that the product has fixed costs of $2,500,000. Table 12-7B shows the effect of a 6 percent increase in volume on costs and Table 12-7C shows the comparative effect on profits. Thus, while the price reduction produced an increase in revenues of $285,000, profits were reduced by $579,000. As Table 8-8 and Fig. 8-6 indicated, for a product with a PV of 0.20 [($6.00 − $4.80)/$6.00], a price reduction of 4.2 percent must be accom-

---

[5]This example is adapted from Clare E. Griffin, "When Is Price Reduction Profitable?" *Harvard Business Review*, 38 (September–October 1960), 125–132.

TABLE 12-7

	Before	After
A. Effect on revenues of a 4.2% price reduction		
Demand, units (Q)	3,000,000	3,180,000
Price (P)	$ 6.00	$ 5.75
Revenues ($P \times Q$)	$18,000,000	$18,285,000
B. Effect on costs of a 4.2% price reduction		
Fixed expenses	$ 2,500,000	$ 2,500,000
Variable costs ($4.80 $\times$ Q)	14,400,000	15,264,000
Total costs	$16,900,000	$17,764,000
C. Effect on profits of a 4.2% price reduction		
Total revenues	$18,000,000	$18,285,000
Total costs	16,900,000	17,764,000
Profits	$ 1,100,000	$ 521,000

panied by a volume increase of more than 26 percent if profits are to remain unchanged.

At the maturity stage of the life cycle, the firm probably should attempt to maximize short-run direct product contribution to profits. Hence, the pricing objective is to choose the price alternative leading to maximum contribution. If competition reduces prices, the firm may, however reluctantly, match the price reduction. On the other hand, it may try to reduce costs by using cheaper materials, eliminating several labor operations, or reducing period marketing costs. All or any of these actions may allow the firm to match competitively lower prices and still maintain target contributions to profit.

For example, assume a competitor has reduced price to $5.75. Since the firm

TABLE 12-8

	Before	After
A. Change in cost structure		
Fixed expenses	$ 2,500,000	$ 2,250,000
Variable costs per unit	4.80	4.60
B. Effect on profits of a 4.2% price reduction and change in cost structure		
Total revenues	$18,000,000	$18,285,000
Total costs	16,900,000	16,878,000
Profits	$ 1,100,000	$ 1,407,000

wishes to meet that $5.75 price, it attempts to maintain profitability by modifying production procedures and reducing marketing period expenditures. The effects on costs are shown in Table 12-8A and the profit effect is shown in Table 12-8B.

PRICING A DECLINING PRODUCT

During the declining phase of a product's life, direct costs are very important to the pricing decision. Normally, competition drives the price down close to direct costs. Only those sellers who were able to maintain or reduce direct costs during the saturation stage are likely to have remained. If the decline is not due to an overall cyclical decline in business but to shifts in buyer preferences, then the primary objective is to obtain as much contribution to profits as possible.

As long as a firm has excess capacity and revenues exceed all direct costs, the firm probably should consider remaining in the market. Generally, firms eliminate all period marketing costs (or as many of these costs as possible) and remain in the market as long as price exceeds direct variable costs. As noted in Chaps. 7 and 8, the direct variable costs are the minimally acceptable prices to the seller. Thus, with excess capacity, any market price above direct variable costs would generate contributions to profit. Indeed, as suggested in Chap. 8, the relevant decision criterion is to maximize contributions per sales dollar generated. In fact, it might be beneficial to raise the price of a declining product to increase the contributions per sales dollar.

FOCUSED PRICE REDUCTIONS

The difficulty of effecting successful price reduction strategies makes across-the-board price cuts very risky. Over the product life cycle, however, there often is a need to consider reducing prices, either because of competitive pressures or because there are price-sensitive buyers in the market. Thus, if the firm can selectively reduce price to attract specific market segments, focused price reductions may be profitable. A requirement for pursuing focused price reductions is the firm's knowledge of the different degrees of price sensitivity across price/market segments *and* the relative costs of serving these segments. Information from pricing research and marketing cost analyses must be available to develop a focused price reduction strategy. Some methods for implementing focused price reductions are offered next.

Base Product Versus Option Prices

By selling the basic product without a multitude of add-on features and options, often the seller can appeal to a price-sensitive market—those who want only the basic product—and to other buyers who are not price sensitive. Many customers will make their purchase decision using the base price alone, and then become less price sensitive to the additional options or accessories that can be purchased separately. The discussion in Chaps. 3 and 4 on how buyers form value judgments suggests that this segregation of perceived losses with differential gains (the features) may lead to positive value perceptions. Some examples include bank practices of separating interest rates and fees, movie theaters separating seat tickets from concessions, automobile sales, and service contracts on consumer appliances.

Channel-Specific Pricing

The experience of off-price retailers and factory outlets documents the success of this approach. High-price designer clothing can frequently be purchased in these outlets at a fraction of the price at which it is sold in upscale stores. There may be some differences in the assortment available and in amenities and services provided; nevertheless, fashion clothing can be purchased at relatively low prices in these stores. The objective of using this strategy is to identify distribution channels that serve price-sensitive customers and offer lower prices through these channels only.

Pricing According to Customers' Perceived Values

The relative success of airlines and hotels in offering similar services to customers at different prices (see the discussion on yield management in Chap. 13) supports the use of this approach. Offering lower prices for demand that occurs during off-peak hours—e.g., long-distance telephone or midnight to 5:00 A.M. utility rates—is a price reduction strategy that not only shifts demand but enhances volume from price-sensitive segments.

Price Bundling

Price bundling is the practice of offering two or more products or services at a price that is lower than the sum of the individual prices. Price bundling is pervasive today and, like any price reduction strategy, can be successfully used in particular circumstances only. We will discuss this price reduction strategy in Chap. 13.

Product Redesign

This strategy is a variation of the unbundling of the base product from the options. The difference is that the product is changed in some way (fewer features, lower grade material, different brand name) and sold as a separate, lower priced product. Again, the objective is to appeal to price-sensitive customers who would normally not buy the original product at its regular price.

SUMMARY

This chapter has developed techniques for establishing prices over a product's life cycle. Contribution analysis was extended to show its adaptability and usefulness for pricing over the life cycle. Since it is advocated that a pricing strategy be planned during the development stage, both price *and* cost forecasting are important to the analysis.

To avoid the common mistake of basing a new product's price on unrealistic introductory production and marketing costs, the experience curve can be utilized to obtain more practical cost estimates. Furthermore, an experience curve can be used to determine when volume increases caused by price reductions will also lead to unit cost decreases.

Finally, it is important for the price setter to be provided proper accounting and financial data. Accountants who prepare data for pricing administrators should tailor their analyses to the life-cycle stage for each product. Product profit–volume charts can facilitate understanding of the implications of each pricing alternative.

This chapter has also demonstrated that price reduction strategies for mature products are likely to also reduce profitability. The need to consider specific focused price reductions instead of across-the-board price reductions was briefly outlined.

DISCUSSION QUESTIONS

1 Describe the pricing environment for each stage of the product life cycle.
   a What are the possible pricing objectives?
   b What are the general pricing strategies for each of these objectives?
   c As a product progresses through the different life-cycle stages, how do these objectives and general pricing strategies change? Why?
   d Carefully discuss the role of competition on the objectives and strategies you developed in parts a and b.
2 During fall 1977, the VCR caught on in the United States consumer market. Prior to this time Sony had priced its Betamax at $1,295. In August 1977, RCA set a suggested price for its model at $1,000. In November 1977, Zenith reduced its price to $995 from $1,295.
   a What do you think was the pricing reaction of Sony? Why?
   b What do you think happened to the prices of VCRs in 1978? Why?
3 In November 1977, Sony reduced the price of its Betamax from $1,295 to $1,095 in response to the competitive price moves by Zenith and RCA described in Question 2. What is your evaluation of the price change?
4 The Scientific Corporation is in the final stages of developing a new product. Preliminary market tests show that potential customers like the product. Based on these market tests and customer surveys, the market research staff has provided the following sales estimates for the first three years of the product's life:

Price	Year 1	Year 2	Year 3
$12	20,000 units	40,000 units	60,000 units
$14	15,000 units	25,000 units	45,000 units
$16	12,000 units	22,000 units	40,000 units
$18	10,000 units	20,000 units	35,000 units
$20	8,500 units	18,000 units	30,000 units

After reviewing the marketing, production, and financial plans for the new product the controller estimates that direct variable costs will average $8.00 for the first 25,000 units produced, $7.00 after the first 25,000 units produced, $6.50 after the first 50,000 units produced, and $5.00 after the first 100,000 units produced. Period fixed costs are expected to be $50,000, $100,000, and $150,000 for the first three years, respectively. Further, it is expected that the Malloy Corporation will be able to market a similar product by the beginning of the second year and with a cost experience similar to that of the Scientific Corporation.

Develop a pricing strategy for the first three years of the product for the Scientific Corporation. Support your strategy with the necessary exhibits and analyses. What is the rationale of your strategy?

SUGGESTED READINGS

Böer, Germain B.: "Additional Applications of Direct Cost Information to Pricing Decisions," in *Direct Cost and Contribution Accounting* (New York: Wiley, 1974), pp. 164–183.

Dean, Joel: "Pricing Policies for New Products," *Harvard Business Review,* 54 (November–December 1976), 141–153.

Lilien, Gary L., and Eunsang Yoon: "An Exploratory Analysis of the Dynamic Behavior of Price Elasticity over the Product Life Cycle: An Empirical Analysis of Industrial Chemical Products," in Timothy M. Devinney (ed.), *Issues in Pricing: Theory and Research* (Lexington, Mass.: Lexington Books, 1988), pp. 261–287.

Monroe, Kent B.: "Pricing New Industrial Products," in Earl L. Bailey (ed.), *Product Line Strategies* (New York: The Conference Board, 1982), pp. 67–72.

Monroe, Kent B.: "Techniques for Pricing New Products and Services," in V. Buell (ed.), *Handbook of Modern Marketing,* rev. ed. (New York: McGraw-Hill, 1986), pp. 32-1–32-13.

Monroe, Kent B., Akshay R. Rao, and Joseph D. Chapman: "Toward a Theory of New Product Pricing," in J. Sheth and G. Frazier (eds.), *Contemporary Views on Marketing Practice* (Lexington, Mass.: Lexington Books, 1987), pp. 201–213.

Robinson, Bruce, and Chet Lakhani: "Dynamic Price Models for New-Product Planning," *Management Science,* 21 (June 1975), 1113–1122.

Sizer, John: "Accountants, Product Managers and Selling Price Decisions in Multi-Consumer Product Firms," *Journal of Business Finance,* 4 (Spring 1972), 70–84.

CHAPTER 13

PRODUCT-LINE PRICING

A fundamental marketing decision problem is the determination of price for a product or service. Among the factors that complicate pricing decisions are cost per unit, competitor and buyer sensitivity to price, objectives of the firm, legal constraints, potential entry or exit of competing sellers, and the total product/service offering of the firm. Each of these factors, with the exception of the total product/service offering of the firm, has been discussed in some detail in the pricing literature. Exclusion of the product/service offering as a factor is the result of the attention given the problem of determining price for a single product or service. But since few firms today offer single products, there is a need to consider the problem of setting prices for multiple product/service offerings.

From a market perspective, many firms have discovered that there are specific price/market segments for their products and that determining prices to differentiate these products is a complex process. Whether to add a midpriced product or change the number of price offerings depends not only on the number of price/market segments but also on whether the objective is to differentiate the products in the minds of buyers (segmentation strategy) or to encourage buyers to trade up to a higher priced product (trading-up strategy). This chapter develops a behavioral approach to determine ways to position products in a product line according to price. Many of the important costing issues relative to multiple product offerings were discussed in Chap. 8 (e.g., the sales dollar mix and the use of common resources to produce, market, or distribute products or services).

NATURE OF THE DECISION PROBLEM

Most firms sell a variety of products or services that require different marketing strategies. Generally, a firm has several product lines—groups of products that are closely related because they are used together, they satisfy the same general needs, or they are marketed together. Within a product line there are usually some products that are substitutes for one another and some that complement the demand for other products in the line. Because of the demand interrelationships as well as the cost interrelationships inherent to such a product line, and because there are usually several price market targets, product-line pricing is one of the major challenges that face a marketing executive.

Although an organization may wish to pursue a pricing policy of high prices only (or low prices only), it still must decide how high (or low) its prices should be and the differentials between different products in the line. In addition, it must decide on the lowest (or highest) price that helps to maintain a consistent price policy. Thus, three types of pricing decisions are required:

1 Determining the lowest priced product and its price *(low-end product)*
2 Determining the highest priced product and its price *(high-end product)*
3 Setting the price differentials for all intermediate products

The pricing problem is compounded because complementarity may exist even if the products in the product line or assortment are functionally substitutable. For example, one researcher discovered that a substitute relationship existed for the product-line brand vs. competitors' brands, but that a complementarity relationship existed between brands within the product line.[1] As noted in Chap. 2, the cross-price elasticity is positive when the relationship is one of substitution but negative when it is complementary. In addition, by adding new items or reducing certain prices, a firm may increase demand for already existing products. Finally, it is known that the lowest and highest priced products are more frequently remembered and noticed, implying a further complementarity.[2] This issue of pricing multiple products to maximize contributions to profits extends to retail firms and to service providers.[3]

The low-end price usually is the most frequently remembered one and probably has considerable influence on the marginal buyer (the buyer who is doubtful but still seriously considering buying). Hence, the lowest priced product is often used as a traffic builder. On the other hand, the highest priced product is also highly visible and, through quality connotations, may also stimulate demand.

Many of the behavioral pricing principles discussed in Chaps. 3–5 provide the price setter with operational guidelines for solving these complex pricing problems. The notion of the acceptable price range may help the firm establish the boundaries of different price/market segments and help determine the prices of the low-end and high-end products in the line. As suggested earlier, the prices of these end products may enhance the salability of the entire product line.

[1]Glen Urban, "A Mathematical Modeling Approach to Product Line Decisions," *Journal of Marketing Research,* 6 (February 1969), 40–47.

[2]Alfred Oxenfeldt, "Product Line Pricing," *Harvard Business Review,* 44 (July–August 1966), 135–143.

[3]John D. C. Little and Jeremy F. Shapiro, "A Theory for Pricing Nonfeatured Products in Supermarkets," *Journal of Business,* 53 (July 1980), S199–209; David J. Reibstein and Hubert Gatignon, "Optimal Product Line Pricing: The Influence of Elasticities and Cross-Elasticities," *Journal of Marketing Research,* 21 (August 1984), 259–267.

In addition to the inherent complementary relationships within a product line, products that are functionally complementary present a pricing problem. For example, the pricing of cameras and film, or the pricing of razors and razor blades, introduces further problems. Clearly, demand for film or razor blades is enhanced by the sale of cameras or razors. Should the firm intentionally set the price of razors and cameras relatively low in order to increase demand for blades and film?

Finally, some buyers may be willing to purchase several products in the line, yet the individual prices for some of the products may exceed the maximum price they are willing to pay. The practice of price bundling (offering several products or services at one price) has been used to overcome this particular problem. We will discuss this pricing practice later in the chapter and offer guidelines for its use.

Conceptual Framework

Generally, a firm produces and distributes multiple products because (1) the demands for the various products are interrelated, (2) the costs of production and distribution are interrelated, (3) both costs and demands are interrelated, or (4) multiple products enable the firm to appeal simultaneously to several diverse market segments (i.e., the products are neither demand nor cost related, but instead they permit the firm to pursue expansion or diversification objectives).

Products are demand related if a change in the price of a product, Q_1, induces the buyer to change the quantity of his or her purchases of other products (Q_2, . . . , Q_n), along with changing purchases of Q_1. Similarly, products are related by production and distribution if a change in the quantity produced and distributed of a product, Q_1, results in a change in the unit costs of other products, $Q_2, \ldots, Q_n$. Thus, if the firm's products are related by both demand and costs, the quantity produced and sold of any particular product affects both the revenues and costs of the other products a firm sells. An adjustment in the price of a particular product to increase net profit for that product thus may or may not increase profits for the entire firm. In such situations, if the firm is interested in *maximizing contributions to profits,* it must consider not only the effect on revenues and costs of the particular product for which price is being adjusted, but also the changes in revenues and costs for all other related products. Despite the fact that most organizations offer multiple products or services, and despite the obvious need to develop solutions for solving this decision problem, little attention has been given to the problem.[4]

Theoretically, the optimal solution for a firm producing multiple products is to equate the adjusted marginal revenue for each product with the adjusted marginal cost for each product. The adjustment required depends on the impact of the product's price and volume changes on the revenues and costs of the other products in the line. Table 13-1 provides the theoretical pricing solutions for the different possible situations. The reason for specifying adjusted marginal revenues and marginal costs is that the level of sales and costs for any one item in the product line may be changed in response to a price-induced volume change of another product

[4]Reibstein and Gatignon, ibid.

TABLE 13-1
THEORETICAL PRICING SOLUTIONS—PRODUCT-LINE PRICING

Situation	Solution*
Products are not related (independent)	$MR_i = MC_i$
Products are demand related only	Adjusted $MR_i = MC_i$
Products are cost related only	$MR_i =$ adjusted MC_i
Products are demand and cost related	Adjusted $MR_i =$ adjusted MC_i
Products are demand related, but there is only a single "cost-generating" product	$MR_i = MC$

*$MR_i =$ marginal revenues for the ith product; $MC_i =$ marginal costs for the ith product.
Source: Developed from Kristian S. Palda, *Economic Analysis for Marketing Decisions* (Englewood Cliffs, N.J.: Prentice-Hall, 1969), p. 140.

in the line. Thus, changing price for any given product may or may not produce the desired result unless prices of the other products in the line are also adjusted.

To observe the nature of the required adjustments, assume a product line wherein products are demand related only, i.e., there are no cost interrelationships. The demand relationships may be either substitutable or complementary, as observed previously. For the moment, consider only two products, A and B, both of which have inverse price–volume demand functions. That is, their own price elasticities are negative, as developed in Chap. 2. Now, if the demand relationship between the two products is complementary, then the cross-price elasticities are negative. But if the demand relationship between the two products is substitutable, then the cross-price elasticities are positive.

It can be shown that the price of product A is

$$p_1 = \frac{\Delta c}{\Delta q_1} + q_1 \left(\frac{\Delta p_1}{\Delta q_1} \right) \pm q_2 \left(\frac{\Delta p_2}{\Delta q_2} \right)$$

where $p_1 =$ price of product A
$\Delta c / \Delta q_1 =$ change in variable costs due to a change in the volume produced and sold of product A
$q_1, q_2 =$ sales volume of products A and B respectively
$\Delta p_1 / \Delta q_1 =$ slope of the demand curve for product A
$\Delta p_2 / \Delta q_1 =$ change in the price of product B induced by a change in the volume of product A

If the products are complementary, the price of product A will be above or below cost, depending on whether $q_2(\Delta p_2/\Delta q_1)$ is less than or greater than $q_1(\Delta p_1/\Delta q_1)$. For substitutable products, the price will always be above marginal cost. Note that a decrease in price for a complementary product that leads to increased demand for that product also will increase demand for the product it complements. The reduced price for the complementary product also leads to a lower marginal revenue for that product. Therefore, the adjustment in the marginal revenue for this product is downward. On the other hand, for substitute products in the line, adjustments to marginal revenues and price are upward.[5] (Later in this chapter, the development of the principles for price bundling will draw on this basic result for the pricing of complementary products in a product line.)

Complicating the application of the theoretical solution is the inability of the firm to obtain sufficient data concerning the demand and cost interdependencies of the products in the line. A further complication arises when issues of price perception are considered. The research literature on buyer reactions to price indicates that the lowest priced product in the product line may affect the quantity sold of all products in the line to a greater degree than the price of any other products.[6] These reactions appear to be related to a principle of Gestalt psychology called *outstandingness:* some objects have certain special qualities that make one's perception of them easier and more lasting than a perception based merely on their physical attributes. Applying this principle and these observations, it can be suggested that the price of the lowest priced product is the price most frequently noticed and most frequently remembered. To complete the use of the principle of outstandingness, it is suggested that the price of the highest priced product in a product line also is relatively more visible to potential buyers than are prices spaced between the lowest and highest prices (end prices).

If the end prices of a product line are relatively more visible to buyers than are other prices in the line, then these end prices may influence sales of all products in the line. That is, end prices may have information content for potential buyers, and these buyers may then transfer their interpretation of this information to the entire product line, e.g., a bargain vs. a quality interpretation. Since end prices can affect demand for all products within a product line, the optimum end prices that will enhance the sale of products in the product line as well as the optimum price for each individual product must be determined.

Product-Line Examples

The discussion thus far has illustrated the concept of a product line with reference to cameras and photographic accessories and to razors and razor blades. In both examples one type of product is a complement to the other type. Sometimes, however, it is convenient to consider only a line of cameras or a line of hand razors.

In the camera example, the manufacturer may have several models, each with different features appealing to different types of camera users. The simplest camera may appeal to the young photographer or infrequent picture taker who wants a

[5]For a more complete theoretical development see Kent B. Monroe and Susan M. Petroshius, "A Theoretical Approach for Determining Product Line Prices," in *Proceedings of the Special Conference on Marketing Theory* (Chicago: American Marketing Association, 1980), pp. 21–24.

[6]Kent B. Monroe, "The Information Content of Prices: A Preliminary Model for Estimating Buyer Response," *Management Science,* 17 (April 1971), B519–B532.

simple "aim-and-shoot" camera. The next camera in the line may have a telescopic lens, and other models may feature 12 or 20 exposures, 35-millimeter film, adjustable focus, or range finder. As the manufacturer expands the line of cameras from the simplest camera to the sophisticated camera used by professionals, each camera appeals to a different market segment, and each differential feature is valued differently by these segments. The pricing problem is to decide on a set of prices that corresponds to what each market segment is willing to pay.

Moreover, the price differentials between camera models must correspond to perceived differences in the separate cameras. For example, if the simplest camera, model A, is priced at $45 and model B, which includes a telescopic lens, is priced at $49, buyers will perceive that $4 is or is not too much to pay for this added feature. But if buyers are willing to pay up to $55 for model B, then a pricing error has been made *unless* it is the seller's intent to "trade buyers up" to model B.

When Chevrolet introduced its Corvair in the early 1960s, the car was priced close to the regular-sized models to encourage the sale of the regular models. On the other hand, Ford priced its compact Falcon to differentiate it from the larger models. Thus, the Falcon outsold the Corvair, but the larger and more profitable Chevrolet models outsold the larger Ford models. The essence of Chevrolet's plan was to use a *trading-up pricing strategy.* That is, Chevrolet priced the Corvair perceptably close to the regular-size models so that customers would notice the additional value for a slightly higher price. On the other hand, Ford's strategy can be characterized as a *price segmentation strategy.* That is, Ford's objective was to price each car model so that customers would perceive each distinctively. Thus, the Falcon was priced well below the regular-size models. In the next section we will develop some principles for segmented and trading-up pricing strategies.

The pricing of hotel or motel rooms is a product-line pricing problem. Most motels or hotels have different-sized rooms, and some rooms face a desirable location such as a pool or park while others face a less desirable location such as a parking lot or a busy highway. Moreover, management must determine a single and a double rate for each type of room. And if suites are available, an additional pricing decision must be made.

Product lines are also prevalent in the industrial sector of our economy. For example, a company selling in the copier market normally sells platemakers, offset duplicators, plate materials, chemicals, and parts and offers service/maintenance contracts. Moreover, the company may have several models of platemakers and several models of offset duplicators, each with different features.

DETERMINING END PRICES AND PRICE DIFFERENTIALS

End-Price Concept

The concept of end prices was briefly developed at the beginning of this chapter. It was suggested that buyers are likely to have a range of acceptable prices for a product, and that if the desired product is priced within this price range, the buyer probably would be favorably disposed to complete the purchase. Also, extending the concept of a price range to a product line provides the concept of an acceptable range of product-line prices.

In effect, then, the existence of high and low price limits represents a price-decision constraint. That is, if a product is priced too low or too high for a particular buyer, there is little chance that he or she will purchase the item unless the parameters of the buyer's decision change. Similarly, if some products are priced outside the acceptable price range and others are priced within this range, there would seem to be less chance that a buyer would buy any product than if all the products in the line were priced within the acceptable price range. In such a situation, the price setter seemingly would want to constrain his or her pricing flexibility to those prices lying within the price range with the highest probability of being accepted.

A recent study revealed that the price characteristics of the product line influence consumer product evaluations.[7] Specifically, the research indicated that the range of prices in the product line influenced consumers' judgments of a particular model in the line. This influence depends on the acceptability of the highest price in the line and the relative position of the specific model being evaluated. Products positioned at the higher end of the product line's prices were evaluated as of higher quality but lesser value than products positioned at the lower end of the line's prices. This result is consistent with the price–perceived quality–perceived value model developed in Chap. 4. That is, both perceived quality and perceived monetary sacrifice increase as price increases, but at least for this study and the prices considered, perceptions of sacrifice increased faster than perceptions of quality. Thus, when adding or deleting a model from a line of products, it is necessary to consider where the model's price lies in relation to the other models' prices. Above all else, this research highlights the need for relationship pricing when pricing a product line.

When extending the analysis to include all potential buyers within a market segment, expected variation among individual buyers must be considered since buyers are not expected to have identical threshold prices. Thus, a given market target would have a distribution of high- and low-threshold prices. A procedure has been developed for determining the mean and variance of this distribution when the decision objective is to determine the end prices of the product line.[8] Knowing the mean and variance of the distribution enables one to determine the particular distribution of either the low end price or the high end price, depending on whether relatively low or high prices were used to stimulate the market responses.

Determining Price Differentials

Chapter 3 presented the concept of the Weber–Fechner law, representing the relation between the measured magnitude of a stimulus and the measured magnitude of response,

---

[7]Susan M. Petroshius and Kent B. Monroe, "Effect of Product-Line Pricing Characteristics on Product Evaluations," *Journal of Consumer Research,* 13 (March 1987), 511–519.
[8]Monroe, op. cit.

$$R = k(\log S) + a \qquad (13\text{-}1)$$

This law has served to justify the use of the logarithmic relationship between a price and a market response as well as the use of the lognormal distribution when the market response is probabilistic.[9] Of interest when determining price differentials is the concept of a constant proportion between just-noticeably different (JND) stimuli. Or, stating the situation in reverse, the prices of two products should not be different unless the products themselves are perceived as different by buyers.

Beginning with the lowest price in the product line, P_{min}, the price of the next product would be determined by adding a constant rate, k, to the P_{min}. Continuing in this manner by adding a constant rate, k, to the previously determined price until each product has been priced results in a set of prices reflecting noticeable differences among products.

The basic assumption of this approach is that the subjective price scale of the buyer resembles a ratio (logarithmic) scale rather than a natural scale. *That is, the differences in prices between products should reflect relative differences rather than absolute differences.* For example, it is often the practice of clothing retailers to carry three price lines of merchandise, with the price difference between lines being a constant amount of dollars. But if the low line is priced at $20 and the medium line is priced at $30, the high line should be priced at $45, not $40, to represent a 50 percent difference in price at each level. This prescription reflects correcting the error of not recognizing the difference between relative and absolute price differences that was discussed in Chap. 3.

Assuming the products in the product line have been ranked in ascending order (i.e., the product designated the lowest priced product is ranked 1, the product designated as the next-to-lowest-priced product is ranked 2, and so on, until the highest priced product is ranked n), then any product can be priced once the P_{min} has been set. The price of the jth ordered product is given as

$$P_j = P_{min}k^{j-1} \qquad (13\text{-}2)$$

where k is the constant rate, $k > 1$, and j is the jth ordered product.

Since it is assumed that there is a given number of products in the line and that the low and high end prices have been determined, the constant rate k is easily determined using the relationship

$$\log k = \frac{1}{n-1}(\log P_{max} - \log P_{min} \qquad (13\text{-}3)$$

or

$$k = (P_{max}\,P_{min})^{1/(n-1)}$$

[9]Ibid.

TABLE 13-2
DETERMINING PRICE DIFFERENTIALS

1. Rank products in ascending order of expected prices, i.e., from low to high price.
2. Determine the low-end price, P_{min}.
3. Determine the high-end price, P_{max}.
4. The price of the jth-ordered product is

   $$P_j = P_{min}k^{j-1}, \qquad k > 1$$

5. Thus, the problem is to determine k:

   $$\log k = \frac{1}{n-1}(\log P_{max} - \log P_{min})$$

   where n is the number of products in the line

TABLE 13-3
PRICE DIFFERENTIAL EXAMPLE

	Price, $	
Model	Theoretical	Actual
A	25.00	25.00
B	35.78	36.00
C	51.19	55.00
D	73.25	79.00
E	104.82	109.00
F	150.00	150.00

P_{min} = \$25.00; P_{max} = \$150.00; $n = 6$

$\log k = \dfrac{1}{5}(\log 150 - \log 25)$

$= \dfrac{1}{5}(2.1761 - 1.3979)$

$= \dfrac{1}{5}(0.7782) = 0.1556$

$k = 1.431$

$P_B = \$25.00\,(1.431) = \$\ 35.78$
$P_C = \ \ 35.78\,(1.431) = \ \ \ 51.19$
$P_D = \ \ 51.19\,(1.431) = \ \ \ 73.25$
$P_E = \ \ 73.25\,(1.431) = \ \ 104.82$

If P_{min} and k are known, the price of any product in the line can be set, thereby determining the price differentials among products. Table 13-2 outlines the procedure for determining price differentials that has just been summarized. Table 13-3 gives a numerical example of the process. As shown in Table 13-3, a firm had six products in a line, and it had decided that the low-end product should be priced at \$25, while the high-end product should be priced at \$150. As the table indicates, by using the three values P_{max}, P_{min}, and n, a constant multiplier of $k = 1.431$ was determined. Applying this constant multiplier to each price beginning with the low price of \$25 produced the "theoretical prices" shown. The firm wanted all of its prices at round values, so each price was adjusted to the actual prices shown. An application of this procedure to pricing hotel rooms follows.

Guidelines for Setting Price Differentials

Since the response of demand to price is uncertain, a probabilistic model may be an effective approach to the product-line pricing problem. Empirical evidence of the logarithmic relationship between price and behavioral response suggests that previously developed methodology can be used to obtain the required response estimate for a set of alternative product-line prices. Further, using an extension of this methodology, end prices can be established.

Once the two end prices are determined, a range of prices can be set for the product line. Given the price range and the number of products in the line, price differences among the products may be obtained by adding a constant proportion to the previously determined price to get the next price in the line.

The correct pricing of a product or service line for a *segmented pricing strategy* should follow these principles:

1 Each product or service should be priced correctly in relation to all other products in the line. Specifically, noticeable differences in the offerings should be equivalent to perceived value differences.

2 The highest and lowest prices in the product line have a special complementary relation to other offerings in the line and should be priced to encourage desired buyer perceptions.

3 Price differentials between products in the product line should get wider as price increases over the product line. This principle follows the behavioral finding that price perception follows a logarithmic scale rather than an arithmetic or linear scale.

If the organization wishes to use a *trading-up strategy* when pricing the product line, it must first decide which products or services are to be designed and priced to be similar to each other. Then the higher priced product should have a feature or observable benefit that would be perceived to be of value by buyers, but the incremental price for this extra feature or benefit should be less than its perceived value. In this situation, instead of a wider price differential between these two products, a smaller price differential should be set. That is, the price differential should be perceived as less than the incremental value obtained by trading up to the higher priced product.

PRICING HOTEL ROOMS—A SPECIFIC APPLICATION

A hotel or motel may be viewed as offering a product line consisting of different types of rooms and different types of occupancy, usually single or double. Most hotels derive a large part of their room business from repeat transients, who are sometimes thought of as satisfied guests. Most hotel guests are willing to pay a reasonable room

TABLE 13-4
GUEST ROOM PRICING

Base rack pricing of hotel guest rooms must consider and evaluate at least the following several interrelated factors:

The property:
  Market and location
  Competition
  Image and position
  Type, quality, facilities, services
  Costs
  Profit objectives

The rooms:
  Type, furnishings, quality
  Size
  Facilities
  Location

The essential elements toward objective consideration and evaluation of these factors are assurance of verified current information; involvement of at least a key, relevant, top management member of the hotel and an "outside" rooms or marketing specialist (although ultimate pricing should be reviewed by both functions) who must arrive at consensual evaluation of each factor by visiting and testing the competition and analyzing their hotel's market position and price–value relationship to competition; evaluation of each guest room, or type, in the hotel, considering all factors and recognizing the advantages/disadvantages of the relative hotel product in the market. Appropriately positioned price ranges are the limits for pricing of specific rooms and types. *Each price in the structure must be associated with a readily distinguishable physical attribute of the room or type.*

The initial base prices thus determined must then be analyzed relative to rate and revenue potentials (considering the number of rooms at each price and relationships of room types and prices) and then tested relative to cost/profit factors and objectives, which may necessitate certain adjustments . . . but which must be done consistently and realistically relative to the market, and associated with tailored selling strategies. All special prices and rate packages should be directly derived from a percentage of the then determined base rack prices utilizing a consistent discount concept.

Note: In the terminology of hotel management, the base rack price of a room is the list price for one night's occupancy.

rate provided they perceive that they have received a fair value for that rate. For example, if a guest is given a $50 room when he or she expected to pay $35, that individual will probably not be dissatisfied if the $50 room is *noticeably worth $15 more than the $35 room of a previous visit.* Thus, the pricing problem is to price each room correctly in relation to other rooms *and* to match the number of rooms at each rate to the demand for rooms at each rate. Table 13-4, the pricing policy statement of a major hotel chain, reflects these points.

To price hotel rooms, four analytical steps should be taken:

1 Analyze demand for rooms.
2 Compare the supply of rooms with room demand.
3 Rank the rooms according to noticeable physical attributes.
4 Establish the room prices.

TABLE 13-5
SAMPLE OCCUPANCY DATA

Room Price, $	Number of Rooms	Average Percentage Paying Price	Cumulative Percentage
46.00	20	5.0	5.0
46.50	20	4.0	9.0
47.00	285	3.0	12.0
47.50	55	8.0	20.0
48.00	20	10.0	30.0
48.50	40	10.0	40.0
49.00	15	20.0	60.0
49.50	10	10.0	70.0
50.00	20	8.0	78.0
51.00	10	7.0	85.0
52.00	10	5.0	90.0
54.00	25	3.0	93.0
56.00	5	1.0	94.0
57.00	10	1.0	95.0
57.50	5	0.5	95.5
58.00	5	0.5	96.0
59.00	10	1.0	97.0
59.50	5	1.0	98.0
60.00	5	0.5	98.5
62.00	15	1.0	99.5
65.00	10	0.5	100.0

Each of these steps will be illustrated with an actual pricing problem.

Analyzing Room Demand

The hotel used in this example has 600 rooms and 21 different single-room rates.[10] To analyze demand, two groups of 10 days each were sampled. The two samples were chosen to be representative in terms of the usual transient occupancy rate—75 percent. On each sample day, the actual number of persons paying each single rate was recorded. These data were converted to the average percentage of persons paying each rate (Table 13-5). From Table 13-5 a demand characteristic curve was developed that showed the cumulative percentage of persons vs. the rate actually paid (Fig. 13-1).

Comparing Room Supply with Room Demand

From the demand characteristic curve and the data of Table 13-5, the demand for each room price was determined. It was reasoned that if 5 percent of the guests

[10]See Elmer Roth, "How to Increase Room Revenue," *Hotel Management,* 67 (March 1955), 52ff.

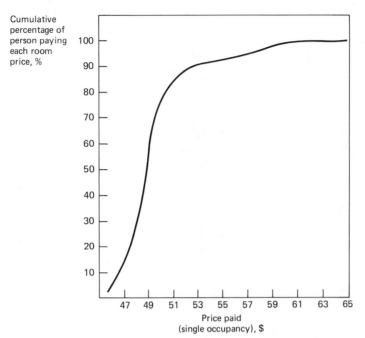

Cumulative
percentage of
person paying
each room
price, %

FIGURE 13-1
Demand characteristic curve.

occupied a $46 room, then 5 percent of 600, or 30 rooms, was the relative demand for a $46 room (Table 13-6). The room data of Table 13-5 were compared to Table 13-6 using Fig. 13-2. As Fig. 13-2 indicates, the actual supply of rooms, particularly at $47, did not match the determined demand for rooms. Indeed, there were too many rooms at $47, an insufficient number of rooms in the $48–$54 range, and too many rooms over $54. In addition, the data indicate that the spacing of room prices was too close, especially at the higher prices.

Ranking the Rooms

All the rooms in the hotel were evaluated and factors of "noticeable differences" were established. As suggested in Table 13-4, the noticeable difference attributes are room size, location in terms of altitude (floor number) and view, and facilities available, such as TV, air conditioning, refrigerator, storage space, size and type of bedding, and accessory furniture. (See also the discussion about hotel room characteristics in Chap. 6.) Each room was coded according to its number of noticeably different factors and assigned a room classification in rank order. It was determined that the hotel had nine noticeably different types of rooms. Hence, it was concluded that there was a greater number of different prices than there were classes of rooms of noticeably different value.

TABLE 13-6
ROOM DEMAND

Room Price, $	Average Percentage Paying Price	Number of Rooms to Meet Demand*
46.00	5.0	30
46.50	4.0	24
47.00	3.0	18
47.50	8.0	48
48.00	10.0	60
48.50	10.0	60
49.00	20.0	120
49.50	10.0	60
50.00	8.0	48
51.00	7.0	42
52.00	5.0	30
54.00	3.0	18
56.00	1.0	6
57.00	1.0	6
57.50	0.5	3
58.00	0.5	3
59.00	1.0	6
59.50	1.0	6
60.00	0.5	3
62.00	1.0	6
65.00	0.5	3

*The number of rooms needed was determined by applying the average percentage paying price to the total of 600 rooms, e.g., 5% of 600 = 30 rooms.

Establishing the Room Prices

Using the nine room classifications, the rooms were ranked according to the number of noticeably different factors. The lowest ranked room class was to be the lowest priced room, and each higher ranked room class would be assigned a higher price.

The lowest ranked and highest ranked room classes were priced first. The lowest price, P_{min}, was established at the traditional minimum rate of $46, and the highest price, P_{max}, was set at the traditional high price of $65.

Once the minimum and maximum single-occupancy prices were set, Eq. (13-3) was applied.

$$\log k = \frac{\log 65 - \log 46}{n - 1} = \frac{1.81291 - 1.66276}{8}$$
$$= 0.018769$$

Taking the antilog of 0.01876 provided the solution $k = 1.044$.

According to the Weber–Fechner law, and given the maximum and minimum price constraints and the number of room classifications, multiplying the minimum

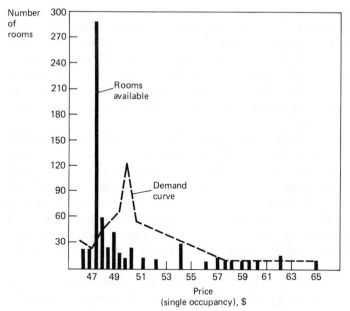

FIGURE 13-2
Room demand at original prices.

price of $46 by 1.044 produces the price for the next room classification, $48.03 ($46 × 1.044 = $48.03). The next price is determined by multiplying $48.03 by the constant k, 1.044, to obtain $50.15. Successive applications of the constant 1.044 produce the theoretical price structure seen in Table 13-7. Management decided to round the theoretical prices to the nearest multiple of $0.25, producing the actual single-occupancy price schedule in the table.

TABLE 13-7
REVISED ROOM PRICE STRUCTURE

Number of Rooms	Single Occupancy		Double Occupancy	
	Theoretical Price, $	Actual Price, $	Double-bed Price, $	Twin-bed Price, $
55	46.00	46.00	49.50	50.00
125	48.03	48.00	51.50	52.00
150	50.15	50.00	53.00	53.50
120	52.37	52.50	56.00	56.50
90	54.68	54.75	58.25	58.75
30	57.10	57.00	60.50	61.00
15	59.62	59.75	63.25	63.75
10	62.25	62.25	65.75	66.25
5	65.00	65.00	68.50	69.00

In setting double-occupancy prices, management wanted one room price below $50 and all room prices below $70. Moreover, management had traditionally priced a twin-bedded double occupancy higher than a double-bedded double occupancy and wanted to continue this policy. Thus, it was decided to differentiate the different types of double occupancy by a constant $0.50. The double-bedded double-occupancy prices were set at $3.50 more than single-occupancy prices, and the twin-bedded double-occupancy prices were set at $4.00 more than single-occupancy prices.

The number of rooms to provide at each price was determined by considering the demand characteristic curve of Fig. 13-2. As nearly as possible, the number of rooms at each price was chosen to match the cumulative percentages given in Fig. 13-2 and Table 13-5. The hotel was constrained by the fact that not enough rooms contained sufficiently different physical attributes to justify a closer alignment of rooms to previous sample data. However, it was felt that by pricing according to perceived room differences, the room and price schedule would receive a high rate of guest satisfaction. Figure 13-3 compares the revised room and price schedule with the estimated demand curve for hotel rooms.

A comparison of Fig. 13-3 with Fig. 13-2 reveals improvements in the new price schedule according to the pricing principles discussed in the previous section.

1 The different prices correspond to different classes of rooms.

2 The highest and lowest priced rooms reflect previous experience about the acceptability of these prices.

FIGURE 13-3
Room demand at revised prices.

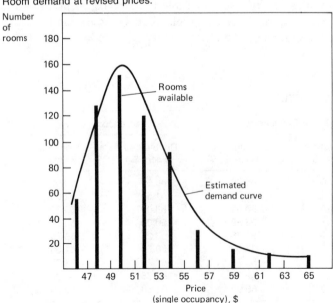

3 Price differentials between classes of rooms get wider as price increases over room classes. The spacing of prices at the high end of the range is greater than at the lower end. Price differentials begin at $2.00 for the lower priced room classes and rise to $3.75 for the higher priced rooms.

4 The number of rooms at each new price more closely approximates the estimated demand at each price.

PRICE BUNDLING

In marketing, one type of product-line pricing that is widespread is the practice of selling products or services in packages, or bundles. Such bundles can be as simple as a restaurant menu offering dinners and the same items à la carte or as complex as a ski package that includes travel, lodging, lift and ski rentals, and lessons. In either situation, some important principles need to be considered when bundling products or services at a special price. Additional examples of price bundling include the following:

Block-booked movies;
Maintenance contracts sold with appliances or technical equipment;
Weekend hotel packages offering lodging and meals at special rates;
Vacation packages combining travel, lodging, and tours at special rates;
Health clubs offering membership packages that include access to individual programs;
Cable TV plans that include premium channels in a special "package rate."

Bundling is ubiquitous and thus seemingly escapes notice. However, because it is so commonplace it has not received recognition as an important marketing strategy. Yet if properly developed and implemented, a price bundling strategy can enhance customers' perceptions of value, provide competitive advantage, lead to cost economies, and effect a profitable pricing strategy. But if bundling is improperly done, it can lead to lost sales, reduced profits, and a deterioration of customer satisfaction.

Essentially, bundling is a segmentation strategy based on the theory that different customer segments value different combinations of products or services differently. Unless the firm's managers understand customer segmentation, it is likely that a successful strategy will not be developed. Some customers find a one-stop purchasing source desirable. Full-service banks attempt to capture such customers by offering full financial services at one institution. However, other customers want a simple checking and saving service only. If the bank forced all customers to pay for full financial services which they neither need nor want, or priced each service separately, neither customer segment would be satisfied. In either situation, the bank would be treating very different customers in a similar manner.

Bundling forces managers to focus on the entire product line and to make judgments about what benefits each product and various combinations of products provide different customer segments. If there are several product or brand managers involved with the different products offered by the firm, then it is not likely that the relationships between the products will be effectively managed.

Rationale for Price Bundling

As observed in Chap. 8, many businesses are characterized by a relatively high ratio of fixed to total variable costs. Moreover, several products or services usually can be offered using the same facilities, equipment, and personnel. Thus, the direct variable cost of a particular offering is usually relatively low, meaning that it has a relatively high PV ratio. The incremental costs of selling additional units therefore are low relative to the firm's total costs.

In addition, many of the products or services offered by most organizations are interdependent in terms of demand, either being substitutes for each other or complementing the sales of another offering. To maximize the benefits received by customers or clients it is appropriate to think in terms of relationship pricing, or pricing in terms of the inherent demand relationships among products and services. *The objective of price bundling is to stimulate demand for the firm's product line in a way that achieves cost economies for the operations as a whole while increasing net contributions to profits.*

Mixed Bundling

In mixed bundling, the customer can purchase products or services individually or as a package. Normally there is a price incentive for the customer to purchase the package rather than acquiring the items comprising the bundle individually. In *mixed-leader bundling,* the price of one product is discounted if the first product is purchased at full price. For example, if cable TV customers buy the first premium channel at full price, they may be able to acquire a second premium channel at a reduction from its monthly rate. Assuming that premium channels A and B are individually priced at $10 per month each, then B might be offered for $7.50 if A is acquired at its regular rate. In *mixed-joint bundling,* a single price is set for the combined group of services. In this situation, the two premium channels would be offered together for one price, e.g., $17.50 per month. As should be obvious with these two examples, the net outlay for the customer buying either bundle is the same, but the seller must weigh several factors in deciding which bundle to offer.

Principles of Price Bundling

Several economic concepts discussed in Chap. 2 and earlier in this chapter provide the basis for developing a set of price bundling principles: consumer surplus, demand elasticity, complementarity, and some ideas from the economics of information. Also, the behavioral concepts of an acceptable price range and value perceptions discussed in Chap. 3 play an important role.

Underlying the notion of bundling is the recognition that different customers have different perceived values for the various products and services offered. In practical terms, these customers have different maximum amounts they would be willing to pay for the products or services. For some customers, the price of the product is less than this maximum acceptable price (upper price threshold), resulting in some consumer surplus. However, for these customers, the price of a second product or service may be greater than they are willing to pay, so they do not acquire it. If the firm, by price bundling, can shift some of the consumer surplus from the highly valued offering to the less highly valued offering, then there is an opportunity to increase the total contributions these offerings make to the firm's profitability. The seller's objective is to influence the sales of the items in the product line so as to enhance the product line's contributions to profits.

Table 13-8 provides an example of this point of shifting consumer surplus.[11] In the example, there are four customers and two products, A and B. Customer 1 is willing to pay up to $8 to acquire product A but only $1 to acquire product B. Thus, customer 1 would be willing to pay up to $9 for the combination of the two products. On the other hand, customer 2 values product A less and would be willing to pay no more than $3 for it. However, customer 2 would be willing to pay up to $6 for product B, or a total of $9 for the combination. Customers 3 and 4 also value the two products differently, with customer 3 willing to spend a total of $15 but customer 4 willing to spend only a total of $7. If the price of A is $7 and the price of B is $4, then customer 1 will buy A only, customer 2 will buy B only, customer 3 will buy both products, and customer 4 will buy neither. However, if the seller offers to sell both A and B as a package (bundle) at a special price of $9, then customers 1, 2, and 3 will buy the bundle. When the products were priced separately, the total revenues were $22, but revenues were $27 with the bundled price.

The ability to transfer consumer surplus from one offering to another depends on the complementarity of demand for these products or services. Products may complement each other because the joint purchase reduces the search costs of acquiring them separately. It is economical to have both savings and checking accounts in the same bank to reduce the costs of having to go to more than one bank for such services. Services may complement each other because acquiring one may increase the satisfaction of acquiring the other. For the novice skier, ski lessons will enhance

[11]This example is adapted from Joseph P. Guiltinan, "The Price Bundling of Services: A Normative Framework," *Journal of Marketing*, 51 (April 1987), 74–85.

TABLE 13-8
ECONOMIC PRINCIPLE OF BUNDLING (INDEPENDENT DEMAND)

	Reservation Prices, $*		
Customer	Product A	Product B	A + B
1	8	1	9
2	3	6	9
3	8	7	15
4	5	2	7

*The *reservation price* is the buyer's highest acceptable price for a product.

the satisfaction of skiing and increase the demand to rent skis. Finally, a full-service seller may be perceived to be a better organization than a limited-service seller, thereby enhancing the perceived value of all services offered.

The preceding example illustrates that one of the basic conditions necessary for bundling to work is that customers must be sensitive to relatively small price reductions, either for one product or for the combination. The degree to which buyers are price sensitive depends on the amount and type of information they have about the products or services that they are considering buying. From economics of information comes the proposition that the more information buyers have, or the easier it is for them to evaluate different offerings, the more price sensitive (elastic) they will be. To observe this relationship between buyers' ability to evaluate products before purchase and price elasticity, we can separate products and services into three classes: search products, experience products, and credence products.[12]

Search products or services have attributes that buyers can readily evaluate before purchase. They can determine an airline's schedule, check on a dentist's fees, or determine the relative quality of a television's reception prior to making a purchase decision. To the extent that buyers do attempt to acquire such information for these

[12]Louis Wilde, "The Economics of Consumer Information Acquisition," *Journal of Business,* 53 (July 1980), S143–158; Philip Nelson, "Comments on 'The Economics of Consumer Information Acquisition,'" *Journal of Business,* 53 (July 1980), S163–165.

TABLE 13-9
SEARCH, EXPERIENCE, AND CREDENCE ATTRIBUTES

	Search Attribute	Experience Attribute	Credence Attribute
Definition	Can be evaluated before purchase	Can be evaluated only after purchase	Usually cannot be evaluated after receipt or use
Examples	Dentist's fees, air travel time, TV picture quality, stereo sound	Food taste, concert performance, dry cleaning, hair permanent	Legal advice, tax advice, health care
Therefore, buyers may be . . .	more aware of substitutes	less aware of substitutes	not able to compare or evaluate alternatives
Sellers likely will . . .	imitate or copy successful features	be less able to imitate or copy successful features	be more likely to customize offerings
Therefore, there will be . . .	more similar substitutes	fewer and less similar substitutes	fewer and more distinctive substitutes
Cross-price elasticity will be relatively . . .	high	moderate	low

products, they are likely to be aware of the attributes of substitute products, and hence more price sensitive than other buyers. As a result, alternative products will appear more frequently than they would if buyers were uninformed (see Table 13-9).

Experience products or services have attributes that can be evaluated only after purchase. Thus, buyers do not know exactly what they are getting when they acquire the product. However, once the product has been purchased and experienced, buyers have an idea of the attributes and the degree to which they are satisfied with the value received. Experience products are likely to be highly differentiated in the marketplace and to be less price elastic than search products.

Finally, *credence products or services* have attributes that buyers cannot confidently evaluate even after one or more purchases. Thus, buyers must rely on the reputation of the product or on external cues such as brand name, store name, or price as signals of quality. Credence products like health care and legal services are therefore least price sensitive.

As noted, demand is likely to be more price elastic for products and services that can be evaluated on the basis of search attributes than for those that can be evaluated only after receipt of the service or not at all. Thus, products or services to be considered for a bundling strategy should have salient attributes that are search-based because one requirement for successful bundling is that at least one of the services be price elastic.

DEVELOPING A PRICE BUNDLING STRATEGY

There are four basic steps to developing a price bundling strategy:

1 Define customer segment targets.
2 Determine bundling objectives.
3 Determine demand conditions for each objective.
4 Determine profitability of alternative strategies.

Defining Customer Segment Targets

As the example summarized in Table 13-8 indicates, there are four basic customer segments: 1 and 2 buy only one of the products under consideration for bundling, i.e., buy A only or buy B only; 3 buys both products (A and B); and 4 buys neither A nor B. Each of these segments has a different buy response curve (see Chap. 6) for the products as well as different distributions of the maximum price they would be willing to pay for the products or services. Thus, it is necessary to determine the price distributions for these different segments using one of the research methods outlined in Chap. 6.

Determining Bundling Objectives

There are three basic bundling objectives. First, the firm could target either segment 1 or segment 2 and attempt to cross-sell. That is, the firm could attempt to convince buyers of A only to also buy B or buyers of B only to also buy A, or it could try to convince both types of buyers to buy the other product. Thus, cross-selling is the attempt to persuade buyers to buy another product on the basis of the product they are currently buying. For example, if men customers of a clothing store typically do not buy shirts when purchasing suits, the store might offer shirts at a reduced price when a suit is purchased.

A second objective would be to target customer segment 4, i.e., acquire new customers for A and B. This objective is much more difficult to achieve simply because the seller must first determine the reasons why these customers do not buy product A or B. Thus, some effort must first be made to determine who these nonbuyers are and why they either do not buy or buy from a competitor. Then the seller would be in a position to determine whether price bundling might be an effective strategy.

The third objective, price bundling to retain current customers who buy both A and B, is least likely to be used. If the seller adopts the cross-selling or retention objective, the benefits will be available to current buyers of A and B. Thus, reducing price to cross-sell or to acquire new customers will lead to a reduction in revenues from current buyers who take advantage of the offer.

Determining Demand Requirements for Each Objective

When cross-selling is the primary objective, the focus is on buyers of A only or B only. To decide whether to use mixed-leader bundling or mixed-joint bundling, the relative unbundled demand for each product is an important consideration. If unit sales volume of one of the products is substantially greater than the other, then mixed-leader bundling should be used. The product with the higher sales volume should be used as the leader. For example, assume A is currently priced at $20 and has a unit sales volume of 10,000. Product B is priced at $10 and has a unit sales volume of 5,000. These two products produce unbundled revenues of $250,000 ($200,000 + $50,000). If the firm offers to sell A at $15 when customers buy B at the regular $10 price, and if all customers take advantage of the offer, the maximum revenues are 15,000 × $15 plus 15,000 × $10, or $375,000. Note that there is more to gain by reducing the price of A to those who buy B at regular price than the reverse arrangement. Potentially, 10,000 customers can be induced to buy B, but only 5,000 can be cross-sold A.

However, if the unit volume sold of A is approximately equal to that for B, then the appropriate strategy to use is mixed-joint bundling. Continuing with the same example, assume that both A and B have unbundled unit sales volume of 7,500. Unbundled revenues are $225,000 (7,500 × $20 + 7,500 × $10). If the seller offers to sell both A and B for $25, and if all customers take advantage of the offer, the maximum revenues will be $375,000 (15,000 × $25). Because the unbundled sales volumes are equal, there is no relative advantage to using one of the products as a leader.

If the objective is to acquire new customers (i.e., customers not now buying either A or B), there is no way to define a leader. We simply do not have sales data for this customer segment. The key then is to determine the relative price sensitivity of these customers for the products in question. Price research as described in Chap. 6 would provide valuable information for this objective. We can also use the notions described earlier from economics to gain some insights as to which products to use in the bundling strategy and how they might be used. Remembering that products or services with attributes that are relatively easy to evaluate are likely to be more price elastic, we might select a product that has these types of attributes as the lead product. Thus, we would use a mixed-leader strategy. The second product must complement the lead product for this strategy to be successful. For example, offering a set of microwave dishes at a reduced price when a microwave oven is purchased would fit these prescriptions. Use of a mixed-joint strategy requires products with attributes that are easy to evaluate, are price elastic, and complement each other.

Determining the Profitability of Alternative Strategies

When examining the relative profitability of bundling strategies it is important to remember that the bundling offer will be available to current customers. This means that the seller will receive less contribution from sales to profits from customers who previously bought both A and B. Further, there will be fewer customers who buy A only or B only (although these customers who buy only A or B will provide the same contribution margin as before). If the unit contribution margins of A and B are different, then the firm's profitability will be enhanced if the larger increase in bundled sales comes from those customers who previously purchased only the lower margin product.

Criteria for Selecting Products to Bundle

It should be clear that developing a bundling strategy requires careful thought and analysis of the consequences of reducing price to enhance volume. As discussed in Chap. 8, a successful price reduction strategy requires that the products have relatively large margins and that sales growth be feasible. Essentially, the products must be in the growth stages of their product life cycles or they must be highly price elastic.

Since the objective is to increase the overall sales level of the firm, the products or services selected for bundling should be relatively small in unbundled sales volume, which will minimize cannibalization. For mixed-leader bundling, the lead product or service must be price elastic, have attributes that are easy to evaluate before purchase, must be the higher volume product or service in the bundle, and should be the lower margin offering. The objective is to use a price reduction in this product or service to generate an increase in its volume, which "pulls" an increase in demand for a lower volume–higher contribution margin offering. The increase in volume of the second product will contribute more to profits than the loss due to the reduced contribution of the lead product.

For mixed-joint bundling, the contributions should be about equal, the unbundled sales volumes should be about equal, their demand should be price elastic, and each should complement the other product. In any case, these products or services should not be high sales volume offerings.

These principles suggest that firms should not pursue price bundling strategies simply because others are doing it. As observed at the beginning of this book, me-too pricing is likely to lead to serious pricing errors. Bundling can be an effective pricing strategy, but it should be applied in a limited way and only after a careful analysis of the nature of the products or services offered and an understanding of customers' perceptions of the value of these offerings.

YIELD MANAGEMENT

A form of segmentation pricing that was developed by the airlines after deregulation is called yield management. Like price bundling, yield management operates on the principle that different segments of the market have different degrees of price sensitivity. Therefore, seats on airline flights are priced differently depending on the time of the flight, day of the week, length of stay in the destination city, when the ticket is purchased, and certain other conditions or restrictions. Besides the airlines, hotels, telephone companies, car rental companies, banks, and savings and loans have used yield management to increase sales revenues through segmentation pricing. It seems likely that retail firms could use yield management to determine when to mark down slow-moving merchandise and when to schedule sales.

Using high-speed computers, the airlines make fare changes daily to reflect changes in demand, changes in seat capacity available between any two cities, and shifts in traffic. (In 1989 United Airlines made about 30,000 fare changes daily.) The objective is to fill seats with the highest possible revenue generated per seat-mile flown. However, realization of this objective is complicated by (1) the existence of a multitude of prices with varying amounts of restrictions that limit the availability of all but the highest priced seat; (2) numerous flights operated by several airlines over different routings, any one of which could be used by passengers to get to their destinations; and (3) varying degrees of demand for the seats on an airline's flight segment over time.

Thus, airlines are faced with determining the best mix of passengers and prices for a particular flight. There are two elements to solving the problem.[13] One is to maintain a reservation-monitoring system that keeps track of what seats are sold and at what prices. Generally, a small number of seats are designated as discount or special fare seats, and these seats usually sell first. However, as the actual time of the scheduled flight approaches, more discount seats may be made available if a large number of seats remain unfilled. For each flight, the airlines have data on the usual number of seats that are likely to be bought just a few days before departure, and if unfilled seats seem likely, then additional low-price seats will be made available. However, if demand for seats on that flight is greater than usual, the airline will stay with the full-fare ticket and not offer additional discount seats. The objective is to

[13]Fred Glover, Randy Glover, Joe Lorenzo, and Claude McMillan, "The Passenger-Mix Problem in the Scheduled Airlines," *Interfaces*, 12 (June 1982), 73–79.

sell as many full-fare seats as possible while minimizing the number of empty seats. Because a seat is a perishable commodity, any revenue above the relatively low direct variable cost of filling that seat is a positive contribution to the operations.

The second element is to evaluate different price–route scenarios to determine the most profitable price/passenger ratio. The profitability of a passenger depends on the length of the trip and the fare class the passenger travels. Although revenue per mile is usually less for passengers traveling long vs. short distances, the total revenue to the airline is greater for these passengers. Associated with each passenger on a given flight segment is the opportunity cost that the passenger occupies a seat that could have been sold at a higher price. For example, suppose a particular flight goes from terminal A to B to C in that order. Suppose a passenger books a seat on the B to C segment. Conceivably, that seat could have been sold to a passenger traveling from A to C with a stop at B. Thus, the plane might have an empty seat on the A to B segment, because the seat from B to C was previously sold. This is why you sometimes hear that a seat from A to C is cheaper than a seat from A to B or from B to C. An empty seat generates no revenues, and the objective is to sell the seat from its original point to its final point.

The unique benefit to a company of the yield management pricing program is continuous monitoring of demand for products. Further, changes in demand are reflected in consequent price changes. If the product is not selling fast enough, then price reductions can be initiated to stimulate sales. Because of a relatively high fixed costs to total variable costs cost structure, these focused price reductions offer leverage for increasing operating profits by their effect on sales volume. As we saw in Chap. 8, with relatively high contribution margins (high PV ratios), small price reductions can be profitable without large increases in volume.

SUMMARY

This chapter has applied some of the concepts developed in Chaps. 2–6 to pricing a product line. Several behaviorally oriented pricing principles were illustrated by an actual problem of pricing hotel rooms.

Chapter 13 has also placed more emphasis on aspects of price determination other than cost. A firm that produces several products sells products that are distinguishable in terms of the products' life cycles, extent of competition, and buyer acceptance of the products and their prices. Hence, as shown in Chap. 10, basing prices on a full-costing formula is arbitrary and does not consider market factors. Finally, a more careful consideration of how price affects buyer perceptions of a firm's product offerings can isolate new pricing alternatives. Development of pricing alternatives based on buyer and market considerations is more difficult than using a cost-oriented approach. But the reward is an opportunity to profitably improve buyer acceptance and satisfaction.

Little has been written previously about product-line pricing except to distinguish between complementary and substitutable items. However, we do know that the pricing structure for a product line can enhance demand for all items in the line even when some or all of the items are functionally substitutable. Such complementary relationships are behaviorally based phenomena and the current interest in price perception research has begun to provide a better conceptual basis for solving product-line pricing problems.

DISCUSSION QUESTIONS

1 Explain and provide examples of the following concepts:
   a Functional substitute.
   b Functional complement.
   c Product line.
2 Explain the product-line pricing problem. What are some of the complexities affecting the pricing of a product line?
3 If you have recently eaten in a restaurant, what do you remember about the prices of the entrées? Can you explain why you remember some of the prices? In general, how would you characterize the prices of this restaurant?
4 Return to Question 6 at the end of Chap. 8. How would you answer parts d and e of that question now? If your answer is different, why did you think it was necessary to change?

SUGGESTED READINGS

Anderson, Lane K.: "Expanded Breakeven Analysis for a Multi-Product Company," *Management Accounting,* 57 (July 1975), 30–32.

Grinnell, D. Jacque: "Product Mix Decisions: Direct Costing vs. Absorption Costing," *Management Accounting,* 58 (August 1976), 36–42, 53.

Guiltinan, Joseph P.: "The Price Bundling of Services: A Normative Framework," *Journal of Marketing,* 51 (April 1987), 74–85.

Oxenfeldt, Alfred: "Product Line Pricing," *Harvard Business Review,* 44 (July–August 1966), 135–143.

Petroshius, Susan M., and Kent B. Monroe: "Effect of Product-Line Characteristics on Product Evaluations," *Journal of Consumer Research,* 13 (March 1987), 511–519.

Reibstein, David J., and Hubert Gatignon: "Optimal Product Line Pricing: The Influence of Elasticities and Cross-Elasticities," *Journal of Marketing Research,* 21 (August 1984), 259–267.

Urban, Glen: "A Mathematical Modeling Approach to Product Line Decisions," *Journal of Marketing Research,* 6 (February 1969), 40–47.

ADMINISTERING THE PRICING FUNCTION

Perhaps the most difficult aspect of the pricing decision is the development of procedures and policies for administering prices. Up to this point in the book, the emphasis has been on the setting of base or list prices. However, the list price is rarely the actual price paid by the buyer. Discounting from list price for volume purchases or early payment, extending credit, charging for transportation—all effectively change the price paid. In this section, we consider such decisions within the analytical framework developed in Chaps. 2–10. Chapters 14 and 15 review the problems of administering prices, and Chap. 16 reviews the various legal issues involved in administering prices.

Pricing decisions and their implementation affect dealer or distributor cooperation and motivation as well as salespeople's morale and effort. Although it is difficult to control prices legally through the distribution channel, it is possible to elicit cooperation and provide motivation to adhere to company-determined pricing policies. Also, since price directly affects revenues of the trade and commissions of salespeople, it can be used to foster desired behaviors by channel members and salespeople. Finally, feedback is essential for a firm in today's dynamic economy. Chapter 15 discusses these management problems and offers approaches to solving them.

One of the most complex and frustrating problems of pricing is justification of price differentials. The need to justify price differentials may arise from litigation initiated by a customer, a competitor, or the government. However, particularly during inflationary periods, customers may request—or demand—justification for a recent price increase. Because it has been traditional to use cost-plus pricing, which incorporates arbitrary overhead allocations, the cost defense has rarely been success-ful in a legal proceeding. Moreover, many firms are hard-pressed to justify price increases to their customers. In fact, the firms' sales personnel are often the least satisfied by such justification attempts. Chapter 16 reviews the major federal legisla-tion in the United States and Canada concerning price discrimination and provides guidelines for justifying price differentials.

DEVELOPING A PRICE STRUCTURE

We now consider the problem of administering base prices throughout the channels of distribution and the markets in which the products are sold. Price administration deals with price adjustments or price differentials for sales made under different conditions, such as

sales made in different quantities;
sales made to different types of middlemen performing different functions;
sales made to buyers in different geographic locations;
sales made with different credit and collection policies;
sales made at different times of the day, month, season, or year.

The discussion of pricing thus far has been oriented toward determining what may be called a base or list price. It is this price, or some reasonable deviation therefrom, that buyers normally encounter. However, there is another vital dimension to prices, called price structure. Price structure involves determining

1 The time and conditions of payment
2 The nature of discounts to be allowed the buyer
3 Where and when title is to be taken by the buyer
4 Who pays for the transportation of the goods and how these charges are determined

Essentially, price structure decisions define how differential characteristics of the product and/or service will be priced. These price structure decisions are of strategic importance to manufacturers, distributors or dealers, and retailers. In establishing a price structure there are many opportunities to antagonize distributors and even incur legal liability. While using the price structure to achieve the desired profit objectives, these dangers must be avoided.

To understand the relative nature of the issue of determining the price structure, consider the problem of developing a price for taxi service. There are a number of ways of pricing taxi services, including

fixed charge to enter the taxi plus a variable fee per mile and/or minute (e.g., $0.50 plus $1.00 per mile traveled, or $1.00 per minute in transit);
fixed charge within the zone of pickup, plus a fee for each zone boundary crossed;
variable fee per mile;
fixed charge per passenger plus any one of the preceding fee schedules;
differential fees for rush hour vs. non–rush hour service.

Or consider the airlines, which may set a ticket price based on one or more of these factors: type of itinerary, time of day, day of week, length of stay at destination, when reservation is made, class of service. There are many ways to price a product or service, depending on the product or service characteristics, who is making the purchase, when the purchase occurs, when payment is made, the volume being purchased, or where the buyer is located. Regardless of its degree of complexity or simplicity, a pricing decision also requires the development of a price structure.

In earlier chapters we noted that the definition of price includes the required monetary outlay by the buyer as well as such complexities as terms of agreement, terms of payment, freight charges, warranty, timing of delivery, and volume of the order. Moreover, offering different products or services in the line with different features or benefits at different prices gives sellers the opportunity to develop prices for buyers who have different degrees of sensitivity to price levels and price differences. Moving from a simple one-price-for-all structure to a more complex pricing structure permits pricing flexibility through price variations based on specific product and service characteristics as well as buyer or market differences. Moreover, a more complex price structure enhances the ability of firms to respond to competitor, buyer, or market changes. This flexibility due to a more complex price structure allows firms to[1]

respond to specific competitive threats or opportunities,
enhance revenues while minimizing revenue loss due to price changes,
manage the costs of delivering the product or service,
develop focused price changes,
be more effective in gaining distributors' cooperation.

Pricing strategy can be linked to overall marketing strategy through price structure, a valuable aspect of both pricing and marketing strategy. The decision makers

---

[1]Andrew A. Stern, "The Strategic Value of Price Structure," *Journal of Business Strategy*, 7 (Fall 1986), 22–31.

need to determine how prices should vary across customers, products, territories, and purchase occasions to meet corporate objectives. To accomplish this goal of differential pricing requires identifying the key factors that differentiate price market segments. Then the elements of the price structure that reflect these factors can be developed. When devising the price structure it is important to recognize that conflicts inevitably will necessitate accepting tradeoffs to achieve the best overall profitable sales mix.

Chapter 14 begins by providing an overview of the different types of discount decisions. Two types of discounts—functional and promotional—will be discussed in greater detail in Chap. 15. After reviewing the different types of discounts, this chapter will discuss the problems of determining quantity discounts, cash discounts and credit policies, and geographical pricing.

AN OVERVIEW OF DISCOUNT DECISIONS

Trade or Functional Discounts

Functional discounts are based on a distributor's place in the distributive sequence and represent payment for performance of certain marketing functions. Although we are accustomed to think of price as a single number, price is usually quoted to distributors as a series of numbers, for example: "30, 10, 5 and 2/10 net 30" or "30, 20, 5, and 2/10 net EOM [end of month]." The first three numbers represent successive discounts from the list or base price. The list price usually designates the approximate or suggested final selling price of a product and is the price usually referred to when discussing the methods of price determination. However, the list price is used to quote and figure the discounts.

In the first quote above, if the list price was $10.00, then the price the dealer pays is $10.00 − 0.30($10.00) = $7.00; then $7.00 − 0.10($7.00) = $6.30; and $6.30 − 0.05($6.30) = $5.98. The 2/10 net 30 part of the quotation states that a 2 percent discount is further allowed if payment is made within 10 days, and in any event the full $5.98 is due within 30 days. If the 30, 10, 5 part of the quotation is for a specific dealer, the 30 will refer to the trade discount for the position the dealer occupies within the distribution channel; the 10 and 5 then refer to discounts allowed for promotional expenses the dealer might incur or other functions performed for the manufacturer.

The justification for trade discounts is that different distributors perform different functions within the distribution channel and should be compensated accordingly. For example, some wholesalers provide storage facilities for the manufacturer, help the retailer set up displays, extend credit to the retailer, and perform personal selling services for the manufacturer. Often it is difficult to fully identify the various functions the distributors perform and therefore to determine a trade discount structure that reflects the services performed. Much of this difficulty is due to the fact that some distributors combine the functions of wholesalers and retailers. It also results from the existence of so many different kinds of wholesalers and retailers.

Promotional Discounts

A promotional discount is given to distributors as an allowance for the distributors' efforts to promote the manufacturer's product through local advertising, special displays, or other promotions. These allowances may take the form of a percentage reduction in the price paid or additional merchandise (e.g., a free case for every dozen cases ordered), or they may be an outright cash payment either to the distributor or to the promotional vehicle, e.g., a local newspaper.

In recent years, sales promotions in the form of special deals to distributors have increased in frequency and magnitude. In some situations, the dollars budgeted for sales promotions now exceed the amount budgeted for advertising expenditures. Unfortunately, until recently, little research effort by industry or academic researchers was available to provide guidance on the proper use of price promotions either to the trade or to final buyers. Our discussion in Chap. 15 on price promotions will address some of the issues relative to this form of temporary price reductions.

Cash Discounts

A cash discount is a reward for the payment of an invoice or account within a specified period of time. At the start of the section, we saw that the terms 2/10 net 30 referred to the cash discount, 2 percent, that could be taken if payment was made within 10 days. The net 30 provides information concerning the length of the credit period the seller is willing to grant; i.e., if the cash discount is not taken because payment did not take place within 10 days, then the entire invoice or account must be paid in full within 30 days.

The cash discount is intimately tied to credit policy and is both a financial and a marketing decision. From the financial viewpoint, the extension of credit incurs costs from two basic sources: (1) the risk of bad-debt losses and (2) resources embedded in accounts receivable that forgo alternative uses. The gains from extending credit revolve around the increase in demand of this pseudo reduction in price.

Quantity Discounts

Perhaps the most common type of discount is the quantity discount. Such a discount is granted for volume purchases (measured in dollars or units), either in a single purchase (noncumulative) or over a specified period of time (cumulative, deferred, or patronage discount). The discount schedule may specify a single product or a limited number of products, or the discount may allow for a complete mix of products ordered in a single purchase or over a period of time.

For example, the following price schedule for reprints of articles applies to the total quantity of reprints ordered at one time, whether for the same or assorted articles, and shipped to one address:

Number of Reprints	English ($US)	Translation ($US)
1	1.00	1.25
2	1.30	1.65
3	1.50	1.90
4–99, each	0.40	0.50
First 100	39.70	49.65
Additional 100's up to 1,000, each	20.00	25.00
First 1,000	215.00	268.75
Additional 100's over 1,000, each	15.00	18.75

Noncumulative quantity discounts such as in this example serve to encourage large orders, which leads to fewer orders over a given time period. This ordering policy benefits sellers in that they have fewer orders to process, ship, and invoice, thereby reducing total costs for these activities. Cumulative discounts do not have these benefits, but they do tend to tie a buyer to a seller over the discount period if the buyer is eager to obtain the discount. However, the nature of a product sometimes makes it advantageous to place small orders, e.g., perishable products and large consumer durables or heavy equipment and machinery. For these kinds of products, buying in small quantities is practical and a cumulative discount schedule is beneficial to both parties.

An Example

To illustrate the nature of these discounts assume that the Stepup Ladder Company produces and sells a line of ladders for commercial and household use. The company produces five different types of ladders that vary in the materials used and ladder length. The suggested list prices of these ladders are $30, $50, $90, $120, and $150. These ladders are sold through hardware distributors to discount department stores and hardware stores. Typical trade discounts are 40, 10, 5. Further, the company quotes a cash discount of 3/10 net 30, and it allows an additional 5 percent discount to distributors for orders of $1,000 or more at list prices.

The Hardware Distributing Company places the order seen in Table 14-1. As the table shows, the total order amounted to $2,700 using list prices. Since the order exceeds $1,000, the quantity discount of 5 percent applied, making the net amount of the order $2,565. The trade discounts are then applied successively in the order shown in Table 14-1C. The total amount of the trade discounts is $1,249.16 ($1,026 + 153.90 + 69.26). Finally, if the order is paid within 10 days of delivery, an additional discount of 3 percent is allowed. Thus, if all discounts are applied, the manufacturer receives $1,276.36 from an order that amounted to $2,700 at list prices.

TABLE 14-1
APPLYING DISCOUNTS

A. The Hardware Distributing Company Order

10 ladders @ $30	$	300
6 ladders @ $50		300
10 ladders @ $90		900
5 ladders @ $120		600
4 ladders @ $150		600
Total	$	2,700

B. Applying the quantity discounts

Total order amount	$	2,700
Discounts, $2,700 × 0.05		135
Net order amount	$	2,565

C. Applying the trade discounts

Net order amount	$2,565.00
Less: 40% discount	1,026.00
	$1,539.00
Less: 10% discount	153.90
	$1,385.10
Less: 5% discount	69.26
Amount due manufacturer	$1,315.84

D. Applying the cash discount

Amount due manufacturer	$1,315.84
Less: 3% discount	39.48
Net remittance	$1,276.36

QUANTITY DISCOUNTS

Several reasons for offering quantity discounts have been presented in the pricing literature. One obvious reason is that sellers can reduce costs in several ways by convincing buyers to place large orders. First, assuming a constant level of demand, fewer orders have to be processed and shipped and fewer sales calls are necessary to generate these large orders. Second, longer production runs may be possible and the manufacturer may now qualify for quantity discounts on raw materials purchases. Third, by shifting to the buyers the cost of carrying finished goods inventory, the seller further reduces operation costs. Fourth, assuming that payment for the goods is prompt, the money available can be reinvested sooner. Fifth, quantity discounts can be viewed as a subtle form of profit sharing between channel members, leading to channel cooperation.[2] The sixth rationale, as demonstrated later, is simply tradition. However, in deciding whether to offer quantity discounts and the type of discount structure to use, the behavioral objectives underlying the policy must be considered. That is, what type of purchasing and ordering behavior by buyers will enhance the profit position of the firm, and what form of price inducement is necessary to achieve such buyer behavior? The framework developed here is designed to help decision makers think through this behavioral issue.

Four decisions must be made when setting up a noncumulative quantity discount schedule:

1 The minimum quantity to be purchased before any discount is applied
2 The number of breaks or additional discounts for larger purchases
3 The maximum quantity qualifying for any additional discount
4 The amount of discount to offer at each quantity level

These decisions have largely been made on the basis of intuition, and the results of such a nonanalytical approach are exemplified by the price structures of four manufacturers selling similar products seen in Table 14-2. Ignoring possible list price differences, the only price advantage in buying from manufacturer A occurs when purchasing 5 to 9 items, because thereafter it becomes more economical to buy from another seller. Further, the relative inconsistency across manufacturers on the price

[2]Abel P. Jeuland and Steven M. Shugan, "Managing Channel Profits," *Marketing Science,* 2 (Summer 1983), 239–272.

TABLE 14-2
PRICING STRUCTURE OF FOUR COMPETING MANUFACTURERS

Price	Volume, Units			
	Manufacturer A	Manufacturer B	Manufacturer C	Manufacturer D
List price	1–4	1–9	1–24	1–49
List price less 5.4%	5 or more			
List price less 7.0%			25–29	
List price less 7.5%		10–24		
List price less 15%				50–99
List price less 16.7%		25–49		
List price less 21.7%		50–99		
List price less 24%				100 or more
List price less 25%		100–249		
List price less 29%		250 or more		
List price less 40%			100–499	
List price less 50%			500–999	
List price less 55%			1,000 or more	

Source: Developed from John F. Crowther, "Rationale for Quantity Discounts," *Harvard Business Review,* 42 (March–April 1964), 121–127.

breaks and discounts offered suggests an intuitive decision process and an unclear conception of the role of a quantity discount schedule.

A Simple Quantity Discount Model

One of the basic points made in Chap. 1 is that ultimately the overall objective of pricing decisions is to influence the purchasing behavior of buyers. That is, the objective of setting a specific price or changing a price or establishing price differentials is to enhance the opportunity of obtaining profitable sales. Thus, the basic purpose of a quantity discount schedule is to enhance demand while reducing the costs of meeting that level of demand. Viewing the quantity discount as a price reduction decision suggests that the elasticity of demand with respect to the percentage discount should be a decision consideration. However, this demand elasticity depends on the relative costs to buyers of balancing their ordering costs with their inventory carrying costs. That is, increasing the size of their orders results in fewer orders being placed within a given time period but also results in buyers carrying a higher level of average inventory over the same time period. Hence, a quantity discount schedule should recognize the potential change in buyers' inventory costs if they change the size of their orders.

The seller must consider the cost of obtaining an order as a function of order size. For example, if customers were to place their entire sets of orders on the first day of the planning period, this purchasing behavior would represent a gain to the seller, who could immediately reinvest these revenues. Further, the seller's total cost of filling orders decreases as the number of orders decreases, i.e., as the volume per order increases.

To see the relative tradeoffs between the increase in buyers' costs and the reduction in the seller's costs consider the following simple model for determining these two costs: *the change in buyer's inventory costs as quantity purchased increases and changes in the seller's costs as the purchase order size increases.*[3] The buyers' cost function is given as

$$\text{TEK}_\text{B} = \frac{Ad}{q} + \frac{qki}{2} \qquad (14\text{-}1)$$

where TEK = total expected inventory costs
A = the cost of placing a single order
d = number of units required during the planning period
q = number of units ordered at one time
k = price of one unit
i = cost of carrying one unit of inventory per period expressed as a fraction of the unit's value

Using differential calculus to find the minimum value for TEK_B as q varies and then solving for q produces the equation for the economic purchase quantity:

[3]John F. Crowther, "Rationale for Quantity Discounts," *Harvard Business Review,* 42 (March–April 1964), 121–127.

$$q_0 = \left(\frac{2Ad}{\text{ki}}\right)^{1/2} \tag{14-2}$$

The seller's cost function is

$$\text{TEKs} = \frac{Ad}{q} - \frac{pkiq}{2} \tag{14-3}$$

where p is the percentage gross margin on an item.

Both the seller's and buyer's optimal annual ordering and inventory costs can be determined before any discount is offered. Then for any larger quantity ordered, it would be possible to determine

1 The increased cost to the buyer
2 The decreased cost to the seller
3 The net decrease in total cost to both parties (i.e., the change in their joint costs)

By splitting the decrease in cost to the seller between both parties, the amount of the possible discount can be determined. The exact proportional split can be determined according to the seller's perceived relative worth of inducing the buyer to purchase in larger quantities.

To be nondiscriminatory, the seller must offer the discount structure to all buyers. Therefore, customers must be classified according to historical average order size, and then the seller may select the order classification to develop the foregoing analysis. The seller then can determine whether more or fewer price breaks would allow a broader appeal to other order-size buyer classifications. The primary advantage of such an approach is that the seller is forced to consider customers and their needs and to balance these needs against the seller's own pecuniary objectives.

An Example[4]

A chemical company offered a product in 55-gallon drums using the following price schedule:

Number of Drums	Price per Gallon, $
1–4	2.57
5–9	2.50
10–19	2.44
20 or more	2.38

[4]This example is adapted from John F. Crowther, "Rationale for Quantity Discounts," *Harvard Business Review,* 42 (March–April 1964), 121–127.

The total purchase cost for five drums purchased singly is $706.75, whereas the total purchase cost for five drums purchased in quantity is $687.50. The discount for a quantity purchase is $19.25, or 2.72 percent. Similarly, the discount allowed for 10 drums is 5.06 percent and that for 20 drums is 7.39 percent. The company's comptroller estimates that it costs the firm $10 to process an order (A) and that an effective interest rate, i, for carrying the product in inventory is 20 percent.

The data in Table 14-3, developed from sales records, indicate that the price break at five drums does not stimulate additional volume per order. Otherwise, customers buying three or four drums would be fewer in number than those purchasing five drums per order. The sales records also indicate that the average customer ordering one or two drums per order purchases four to five drums per year.

Thus, if the small buyers' economic purchase quantity is assumed to be 1.25 drums (q_0) and if their yearly demand (d) is 4.5 drums, then from Eq. (14-2)

$$1.25 = \left(\frac{2A \times 4.5}{\$140i}\right)^{1/2}$$

(The actual purchase cost of a drum is $141.35, but it is rounded to $140 for simplicity.) Solving this equation produces

$$\frac{A}{i} = \$24.31$$

which would result if a small customer's ordering cost was about $3, with an interest rate of about 12.5 percent. By using Eq. (14-1) it is possible to determine the small buyers' costs as a function of order size, q:

TABLE 14-3
FREQUENCY DISTRIBUTION OF ORDER SIZE

Number of Drums per Order	Number of Shipments in Sample Period
1	3,073
2	910
3	336
4	271
5	254
6	183
7	38
8	89
9	68
10	158
11 or more (usually more than 20)	6,630
Total	12,010

$$\text{TEK}_B = \frac{\$3 \times 4.5}{q} + \frac{\$140 \times 0.125 \times q}{2} = \frac{\$13.5}{q} + \$8.75q$$

For an order size q of one to four drums, the total cost, TEK_B, would be as follows:

q	TEK_B, $
1	22.25
2	24.25
3	30.75
4	38.38
5	45.67

And for an order size of five drums, the cost is $45.67 despite the price per drum falling to $137.50. Thus, the small buyer would pay $23.42 more in inventory costs to place one order for five drums as opposed to placing five orders for one drum each.

The seller's cost of serving the small buyer can be computed using Eq. (14-3) where $p = 40$ percent margin:

$$\text{TEK}_S = \frac{\$10 \times 4.5}{q} - \frac{0.4 \times \$140 \times 0.2q}{2} = \frac{\$45}{q} - \$5.60q$$

For an order size q of one to three drums, the seller's cost, TEK, would be as follows:

q	TEK_S, $
1	39.40
2	11.30
3	−1.80

Thus, for an order size of three drums, the seller's savings is $41.20 [or $39.40 − (−$1.80)], whereas the buyer's added costs are $8.50 ($30.75 − $22.25). Now, if the average yearly demand for the small buyer is four and a half drums, then the yearly purchase cost is $636. If the small buyer can be persuaded to purchase three drums at a time, then the seller saves $41.20/$636, or 6.48 percent, but the buyer incurs an additional cost of \$8.50/\$636, or 1.34 percent. Thus, with a discount of 3.5 percent for quantity purchases of three drums, the seller gains about 3 percent and the buyer gains about 2.15 percent.

However, the seller recognized that buyers of four drums per order will also receive a discount of 3.5 percent, reducing the seller's savings. But, on the other hand, the data of Table 14-3 revealed little to be gained by offering an additional discount for purchases of 10–19 drums per order. Hence, the seller's new price schedule:

Number of Drums	Price per Gallon, $
1–2	2.57
3–19	2.48
20 or more	2.38

It is important to remember that if the seller offers a quantity discount to induce the buyer to increase the size of the purchase order, then the lower price obtained for taking the quantity discount may lead to lower total inventory costs by reducing the quantity $qki/2$ in Eq. (14-1). Thus, the buyers' total costs will drop at the price break. Further, if the seller reduces price to induce greater order quantities but does not increase total demand over the planning period, then the savings, in Eq. (14-3), $pkiq/2$, will diminish since price k will have decreased and the profit margin p must also fall. Hence, the seller's cost function will jump at the quantity break point. Figures 14-1 and 14-2 illustrate these points.[5]

The dashed lines in each figure indicate the relevant cost curve as the buyer and seller attempt to determine the optimal purchasing schedule and discount schedule. In Fig. 14-1, the buyer's costs follow the TEK_1 cost curve until the first price break at b_1. Then for quantities between b_1 and b_2, the relevant cost curve is TEK_2. Finally, for quantities greater than b_2, the buyers' cost curve follows TEK_3. For the seller, as indicated, the relevant cost curve jumps at the price breaks. Thus, the cost curve before the first price break is TEK_1. For quantities between b_1 and b_2, the relevant cost curve is TEK_2, and for quantities greater than b_2, the relevant cost curve is TEK_3.

This process of determining the optimal quantity discount schedule requires negotiations between buyer and seller. That is, as a quid pro quo, the seller and buyer could negotiate the minimum joint cost function between them rather than each seeking unilaterally to optimize the operations. Dolan has developed a quantity discount model that demonstrates that this joint cost function can be reduced by

[5]For a model developing the solution technique to this problem see Kent B. Monroe and Albert J. Della Bitta, "Models for Pricing Decisions," *Journal of Marketing Research*, 15 (August 1978), 413–428.

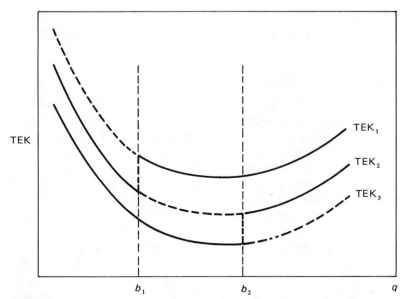

FIGURE 14-1
Economic order-size curves—two price breaks (buyer).

FIGURE 14-2
Economic order-size curves—two price breaks (seller).

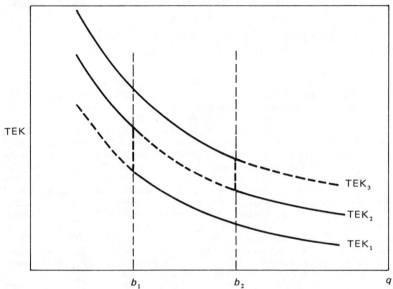

introducing several price breaks. That is, the more complex the price discount structure, the more effective the seller can be in gaining the buyer's cooperation.[6]

Some Additional Managerial Issues

The discussion thus far has presented a method and thought process for developing a rational quantity discount schedule. However, once a discount schedule has been developed, there is a tendency to retain it although conditions in the marketplace change. However, it is imperative that any pricing policy be modified as market and internal conditions change. For example, many discount schedules are based on the dollar volume purchased. Yet as prices are increased without a corresponding change in the discount schedule, more buyers qualify for a discount or for additional price breaks, leading to additional discounts being offered even if there is no change in the size of purchases.

A second problem may occur when two buyers merge either in terms of actual ownership or in terms of forming a buying group. In either situation, the seller may again give more discounts than previously even though there is no increase in purchase volume. Third, as industrial buyers become more proficient at the use of the computer to determine how to track and use different vendor discount structures, they are able to selectively vary volume purchases across vendors. This situation is likely to occur when the competing sellers do not have a carefully rationalized discount structure like that demonstrated in Table 14-2.[7]

Finally, another issue that has evolved over the past few years concerns the possibility that buyers will find it profitable to buy in very large quantities at a relatively low per unit cost and then ship the goods to other markets for resale. Indeed, there has been documentation that cameras produced in Japan and shipped overseas to other countries have been reshipped to Japan and sold profitably to Japanese consumers at prices lower than those of cameras shipped directly from the Japanese producer to the Japanese retailer. This particular issue illustrates a classic

---

[6]Robert J. Dolan, "A Normative Model of Industrial Buyer Response to Quantity Discounts," *Proceedings of the 1978 AMA Educators' Conference* (Chicago: American Marketing Association, 1978), pp. 121–125. Several quantity discount models developed in the past few years address some of the issues outlined in this discussion: Paul A. Rubin, David M. Dilts, and Beth A. Barron, "Economic Order Quantities with Quantity Discounts: Grandma Does It Best," *Decision Sciences,* 14 (April 1983), 270–281; R. R. Britney, P. J. Kuzdrall, and N. Fartuch, "Note on Total Setup Lot Sizing with Quantity Discounts," *Decision Sciences,* 14 (April 1983), 282–291; James P. Monahan, "Quantity Discount Pricing Model to Increase Vendor Profits," *Management Science,* 30 (June 1984), 720–726; Chandrasekhar Das, "A Unified Approach to the Price-Break Economic Order Quantity (EOQ) Problem," *Decision Sciences,* 15 (Summer 1984), 350–358; Rajiv Lal and Richard Staelin, "An Approach for Developing an Optimal Discount Pricing Policy," *Management Science,* 30 (December 1984), 1524–1539; Hau L. Lee and Meir J. Rosenblatt, "A Generalized Quantity Discount Pricing Model to Increase Suppliers' Profits," *Management Science,* 32 (September 1986), 1177–1185; S. K. Goyal, "Comment on: 'A Generalized Quantity Discount Pricing Model to Increase Suppliers' Profits,'" *Management Science,* 33 (December 1987), 1635–1636; Prafulla N. Joglekar, "Comments on 'A Quantity Discount Pricing Model to Increase Vendor Profits,'" *Management Science,* 34 (November 1988), 1391–1398; Robert J. Dolan, "Quantity Discounts: Managerial Issues and Research Opportunities," *Marketing Science,* 6 (Winter 1987), 1–22.

[7]Some useful prescriptions for handling these issues are given in Ashok Rao, "Quantity Discounts in Today's Markets," *Journal of Marketing,* 44 (Fall 1980), 44–51.

example of price discrimination failing when buyers paying a lower price can ship the product back to the higher priced market. In devising a quantity discount price schedule, the seller must periodically examine the discount structure to determine whether any of these flaws exist.[8]

Pricing Special Orders

The contribution per resource unit criterion developed in Chap. 8 can be used even when a firm is not operating at capacity or is faced with the shortage of critical resources. Essentially, use of the CPRU when establishing prices provides a means of maintaining consistency over customers, product lines, or special orders. A special order is defined as an order placed by an established customer for a quantity different from the normal one, a one-time-only order for a substantial quantity placed by a nonregular customer, or an order placed for a product not usually produced by the firm but which the firm has the capacity to produce. In each of these situations, the firm must establish a price that is consistent with prices for regular products and customers and is acceptable to the originator of the special order. The CPRU criterion is useful in pricing such a special order.

To illustrate the application of the CPRU to pricing special orders, assume that the firm normally sells a product in a standard order of 500 units. The basic cost and contribution data for a standard order are given in Table 14-4A. On a standard order of 500 units, the firm spends 10 hours to set up the production equipment to make the production run. Labor costs per hour for a production setup are $7. The standard hourly rate for the machines used in the process is $4.50 and 5 units can be produced per hour. Therefore, an order of 500 units requires 100 hours of machine time. A standard order of 500 units currently is priced at $10 per unit or $5,000 per order.

Suppose a nonregular customer approaches the firm with an offer for a one-time-only order for 1,000 units. This potential customer is aware that a standard order is 500 units at a price of $10. However, the customer asks for a price quotation. Obviously, the customer is seeking a lower price than $10 per unit. The firm has the capacity to handle this special order but wishes to be consistent in its price quotation to be able to justify such a lower price to regular customers should they object.

The data of Table 14-4A indicate that the CPRU per production hour is $27.09 for a standard production run (order) of 500 units. The data of Table 14-4B show the calculations for determining the selling price that meets the two objectives of (1) a lower per unit price and (2) maintaining the CPRU. The price that satisfies these objectives is $9.66 per unit for an order size of 1,000 units.

It is important to note that this price will not necessarily be attractive to the buyer. Nor does the price of $9.66 imply that the seller could not get more from the customer for a 1,000-unit order. But the price does provide management information on the costs and the necessary markup to achieve a specific profit objective. Alterna-

[8]James B. Wilcox, Roy D. Howell, Paul Kuzdrall, and Robert Britney, "Price Quantity Discounts: Some Implications for Buyers and Sellers," *Journal of Marketing,* 51 (July 1987), 60–70.

TABLE 14-4
CPRU PRICING OF A SPECIAL ORDER

A. Data for Standard Order (500 Units)			
1. Revenue at $10.00 selling price			$ 5,000
2. Variable costs			
Setup cost (10 hours @ $7/hour)		$ 70	
Machine cost (100 hours @ $4.50/hour)		450	
Materials ($3.00 per unit)		1,500	
Total			2,020
3. Contribution			$ 2,980
4. Total hours (10 hours + 100 hours)			110
5. CPRU per hour (3 ÷ 4)			$ 27.09

B. Data for 1,000-Unit Orders			
1. Desired CPRU per hour		$ 27.09	
Time required (hours):			
Setup	10		
Machine (100 × 2)	200		
2. Total hours		210	
3. Required order contribution (1 × 2)			$5,688.90
4. Variable costs			
Setup cost (10 hours @ $7/hour)		$ 70.00	
Machine cost (200 hours @ $4.50/hour)		900.00	
Materials (3.00 per unit)		3,000.00	
Total			3,970.00
5. Required sales volume for 1,000 units (3 + 4)			$9,658.90
6. Unit selling price (5 ÷ 1,000)			$ 9.66

tive selling prices can be developed that take into consideration specific demand, competition, and other market factors. Essentially, the CPRU criterion as applied to the pricing of special orders gives management a specific price alternative for a given profit contribution objective. (It should also be noted that developing a CPRU pricing mechanism with time as the critical resource is common for many types of service firms including consulting, lawyers, plumbers, car repairs, cleaning and janitorial firms, and other types of "special order" sellers.)

Legal Considerations

Quantity discounts have been regularly scrutinized by the Federal Trade Commission for possible Robinson–Patman Act violations. It is the responsibility of the seller to prove that the noncumulative discount schedule has been offered to all competing buyers on the same basis and can be justified because of demonstrable cost savings. However, in the past, primarily due to inadequate cost data, the cost defense has had little success. Hence, there are strong reasons for removing intuition and arbitrary decision rules from such pricing decisions. The more rational approach to developing quantity discount decisions illustrated here would provide a stronger economic defense of a discount schedule. The use of marketing and distribution cost analyses to develop a cost-justified quantity discount schedule was illustrated in Chap. 9.

Cumulative quantity discounts are quite difficult to justify because they invariably favor large-volume purchasers and are therefore discriminatory to small purchasers. However, this price discrimination is unlawful only if potential or real injury to competition can be shown (providing there are measurable cost savings involved).

CASH DISCOUNTS AND CREDIT DECISIONS

As observed previously, a cash discount is a reward for the payment of an invoice or account within a specified amount of time. For example, assume that after the trade and promotional discounts have been applied, the invoice indicates the amount due is $456. Further, the invoice indicates the credit policy of the seller is 2/10 net 30. If the buyer pays within 10 days, the correct remittance is $446.88 (98 percent of $456). If the cash discount is not taken because payment was not made within 10 days, then the full amount, $456, must be paid within 30 days. From a decision perspective, the seller must determine

1 The amount of cash discount (2 percent in our example)
2 The length of the credit period (the total time the bill is outstanding, which equals 30 days in the example)
3 The amount to spend on attempting to collect overdue accounts
4 The customers to whom to offer credit terms
5 The magnitude of the line of credit

Cash discounts and credit decisions have traditionally been considered the purview of finance, and this viewpoint has persisted because of the practice of making these decisions in the light of industry and historical practice. Closer analysis of the elements of credit policy decisions suggests that demand is affected by these decisions and therefore that a more active decision approach can have positive effects on a firm's demand. Moreover, it has been recognized that terms of trade are an important factor influencing the degree of channel cooperation or conflict.[9]

An active approach to determining credit policy requires analyzing the relationship between demand and (1) the credit period, (2) the amount of the cash discount, and (3) collection expenditures. Other things remaining the same, we would expect demand to increase with a lengthening of the credit period. That is, for a given list price, a movement away from an "all sales cash" policy to allowing purchases on account would result in an increase in demand, which would grow with the number of days an account is allowed to be outstanding. In addition, increasing the amount

---

[9]Michael Levy and Dwight Grant, "Financial Terms of Sale and Control of Marketing Channel Conflict," *Journal of Marketing Research,* 17 (November 1980), 524–530.

of the cash discount or lengthening the time period that the discount applies will normally result in increases in demand. In either decision the key information is the elasticity of demand with respect to changes in these variables.

Reasons for Cash Discounts

Among the reasons cited for using cash discounts are the following:

1 To encourage prompt payment of invoices, thereby keeping the seller's cash flow in a more rapid turnover condition. As was discussed in Chap. 10, cash is an asset and the more times it is turned over (used successively), the better the firm's pricing flexibility.

2 To reduce credit risks and the cost of collecting overdue accounts. Since buyers are rewarded for prompt payment, in theory there will be fewer overdue invoices.

3 To follow industry or historical practice. One manufacturer in the clothing industry recently was puzzled over the custom of offering a cash discount of 8/10 net EOM. An examination of sales records revealed that the firm had granted about $500,000 in cash discounts on $7,000,000 in sales. It simply had been following the same discount policy established many years earlier. (As suggested previously and amplified later, cash discount and credit policies should be reviewed periodically to determine their appropriateness for current and future market conditions.)

Problems with Cash Discounts

Cash discounts tend to be taken regularly by buyers because of the amount of savings involved. In the example of the clothing manufacturer mentioned previously, if we assume that the cash discount is taken by the tenth day of the month, then the seller has the use of the money 20 days sooner than if payment was made by the end of the month. In essence, the clothing manufacturer was willing to pay the retail buyers an interest rate of 144 percent on an annual basis for the privilege of using the money 20 days earlier. (In a 360-day year, there are 18 periods of 20 days. Thus, $(360/20)8\% = 144\%$.] Clearly, it may be more economical for a firm to borrow money on a short-term basis than to offer cash discounts.

A second problem occurs when large buyers take the cash discount as a matter of routine, even though payment is not made within the discount period. In such circumstances, many sellers are reluctant to press the issue and the effective interest rate they are granting these buyers is even higher. Hence, the problem of equitably policing the discount policy is often a difficult one. Further, permitting such variances in the cash discount policy is unlawful. Cash discounts are legal under the Robinson–Patman Act so long as they are offered under the same terms to all competing buyers.

Third, during periods of inflation, it has been observed that many firms experience a slowdown in the payment of bills by customers. Apparently, higher interest rates and inflationary pressures lead to a lengthening of the payment period. By forgoing the cash discounts, customers are using suppliers' funds as a source of capital. Unless the seller is indifferent to this change in payment practices, the lengthening of the payment period could lead to a conflict within the marketing channel. Indeed, pharmaceutical wholesalers believe that sales terms are among the most important aspects of customer service and affect purchase behavior.[10]

Cash Discount Models

The extension of credit involves two costs. The first stems from the risk of bad-debt loss, and the second results from leaving in accounts receivable resources that are forgoing returns from alternative uses. But the gains from extending credit revolve around the increase in the long-run sales rate. Therefore, an appropriate credit and cash discount policy requires the balancing of the sacrifice in alternative returns and potential bad-debt losses against the loss in profits because of lost sales.

Conceptualization of the Problem[11]   To develop insights into the decision problems, we will analyze the relationship between the rate of demand and (1) the credit period and (2) the cash discount. If we can initially hypothesize some of the characteristics of these relationships, it will be easier to make intuitive decisions. To do so, other factors affecting the demand for the firm's products will be considered constant. Finally, to simplify, we will assume all sales are credit sales.

Other things being equal, we would expect demand to increase with a lengthening of the credit period. That is, as the firm moves from an "all sales cash" policy to an extension of sales on credit, demand would increase up to a limit. As illustrated in Fig. 14-3, demand would increase to T_0. It should be emphasized, though, that a credit period equal to T_0 does not imply a profit-maximizing credit period. Although it is unlikely that the elasticity of demand with respect to changes in the credit period will be known, the relationship seen in Fig. 14-3 appears to be reasonable.

To analyze the relationship between the size of the cash discount and demand, it is important to recognize that offering a cash discount is equivalent to reducing the price of a product. Thus, an increase in the cash discount (cd) should result in an increase in the rate of demand. Figure 14-4 illustrates the relationship between demand and cash discount. Clearly, as the cash discount approaches 100 percent, the price approaches zero.

A second aspect of the cash discount decision is determining the length of the discount period. Generally, it would be expected that for a given cash discount, a lengthening of the cash discount period would lead to an increase in the rate of demand.

---

[10]Michael Levy, "Toward an Optimal Customer Service Package," *Journal of Business Logistics,* 2 (1980), 87–109.

[11]The original conceptualization of the problem was formulated in William Beranek, *Analysis for Financial Decisions* (Homewood, Ill.: Richard D. Irwin, 1963). More recent developments can be found in Monroe and Della Bitta, op. cit.; Levy and Grant, op. cit.; Ned C. Hill and Kenneth D. Riener, "Determining the Cash Discount in the Firm's Credit Policy," *Financial Management,* 8 (Spring 1979), 68–73; and Donald H. Wort and J. Kenton Zumwalt, "The Trade Discount Decision: A Markov Chain Approach," *Decision Sciences,* 16 (Winter 1985), 43–56.

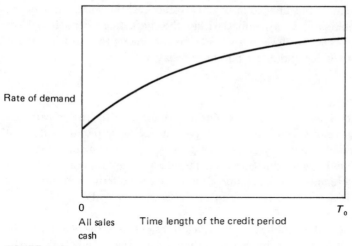

FIGURE 14-3
Relations of demand to the length of the credit period.

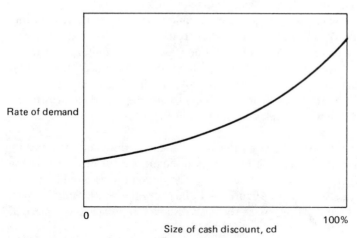

FIGURE 14-4
Relations of demand to the size of the cash discount.

Some Simple Models   A number of models deal with the problem of developing an optimal cash discount and credit policy structure. As a point of departure, denote contribution to profits as total revenues minus total costs:

$$PR = p_0 Q - VC(Q) \qquad (14\text{-}4)$$

where PR = profits
   p_0 = unit price
   Q = number of units produced and sold
   VC = unit variable costs

Assume that price, the cash discount, the credit period, and the rate of expenditures on collections are given: $p = p_0$, cd $=$ cd$_0$, $T = T_0$, and $E = E_0$. Assume that credit terms allow for a cash discount if payment is made by the tenth day of the month following the month the sales were made. From Eq. (14-4), the adjusted profit function is

$$PR_1 = (1 - cd_0)p_0 Q - VC(Q) \qquad (14\text{-}5)$$

Thus, the adjusted contribution to profit is lower by the amount $cd_0 p_0$. The effect of an increase in cd is virtually equivalent to a lower price for the firm's output. Therefore, demand will increase depending on the price elasticity of demand. The effect on profits depends on whether the incremental revenue due to this "price reduction" is greater than the incremental cost of the greater volume of output. As noted, the net price $(1 - cd_0)p_0$ is less because of the discount, making adjusted profits less. Thus, for a cash discount to be profitable, the elasticity of demand to the cash discount must lead to a demand rate that is sufficiently great to overcome the lower per unit profit. (See discussions on price reduction strategies in Chaps. 8 and 11.)

Now consider a situation where a given proportion of total sales volume does not take the cash discount but instead pays in full at the end of the month. This situation means that some receivables will be outstanding between the tenth and thirtieth of each month, thereby requiring additional resources and forgoing the returns that these resources could obtain if allocated to the next best opportunity. Denote this alternative rate of return as i per dollar per month. If ΔA are the resources required to carry nondiscounting customers from day 10 to day 30, then the firm forgoes the amount $\frac{2}{3}i\Delta A$ each month by permitting nondiscounting. Since these customers do not receive the discount cd_0, profits serving these customers will be larger than in Eq. (14-5). But allowing a 30-day credit policy means there is the opportunity cost as given above. Hence, contributions to profits are

$$PR_2 = p_0 Q - VC(Q) - \frac{2}{3}i\Delta A \qquad (14\text{-}6)$$

It is again obvious that the only way greater profits can result from this policy is for the credit policy to generate an increase in demand to offset the additional costs of credit extension. Further, if the firm permits a credit period that is longer than the discount period, then optimal nondiscounting requires

$$PR_2 - PR_1 > 0 \qquad\qquad (14\text{-}7)$$

These basic models can be extended to include analysis for determining the optimal length of the nondiscount credit period as well as deciding on optimum level of collection expenditures. However, it should be apparent that to offer either a cash discount or extended credit terms is optimal only as long as demand is sufficiently sensitive to these decision variables to offset additional costs (or reductions in unit profitability).

Extending the Model

As we noted when discussing quantity discount models, it is necessary to develop the decision approach to include not only the seller's optimal behavior but also the buyers' optimal behaviors. Customers are likely to have different internal costs of capital and therefore to respond differently to an established cash discount and credit policy. Moreover, as the relative cost of capital increases over time or over different types of customers, some customers are likely to stretch out their payments. As discussed in Chap. 9, some of these slow-paying customers may actually be costing the seller more money than is earned by making the sale. Hence, an important question is how to construct and/or change the cash discount and credit policy to recognize this problem without creating undue conflict within the marketing channel.

Using the formulation given earlier and considering only the seller's objective, it can be shown that the optimal sales terms for the seller can be obtained only at the expense of the buyers. That is, the seller will determine the lowest possible cash discount that maximizes its profits. However, given this minimum cash discount, the optimal behavior of the buyers is to either pay the invoice immediately or forgo any discount and delay payment as long as possible. Thus, there would be no discount policy sufficiently attractive to the buyers to induce them to pay within 10 or 20 days from invoice date.[12] That is, the optimal terms of sale would be either a cash discount at the time of purchase if the buyers have a cost of capital lower than the seller or no cash discount and an extended credit period if the seller has the lower cost of capital. Obviously, industry practice does not conform to either possibility.

Once we recognize that some buyers may have a lower cost of capital than the seller and that some buyers have a higher cost of capital, then it becomes obvious that a flexible cash discount policy is necessary. In this way a seller will have a cash discount schedule that is more likely to induce buyers to pay early because it is advantageous for them to do so. Such a cash discount schedule might look like the one illustrated in Table 14-5A. Note that different cash discounts are available depending on the length of time before payment is made. Note also that the implicit interest rate the buyer is paying by delaying payment beyond 10 days, or 15, 20, or 25 days increases the longer payment is delayed. The cost of delaying payment

---

[12]Levy and Grant, ibid.

TABLE 14-5
DEVELOPING A FLEXIBLE CASH DISCOUNT AND CREDIT POLICY

Terms	Cash Payment, $	Implicit Interest to Buyer by Delaying Payment, %*
A. Original schedule		
2/10	98.00	. . .
1.7/15	98.30	21.6
1.3/20	98.70	28.8
0.8/25	99.20	36.0
Net 30	100.00	50.4
B. Revised schedule		
3/10	106.60	. . .
2.5/15	107.25	36.0
1.8/20	108.02	50.4
1.0/25	108.90	57.6
Net 30	110.00	72.0

*The implicit interest is determined by noting that the buyer accepts a 0.3% less discount for an additional five days of nonpayment: (360/5) 0.3% = 21.6%
Source: Developed from Michael Levy and Dwight Grant, "Financial Terms of Sales and Control of Marketing Channel Conflict," *Journal of Marketing Research,* 17 (November 1980), 524–530.

increases to reflect a perception that there is an increase in risk of nonpayment to the seller.

Now assume that the seller wishes to increase prices and at the same time adjust the cash discount and credit policy to reflect an increase in the cost of capital because of higher interest rates. Table 14-5B shows that list prices have been raised 10 percent, but that the sales terms have been adjusted to reflect a net price increase of approximately 8.9 percent at day 10. Also note that the costs of delaying payment are higher than previously to reflect this increase in capital costs.

The primary advantage of the models is that they force us to reconsider the influence of decision variables on demand and to turn away from tradition as a means of making basic pricing decisions. Furthermore, recognition of the effects on demand of these decisions suggests the need for greater involvement by marketing personnel in these heretofore financial decisions. Further, these models indicate that traditional cash discounts of a given magnitude, e.g., 2 percent, are not likely to be optimal policy. Thus, existing policies of cash discount and credit extension should be more flexible and should be periodically reexamined as market conditions change. Finally, it should be noted that a cash discount is not a cost per se but a price reduction. As developed in Chaps. 8 and 11, a price reduction strategy can be profitable only when there is an opportunity for sales growth to occur (i.e., demand is price elastic) and a relatively high contribution margin product. Indeed, it has been shown that the lower a product's variable costs (i.e., the higher the contribution margin), the higher is the feasible cash discount.[13]

A Behavioral Note

If it is assumed that the motive for extending a cash discount is to increase the number of buyers making prompt payments, the method of relating the policy to customers should be considered. Research suggests that people seek out positive alternatives; choosing among negatives seems like no choice at all.[14] Further, as discussed in Chap. 3, people value perceived gains differently than perceived losses. Consider one way the cash discount and credit policy may be framed on an invoice:

> Terms: 2/10; net 30. Invoices outstanding more than 30 days will be assessed a service charge of 10%.

On a bill for $100, the buyer is faced with paying $98 in 10 days, $100 within 30 days, or $110 later. That is, the buyer is offered a *reward* (gain) of $2 for early payment and threatened with a *penalty* (loss) of $10 for late payment.

Now suppose the invoice states the charge is $110 but offers the buyer a $12 reward (gain) if payment is made in 10 days or a $10 reward (gain) if payment is made between the tenth and thirtieth days. In this case, the buyer is offered a choice between two positive alternatives—paying early and gaining $12 or paying a little later and gaining $10. In the original statement, the buyer was offered a choice among a positive alternative (gain $2 if paying early), a neutral alternative (paying within 30 days), or a negative alternative (paying a penalty of $10 if paying late).

Apart from the economic reason for making early payment—savings—the idea of presenting a cash discount and credit policy to the buyer in terms of positive choices may increase the chance of early payments. Developing positive feelings on the part of buyers will increase their desire or willingness to respond favorably to the cash discount and credit policy. Early payment is the behavioral objective of a cash discount and communicating rewards or gains as opposed to penalties or losses creates a more favorable attitude and behavioral tendency. Moreover, to take advantage of a positive frame of reference, the seller may wish to present the actual dollar alternatives on the invoice. That is, the invoice could indicate that the buyer gains $12 if paying within 10 days. This procedure is similar to the notion of transaction value induced by a sales promotion (discussed in Chap. 3). Given computerized billing systems available, such a communication procedure is very feasible. Indeed, one of the critical ingredients of implementing a price structure is the communication of the structure to buyers in a way that fosters the desired buyer behavior.

---

[13]Hill and Riener, op. cit.
[14]See Jerald M. Jellison and John H. Harvey, "Determinants of Perceived Choice and the Relationship between Perceived Choice and Perceived Competence," *Journal of Personality and Social Psychology,* 28 (1973), 376–382; Jerald M. Jellison and John H. Harvey, "Why We Like Hard, Positive Choices," *Psychology Today,* 9 (March 1976), 47–49.

GEOGRAPHICAL PRICING DECISIONS

One of the most significant costs in marketing arises from the transportation of goods from points of origin to points of destination. We normally think of marketing as primarily related to the stimulation of demand. However, a necessary corollary activity is to supply the various markets with the demanded products. The costs of performing this supply activity range well into billions of dollars annually for transportation alone. The way that sellers solve the transportation problem affects their marketing programs by influencing the range of geographic market areas they serve, the degree to which they may be vulnerable to price competition in some markets, their profit margins, their ability to control resale prices, and the effectiveness of their personal salespeople.

From a pricing perspective, part of the decision problem revolves around whether sellers wish to account for their shipping costs in their price structure. If they do, there are two general methods they can use: the f.o.b. origin pricing method and the delivered pricing method. A second aspect of the decision problem is to determine relative competitive advantage considering both list price and transportation costs in various geographic markets. These two issues will be discussed in this section.

F.O.B. Origin Pricing

F.O.B. origin pricing means the seller quotes prices from the point of shipment. Free on board (f.o.b.) means it is the buyer's responsibility to select the mode of transportation, choose the specific carrier, handle any damage claims, and pay all shipping charges. Thus, the net return to the seller is the same for all buyers purchasing in the same quantities and with the same trade status, regardless of their locations. The seller's freedom from responsibility for transportation and provision of the same net return for every similar sale are the primary advantages of the f.o.b. origin method.

However, unless all sellers are located in geographical proximities, product demand is relatively inelastic, and there is a degree of product differentiation, sale of a product becomes increasingly difficult the further away a market is located. Also, because the cost to distributors varies with their distance from the seller, it becomes increasingly difficult to control and maintain resale prices. Finally, the seller's salespeople will find it increasingly difficult to quote an accurate cost to customers since the costs will vary with distance and with the transportation method(s) selected by the buyer.

Delivered Pricing

In delivered pricing, the price quoted by the manufacturer includes both the list price and the transportation costs. In such cases, the prices are quoted as *f.o.b. destination,* meaning the manufacturer bears the responsibility of selecting and paying for the method of transporting the product.

Single-Zone Pricing In single-zone pricing, the seller receives a different net return (delivered price minus transportation costs) when transportation costs for customers vary. That is, the seller quotes one list price plus transportation costs to all buyers regardless of their location. On the other hand, buyers pay a uniform delivered price regardless of their location relative to the seller. In essence, then, all buyers pay the same "average transportation cost."

Multiple-Zone Pricing In a multiple-zone pricing system, delivered prices are uniform within two or more zones. Most retail mail-order catalogs use a multiple-zone pricing system. That is, buyers must determine which concentric circle (zone) around the catalog's distribution center they are in to determine the shipping costs per pound for their order. The differences in price between zones depend on distance from the shipping point, competition, and demand in geographic market segments.

Zone systems generally make it easier to sell in distance markets, since prices are determined by "average" transportation costs. Within any zone, therefore, it is easier to control resale prices and increase the ability of salespeople to quote prices. Using multiple zones enables the seller to geographically segment markets if there are varying price elasticities and thus to determine several satisfactory prices. Multiple-zone systems also facilitate dealing with variations in strength and type of competition.

But there are some drawbacks. The seller does not receive the same net return per sale since the net return varies with the actual shipping costs. Moreover, the demand center for the firm may shift geographically, leading to, for example, more shipments going to more distant buyers than before. However, a properly designed information system can monitor these market shifts and alert the firm to change its pricing structure. Within any zone, some buyers are paying more and some are paying less than the actual cost of transportation, because the cost is averaged for any zone. Moreover, buyers located on the boundaries of zones may pay more than nearby buyers because they have arbitrarily been positioned in a different price zone. Finally, zone-pricing methods require the seller to choose the mode of transportation, select the carrier, handle the damage claims, and pay the freight bills. Each of these responsibilities may become an increased burden to the selling firm.

F.O.B. with Freight Allowed Another form of delivered pricing is f.o.b. with freight allowed. The buyer arranges and pays for the transportation but deducts these transportation costs from the invoice total and remits the net amount. Thus, by arranging cheaper transportation methods, e.g., using a private fleet of trucks, the buyer pays a lower total price. However, the seller receives varying net returns and the resale prices may also vary.

Basing-Point Pricing In another variation of delivered pricing, the delivered price is the product's list price plus transportation costs from a basing point to the buyer. The basing point is a designated city where the product is produced. But in basing-point pricing the product may actually be shipped from a city other than the basing point. Firms or plants at the basing points receive the same net returns, whereas firms or plants not at the basing point receive different net returns from different sales. This variation in net returns is due to the difference between actual shipping costs and the transportation factor used in the price quotation.

Figure 14-5 illustrates the principle of basing-point pricing. All three mills, X, Y, and Z, quote the same delivered price to customer A, $120, which is determined by adding the $100 base price at mill X to the freight charge of $20 from mill X to customer A. To quote the $120 delivered price, mill Y must absorb $10 of freight charges (called freight absorption), whereas mill Z collects $10 of phantom freight.

One or more basing points can be used for any transaction, depending on whether the pricing method used is a *single basing-point system* or a *multiple basing-point system.* Further, the system may be a company system used by a firm with several geographically dispersed production plants or an industry-wide system used by most firms in the industry. An industry-wide system may develop as a result of an industry tradition of using particular basing points or it may evolve from a practice of price leadership where firms follow the basing-point pricing practices of the price leader. An industry-wide system may also be the result of collusion by the firms involved.

In a multiple basing-point system several locations are designated as basing points. On a particular sale, the basing point chosen is the point that yields the lowest delivered cost to the buyer. With a multiple basing-point system, both the basing-

FIGURE 14-5
Basing-point pricing system.

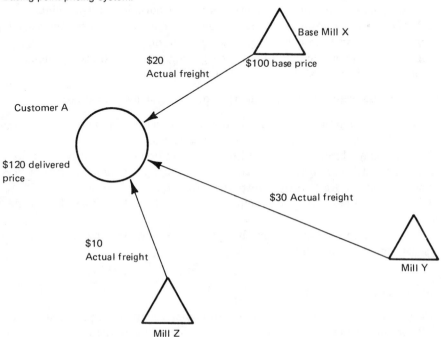

point plant or firm and the plants or firms not located at a basing point receive varying net returns from different sales.

There are advantages and disadvantages in both types of multiple basing-point systems. The advantages of a company-wide basing-point system are:

1 It eliminates price competition between the firm's different production facilities. The buyer pays the same price no matter where he or she is located or what the origin of the shipment is.

2 It allows the firm to balance shipments from the different plants and thus ensure that plants receive enough shipments to keep them operating at a desirable level of capacity.

3 It simplifies price quotations in that a schedule of delivered prices need be prepared only for the basing points and not for every production facility.

The disadvantages of a company-wide basing-point system are:

1 Customers who discover they pay more for transportation than the actual costs will be unhappy. This unhappiness will be more pronounced when they discover that other customers pay less than the actual cost of transportation.

2 It may result in a large amount of freight absorption.

3 The return to the seller varies on each sale.

4 The price discrimination features of company-wide basing-point pricing may produce legal difficulties.

The advantages of an industry-wide basing-point pricing system are:

1 Price competition based on differences in transportation costs is eliminated.

2 It permits a firm to secure greater volume since large transportation costs do not prevent the firm from expanding its geographic market area.

3 Any firm or plant can sell in a larger geographic area since transportation costs are not a factor in buyers' purchasing decisions.

Among the disadvantages of an industry-wide basing-point system are:

1 Buyers who find they are paying for transportation costs from producing plants that do not originate the shipment will be dissatisfied.

2 Buyers may object to the lack of price competition in transportation costs.

3 Since the delivered price is the same regardless of shipping point, there is less incentive to use the least costly transportation.

4 The reduced basis for price competition may lead to higher and less flexible prices.

5 It may lead to excessive freight absorption for a seller, varying sales returns to the seller, and legal difficulties.

Legal Considerations

There is a long history of legal questions surrounding geographical pricing practices. F.O.B. origin pricing is legal. But in zone-pricing systems, there is an inherent element of price discrimination since some buyers pay more than the cost of transportation while other buyers pay less. Sellers who practice single-zone pricing have not been prevented from maintaining a uniform delivered price. Apparently, since there are no price differences at the point of *destination* with this system, the Federal Trade Commission and the federal courts have not viewed the system as discriminatory.

Multiple-zone systems have had difficulty only when all firms have had similar zone-pricing systems. Indeed, the Federal Trade Commission has taken the position that when competing firms establish zone systems with identical boundaries and identical price differentials, collusion is likely to be present.

Basing-point pricing has had considerable difficulty under the Robinson–Patman Act and the Federal Trade Commission Act. These difficulties stem primarily from the fact that different firms or plants receive varying net returns from different sales under similar circumstances without real cost justifications. Although such sales are generally held to be price discriminatory, unless there appears to be clear-cut evidence of conspiracy, it is relatively unlikely that the Federal Trade Commission will initiate proceedings against delivered pricing systems.

Despite the position of the Federal Trade Commission, basing-point pricing is patently unfair to at least some customers. The unfairness of the system can eventually lead to customer dissatisfaction. In a competitive environment, dissatisfied customers will seek out alternative sources of supply from domestic or foreign sellers.

USING PRICE STRUCTURE TO GAIN COMPETITIVE ADVANTAGE

One of the key points of this chapter is that the development of a more complex price structure provides for pricing flexibility and enhances a firm's ability to respond to competitor, buyer, or market changes. Indeed, the discussion on quantity and cash discounts has suggested that there may be profit opportunities to developing more complex discount structures. The purpose of this section is to illustrate the opportunities of using price structure to either gain competitive advantage or diminish a competitive disadvantage. The problem of handling freight costs will be used to develop the example.

As should be apparent from the preceding discussion on geographical pricing, the relative distances from competing sellers to a customer may play a role in the customer's purchase decision, particularly if the products sold by the two sellers are perceived to be similar. Indeed, if the buyer perceives that there is relatively little difference in the products offered by the two sellers, then the purchase decision is likely to be determined by the relative costs of buying from each seller. Thus, the buyer will assess the total cost of acquiring the product from each seller.

For the moment assume that one seller (A) enjoys a manufacturing cost advantage over another seller (B) and that this translates into a list price of $15 per ton less than B's price. However, assume B is located closer to the buyer and enjoys a relative advantage in terms of freight costs. In Table 14-6A, the price advantage of

TABLE 14-6
EVALUATING RELATIVE COMPETITIVE ADVANTAGE: PRICE AND FREIGHT COSTS

Order Size, Tons	Price Advantage, $/Ton	Freight Dis- advantage, $/ Ton	Net Advantage, $/Ton	Relative Advantage, $/ Order
A. Seller A vs. Seller B				
5	15	−16	−1	−5
10	15	−14	+1	+10
15	15	−12	+3	+45
20	15	−10	+5	+100
25	15	−9	+6	+150
B. Seller A vs. Seller C				
5	−15	+16	+1	+5
10	−16	+14	−2	−20
15	−17	+12	−5	−75
20	−18	+10	−8	−160
25	−19	+9	−10	−250

A is assumed to be \$15 at all feasible order sizes. But the freight disadvantage encountered by A declines per ton as the feasible order size increases through economies of larger shipments. As indicated in Table 14-6A, seller A has a relative advantage at all order sizes except the smallest one. Moreover, this relative advantage increases as order size increases. Thus, if the customer is small in terms of usual order size, it is more likely to place its orders with seller B. However, at all order sizes above 5 tons, the buyer is likely to order from seller A.

In Table 14-6B, seller A faces a price disadvantage relative to a third seller (C), but being closer to the buyer enjoys a relative freight cost advantage. Further contributing to the price disadvantage is the fact that seller C offers a quantity discount of \$1/ton at each of the larger order sizes, thereby increasing seller A's relative price disadvantage. Thus, seller A would enjoy a competitive advantage at the lowest feasible order size but would be at a disadvantage at all other order sizes. If seller A decided to match the quantity discount schedule of seller C, then its relative disadvantage would be the same as depicted in Table 14-6A for seller B.

This simple illustration shows that when a price structure is kept simple, it is relatively more difficult to take advantage of differential characteristics that may lead to a competitive advantage, or it is more difficult to diminish or remove a competitive disadvantage. However, by using distance between seller and buyer and by understanding the buyers' relative costs of carrying inventory and costs of capital, a price structure can be developed that affords the seller an opportunity to develop differential prices that reflect differential buyer, market, and product or service characteristics. Moreover, such a price structure provides for additional flexibility when responding to market, buyer, or competitor changes.

SUMMARY

This chapter introduced the problem of administering the prices of products and services. This problem usually begins with a decision on the price to offer buyers. The price setter must also consider adjusting prices for sales made in different quantities, sales made to different types of buyers in different geographic markets, sales made with different credit and collection terms, and sales made at different times.

Chapter 14 considered the decision problems connected with developing a quantity discount schedule and with setting cash discount and credit policies. Generally, quantity and cash discount decisions have been made on the basis of convenience and tradition. One consequence of such nonanalytical decision making has been the inability to defend such pricing decisions when faced with legal or buyer scrutiny. However, if the motive for offering quantity and cash discounts is to influence the behavior of buyers, e.g., to order more at a time or to pay early, then analysis underlying these decisions must begin with buyers. For both types of decisions, the problem is determining what "price breaks" will motivate buyers to behave in a manner favorable to the firm. The seller must then balance these price breaks against the costs of providing them. When a firm sells to many different types of buyers, it must set the price breaks or rewards to avoid discrimination on the basis of price to buyers. Hence, price administration is fraught with legal complications.

Geographical pricing involves large dollar amounts, and there is a lack of understanding of its difficulties and importance. As with quantity and cash discounts, the determination of a geographical pricing policy should begin with a consideration of the buyers. Transportation charges vary with many factors including weight and distance. Geographical pricing practices are concerned primarily with the effect shipping distances have on delivered prices. Again, developing a geographical pricing policy solely on the basis of convenience and tradition will ignore real differences in buyers and in the costs of serving them. Dissatisfied customers are no basis for long-run profitability.

DISCUSSION QUESTIONS

1 Briefly discuss the different types of decision problems in price administration.
2 Explain what is meant by
  a Price structure.
  b Base or list price.
  c Functional discount.
3 Explain the difference between a cumulative quantity discount and a noncumulative quantity discount.
4 Explain and illustrate the decision problems encountered when developing a quantity discount schedule.
5 Explain and illustrate the decision problems encountered when establishing a cash discount and credit policy.
6 What are the behavioral objectives involved in establishing trade discount, quantity discount, and cash discount policies? What can a price administrator do to reach these behavioral objectives?

7 Explain and illustrate the decision problems encountered when establishing a geographical pricing policy.
8 Explain what is meant by
 a Free on board origin.
 b Free on board destination.
 c Delivered pricing.
 d Zone pricing.
 e Basing-point pricing.
 f Phantom freight.
 g Free on board with freight allowed.
9 If the list price is $600 and the seller quotes a chain discount of 30, 10, 5, with a cash discount of 3/10 net 30, what is
 a The total trade and promotional discount amount?
 b The cash discount amount?
 c The correct remittance if all discounts are taken?
10 Discuss the legal implications of determining a geographical pricing policy.
11 In the mid-1970s, the United States economy was beset by a relatively high rate of inflation. Manufacturers were faced with problems as they frequently increased their prices to reflect rising costs of labor and materials. Manufacturers also incurred the expense and the problem of informing customers and salespeople of these price changes. One West Coast manufacturer handled this pricing problem by establishing what was believed to be the price that should be charged about a year later. Customers were then offered relatively large discounts, so that the actual price paid reflected what the firm believed the current price should be. Then as production costs increased, the firm reduced the amount of the discounts available to customers, until it was time to increase the list price again. What do you believe to be the advantages and disadvantages of such a pricing policy? What do you think would be competitor and buyer reaction?

SUGGESTED READINGS

Dolan, Robert J.: "Quantity Discounts: Managerial Issues and Research Opportunities," *Marketing Science,* 6 (Winter 1987), 1–22.

Levy, Michael, and Dwight Grant: "Financial Terms of Sale and Control of Marketing Channel Conflict," *Journal of Marketing Research,* 17 (November 1980), 524–530.

Monroe, Kent B., and Albert J. Della Bitta: "Models for Pricing Decisions," *Journal of Marketing Research,* 15 (August 1978), 413–428.

Rao, Ashok: "Quantity Discounts in Today's Markets," *Journal of Marketing,* 44 (Fall 1980), 44–51.

Stern, Andrew A.: "The Strategic Value of Price Structure," *Journal of Business Strategy,* 7 (Fall 1986), 22–31.

Wilcox, James B., Roy D. Howell, Paul Kuzdrall, and Robert Britney: "Price Quantity Discounts: Some Implications for Buyers and Sellers," *Journal of Marketing,* 51 (July 1987), 60–70.

CHAPTER 15

PRICING TO AND THROUGH THE CHANNEL

In our previous discussions of variables to consider and pricing methods to follow, it was implicitly assumed that the price setter could control the prices paid by the ultimate buyers. Such an assumption is valid only when the manufacturer sells directly to the final user. Although this assumption predominates the thinking in economic price theory, in practice it is clearly the exception rather than the rule. In fact, one recent research effort indicated that the power to control distribution channels in the industry was a basic factor in the setting of prices. For example, in the grocery industry, almost all major supermarket chains now demand that manufacturers pay "slotting allowances," i.e., rent for shelf space.[1]

When the manufacturer sells products through several independent businesses before the final purchase by a user, control over the way the products are ultimately marketed is usually relinquished. However, because of the importance of the marketing methods used, the manufacturer has a vested interest in the way the products are sold as they move through the channels of distribution. Thus, the manufacturer seeks means to influence the way distributors market the products, including the setting of resale prices.

In Chaps. 3 and 4 we saw how prices influence buyers' perceptions of value. It was suggested that certain prices anchor, or frame, buyers' responses, e.g., the end prices of a product line, the price of the brand last purchased, and the price of the

---

[1]Thomas V. Bonoma, Victoria L. Crittenden, and Robert J. Dolan, "Can We Have Rigor and Relevance in Pricing Research?" in Timothy M. Devinney (ed.), *Issues in Pricing: Theory and Research* (Lexington, Mass.: Lexington Books, 1988), pp. 337–359; "Want Shelf Space at the Supermarket? Ante Up," *Business Week,* August 7, 1989, pp. 60–61.

leading brand. It was also pointed out that the price differences between products in a product line, as well as those between national and private brands, between different national or private brands, or following price changes, serve to influence buyers' perceptions. In addition, for some products and under certain conditions a positive price–perceived quality relationship exists. Thus, since prices and price differences may affect perceptions and purchase behavior by ultimate buyers, the manufacturer is naturally concerned about how these prices are presented to buyers.

Suppose a manufacturer has determined what is believed to be an optimal pricing strategy. Can he or she then ensure that the price to the ultimate buyer is the price decided upon? The possibility that the product will be sold through several channel levels before the point of final resale complicates this issue, and if the common resale pricing practice is to apply a percentage markup over cost, any pricing deviations during the product's flow through the channel will not produce the desired final selling price.

Part of the problem of controlling price through the channel lies in the setting of discount policy for distributors. Where there is competition from rival sellers for distributor support, the price paid for distributor cooperation must reflect not only the marketing functions distributors perform but also the competitive environment. That is, the manufacturer must consider not only competition from other manufacturers but also the competition the distributors face at each level in the channel. For example, if competition at the distributors' level has pared the distributors' margins, then to gain the distributors' support for the manufacturer's policies, it may be necessary to increase the trade or functional discount.

Pricing decisions and the policies that are derived from them have impact on dealer cooperation and motivation as well as on sales force morale and effort. Although it is legally difficult to control prices through the distribution channel, it is possible to motivate people to adhere to company-determined pricing policies. Since price directly affects the revenues of the trade and salespeoples' commissions, it can be used to foster desired behaviors by channel members and salespeople.

To use price as a means of influencing channel members, the seller may offer trade discounts or special price promotions and deals. As defined in Chap. 14, a trade or functional discount is offered to members of the distribution channel because they provide certain marketing services (functions) for the seller. Although the offering of a functional discount may seem easy, in fact this discount decision is fraught with managerial and legal difficulties. Similarly, the strategy of price promotions and short-term price deals is more complex than is apparent. Judging by the number of legal cases and complaints by distributors, there is much to be concerned about in making trade discount and price promotion decisions. This chapter discusses these managerial problems and suggests approaches for their solutions.

TRADE OR FUNCTIONAL DISCOUNTS

Trade or functional discounts are based on a distributor's place in the distributive sequence and represent payment for performing certain marketing functions. The justification for trade discounts is that different distributors perform different functions within the distribution channel and should be compensated accordingly. For example, some wholesalers provide storage facilities for the manufacturer, help the retailer set up displays, extend credit to the retailers, and perform personal selling services for the manufacturer. Often it is difficult to fully identify the various functions the intermediaries perform and therefore it is difficult to determine a trade discount structure that reflects those services. Much of this difficulty arises because some distributors are wholesalers as well as retailers and because there are many different kinds of wholesalers and retailers.

Legal Status of Functional Discounts

Since functional discounts are not specifically mentioned in the Robinson–Patman Act, their legality has not been completely resolved. However, the general interpretation is that these discounts are lawful if they are offered to all competing buyers of the same distribution class on the same terms and if the discounts accurately reflect cost savings to the seller.

Primarily, the legal question is whether a particular discount is valid for particular kinds of buyers. Since the Robinson–Patman Act fails to specifically mention functional discounts, the validity of these discounts is determined by case law under Section 2(a), wherein it is unlawful to discriminate in price when the effect may be to lessen or injure competition. The legal test is whether the price difference due to a functional discount has an adverse competitive effect. Thus, *the validity of a functional discount derives solely from the doctrines and facts of competitive effect, not from any general principles governing functional discounts.* [2]

If the purchasers do not compete with each other, then there is no probable adverse competitive effect. Thus, a functional discount to an original equipment manufacturer can probably be justified since the item becomes a part of a larger and distinct product. A functional discount to auto manufacturers when buying automobile tires for new cars generally can be justified. However, if the automobile manufacturer buys the tires for resale to car dealers as replacement parts, then the automobile manufacturer may be in competition with the tire manufacturer's own distributors. In this situation, the functional discount to the automobile manufacturer would probably not be valid.

Traditionally, wholesalers are given larger discounts than retailers because it is recognized that these two types of distributors are on different functional levels. Economically, distributors positioned higher up the distribution channel, such as wholesalers, have a need to buy at lower prices than direct-buying retailers in order to survive. This traditional discount is valid if it does not lessen the ability of the direct-buying retailers to compete with the wholesalers' retail customers. Although direct-buying retailers are, in effect, performing all or most of the wholesaler's

[2]William E. Beringer, "The Validity of Discounts Granted to Dual Function Buyers under the Robinson–Patman Act," *The Business Lawyer,* 31 (January 1976), 783–800.

function, it would probably be construed that competition might be harmed if they set lower prices because of a more favorable discount afforded them.

Parenthetically, it should be clear that there is no requirement that wholesalers and retailers be priced differently. Wholesalers and retailers can be offered the same prices. When there are no price differences, there is no price discrimination, even though there may be adverse competitive effects. (This point is discussed in greater detail in Chap. 16.)

Dual-Function Discounts

The preceding observations refer to *single-function buyers,* i.e., buyers who perform essentially the same marketing services irrespective of the level or position in the distribution channel. However, there is a question of the validity of a functional discount for a particular service (function) performed by one buyer when that buyer and the competitors of that buyer perform other functions for which no one receives a discount. Buyers who perform more functions than their competitors and who receive a discount for these additional functions are referred to as *dual-function buyers.*

To illustrate the nature of a dual-function discount system, consider the Purolator case.[3] Figure 15-1 is a flow chart of the distribution system used by Purolator, a manufacturer of automotive filters in the replacement parts market. Purolator sold only to warehouse distributors. However, there were two types of warehouse distributors: type I distributors, who had only a single warehouse location, and type II distributors, who had either branch warehouse locations or affiliated jobbers. The type II distributors sold either to independent jobbers or to their affiliated jobbers. Type I distributors sold only to independent jobbers. All jobbers sold to dealers and fleet operators.

The amount of functional discount Purolator gave to its warehouse distributors depended on (1) whether or not the distributor had either branch locations or affiliated jobbers and (2) the type of customer, dealer, or fleet operator to whom the filters were resold. Purolator offered a 4 percent discount to the type II distributors. The type II distributors performed an additional distribution function that the type I distributors did not perform.

The Federal Trade Commission held that the additional 4 percent discount to the type II distributors injured competition because it subsidized their internal operation. Purolator had offered evidence that the reshipping operations of the type II distributors (from their central warehouse to the affiliated branches) increased the operational costs of these distributors, and the discount was granted to offset these costs. The commission noted that the affiliated warehouse distributors had selected their method of operation and that customers' internal costs could not justify a price difference. As with single-function discounts, dual-function discounts are valid only if there are no probable adverse competitive effects.

---

[3]Purolator Products, Inc., 65 F.T.C. 8, CCH Trade Reg. Rep. P 16, 877 (1964), *aff'd,* 352 F.2d 874 (7th Cir. 1965).

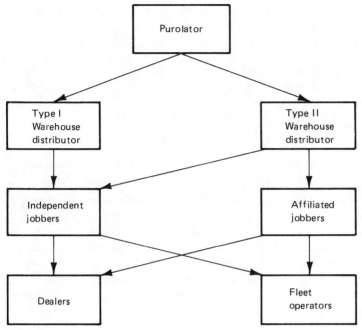

FIGURE 15-1
Purolator's distribution system for automotive filters.

Guidelines for Setting Functional Discount Policy

As the discussion on the legal status of functional discounts indicates, the policy of offering price concessions to members of the distribution channel can be cumbersome and legally complex. It should be clear that traditional policy is no excuse or defense for a discount policy that is legally challenged. Today, with the additional complexities of vertically integrated distribution systems, it is incumbent on sellers to carefully analyze functional discount policies.

When establishing a functional discount pricing structure, the seller should determine

1 The functions the distributors should perform for the seller
2 The costs to the distributors for performing these functions
3 The relative costs of selling to different types of distributors
4 The trade status of each buyer, i.e., the buyer's position in the distribution sequence
5 The extent of competition among buyers at all levels in the distribution sequence
6 For combination wholesaler–retailer buyers, the sales that are wholesale and the sales that are retail [By segregating the wholesaler–retailer's purchases between the wholesale and retail function and allowing a wholesale discount on legitimate

wholesale purchases only, the seller is demonstrating compliance with Section 2(a) of the Robinson–Patman Act.]

7 The savings in cost of serving the various distributors (see Chap. 9)

Above all, "any supplier who extends a functional discount—whether to a dual- or a single-function buyer—needs to get and keep reasonable proof that the functional classification is lawful and that all the purchases for which the functional discount was given do in fact fit the classification."[4]

PRICE PROMOTIONS AND DEALS

Advertising and personal selling have received considerable attention as methods of stimulating demand for products and services. However, until recently, the activities of sales promotion have not been as well studied, yet they represent an important aspect of marketing. Major forms of sales promotion include cents-off deals, two-for-one offers, sampling, coupons, refunds, rebates, premiums, sweepstakes, and contests. "According to new thinking, couponing should be thought of as primarily a price promotion. 'Couponing is the best way to deliver a short-term price incentive directly to the consumer' . . . according to Don Pratt, president, Newspaper Co-op Couponing."[5] Temporary price reductions may be used to

1 Generate new interest in an old product

2 Accelerate demand for products or flush out old merchandise to make room for new merchandise

3 Introduce a new product (Often, introductory lower prices, coupons, or rebates may be used to introduce a new product. By stimulating trial of new products, promotions reduce some of the retailers' risk in stocking new brands.)

4 Meet specific competitive situations in different geographic locations, for limited time periods, for specific products or services

5. Help sellers adjust to fluctuations in supply and demand without changing list prices (In recent years, automobile manufacturers have used rebates, special deals, low financing terms to encourage sales in slow-selling periods. The list prices are not changed as a defense against possible governmental price controls or future increases in costs or to avoid the costs of preparing new price lists and promotional literature.)

6. Help small sellers compete against national brands with large advertising budgets (Normally promotion costs are variable with sales and therefore occur as the sales are made, whereas advertising requires a fixed cash commitment. Small sellers without the cash resources for a large advertising budget may use variable promotional costs to compete more effectively.)

7. Enhance advertising by conveying some message about the product's features and benefits as well as the price and deal information

[4]Beringer, op. cit., p. 794.
[5]Louis J. Haugh, "Record Couponing Reflects New Price Promo Philosophy," *Advertising Age,* October 17, 1977, pp. 62–63.

Incidence of Price Promotions

In recent years, manufacturers and retailers have made increasing use of coupons, rebates and refunds, short-term price reductions, and free samples to stimulate short-term demand for their products and services. However, despite the popularity of these price deals, it is not at all clear that a majority of these deals are profitable. As indicated in earlier chapters (see especially Chaps. 8 and 11), for a price reduction to be profitable it is necessary that the product or service have a relatively high contribution margin and that the price reduction stimulate substantial sales growth. But if the short-term price reduction can be focused to appeal to a market segment not previously buying the product while maintaining full-price sales to most previous buyers, then the incremental sales resulting from the price deal may enhance profits.

Simply offering a coupon, rebate, or price-off deal to current buyers in the hope of stimulating a substantial increase in unit sales is likely to reduce profits unless mostly new buyers take advantage of the deal. Thus, *the underlying objective of a price promotion to final customers should be to focus on a price/market segment that is more price sensitive or deal responsive than existing buyers.* Essentially, then, price promotions to final customers simply become an aspect of segment pricing.

Effect of Price Promotions on Buyers' Perceptions

Discounting through price promotions has become quite important in the market-place because it is viewed by consumers as an acceptable method of reducing price. Since the objective of a price discount is to enhance unit sales of the product or, if used to increase store traffic, to enhance total sales of the store, the tradeoff between lower unit margin and increased sales volume determines whether there will be a positive impact on profits. However, if buyers do not perceive that there is a "deal" or that there is an enhancement in value, the discount strategy may not have the desired impact on revenues. Thus, an incorrect price discount decision can be detrimental in terms of lost sales and profits.

A research effort, using the price–perceived value framework developed in Chap. 4, explored the differential impact of offering a price reduction using several different ways to "frame" the promotion offer. Use of a price promotion frame that featured both the "regular" price and the lower "sale" price led to significant increases in perceived value. The results also indicated that buyers evaluate the worth of an offer based on their perception of how good a deal they are getting and that they evaluate deals differently depending on whether coupons or rebates are offered. Generally, a product promoted with a rebate was perceived as lower in quality and value than a promotion using either a coupon or a regular price–sale price frame.[6] It may be that consumers tend to look upon products that offer rebates as lower quality products and/or that they consider the offer to have lower value because of the extra

[6]Joseph D. Chapman and Kent B. Monroe, "The Framing Effects of Alternative Price Promotion Methods on Buyers' Subjective Product Evaluations," Working Paper, Department of Marketing, Virginia Polytechnic Institute and State University, Blacksburg, September 1989.

effort associated with the redemption of the rebate. Also, there is some evidence that immediate rewards (gains) are more highly valued than delayed rewards.

Price Promotion as Price Discrimination

As will be documented later, not all buyers of a product on price promotion take advantage of the promotion. Redemption rates for coupons and rebates indicate that many buyers do not redeem coupons or follow through and take the rebate that is offered. In 1979, of the 81.2 billion coupons distributed, 4.2 percent were redeemed. In 1986, of the 202.6 billion coupons distributed, 3.6 percent were redeemed. And in 1988, of the 252.7 billion coupons distributed, fewer than 4 percent were re-deemed. The average value of the coupons redeemed was 44 cents, and the total value of the redeemed coupons was \$4.657 billion.[7] One obvious reason for this lack of redemption, or follow through, is that the perceived cost of redeeming coupons or qualifying for the rebate is larger than the perceived value of the coupon or rebate. Since buyers who do not take advantage of the price promotion pay the regular price, by offering a coupon or rebate the seller has effectively segmented the market into two price segments.

The practice of charging different prices for the same product to different seg-ments is price discrimination.[8] However, if a coupon or rebate is available to all buyers—and some buyers choose not to take advantage of it—this price discrimina-tion is passive and the seller is not legally culpable. For this type of segmented pricing to be profitable, some additional conditions must prevail. First, the segments must be separable to some degree. This separation must either be due to some natural separation, such as geographic region or location, time of purchase, or category of buyer, e.g., business buyer vs. consumer. Second, these segments must have different degrees of price sensitivity and/or different variable purchasing costs. Third, the variable costs of selling to these segments must not be so different that the effect of the lower price is canceled by increased selling costs.

Price Promotion Decision Variables

To understand the complexity of developing a price promotion policy, it is useful to review the types of decisions that need to be made before a promotion can be implemented. Despite the facts that over \$125 billion was expected to be spent on promotions in 1989, that these promotional expenditures have been growing at the rate of 20 percent, and that in 1987 promotion's share of the marketing budget was 60 percent,[9] little attention has been placed on designing the best price promotion

[7]"Coupons," *Progressive Grocer,* 63 (September 1984), 186–188; *Progressive Grocer,* 66 (September 1987), 25–26; *Advertising Age,* 60 (March 13, 1989), 70.

[8]Chakravarthi Narasimhan, "A Price Discrimination Theory of Coupons," *Marketing Science,* 3 (Spring 1984), 128–147.

[9]"Shops See Surge in Promo Revenues," *Advertising Age,* 60 (February 20, 1989), 60.

policy for a seller. The following questions indicate the need to put more planning effort into this activity.

1 Should a price promotion be offered? The first question is simply whether the seller should offer a coupon, rebate, cents-off deal, or promotional discount to dealers. This decision cannot be made without considering the following decisions issues.

2 To whom should the deal be offered, dealers or final customers? Offering a price promotion to dealers or distributors in anticipation that the deal will be offered to final customers is not the same as offering it directly to final customers. Dealers may choose to reduce their prices the full amount, less, or not at all. Further, they may buy excess amounts of the deal merchandise, relative to actual demand, and sell some units at full price after the deal period is over. This activity is known as *forward buying.*

3 When should the promotion be offered? This question refers not only to the specific time of the year but also to whether to offer the deal during peak or slack selling seasons. For example, should ketchup manufacturers offer price promotions during the peak outdoor cooking season (May–September) or during the winter months?

4 How frequently should a promotion be run? If a product is offered frequently on some form of price deal, customers may come to expect the deal and buy only on deal. The effect is that the product is rarely sold at full list price, and the advantage of price segmentation is lost.

5 How long should the promotion be run? This decision is related to the issue of promotion frequency, peak vs. slack selling periods, and the length of buyers' repurchase periods. Many consumer coupons have no expiration date, thereby extending the promotion period indefinitely and making it difficult to measure the effectiveness of the coupon promotion.

6 How many units should be covered by the promotion? When deals are offered to the trade, there often is a restriction on the amount that a dealer can order on deal. This restriction may be related to the dealer's usual order size for the length of the promotion period and may be some proportion of this usual demand level. Also, some manufacturers may produce a specific type of product especially for the promotion. For example, one luggage company produced a special overnight bag solely for their winter luggage sales promotion and offered it at a "special" price.

7 What products and/or sizes should be promoted? Should a coffee producer offer a coupon on all package sizes of coffee or on the 1-pound size only? Should a luggage manufacturer feature all of its luggage or only certain models in the promotion?

8 How much should the price be reduced? What should the amount of the rebate be? What should the value of the coupon be? As discussed in Chaps. 3 and 4, the degree of buyer sensitivity to the price reduction, or the degree to which buyers perceive additional transaction value, will have an impact on the success of the promotion. The important issue here is how much of a price difference is necessary to induce buyers to take advantage of the offer, i.e., to perceive there is additional value in the offer.

As should be apparent from the foregoing list and brief commentary, a variety of issues need to be considered before developing and implementing a price promotion. In the sections that follow, we will discuss this complex and important decision problem. But first we need to consider what we know about who takes advantage of price promotions.

Who Responds to Price Promotions?

Presumably, one of the advantages of price dealing is that the results are directly observable in terms of increased sales and market share. The basic attractiveness of the price deal is that it can stimulate sales by appealing to the bargain-mindedness of buyers or to their satisfaction from being careful and smart shoppers. However, although price deals have been widely used by manufacturers and retailers, there is little conclusive evidence available on the characteristics of deal-prone buyers or their reasons for using these deals.

Coupons are documents that entitle the holder to a reduced price, or to x cents off the actual purchase price of a product or service. For years, coupons have played a substantial role in the promotion and purchasing of products. Indeed, the coupon is "epidemic, omnipresent, and suddenly a controversial marketing tool, alternatively commanding our respect through the sheer volume of its use and inciting our suspicion over its effectiveness."[10] During the 1980s, the use of rebates grew substantially, becoming an important price promotion tool. At the same time couponing has increased, leading to an estimate that over 2,000 manufacturers' coupons are distributed to each household each year.[11] However, the clutter of coupons has led to an overall decline in the rate of coupon redemption over the past few years.

Similarly, the number and frequency of retail promotions increased during the 1980s. Indeed, many large packaged goods companies in the United States now spend more dollars on promotions than on brand advertising.[12] Because of this increasing and widespread use of promotions and emphasis on price reductions, the profitability of price promotions has become an important managerial issue. Although little has been published previously concerning the source of increased sales due to promotions or the costs associated with these promotions, there is some emerging information on who uses coupons and who is likely to purchase on deal. Because of the segmentation issue raised earlier, to develop more effective price promotions it is very important to determine who responds to them.

In a national telephone sample, the A. C. Nielsen Company found that the main

[10]Robert D. Hisrich and Michael P. Peters, "Coupon Mania Presents Opportunities and Problems for Manufacturers, Users," *Student Edition: Marketing News,* December 1984, p. 9.

[11]Linda L. Price, Lawrence F. Feick, and Audrey Guskey-Federouch, "Couponing Behaviors of the Market Maven: Profile of a Super Couponer," in Michael J. Houston, (ed.), *Advances in Consumer Research,* Vol. 15 (Provo, Utah: Association for Consumer Research, 1988), pp. 354–359.

[12]"Sales Promotion Spending Closing in on Advertising," *Marketing News,* 20 (July 4, 1986), 8.

appeal of a coupon is its money-saving feature, followed closely by the consumer's inclination to use a coupon to try a new product at a "reduced" price. Further, it was shown that the households which reported the highest levels of coupon usage were those with higher incomes, larger families, and larger weekly expenditures for groceries.[13]

Three panel studies have investigated the characteristics of consumers who are responsive to "deals." Webster determined that only the age of the housewife was significantly related to deal-proneness; deal-proneness tended to increase as the housewife's age increased.[14] Montgomery found that a housewife's brand loyalty was inversely related to dealing activity; that venturesomeness, media exposure, and gregariousness were directly related to dealing activity; and that opinion leadership, interest scores on health, raising children, and food buying, and presence of children did not seem to relate to dealing activity.[15] Massy and Frank found that households responsive to deals were characterized by higher housewife educational attainment, but housewife employment/unemployment, household income or size, and age of housewife were not significantly related to deal responsiveness.[16]

Schiffman and Neiverth reaffirmed earlier findings that demographic characteristics are weak indicators of consumer dealing behavior.[17] They also found support for the inverse relationship between deal-proneness and brand loyalty in that a significantly greater portion of the coupon users were either multibrand users or loyal users of the deal brand. A little later, the *Ladies Home Journal* reported that 60 percent of the women surveyed regularly took advantage of cents-off coupons, with 80 percent being interested in them.[18]

In a comparison of coupon-prone and non–coupon-prone households, Bawa and Shoemaker found that the coupon-prone households tended to have a more educated husband and a somewhat more educated wife. In addition, the coupon-prone households tended to have a higher average income than the non–coupon-prone households. This finding is consistent with earlier findings of Teel, Williams, and Bearden.[19]

Several other findings of Bawa and Shoemaker are of interest to the question of who redeems coupons. People living in urban areas were more likely to be heavy

[13]"What Consumers Think of Coupons," *The Nielsen Researcher,* 30, no. 6 (1972), 3–10.

[14]Frederick E. Webster, "The 'Deal-Prone' Consumer," *Journal of Marketing Research,* 2 (May 1965), 186–189.

[15]David B. Montgomery, "Consumer Characteristics Associated with Dealing: An Empirical Example," *Journal of Marketing Research,* 8 (February 1971), 118–120.

[16]William F. Massy and Ronald E. Frank, "Short Term Price and Dealing Effects in Selected Market Segments," *Journal of Marketing Research,* 2 (May 1965), 171–185.

[17]Leon G. Schiffman and Clifford J. Neiverth, "Measuring the Impact of Promotional Offers: An Analytic Approach," in Thomas V. Greer (ed.), *Increasing Marketing Productivity and Conceptual and Methodological Foundations of Marketing,* combined Spring and Fall 1973 conference proceedings (Chicago: American Marketing Association), pp. 256–260.

[18]Louis J Haugh, "Women Cool to Promotions, 'LHJ' Tells Premium Executives," *Advertising Age,* October 10, 1977, pp. 10, 102.

[19]Kapil Bawa and Robert W. Shoemaker, "The Coupon-Prone Consumer: Some Findings Based on Purchase Behavior Across Product Classes," *Journal of Marketing,* 51 (October 1987), 99–110; Jesse E. Teel, Robert H. Williams, and William O. Bearden, "Correlates of Consumer Susceptibility to Coupons in New Grocery Product Introductions," *Journal of Advertising,* 9, No. 3 (1980), 31–35.

coupon users. Also, households with strong brand preferences were more likely to be light users of coupons. Similarly, households that are more prone to use coupons tend to be significantly less store loyal.

Some other recent evidence suggests that there is a group of heavy coupon users and that they account for a large proportion of total coupon redemptions.[20] This study found the following information concerning coupon redemption:

1 A higher percentage of redemptions was by nonloyal buyers and by buyers of low-share brands. Apparently, loyal buyers of high-share brands were less likely to redeem coupons. Thus, distributing coupons in a product category characterized by a large proportion of brand-loyal buyers is likely to be less productive.

2 Higher coupon values were more likely than lower values to be redeemed by nonbuyers. The lower coupon values were more likely to be redeemed by loyal and semiloyal buyers. Thus, unless the objective is to gain new triers, offering a higher coupon value may not be profitable.

3 Direct-mail approaches produced more redemptions by nonbuyers than did other approaches, such as freestanding inserts in newspapers.

4 The only significant demographic finding was that in the heavy coupon user group there was a lower incidence of female heads of households employed full time. Also, heavy coupon users were more likely to be nonloyal or semiloyal buyers, i.e., brand switchers.

The foregoing findings about brand loyalty, store loyalty, and coupon redemption have several important managerial implications. The heavy coupon users tend to be low in both brand and store loyalty. They tend to be better educated, have higher incomes, and live in urban areas. This segment of coupon users appears to have a relatively high response elasticity to coupons, and are likely to be responsive even for low-value coupons. However, the light coupon users tend to be store and brand loyal; they are older, less educated, have lower incomes, and are located in nonurban areas. Since they do not respond well to normal coupon offerings, it is likely that coupons with higher face values, or free samples, or in-store promotions would be more effective promotion vehicles.[21]

The Strategy of Price Deals

Price deals have been popular since the late 1800s, when C. W. Post offered a box of Grapenuts, a new product, for one cent. Price dealing and promotion have been increasing in popularity ever since. This popularity of price deals has led to questions of when is it best to offer a price deal, how many price deals a product should have in a given time period, and what the optimal duration of a price deal is. Consumer advocates have also noticed the increased use of price deals and have expressed some

[20]Steve Kingsbury, "Study Provides Overview of Who's Redeeming Coupons—and Why," *Marketing News,* 21 (January 2, 1987), 56.

[21]Bawa and Shoemaker, op. cit. See also Kapil Bawa and Robert W. Shoemaker, "Analyzing Incremental Sales from a Direct Mail Coupon Promotion," *Journal of Marketing,* 53 (July 1989), 66–78.

alarm at the possible fraudulent use of price deals. However, temporary price reductions remain a legitimate price tactic.

An early study revealed a number of strengths and shortcomings of price deals:[22]

1 Off-season price reductions were more profitable.

2 Too frequent price promotions may make consumers more price conscious.

3 Deals were not very effective in countering new competitive brands, nor were they necessarily more effective when accompanied by product or package innovations.

4 Price deals were more effective for new brands.

5 Price deals were not cures for generally "sick" products.

A price deal may be offered to consumers only, with appropriate dealer compensation for participating, or to dealers, presumably leading to expanded distribution, better product displays, or other conditions encouraging consumer purchasing. Often, however, the consumer or trade deals fail to realize the objective of greater sales volume because the retailer may not or cannot fully comply with the special deal.

The evidence on price deals suggests that many sellers misuse this pricing strategy. Some sellers run price deals during the peak selling season, thereby providing a price discount at a time *when demand is heavy* and relatively less price sensitive. Other sellers run frequent price deals and find it is most difficult to sell the product at its "regular" price because the buyers have either stocked up or are waiting for the next deal.

Other problems in developing a price deal strategy include the following:

1 Approximately 25 percent of the coupons redeemed do not have a corresponding purchase, costing manufacturers approximately $250 million per year.[23] Fraudulent claims by grocers for supermarket coupons have been estimated to total 15 percent of all claims.[24] Quaker Oats has developed a coupon redemption center and, using computers, processes over 800,000 coupons a day. This system, by using a 100 percent count, is able not only to detect coupon redemption fraud but also to analyze redemption rates, reduce coupon processing costs, and reimburse retailers several weeks quicker than previously.[25]

2 Refunding and coupon clipping have become a hobby. Today, there are many bulletins and newsletters published that alert members to all the new offers currently available, provide for an exchange of coupons and labels or other proofs of purchases, and offer information on the latest trends. In addition, couponing groups hold conventions for their members. According to a representative of The Nestlé Co., Inc., these couponers and their newsletters are "the bane of our existence." And

[22]Charles Hinkle, "The Strategy of Price Deals," *Harvard Business Review,* 43 (July–August 1965), 75–85.

[23]"Computers Help Foil Coupon Fraud," *Marketing News,* 20 (August 15, 1986), 1, 22.

[24]Louis J. Haugh, "Record Couponing Reflects New Price Promo Philosophy," *Advertising Age,* October 17, 1977, p. 63.

[25]"Computers Help Foil Coupon Fraud," op. cit. See also Lynn G. Coleman, "Con to Explain Pros of Coupon Security," *Marketing News,* 23 (April 24, 1989), 2, 6.

a spokesperson for a major soup company indicated that coupons meant to be used in one part of the country show up in other areas and ruin test markets.

3 Competitors often react quickly to counter an offer or even offer a more attractive deal.

4 Many deals require changing the retail prices. At one chain store, price deals required the changing of prices on 44 different brands of products on the same day.

5 The distributor often is offered an insufficient allowance to justify price changes or special promotional efforts. One deal offered the retailer 60 cents per dozen on a slow-moving item if each retailer would set up a special display and reflect the allowance in a lower retail price. The retailers did not believe that 5 cents per item was a sufficient inducement, and the deal allowance failed.

6 Many offers create utter confusion to retailers and distributors. One instant coffee producer offered an allowance of $2.40 per case, encouraging retailers to change the retail price from $3.35 to $3.15. However, before this deal expired, the producer offered a larger size jar containing 2 ounces of coffee "free" at the regular retail price of $3.35. Distributors did not know whether to reprice the original deal back to $3.35 or continue to offer the regular jar at $3.15 and simultaneously the "2-ounce free" jar at $3.35, with the resulting confusion for consumers. Such confusion leads to mistrust and wariness by consumers about the truthfulness of special deals. Moreover, distributors become less accepting of such deal opportunities.

7 In the past few years, regulations have come into force to counter potential and actual deception in the use of price deals. Price deals often had been used to camouflage price increases. For example, a box of 125 paper tissues had been retailed at $1.33. The manufacturer then offered a box of 150 tissues with this legend on the box: "This box normally contains 125 sheets. Our 25 percent FREE BONUS OFFER gives you 150 sheets at no increase in price—a true bonus value." The retail price was $1.38.

What had happened was that in the previous six months the manufacturer had raised the wholesale price of the 125-count box of tissues three times. The manufacturer then provided the bonus offer of 150 sheets for the new price of 125 tissues. The astute reader has perhaps also noticed that the "25 percent bonus" offer was only 20 percent [100(25/125)].

Figure 15-2 illustrates the way the price increase was concealed. The issue of deception arises in respect to the comparative frame of reference for claiming a "free bonus offer." From the seller's perspective, the representation is true when compar-

FIGURE 15-2
Using a bonus offer to conceal a price increase.

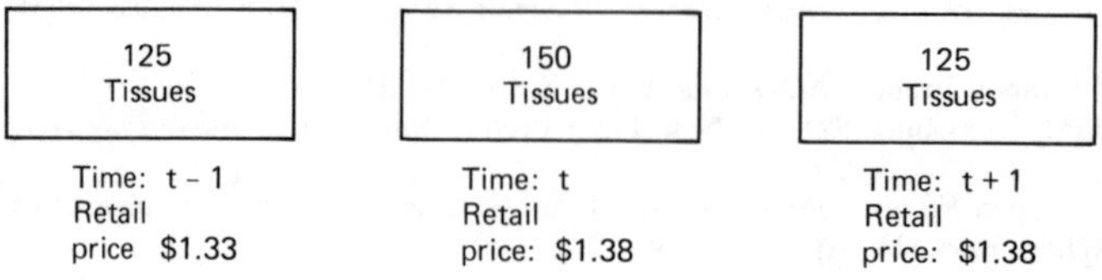

125 Tissues	150 Tissues	125 Tissues
Time: t − 1 Retail price $1.33	Time: t Retail price: $1.38	Time: t + 1 Retail price: $1.38

ing the offer at time t with the *planned* offer at time $t + 1$. But from the buyer's perspective, the representation is false when comparing the offer at time t with the *previous* offer at time $t - 1$.

To counteract such difficulties, the Federal Trade Commission has published guidelines and regulations governing "cents-off," "economy-size," and other savings representations. Moreover, many states have prosecuted firms for deceptive comparative price advertising. In one case, Maryland charged a local department store chain with falsely advertising mattresses for sale at prices drastically reduced from "regular" prices that never existed. For example, the state indicated that the store offered a nationally branded mattress in a newspaper advertisement as reduced from a "regular price" of $420 to $188.99. The state's lawsuit contended that the mattress had been offered at prices between $188.99 and $209.99 during 36 of the previous 40 weeks. Further, the mattress had never been sold at the $420 price. While the store admitted no wrongdoing, it agreed to pay a $500,000 penalty to settle the lawsuit. In a similar type of lawsuit, a department store chain in New York agreed to a $250,000 penalty after the state contended that it had falsely advertised sale prices of up to 50 percent off "regular prices" when the items, in fact, had never been sold at those regular, higher prices.[26]

8 For many manufacturers and retailers, sales, deals, coupons, rebates, and other forms of promotions have become almost the normal way of doing business. As a result of the almost constant promotions, buyers have been conditioned to wait for a sale or deal before buying. Indeed, one of the negative consequences of this frequent discounting by sellers is that buyers' reference prices are established at the lower deal prices and they resist buying when prices return to regular levels (see Chap. 3).[27] Moreover, instead of the 15–20 percent off for a promotion, deeper and deeper discounts of 50 percent and more have become standard practice. One negative result is that buyers have become conditioned to look for the deal (transaction value; see Chap. 3) rather than the product's benefits (acquisition value). "There is a new brand called 'deal' and it has growing loyalty."[28] Another negative result is that sellers become tempted to use the deceptive practices illustrated here.

Estimating the Profitability of Price Promotions

As indicated, sellers have become trapped into offering more and more price deals at larger and larger amounts off. One reason for this entrapment is that they have failed to recognize that price is the ratio of what a buyer receives in the way of product or service benefits relative to what the buyer gives up in the form of money

[26]"Hecht Co. Agrees to Settle Suit Over Advertising of Mattresses," *Washington Post,* July 29, 1988 p. G.1; "Sibley's $225G Payment Settles Ad Investigation," *Syracuse Post-Standard,* April 28, 1989, p. 1.

[27]James M. Lattin and Randolph E. Bucklin, "Reference Effects of Price and Promotion on Brand Choice Behavior," *Journal of Marketing Research,* 26 (August 1989), 299–310.

[28]Michael L. Rothschild, "A Behavioral View of Promotion Effects on Brand Loyalty," in M. Wallendorf and P. Anderson (eds.), *Advances in Consumer Research,* Vol. 14 (Provo, Utah: *Association for Consumer Research,* 1987, pp. 119–120; Francine Schwadel, "The 'Sale' Is Fading as a Retailing Tactic," *The Wall Street Journal,* March 1, 1989, p. B1.

or other goods (see Chap. 1). Sellers have attempted to create more value by offering price discounts. Yet, as observed in earlier chapters, price reductions have limited capability to enhance profits. However, the analytical tools provided in earlier chapters offer ways to establish the relative profitability of price promotions. Often the strategy of a price promotion is discussed in terms of its ability to increase market share. Yet if the increase in market share is of a short-term nature, due perhaps to some buyers accelerating their purchases (forward buying) or to others switching because of the deal, this short-term increase in volume may actually occur at a sacrifice in margin.

Coupon Profitability   The issues and problems of couponing and dealing reviewed thus far lead to some important questions about when couponing might be a profitable activity. Assume that the brand for which a coupon will be distributed is A, and that all other competing brands are C. The first question that needs to be answered is: How many customers who usually buy A will redeem the coupon? The coupon is a reduction in price for these buyers and a loss in revenue for this firm. The proportion of loyal buyers who redeem the coupon is difficult to estimate because it is likely that unless the coupon has a fixed expiration date, the redeeming household will not immediately redeem it. One study found that 70 percent of the redeeming households did not redeem the coupon on their first purchase opportunity.[29]

Second, how many customers who usually buy C redeem A's coupon? Customers who switch to A because of the coupon represent a gain in revenues for the firm. However, the evidence reviewed previously indicates that loyal buyers are least likely to redeem coupons of nonpreferred brands. Hence, if the market is comprised of a large proportion of brand-loyal buyers, there will be little gain from this loyal segment of brand C buyers.

The third question is, How many nonloyal buyers will redeem the coupon? Again, nonloyal buyers who switch to A because of the coupon represent a gain in revenues. The fourth question is, How many of the C-loyal and nonloyal buyers will repeat purchase brand A and how many repeats will occur? This question addresses the issue of whether the coupon promotion is able to sustain an increase in market share once nonloyal A buyers try A because of the coupon. While previous research tended to suggest that promotions led to lower repeat purchase rates, recent evidence suggests that this may not necessarily be so. If the promotion attracts a proportionately larger number of switchers, these buyers are not likely to continue purchasing the brand after the deal, thereby lowering the observed repeat purchase rate.[30]

Given that the firm decides to issue a coupon for brand A, the last question is, What will be the value of the coupon, i.e., the percentage off the regular price expressed in dollars and/or cents? If there is a large segment of brand C loyal buyers,

[29]Kapil Bawa and Robert W. Shoemaker, "The Effects of a Direct Mail Coupon on Brand Choice Behavior," *Journal of Marketing Research,* 24 (November 1987), 370–376.
[30]Scott Neslin and Robert W. Shoemaker, "An Alternative Explanation for Lower Repeat Rates after Promotion Purchases," *Journal of Marketing Research,* 26 (May 1989), 205–213.

then a high-value coupon (e.g., 50 cents) is more likely to bring in new users but not repeat purchasers. If there is a large segment of switchers, then a low-value coupon (e.g., 15 cents) may be sufficient to attract new customers but again not many repeat purchasers. Also, a low-value coupon is likely to attract some current customers, but at a lower margin.[31] In a recent study, it was reported that more than 84 percent of the sales increase attributable to a promotion was due to brand switching. Purchase acceleration accounted for less than 14 percent of the sales increase, and less than 2 percent was due to buyers stockpiling the product while it was on promotion.[32] Thus, the current evidence on who redeems coupons can be used to develop a framework for determining whether to use coupons as a promotional tool and, if used, the actual value of the coupon. As expected, the incremental gain in revenues must be compared to the additional costs associated with the development, distribution, and redemption of the coupons.

Profitability of Segmented Pricing   Earlier in this chapter it was pointed out that not all buyers of a product redeem coupons or purchase a product on price promotion. This situation, where some buyers pay a higher price for a product than others, was called passive price discrimination. Essentially, this form of buyer inertia results in the firm's being able to sell to two markets that have different degrees of price sensitivity. If the firm does not engage in price promotion activity, then it must set one price, which probably is lower than the price that the low–price-sensitive buyers are willing to pay but higher than many of the high–price-sensitive buyers are willing to pay. Another problem noted is that some of the loyal, low–price-sensitive buyers will take advantage and buy when the product is on promotion, creating some leakage from the low–price-sensitive market to the high–price-sensitive market. To analyze the firm's pricing options, some additional information about the degree of price sensitivity in each market segment, the degree that some leakage will occur when the product is on promotion, the costs of implementing the price promotion, and the variable costs associated with the production, marketing, and distribution of the product is needed. As pointed out in Chaps. 7–9, fixed-period costs unrelated to this decision are not pertinent to the analysis.

Table 15-1 illustrates the type of analysis that can be conducted when the needed information is available. The information in the table assumes that if the firm decides to pursue a one-price policy, i.e., use no price promotions, then the price set must be lower in order to generate volume. However, with a price promotion offered for a limited amount of time, it may charge a higher regular price because there is a low–price-sensitive market segment. The price promotion is designed to appeal to the high–price-sensitive market segment, which will buy only when the product is offered at a price deal. The table compares the no-promotion pricing policy with the

[31]Robert W. Shoemaker and Vikas Tibrewala, "Relating Coupon Redemption Rates to Past Purchasing of the Brand," *Journal of Advertising Research*, 25 (October–November 1985), 40–47.

[32]Sunil Gupta, "Impact of Sales Promotions on When, What, and How Much to Buy," *Journal of Marketing Research*, 25 (November 1988), 342–355.

TABLE 15-1
ESTIMATING PROFITABILITY OF PRICE PROMOTIONS

		Promotion			
		No Leakage		25% Leakage	
	No Promotion	No Promotion	Promotion	No Promotion	Promotion
Price	$ 2.50	$ 2.90	$ 1.90	$ 2.90	$ 1.90
Variable costs	1.25	1.25	1.25	1.25	1.25
Contribution	1.25	1.65	0.65	1.65	0.65
Volume (000's)	1,000	850	600	640	660
Revenues (000's)	$2,500	$ 2,465	$1,140	$1,856	$1,254
PV	0.50	0.57	0.34	0.57	0.34
Total contribution (000's)	$1,250	$1,402.50	$ 390	$1,056	$ 429
		$1,792.50		$1,485.00	
Promotion costs (5% of sales) (000's)		57.00		62.70	
Net contribution (000's)	$1,250	$1,735.50		$1,422.30	

price promotion policy under two conditions of market leakage. In the first situation, there is no leakage, i.e., no buyers willing to pay $2.90 would wait to buy the product on sale at $1.90. In the second situation, it is assumed that 25 percent of buyers willing to pay $2.90 do take advantage of the deal and purchase at the $1.90 price. Further, 25 percent of those buyers willing to pay $1.90 either do not buy or buy from another seller.

As the example shows, even with a 25 percent leakage, under the demand assumptions made, the two-price policy (higher regular price with lower promotion price) contributes more to fixed costs and profits than a one-price policy. Moreover, the additional costs associated with implementing the promotion, assumed to be 5 percent of sales generated by the promotion, are explicitly considered in the analysis. Clearly, to develop a price promotion policy it is important to consider not only the incremental sales generated by the short-term price reduction but also the regular sales that are cannibalized by the price promotion. As with any price reduction, there will be a gain in revenues due to the increased sales and a loss in revenues attributable to salable units sold at a lower price than necessary. Given that the current evidence indicates that, for mature products, an increase in market share due to a price promotion is not likely to be sustainable, careful analysis of these gains and losses in revenues as well as the incremental increase in costs is a necessary part of the decision process.

In essence, the two-price policy (regular price and short-term price reductions) is a variation of the product-line pricing problem introduced in Chap. 13. That is, the firm, over time, is offering two differentially priced products to appeal to two different price/market segments.

PRICING TO GAIN STRATEGIC ADVANTAGE IN DISTRIBUTION NETWORKS

As indicated earlier, one of the means of gaining distributor cooperation and motivation to improve the sales performance of the manufacturer's products is the offer of trade or functional discounts and promotional discounts or allowances. Other types of incentive programs involve the compensation plans of the manufacturer's sales force as well as incentive plans for the distributing firm or its sales force. Unfortunately, the discount plans or incentive plans are often offered as short-term efforts to improve sales performance and are not part of an overall strategic marketing and pricing plan. The purpose of this section is to offer some guidelines for using price to gain a strategic advantage in the distribution network.

When a distributor pricing plan is ad hoc and not part of the overall strategic plan some undesirable consequences may result. For example, one manufacturer attempting to increase market penetration offered distributors an additional functional discount of 5 percent. The purpose of this additional discount was to motivate the distributors to become more aggressive in promoting the manufacturer's products and gaining new customers. However, the distributors simply passed the additional discount on to their customers in the form of lower prices. The net result was that sales overall remained stable, no new customer accounts materialized, and a price war developed as competitors responded to the lower selling prices. As demonstrated in Chap. 8, this form of price reduction reduced margins without generating the necessary sales growth for profit enhancement.

Another manufacturer offered its sales force an incentive of a two-week vacation at an exotic resort for the largest increase in sales over the same quarter from last year. However, when the incentive program expired, sales dropped dramatically. Since the company had used a rebate program to encourage the sales increase that occurred during the sales incentive contest, most distributors simply had stocked up on inventory. (This practice of buying excess inventory because of a temporary price reduction, called forward buying, often occurs when distributors are offered short-term deals.) Thus, the manufacturer paid additional sales bonuses to its sales force, offered price reductions to distributors in the form of rebates, and experienced no real gains in sales. Moreover, the sales force experienced a decline in compensation after the incentive program because of the dramatic drop in sales during the time the distributors were selling off their excess inventory.

In earlier chapters, an important thesis was that sellers need to offer superior value to their customers in order to gain competitive advantage. In like manner, manufacturers need to provide their distributors with the opportunity to gain superior value with the resale of the manufacturers' products. Manufacturers who are able to gain a channel position advantage by offering distributors superior value are likely to gain eventual competitive advantage in the final selling markets. Thus, the manufacturer must not only seek to provide superior value to the final customer but also, through the use of discounts, dealer support, and incentive programs, develop a long-term partnership with its distributors. As one manufacturer indicated, we are "in partnership with [our] customers in pursuit of profits for them." Only then can we "make the maximum contribution to [our] company's profits."[33]

Guidelines for Enhancing Distributor Performance

The guidelines that are outlined in this section extend some basic principles that were developed in earlier chapters as well as offering some principles directly related to channel management. For effective distributor performance, manufacturers need to[34]:

1 Recognize the strategic importance of (perceived) product quality and brand reputation (see Chaps. 3–5)
2 Recognize the strategic importance of financial terms of trade (functional, cash, quantity discounts; see Chap. 14 and this chapter)
3 Recognize that incentive programs need to be an integral part of the price-channel strategy; such incentive programs should
   a be institutionalized with a few well-understood major annual efforts aimed at improving distributor performance
   b be simple and easy to implement
   c be tied to "real" sales increases, not the building of distributor inventories
   d encourage activities that have long-term benefits, e.g., sales training programs
   e help distributors improve their own financial performance
   f direct the incentive programs to the distributor firm and not to the distributors' sales force (enhances distributor management control without interference from the manufacturer)

    Thus, the focus of the seller is on ways to enhance the total value to its dealers and distributors. Overall, the goal is to increase the profits of the dealer or distributor to gain cooperation and a sharing of these profits by seller and distributor.

An Example

To illustrate how aspects of a manufacturer's product, distribution, and pricing strategic plan can be integrated into effective channel performance consider the Sullivan Equipment Company's experience. This company sold a wide range of industrial products used in a variety of manufacturing processes. Because of the technical nature of their products and variety of applications, distributors often did not have the capability to effectively sell the firm's products. Moreover, Sullivan had stressed product quality and enjoyed a reputation for technically superior products at relatively higher prices. As a result, many distributors found it

   [33]John C. Narver, "Price, Differentiation, and Channel Control," in L. P. Bucklin and J. M. Carman (eds.), *Research in Marketing: Distribution Channels and Institutions,* Vol. 8 (Greenwich, Conn.: JAI Press, 1986), pp. 225–249.
   [34]James A. Narus and James C. Anderson, "Strengthen Distributor Performance through Channel Positioning," *Sloan Management Review,* 29 (Winter 1988), 31–40.

TABLE 15-2
SELECTED ELEMENTS OF SULLIVAN'S DISTRIBUTION PLAN

Plan Element	Sullivan	Industry Average
Functional discount	35%	30%
Cash discount	2/10 net 30	2/10 net 30
Quantity discount	3% on orders of 25–49 units 5% on orders of 50–99 units 7% on orders of 100+ units	2% on orders of 50–99 units
Life-cycle costs	$350	$450
Suggested list price (example)	$50	$35
Incentive program		
Sales force	Commission based on contributions of sales; only distributor sales to final customers were used to determine bonus	Commission based on dollar sales to distributors
Distributors	Special discounts for off-season sales; end-of-year bonus based on actual sales increase over the year	Rebates made on sales during peak sales period

easier to sell lower priced, less technically superior products and did not make strong efforts to sell Sullivan's products. Finally, recognizing this lack of distributor effort, Sullivan's management developed a new approach to improve their distributors' performances relative to their product lines. Table 15-2 summarizes some of the pricing-related changes implemented relative to the averages of competing manufacturers.

In addition to the items listed in Table 15-2, the company hired and made available to the distributors technical specialists to assist in sales presentations and handling customer queries, developed more informative sales and technical information brochures for the distributors and final customers, provided training programs for the distributors' salespeople, and developed annual incentive programs aimed at their own sales force and the distributor firms. These annual incentive programs were used during the normal slow-selling months of the year.

Besides offering slightly better discount programs to the distributors, Sullivan's sales brochures and training programs stressed the nature of value analysis and life-cycle costing to demonstrate to customers the superior value they received despite the higher list prices (see Chap. 5). The better discounts offered to the distributors coupled with higher prices produced better margins for the distributors and enhanced Sullivan's relationships with the distributors. Several years after implementing this distributor program, the firm had become the sales leader and had a widespread favorable reputation among the distributors and final customers.

SALES COMPENSATION PLANS

Not only must the manufacturer be concerned with obtaining cooperation from distributors, but care must also be exercised to gain the sales forces' cooperation. Many companies have indicated that greater care is needed when explaining changes in prices or price policy to the sales force than when explaining these changes to customers.

As pointed out in Chap. 1, many pricing changes recently enacted by business firms have reduced the flexibility of the sales force and have increased sales force dissatisfaction. Moreover, the increased accent on profit margins and pruning products and services makes it incumbent on management to develop compensation plans that reward rather than penalize the sales force.

By using the costing principles developed in earlier chapters, a sales compensation plan can be developed that rewards salespeople in terms of their contributions to profit. The segment contribution analysis developed in Chap. 9 can be used to evaluate the economic rationale of sales compensation plans.

A compensation plan that companies increasingly are turning to is one based on contribution to profits. Such a plan rewards salespeople to the degree that they help the firm reach its profit goal, and it discourages them from putting their effort into easy-to-sell, low-margin products. Moreover, when companies move away from a varying-price policy to a one-price policy, such a compensation plan gives the salesperson incentive to avoid shading or reducing prices as a means of soliciting sales. Finally, a compensation plan based on profit contributions will influence salespersons to restrict selling expenses, which will improve their sales performance.

A compensation plan that properly motivates the sales force can be effective in managing the product–sales mix. Again, it is important to recognize that pricing policy is intricately related to all parts of the marketing management function.

SUMMARY

This chapter has shown the relationship of the pricing function to three major marketing decision variables—distribution and channel decisions, promotion management, and sales force management. Previously, Chaps. 12 and 13 linked the pricing decision to product management and Chap. 14 discussed the relationship between pricing and transportation decisions.

Price was defined in Chap. 1 as a ratio of the quantity of goods and services provided by the seller to the quantity of goods and services given up by the buyer. There are many options available to the seller when price must be changed. The seller can change the product's performance or attached services, the discount structure, the methods of distribution, or the sales promotion methods. Thus, price as the only revenue-generating marketing variable is intimately linked to the other marketing variables. The seller, therefore, has many alternatives available when making either short-term or permanent price changes.

As a final note, it should be remembered that the ultimate objective of a pricing decision is to influence buyer behavior. Thus, the decision should come less from traditional practice than from the analysis of what pricing alternatives will positively influence buyers. The purpose of this chapter has been to demonstrate that the underlying rationale for pricing decisions is also useful when making distribution, promotion, or sales management decisions.

DISCUSSION QUESTIONS

1 a Discuss the problem of controlling prices through the distribution channel.

  b What are some legal ways of developing price controls?

  c Why would a manufacturer be concerned with controlling the price through the channel?

2 a Distinguish between single-function and dual-function buyers.

  b Why is this distinction important?

3 What should a manufacturer do to establish a legally valid functional discount pricing structure? Why?

4 a Why would a firm reduce prices temporarily?

  b What are some alternative ways to temporarily reduce prices?

  c What are some of the problems of establishing a special price promotion?

5 If a manufacturer paid close attention to the behavioral aspects of price as discussed in Chap. 3, what behavioral principles would you suggest be used when developing a price–deal strategy?

6 a What are some ways in which a seller might use price deals deceptively?

  b Can you formulate any prescriptions for avoiding such deceptions?

7 a Look through several magazines, particularly magazines such as *Readers' Digest, Ladies Home Journal, Woman's Day,* and *Family Circle.* List the number of different types of deals—coupons, refunds, premiums—that you find.

  b Look through several Sunday newspapers and the Wednesday or Thursday food section of your newspaper. List the number of different types of deals—coupons, refunds, premiums—that you find.

  c If you took advantage of all the coupons you found, how much would you save?

  d Compare the weekly advertisements of several grocery stores in your area for at least a month. Are any national brands featured as specials by rival supermarkets? Are they the same brands?

  e Why do you suppose rival supermarkets would feature the same national brands as price specials?

SUGGESTED READINGS

Bawa, Kapil, and Robert W. Shoemaker: "The Coupon-Prone Consumer: Some Findings Based on Purchase Behavior Across Product Classes," *Journal of Marketing,* 51 (October 1987), 99–110.

Beringer, William E.: "The Validity of Discounts Granted to Dual Function Buyers under the Robinson–Patman Act," *The Business Lawyer,* 31 (January 1976), 783–800.

Bonoma, Thomas V., Victoria L. Crittenden, and Robert J. Dolan: "Can We Have Rigor and Relevance in Pricing Research?" in Timothy M. Devinney (ed.), *Issues in Pricing: Theory and Research* (Lexington, Mass.: Lexington Books, 1988), pp. 337–359.

Farris, Paul W., and John A. Quelch: "In Defense of Price Promotion," *Sloan Management Review,* 29 (Fall 1987), 63–69.

Monroe, Kent B., and Albert J. Della Bitta: "Models for Pricing Decisions," *Journal of Marketing Research,* 15 (August 1978), 413–428.

Narus, James A., and James C. Anderson: "Strengthen Distributor Performance through Channel Positioning," *Sloan Management Review,* 29 (Winter 1988), 31–40.

CHAPTER 16

LEGAL ASPECTS OF PRICING STRATEGY

As should be apparent from the preceding two chapters, the development of a price structure to implement a pricing strategy not only is a difficult and complex task, but it is fraught with potential for violating federal and state laws. Some of the legal implications of pricing were briefly discussed in Chaps. 9 (justifying price differentials), 14 (quantity and cash discounts and geographical pricing), and 15 (functional discounts and price promotions). In fact, the legal aspects of pricing strategy comprise one of the most difficult parts of marketing strategy and have left many businesspeople not only frightened of making pricing decisions but often, at the same time, vulnerable to legal action because of their pricing activities.

As will be elaborated upon in Chap. 20, there is a need for firms to establish a pricing administration function within their organizations. The pricing administrator or manager coordinates the many facets of pricing products and product lines as well as the interrelationships of price to advertising and promotion, channel management, and sales management. One of the important advantages of a price administrator is the provision of a means of overseeing the legal implications of various pricing strategies and tactics.

This chapter offers a broad view of the myriad set of federal laws that exist in the United States affecting pricing management. Given the increasing importance of international marketing, some commentary is also provided concerning the Combines Investigation Act of Canada as well as various legal situations in Europe.

First, this chapter surveys the main federal laws affecting pricing in the United States. For the most part, the discussion will be brief, with no examination of major landmark cases. The objective is not to provide a legal opinion on what is a legal or illegal pricing decision or action; this is the function of legal counsel. It has been the author's experience that most people involved in pricing at various firms have had neither formal training in pricing nor exposure to the real complexities of the legal environment for pricing. Consequently, many of these people come dangerously close to violating federal and state statutes on a regular basis. Because many pricing behaviors in firms and industries have become more or less traditional, little attention is given to the possibility of illegal pricing strategies and tactics. During the 1980s, the federal government pursued a laissez-faire approach to the regulation of business activity. However, as the Bush administration began its activities in 1989, there were indications that attention to various business activities will be renewed on the legal front.[1] Moreover, there are clear signals that attorneys general in a number of states are increasing their attention to the effect of pricing on consumer welfare. Thus, there is a need to be knowledgeable and attentive to the legal aspects of pricing decisions.

One of the most complex and frustrating areas of pricing is the justification of price differentials. This problem may arise (1) when a customer believes that he or she has been illegally charged a price higher than the price charged to other customers for the same product; (2) when a competitor believes that a rival's prices are lower in markets where they both compete than in markets where they do not compete; (3) when the government believes that competing customers of a seller are charged different prices; and (4) when price changes must be justified to customers, sales force, or a price control board.

Conditions 1, 2, and 3 generally arise as a result of legal proceedings after a charge of illegal price discrimination. The fourth condition prevails more frequently during inflationary periods. For example, during the double-digit inflation of the 1970s, price increases had to be cost-justified to a price control commission, and even when the price control commission approved such price increases, firms often found it necessary to justify price changes both to their sales force and to their customers. "We ask them [sellers] to justify [every price increase]," said Peter Tremblay, purchasing agent for Gillette Co.[2] (And the firm's sales personnel were often the least satisfied by such justification attempts.)

A second major purpose of this chapter is to illustrate how price differentials may be justified when a firm is faced with either litigation or disgruntled customers and sales force. Although other legally defensible approaches will be discussed, cost justification of price differentials seems to have wider application than the other approaches. A cost justification study for differential prices can be used to prevent further litigation, soothe disgruntled customers, and develop a sound price structure. Other legal defenses are suitable primarily within the legal arena.

The chapter begins by surveying the legal environment for pricing decisions. A brief summary of major federal legislation and the current atmosphere for enforcement will be presented. Then the nature of price discrimination will be discussed. The provisions of the Robinson–Patman Act will be summarized, and a brief inter-

---

[1]"Putting the 'Anti' Back in the Antitrust Div.," *Business Week,* June 19, 1989, pp. 64–70.

[2]Terry Kirkpatrick, "Purchasing for a Corporation: Buyer Fights Nightmare of Inflation," *Roanoke Times and World-News,* August 13, 1978, p. D1.

pretation of its litigation history will be offered. A section on the cost justification defense including guidelines for a cost justification study will follow. Finally, issues relative to controlling prices through the distribution channel will be discussed.

AN OVERVIEW OF MAJOR FEDERAL LAWS AFFECTING PRICING

As was apparent in Chaps. 8, 11, 14, and 15, the short-term effects of price reductions on profits are unlikely to be positive. Yet many firms attempting to gain volume or market share often resort to price reductions. Other competing firms feel compelled to follow these price reductions, and often undercut the original price-reducing firm. Pressure, real or perceived, sometimes prompts firms to grant certain buyers a favored status by giving them additional discounts for their business. To counteract these pressures to reduce prices and to stabilize profits some businesses have attempted, either by overt or covert actions, to stabilize prices and market share. In other situations, a large firm has intentionally reduced prices in one market area, or to a specific set of customers, in order to reduce competition or to drive a competitor out of business. Moreover, it was suggested in earlier chapters that there are typically several price/market segments distinguished by different degrees of sensitivity to prices and price differences. Thus, there is the opportunity to set different prices or to sell through different channels to enhance profits.

Each of these possible strategies or tactics is covered by some form of federal legislation and regulation. In fact, there are laws concerning *price fixing* among competitors, *exchanging price information or price signaling* to competitors, pricing similarly to competitors *(parallel pricing), predatory pricing,* and *price discrimination.* In this section we briefly consider the laws that cover these activities.

Price Fixing

The Sherman Anti-Trust Act (1890) specifically addresses issues related to price fixing, exchanging price information, and price signaling. It also has an effect on the issue of predatory pricing. Section 1 of the act prohibits all agreements in restraint of trade. Generally, violations of this section are divided into per se violations and rule of reason violations. *Per se violations* are automatic. That is, if a defendant has been found to have agreed to fix prices, restrict output, divide markets by agreement, or otherwise act to restrict the forces of competition, he or she is automatically in violation of the law and subject to criminal and civil penalties. There is no review of the substance of the situation, i.e., whether there was in fact an effect on competition. In contrast, *rule of reason violations* call for an inquiry into the circumstances, intent, and results of the defendants' actions. That is, the courts will examine the substantive facts of the case including the history, the reasons for the actions, and the effects on competition and the particular market. The current attitude of federal and state agencies and courts is that price fixing is a per se violation and criminal sanctions should be applied to the guilty persons.

In two recent Supreme Court decisions, the abhorrent view of price fixing was extended to the attempt to control *maximum prices* that may be charged. The Maricopa County Medical Society and its physician members agreed to establish a maximum fee schedule for health services. The Court, in 1982, declared that agreements to fix maximum prices were as repugnant to the Sherman Act as agreements to set minimum prices. Also in 1982, the Court declared that a chiropractic association's attempt to control prices through a peer review committee was in violation of the Sherman Act. Thus, the attempt of a professional association to set prices is an illegal pricing practice. In effect, all overt interferences with the independence of the pricing mechanism are prohibited. "No marketer may safely tamper with the independent pricing mechanism without inviting judicial action."[3]

Section 2 of the act prohibits the practice of monopolizing, i.e., the wrongful attempt to acquire monopoly power. Thus, having a monopoly is not illegal, but the deliberate attempt to become a monopoly is illegal. The issue here in recent cases has been not whether a firm had acquired a monopoly per se but the methods of achieving such market power. Thus, the courts have become increasingly aware of a firm's need to develop a strong competitive position in the markets it serves, and that a strong competitive position may translate into a dominant market share. However, if a dominant market share leads to above-market average prices, some form of legal or regulatory action may take place (e.g., the dominance of some airlines in hub cities has recently been questioned).

Exchanging Price Information

Many trade associations collect and disseminate price information from and to their members. A legal problem arises when there is an apparent agreement to set prices based on the exchanged price information. Moreover, if members discuss prices and production levels at meetings, and if prices tend to be uniform across sellers, then it is likely that the exchange of information led to some form of price fixing. Again, the legal issue is whether the exchange of price information seems to have the effect of suppressing or limiting competition, which is a violation of Section 1 of the Sherman Act.

The exchange of price information may be lawful when it can be shown that the price information is about past prices, not future prices, where individual firms are not identified, where the data are publicly available to non–trade association members, and where meetings did not include discussions of price and production policies. Care must be exercised when competing sellers exchange price information. The trend in litigations recently has been to make such exchanges more difficult to prove that they do not violate Section 1.

Parallel Pricing and Price Signaling

In many industries and markets, one firm may emerge as a price leader. That is, the firm often is the first to announce price changes, and most rival sellers soon follow

³Ray O. Werner, "Marketing and the Supreme Court in Transition, 1982–1984," *Journal of Marketing,* 49 (Summer 1985), 97–105.

the price changes made by the leader. At other times, another firm may initiate the price changes, but if the price leader does not introduce similar price changes, the other firms as well as the initial firm adjust their prices to correspond to the price leader's prices. The legal question here is whether these somewhat concerted price changes constitute a tacit, informal, and illegal agreement in violation of Section 1.

Recent court actions seem to indicate that parallel pricing per se is insufficient to prove a violation. Rather, parallel pricing *plus* evidence that the defendants acted in a concerted way, and that they communicated in some way to achieve a common understanding over prices, must be present.

Recently, some questions have been raised as to whether the public announcement of prices and price changes has been used by sellers to signal prices and to achieve this common understanding about prices. That is, do sellers achieve this common understanding about prices through public announcements about their prices and price changes? If so, then a violation of Section 1 may exist. For example, if one company announces a price increase effective 60 days later, some lawyers have suggested that the announcement serves as a signal to competition. The suggestion seems to imply that if others follow with similar announcements, then the price increase will remain in effect; if others do not follow, the price increase will be rescinded. As the discussion in Chap. 3 indicated, announcing price increases ahead of the effective date provides time for customers, distributors, and the sales force to adjust their price frame of reference. However, what may be an effective managerial practice could be interpreted as a mechanism for attempting to achieve a common understanding among rival sellers.

The ramifications of price signaling from a legal perspective remain to be determined by legislative action, litigation, or further debate.

Predatory Pricing

Predatory pricing is the cutting of prices to unreasonably low and/or unprofitable levels to drive competitors from the market. If this price cutting is successful in driving out competitors, then the price cutter may have acquired a monopoly position via unfair means of competition—a violation of Section 2 of the Sherman Act.

There is considerable controversy about predatory pricing, particularly how to measure the effect of a low-price strategy on the firm's profits and on competitors. Predatory pricing occurs whenever the price is so low that an equally efficient competitor with fewer resources is forced from the market or is discouraged from entering it.[4] The primary effect on the smaller seller is a drain on cash resources, not on profits per se. As argued in Chap. 12, if the cash inflow from the sale of products or services does not exceed the cash outflow, the firm cannot recover its investment in the product. Moreover, if the cash inflow does not cover the firm's cash outflow, then the cash drain prohibits it from investing in new products and other types of business activity. Thus, much of the controversy surrounding measuring the effects of an alleged predatory price relates to the proper set of costs to be used to determine the relative profitability of the predator's actions.

[4] John Dearden, "Taming Predatory Pricing," *Financial Executive,* January 1983, pp. 38–44.

Recently, the courts have been adopting the rule that predatory pricing exists if the price does not cover the seller's average variable or marginal costs. However, the intent of the seller remains an important consideration in any case.[5] For example, in 1976 the Federal Trade Commission (FTC) issued a complaint that General Foods had sold its regular blend Maxwell House coffee at unreasonably low prices, sometimes below cost (predatory pricing), and that it had engaged in discriminatory pricing as well as promotional and advertising practices. At the time, Maxwell House enjoyed a market share of 45–50 percent in the eastern United States. In January 1982, an administrative law judge for the FTC ruled that General Foods' actions were legitimately defensive. Essentially, the judge recognized that coffee consumption had been declining, that a major competitor, Procter & Gamble, had entered the eastern market with a nationally recognized brand, Folger, and that for a mature product like coffee, sales growth would occur only if market share was taken from rival sellers. Thus, General Foods had a legitimate defense: it had engaged in these activities to prevent losing market share to Procter & Gamble by letting the competitor enter this regional market. Generally, the climate by the late 1980s was more attuned to analyzing the relationship between a firm's price and its average variable costs. Thus, there now seems to be greater opportunity for competitors to be more aggressive in their pricing decisions.[6]

Other Important Laws

The Clayton Act (1914) was passed to correct certain defects and omissions of the Sherman Act. It prohibits anticompetitive mergers, tying arrangements, exclusive dealing agreements, interlocking directorates, and the acquisition of stock in competitor companies. It was felt that certain mergers, interlocking boards of directors, and the buying of a competitor's stock would lead to dangerous oligopolies and the control of market prices. Also, Section 2 of the act prohibited predatory price discrimination.

As noted earlier, except for the per se violations, the Sherman Act is not violated unless substantial adverse effects on competition can be proved. With the Clayton Act an action that has the *potential* of substantially lessening competition may be illegal. Thus, the Clayton Act made an important distinction between actual harm to competition and the potential for such harm to occur.

The Federal Trade Commission Act (1914) established the Federal Trade Commission, prohibited "unfair methods of competition in commerce, and unfair or deceptive acts or practices in commerce" (Section 5). Unfair methods of competition include acts or behaviors that violate the Sherman or Clayton Act. However, if for a technical reason an action is beyond the scope of either of these two acts, the FTC may invoke Section 5 if there are indications that the action has had or has potential to have substantial anticompetitive effects.

[5]Louis W. Stern and Thomas L. Eovaldi, *Legal Aspects of Marketing Strategy* (Englewood Cliffs, N.J.: Prentice-Hall, 1984), pp. 257–263.
[6]Susan S. Samuelson and Thomas A. Balmer, "Antitrust Revisited—Implications for Competitive Strategy," *Sloan Management Review,* 30 (Fall 1988), 79–87.

The FTC was created by Congress to protect the competitive structure from monopoly tendencies and to protect businesses from unfair methods of competition. In 1938, Congress passed the Wheeler–Lea Act as an amendment to the Federal Trade Commission Act, broadening the FTC's purpose to include protection of the public from deceptive business practices. The amendment also prohibited false and misleading advertising and provided more stringent penalties and enforcement procedures. In 1950, Section 15 of the Federal Trade Commission Act was amended to strengthen the FTC cease and desist order by providing that a separate violation could be found for each day the violation of a final order continued. The penalty for each such violation could be up to $5,000. Thus, the FTC has the authority to eliminate deception and to provide consumers with information that will help them make intelligent purchase decisions.

THE NATURE OF PRICE DISCRIMINATION

Both the Clayton Act and the Robinson–Patman Act prohibit illegal price discrimination, but neither prohibits price differences, as is often believed. In fact, price discrimination can be found in many markets. Although, price discrimination in selling to ultimate consumers is assumed by the Federal Trade Commission, the courts, lawyers, and marketers to be legal, many cases of permissible and accepted price discrimination involve ultimate consumers. As was pointed out in Chap. 15, whenever some buyers are willing to pay a higher price, or do not take advantage of the opportunity to buy at a lower price, there is some form of price discrimination. But there are also some recognized acceptable price differences for the same product or service that reflect differential price sensitivity or ability to pay. For example, it is readily accepted that many retirees, with limited fixed incomes, should be offered discounts or other opportunities to pay less for some products or services. Also, there are discounts for professional association members as a benefit of membership, and for students and educators, for when purchase is made, e.g., matinee performances. Moreover, when businesses sell to businesses, the Robinson–Patman Act indicates certain situations in which it is lawful to discriminate on the basis of price.

Economically, price discrimination occurs whenever there are price differences for the same product or service sold by a single seller that are not justified by cost differences or by changes in the level of demand. Price discrimination also occurs when two or more buyers of the same product or service are charged the same price despite differences in the cost of serving these buyers.[7] Thus, to know whether price discrimination exists, in the economic sense, between two or more buyers, it is necessary to know both the price and the total relevant costs applicable in each instance of possible discrimination.

As indicated by the definition of price in Chap. 1, price discrimination may arise in a variety of ways. The product sold to some buyers may be physically different or of different quality. There may be differences in services that accompany the products, e.g., delivery, storage, credit extension, sales force efforts. Some buyers

[7]*The Attorney General's National Committee to Study the Antitrust Laws* (Washington, D.C.: Office of the *Federal Register,* National Archives and Records Service, 1955), pp. 333–336.

may qualify for volume, cash, or trade discounts. Hence, whether there is price discrimination in the economic sense depends on the factual detail surrounding the transactions.

However, the legal basis for price discrimination goes beyond these economic tests. Indeed, the Robinson–Patman Act sets out conditions beyond cost differences in which price discrimination may legally exist. We turn now to an overview of the Robinson–Patman Act.[8]

PROVISIONS OF THE ROBINSON–PATMAN ACT

Section 2 of the Clayton Act sought to prevent sellers from cutting prices in areas where strong competition existed while maintaining higher prices in areas with little or no competition. Essentially, the act was aimed at preventing local price cutting. However, Section 2 was also interpreted as applying to price discrimination among competing buyers.

During the 20 years following passage of the Clayton Act in 1914, chain stores grew rapidly and increased their buying power. As a chain's buying power increased, some chain buyers began coercing price concessions to their advantage. This type of price discrimination was thought to threaten the survival of independent wholesalers and retailers, and Section 2 was insufficient to protect these independent distributors. Hence, in 1936, Congress passed the Robinson–Patman Act as an amendment to the Clayton Act.

Section 2 of the Robinson–Patman Act amends Section 2 of the Clayton Act and is divided into six parts. Section 2 of the Robinson–Patman Act contains civil prohibitions and Section 3 lists criminal prohibitions.

Section 2(a) is the backbone of the act. It prohibits sellers from charging different prices to different buyers for similar products where the effect might be to injure, destroy, or prevent competition, in either the buyers' or sellers' markets. It also provides a defense when a price discrimination can be cost-justified by the seller and offers other limited defenses and exceptions.

Section 2(b) places the burden of proof on the person charged with a price discrimination violation under Section 2(a). Section 2(b) also provides a defense if the seller can prove that the lower price was made to equal a lawful low price of a competitor.

Section 2(c) prohibits the seller from paying and the buyer from receiving any brokerage fee, commission, or other form of compensation for a transaction.

Sections 2(d) and 2(e) prohibit a seller from granting discriminatory allowances [2(d)] or services and facilities [2(e)], unless such allowances or services are available on proportionately equal terms to all competing customers.

Section 2(f) makes it unlawful for a buyer knowingly to induce or receive an illegal price discrimination.

---

[8]For an excellent presentation of economic and legal bases for price discrimination in utility rate-making, see *Legal Memorandum of Assistant General Counsel,* Litigation Division on Discriminatory and Preferential Practices under the Postal Reorganization Act, Washington, D.C., Postal Rate Commission, Docket No. *mc* 73-1, April 15, 1974.

Section 3 prohibits a seller from providing secret allowances to a favored buyer. The section also forbids territorial price reductions or sales at unreasonably low prices for the purpose of destroying competition or eliminating a competitor. Section 3 is a criminal statute in that it makes it a crime for any person to be a party to its prohibition. Maximum penalties include a $5,000 fine and imprisonment for a year. However, the U.S. Supreme Court has held that Section 3 is not an antitrust statute and therefore does not provide for liability for treble damages by private litigants if a conviction occurs.

Jurisdictional Defenses—Section 2(a)[9]

Unlike economic price discrimination, a price differential is not illegal price discrimination per se; certain requirements specified in Section 2(a) must be met. In any price discrimination litigation, the seller first may attempt to prove that the act does not apply to the price differences at issue. Primarily, a *jurisdictional issue* is a legal matter and does not include the actual issue of the price differentials.

Before a violation of Section 2(a) can be shown, the following jurisdictional requirements must be present. It must be shown that

1 The same seller
2 Charged different prices
3 To two or more different purchasers
4 For use, consumption, or resale within the United States or any territory

Furthermore, it must be shown that

5 There were two or more sales
6 Reasonably close in time
7 Involving commodities
8 Of like grade, quality, and quantity
9 And that at least one sale was "in commerce"

Each of these jurisdictional requirements will be discussed in turn.

The Same Seller   Although this requirement seems uncomplicated, it has presented some thorny problems. Primarily the problems occur when parent corporations sell through independent subsidiaries or distributors and when at least one of the purchasers bought directly from the parent while unfavored customers bought from an independent distributor or subsidiary.

Legally, it must be shown that the distributor or subsidiary possesses sufficient autonomy insofar as distribution policies are concerned. That is, the issue is not ownership per se but rather whether there is managerial autonomy in the marketing

---

[9]In the commentary that follows, specific court cases will not be cited. Excellent overviews of the Robinson–Patman Act that include case citations are Earl W. Kinter, *A Robinson–Patman Primer* (New York: Macmillan, 1970); Paul H. LaRue, "Meeting Competition and Other Defenses under the Robinson–Patman Act," *The Business Lawyer,* 25 (April 1970), 1037–1051; and Stern and Eovaldi, op. cit., pp. 263–276.

activities of the subsidiary or distributor. There are no specific guidelines on how a firm can determine whether sufficient marketing control resides with the distributor or subsidiary to legally define the parent and the distributor or subsidiary as separate sellers. However, if legal autonomy is proved, then the alleged discrimination did not result *from sales by the same seller* and illegal price discrimination is not present.

An offer to sell or a bid that is not accepted does not result in a discriminatory price. Further, refusal to sell ordinarily is not a violation of the Robinson–Patman Act. Primarily, either an unaccepted offer to sell or a refusal to sell does not result in two sales and a resulting price difference between purchasers.

A Price Difference   Within the legal setting, price has been defined simply as what the buyer has actually paid the seller as consideration, i.e., what the seller gives up to acquire the goods and services. Thus, the U.S. Supreme Court has held that a difference in price is prima facie (at face value) evidence of price discrimination. Thus, if the seller has one price for all customers and they pay transportation expenses, there is no violation of Section 2(a).

Because, price discrimination legally is equivalent to price differentiation, equal prices are not unlawful. As was indicated in Chap. 15, a firm may sell at the same price to wholesalers, retailers, and consumers. However, when there are differing terms or conditions of sale, an illegal, indirect price discrimination may occur.

It is important to recognize that the pricing activity under examination for a possible violation must be something other than a reasonable policy of price flexibility. An important issue is whether the price difference and the amount of goods sold at different prices are substantial enough to have a serious anticompetitive effect to the detriment of the public interest. As observed in our definition of price in Chap. 1 and as discussed in Chaps. 14 and 15, there are many ways to differentiate price besides the direct dollar quotation. Promotional, trade, cash, and quantity discounts, rebates, premiums, or free goods, guarantees, provision of delivery, warehousing, and credit all affect how much the buyer actually receives. Differences in these terms and conditions of sale have been held to result in indirect price discrimination within the domain of Section 2(a). Moreover, under Sections 2(d) and 2(e), these terms and conditions of sale must be available to all competing customers on proportionately equal terms.

Two or More Purchasers   Similar to the requirement that there be a single seller, it must also be shown that the alleged price discrimination was between two or more purchasers. Again, this issue arises when a manufacturer used more than one channel of distribution. That is, the manufacturer may sell direct to some customers and through distributors or subsidiaries to other customers, who compete on the same level as the direct-buying customers.

It has been held that in some cases in which the manufacturer also deals directly with the distributor's or subsidiary's customers, these customers are also *indirect purchasers* of the manufacturer in the eyes of the law, and they may therefore pay a higher, discriminatory price than competing direct-buying customers. As in the situation of the same seller, this legal issue revolves around the question of managerial control. But although a subsidiary or distributor may be legally autonomous within the purview of the same-seller requirement, it is possible that the manufacturer may have sufficient contact with the indirect customers to establish the requirement of two or more purchasers. Indeed, this was one of the legal issues prevailing against Purolator, as discussed in Chap. 15.

Perhaps the safest approach is to have no contact between a manufacturer and its distributor's customers. Such an approach would rule out the use of "missionary" salespeople, who arrange store displays, check retailer's inventory, and occasionally take orders. Furthermore, this "hands-off" approach would prevent controlling wholesalers' or retailers' selling prices. The legal precedents in this area are inconclusive and, at this time, raise additional questions about the definition of legally acceptable distribution control.

Geographical Requirement   Section 2(a) cannot be applied to sales made for use, consumption, or resale in a foreign country. That is, export sales are exempt but import sales are not exempt from the provisions of Section 2(a). However, Sections 2(c), 2(d), and 2(e) have been applied to export sales.

Two or More Sales   The different-purchasers requirement has been interpreted to mean that both sets of transactions consist of sales. It has been held that consignments are not "sales" for the application of the act. The issuance of a loan, the making of a gift, and terms of leases are not "sales." Furthermore, refusing to sell is not per se an unlawful price discrimination. Hence, price discrimination that involves nonsale transfers of property or refusal to sell is not prima facie evidence of unlawful price discrimination.

Contemporaneous Sales   Since discrimination occurs when there is a price differential for similar transactions under comparable conditions, the act is operative only if sales are reasonably close in time. The courts have ruled that price differences must be reasonably close in time and must involve delivery of the products also reasonably close in time. Thus, two contracts for future delivery at different times will not necessarily be in violation since delivery does not occur at the time of the contract agreement.

Also, Section 2(a) permits "price changes from time to time . . . in response to changing [market] conditions." Included in such price changes are obsolescence of seasonal goods, perishable products, going-out-of-business sales, closing-out-a-line sales, and court-sanctioned distress sales.

Tangible Commodities   It has consistently been found that Section 2(a) applies only to tangible products and does not encompass price differences for real estate, services, or contract rights or privileges. Thus, the courts have said that the word *commodity* is restricted to products, merchandise, or other tangible goods.

Products of Like Grade and Quality   Jurisdiction is not present when it is demonstrated that the products involved are of different grade and quality. Basically, the defendant must show that there are substantial physical differences affecting consumer preference or marketability. However, brand differences alone are not a sufficient defense.

Recently, the courts have seemingly applied some current marketing thinking and have considered customer preferences for the products in question. Thus, if there is substantial customer preference for a variation in design, and if the customer is willing to pay a higher price for the product, then the two products are not of like grade and quality. These design variations should not be decorative features that have no demonstrable effect on consumer demand.

The effect of using different labels or brand names was argued in the landmark Borden case.[10] The Borden Company had been producing private-label evaporated milk for about 20 years when the FTC issued a complaint on April 22, 1958. Borden was charged with price discrimination by selling milk of "like grade and quality" to different purchasers at higher prices than to the private-label purchasers. It was readily admitted that there were no physical differences between the Borden brand and the private brands of evaporated milk. However, Borden contended that the Borden brand commanded a higher market price because of consumer acceptance. Hence, the Borden brand of evaporated milk was a different product than the private brands.

The hearing examiner, the full Federal Trade Commission, and the U.S. Supreme Court all concluded that Borden's evaporated milk and the private brands that Borden produced were of like grade and quality. However, the U.S. Supreme Court remanded the case back to the Appeals Court to make a final determination of the issues of injury to competition and cost justification.

The Fifth Circuit Court of Appeals rendered the final decision on July 4, 1967. It was the court's opinion that Borden's policy of selling private-brand milk did not result in injury to competition, and the case was resolved in favor of Borden. The court did not take a position on the cost justification issue.

In finding no competitive injury the court recognized the value of a premium brand:

> Where a price differential between a premium and nonpremium brand reflects no more than a consumer preference for the premium brand, the price difference creates no competitive advantage to the recipient of the cheaper private brand . . . [the price difference] represents merely a rough equivalent of the benefit by way of the seller's national advertising and promotion which the purchaser of the more expensive branded project enjoys.[11]

Thus, the court recognized that when the buyer perceives there is a difference between two branded products, then there is a valid difference, so long as the "price difference is reasonable." What constitutes a reasonable price difference has not been established.

---

[10]This case has spawned a number of articles including Jacky Knopp, Jr., "Branding and the Robinson–Patman Act," *Journal of Business,* 39 (January 1966), 24–34; Morris L. Mayer, Joseph B. Mason, and Einar A. Orbeck, "The Borden Case—A Legal Basis for Private Brand Price Discrimination," *MSU Business Topics,* 18 (Winter 1970), 56–63; Thomas F. Schutte, Victor J. Cook, Jr., and Richard Hemsley, "What Management Can Learn from the Borden Case," *Business Horizons,* 9 (Winter 1966), 23–30.

[11]*The Borden Company v. FTC,* 381 F.2d 175 (5th Cir. 1967).

One Sale in Commerce   Section 2(a) provides "that it shall be unlawful for any person engaged in *commerce,* in the course of such *commerce . . .* to discriminate in price . . . where either or any of the purchasers . . . are in *commerce"* (italics added). Hence, it is a jurisdictional defense that the alleged discrimination did not involve a sale "in commerce." Generally, the courts have held that for a sale to be "in commerce" the product must cross a state line. Legally, a firm is not engaged in commerce if it sells its products only in the state where they are produced. Thus, the use of local plants selling their products only in the producing state has become a recognized way of avoiding the prohibitions of Section 2(a).

In 1983, the Supreme Court extended the coverage of the Robinson–Patman Act to include governmental agencies that are not purchasing goods for "traditional" purposes. Sales to governmental agencies cannot be made at lower prices than sales to buyers in the private sector if the agencies are reselling the products at prices lower than private firms. This extension of the Robinson–Patman Act to governmental agencies raises questions about universities that may buy personal computers at low prices for resale to their students. Moreover, an agency that bargains for such low prices may be charged with knowingly inducing price discrimination in violation of Section 2(f).

The "No Statutory Injury" Defense

Section 2(a) provides another jurisdictional defense in that price discrimination is illegal if the effect is to injure, destroy, or prevent competition. As pointed out in the discussion on the Borden case, the Appeals Court determined that no competitive injury had resulted from the price differentials. As with Borden, many Robinson–Patman defendants have prevailed by showing no injury to competition.

The "Guidelines for Setting Functional Discount Policy" in Chap. 15 included a recommendation for knowing the buyer's position in the distribution sequence. This knowledge enables the seller to determine whether differential prices to different channel members would have the effect of injuring competition. For example, suppose manufacturer M sells to two distributors, D_1 and D_2. However, D_1 in turn sells to retailer R_1, and D_2 also sells to retailer R_2, who sells to final consumers in a separate market area. Figure 16-1a illustrates this possibility.

If M charges D_1 and D_2 the same price, then there is no discrimination at the distributor level and no competitive injury. However, since D_2 competes with R_1, it is possible that D_2 could sell to consumers in market A at a price lower than R_1's price. If the price advantage harms the competitive position of R_1, then illegal price discrimination exists.

If the price to D_1 was lower than the price to D_2, then there is no illegal price discrimination since D_1 and D_2 do not compete for the same customers. However, if the lower price to D_1 permits R_1 to sell in market A at a price lower than D_2's price, *and* if D_2's competitive position is harmed, then there is illegal price discrimination by the manufacturer. Note, however, that if prices to R_1 and R_2 differ because of the manufacturer's pricing policy, there is no illegal price discrimination to these two retailers, since R_1 and R_2 do not compete with each other.

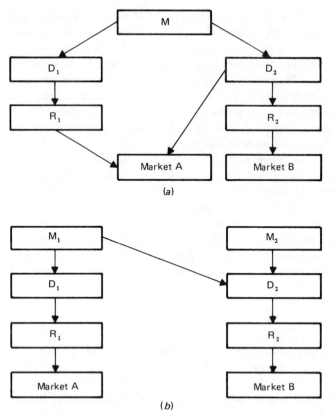

FIGURE 16-1
Hypothetical distribution systems.

Each of the foregoing situations in which a possible competitive injury existed is called a *secondary-line injury case.* That is, competitive injury due to a manufacturer's pricing policy occurs somewhere in the distributive sequence. For secondary-line injury to occur at some level of distribution, it is necessary that competing buyers purchase the same product at different prices and that the disadvantaged buyer's competitive position be injured. The important issue here is whether competition has been injured.

Now consider the situation depicted by Fig. 16-1b. M_1 competes with M_2 for the purchases of D_2. There is no other competition at lower levels of the distribution system. Suppose M_1's price to D_2 is lower than the price to D_1. Since M_2 does not sell to D_1, it is possible that M_2's competitive position can be harmed. Indeed, it is not necessary that M_1's price to D_2 be lower than M_2's price to D_2 for a possible finding of competitive injury to prevail. This second example is called a *primary-line injury case.* Primary-line cases usually involve area price reductions at the seller's level of competition. Normally, injury may be shown whenever predatory intent can be proved or inferred.

Even if one or more of the nine jurisdictional requirements discussed in the previous section are present for a determination of price discrimination, the defendant may prevail by proving no competitive injury. As we have discussed, injurious price discrimination can occur at the seller's level (primary-line injury) or at a lower level in the distribution sequence (secondary-line injury). Furthermore, a seller's attempt to match a lower competitive price in one market area while maintaining higher prices elsewhere may lead to an inference of predatory intent to harm competition. Clearly, the legal complexities of establishing the presence of price discrimination within the domain of Section 2(a) makes pricing a difficult managerial task.

The Affirmative Defenses

Even when an alleged price discrimination charge has withstood the jurisdictional defenses just outlined, the seller may still show justification using one of three affirmative defenses: meeting competition, changing market conditions, or cost justification. These defenses may be utilized when it has been established that the price differences constitute price discrimination under the Robinson–Patman Act. Since it has been established that the act has jurisdiction over price differences, there is a prima facie case of price discrimination, i.e., the seller is guilty until proven innocent.

Defense of Meeting Competition   A seller may reduce prices in a good-faith attempt to meet an equally low and lawful price of a competitor. The meeting of competition is a complete defense under Section 2(b), but there are strict rules for when such a defense should be used.

First, the defense is not available if the defendant knew, or should have known, that the competitor's price was unlawful. The seller must show that there was reason to believe that the competitor's price was lawful.

Second, the seller's price discrimination must have been temporary, not part of a permanent price schedule. That is, the seller may reduce a price to hold a customer or gain a new customer, but this new, lower price must be temporary and not part of a plan to systematically charge higher prices to some customers.

Third, "an equally low price of a competitor" must be for a given quantity. The competitor's product need not be of like grade and quality, but the products in question must be competitive, and the prices must be for a similar quantity.

Fourth, the seller's lower price must be available to specific customers. That is, the price concession must be limited to those specific customers to whom a competitor has offered the lower price.

Fifth, the statute expressly permits reducing prices to *meet* a competitor's lower price, but the competitor's price cannot be bettered. That is, the seller's price cannot be reduced below the competitor's price. As simple as this condition seems, it becomes complicated when the products are premium and nonpremium products, e.g., beer or gasoline. Where historically there has been an established range of price differences between a premium and a nonpremium product, meeting competition means preserving the established price differentials.

For a seller facing a price discrimination charge, the evidence necessary for a successful meeting-competition defense includes

1 Existing market conditions and foreknowledge of competitors' low prices
2 A good-faith effort to verify the competitors' low prices
3 Facts indicating it was reasonable to believe the reports of competitors' low prices to be true
4 A belief that business would be lost without the price reduction

Changing-Conditions Defense   Section 2(a) provides that prices may be changed to reflect changing market conditions or changes in the marketability of the product. The section also lists a number of applicable examples: "actual or imminent deterioration of perishable goods, obsolescence of seasonal goods, distress sales under court process, or sales in good faith in discontinuance of business in the goods concerned."

Few defendants have attempted to use this defense. As with the meeting-competition defense, there are strict rules for using the changing-conditions defense:

1 The specific market change or change in marketability must be a departure or variation from usual market conditions. These market changes must not result from behavioral changes by a competitor or by the defendant.
2 The market must resemble the provisions of the statute, i.e., the defense is confined to sales of products whose marketability has been affected by obsolescence or by changes in buyer preferences.

Cost-Justification Defense   Earlier in this chapter, it was observed that price differences not warranted by cost differences constituted economic price discrimination. Section 2(a) provides for a complete defense if the price differentials "make only due allowance for differences in the cost of manufacture, sale, or delivery resulting from the differing methods or quantities in which such commodities are to such purchasers sold or delivered." Thus, the Robinson–Patman Act provides for a defense based on economic principles.

Despite congressional intent, it has not been easy for a seller to justify price differentials on the basis of cost differences. Cost defenses have been successful, and many investigations by the Federal Trade Commission have been closed upon showings of cost justification. Yet the cost-justification defense has been used infrequently relative to the total number of cases litigated under the act.

There are a number of reasons why the cost-justification defense has had limited use. First, there are limited areas of business operations that provide recognizable cost savings of serving particular customers. If a manufacturer produces to maintain inventory and sells from inventory, there are no demonstrable savings from manufacturing. Since it is impossible to causally relate any order, large or small, to the manufacturing process, volume discounts cannot be justified because of "production economies of scale." Only if the seller produces to fill specific orders can manufacturing costs be a part of the cost justification.

Second, the Federal Trade Commission has consistently accepted actual costs only. Incremental or marginal costs have been unacceptable, as have investment and opportunity costs.

Third, there is a lack of officially sanctioned accounting standards for performing a cost-justification study. As noted, manufacturing costs cannot be used as cost justification of price differences. Thus, the primary area of study is marketing and distribution. However, as shown in Chap. 9, little attention has been devoted to developing and utilizing standards for marketing and distribution cost analysis.

Fourth, a cost-justification defense is usually expensive and, because of the inexactness of marketing and distribution cost analysis, unpredictable. Moreover, since the cost studies used as a defense invariably follow the discrimination citation, there was an obvious lack of good faith in setting price differentials based on cost differences.

GUIDELINES FOR JUSTIFYING PRICE DIFFERENTIALS

As the foregoing summary indicates, there are a number of ways to defend price differentials successfully. However, a careful reading of the litigation history of the Robinson–Patman Act reveals a woeful lack of attention to the pricing function by many firms. Most defenses to a price discrimination charge have relied on hastily developed studies that, when subjected to cross-examination, have failed to justify the price differentials.

Despite its relative lack of use, the cost-justification defense remains one of the most viable defenses available. However, it is necessary for firms to develop cost accounting techniques for analyzing marketing expenditures and to refrain from lumping marketing and distribution costs into a general overhead category such as selling, general, and administrative overhead. The basic approach to marketing cost accounting was outlined in Chap. 9.

Any seller who, in the normal course of business, charges different customers different prices should not leave to chance the matter of complying with the Robinson–Patman Act. From a policy perspective it is necessary to have clearly defined policies and procedures.

Administrative Guidelines[12]

Minimally, these policies and procedures should

1 Provide a published price list that includes the price breaks and discount eligibility criteria
2 Establish all discount schedules on a cost-justified basis
3 Communicate to all sales personnel the policy of adhering to the established price lists and discount schedules
4 Provide for specific procedures when departing from the established prices and discount schedules
5 Develop a program for cost-justifying discount schedules and other sources of price differentials
6 Instruct sales personnel to obtain, whenever possible,

---

[12]These guidelines are adopted from Ronald M. Copeland, "The Art of Self-Defense in Price Discrimination," *Business Horizons,* 9 (Winter 1966), 71–76; LaRue, op. cit.; John E. Martin, "Justifying Price Differentials," *Management Accounting,* 47 (November 1965), 56–62.

a Copies of competitors' offers, price lists, discount schedules, and invoices from customers
b Signed statements from customers about claimed price concessions provided by competitors
c Memoranda of conversations with customers who report competitive offers
d A list of customers lost because of lower competitive offers
7 Provide for periodic review of all price concessions granted to meet competition

Cost-Justification Guidelines

To cost-justify price differences the seller should develop a marketing and distribution cost accounting system. Such an accounting system should utilize a computer to prepare reports showing the cost and price differences of serving different types of customers. Marketing and distribution costs should not be averaged but should be traced objectively and directly to the activities that give rise to these costs.

Cost justification studies should

1 Be made before price lists and discount schedules are established
2 Be periodically reviewed to determine effects of cost changes
3 Analyze only those costs that vary among customers
4 Include marketing, accounting, and legal personnel
5 Include only the seller's costs
6 Group customers according to similarities of marketing to them and according to similarities of their purchasing behavior
7 Classify relevant costs into their variable and fixed components
8 Compare cost differences to the price lists and discount schedules to determine the legal basis of the price differentials

In addition to providing for legal defense to a price discrimination charge, these administrative and cost-justification guidelines provide management with useful knowledge for making pricing decisions. The value of good intelligence reports from salespeople and the value of marketing and distribution cost studies is that they provide useful guidance for developing overall marketing strategies.

RESALE PRICE MAINTENANCE

As discussed in Chap. 15, a concern of suppliers, particularly manufacturers, is that the price to the final buyer be in accord with the suppliers' overall marketing strategies. Resale price maintenance is the specification by the supplier of the prices below or above which channel members may not sell the supplier's products. The issue revolves around the extent to which manufacturers may control prices at which their products are resold. Prior to the passage of the Consumer Goods Pricing Act of 1975, the practice of fixing prices vertically in the channel had been exempted from antitrust laws by the Miller–Tydings Act of 1937. In effect, prior to 1975, state laws permitting resale price maintenance contracts ("fair trade") were exempt from the federal antitrust laws. Manufacturers had been given legal permission to use coercive power to control prices in their channels of distribution. In 1975, Congress repealed this exemption to price fixing from antitrust violations.

As noted previously, price fixing is illegal per se. Thus, whether the price agreement is horizontal—i.e., between rival sellers—or vertical—i.e., between a manufacturer and members of the distribution channel—it is illegal. Attempts to enforce prices at points of resale through any form of coercive act or threat is illegal per se. Recently, Panasonic agreed to a large financial settlement with the attorneys general of the states of New York and Maryland after attempting to coerce retailers to agree not to discount their consumer electronic products. The alleged coercive attempts included refusals to sell and "backroom persuasion."

The current environment surrounding the status of resale price maintenance is somewhat murky. Congress has attempted to pass some form of a resale price maintenance bill, typically labeled as a "fair trade" bill. The courts have not fully established a set of consistent legal precedents about when a supplier may have a legally defensible resale price maintenance program. However, it does seem clear that if the resale price maintenance program involves a conspiracy or combination to fix prices, involves written agreements, and uses coercion—implied or actual—to enforce the maintenance program, it is probably a per se violation of the Sherman Act.

Perhaps the most important point of a resale price maintenance program is that the supplier act unilaterally.[13] There can be no attempt to force dealers to register complaints or enact boycotts if rival dealers do not conform to the pricing policy. Further, there can be no form of coercion, such as nonrenewable contracts for nonconforming pricing behavior, or termination and then reinstatement of discounting dealers. Legal means of obtaining dealer cooperation about prices include establishing a "partnership," as discussed in Chap. 15, printing the retail price on the product or package, advertising the suggested retail price, announcing suggested retail prices in catalogs or sales brochures, and supporting the advertising efforts of dealers who feature the suggested retail prices.[14] However, it must be abundantly clear that the dealers are free to deviate from the printed or suggested prices should they feel it in their best interests to do so. Dealers cannot be compelled to follow a specific recommended price of the supplier.

DECEPTIVE PRICE PROMOTIONS

The Wheeler–Lea Amendment to the Federal Trade Commission Act gave the FTC jurisdiction over business practices that tend to mislead and deceive consumers. In Chaps. 3 and 4, the various ways consumers perceive prices and the effects of these perceptions on value judgments and purchase behaviors were explained. Further, in Chap. 15, the use of fraudulent advertised regular prices to influence consumers' formation of reference prices for making price comparisons was discussed. Thus, given the complex and important role that price plays in purchasing decisions, clearly the advertising and promotion of "special" prices, cents-off deals, sales, and other forms of price promotion have the capacity to attract buyers to the store to

[13]Mary Jane Sheffet and Debra L. Scammon, "Resale Price Maintenance: Is It Safe to Suggest Retail Prices?" *Journal of Marketing,* 49 (Fall 1985), 82–91.

[14]Virginia G. Maurer and Michael Ursic, "Resale Price Maintenance: A Legal Review," *Journal of Public Policy & Marketing,* 6 (1987), 171–180.

purchase the items being promoted. Indeed, a number of European countries, Canada, and Australia have established regulations to check the deceptive effects of price promotions.

Normally, promotion prices either explicitly or implicitly claim or imply that the seller's price is lower than some comparative price for the item being promoted. The comparison may be to a previous or former price, a manufacturer's suggested selling price, a usual price in the market area, or, as in an introductory offer, a future price. Because consumers vary greatly in their knowledge of usual or regular prices (see Chap. 3) and in their search for product and price information, they often have no factual basis for determining the truthfulness of such claims.

Price promotion offers can be viewed as a healthy aspect of price competition which directly or indirectly helps buyers save money. But when such offers are false or misleading, they become an unfair practice that is detrimental to both competition and consumers. And when they have the capacity to confuse or mislead consumers, they are simply undesirable. One survey taken in Norway, Sweden, Denmark, and Finland indicated that comparison price promotions tended to confuse significant numbers of consumers.[15] This capacity to confuse and mislead consumers has led to increased concern about the widespread use of sales and price promotions by businesses. In addition to the FTC's efforts to define deceptive price advertising, other countries have enacted laws and regulations governing such business practices.

In Australia, the Commonwealth Trade Practices Act 1974 prohibits

- Misleading or deceptive conduct in trade or commerce
- Misrepresentations about the benefits of goods or services
- False or misleading claims with respect to the prices of goods or services

In Belgium, the Business Practices Act of 1971 permits price reductions only with reference to previous and usual prices. To be "usual," a price must have been charged for at least one month before its reduction. Moreover, the effective date of a reduced price must be displayed.

The Danish Marketing Practices Act of 1974 requires that terms like "sale" or "now only" be used only when it can be proved that the goods were previously sold from the same place of business at higher prices. Other countries, including West Germany, France, Japan, Finland, New Zealand, Norway, Sweden, Switzerland, and the United Kingdom, all have some prohibitions or regulations concerning price promotions. Moreover, there seems to be increasing concern with the negative aspects of price promotions in these countries. Thus, as firms expand their international marketing activities, there is a clear need to be conscious of the legality of price promotion practices.

THE COMBINES INVESTIGATION ACT OF CANADA

As free trade between the United States and Canada increases, it becomes important to understand some of the regulations concerning pricing in Canada. In Canada, the

---

[15] *Bargain Price Offers and Similar Marketing Practices,* Report by the Committee on Consumer Policy (Paris: Organization for Economic Co-operation and Development, 1979).

Combines Investigation Act is the basic law dealing with all types of restrictive business and unfair marketing practices. The act prohibits

1. Bid rigging (Section 32.2)
2. Unfair price discrimination (Section 34.1a)
3. Regional price differences (Section 34.1b)
4. Predatory pricing (Section 34.1c)
5. Misleading price advertisements (Section 36.1)
6. Double ticketing, i.e., displaying two prices on an item (Section 36.2)
7. Bait-and-switch selling (Section 37.2)
8. Sales above advertised prices (Section 37.1)
9. Resale price maintenance (Section 38)

In addition, the act requires that promotional allowances be on a proportionally available basis (Section 35.2). Although there are many similarities between the United States and Canada in terms of the basic prohibitions of unfair or misleading business practices, there are some important differences in terms of the requirements for prevailing in litigation and the types of defense allowed. *It is crucial for business firms to seek to understand the laws and regulations prevailing in each country in which they seek to do business.*

SUMMARY

The chapter has provided an overview of the legal environment for managing the pricing function. Litigation history yields few clear guidelines for developing lawful price structures but clearly suggests one must be prepared. Indeed, those firms that have prevailed against price discrimination charges often could demonstrate an underlying analytical foundation for their pricing practices. At the very least, price analysis of a firm's pricing practices is a good-faith attempt to comply with the requirements of the Robinson–Patman Act.

This chapter has also integrated material from Chaps. 3, 4, 8, 9, 14, and 15. The importance of knowing both the direct and traceable costs of manufacturing and marketing activities has been shown. Arbitrary allocation of marketing costs, with no clear understanding of how these costs vary when serving different types of customers, usually fails to justify price differentials. In Chaps. 14 and 15, we repeatedly argued against tradition as a basis for establishing discount policies. Given the dynamic nature of our economy, the guidelines in this chapter also stress a planned, periodic review of all prices and underlying analyses. Regardless of the legal benefits of such control, reviews are simply sound management practice.

Another benefit of an analytical base for making pricing decisions is that it facilitates explanation of the necessity for price changes to sales personnel, customers, or a price control board. During periods of inflation, price increases generally are expected, but the frequency and amount of these increases often exceed the expectations of salespeople, distributors, and customers. To help these people adapt to the price increases, a reasoned justification is useful. Additional prescriptions for pricing management are given in Chap. 20.

DISCUSSION QUESTIONS

1 Contrast the meaning of price discrimination from the economic point of view with the legal view represented in the Robinson–Patman Act.

2 Develop additional examples of permissible price discrimination, i.e., when it is legal and/or acceptable for buyers to pay different prices for essentially the same product or service. Do you feel that these forms of price discrimination are justifiable?

3 What is a jurisdictional defense? What are the 10 jurisdictional requirements for price discrimination as set forth in the Robinson–Patman Act?

4 What is the importance of the Borden case for marketing?

5 What is a primary-line injury case? What is a secondary-line injury case?

6 Explain the meaning of the "no statutory injury" jurisdictional defense.

7 What are the affirmative defenses to a charge of price discrimination?

8 What are the necessary conditions for the following defenses to a charge of price discrimination:

a Meeting competition.

b Changing conditions.

c Cost justification.

9 What is the rationale for the proposed administrative and cost-justification guidelines given in the chapter? How do these guidelines help a pricing administrator manage the pricing function?

SUGGESTED READINGS

Dearden, John: "Taming Predatory Pricing," *Financial Executive,* January 1983, pp. 38–44.

Ford, Gary T., and John E. Calfee: "Recent Developments in FTC Policy on Deception," *Journal of Marketing,* 50 (July 1986), 82–103.

Kinter, Earl W.: *A Robinson–Patman Primer* (New York: Macmillan, 1970).

LaRue, Paul H.: "Meeting Competition and Other Defenses under the Robinson–Patman Act," *The Business Lawyer,* 25 (April 1970), 1037–1051.

Maurer, Virginia G., and Michael Ursic: "Resale Price Maintenance: A Legal Review," *Journal of Public Policy & Marketing,* 6 (1987), 171–180.

Samuelson, Susan S., and Thomas A. Balmer: "Antitrust Revisited—Implications for Competitive Strategy," *Sloan Management Review,* 30 (Fall 1988), 79–87.

Sheffet, Mary Jane, and Debra L. Scammon: "Resale Price Maintenance: Is It Safe to Suggest Retail Prices?" *Journal of Marketing* 49 (Fall 1985), 82–91.

Stern, Louis W., and Thomas L. Eovaldi: *Legal Aspects of Marketing Strategy* (Englewood Cliffs, N.J.: Prentice-Hall, 1984).

Werner, Ray O.: "Marketing and the Supreme Court in Transition, 1982–1984," *Journal of Marketing,* 49 (Summer 1985), 97–105.

SPECIAL TOPICS ON PRICING

Chapters 17 to 19 discuss some specific aspects of pricing. Chapter 17 presents a brief overview of the problem of developing bids to meet special orders for products or services. The chapter provides applications of costing and discusses specific considerations of competitive strategy. Chapter 18 reviews some of the particular problems of developing prices for services and offers specific illustrations concerning financial services and the pricing of online information services. Chapter 18 also provides an introduction to the setting of prices for international markets.

In the past decade, there has been considerable research on the development of pricing decision models. Chapter 19 surveys these modeling activities and offers suggestions for additional efforts to improve price decision making.

six

SPECIAL TOPICS ON
PRICING

CHAPTER 17

DEVELOPING COMPETITIVE BIDS

In business marketing and in selling to the government, firms often compete by submitting bids that detail the services and product specifications to be offered at a stated price. Sealed or closed bidding takes place when two or more bidders submit independent bids for the rights to property or to render a service. The auction is a special type of competitive bidding.

This chapter presents an overview of the problem of developing fixed-price bids for providing products or services on an order basis. After discussing a procedure for determining whether to submit a bid, the chapter considers cost estimation, determining the probability of winning the contract, and determining the best bid. The chapter concludes by introducing important variations to the basic fixed-price competitive bidding model.

FIXED-PRICE COMPETITIVE BIDDING

Competitive bidding is a fascinating, challenging, and difficult job involving judgmental assessment of customers and competitors as well as scientific analysis. The theory of fixed-price competitive bidding has received considerable attention from management scientists. It covers such situations as (1) deciding what price to bid when the number of competing bidders is known and when the identity of competitors is known, (2) deciding what price to bid when the number and identity of competitors are unknown, (3) deciding whether to submit a bid at all, and (4) deciding how many contracts to bid on simultaneously when a company cannot afford to win them all.

Normally, when all other factors such as quality and service are equal, the low bidder is awarded the contract. Thus, the decision problem is to submit a bid that will help the firm achieve its objectives and be lower than competing bids. What to bid depends largely on the objectives of the firm. Some possible objectives are

1 To maximize immediate profits
2 To maximize long-run profits
3 To achieve a stated return on investment
4 To minimize risk of losses
5 To minimize the profits of competitors

In the basic decision models, it is generally assumed that the firm is interested in achieving immediate profits. Since it is also assumed that the lowest bid gets the award, the chances of the firm winning the bid decrease as the bid price increases. Yet if the firm does not get the bid its profits are zero. Thus, the amount of profits to be earned from any particular bid is uncertain and probability theory is used to determine the optimal bid. The theory of competitive bidding assumes the bidder's objective is to maximize expected profits.

An example would perhaps make this point clearer. Suppose that on a particular contract a firm determines that its costs for fulfilling the contract would amount to $50,000. Further assume that the probability of being awarded the contract is 0.70 if the bid is $60,000 but only 0.40 if the bid is $90,000. Which bid should the firm submit if it wishes to maximize expected immediate profits? If a bid of $60,000 is submitted, expected immediate profits are $7,000 [0.70 × ($60,000 − $50,000)]. If a bid of $90,000 is submitted, expected immediate profits are $16,000 [0.40 × ($90,000 − $50,000)]. Thus, in this simple example, the firm should bid $90,000 on the contract. Table 17-1 shows this example in greater detail.

In practice, the greatest difficulty in competitive bidding is to develop the required information to estimate the probabilities of winning the contract at various prices.

TABLE 17-1
COMPETITIVE BIDDING EXAMPLE

Bid (B)	Cost (C)	Immediate Profits (B − C)	Probability of Contract (P)	Expected Immediate Profits [P × (B − C)]
$ 30,000	$50,000	$−20,000	1.00	$−20,000
40,000	50,000	−10,000	0.90	−9,000
50,000	50,000	0	0.80	0
60,000	50,000	10,000	0.70	7,000
70,000	50,000	20,000	0.60	12,000
80,000	50,000	30,000	0.50	15,000
90,000	50,000	40,000	0.40	16,000
100,000	50,000	50,000	0.30	15,000
110,000	50,000	60,000	0.20	12,000
120,000	50,000	70,000	0.10	7,000
130,000	50,000	80,000	0	0

Usually a firm has some idea of the costs that will be incurred if the bid is awarded. It must also estimate the number of bidders submitting a bid since the probability of winning a bid is also a function of this number. The firm must also estimate what competitors are likely to bid since competitors will keep their intentions as secret as possible. Therefore, the company must rely on past bidding information when relevant, on conjecture, and perhaps on trade rumors.

AUCTIONS

Another form of bidding is the situation in which several buyers compete for the opportunity to acquire a particular resource, e.g., oil-drilling rights, a valuable work of art, the contract rights to a professional athlete. In some respects, the nature of a fixed-price competitive bidding situation resembles that of some auctions in which the basic roles of buyers and sellers are reversed.[1] In an auction, the seller, or bid taker, must develop a strategy that allows him or her to maximize the expected revenue from the auction. These revenues depend on how the bidders bid, and their bidding behavior depends on a variety of factors. For example, the bid taker announces auction rules that specify how the bidding will be conducted and how the bidding determines who pays how much and to whom. These rules may also affect the number of bidders in the auction. Other important factors affecting the auction outcome are the amount and type of information that each bidder has about the underlying situation, the bidders' perceived value in acquiring the object or service being auctioned, and whether it will be a single-bid or multiple-bid auction.

PREBID ANALYSIS

When offered a contract opportunity, a firm should first perform an analysis to determine whether to prepare a bid. By being selective in its bidding, a company can save time and money that would be spent on bid activities such as cost estimation, engineering proposals, purchasing (there will be fewer requests for subcontract quotes), and printing the bids. The Cleveland Pneumatic Tool Company developed a procedure for screening bid opportunities that permits it to avoid costly bid proposals.[2]

The Cleveland Pneumatic Tool Company has a screening committee that evaluates a bid opportunity in terms of potential growth, engineering capability and facilities needed, and potential competition. As an executive of the firm pointed out, "The important thing is developing a philosophy of the kind of business you're in, where you want to be, and what your sales curve growth should be. Look at your present capabilities and future markets . . . in determining whether to bid."[3]

[1] Richard Engelbrecht-Wiggans, "Auctions and Bidding Models: A Survey," *Management Science,* 26 (February 1980), 119–142.

[2] "Evaluation System Boosts Job Shop's Bidding Average," *Steel,* September 21, 1964, pp. 46–47.

[3] Ibid., p. 47.

Determine Bid Objectives

Whether to bid and what to bid depend largely on the firm's objectives. As already indicated, the objective may be the typical economic objective of profit maximization, either in terms of return on investment or absolute profits, or it may be to keep labor busy, gain entrée into a new business, or overcome a survival crisis. A bidder should define objectives carefully before evaluating bid opportunities. Whenever possible, the objectives of potential competitive bidders should also be analyzed. This information will be useful in assessing the chances of winning the contract.

Develop Evaluation Criteria

To evaluate a bid opportunity the firm needs benchmarks, or criteria. Among these criteria would be

1 Labor skills and engineering capability required
2 Available plant capacity
3 Follow-up bid opportunities
4 Design content
5 Competition
6 Degree of familiarity with the bid project
7 Delivery requirement
8 Experience curve factor

It is necessary to determine whether the firm has the *necessary labor skills and engineering capability* to complete the bid project as specified. If major extensions of skills are required, the firm must consider the cost of acquiring these capabilities.

Available plant capacity is an important factor. To bid on a contract requiring 20 percent of a firm's capacity when the firm is already operating at 90 percent would usually be considered inappropriate. On the other hand, a company operating at 60 percent capacity would probably be quite interested in this bid opportunity.

The firm should also consider whether it has capacity for future business that might result from winning the contract. For example, if the firm's business has been growing normally, it might not be able to accommodate this normal growth in the next few years if current slack capacity is devoted to the contract.

Many bid opportunities provide the possibility that *follow-up orders* will be secured after the first contract has been fulfilled. Winning a federal government contract, e.g., to develop a new defense system, gives the winning bidder an expertise that would be important in future bids to supply more components for the defense system. Moreover, winning a contract may make other potential buyers aware of the firm's expertise and capabilities.

Jobs with low *design content* may not fully utilize a company's design engineering talent. A precision, design-oriented company would want to keep its engineers occupied developing new processes or special materials and would be less interested in jobs requiring little design effort.

To determine the chances of winning a bid, it is important to consider the number and identity of *probable competitors* for the contract. In general, the more profitable a bid opportunity seems to be, the greater the number of competitive bids that will be submitted.

In high-technology fields, great significance is placed on the *degree of familiarity* the firm has with the bid project. Often the firm's degree of competency is an important factor in winning an award. It is known that aerospace companies prepare for future bids by adding skills and experience in advance.[4]

A fundamental factor in awarding contracts is whether a bidder can *deliver the project on time*. Indeed, the federal government will invalidate a bid if it appears that the bidder may not be able to deliver as specified. The firm must also consider the effects on permanent customers if an awarded contract is given priority in production.

Finally, the firm should consider whether the quantity of items specified in the bid will allow a cost savings based on the *experience curve*. For example, if the contract results in a doubling of cumulative production volume, then the cost savings will extend to all similar products. Hence, the contract could make the firm more cost competitive in its traditional markets.

Develop a Screening Procedure

The eight criteria previously outlined must be analyzed to measure the value of a bid opportunity. One procedure would be to assign a weight to each of these factors according to their relative importance to the firm. Then, for a particular bid, the relative merits of each factor could be assigned a rating of high, medium, or low. These ratings might then be assigned quantitative values, e.g., 10, 5, 0, so that a project using existing labor skills would get a rating of 10. The product of each factor's weight and rating could be summed to give an overall score. The firm would then compare the score to other previous bids or to a predetermined minimum acceptable value. If the bid opportunity passes this prebid analysis, then the firm would proceed to develop a bid.[5]

Table 17-2 illustrates this screening procedure. In this case, a minimum score of 650 is necessary before the firm will prepare a bid. In the bid opportunity presented in the table, the firm would be able to use existing labor skills and design engineers. Moreover, the firm is familiar with the project requirements because of past and present projects, and it could obtain cost reductions of current projects because of the experience factor. Hence, each of these criteria receives a high evaluation and a weight of 10. Thus, despite the lack of follow-up opportunities, the bid opportunity scored high on a sufficient number of factors to warrant preparing a bid. The development of such a screening procedure has improved the bidding success of the Cleveland Pneumatic Tool Company.[6]

[4]Stephen Paranka, "The Pay-Off Concept in Competitive Bidding," *Business Horizons*, 12 (August 1969), 77–81.

[5]Stephen Paranka, "Competitive Bidding Strategy," *Business Horizons*, 14 (June 1971), 39–43.

[6]"Evaluation System Boosts Job Shop's Bidding Average," op. cit., p. 47.

TABLE 17-2
EVALUATION OF A BID OPPORTUNITY

| Prebid Factor | Weight | Rating | | | Score |
		High, 10	Medium, 5	Low, 0	
Labor skills	20	10	. . .	. . .	200
Plant capacity	20	. . .	5	. . .	100
Follow-up	10	. . .	. . .	0	0
Design content	5	10	. . .	. . .	50
Competition	10	. . .	5	. . .	50
Familiarity	15	10	. . .	. . .	150
Delivery	10	. . .	5	. . .	50
Experience	10	10	. . .	. . .	100
Total	100				700

Minimum acceptable score: 650

COST ESTIMATION

Cost estimation involves the familiar procedures for costing discussed in Chaps. 7–10. It is vital that the components of cost as illustrated in Fig. 8-1 be classified and separated to permit an analysis of the implications of alternative bids. As discussed earlier, the direct-cost data set a price floor below which the firm will not want to make a bid. A firm operating well below capacity may choose to bid less than full cost, whereas, when operating near capacity, it may choose to submit a full-cost-plus-profit bid. In any event, the firm should avoid arbitrary cost-estimating formulas and instead prepare careful cost estimates based on realistic activity levels.

ESTIMATING THE PROBABILITY OF WINNING

As the example at the beginning of this chapter indicated, the theory of competitive bidding relies on the use of probabilistic models. A key factor in submitting a bid is to estimate the chances of winning the contract. Assuming that the lowest bid will win the contract, as is true in most governmental bidding situations, the problem is predicting how competitors will bid. Probabilistic bidding models assist a firm in determining a bid price that optimizes the combination of probability of winning and profit if it does win. Evidence shows that firms that use probabilistic bidding models have a better record of successful bids than firms that do not.[7]

There are a number of approaches to estimating the chances of winning. The *winning-bid approach* simply uses the history of competitors' winning bids. The *average-opponent approach* uses the history of competitors' winning and losing bids to represent the bidding behavior of an average opponent. The *specific-opponent*

[7] Paranka, "The Pay-Off Concept in Competitive Bidding," op. cit.

approach uses the past bidding behavior of specific competitors. Each of these approaches will now be illustrated.[8]

The Winning-Bid Approach

The estimation of the probability of winning is based on two assumptions: (1) that there is a constant relationship between competitors' estimates of direct costs and the bidder's direct cost estimates and (2) that competitors will act in the future as they have acted in the past. The second assumption can be relaxed by allowing decision makers to incorporate their subjective feelings in the analysis. To reflect the first assumption in the following discussion, all bids will be expressed as a percentage of the bidder's estimated direct costs. For example, with direct costs of $100,000, a bid of 120 percent is actually a bid of $120,000.

[8]A more complete discussion of these approaches is in John F. Kottas and Basheer M. Khumawala, "Contract Bid Development for the Small Businessman," *Sloan Management Review,* 14 (Spring 1973), 31–45.

TABLE 17-3
WINNING-BID APPROACH

Bid as a Percentage of Direct Cost (*B*)	Number of Competitors' Winning Bids Exceeding *B*	Fraction of Competitors' Winning Bids Exceeding *B*
90	100	$\frac{100}{100} = 1.00$
95	100	$\frac{100}{100} = 1.00$
100	95	$\frac{95}{100} = 0.95$
105	88	$\frac{88}{100} = 0.88$
110	75	$\frac{75}{100} = 0.75$
115	50	$\frac{50}{100} = 0.50$
120	30	$\frac{30}{100} = 0.30$
125	16	$\frac{16}{100} = 0.16$
130	5	$\frac{5}{100} = 0.05$
135	2	$\frac{2}{100} = 0.02$
140	0	$\frac{0}{100} = 0$

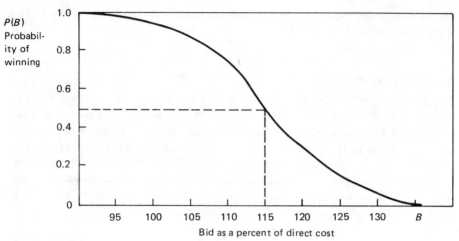

FIGURE 17-1
Winning bid approach.

To utilize the winning-bid approach requires only a knowledge of the history of previous winning bids. As seen in Table 17-3, the first step is to calculate the ratio of each winning bid to the firm's direct costs on that bid. Then, for selected bids, the fraction of competitors' winning bids that exceeds these bids is determined. Figure 17-1 illustrates the development of the data in step 2 into a probability curve. For example, a bid of 115 percent would have a 0.50 probability of winning.

As shown, the winning-bid approach is a relatively simple way of estimating the probability of winning $[P(B)]$. Since it utilizes only the history of winning bids, it is best used when this history is the only available information.

The Average-Opponent Approach

The average-opponent approach is more sophisticated in that it considers the number of competitors presenting bids. Although it does not require knowledge about specific competitors, it does consider all past winning and losing bids. The probability of underbidding the average opponent $[P_A(B)]$ is determined by calculating the fraction of all previous bids which exceeded selected bid values, as seen in Table 17-4. Figure 17-2 illustrates the development of these data into the probability curve for $P(B)$.

As Table 17-4 and Fig. 17-2 show, the probability of winning (underbidding) decreases as the number of competitors increases. By assuming each opponent to be average, the $P(B)$ is equal to the product of the chances of underbidding each of the N opponents with a bid of B:

$$P(B) = [P_A(B)]^N \tag{17-1}$$

TABLE 17-4
AVERAGE-OPPONENT APPROACH

Bid as a Percentage of Direct Cost (B)	Fraction of Previous Bids Exceeding B	Probability of Underbidding N Average Opponents $[P_A(B)]^N$ (Number of Opponents $= N$)				
		1 $P_A(B)$	2 $P_A(B)^2$	4 $P_A(B)^4$	8 $P_A(B)^8$	16 $P_A(B)^{16}$
95	$\frac{100}{100}$	1.00	1.00	1.00	1.00	1.00
100	$\frac{95}{100}$	0.95	0.90	0.81	0.66	0.44
105	$\frac{90}{100}$	0.90	0.81	0.66	0.43	0.19
110	$\frac{85}{100}$	0.85	0.72	0.52	0.27	0.07
115	$\frac{75}{100}$	0.75	0.56	0.32	0.10	0.01
120	$\frac{60}{100}$	0.60	0.36	0.13	0.02	0
125	$\frac{40}{100}$	0.40	0.16	0.03	0	0
130	$\frac{20}{100}$	0.20	0.04	0	0	0
135	$\frac{5}{100}$	0.05	0	0	0	0
140	$\frac{2}{100}$	0.02	0	0	0	0

Indeed, as the number of opponents increases, there is a rapid decrease in the chance of winning. For example, if the bid, B, is 115 and if there is only one other bidder, then the probability of winning the bid is $P(B) = P_A(B) = 0.75$. But if there are two opponents, then $P(B) = P_A(B)^2 = (0.75)^2 = 0.56$. With four opponents, $P(B) = P_A(B)^4 = (0.75)^4 = 0.32$. Table 17-4 and Fig. 17-2 show these results as well as the $P(B)$ for $N = 8$ and 16.

It should also be noted that the fewer the opponents, the greater is the opportunity for a winning bid to contribute to profit and overhead. For example, when there is only one opponent, four bids greater than 100 percent have better than a 50 percent chance of winning (120, 115, 110, 105). However, with four opponents, only bids of 110 and 105 have better than a 50 percent chance of winning and making a contribution to profits.

If, for a particular contract, it is not known exactly how many competitors will bid, the probability of the number of different opponents must be estimated. One approach is to calculate the proportion of times that different numbers of competitors have bid on a contract. If f_i is the proportion of time and there are i competitors, the chances of winning can be estimated using

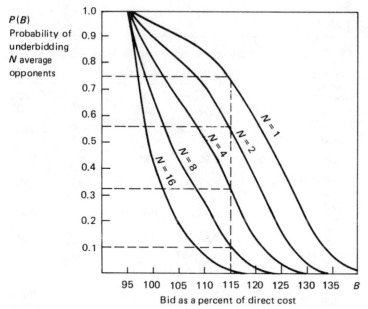

FIGURE 17-2
Average opponent approach.

$$P(B) = f_0 + f_i P_A(B) + f_2 [P_A(B)]^2 + \cdots + f_N [P_A(B)]^N \qquad (17\text{-}2)$$

where f_0 is the estimated probability that there will be no competitors. (The sum of the f_i should equal 1.) Suppose it is calculated that $f_0 = 0.1, f_1 = 0.4, f_2 = 0.3$, and $f_3 = 0.2$, and as given in Table 17-4, $P_A(120) = 0.60$. The chances of winning the contract with a bid of 120 is

$$
\begin{aligned}
P(120) &= 0.2 + 0.4(0.60) + 0.3(0.60)^2 + 0.2(0.60)^3 \\
&= 0.2 + 0.4(0.60) + 0.3(0.36) + 0.2(0.22) \\
&= 0.2 + 0.24 + 0.11 + 0.04 \\
&= 0.59
\end{aligned}
$$

The advantage of the average-opponent approach is that it allows for consideration of the number of bidders for a contract. When economic conditions are slow
or the contract is lucrative, the expected number of bidders generally increases. This,
along with the fact that $P(B)$ is sensitive to the number of bidders, makes the
average-opponent approach more refined than the winning-bid approach. However,
a more sophisticated approach would be to consider the bidding behavior of specific
competitors.

The Specific-Opponent Approach

If the firm knows both the specific opponents that will bid on a contract and their history of previous bidding behavior, the specific-opponent approach may be used. It is now necessary to estimate the chances of underbidding each opponent. Thus, the fraction of each competitor's bids that exceeds selected bid values must be calculated. To win the contract, the firm must bid lower than all competitors. The probability of underbidding all competitors is determined by multiplying the probabilities of underbidding each competitor.

$$P(B) = P_1(B) \times P_2(B) \times P_3(B) \times \cdots \times P_N(B) \qquad (17\text{-}3)$$

Table 17-5 and Fig. 17-3 illustrate the specific-opponent approach when there are three rival competitors. Table 17-5 is constructed by computing the fraction of times a specific bid was exceeded by a given competitor relative to the total number of times the opponent was a competitor. For example, a bid equal to direct costs (100 percent in column B) was exceeded by competitor 1, 95 percent of the time.

In the usual bidding situation, potential bidders file an intention to bid and pay a fee for the project specifications by a specific date. Competitors who fail to file by the specified date are not eligible to bid. However, it is not certain that all eligible bidders will actually submit a bid. Thus, Eq. (17-3) needs to be modified by

$$P(B) = P_{S1}(B) \times P_{S2}(B) \times P_{S3}(B) \times \cdots \times P_{SN}(B) \qquad (17\text{-}4)$$

FIGURE 17-3
Specific opponent approach.

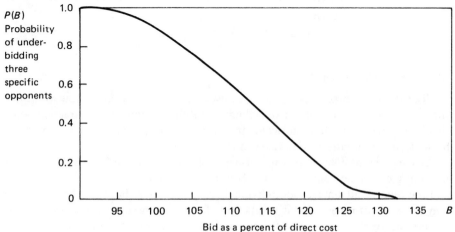

$P(B)$
Probability of under-bidding three specific opponents

Bid as a percent of direct cost

TABLE 17-5
SPECIFIC-OPPONENT APPROACH

Bid As a Percentage of Direct Costs (B)	Probability of Underbidding Competitor i ($i = 1,2,3$)			Overall Probability of Underbidding
	1	2	3	
95	1.00	1.00	1.00	1.00
100	0.95	0.98	0.95	0.88
105	0.90	0.95	0.85	0.73
110	0.85	0.88	0.80	0.60
115	0.75	0.80	0.70	0.42
120	0.60	0.65	0.62	0.24
125	0.40	0.45	0.40	0.07
130	0.20	0.22	0.15	0.01
135	0.05	0.10	0.05	0
140	0.02	0.05	0.01	0

where

$$P_{Si}(B) = p_i P_i(B) + (1 - p_i), \qquad i = 1, 2, \ldots, N \qquad (17\text{-}5)$$

The $P_{Si}(B)$ is the probability of underbidding specific competitor i with bid B and p_i is a fraction of times potential competitor i actually has submitted a bid when eligible to submit a bid. For example, suppose there are three potential competitors and that the fraction of times they previously submitted bids is $p_1 = 0.5, p_2 = 0.8,$ $p_3 = 0.6$. The probability of winning with a bid of 120 is determined using Table 17-5:

$$P_{S1}(B) = 0.5(0.60) + (1 - 0.5) = 0.80$$
$$P_{S2}(B) = 0.8(0.65) + (1 - 0.8) = 0.72$$
$$P_{S3}(B) = 0.60(0.62) + (1 - 0.6) = 0.77$$
$$P(B) = 0.80(0.72)(0.77) = 0.44$$

Utilizing Subjective Estimates

Each of the three preceding approaches uses historical data only. However, often the decision maker has subjective feelings or intuition about the contract situation that is not revealed in the historical data. Each of these approaches may be modified by subjective estimates as described in this section.

An experienced contractor will normally have substantial information about the prevailing economic conditions, the slack plant capacity of potential competitors, and the relative advantages an individual competitor may have, or the contractor may know about potential new competitors for which there are no historical data. In both the average-opponent and specific-opponent approaches the decision maker can modify the f_i or the p_i to reflect the perceptions of the current bidding situation.

Moreover, the bidder can modify the $P_A(B)$ or the $P_{Si}(B)$ to reflect the perceptions of the bidding situation.

For example, when economic conditions are slack and plant capacity utilization is low, a firm can expect more competitive bids at or near estimated direct costs. But when many or all competitors are operating close to plant capacity, the firm can expect fewer bids, and these bids are more likely to be higher than estimated direct costs. Sewall described the use of an operational procedure for a New York contractor to handle such a situation.[9]

Combining the Specific- and Average-Opponent Approaches

Often the firm knows some of its potential competitors but has reason to believe other, unknown competitors will enter the bidding competition. The chances of underbidding the known competitors can be determined using Eq. (17-4) or (17-5). The unknown competitors' behavior must be estimated using Eq. (17-1) or (17-2). To win, the firm must underbid all competitors. The probability of doing this can be estimated[10] using

$$P(B) = P_{KC}(B) \times P_{UC}(B) \tag{17-6}$$

where $P_{KC}(B)$ = probability of underbidding all specific, known competitors
$P_{UC}(B)$ = probability of underbidding all unknown competitors as an average opponent

Problem of Determining Reasons for a Winning Bid

The structure of fixed-price competitive bidding in essence assumes that the lowest bid in competitive bidding or the highest bid in an auction is selected. However, as developed in Chaps. 3–5, buyers and sellers often have complex reasons for making purchase decisions or, in the case of an auction, selling decisions. That is, the bid taker may be attempting to maximize the perceived value of the decision by trading off price with other product service attributes. For example, in evaluating the bidding situation for performing offshore oil drilling, the Western Oceanic contract drilling company found out that the safety record of the bidding company's rigs was an important consideration to the oil companies.[11] Also, superstar athletes occasionally turn down better financial offers to accept the offer of a team in a preferred geographical location. (In 1988, pitcher Bruce Hurst spurned equal or better financial offers from the Boston Red Sox and St. Louis Cardinals to sign with the San Diego Padres. He indicated that a western city was an important consideration for this decision.)

[9]Murphy Sewall, "A Decision Calculus Model for Contract Bidding," *Journal of Marketing,* 40 (October 1976), 92–98.
[10]See Sewall, ibid., for an application of this approach.
[11]Gabriel M. Gelb, "Conjoint Analysis Helps Explain the Bid Process," *Marketing News,* 22 (March 14, 1988), 1, 31.

As argued in Chap. 6, it is important that a firm bidding for contracts or participating in auctions undertake pricing market research and develop a continuing price information system. Many times after a bid has been turned down, it is difficult to know the extent to which the firm lost out because of price, or other factors, or some combination of factors. In business marketing, the salespeople involved with the buying company need to try to determine reasons why the bid was lost. However, this particular method of feedback depends on an honest report to the salesperson from the customer and an accurate report back from the salesperson to the bidding management team. The purchasing company wants to maintain relationships and to be sure the company will bid on another contract, and the salesperson wishes to ensure that he or she is not blamed for the lost business. Hence, there is the possibility that the purchasing company will minimize the price differential and the salesperson may overstate the price differential between the winning and losing bids.[12]

Another research approach for postbid analysis is to conduct interviews with clients to elicit information about the bid selection and the reasons for the selection of the winning bid. However, like the salesperson asking for feedback, the customer too may attempt to rationalize the selection.

The techniques of tradeoff or conjoint analysis described in Chap. 6 are better for getting information on the bidding process. As mentioned earlier, the Western Oceanic drilling company conducted a conjoint analysis to determine the important factors for oil companies awarding drilling contracts. A small interview sample of drilling superintendents and purchasing agents ranked various combinations of price, safety, and other important performance factors. Based on the conjoint analysis, a number of important decisions were made about when and what bids should be made. As a result of these decisions, the utilization rate for Western Oceanic's drilling rigs went from 39 to 93 percent.[13]

DETERMINING THE BEST BID

Probabilistic bidding models assist the firm in determining a bid price that optimizes the combination of the probability of winning and of making a profit if the bid wins. The optimal bid is the bid that offers the highest expected contribution to profit and overhead. The expected contribution of a bid $E(B)$ is determined by multiplying the probability of winning with a bid, $P(B)$, by the difference between the bid price and the estimated direct costs $(B - C)$:

$$E(B) = (B - C) \times P(B) \qquad (17\text{-}7)$$

Table 17-6 and Fig. 17-4 illustrate the relationship between the probability of winning and expected contribution. As indicated in Table 17-6 and Fig. 17-4, the

[12]John P. Tully, "Field Information for Competitive Bidding," in Earl L. Bailey (ed.), *Pricing Practices and Strategies* (New York: The Conference Board, 1978), pp. 58–61.
[13]Gelb, op. cit.

TABLE 17-6
EXPECTED CONTRIBUTIONS IN RELATION TO SIZE OF BID

Bid as a Percentage of Direct Cost (B)	Probability of Bid Winning [$P(B)$]	Contribution Margin, % ($B - C$)	Expected Contribution from Bid, % [$E(B)$]
80	1.00	−20	−20
85	1.00	−15	−15
90	1.00	−10	−10
95	1.00	−5	−5
100	0.88	0	0
105	0.73	5	3.65
110	0.60	10	6.00
115	0.42	15	6.30
120	0.24	20	4.80
125	0.07	25	1.75
130	0.01	30	0.30
135	0	35	0
140	0	40	0

maximum expected profit occurs with a bid of 115. The expectation curve in Fig. 17-4 shows the expected profit contribution corresponding to each bid. The optimal bid is 115, or 15 percent above the direct cost. Zero expectation will always occur at a bid equal to direct cost. A bid below direct costs will always have a negative expectation, and bids above direct costs will range upward from zero to an upper value and then taper off, reaching zero again for bids far above direct costs.

Sometimes a firm wants to maximize expected contributions, but only with some minimum probability of winning the bid. For example, assume that a firm wishes to have a probability of winning the contract of at least 0.60. The firm is in need of some work, has sufficient short-term financial resources, and does not feel the need to maximize its expected contributions. As shown in Table 17-6, a bid of 110 is the best bid since the expected contribution of 6 percent is the best under the probability of winning constraint.

On the other hand, a firm operating near capacity will consider new business only if it has higher than usual contributions. If, for example, the firm decides that a contribution of 20 percent is the lowest it will accept, then a bid of 120 maximizes the expected contribution, subject to the contribution margin constraint.

As these examples indicate, frequently a firm will change its bidding objectives depending on the overall bidding situation. Regardless of the objective selected, the firm ultimately must trade off the chances of winning against maximizing expected contributions to select the best bid. The procedures outlined here allow management to consider the firm's objectives, its market and financial positions, current and future competition, and current and future opportunities to select the best bidding strategy. Moreover, these procedures allow for management to *subjectively* change the data to reflect current perceptions of the bidding situation.

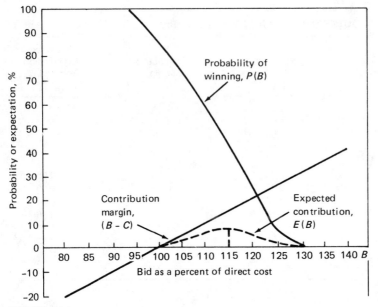

FIGURE 17-4
Relation between probability of winning and expected contribution.

CONTINGENT CONTRACTS

Often, neither the bidding firm nor the bid-taking organization has complete information about the costs of performing the service or developing and providing the
product or the value to be derived from receiving the service or using the product.
As illustrated by the EMS example in Chap. 5, the cost of providing the service as
well as the value of the service cannot be determined exactly at the time the contract
is bid and awarded. Thus, contingency contracts are used to share the risks when
these types of uncertainties occur in the contractual relationship. Another aspect of
the risks involved in these situations is that the parties involved have different
amounts of information available when making the decision. Presumably the performing organization has more and better information about its capabilities and
costs, and the purchasing organization has better information about the relative
value of the product or service to it.

One form of contingency contract is a cost-plus contract. The issue here is one
of determining the amount of "guaranteed" profit for the performing organization.
However, there is considerably more risk to the purchasing organization because
there are no incentives to prevent cost overruns since the performing firm has a
guarantee for a certain level of profit. (The government has been beset by such
contracts in recent years.) An incentive or risk-sharing contract would provide some
relief from a cost-plus contract. For example, the performing firm might agree to
pay for 20 percent of the cost overrun. Another example of a contingency contract
is the EMS contract in which the engineering firm guaranteed the school system
energy savings at the risk of forfeiting its fee. (See the EMS example in Chap. 5.)

In a contingency-value contract, the bidding firm uses the amount of the incentive built into the bid as a signal of its performance capabilities. That is, other things remaining the same, the more of the cost overrun the firm is willing to share, the greater is the likelihood that its cost estimates will be correct. Thus, the contingency terms offered by the bidding firm help the bid-taking organization screen bids that have been submitted.[14]

BIDDING WITH CAPACITY CONSTRAINTS

A firm may be offered the opportunity to bid on a project when it is operating near full capacity. In such a situation, the contribution margin criterion is insufficient to help the firm set its bidding strategy. When operating at or near full capacity, the firm is in a position to allocate its resources to *maximize contributions per resource unit.* Chapter 8 developed this criterion and showed its application to product-line pricing. When capacity constraints exist, the bidding firm should substitute the contribution per resource unit criterion for contribution margin in the analytical procedures developed in this chapter, and then proceed as usual.

SUMMARY

This chapter has presented an overview of the problem of developing bids for providing products or services on an order basis. Applications of direct costing and considerations of competitive strategy and capacity constraints have been explored. The most serious limitation of a probabilistically developed bidding strategy is the assumption that competitors will follow the same bidding behavior in the future that they followed in the past. There is no guarantee that this assumption will prevail. Hence, it is important that any analytical procedure provide for management to change the data based on subjective criteria that reflect its perceptions. The procedures outlined in this chapter permit such subjective adaptation.

Overall, a probabilistic bidding model provides a guide for management in

1 Evaluating the chances of winning a particular contract
2 Recognizing the profit potential that can be expected under various bidding situations
3 Identifying projects in which the expense of preparing and submitting a bid is not economically justified

Competitive bidding models provide management with useful and objective procedures for developing appropriate pricing strategies.

DISCUSSION QUESTIONS

1 What is the most difficult part of preparing a competitive bid? Why?
2 Why should a firm perform an analysis to determine whether to prepare a bid?

---

[14]William Samuelson, "Bidding for Contracts," *Management Science,* 32 (December 1986), 1533–1550.

3 a Describe the steps involved in prebid analysis.

  b Assume that a prebid analysis has produced the result given in Table 17-2. To what extent should this prebid analysis influence the bid that will eventually be made? Why?

  c Suppose that the evaluation shown in Table 17-2 led to an assigned weight of 10 for the follow-up factor. What would be the total score for the bid now? Would this high score on follow-up affect your answer on how the prebid analysis might influence the bid that will eventually be made? Why or why not?

4 A firm was preparing a bid on a government contract for an electronic part in a new missile guidance system. The contract was for 10,000 units. The company determined that five other companies are likely to bid on the contract. Two of these potential bidders have never bid against the firm before, but management believes that these new bidders will be similar to previous opponents on other government contracts. Direct costs for producing one of these electronic parts is estimated to average $100 if the firm wins the contract. Moreover, it is likely that the government will ask for another round of bids on this electronic part within 18 months after this current contract is settled. The firm believes that the 10,000 units can be produced and delivered within 15 months of the contract award. Assume that the data given in Tables 17-4 and 17-5 are relevant for this firm's initial bid. Prepare an analysis for this bid opportunity. What bid would you recommend? Why?

SUGGESTED READINGS

Engelbrecht-Wiggans, Richard: "Auctions and Bidding Models: A Survey," *Management Science,* 26 (February 1980), 119–142.

Engelbrecht-Wiggans, Richard: "On a Possible Benefit to Bid Takers from Using Multi-Stage Auctions," *Management Science,* 34 (September 1988), 1109–1120.

Kottas, John F., and Basheer M. Khumawala: "Contract Bid Development for the Small Businessman," *Sloan Management Review,* 14 (Spring 1973), 31–45.

Paranka, Stephen: "The Pay-Off Concept in Competitive Bidding," *Business Horizons,* 12 (August 1969), 77–81.

Paranka, Stephen: "Competitive Bidding Strategy," *Business Horizons,* 14 (June 1971), 39–43.

Samuelson, William: "Bidding for Contracts," *Management Science,* 32 (December 1986), 1533–1550.

Sewall, Murphy: "A Decision Calculus Model for Contract Bidding," *Journal of Marketing,* 40 (October 1976), 92–98.

CHAPTER 18

EXTENDING THE
CONCEPTS OF STRATEGIC
PRICING

As mentioned in Chap. 1, the economies of North America have increasingly been shifting from their product-based history to a service base. In part, this change has resulted from a level of income for a majority of people that allows for more leisure activities. But this shift also reflects some important changes in life styles and values. There has been a growing emphasis on education, on health and personal care, on private and publicly funded care and assistance programs, on entertainment and travel, on financial and insurance services, and on various types of advising and counseling services, to name some wide-ranging examples.

Another trend noted in Chap. 1 is the "globalization" of markets, the increasing foreign competition in domestic and overseas markets. The development of free-trade agreements, such as that between the United States and Canada, the unification of the Western European economy scheduled for 1992, the future industrialization of the Third World and, in particular, the Pacific Rim countries, have increased pressure to correctly price products and services.

Unfortunately, the pricing problems associated with pricing services and with international marketing have rarely been written about, although services are provided and firms are engaged in exporting to and locating in foreign countries. Prices are set, products and services are sold, and profits and losses occur. The pricing principles developed in this book apparently can be applied to services and to international marketing, but some important nuances in this area suggest that additional care must be exercised when developing prices and price structures in these market situations. Indeed, the principles developed in this book are more applicable in pricing services and in international marketing than are the traditional principles and practices criticized in this book.

Over time, service marketing has spawned a lengthy list of terms that euphemistically replace the word "price." For example, we pay a postage *rate* to the U.S. Postal Service. *Fees* are paid to doctors and dentists. We pay *premiums* for insurance coverage, *rent* for apartments, *tuition* for education, and *fares* for taxis, buses, and airlines. We pay *tolls* to cross a bridge and *admission* to a sporting event, concert, movie, or museum. Banks may have *user fees* for credit charges, *minimum required balances* for checking account, *rents* for safety deposit boxes, and *fees* or *interest charges* for automatic teller machine (ATM) use or cash advances. Moreover, in international marketing, *tariffs* and *duties* are paid to import goods to another country.

As we wade through this variety of terms, we often fail to recognize that the setting of a rent, interest rate, premium, fee, admission charge, or toll is a pricing decision exactly like the pricing of a product purchased in a store. Moreover, most organizations that set these fees, rates, etc., must also develop a price structure. That is, for all the services offered, issues related to discounts, terms of payment, different types of client, etc., must be settled exactly as discussed in Chaps. 14 and 15. Moreover, a proactive pricing approach is a strategic necessity, and the price setter, just as for products, must understand how pricing works, how customers perceive price, and how customers develop perceptions of value.[1]

Another important prescription for service marketing is that the price setter must understand the behavioral objectives of the price decision. That is, whether the financial goal is to make a profit or to break even (say for the U.S. Postal Service or the YMCA), the price setter must understand how price is used to influence buyers' behavior so the financial goal can be achieved. For example, an apartment complex had determined its rents for one-, two-, and three-bedroom units by adding a constant differential to the basic rate for a one-bedroom unit. That is, a one-bedroom unit was rented for $450 per month, and the rents for the two- and three-bedroom units were $500 and $550 respectively. However, given the limited supply of three-bedroom units, there was always a long waiting list for these units. Finally, the manager decided to raise the rent for a three-bedroom unit by $5 per month each time a new renter began renting a three-bedroom unit. Before long the rent for a three-bedroom unit was approaching $600 per month and the manager realized that he had to set the rents not by some flat amount but by the differential value various people placed on one-, two-, and three bedroom units. That is, he realized that he had a "product-line" and needed to set rent differentials consistent with the different value perceptions of potential renters.

Similarly, the athletic department of a major university recognized that it needed to increase revenues from revenue-producing sporting events to help defray the increasing costs of running the athletic program. Recognizing that several football games were usually sold out and that others barely sold 50 percent of the seating capacity, the marketing manager developed several different season ticket plans as well as a differential per game admission fee to reflect the differential perceived value of the attendees for the various football games. Average attendance increased from

---

[1] See Kent B. Monroe, "The Pricing of Services," in Carol Congram and Margaret Friedman (eds.), *The Handbook of Service Marketing* (New York: AMACOM, 1990).

60 percent of capacity to 78 percent of capacity in the first year and to 86 percent in the second year. Net revenues for the admission fee plan substantially increased from previous years.

There are three major sections in this chapter. First, the problems and issues of pricing services will be discussed. Pricing examples from financial services, on-line information services, and higher education will be presented to illustrate the extension of the principles of strategic pricing to services. Second, the unique problems and issues related to pricing for export will be discussed. Finally, one of the difficulties associated with global marketing is determining how to develop prices for goods produced in one country by one division of a firm but imported by another division into another country for either additional production activities or final sale. The problem of international transfer pricing is an extension of the complex issue of transfer pricing. Therefore, the third section of this chapter briefly reviews the problems and alternative solutions to the transfer pricing problem.

THE PRICING OF SERVICES

One important characteristic of most services is that they are primarily retailing-type activities. That is, the seller or provider of the service deals directly with the final buyer or user. In fact, in many cases, the work or performance of the seller *is* the service. The final buyer may be a business firm, a government agency, an institution, or an individual. Unlike retailers of tangible goods, service retailers generally cannot rely on a manufacturer to produce the offering or to provide assistance in determining the service's price. Moreover, service providers cannot buy service units in case lots or other standard packaging form for resale to purchasers. In effect, service retailers produce and distribute the service to purchasers or users.

Services are distinct in that relevant costs for profitability analysis are determined by an approach different from the usual standard costing systems. As developed in Chaps. 7–9, relevant costs for pricing purposes are identified by focusing on the activity or function being performed rather than thinking in terms of production variable costs such as materials and direct labor. Because many service organizations have little or no direct material costs, and some, such as the airlines or hotels and restaurants, have proportionately fewer direct labor costs, it becomes very important to focus on those costs that are attributable to the provision and sale of the particular service activity.[2]

Another unusual characteristic of services is that most consumers are unable to assess the price–quality relationship prior to purchase, and often they cannot assess it even after purchase and use.[3] As indicated in Chaps. 2–4, the more knowledgeable people are about the relationship between price and quality, the more likely are they to be sensitive to price differences. Moreover, for some services, such as medical care and legal counsel (i.e., credence good; see Chaps. 2 and 13), the inability to evaluate

---

[2]John Dearden, "Cost Accounting Comes to Service Industries," *Harvard Business Review,* 56 (September–October 1978), 132–140.

[3]Joseph P. Guiltinan, "A Conceptual Framework for Pricing Consumer Services," in Mary Jo Bitner and Lawrence A. Crosby (eds.), *Designing a Winning Service Strategy* (Chicago: American Marketing Association, 1989), pp. 11–15.

the service even after acquisition makes service buying more risky.[4] In such situations, it is more likely that buyers will be less sensitive to price, and will ascribe quality on the basis of the price charged.

PRICING FINANCIAL SERVICES

Customers of financial services pay not only in "hard" money, such as coins and currency, checks, drafts, and credit, but also indirectly in the forms of balances that are kept on deposit. If customers are required to leave a non–interest-bearing balance on deposit, or balances that earn less than market rate of interest (the rate of interest they could get elsewhere), then value is given to the institution, because it can invest these balances to earn additional revenues. This concept of *fees and balances* is unique to financial institutions and is fundamental to the pricing of financial services.

Some consumers think that if they maintain a $500 minimum balance in their checking account, the bank provides free checking, but in reality the balance required to avoid a monthly fee is the bank's way of charging for the checking service. Or consider one bank's recent pricing plan, which provided "free" traveler's checks, free checks, and a reduced monthly charge for a safety deposit box if the customer maintained a minimum of $10,000 on deposit in the bank in savings and checking accounts, IRA accounts, or certificates of deposit (CDs). What this plan was attempting to do was to get more customers to use the bank as a "full financial service" institution. Note that this plan, in essence, is a price bundling offer (see Chap. 13), in that several services are offered for one bundle price. Indeed, many banks have been attempting to determine the advantages of offering multiple services for one bundle price or of unbundling their services and offering them at individual prices.

Whether to charge explicit fees for financial services or require balances on deposit should be considered from the perspective of a bank's customers. As indicated in Table 18-1 the argument for fees vs. that for balances depends on how customers perceive the relative differences between these two ways of pricing financial services. Point 3 stems from the 1980 Depository Institutions Deregulation and

[4]Patrick E. Murphy and Ben M. Enis, "Classifying Products Strategically," *Journal of Marketing,* 50 (July 1986), 24–42.

TABLE 18-1
ARGUMENTS FOR FEES VERSUS BALANCES—CUSTOMER'S POINT OF VIEW

	Fees	Balances
1.	Customer earns a return on money rather than paying for services	Customer is unable or not inclined to earn a market return on money
2.	Customer can apply fees against tax obligation	Customer cannot apply fees against tax obligation
3.	Fractional reserve system requires a percentage of deposits held	Financial institution does not have a large reserve requirement

Monetary Control Act, which requires a bank to hold in its vaults or at a Federal Reserve Bank up to 12 percent of its total deposits as a reserve. These funds cannot be invested by the bank and therefore are not available to accrue interest for customers. If the institution does not have many transaction accounts, such as demand deposit accounts (e.g., checking), then the bank's normal vault cash may be sufficient to meet the reserve requirement.

To determine the appropriate relationship between a balance pricing system and a fee pricing system, a financial institution must evaluate four interrelated components: (1) the price or fee, (2) the annual equivalent of a monthly fee, (3) the earnings credit rate (what the institution would need to pay to obtain the deposit balance in the market), and (4) adjustments for nonearning assets (i.e., the ratio of nonearning assets to earning assets, e.g., reserve requirements).[5]

Equating Fees with Balances

Equation (18-1) is used to determine the relationship between fees and balances.[6]

$$\frac{\text{Fees} \times \text{constant}}{\text{Earnings rate} \times \text{adjustments}} = \text{balance equivalent} \qquad (18\text{-}1)$$

or

$$\frac{F \times C}{E \times (1 - A)} = B \qquad (18\text{-}2)$$

where F = fees or price
C = annualization constant
E = earnings credit rate
A = adjustments expressed as a percentage
B = balance equivalent

As an example, consider NOW (negotiated order of withdrawal) accounts, which pay explicit interest on transaction balances (i.e., the amount of money in the account). These accounts are similar to interest-bearing checking accounts. In pricing them, the financial institution must determine the relative indifference point between a monthly fee and an average monthly balance on deposit. In essence, this is a form of break-even question, i.e., the break-even point between a fixed monthly charge and a required average deposit balance must be determined.

Assume the bank currently charges a monthly fee, F, of $10, pays a monthly interest on the transaction account of 5 percent, and earns 9 percent on the balance in a money market, and assume that the adjustment for nonearning assets is 10

[5]G. Michael Moebs and Eva Moebs, *Pricing Financial Services* (Homewood, Ill.: Dow Jones–Irwin, 1986).
[6]Ibid., p. 103.

percent. Because the account is tallied monthly, the annualization factor is 12. Applying Eq. (18-2),

$$\frac{\$10 \times 12}{(9\% - 5\%) \times (1 - 10\%)} = B$$

$$\frac{\$120}{0.036} = \$3,333 = B$$

Note that the interest paid to the customer on the monthly balance must be deducted from the interest the institution earns by investing that money in the money market. The bank can now offer two pricing alternatives to customers. The customer can elect to pay a $10 service charge per month or to maintain a minimum balance of $3,333 in the account and pay no monthly service charge. A survey determined that the average NOW balances were $2,886 in banks and $1,101 at savings institutions.[7]

Determining the relationship between a required balance and a fee represents only one aspect of the development of a pricing structure for a NOW account. Many other pricing questions must be asked:

1 Should there be a charge for each draft or check written, and if so, what should it be?

2 How much should be charged for each deposit transaction?

3 How many checks or drafts may be written before a charge or fee is applied?

4 How much should be charged for "excessive check" usage?

5 What should be charged for returned canceled checks?

6 What should a stop-payment order cost?

7 How much should be charged for insufficient funds?

8 What should personalized checks cost?

9 Should a customer pay for help in balancing a checkbook, and if so, how much?

10 What should the minimum NOW account balance, below which no interest will be paid to the depositor, be?

As with product pricing, the decision maker must weigh the institution's costs and revenues for the service against the benefits perceived and valued by the customers.

If in this example the customer used a non–interest-bearing checking account with a monthly service charge of $10, the equivalent monthly balance would be

$$\frac{\$120}{0.09 \times 0.90} = \$1,481$$

---

[7]James W. Kolari, Peter S. Rose, and P. Rajan Varadarajan, "NOW-Account Strategies of Depository Institutions: A Recent Survey of the Goals, Pricing Policies, Costs, and Returns in New England," *Journal of Business Research,* 14 (October 1986), 441–457.

Note that because the customer receives no interest on the balance in the account, the required monthly balance is substantially less than for the NOW account. Depending on the actual figures for these components and the behavioral objectives for the bank, the alternative fee vs. balance relationship can be adjusted. For example, if the bank wants more people to leave larger balances in their transaction or demand-deposit accounts, then raising the monthly fee reduces the required average deposit balance. More people will then be able to qualify for the perceived "free" service, enhancing their perceptions of value (see Chap. 4). This decision will also depend on the amount and type of competition in the markets in which the financial institution operates.

Because of the intense competition for depositors among different types of financial institutions since deregulation, some questions have been raised about certain banking practices. Consumers have become confused when the banks advertise interest rates paid for certificates of deposit, money market accounts, or savings accounts. The limitations—early withdrawal penalties, minimum balance requirements, and interest compounding methods, e.g.—simply are not clear. In 1989 Congress began hearings on a proposed truth-in-savings bill to eliminate such confusion. The bills being considered would require banks to disclose their bank deposit rates, minimum balance requirements, fees, and penalties. Further, bank advertisements would have to disclose the actual compounding interest rate the banks are using and the annualized percentage rate (APR).

Pricing Strategy for Automated Tellers

Automated teller machines (ATMs) have become widespread and are used by many banks to increase their service hours while minimizing the demands on tellers for many routine transactions. The typical pricing approaches have been to charge nothing for the service, to charge by transaction, to charge a monthly or annual card fee, or some combination of these elements. Indeed, the most typical pricing approach when introducing an ATM has been to offer it "free." Later, when attempting to recover some of the costs associated with the ATM, banks have considered charging a fee of some sort. However, the issue now becomes one of determining the relative perceived value to the customers of having an ATM card vs. standing in line for a teller during normal banking hours.

As was shown in Chap. 5, placing a price or fee on an item conveys value to the customer. One way that has been suggested to convey the value of the ATM and at the same time encourage more routine transactions at the ATM is to charge a monthly or annual fee and to grant a credit for each transaction at the ATM until the fee has been completely rebated.[8] Thus, by charging a fee for an ATM card, the bank has an opportunity to reward customers for not tying up tellers with routine transactions. The bank gains when the tellers are used for functions that

---

[8]Catherine Bond Nease, "A Positive Pricing Strategy for ATMs," *Bank Marketing,* February 1989, pp. 26–29.

generate more revenue than cashing a check, taking a deposit, or receiving a bill payment.

Pricing Bank Card Services

Another popular service provided by banks and other financial institutions is the extension of credit through Mastercard, Visa, or similar credit and debit cards. To develop a pricing structure for this service, the price setter must balance the costs of providing the service against the benefits provided to the cardholders and to the merchants who accept the card in lieu of money. Essentially, the bank provides two services to the cardholder: (1) a transaction service, i.e., providing a mechanism to complete a purchase without using money, and (2) a credit service, i.e., the extension of a short-term line of credit before paying for the transactions. For the merchants, the bank provides a transaction service and a collection service. Moreover, when the cardholder completes a transaction outside the bank's service area, there is an interchange service provided between the banks using the particular charge card system. Today, the most popular pricing mechanism for the bank charge cards seems to be an annual fee plus an interest charge on unpaid balances, as well as a fee for providing cash advances. There is also a fee assessed for using an interbank system different from the one of which the bank is a member. Merchants typically pay a discount based on the amount of money that the bank transfers to their account from the credit card transactions.

Before banks instituted some form of annual or monthly fees, people often held a number of bank cards. That is, since there was no penalty or fee for using the card as long as the credit amount outstanding was paid in full each month, by judicious use of these cards customers could receive interest-free credit extensions of 45 days or more. Essentially, these people were active users of bank cards but did not pay for the service.

From the banks' perspective, there is a fixed cost of maintaining each active card account, a variable cost for each transaction (i.e., number of entries or transactions), and a cost of extending credit to the cardholder. There is also the initial cost of establishing the account and periodically issuing a card to the cardholder. The pricing issue is how to develop a pricing structure that allows the bank to recover its costs of offering the service as well as earning a reasonable profit for the service, while at the same time offering customers enough perceived value of the benefits derived to encourage them to use the cards for their transactions.

One pricing structure would cover the fixed costs of maintaining the account by charging either a flat annual fee or a fixed charge per month and would cover the variable costs of the transactions and credit extensions by charging some form of a variable fee. The variable costs of the transaction service might be recovered by assessing a fee of x cents per line entry, and the variable cost of credit might be recovered by assessing a small percentage (e.g., 1 percent) against the average daily balance. Another possibility would be to establish an average deposit balance requirement in savings or demand–deposit accounts to avoid having a monthly credit card fee assessed.

As suggested in the discussion of ATM pricing strategy, selecting the appropriate pricing structure depends on understanding how customers value the credit card service, how they use the card, and the financial institution's behavioral objective for pricing the card service. Also, if the institution would like to change customers from a credit card to a debit card (amount of the purchase is deducted from the person's bank account), then it must understand customers' purchase and payment behaviors and then devise pricing strategies that reflect this understanding. To simply offer a credit card service for free, or to suddenly establish an annual and/or monthly fee schedule without understanding the consumers who use the cards, would be a mistake.[9] Moreover, establishing a means for analyzing different types of consumers who use credit cards would lead to a better understanding of which customers use the service without paying for it, i.e., which customers' service costs are greater than the revenues the bank generates for providing the service. As pointed out in Chap. 9, customer profitability analysis is an important aspect of developing profitable pricing strategies, whether for a product or service organization.

PRICING ON-LINE INFORMATION SERVICES

During the past decade, the ability to retrieve information from data bases for personal or business use has grown at a dramatic rate. However, the pricing of on-line information services has not kept up with the rapid changes in technology and customer-use behavior. For information service providers to become proactive pricers, they must understand how pricing works and how customers perceive prices and price changes.

To apply these two prescriptions in the context of on-line service pricing, it is necessary to determine first what it is that buyers are purchasing when they query an on-line service and second why they want the "product." People buy on-line services because they need information to solve a problem or make a decision. The information has little intrinsic value; its value is relative to the nature of the problem or decision that an individual or organization is facing.[10] In this context, information has value only when it serves to reduce the uncertainty or risk of making a decision or pursuing a course of action without that information. (In some situations, an on-line search will reveal that no other information exists, which can also have value. For example, a researcher performing a bibliographic search and finding no articles on a specific topic has received the knowledge that no other researcher has published research on this topic, which indicates that the researcher is involved in pioneering work.)

As argued in Chaps. 3–5, perceived value represents a tradeoff between customers' perceptions of benefits to be received by using the information relative to the

[9]Robert W. Johnson, "Pricing of Bank Card Services," *Journal of Retail Banking,* 1 (June 1979), 16–22.

[10]R. M. Haynes and T. Erickson, "Added Value as a Function of Purchases of Information Services," *Information Society,* 1, No. 4 (1982), 307–338.

perceived costs of acquiring the information. Although the price of the information to be acquired by using the on-line service is known in terms of the pricing structure used by the distributor or vendor, the buyer rarely knows prior to search what the information to be received will actually cost.[11] For example, if the pricing structure is a fixed charge per hour of connect time plus a print charge, the buyer does not know a priori either the amount of time the search will take or how much information will be printed out. Similarly, the buyer has no way of anticipating the benefit of the information to be acquired until after it has been received.

Current Pricing Approaches

Under current pricing structures, it is difficult for the buyer or purchase decision maker to determine with any reasonable degree of accuracy the relative tradeoff between price or acquisition cost of the information and the benefits to be received by initiating an on-line query. Therefore, it is more likely that users of on-line services are those who have used the service and have received benefits from such use. Further, an individual's sensitivity to risk, or the uncertainty that the information search will be productive, will also play a role in the decision.[12] Finally, how individuals view the factors of perceived need, relative cost, perceived benefits, and uncertainty about outcome will depend on their location in the organization and individual personal differences.

It is likely that a technical specialist or researcher will evaluate these factors differently from a person in the purchasing department. Thus, it is extremely important to determine who makes the decision to purchase an on-line service and to obtain a better understanding of how such people perceive the relative benefit vs. acquisition cost tradeoff. It is also important to know how such individuals assess the risk of the outcome of the information search.

Comparing the prescriptions given here with the way that on-line services have usually been priced makes it clear that the item of value, information, is not what has been priced. Rather, customers of on-line services have been paying for the *amount of time that they are connected to the system.* It is little wonder then that users have developed search strategies designed to minimize the amount of connect time while maximizing the amount of information received. Using faster machines, microcomputers, and search software has led to an ability to minimize the connect time while obtaining the desired information. Further, the purchaser with less sophisticated equipment and less search experience may spend more time searching and actually obtain less information for the effort. The irony of all this is that the item of value, information, is not priced, but that which does not enhance the value to the searcher, connect time, is the pricing mechanism.

[11]Arnold A. J. Jansen, "Towards a New Pricing Structure for Online Databases," *Journal of Information Science,* 10 (1985), 125–130.
[12]Ronald G. Dunn and Harry F. Boyle, "On-Line Searching: Costly or Cost Effective? A Marketing Perspective," *Journal of Chemical Information and Computer Services,* 24, No. 2 (1984), 51–54.

What needs to be stressed is that the reason for prescribing "target the purchaser" is that it is necessary to know how customers behave relative to price and price changes. Under the current pricing system, since there is no a priori way to assess the relative value of an information search, the customers' behavior goals are either to minimize connect time or to maximize information acquisition relative to a predetermined time constraint. This behavior is equivalent to shoppers attempting to minimize the amount of time shopping for a product or to maximize the number of products they can purchase within a predetermined time limit. Neither shopping objective is likely to enable the buyer to maximize the value received from such a purchasing trip.

Developing a New Pricing Structure

From the seller's perspective, the pricing objective may be to maximize profits by a specified time. If, at any period of time, the cost structure for an on-line service provider is one of high fixed costs relative to the variable cost of providing the service to a searcher, then this profit goal can be simplified to one of maximizing revenues, since costs will not be incrementally much greater due to the search activity. Rather than attempting to enhance revenues by increasing the connect-hour rate or the print charges, the provider needs to find a mechanism for setting price relative to the perceived value of the information to the searcher. Otherwise, the searcher acts to minimize the connect time rather than maximizing the amount of information acquired.

It should be clear that it is necessary to change from charging for time to charging for the amount of information acquired from a search. The basic mechanism should consist of two types of charges: (1) a fixed fee per inquiry or specific activity, and (2) a variable price per unit of information received by the searcher. (Depending on the mechanism used to provide the information to the searcher, such as on-line printing, there would also need to be a fixed and variable rate structure to represent the costs to the provider and the value to the searcher of receiving the information via an on-line print.) The fixed fee component of the pricing mechanism enables the provider to recover the costs incurred of having the service available regardless of the length of the search in terms of time or amount of information provided. The variable portion of the charges relates to the variable cost of providing the connection over the time period and the relative value to the searcher of the information received. Moreover, assessing a fixed charge and a charge for the portion of the variable fee that relates to the variable cost of providing the connection is a way to collect revenues even when the search uncovers no information. As indicated earlier, such a result does have value to the client.

The pricing mechanism can also be changed to develop a variable pricing structure offering subscription rates (with clearly defined rules of membership), volume discounts, and peak-load and off-peak-load prices. A variable pricing structure can take into account differential perceived value by setting differential rates based on the type of file queried, the type of search utilized (e.g., bibliographic vs. factual database), and perhaps the nature or type of organization doing the search (e.g., university vs. business firm).[13] An important point to remember is that the markets for these services are not homogeneous and that a differential pricing structure can be developed that recognizes differences in buyers' sensitivities to prices due to differences in the perceived value of the information to be received. Developing a pricing structure that reflects an understanding of how buyers perceive the value of information and that encourages buyers to utilize the on-line service to acquire valuable information should be the pricing goal of on-line service organizations and distributors.

As with financial institutions, information service and telecommunication firms need to avoid "me-too" pricing strategies and tactics. It is important that a careful analysis of the organization's objectives, costs of providing specific products and services, competitors' offerings and costs, and the value perceptions of prospective and served customers be completed before establishing specific strategies. Different offerings compete in different markets facing different competitive environments while satisfying different requisites sought by customers. Thus, each product or service must be priced as an individual offering that is inherently related to the other offerings in the service line.

PRICING ISSUES IN HIGHER EDUCATION

At first glance, it may seem incongruous to discuss the pricing of higher education. However, although public and private universities and colleges are not-for-profit organizations, they nevertheless offer multiple "products" to different market segments at different "prices." Many universities and colleges have traditionally offered a bundle of services at one price or level of tuition, although there is evidence that departures have occurred with differential tuition rates for undergraduate and graduate education and for some professional schools or colleges, such as medicine, law, veterinary medicine, and business. Moreover, offering fellowships and scholarships on the basis of merit or financial need to some students reflects the offering of a price discount. Hence, some students pay the full price while others pay a discounted price that may even be a complete remission of all fees and tuition. Once we recognize that colleges and universities engage in pricing decisions, that they offer a wide range of services, and that different educational programs vary in costs and in students' perceptions of value, then we are in a position to analyze the appropriateness of current pricing approaches by higher education.

Services Provided by Higher Education

Although most institutions of higher education grant degrees to students, this is only one of five basic services they perform. In fact, universities and colleges (1) dissemi-

[13]Frances H. Barker, "Pricing of Information Products," *Aslib Proceedings,* 36 (July/August 1984), 289–297.

nate information, (2) provide counseling, (3) provide credentialing, (4) engage in coercion, and (5) permit club or social membership.[14]

Information   One of the major functions of colleges and universities is to disseminate information in the forms of lectures, written papers and books, and other means of communication to students and other interested parties. Although much of undergraduate education is still offered via the traditional lecture–discussion system with reading and other types of assignments supplementing the lectures, current technology now offers a challenge to this system. One of the interesting implications of the new delivery systems is the underlying costs associated with developing, implementing, and maintaining such systems, and the means of handling the faculty–technology interface. From a pricing perspective, the costs of such systems and the value delivered to students must be considered when determining prices for courses or credit-hours earned.

Counseling   Students are counseled by faculty and by special counseling departments on academic matters such as course selection, on major program requirements, for personal and psychological needs, and for career and job placement activities. Not all students use these various counseling services, but some use them quite heavily. To the extent that these services are bundled into the tuition and fees, some students are subsidizing others for the receipt of these services. A decision to unbundle these services (as most institutions unbundle room and board) and price them separately would provide an opportunity for those who use the services to pay for them.

Credentialing   The awarding of a diploma with a degree in a specific area of study certifies to the public that a person has attained a certain level of achievement. However, prior to the awarding of the diploma, the faculty and administrative structure, through an intricate system of exams and grading and the monitoring of cumulative performance, certify the person's achievement. As long as students meet course distribution requirements and maintain a minimum grade point average, the university certifies them with the awarding of a diploma. The monetary value of this certification has been documented with the numerous studies quantifying the relative lifetime earning power of a college graduate vs. a high school graduate. Given the value of the certification or credentialing, there is a question as to whether a college education is fairly priced relative to those who do not go to college and subsidize public universities through their taxes.

Coercion   The coercion function is performed through the system of requirements, fixed time periods for study, examinations, fixed enrollment periods, etc. Although many students are forced to at least perform at some minimum level of

[14]W. K. S. Wang, "The Dismantling of Higher Education," *Improving College and University Teaching,* 29, No. 2 (1981), 55–60.

achievement, if there were other forms of motivation they might perform at levels closer to their abilities.

Membership The membership function is accomplished in two ways. First, most universities limit who may attend and take courses. To be admitted to a specific university or college grants some measure of exclusivity of membership. Second, through the various clubs and social organizations students interact with other students and with members of the faculty and staff. However, not all students join these clubs and organizations, nor do they partake of various extracurricular activities equally. Yet, through the mechanism of student activities fees, all students pay, to some extent, for these membership opportunities.

The foregoing discussion is not meant necessarily to be a criticism of the current tuition and fees system used by most universities and colleges. What is intended, however, is to develop a recognition that universities and colleges, to varying degrees, have a multiple-prices system, which does not always recognize the different price/market segments for the services provided by these institutions. As universities move to nontraditional educational programs, such as adult education and lifelong learning, and to new delivery systems, such as satellite television courses transmitted to remote locations, there is a need to scrutinize all aspects of the pricing systems and to develop a set of prices that enables them to generate revenues that cover costs while providing for a value-oriented set of prices. The unbundling of the university system is one option that deserves careful consideration.[15]

Current Pricing Approaches

Considering price only from the perspective of generating revenues, the institutions of higher education have three main "products": instruction, research, and donations.[16] Tuition is the price for instruction. For sponsored research, the price typically is the amount of direct and indirect costs associated with conducting the research. When some research sponsors balk at paying indirect costs, some form of negotiated price results. For a donor to be recognized for the contribution made to the university, it normally has to be of a certain minimum magnitude. For example, establishing a professorship in the donor's name might require a donation of $250,000, while establishing an endowed faculty position (chaired professorship) might require a donation of $1 million, and the naming of a college or school within the university might require a contribution of $10 million.

As in the private business sector, there are forces that affect discretion in the setting of prices for each of these products. Universities that have a strong public

[15]See J. P. O'Neill, "An Experiment in Unbundling Services for Adults," in R. K. Loring, C. LeGates, M. J. Josephs, and J. P. O'Neill, *Adapting Institutions to the Adult Learner: Experiments in Progress* (Washington, D.C.: American Association for Higher Education, 1978); Wang, op. cit.; W. K. S. Wang, "The Beginnings of Dismantling," *Improving College and University Teaching,* 29, No. 3 (1981), 115–121.

[16]Timothy Warner, "Priorities, Planning, and Prices," in Larry H. Litten (ed.), *Issues in Pricing Undergraduate Education: New Directions for Institutional Research* (San Francisco: Jossey-Bass, 1984), pp. 35–46.

image for offering a high-quality education will be granted an opportunity to set higher tuition rates, require higher donation levels to receive recognition for the contribution, and perhaps be more successful in negotiating research cost recovery. If the university is the only multipurpose institution in the market area, its market position is relatively stronger, and this position can affect its ability to set tuition and research cost recovery levels. Finally, its long-term goals in terms of educational programs, research objectives, and donation levels will influence its current and future pricing strategies.

There are at least six different approaches to the setting of tuition levels used by universities and colleges. Most institutions probably use some combination of two or more of these approaches to determine tuition. Under *proportional cost pricing,* tuition is set to cover a predetermined proportion of the institution's operating budget. *Mandated pricing* follows the preferences and requirements of a legislative body. At Virginia Polytechnic Institute and State University, the state legislature has mandated that tuition or instructional fees cover 35 percent of instructional costs. Thus, proportional pricing has been mandated by the legislature.

Some institutions use an external index like the Consumer Price Index to set tuition rates. Thus, under *externally indexed pricing,* tuition follows the general trend of the external index used. Using *peer pricing,* an institution sets tuition relative to a peer institution or an average of a set of peer institutions. In *value-oriented* pricing, tuition is set relative to the perceived market value of the degree or program. Many business schools offer executive development programs at relatively higher prices because of the value business people place on these education programs. Indeed, low-price programs rarely do well with executives because of the perception that there is a price–quality relationship. Institutions that use *residual pricing* set tuition so that total tuition income is sufficient to balance the operating budget. At times, particularly for private institutions, income from investments through the endowment fund is lower than forecasted and the institution faces a budget crisis through this income shortfall.

Proportional Cost Pricing   Given the prescription that an organization should know its costs when establishing prices, additional discussion on costing issues for pricing higher education is warranted. Because higher educational institutions are normally not-for-profit organizations, developing an appropriate cost basis for setting prices is vital. Depending on the nature of the institution, the problem of determining the costs of the educational mission can be relatively straightforward or highly complex.

For a strictly undergraduate institution that emphasizes teaching, the institution's operating costs are basically education costs. But for a multipurpose university with undergraduate, graduate, and professional degree programs as well as an emphasis on teaching, research, and short-term educational programs, the problem of joint and common costs becomes cumbersome. For example, consider a college or school of business that offers several undergraduate majors, an MBA program, specialized M.S. degrees, a doctoral program, an executive development program, and perhaps an evening or weekend program for part-time MBA students. If, during the course of an academic year, a faculty member teaches an undergraduate course, an MBA course, and a doctoral seminar and offers an executive training course, how should that person's salary be allocated to these different "products"? And, to further complicate the issue, what if this person also engages in research activities and performs some counseling of students as an advisor?

Although government-mandated formulas for determining the costs of government-sponsored research have led to arbitrary rules for allocating joint and common costs, for the purposes of pricing decisions, such costs are incorrect. Note that this dilemma is no different from the multiple–product-line business firm discussed throughout this book. And the solution for determining the relevant costs for pricing is essentially the same: determine the attributable costs for each activity and determine the way these costs behave as the activity or function is being performed.

Again, consider a school or college of business. Costs that are associated with the central administration or other programs outside the school are irrelevant. Costs that are associated with the school's administration or that can be *objectively* traced to the school are relevant to the analysis.

Once this pool of relevant costs has been determined, the school's various programs and the unique costs associated with these programs need to be identified. For example, the administration costs associated with the dean's office and any other centrally administered functions need to be separated from specific program costs. The salaries of the MBA director and staff would be assigned to the MBA program. Salaries of the marketing faculty would be assigned to the marketing programs except when they teach in other programs such as the MBA program. Then a proportion of the faculty member's salary would be assigned to the costs of the MBA program as well as staff assistance costs required when teaching the MBA course.

In like manner, the revenues generated by the students' tuition payments should be assigned to the programs that offer the courses taken by these students. In this way, a cost and revenue figure for each program could be generated that would be, as in business, helpful for diagnosing unprofitable operations as well as developing differential program prices. For example, it is well known that engineering and science programs generally are more costly to provide than are humanities or liberal arts programs. Universities need to consider the degree to which an English major subsidizes an engineering student by paying the same tuition over the same four years in college. Moreover, the economic value of an engineering degree in terms of future earnings is much higher than that of the English major. The unbundling of education prices needs to be considered, just as financial institutions have begun to unbundle financial services. Differential pricing makes sense whenever a multiple product or service line is offered to different markets for these offerings.

Price Discounting Price discounting is simply the reduction in tuition through a scholarship or fellowship, whether based on financial need or merit. In recent years, as the price of a college education has increased faster than the general rate of inflation, colleges have intensified their efforts to maintain general enrollment levels while at the same time competing for academically gifted students. These efforts have led to the granting of more awards of financial aid and establishment of more special merit scholarship programs. Indeed, many universities determine the student's ability to pay through a financial aid formula. The effect of applying these formulas is that some students pay full tuition, some students pay partial tuition at different monetary levels, and some students pay no tuition. Through these various price discount programs, the full-paying students subsidize partial-paying students just as English majors subsidize engineering students. Moreover, as additional money is placed in financial aid programs or merit scholarship programs, tuition must increase faster to recover the costs of price discounting. Moreover, as the scope and size of these price discount programs grow, so do the administration costs associated with them.

Another problem associated with price discounting surfaced in August 1989, when it was announced that the U.S. Justice Department was investigating about 20 universities and colleges for violations of the Sherman Anti-Trust Act. Apparently, representatives of these institutions would meet or otherwise communicate with one another concerning the amount of financial aid a prospective student would be offered from each school. Allegedly, if a student had applied to and was accepted for admission at more than one of these institutions and qualified for some financial aid, the institutions would agree on the amount of financial aid the student would be offered. Thus, when the letter of acceptance was received by the student from each institution, the amount of financial aid offered would be an identical dollar amount. The purpose of this agreement between the institutions was to reduce the amount of price competition among them for students. If the price discount via a financial aid offer was equal across the institutions, presumably the student would base the choice on reasons other than price. Although educational institutions are exempt from some provisions of the antitrust laws, they are not exempt from restraining trade via price fixing.

As with a profit-oriented business, universities and colleges need to review their price discounting to determine the relative merit of these strategies. Similar to the increased use of price promotions by manufacturers and retailers, increasing price discounting by colleges and universities has serious long-term financial, marketing, and legal implications that should be carefully reviewed.

PRICING FOR EXPORT MARKETING

During the 1980s, the United States economy was characterized by an increasing trade deficit. That is, the country was importing more foreign goods than it was exporting American goods. As a result of this trade imbalance, both federal and state governments applied pressure on U.S. firms to expand their exporting activities. Indeed, government trade missions to China, other Pacific Rim countries (Japan, Korea, Taiwan, Singapore, Thailand), Eastern and Western Europe, and elsewhere, were conducted to find opportunities for U.S. businesses to export. Further, the United States–Canada trade agreement and the 1992 unification of the European economy introduced new opportunities and problems for exporting. Despite pressures for internationalizing business activities, little written information exists on export pricing. The purpose of this section is to identify some of the problems and issues associated with export pricing.

Six factors bear on the pricing of exports:[17]

1 The nature of the product or industry
2 The location of production facilities
3 The distribution system
4 The environment of the foreign market
5 Government regulations
6 The attitude and capability of the organization's management

Product

A product that has a technological edge, thereby limiting the number of local or foreign competitors, enhances pricing flexibility. In addition, if the importing country has few import barriers or other regulations, pricing flexibility is further enhanced. On the other hand, with other foreign competitors using low price as an entry tactic, pricing flexibility is diminished. Further, if the raw materials used to produce the product are subject to market price fluctuations, then increased price review and flexibility are required. Essentially, then, the amount of pricing flexibility or discretion a firm has in exporting depends on the degree of the product's competitive advantage in terms of value delivered, limited amount of government controls, and lack of price-oriented competition from other exporting countries.

Location of Production

One of the developments of the 1980s was the strategy of many companies to build production and assembly operations abroad to take advantage of raw material sources, lower labor costs, and favorable exchange rates. At the same time, with the weakening of the U.S. dollar, many European and Japanese firms were investing in production and assembly operations in the United States. Also, with the coming of the United States–Canada trade agreement, many Canadian companies were investing in operations in the United States. One of the issues of multinational production plants is how to price products transferred from one division in one country to another division in another country. This issue of international transfer pricing will be discussed later.

Distribution System

The channels of export distribution have an important effect on pricing control. If a firm transfers its products to a subsidiary operating in another country, greater

---

[17]S. Tamer Cavusgil, "Unraveling the Mystique of Export Pricing," *Business Horizons,* 31 (May–June 1988), 54–63.

pricing control exists than if an independent distributor is used. Executives have reported that distributors often mark up the prices substantially beyond the manufacturer's intent—up to 200 percent in some instances.[18] This problem is compounded if the firm uses several levels of distributors in reaching its final foreign market. Hence, many firms use as direct a method of distribution as possible.

Distribution costs are also affected by the size of the distribution systems, which in many countries are underdeveloped relative to North America. Many distributors and retailers are small businesses trading in small volumes. For example, the Campbell Soup Company discovered that English grocers typically purchased 24-can cases of assorted soups rather than 24-can cases of one soup. Each case had to be hand-packed for shipment. Further, the typical case in the United States contains 48 cans of soup. Because of the generally small orders, the frequency of orders in England was larger than in the United States, and more sales calls were required per customer.[19]

Transportation costs of moving goods to other countries and associated costs of packing, handling, and insurance are standard in the export business. Because import tariffs and taxes are based on the total landed costs, these additional transportation and associated costs further escalate the final price in international markets. *Price escalation* refers to the higher prices for the same goods in international markets relative to domestic markets. These higher prices reflect additional shipping costs, tariffs, taxes, larger distributor margins, longer distribution channels, and exchange rate fluctuations.

Environmental Factors

A variety of environmental factors affects export pricing. Market entry and effectiveness of prices hinge on economic factors such as exchange rates, rates of inflation, and governmental price controls.[20] Because several of these factors are cyclical in nature, many firms build compensating adjustments into their pricing. When an exporter's own currency is undervalued, a pricing advantage is obtained; when it is overvalued, the exporter faces a pricing burden. For example, when the U.S. dollar weakens relative to the Japanese yen, significant erosion of Japan's pricing advantage in the U.S. market occurs.

Today, all major currencies float freely relative to one another, making it difficult to forecast the value of any one currency. As a result, many companies insist that terms of trade be in the selling company's national currency. Also, many companies engage in hedging in the money market. Especially when writing long-term contracts, companies must factor into the contract changes in the currency exchange rates as well as inflation. Otherwise, the company may end up providing large and

---

[18]Ibid.

[19]Philip R. Cateora, *Strategic International Marketing* (Homewood, Ill.: Dow Jones–Irwin, 1985), p. 199.

[20]Victor H. Frank, Jr., "Living with Price Controls Abroad," *Harvard Business Review,* 62 (March–April 1984), 137–142.

unintended discounts (see our earlier discussion in Chap. 14 about reviewing quantity discount structures due to inflationary effects).

Attitude Toward Export Marketing

Many small and medium-sized U.S. companies view exporting as a cure for excess production or as a safeguard against difficulties in the domestic market. As a result, top management does not put much effort into the exporting aspect of the business. Managers therefore use simple pricing approaches such as full costing as opposed to a more market-oriented approach. Pricing tends to be inflexible and problems often develop because of this approach.

On the other hand, successful exporting companies tend to be flexible in their pricing and are likely to use an adaptive, incremental pricing strategy. In this approach, domestic marketing and promotion costs are ignored, as are domestic overhead costs and fixed plant and equipment costs. Exports are viewed as incremental business, and only relevant costs (variable and fixed) of the international business are considered. Consequently, these companies are highly flexible in their pricing and are able to adapt to changing competitive and environmental conditions in different countries. For example, the Micro Power Division of the Ray-O-Vac company produces batteries for hearing aids and watches. Exports account for 20 percent of the business, and they sell in Europe and the Far East. The firm operates wholly owned subsidiaries in each major market and treats each subsidiary as a separate profit center. Subsidiary managers are able to adjust prices daily as exchange rates or competitive pressures change, or as needed to gain new business.

As in domestic marketing, executives need to be proactive in their pricing for export marketing. Managers need to escape from the perceived certainty of the cost-plus security blanket. Export products need to be priced according to the dynamics of the market conditions in which they are sold. What is required is pricing flexibility, a willingness to consider incremental profits, and changing prices as competition, exchange rates, and other market variables change.

Additional Pricing Issues

Selling in international markets continues to give rise to new pricing issues. In some situations, importing countries do not have the cash to purchase needed capital equipment or have severe restrictions against money flowing across their national borders. Two strategies to resolve these two issues are leasing arrangements and countertrades. A third issue that has emerged, particularly as newly developing countries (NDCs) attempt to make significant progress in world trade, is "dumping," or selling products below cost in international markets. We briefly discuss these three issues next.

Leasing   One way to alleviate the high cost of purchasing capital equipment, particularly for foreign firms that do not have strong financial capability, is leasing. Leasing in international markets is similar to that in the United States. Leases typically run for one to five years, have either monthly or annual payments, and include servicing, repairs, and replacement parts. As discussed earlier, in countries beset with rampant inflation, lease contracts can incur losses in the latter part of their time periods. Further, there exists the possibility of currency devaluation, risk of political turmoil affecting the lease, and, in cases of expropriation, even outright loss of the equipment. However, despite these disadvantages, leasing remains an important aspect of international pricing.

Countertrades   Countertrade covers those transactions where payment is made in kind rather than in currency. It has become a popular method of payment in Eastern European countries, China, and some of the developing countries. Countertrade includes four types of transactions: barter, compensation deals, counterpurchase, and buyback.

Barter is the direct exchange of goods in a transaction. Perhaps one of the most notable recent barter transactions was the agreement between Occidental Petroleum and the Soviet Union. Occidental Petroleum agreed to ship superphosphoric acid to the Soviet Union in exchange for ammonia, urea, and potash. The agreement was for 20 years and was estimated to be valued at $20 billion. In such a barter situation, the exporting company, in this case Occidental Petroleum, must be able either to use the acquired products or to find markets for them. Obviously, an additional problem is establishing the relative value of the goods being exchanged, and firms involved in bartering often rely on barter houses to establish the value of the goods and to locate potential buyers for the goods.

In a *compensation deal,* part of the payment is in currency and part is in goods. The basic advantage of a compensation deal is that there is an immediate cash settlement for a portion of the transaction. The remainder of the cash is received after the goods that were a part of the compensation are sold.

Counterpurchase involves two transactions. First the selling company negotiates a cash settlement for the goods being exported. Then the company agrees, in a separate contingent transaction, to purchase goods from the buyer equal to the amount of the initial sale. For example, McDonnell Douglas agreed to sell or buy $25 billion of Yugoslavian goods in exchange for a sale of 22 DC-9 airplanes worth $100 billion to Yugoslavia. McDonnell Douglas then arranged to sell the variety of goods, such as hams, glassware, and leather goods, to department store buyers.

In a product *buyback agreement,* the seller agrees to buy back, at a later time, output produced with the equipment originally sold. For example, a clothing manufacturer may agree to buy back a certain amount of the clothing produced in a plant established in a foreign country by the manufacturer. In effect, the exporting firm transfers technology (a manufacturing plant) to a foreign country and then agrees to buy some portion of the plant's output when it is fully operational. However, one major problem has surfaced with such arrangements: eventually the foreign plant produces goods that directly compete with the manufacturer's own goods in world markets. This particular problem is now plaguing U.S. automobile parts manufacturers as plants established in Asian countries are competing directly with the U.S. companies for the sale of automobile parts.

Dumping   As should be apparent from the preceding discussion, prices in export markets are often different from those in domestic markets for the same products. Dumping is defined as the practice of selling products in foreign markets at prices below the costs of providing the products in those markets. Most countries have legislation against dumping, and when it is determined that dumping has occurred, a countervailing duty (tax) is imposed to effectively raise the import price of the product. When foreign countries provide subsidies to their domestic companies for exporting goods, it becomes relatively easy to sell below cost in foreign countries and still make a profit. For example, Pakistan has provided a 15 percent subsidy for Pakistani companies exporting to other countries. Thus, even setting prices 5 percent below cost allows a profit to be made on the exporting activity.

INTERNATIONAL TRANSFER PRICING

As noted, one of the developments relative to global marketing is the tendency of multinational companies to develop manufacturing and marketing subsidiaries in foreign countries. Depending on the relative advantages, a multinational company (MNC) might produce the products at home and export them to foreign markets, or they might produce the products in foreign countries for sale in the producing country, or they might produce in a foreign country for sale in the home country or other countries.

There are many reasons for considering a multinational operation, including (1) improving competitive position in current markets, (2) opening new markets, (3) increasing profits, (4) minimizing the effects of tariffs or import quota restrictions, (5) obtaining better raw material sources, (6) reducing production costs, particularly in low–labor-cost countries, and (7) minimizing tax obligations. However, to expand worldwide, a firm's management must take a global perspective of all the firm's operations. Each subsidiary must be treated as a separate profit center, and divisional managers are expected to coordinate all aspects of the firm's operations in domestic and international markets.

Subsidiary managers need to have the capability to make decisions that allow them to maximize the profits their operations contribute to the MNC. That is, such managers need to be able to decide what products to produce and sell in their markets, what prices to charge their customers as well as other subsidiaries of the MNC, what resources to acquire, etc. In this way the manager is held accountable for the relative success of the subsidiary being managed. However, delegating this authority creates an important dilemma for the MNC. When a product is transferred from one subsidiary or division to another, what price should be used for the transfer? Should the transfer price be the prevailing world market price? Should the transfer be at full cost, variable cost, cost plus some markup, or opportunity cost?

A *transfer price* is the price charged by the selling department, division, or subsidiary for a product or service to another buying department, division, or subsidiary of the same organization. There are several traditional methods for determining a transfer price. By using one of the cost methods (full, variable, or cost plus), the product can be transferred at either actual or standard costs. By using the market price method, the transfer price is that which a significant external party pays for similar quantities of the product. A negotiated transfer price is determined by a bargaining process between the buying and selling divisions. The choice of the appropriate transfer pricing method should consider the effect the method has on the firm's overall profit level, how well it allows for an evaluation of subsidiaries and their managers, its effect on the decision making of top management, and the degree to which it promotes autonomy for the subsidiary or division.

International transfer pricing occurs when the buying and selling divisions are in different countries. Moving products across national borders creates additional complexities that need to be considered. One of the important issues is the taxes to be paid to both the exporting country and the importing country. For example, suppose that a firm has a subsidiary in country A with a low corporate income tax and a subsidiary in country B with a high income tax structure. Setting a low transfer price for products transferred from the subsidiary in country B to country A will lower the MNC's tax liability. However, national tax authorities, being aware of such possibilities, may attempt to restrict such options. A second problem arises when a country restricts the movement of cash from its borders. Such a situation may require multiple transfers in order to get the subsidiary's profits into the MNC's home country.

A third complication is the existence of high import duties, tariffs, or custom fees. A subsidiary can reduce the MNC's import duties by lowering the transfer price when exporting to a subsidiary in a high-tariff country. Because of the possibility of firms reducing their tax and tariff payments through transfer pricing, governments watch such activities very carefully.

To develop an appropriate international transfer pricing policy, it is important that the transfer pricing policy[21]

1 Allow for proper profit measurement of the subsidiary or division's operations
2 Provide correct information as a guide to top-level management decisions
3 Lead to an increase in the firm's overall profit rate
4 Motivate divisional or subsidiary managers to become as efficient as possible and to maximize their contributions to the corporation's overall profits
5 Minimize international transaction costs by minimizing tax liabilities, tariff obligations, unfavorable exchange rates, and conflict with governmental agencies in all countries

As with any pricing policy, a transfer pricing policy should be developed with specific behavioral and profit objectives in mind. Such a policy must be flexible but at the same time have a solid analytical basis.

SUMMARY

This chapter has extended the discussion of developing profitable pricing strategies and tactics to areas that have not received much attention. Even though services

[21]Wagdy M. Abdallah, *International Transfer Pricing Policies* (New York: Quorum Books, 1989).

have become dominant in the U.S. economy, there has been relatively little discussion of appropriate pricing methods. In earlier sections of this book some of the principles were applied to services. For example, contingency value pricing for an engineering consulting firm was developed in Chap. 5. The pricing of hotel rooms was discussed in Chap. 13, as was yield management used by both airlines and hotels. Additional issues of service pricing were developed in this chapter. However, the underlying pricing principles remain the same, whether the service provider is profit oriented or is a not-for-profit organization.

These principles will be summarized in Chap. 20, but as should be apparent from the perspective developed in this book, pricing needs to be carefully developed by all organizations, regardless of profit motivation. There is a definite need to move from tradition as a basis for setting prices to a careful analysis of the customers being served, their value perceptions and reasons for purchasing, the organization's relevant costs of serving these customers, the organization's pricing objectives, and the organization's competitive market position. Also, service organizations, like the financial and educational service institutions discussed in this chapter, need to carefully consider unbundling their service offerings and to be more aware that they are providing multiple service lines to different price/market segments. An important reminder is that price competition does not mean simply meeting or beating lower prices of competitive offerings. Following a price reduction strategy as a means of competing has some very restrictive requirements for being successful (see Chaps. 8 and 11). Unless these price reductions are focused and offered to specific price-sensitive markets, the net result is likely to be less profits than before or less revenue than is needed to cover operational costs. Focusing on the value–price relationship of service offerings rather than simply minimizing the price charged will be of more long-run significance.

Finally, issues of export pricing in international markets and transfer pricing were briefly discussed. The underlying principles of pricing for export are the same as those prescribed for domestic product and service pricing, although there are additional complexities in marketing in foreign countries to be considered.

DISCUSSION QUESTIONS

1 Summarize the unique differences between producing and marketing
   a Services as opposed to products.
   b Products in domestic markets as opposed to foreign markets.
   c Products for other divisions or subsidiaries of a firm.
2 Using the differences developed in the answer to Question 1, explain the implications for developing pricing strategies and prices for services, for export marketing, and for interdivisional product transfers.
3 What are the similarities of pricing products and services and pricing for export as opposed to the differences developed in the answer to Question 2?
4 Go to a bank or other financial institution and obtain information on all of the services the institution provides to its customers and the various prices, fees, charges, or balance requirements associated with these services. Are any services bundled for a specific package or bundle price?

5 What are the various fees that students pay as a part of their billing to attend your college or university? Are there any additional fees, e.g., to graduate or to use the placement service? If not, do you think there should be fees that are user-oriented rather than simply across-the-board flat fees for all students? What do you think of differential tuition for in-state vs. out-of-state students in public universities and colleges?

6 Write a research report on the implications for pricing of the trade agreement between the United States and Canada or of the unified European economy by 1992.

7 Write a research report on the pricing strategies and practices of Japanese firms.

SUGGESTED READINGS

Abdallah, Wagdy M.: *International Transfer Pricing Policies* (New York: Quorum Books, 1989).

Benke, Ralph L., Jr., and James Don Edwards: *Transfer Pricing: Techniques and Uses* (New York: National Association of Accountants, 1980).

Cavusgil, S. Tamer: "Unraveling the Mystique of Export Pricing," *Business Horizons,* 31 (May–June 1988), 54–63.

Conant, Jeffrey S., Michael P. Mokwa, and John J. Burnett: "Pricing and Performance in Health Maintenance Organizations: A Strategic Management Perspective," *Journal of Health Care Marketing,* 9 (March 1989), 25–36.

Dearden, John: "Cost Accounting Comes to Service Industries," *Harvard Business Review,* 56 (September–October 1978), 132–140.

Frank, Victor H., Jr.: "Living with Price Controls Abroad," *Harvard Business Review,* 62 (March–April 1984), 137–142.

Guiltinan, Joseph P.: "A Conceptual Framework for Pricing Consumer Services," in Mary Jo Bitner and Lawrence A. Crosby (eds.), *Designing a Winning Service Strategy* (Chicago: American Marketing Association, 1989), pp. 11–15.

Johnson, Robert W.: "Pricing of Bank Card Services," *Journal of Retail Banking,* 1 (June 1979), 16–22.

Litten, Larry H. (ed.): *Issues in Pricing Undergraduate Education: New Directions for Institutional Research* (San Francisco: Jossey-Bass, No. 42, June 1984).

Moebs, G. Michael, and Eva Moebs: *Pricing Financial Services* (Homewood, Ill.: Dow Jones–Irwin, 1986).

Monroe, Kent B.: "The Pricing of Services," in Carol Congram and Margaret Friedman (eds.), *The Handbook of Services Marketing* (New York: AMACOM, 1990).

Nease, Catherine Bond: "A Positive Pricing Strategy for ATMs," *Bank Marketing,* February 1989, pp. 26–29.

Samiee, Saeed: "Pricing in Marketing Strategies of U.S.- and Foreign-Based Firms," *Journal of Business Research,* 15 (February 1987), 17–30.

Shay, Robert P.: "Bank Credit Card Pricing: Is the Market Working?" *Journal of Retail Banking,* 9 (Spring 1987), 26–32.

Walters, Peter G. P.: "A Framework for Export Pricing Decisions," *Journal of Global Marketing,* 2, No. 3 (1989), 95–111.

CHAPTER 19

PRICING DECISION MODELS

During the 1980s, a relatively large number of pricing models were developed by researchers in marketing. Coupled with the behavioral pricing research reviewed in Chap. 3, these models have contributed to a new excitement in pricing research. While great strides have been made, considerably more progress is possible. One of the objectives of this chapter is to suggest necessary model development and validation to continue the progress made over the past decade.

In previous reviews of pricing model development and the commentaries on these reviews, criticism has been offered and suggestions have been made to further model development in pricing.[1] To help assess the progress that has been made as well as prescribing further research efforts, it is useful first to review the nature of these previous assessments of model development in pricing.

The 1978 review by Monroe and Della Bitta found serious deficiencies in pricing models. Primarily, the assumptions of most models were neither clearly specified nor realistic. This problem seemed to stem from the historical reliance on the precepts of classical economics, particularly in terms of buyer behavior. Also, the information

---

[1]Previous reviews on pricing decision models include Kent B. Monroe and Albert J. Della Bitta, "Models for Pricing Decisions," *Journal of Marketing Research,* 15 (August 1978), 413–428; Thomas Nagle, "Economic Foundations for Pricing," *Journal of Business,* 57 (January 1984, pt. 2), S3–S26; Vithala R. Rao, "Pricing Research in Marketing: The State of the Art," *Journal of Business,* 57 (January 1984, pt. 2), S39–S60; and Kent B. Monroe and Tridib Mazumdar, "Pricing-Decision Models: Recent Developments and Research Opportunities," in Timothy M. Devinney (ed.), *Issues in Pricing: Theory and Research* (Lexington, Mass.: Lexington Books, 1988), pp. 361–388. Commentaries on the Nagle and Rao reviews also appeared in the special January issue of the *Journal of Business* by Chakravarthi Narasimhan and Artur Raviv on Nagles' review, and by Shmuel S. Oren and John R. Hauser on Rao's review. This chapter is based, in part, on the Monroe and Mazumdar review cited here.

required to implement or empirically validate these models included detailed knowledge of the firm's demand curve and its elasticity as well as its cost structure. Finally, the underlying relationships often were not clearly specified, and most models did not take into account existing research evidence on buyers' use of price information.

By 1984, a number of positive developments were noted by Rao, particularly in the area of new-product pricing models in a dynamic framework. Nevertheless, formidable problems associated with empirical validation of the models remained. Concern was also expressed that recent behavioral evidence was not incorporated in the structure of these models. Recent research on pricing was characterized as disjointed, and a call for practical research on pricing decisions was made. On this latter point, it was suggested that a good description of pricing practices would be beneficial to the development of better pricing theory. Other areas needing research included product-line pricing, the role of price in consumer choice, competitive pricing models, and empirical validation of pricing models.

Comments on Rao's review clarified some of the distinctions between a marketing approach and an economic approach to developing pricing models. An important issue concerns viewing price as a decision variable (marketing) rather than as a given (economics) (see Chap. 2). Moreover, the models from economics rarely are validated or calibrated for the acquisition of empirical data. Caution was advised against uncritically adopting economic concepts, methods, and assumptions for the development of marketing-oriented pricing models. In particular, it was prescribed that the assumptions of economics be scrutinized and adapted in light of empirical evidence amassed in marketing and consumer behavior.

A review by Nagle warned against expecting too much from economic theory as a basis for pricing models. Simply, economic pricing models are abstractions that hold many real variables constant and, consequently, rarely provide useful prescriptions or descriptions of pricing practice by either buyers or sellers. As developed in Chap. 2, economic theory is more concerned with the behavior of aggregates or markets, and particularly how persistent and widespread behavior leads to certain stable results called equilibrium. However, some recent developments in economic theory that were discussed in Chap. 2 offer useful insights for pricing theory.

The commentaries on Nagle's review offered additional suggestions on the use of economics in pricing research. Both commentaries pointed out the relative newness of these approaches and the limitations that currently exist in terms of useful contributions. These commentaries clearly focus on the economic foundations for pricing, but a strict economic orientation to the development of pricing models ignores other relevant and important foundations for developing pricing theory. Economic concepts and analytical methods can be useful, but at the same time the trap of overreliance on the mathematical elegance of the structure at the expense of real progress in knowledge development must be avoided.

As indicated, numerous pricing models have been developed in recent years. These models have attempted to capture the dynamic interrelationships between cost- and demand-related factors, the effects of competitive actions, the effects of price promotion and deals, the role of price in individual choice decisions, and the relationship of price with other marketing mix variables. However, despite these efforts, practitioners and academic researchers continue to experience difficulty in using and evaluating the models.

This chapter will present some criticisms of the present state of pricing models; nevertheless, the overall purpose is to encourage the development of pricing models. A constructive way to accomplish this goal is to identify a few selected areas in pricing that have received attention, isolate their underlying theoretical assumptions, and delineate the scope and boundaries of their applicability.

We begin with a general framework for pricing decisions. Some of the important factors influencing the pricing decision and the interrelationships among these factors will be identified. Then a classification scheme will be developed to categorize the various pricing models according to their objectives and variables. The chapter will then review the models in this book and several other selected models and offer a critique of their premises and assumptions. Finally, an agenda for future pricing model research will be offered.

A CONCEPTUAL FRAMEWORK FOR PRICING DECISIONS

A major challenge in making sound pricing decisions lies in resolving the complex interactions among the internal and external factors that need to be considered. If one accepts the importance of customers' perceptions, then the selection of the pricing strategy should flow directly from demand-related factors like customers' perceptions of value, existence of distinct price/market segments based on buyers' preferences and price sensitivities, and demand interrelationships among multiple product offerings. Guided by an overall marketing and pricing strategy, the firm should develop a set of feasible pricing alternatives, taking into account cost-related factors, anticipated competitive reactions, prevalent trade practices in the distribution channel, and corporate objectives within a legal and public policy framework.

Setting prices is complex and difficult not only because of the large number of variables influencing the decision, but also because of the interrelationships among them. The difficulty these interrelationships present when specifying and estimating cost and demand functions was demonstrated in a value-maximizing model.[2] In particular, the difficulties are apparent when (1) previous period cost and demand functions enter the model endogenously and (2) competing products and the marketing mix variables of other products in the line influence the impact of the product's price. What this model illustrates is the need to partition the complex decision problem into a number of smaller problems in order to obtain reasonable mathematical solutions. Thus, no single modeling effort can be expected to address the entire decision problem. Rather, each pricing model should be evaluated in terms of its ability to formulate and solve specific pricing issues. The next section classifies pricing models on the basis of their objectives and the variables considered relevant for the particular pricing problem.

[2]Rao, ibid.

CLASSIFICATION FRAMEWORK

Despite considerable diversity in previous modeling efforts, patterns emerge in terms of model objectives and variables included. The pricing models can be broadly classified into six categories. A brief description of each category is provided here.

Single-period pricing models are concerned with solving specific marketing problems with an objective of selecting a price that maximizes single-period profits. Although a number of diverse models fit this category, their distinctive feature is the assumption that the variables of interest do not change over time.

On the other hand, the *dynamic pricing models* have explicitly examined changing cost and demand functions over time. These two time-dependent functions are combined to develop a pricing strategy that maximizes the present value of the firm's profit stream. Within this framework, various models have been proposed that incorporate the effects of competitive entry, product obsolescence, and situations where the product's value changes with increased adoption.

The *price promotion/discount models* primarily have treated the issue as an inventory management problem. In these models, the sellers' concern is to dispose of inventory with the help of price inducements and the buyers' objective is to balance the savings of buying on deal against the additional time and storage costs.

The *product-line pricing models* examine the cost and demand interdependencies of products in the line in order to maximize the firm's total profits. The major variables of interest include the own-price and cross-price elasticities among products on the demand side and the sharing patterns of input resources on the cost side. In this classification a variety of models incorporating nonlinear price–volume schedules and the effects of price differentials have been proposed.

The models capturing the *interaction between price and other marketing mix variables* have received limited attention. In general, these models have examined how product characteristics, advertising, product warranties, channel competition and structure, and sales force pricing authority affect pricing decisions and profits.

The role of price in *individual-choice decisions* is an area that has generated considerable interest. The basic issues being addressed by researchers include whether price enters at the value (utility) formation stage or serves as an external constraint on buyers' income. Researchers have also examined how buyers' reference prices are formed and how these reference prices affect purchase decisions.

In the next section, each of these modeling areas is examined in greater detail.

REVIEW OF SELECTED PRICING MODELS[3]

Single-Period Models

The classical condition for maximizing profits has been developed in microeconomics as

---

[3]A number of pricing models are reviewed. However, because the review is brief, the original papers should be considered for a more thorough understanding.

$$MR = \left(1 + \frac{1}{e_p}\right)p^* = MC \qquad (19\text{-}1)$$

where MR = marginal revenue
   MC = marginal cost
   e_p = price elasticity of demand
   p^* = price at which a monopolist maximizes single-period profits

By rearranging terms, the optimal price for a monopolist is

$$p^* = \left(\frac{e_p}{1 + e_p}\right) MC \qquad (19\text{-}2)$$

Despite the apparent simplicity of this formulation, its application is restricted for at least three reasons. First, the most critical reason is the difficulty in formulating and validating the necessary demand and cost functions. Second, this optimality criterion is restricted to a product that is price elastic, i.e., price elasticity is less than -1 (see Chap. 2). Third, the criterion does not consider changes in demand and costs over time, nor does it include the effects of other marketing mix variables.

Nevertheless, researchers have used this basic maximizing principle to analyze and model different pricing problems. Kunreuther and Richard compared the impact of centralized and decentralized pricing and inventory decision making on retail store profits.[4] In a centralized decision system, the pricing and purchase decisions are made simultaneously, whereas in a decentralized system, the decisions are made sequentially (i.e., the pricing decision assumes zero inventory costs). The centralized system was shown to be more profitable when demand was price elastic, order sizes were small, and ordering costs were relatively high.

A Bayesian decision approach led to the conclusion that the price at which expected demand equals quantity produced at the minimum average cost maximizes the firm's expected profits.[5] To apply this model, subjective probabilities are assigned to different price–quantity combinations. The model assumes the market is relatively free of competition, facilitating the revision of the prices as suggested by the model.

Another model for low-priced, frequently purchased products uses the concepts of perceived value and upper price threshold to determine consumers' brand switching behavior in response to simultaneous competitors' price changes.[6] The model has two assumptions that need to be mentioned. First, buyers are assumed to be able to detect any price change and to alter their purchase behaviors so long as the new price does not exceed their perceived value. Current behavioral price research raises the

   [4]H. Kunreuther and J. F. Richard, "Optimal Pricing and Inventory Decisions for Non-Seasonal Items," *Econometrica,* 39, No. 1 (1971), 173–175.
   [5]J. Braverman, "A Decision Theoretic Approach to Pricing," *Decision Sciences,* 2 (January 1972), 1–15.
   [6]Hani I. Mesak and Richard C. Clelland, "A Competitive Pricing Model," *Management Science,* 25 (November 1979), 1057–1068.

question of whether buyers are able to remember previous prices paid for frequently purchased goods (see Chap. 3). The ability to detect price changes presumes that buyers know previous prices paid. Moreover, how much of a price difference is necessary before buyers shift their purchase behavior (price differential threshold) is a behavioral issue not addressed in the model. Second, the model assumes that only price changes induce buyers to switch brands. Nonetheless, the researchers show that their competitive pricing model had better predictive accuracy than an alternative model used by the company.

Several models consider the issue of price segmentation and price discrimination. A model extending the traditional segmented pricing approach allows buyers in a high-price segment to move to a low-price segment by incurring a transaction cost.[7] When market segments are not perfectly sealed, it was shown that a price differentiation strategy would still be profitable when buyers in the high-price market segment incur high transaction costs when shifting to a low-price market. (See discussion on gray markets in Chap. 15.) Conversely, when these transaction costs are relatively low, a price differentiation strategy may be ineffective. By using this model, it is also possible to determine the amount of leakage from the high-price market to the low-price market before a price differentiation strategy becomes unprofitable.

Another model, although dynamic in nature, examines the necessary static conditions for optimality when a market can be segmented in terms of desired quality and levels of market penetration.[8] After assuming different price sensitivities of buyers in different quality segments and assuming one dimension of quality, an optimal pricing equation is developed. This pricing equation assumes the buyers' objective is to maximize their consumer surplus (see Chap. 2) subject to the market penetration level. In essence, the model assumes that buyers are price conscious regardless of their quality orientation, possibly a contradictory assumption.

A third model estimates optimal retailer markups when buyers can be segmented in terms of purchase frequency and price consciousness.[9] Although the authors use the term price awareness, the more appropriate term is price consciousness (see Chap. 3). Three critical assumptions about buyer behavior are made:

1 Prices of frequently purchased products are more likely to be remembered.
2 Buyers use these remembered prices to infer overall store price levels.
3 Shoppers choose stores on the basis of "low-price" image.

Given these assumptions, frequently purchased products should be priced with relatively lower markups to maximize store patronage. Shoppers who are not price conscious are presumed to be convenience oriented. Thus, items purchased frequently by convenience-oriented shoppers should have higher markups.

---

[7]Eitan Gerstner and Duncan Holthausen, "Profitable Pricing When Market Segments Overlap," *Marketing Science,* 5 (Winter 1986), 20–36.

[8]Stephen A. Smith, "New Product Pricing in Quality Sensitive Markets," *Marketing Science,* 5 (Winter 1986), 70–87.

[9]Thomas T. Nagle and Kenneth Novak, "The Roles of Segmentation and Awareness in Explaining Variations in Price Markups," in Timothy M. Devinney (ed.), *Issues in Pricing: Theory and Research* (Lexington, Mass.: Lexington Books, 1988, pp. 313–332.

There are two major difficulties with the structure of these assumptions. First, research on patronage behavior suggests that shoppers can be typed into other categories as well. Thus, a segmentation strategy based on either price-oriented (economy segment) or convenience shoppers will not tap a major portion of the market. Second, research on shoppers' ability to remember prices suggests that this ability even for frequently purchased goods is not as high as the model assumes.

The authors' attempt to validate their model empirically underscores the difficulty faced by researchers attempting to validate their pricing models. They were able to use actual price, cost, and other relevant store data from one grocery chain in one area. These data were supplemented by aggregate brand usage data from Simmons Market Research Bureau. Another difficulty they encountered was in operationalizing the concept of buyer price sensitivity. Differences in buyer price sensitivities were represented by a set of demographic and product use variables and not measured directly. Previous research on buyers' ability to remember prices has not been successful in relating demographics or use to the ability to remember prices (see Chap. 3). Despite these difficulties, it is important to encourage modelers to face the very necessary step of empirically validating their models.

Dynamic Pricing Models

Pricing over the life of a product has generated considerable attention from researchers in recent years. The two major concepts used in life-cycle pricing are (1) diffusion of innovation to capture the dynamics of demand and (2) the experience curve to model cost dynamics.

Following the theory of adoption of innovations, an early model developed a quadratic sales function, the parameters of which express the rate of innovation adoption, imitative effects, and the total market potential.[10] Following these initial efforts, the next model combined the experience curve concept with diffusion of innovation for a multiperiod pricing model.[11] A test of this model using six consumer durable products suggested that the single-period profit maximization rule will not result in optimizing the profit stream of a product over its life cycle.[12]

These earlier models were extended in two important ways.[13] First, repeat-purchase situations were considered to apply to nondurable products. Second, the firm's objective was assumed to be maximization of the net present value of the profit stream. The optimal multiperiod price can be expressed as

[10]Frank M. Bass, "A New Product Growth Model of Consumer Durables," *Management Science,* 15 (January 1969), 215–227.

[11]Bruce Robinson and Chet Lakhani, "Dynamic Price Models for New-Product Planning," *Management Science,* 21 (June 1975), 1113–1122.

[12]Frank M. Bass, "The Relationship Between Diffusion Rates, Experience Curves, and Demand Elasticities for Consumer Durable Technical Innovations," *Journal of Business,* 53 (July 1980), 551–567.

[13]Robert J. Dolan and Abel P. Jeuland, "Experience Curves and Dynamic Demand Models: Implications for Optimal Pricing Strategies," *Journal of Marketing,* 45 (Winter 1981), 52–62; Abel P. Jeuland and Robert J. Dolan, "An Aspect of New Product Planning: Dynamic Pricing," in A. Zoltners (ed.), *TIMS Studies in the Management Sciences,* Special issue on marketing planning models (Amsterdam: North Holland, 18 (1982), 1–21.

$$P^*_{(t)} = {}^*P_{m(t)} + dP_{(t)} \qquad (19\text{-}3)$$

where $P^*_{m(t)}$ = optimal price, from Eq. (19-2)
   $dP_{(t)}$ = an adjustment expressed as a function of the price elasticity, innovative and imitative effects, market potential, and discount rate

A number of interesting implications arise from this optimal price solution:

1 For a single time period, the solution is identical to the classic solution given in Eq. (19-2). In such a situation, the optimal prices decline continuously over time following the experience curve.
2 When future profits are not discounted three situations are important:
   a For durable goods where the imitation effect is important for adoption, the optimal price path follows a pattern of low introductory price, increasing to a peak high price, and declining thereafter.
   b For durable goods where the imitation effect is unimportant, an introductory high price (skimming) followed by a monotonic decline in price is optimal.
   c For nondurable goods with frequent repeat purchases, the optimal price path would be an introductory low price (penetration) followed by a monotonically increasing price.
3 As the discount rate increases, the present-value factor becomes less important. Eventually, for a discount rate of infinity, the optimal multiperiod pricing strategy is identical to the myopic optimal solution.

Other researchers have offered several extensions and modifications of the model. One model examined two different effects of adoption on demand.[14] First, following adoption, demand increases due to strong word-of-mouth effects. In this situation, the optimal pricing strategy is similar to strategy 2a above. However, when increases in adoption cause market saturation and a subsequent decrease in demand (for durable goods with a finite market size), the optimal strategy is 2b above.

In an attempt to validate the dynamic pricing model, a computer simulation led to the conclusion that multiperiod prices should decline over the product's life and will always be less than the single-period optimal price.[15]

This brief overview is indicative of considerable advancements made in dynamic pricing models. However, additional research is necessary to solve some difficult problems. First, the dynamic pricing model needs to be validated and the parameters estimated. For a truly innovative product, the task of estimating eventual market potential, innovative and imitative effects, and repeat-purchase rates is extremely difficult, if not impossible. The development of some realistic measures of these variables will be necessary for this task.

Although it is convenient to assume a monopolistic market structure, competition has a strong impact on pricing over a product's life cycle. Recently, researchers have attempted to grapple with the competition effect. A comparison of skimming and

[14]Shlomo Kalish, "Monopolist Pricing with Dynamic Demand and Production Cost," *Marketing Science,* 2 (Spring 1983), 135–159.
[15]Frank M. Bass and Alain V. Bultez, "A Note on Optimal Strategic Pricing of Technological Innovations," *Marketing Science,* 1 (Fall 1982), 371–378.

penetration strategies in a duopolistic (two-seller) market illustrated the usefulness of simulation techniques and a game-theoretic approach; however, the results were not generalizable.[16] Using a non–zero-sum differential game, another model developed an optimal pricing and advertising policy for an oligopolist.[17] Another model, also using differential game theory, analyzed the dynamics of price and market share over the life of a product.[18] The results suggest that with the experience effect operating, and with a decline of price sensitivity of buyers coupled with a declining growth rate of demand, a strategy of maximizing sales volume in the introductory stage gives a firm a competitive advantage. Another model assumed a duopolistic market situation and applied game theory to examine the use of penetration pricing (introductory pricing strategy) to forestall competitor entry.[19] The model suggests that a monopolist may delay competitor entry by starting with a low price (and assumed high output levels), and then increasing price over the product's life while reducing output levels. Of course, what this monopolist does with the initial capacity that required a substantial investment for the introductory period is not addressed by the model.

A third issue to be resolved is the assumption of constant price elasticity over the life of the product. Given the empirical research on this issue, the need to incorporate changing price sensitivities over the life cycle is a necessary complexity.[20]

Although it is evident that much additional work needs to be done, the research on dynamic pricing models has made substantial progress. It is clear that the foregoing models still have not considered the dynamics of buyer behavior over a product's life cycle. For example, for frequently purchased products, behavioral research has yielded evidence that an introductory low price followed by a price increase may lead to a substantial dampening of demand over time (see Chap. 3). Such a pricing strategy may actually enhance buyers' price sensitivities and reduce market potential. Moreover, for durable products there is the possibility that multiple price/market segments with different price sensitivities and different market potentials exist.

Price Promotion and Discount Models

In recent years, manufacturers and retailers have made increasing use of coupons, rebates, short-term price reductions, and free samples to stimulate short-term demand for their products. Despite the popularity of these price deals, it is not at all

[16]Darral G. Clarke and Robert J. Dolan, "A Simulation Analysis of Alternative Pricing Strategies for Dynamic Environments," *Journal of Business,* 57 (January 1984, pt. 2), S179–S200.

[17]Gerald L. Thompson and Jinn-Tsair Teng, "Optimal Pricing and Advertising Policies for New Product Oligopoly Models," *Marketing Science,* 3 (Spring 1984), 148–168.

[18]Birger Wernerfelt, "The Dynamics of Prices and Market Shares over the Product Life Cycle," *Management Science,* 31 (August 1985), 928–939.

[19]Ram C. Rao, "Strategic Pricing of Durables under Competition," in Timothy M. Devinney (ed.), *Issues in Pricing: Theory and Research* (Lexington, Mass.: Lexington Books, 1988), pp. 197–217.

[20]Gary L. Lilien and Eunsang Yoon, "An Exploratory Analysis of the Dynamic Behavior of Price Elasticity over the Product Life Cycle: An Empirical Analysis of Industrial Chemical Products," in Timothy M. Devinney (ed.), *Issues in Pricing: Theory and Research* (Lexington, Mass.: Lexington Books, 1988), pp. 261–287.

clear that a majority of them are profitable. As we saw in Chap. 15, a number of perplexing issues must be resolved if an optimal discount structure is to be developed.

An early model handled the discount decision as an inventory management problem of the seller.[21] The seller's objective was to minimize the opportunity costs for excessive quantity sold at a reduced price and lost sales due to merchandise being unavailable for sale. The model determined the optimal quantity to be offered on deal and the optimal size of the discount. Another approach used a brand-switching model when competing brands offer temporary price reductions.[22] There were two price/market segments (price-conscious and quality-conscious buyers) and two brands (private and premium brands). The model developed a schedule of when to promote, depending on competitive reaction to maximize incremental sales revenue.

Price promotion models took a different perspective by considering households as production units. In this view, households are postulated to include the value of their time in their buying decisions. Thus, buyers are postulated to make cost–benefit assessments and evaluate the benefits of the deal against the time and storage costs incurred when buying on deal. One approach combined both the consumers' and retailer's perspectives to develop a comprehensive model.[23] At the core of the model lies an assumption that the inventory costs are transferred from the retailer to customers. The optimal quantity to purchase on deal was determined to be proportional to the magnitude of the deal and the consumption rate but inversely related to buyers' holding costs. Also, the optimal purchase period was positively related to the deal magnitude but negatively related to buyers' holding costs.

In the retailer model, the retailer's objective is to minimize total cost per inventory cycle. Based on the optimal solutions, the following are implied:

1 The deal magnitude increases with the retailer's setup cost and buyers' holding costs but decreases with demand and retailer's holding costs.

2 The retailer's optimal reorder time is directly proportional to the deal magnitude but inversely proportional to buyers' holding costs.

3 Dealing costs increase with demand, setup costs, and retailer's holding costs.

4 Dealing frequency is positively related to rate of demand and holding costs of both sellers and buyers but inversely related to retailer's setup cost.

A more recent model develops the conditions for optimal discounts and frequencies for a monopolist selling to two market segments, loyal and nonloyal.[24] The conclusions indicate that a product with a greater share of loyal customers should offer lower discounts less frequently. Assuming loyalty for an established product

[21]David A. Goodman and Kavin W. Moody, "Determining Optimum Price Promotion Quantities," *Journal of Marketing,* 34 (October 1970), 31–39.

[22]Yoram Kinberg, Amber Rao, and Melvin Shakun, "A Mathematical Model for Price Promotions," *Management Science,* 20 (February 1974), 948–959.

[23]Robert C. Blattberg, Gary D. Epen, and Joshua Lieberman, "A Theoretical and Empirical Evaluation of Price Deals for Consumer Nondurables," *Journal of Marketing,* 45 (Winter 1981), 104–115.

[24]Chakravarthi Narasimhan, "A Model of Discounting for Repeat Sales," in Timothy M. Devinney (ed.), *Issues in Pricing: Theory and Research* (Lexington, Mass.: Lexington Books, 1988), pp. 171–192.

develops over time, a new product would need more frequent and deeper discounts. It seems that this observation would generalize to products that have low market share (low loyalty segment) as well.

In the past few years considerable progress has been made in the development of price promotion and discount models. However, additional opportunities exist for understanding buyers' behaviors and reactions to deals and discounts. As developed in Chaps. 3 and 4, research in the area of comparative price advertising, framing, and reference prices would provide additional insights for model developers.

Product-Line Pricing Models

There are several reasons why prescriptions for single-product pricing may not generalize to a multiple-product situation. First, products in the line may be related on the demand side (substitutes or complements). Second, there may be cost interdependencies, such as shared production, distribution, and marketing expenditures. Third, several products may be sold as a bundle, thereby creating complementarity among them. Fourth, the price of a product in the line may influence buyers' subjective evaluations of other products. Finally, there may be some overriding corporate objective that influences prices of other products (e.g., in a regulated industry or a not-for-profit organization).

Although interest in single-product pricing models has been predominant, there have been some efforts to model the multiple-product problem. An early model examined the interdependencies of prices, advertising, and distribution among brands in a product-line context.[25] Using store audit data for three product lines of related, frequently purchased goods, a procedure for measuring the own- and cross-price elasticities for each marketing variable was developed.

A single-period profit-maximizing pricing solution under demand and cost interdependencies among products in the line was developed.[26] However, the model is restricted by three assumptions. First, the linear cost function precludes scale economies in production, distribution, or marketing. Second, the fixed-cost components are separable, making the model a maximizing contribution to profits model. Third, the effects of competition are excluded.

Another model examined the interactions between customers and retail store when several products carried by the store are interrelated.[27] By maximizing the store's single-period profit function subject to consumers receiving a given level of utility, the optimal prices are determined by the products' own- and cross-price elasticities, the nature of demand, and the gross margins. No empirical evidence was provided for the validity of the solution.

Three nonlinear stochastic sales response functions were considered in the devel-

---

[25]Glen Urban, "A Mathematical Model Approach to Product Line Decisions," *Journal of Marketing Research,* 6 (February 1969), 40–47.

[26]Monroe and Della Bitta, op. cit.

[27]John D. C. Little and Jeremy F. Shapiro, "A Theory for Pricing Nonfeatured Products in Supermarkets," *Journal of Business,* 53 (July 1980, pt. 2), S199–S209.

opment of an optimal pricing model for demand-related products.[28] The optimal solution is similar in structure to the expression in Eq. (19-2) for a deterministic demand situation:

$$P_i^* = \left(\frac{e_i}{1 + e_i}\right) MC_i - \left(\frac{e_{ij}}{1 + e_i}\right) * \left[\frac{(Q_j \ (P_j - MC_j)}{Q_i)}\right] \qquad (19\text{-}4)$$

The substantive implication of Eq. (19-4) is that the optimal price of a product in a demand-interdependent product line is the single-product optimal price [the first expression in Eq. (19-4)] corrected by an adjustment factor (the second expression in the equation). The adjustment factor is a function of the product's own-price and cross-price elasticities, demand for the products in the line, and the price and marginal costs of the other products in the line. For a stochastic sales response function, the adjustment factor is also dependent on the variances of the disturbance terms. When tracking UPC scanner data for the sale of eggs over 25 weeks, the most realistic estimates were obtained when cross-elasticities were included in the model.

Saghafi has pointed out several shortcomings of previous product-line models:[29]

1 The firm's objective is assumed to be profit maximization.
2 Average production costs are assumed to be constant.
3 It is assumed that products are in a product line.
4 It is assumed that the firm is always operating in the elastic portion of the demand curve.

For a traditional single-period profit-maximizing firm operating under economies of scale, it was determined that the firm would be better off if it produced one product rather than the two substitute products. However, if the products were complements, then both products should be produced, but the products need not be operating in the elastic portion of the demand curve. If the firm is a return-to-cost maximizer, and if the products are demand independent, then the product line should be produced. It was also shown that under specific objectives, regardless of demand interdependencies, a simultaneous product-line pricing strategy should be adopted. As in the other models reviewed here, it is apparent that a necessary piece of information for pricing a product line is the own- and cross-price elasticities for the products, which is not always easy to find.

Price and Other Elements of the Marketing Mix

Although price interacts with the other elements of the marketing mix to influence demand, few efforts have been made to model these interactions. There are some

[28]David Reibstein and Hubert Gatignon, "Optimal Product Line Pricing: The Influence of Elasticities and Cross-Elasticities," *Journal of Marketing Research,* 21 (August 1984), 259–267.

[29]Massoud Saghafi, "Product Line Pricing under Different Firm-Specific Objectives," Working Paper, University of Southern California, Los Angeles, 1987.

models based on the interaction of product and advertising with price, and, more recently, the interaction of distribution with price has been modeled.

Product and Price   The interrelationship between product and price has been studied using the economics perspective as well as the behavioral perspective. Within the economics paradigm, a product is viewed as a bundle of utility producing characteristics, and buyers are assumed to judge the utility of the product independent of price. Recognizing the discrete nature of product characteristics, the hedonic approach (utility producing) was introduced into the marketing literature. According to the hedonic approach, a product's price is determined by utility or satisfaction-producing characteristics. The contribution each characteristic makes to price can be estimated by a regression between prices and product characteristics. The regression equation can then be used to predict the price that people are willing to pay for different levels of various product characteristics.

By assuming a linear relationship between price and the product characteristics, the contributions of different characteristics of breakfast cereals to their prices has been demonstrated.[30] A loglinear hedonic price function has been used to explain about 70 percent of the variation in automobile prices. However, the predictive power of the hedonic approach depends primarily on the careful selection of appropriate product characteristics.[31] It is also possible that the difference between actual and hedonic prices occurs because of buyer inertia, buyers' lack of complete information, and other imperfections in the marketplace. This issue of information asymmetry between buyers and sellers was discussed in Chap. 2.

Price and Advertising   Research involving the interaction between price and advertising has raised some important managerial and public policy issues. Depending on the perspective taken, advertising serves to either increase or decrease buyers' sensitivities to price. If advertising primarily differentiates the product, then the more successfully this function is performed, the less concerned buyers become about price. The opposing perspective maintains that the increased information from advertising makes buyers more knowledgeable and therefore more price sensitive. Research on the impact of advertising on buyers' price sensitivities supports both positions. In a recent field experimental study with a frequently purchased consumer product, price elasticity decreased with increased levels of advertising.[32] It was also found that the decrease in price elasticity was more pronounced among buyers in the high price-sensitivity segment than it was for buyers with less price sensitivity.

Other researchers have developed models for optimal price and advertising strategies over time. Assuming demand to be a function of both price and advertising, a

[30]Karen J. Morgan, Edward J. Metzen, and S. R. Johnson, "An Hedonic Index for Breakfast Cereals," *Journal of Consumer Research,* 6 (June 1979), 67–75.

[31]Manoj Agarwal and Brian T. Ratchford, "Estimating Demand Functions for Product Characteristics: The Case of Automobiles," *Journal of Consumer Research,* 7 (December 1982), 249–262.

[32]Lakshman Krishnamurthi and S. P. Raj. "The Effect of Advertising on Consumer Price Sensitivity," *Journal of Marketing Research,* 22 (May 1985), 119–129.

model that maximizes the present value of the seller's profit stream was developed.[33] In this model, as well as in most of the price–advertising models, the effect of advertising is assumed to decay over time but can be replenished by current advertising. One conclusion was that maintaining a constant price and a constant level of advertising throughout the planning period is optimal.

Recently, a dynamic pricing and advertising model for a new consumer nondurable product was developed.[34] Three distinctive features of the model are worth noting. First, the initial trial is assumed to be random because of the uncertainty surrounding the product's performance. Second, the pricing and advertising decisions are assumed to be probabilistic functions of the rate of market penetration. Third, the market is segmented between triers and nontriers. The model indicates that if demand is insensitive to price, then a penetration introductory pricing strategy would be optimal only if advertising in the repeat-purchase market helps to differentiate the product. When the new customer segment is price sensitive, but this sensitivity declines as the product matures, then a penetration strategy would be preferable. A skimming strategy would be appropriate if the new market demand initially is not price sensitive, but the repeat purchase segment becomes price sensitive.

An important issue developed by this model is the price sensitivity of repeat buyers. Because sales growth is dependent on repeat purchases, the price sensitivity of this segment dominates the firm's strategy. Why would the relatively large number of triers attracted by a low introductory price become less price sensitive after trying the product? If they like the product and recognize that it offers value to them, or if advertising persuades them that the product is useful to them, then perhaps, within some range of higher prices, these buyers will continue to buy as the price increases. However, if the initial low price becomes the reference price for future purchases, then it is likely that these initial triers will become more rather than less price sensitive. Evidence from behavioral price research indicates that this lower reference price may serve to increase price sensitivity as the product's price increases (see Chaps. 3 and 4). Also, this model requires knowledge of price sensitivities prior to the product's introduction to the market, a most difficult requirement.

Price and Distribution   There has been little research on the interaction between price and distribution. One study investigated the effect of delegating pricing responsibility to the sales force.[35] The study concluded that a necessary condition for salespeople to be given pricing responsibility is for them to have better information about the selling environment than does upper management.

[33]U. P. Welam, "Optimal and Near Optimal Price and Advertising Strategies for Finite Horizons," *Management Science,* 28 (1982), 1313–1327.

[34]George E. Monahan and Kofi O. Nti, "Optimal Pricing and Advertising for New Products with Repeat Purchases," in Timothy M. Devinney (ed.), *Issues in Pricing: Theory and Research* (Lexington, Mass.: Lexington Books, 1988), pp. 145–170.

[35]Rajiv Lal, "Delegating Pricing Responsibility to the Salesforce," *Marketing Science,* 5 (Spring 1986), 159–168.

Two additional research efforts consider the interaction between price and distribution. One model examined the effects of product assortment and shopper types on a store's markup decisions.[36] The objective of the model is to study the effect of price when shoppers select an outlet before choosing a product. The underlying premise is that the price set by the store depends on the store's assortment. Implicitly, the model assumes that the existence of different price/market segments provides the store's motivation to offer an assortment of products. Moreover, the different price segments differ in the degree to which buyers are sensitive to prices.

The model develops two effects of product-line pricing. In the segmentation effect, prices are set so that buyers will perceive the prices of the different products as different. Thus, the prices must be set far enough apart to preclude buyers in a particular price/market segment from selecting a product outside the price segment. In the trading-up effect, the goal is to set prices so that buyers will not perceive that prices between products are different. (A distinction must be made between noticing that two prices are *numerically different* and perceiving that two prices are *dissimilar.*) Although the model indicates that the segmentation effect dominates the trade-up effect, this result depends on the assumption made about the relative size of the acceptable price range for each market segment.

Efforts to empirically validate the model's prediction are noteworthy, not only for the attempt but also as an illustration of the wide differences between the real world of price setting and current modeling efforts. An important finding of the empirical effort is that outlets seldom offer identical products, even when carrying the same brand. Moreover, these outlets find a variety of ways to differentiate their offerings from competitors. Another finding of interest is that the price of an item within an outlet was not significantly correlated with prices of other items in the store. This last point means that inferring the overall price level of a store on the basis of a small sample of items offered for sale may be based on an incorrect assumption.

Another model offers a framework for studying the pricing behavior of channel members under different channel structures and in a duopolistic situation.[37] The model provides a structure for understanding the motivation to vertically integrate a channel but does not consider the effect of price on final demand. In effect, the assumption that the profit-maximizing behavior of channel members causes specific market prices ignores the ability of the final buyer (the end user) to refrain from buying if the price is unacceptable. The model demonstrates the destructive nature of price cutting as a competitive reaction. Unfortunately, it is not clear that distributors in reality do recognize this point. The conclusion that it is imperative to know how pricing decisions are made in practice if we are to further the theory of price setting is an important point.

[36]Steven M. Shugan, "Pricing When Different Outlets Offer Different Assortments of Brands," in Timothy M. Devinney (ed.), *Issues in Pricing: Theory and Research* (Lexington, Mass.: Lexington Books, 1988), pp. 289–311.

[37]Steven M. Shugan and Abel P. Jeuland, "Competitive Pricing Behavior in Distribution Systems," in Timothy M. Devinney (ed.), *Issues in Pricing: Theory and Research* (Lexington, Mass.: Lexington Books, 1988), pp. 219–237.

Price and Individual Choice

The role that price plays in influencing individual purchase decisions was developed in detail in Chaps. 3 and 4. Therefore, this area will not be considered further in this chapter.

SUMMARY

As noted at the beginning of this chapter, model building in pricing has made substantial progress in the past decade. This brief and selected review has covered a range of pricing issues, many of which had not been subjected to model development prior to 1980. Moreover, the interest in pricing research, both in model development and in empirical efforts, continues to grow. These changes are welcomed and necessary if knowledge in pricing is to proceed. Nevertheless, despite notable advancements, some criticisms from previous reviews remain and need to be addressed by researchers in pricing.

The authors of the models reviewed in this chapter have been aware of the need to clarify their assumptions, although there remains room for improvement. Pricing model developers for the most part have not scrutinized traditional economic assumptions in the light of empirical evidence in marketing and consumer behavior. Thus, we find assumptions of a monopolist selling to many small buyers who are perfectly informed after one purchase. Prescriptions based on such models have no hope of being adopted either by price setters or by public policy makers. Moreover, the enormous difficulties of attempting to empirically validate such theories will lead to the models being relegated to the category of interesting intellectual exercise. Pricing necessarily must incorporate information, assumptions, and methods from the areas of economics, marketing, psychology, sociology, finance, accounting, and other disciplines as relevant to the issues under scrutiny.

A second area of concern is the low attention paid to the existing and growing base of empirical knowledge on how buyers acquire, retain in memory, and use price information. Many of the models continue to rely on the assumption that buyers have current and past price information available to them or are able to extract such information from memory without error. Further, there is the assumption that buyers are able to acquire complete information about the products' attributes with one purchase. Once it is assumed that buyers do have price information, it is also assumed that the "rational" buyer seeks to minimize the price paid, i.e., to equate the marginal utility of acquiring one more unit of the product to its price. Such assumptions may be necessary to extract optimal solutions from the model, but they do not conform to the empirical realities about buyer behavior.

Another important issue is the relative lack of empirical validation for the models that have been proposed. It is difficult to obtain data that conform to the structure of the theoretical formulation. One source of this difficulty relates to the criticisms of model development just discussed. However, another critical difficulty concerns the inability or unwillingness of business firms to permit researchers access to data that may be closer to the needs of the model being tested than retail shelf or checkout observations. To enable academic researchers to focus on the pricing issues of concern to management, management must be willing to be accessible to academic researchers and their data needs. For a variety of reasons, management traditionally has not been amenable to the needs of academic researchers in the area of pricing.

As these criticisms suggest, there are many opportunities for researchers in the area of pricing. Researchers with a behavioral orientation can investigate issues relating to how buyers acquire, remember, and use price information for evaluating product alternatives and for choosing among these alternatives. Researchers with a quantitative modeling orientation have ample opportunities to use the evidence from behavioral researchers, adapt the many important and useful concepts and theories from economics, and develop models that can help advance pricing knowledge. Researchers who are methodologically oriented need to work on the problems and issues related to empirical validation of the models. Researchers with established relationships with managers need to engage in descriptive research to provide better information about the variety of pricing environments that exist in the world of business.

The ability to solve current and future pricing problems will require (1) new attitudes toward pricing by business and academics and (2) the establishment of price research programs to provide information on (a) buyers' use of price information, (b) cost, volume, and profit implications of price decisions, and (c) an integration of price in product and market life-cycle strategies. The need for research attention to pricing is critical because pricing is an important and complex aspect of business management and buyer behavior.

DISCUSSION QUESTIONS

1 Select one of the pricing decisions discussed in Chaps. 12–15. Carefully review the nature of that decision problem. Review some recent pricing decision models for that decision problem. To what extent have these decision models captured the essence of the decision problem?

2 Select several product categories of interest, e.g., watches or sports equipment. Then visit several stores that sell this product category. Determine the brands, models, or sizes of the products in the category sold by each store. How similar are the offerings across stores, including the prices? What conclusions, if any, can you draw about the manufacturers' product-line pricing decisions? What conclusions can you draw about the ability of the manufacturers to control (managerially) retail prices for their products? Now review some of the decision models for product-line pricing. How do these models correspond to what you found in your survey?

3 Review Chaps. 2 and 3. Then review the models for one of the decision areas discussed in Chap. 19. What observations can you make about how these models are able to relate to both the sellers and buyers involved in the pricing of products and services?

4 What are some problems that pricing model developers need to overcome to make their models more applicable to decision makers?

SUGGESTED READINGS

Devinney, Timothy M. (ed.): *Issues in Pricing: Theory and Research* (Lexington, Mass.: Lexington Books, 1988).

Monroe, Kent B., and Albert J. Della Bitta: "Models for Pricing Decisions," *Journal of Marketing Research,* 15 (August 1978), 413–428.

Rao, Vithala R.: "Pricing Research in Marketing: The State of the Art," *Journal of Business,* 57 (January 1984, pt. 2), S39–S60.

RECOMMENDATIONS

This last section of the book offers some prescriptions for improving pricing decisions. Chapter 20 begins by outlining four basic rules for developing a positive approach to pricing. These rules summarize the analytical prescriptions contained in Chaps. 2–11. The chapter also discusses the different types of information that can be used when considering the profit implications of pricing alternatives and suggests the appropriate use of each.

The chapter also recommends that pricing be included in a firm's marketing planning in an adaptive manner. An adaptive or flexible approach to pricing is necessary to help both for-profit and not-for-profit organizations adjust to current and future economic pressures. Finally, the chapter provides a set of guidelines for developing and maintaining an effective approach to solving pricing problems.

CHAPTER 20

GUIDELINES FOR BETTER
PRICING DECISIONS

This book has systematically presented the factors to consider when setting price and has shown how pricing alternatives can be developed and analyzed. As was observed in Chap. 1, many contemporary pricing practices are reactions to environmental pressures that have evolved over a number of years. In reaction to these environmental pressures, we have witnessed a near-revolution in pricing practices with implications for capital spending, the inflation rate, the development of global markets, and the application of regulatory and legal policies.

As the reader may have perceived, this book has not emphasized descriptions of current or past pricing practices. Rather, the book has sought to outline and prescribe approaches to the setting of prices that reflect the current and future realities of a modern global economy. Indeed, many businesses have changed their approach to pricing. Perhaps the foremost change has been the elevation of the pricing decision to a more central position in corporate headquarters. Also, business organizations are establishing strategic pricing groups, and service organizations are recognizing the importance of price for their success. Moreover, price has been recognized to be a key influence on investment decisions because of the direct link between price and net cash flow into the organization.

This chapter reviews some of the basic prescriptions for improving the pricing function of an organization and presents a set of guidelines for developing and maintaining an effective organizational approach to solving pricing problems. The chapter first summarizes the analytic framework provided in Chaps. 2–11 then presents some criteria for making pricing decisions. It concludes with a set of guidelines for improving the pricing function of the organization.

FOUR BASIC RULES FOR PRICING

The four rules listed here are intended to capture the essence of the analysis necessary to determine and evaluate pricing alternatives. The order in which the rules are presented does not imply a hierarchy of importance—each rule is equally important.

Know Your Costs

An initial prescription is to determine the basic cost data necessary for the pricing decision. As stated in Chaps. 7–9, it is necessary to know which costs vary directly with changes in levels of activity and the underlying causes of the changes in costs. It is also necessary to identify the costs that are directly related to the product being costed but do not vary with activity levels—direct period or fixed costs. Furthermore, marketing and distribution costs should be objectively traced to the products and not simply lumped into a general overhead category.

Valid cost data provide an objective basis for choosing between pricing alternatives, determining discounts, and establishing differential pricing alternatives. Furthermore, objective cost studies that are completed before the pricing decisions provide the firm with a valid legal justification for its price structure. The costing approach developed in this book provides a mechanism for obtaining objective, valid cost data. It is based on the idea of considering the relevant activities and functions performed by the various operating units, and not on production plus all other costs. As indicated in Chap. 9, this activity accounting approach is recognized today as closer to the realities of modern business enterprise. Finally, as shown in Chap. 10, when it is necessary to develop full-cost data, the firm should avoid arbitrary allocation formulas based on inappropriate allocation bases. Again, well-executed cost studies will usually provide a more valid way of allocating period expenses not directly related to the appropriate activity levels.

As shown in Chap. 11, the experience curve can be a valuable analytical tool for understanding the dynamics of a product's, firm's, or industry's costs. However, the experience curve is limited in its usefulness and requires careful monitoring and estimating of the firm's costs over the various activities and functions performed.

Know Your Demand

This second prescription suggests that the firm understand fully the factors influencing the demand for its products and services. Demand analysis is not as objective or as quantifiable as cost analysis, but it is critical. The emerging discipline of buyer behavior has provided considerable information on consumer behavior and has begun to provide information on industrial buying behavior. From the perspective of this book, the key question is the role of price in the purchaser's decision process. As Chaps. 3–5 indicated, price and price differentials influence buyer perceptions of value. In fact, many companies have achieved positive results from differentially pricing their products and services. A vice president of a large data processing company observed, "We try to find a market position where our product has a unique application."

Coupled with knowing how price influences buyers' perceptions of value, it is necessary to know how buyers use the product or service. Is the product used as an input in the buyer's production process? If so, does the product represent a significant or insignificant portion of the buyer's manufacturing costs? If the product is a major cost element in the buyer's production process, then small changes in the product's price may significantly affect the buyer's costs and the resulting price of the manufactured product. If the final market is sensitive to price increases, then a small price increase to the final manufacturer may significantly reduce demand to the initial seller of the input material. Thus, knowing your buyers means also understanding how they react to price changes and price differentials, as well as knowing the relative role price plays in their purchase decisions. As prescribed in Chap. 1, the successful proactive pricer targets the relevant purchasing decision maker.

Further, as was suggested in Chaps. 14–16, the seller should know the different types of distributors and their function in the distribution channel. This is particularly important when the manufacturer sells both to distributors and to the distributors' customers.

Know Your Competition and Your Market

In addition to the influence of buyers, there are a number of other significant market factors influencing demand. It is important to understand the operations of both domestic and foreign competitors, their rate of capacity utilization, and their products and services. As described in Chap. 11, the current rate of capacity influences product supply. In many markets, the dynamic interaction of supply and demand influences prices. Moreover, changes in capacity availability due to capital investment programs will influence supply and prices.

A second important aspect of knowing the market is the need to determine price–volume relationships. Chapter 6 discussed methods of estimating demand and behavioral influences on demand. Chapters 12 and 17 stressed the importance of knowing price–volume relationships when setting prices or determining competitive bids. Finally, as shown in Chap. 8, when scarcity of resources and/or capacity is present, knowing price–volume relationships facilitates the use of price to allocate these scarce resources over products and to customers.

Know Your Objectives

Many firms stress the profit objective of return on investment. Other firms stress the objective of maintaining specified profit margins. Still other firms seek to achieve market-share goals. As shown in Chap. 10, it is not necessary for each product to maintain the same profit margin in order to achieve a particular return on investment. Similarly, different margins on products may still produce an overall desired corporate profit goal. Finally, firms stressing market share may utilize the experience curve factor developed in Chap. 11 and build profits by reducing prices.

The important point to remember is that differences in corporate profit objectives eventually will lead to differences in prices and the role of price in influencing actual profits. Thus, imitating or following the pricing practices of other companies is not necessarily in the best interests of any firm. Ultimately, regardless of the financial goal, profits or break-even, the pricing objective is behavioral in nature. That is, whether buyers buy more, whether nonbuyers decide to buy, whether buyers decide to purchase less frequently but in greater volume per order, or whether buyers decide to pay earlier is influenced by the prices and price structure of the seller. Further, the degree that distributors and dealers are cooperative and motivated to sell the firm's products depends largely on the financial incentives provided by the suppliers' prices and price structure. Also, the sales force's motivation to help the firm achieve its financial objectives depends on their understanding and acceptance of the pricing strategy being followed. Price has an important role in the development of incentives of distributors, salespeople, and buyers to perform in ways that will be beneficial to the firm. Thus, it is important that the seller develop a positive attitude toward pricing, leading to a proactive pricing approach.

CRITERIA FOR PRICING DECISIONS

Following the preceding four rules should enable a firm to have a balanced approach to pricing. That is, costs, demand, competition, and corporate profit objectives will all have a place in the analysis. Hence, when a firm is operating at normal capacity, and internal and external environmental factors are stable, prices can be determined with a degree of confidence. However, as observed throughout the book, the current and future economic environment has made pricing a more complex and important decision. The price setter therefore must develop a more analytical decision process.

Throughout this text, a contribution approach to pricing has been emphasized. A contribution analysis produces several types of data: profit–volume ratio, contribution dollars, contribution per scarce resource unit, target selling price. In this section, the appropriateness of each of these types of data is evaluated for situations in which a firm is not operating under normal conditions.

When Operating below Normal Capacity

As suggested when discussing whether to submit a bid and at what price, a firm operating at 55 percent capacity needs additional business that can make some contribution to overhead and profits. Hence, maximizing contribution dollars represents the key criterion for pricing new orders or for increasing the demand for existing products. The primary concern of management should be to generate enough contribution dollars to bring its operating level above the break-even point. Thus, the key pricing decision criterion is to maximize contribution per sales dollar generated.

By using either a minimum PV ratio or gross margin, a firm may turn away business because its prices are too high. Adhering to a target selling price may also lead to overpricing the market. When operating below normal capacity, the goal is to generate sufficient product volume to cover all costs and also earn a profit. By stressing the dollars of contribution earned per sales dollar, the firm is in a position to achieve some minimal level of profits.

When Operating at or Near Maximum Capacity

When a firm is operating at capacity, its situation is essentially the same as when resources are scarce. And, as demonstrated in Chap. 8, the appropriate decision criterion is to maximize the contribution per scarce resource unit. Any other criterion may produce lower contributions to profit.

When Operating at Normal Capacity

Under normal operating conditions, a firm should seek primarily to maximize dollar contributions consistent with target return on investments. As shown in Chap. 10, because of the different ways variable and fixed capital are mixed to produce different products, it is not necessary for each product to have equal profit–volume ratios or contribution margins. And since there are no scarce resource constraints in normal circumstances, the CPRU criterion is also inappropriate.

Summary

It is important to realize there is no one right way to determine price. Pricing simply cannot be reduced to a formula—there are too many interacting factors. Successful pricing requires considering all internal and external factors and adapting to changes as they occur. Successful pricing is adaptive pricing.

ADAPTIVE PRICING

Adaptive pricing explicitly recognizes the role of costs, corporate goals, and competition, as well as the effect of price and the total interaction of the marketing mix variables on demand when making pricing decisions. Moreover, adaptive pricing provides for a formal mechanism to adapt to environmental changes.

Adaptive pricing provides for the formal use of (1) plans and standards of controls, (2) review and analysis of deviations between planned and actual results, and (3) an information feedback system providing for revision of plans, standards, and policies. The decision to commit resources involves analyzing a variety of variables that interact with price: (1) product characteristics, (2) price–product quality relationships, (3) the distribution organization for marketing the products, (4) advertising and other communicative efforts, (5) the quality and nature of services to offer with the products.

Changes in demand, legal and regulatory changes, and changes in competitor strategies and products influence the firm to develop adaptive policies with respect to product, quality, price, personal selling, advertising, and service. These decisions influence the quantity and type of fixed investments and the level and behavior of other costs. The decision process involving these variables must consider several alternative dimensions for each variable. To limit the costs of generating, processing, and transmitting information, goals and tasks are determined for each of several levels in the firm. That is, operating divisions are given targets, and if these targets are reached, the overall position of the firm is enhanced. For example, a product manager may be given a market share target determined by considering the market potential and the managerial judgment of the share of the market the product may be expected to capture. Given the market potential and the target market share, the expected sales volume can be determined, leading to a determination of the necessary capacity and therefore necessary investment.

The major features of adaptive pricing are

1 Demand and the responsiveness of demand to the marketing mix variables are explicitly considered.

2 The constraining influences of competitive products and services and legal and regulatory forces are recognized.

3 The necessity to develop a mechanism for adapting to changing market and environmental forces is considered.

Hence, a pricing goal per se exists only in the context of an adaptive marketing plan. The adaptive marketing plan should determine investments and cost behavior rather than existing investments and cost behavior determining pricing and marketing decisions.

PROVIDING A BASIS FOR PRICING DECISIONS

The discussion in Chap. 1 detailed reasons why many firms' current pricing strategies are inappropriate. Firms can perform a number of activities to develop strategies that may be more consistent with the actual decision environment.

Determine Consistent Objectives

As suggested, objectives such as improving margins, avoiding bottlenecks, and improving cash flows may not be mutually consistent. As shown in Chap. 8, focusing on high-margin products may increase bottlenecks because of the resources required and may lead to cash flow reductions because of the sales decline of low-margin, high-volume products. A clear and consistent statement of pricing objectives is necessary as a basis for appropriate pricing strategies.

In addition, the impact of short-run objectives on long-run profits must be recognized. When identifying "weak" products, managers should consider potential sales growth and the annual cash flow generated per dollar of assets invested in the product. Further, if shortages are expected to persist in the long run, the appropriate objective would be to maximize contributions per critical resource unit.

Establish a Pricing Research Program

The effects of price changes and price differences on buyer behavior is the least understood and the least studied area of marketing research. As shown in Chap. 3, the lack of appropriate information in this area has led to many inappropriate pricing strategies. Further, to understand the profit implications of these price effects, a pricing research program should also be able to provide information on the cost effects of price changes. (See Chap. 6.)

Demand Effects of Price Changes   The objective of this research is to determine the sensitivity of the market to price changes and price differences. Clearly, the seller should know the sensitivity of buyers to price changes, but the seller should also know the sensitivity of buyers' customers to price changes. The seller should be concerned about how buyers use price in their purchasing decisions, whether they assume quality on the basis of price, and whether perceived end prices affect the evaluation of the product line. Further, considerations of cross-elasticity of demand for the product line, including the behavioral perception of complementarity, should be investigated. (See Chaps. 2–6.)

Cost Effects of Price Changes   Whereas the effect of price changes on demand concerns market or external reactions, the cost effects of price changes are internal considerations. As discussed in Chap. 8, a multiple-product firm has cost and demand interdependencies. Dropping low-margin products or curtailing volume by increasing prices can have unanticipated results. First, eliminating a product shifts its common cost burden to other products. Second, severe reductions in output demand may remove the firm's eligibility for quantity discounts when purchasing production inputs. Therefore, it is important that the firm properly classify costs into those costs that are tangibly traceable to and generated by a given product and those costs that are common. Furthermore, since for pricing purposes only future costs are relevant, the firm must develop adequate bases for forecasting future costs. (See Chaps. 6 and 11.)

GUIDELINES FOR BETTER PRICING DECISIONS

The purpose of this book has been to develop a consistent, analytical approach to pricing. The emphasis has been on developing positive attitudes toward the pricing decision and to demonstrate that price is a critical decision variable in the marketing mix. Further, it has been shown how appropriate pricing strategies can be developed with the help of adequate information and analysis. The following guidelines are offered for those organizations interested in improving their pricing decisions.

Set Consistent Objectives

1 Make sure that operating objectives are clearly stated, operational, and mutually consistent.

2 When there are several objectives, develop priorities, or otherwise clarify the relationships between the objectives.

3 Make sure that everyone concerned with a pricing decision, at any level in the firm, understands the relevant objectives.

4 Translate the operating and financial objectives into buyer and market behavioral objectives.

Identify Alternatives

1 Identify enough alternatives to permit a sensible choice between courses of action.

2 Avoid traditional thinking; encourage creativity.

3 Consider all feasible alternatives regardless of past success or failure.

Acquire Relevant Information

1 Be sure that information about buyers, distributors, and competitors is current and reflects their current and future situations.

2 Make sure information applies to the future and is not just a report of the past.

3 Involve market research people in the pricing problem.

4 Make sure cost information identifies which costs will be affected by a particular pricing alternative.

5 Communicate with and involve accounting staff with the cost aspects of a pricing decision.

6 Analyze the effect a particular alternative will have on scarce resources, inventories, production, cash flows, market share, volume, and profits.

Make the Pricing Decision

1 Make full use of the information available.

2 Correctly relate all the relevant variables in the problem.

3 Check whether the pricing decision is sensitive to the assumptions made about those elements important to the decision.

4 Consider all human and organizational problems that could occur with a given pricing decision.

5 Consider the long-run effects of the pricing decision.

6 Base the pricing decision on the life cycle of each product.

7 Consider the effect of experience in reducing costs as the cumulative production and sales volume increase.

Encourage Feedback and Maintain Control

1 Develop procedures to ensure that pricing decisions fit into the firm's overall marketing strategy.

2 Provide for a feedback mechanism to ensure that all who should know the results of individual price decisions are fully informed.

To summarize, pricing decisions should be logically made and should involve rigorous thinking, with minimal difficulty from human and organizational factors. Further, it should be recognized that judgment and prediction are needed about the future, not the past. Finally, pricing decisions should be made within a dynamic, long-run marketing strategy.

DISCUSSION QUESTIONS

1 Assume that you are the price administrator for a corporation and you wish to implement the four basic rules for pricing given in this chapter. What steps would you take to put these rules into action?
2 Comment on the applicability of the following types of data for pricing purposes:
   a Profit–volume ratio.
   b Contribution dollars.
   c Contribution per scarce resource unit.
   d Target selling price.
3 What is "adaptive pricing"?
4 Review the "Guidelines for Better Pricing Decisions" given in this chapter. Explain the rationale for each guideline.

PRICE DEFINITIONS

Acceptable price range   Those prices that buyers are willing to pay for a good or service. See Price thresholds.

Acquisition value   The buyers' perceptions of the relative worth of a product or service to them. It is formally defined as the subjectively weighted difference between the most a buyer would be willing to pay for the item less the actual price of the item.

Adaptation-level price   The price a buyer uses as the basis of a comparison with a product or service's actual price. See Reference price.

Amortization   An accounting charge that is a write-down of limited-term or intangible assets, such as goodwill.

Anchor   Reference price or product in consumers' comparisons.

Anchoring effect   When buyers make comparisons of prices or products against a reference price or product, the result typically is weighted toward the anchor (q.v.), creating an anchor bias, or anchoring effect.

Assimilation–contrast effects   When comparing prices against a reference price, buyers first judge whether the price being evaluated belongs in the same category as the reference price. If the price is judged to be in the same price category as the reference price, then the buyer judges that it is similar (assimilation effect). If the buyer judges that the price belongs to another price category, then the buyer evaluates it as different (contrast effect).

Auction   A form of selling in which buyers bid the price they are willing to pay to acquire a product or service. Normally, given the rules for bidding at a particular auction, the buyer who bids the highest price is given the opportunity to buy the item.

Average fixed cost   Total fixed cost divided by the number of units produced and sold.

Average revenue   Total revenue divided by the number of units sold.

Average total cost   Total cost divided by the number of units produced and sold.

Average variable cost   Total variable cost divided by the number of units produced and sold.

Barter   The practice of exchanging goods and services for other goods and services rather than money.

Basing-point pricing   A variation of delivered pricing (q.v.). The basing point is a city where the product is produced and from which transportation charges are determined. But in basing-point pricing the product actually may be shipped from a city other than the basing point.

Bottlenecks   Constraints that slow up or halt production and/or distribution of a product. The scarcity of a resource, e.g., equipment, skilled labor, or raw material, can effectively slow down the process.

Break-even analysis   A method of examining the relationships among fixed costs, variable costs, volume, and price. The objective of the analysis is to determine the break-even point (q.v.) at alternative prices and a given cost structure.

Break-even point   The sales volume at which total revenues are equal to total costs.

Buyers' costs   The costs that buyers incur when acquiring and using products and services. Such costs include the price of the item being acquired, cost of information search, shipping costs, transportation and installation costs, and postpurchase costs that may affect buyers' perceptions of the value of the item being acquired.

Cash discount   A reward for the payment of an invoice or account within a specified amount of time.

Cash on delivery   Commonly referred to as C.O.D. The practice of collecting for the price of the merchandise plus the relevant transportation charges at the time of delivery.

Clayton Antitrust Act (1914)   Specifically outlawed discrimination in prices, exclusive and tying contracts, intercorporate stockholdings, and interlocking directorates "where the effect . . . may be to substantially lessen competition or tend to create a monopoly."

Common costs   Costs that cannot be traced to a product or segment (similar to overhead costs). Also called general costs.

Competitive bidding   Firms submit offers (or bids) that detail the services and product specifications to be delivered at a stated price.

Competitors' costs   Those costs that a firm incurs when producing, marketing, and distributing a product that competes with another firm's product or service. Understanding competitors' costs is essential when developing competitive prices.

Conjoint analysis   A research method used to determine prospective buyers' relative preferences for different product attribute combinations including price.

Consumers' surplus   The difference between the maximum price that consumers are willing to pay and the amount they actually pay. At a price where the amount of utility equals market price, consumers who would pay only the market price and thus receive a surplus.

Contingency contract   Agreement to deliver goods or services at a price to be determined either by the actual costs incurred while performing the service or producing the product or by the measured value realized after the service has been performed or the product has been used.

Contingency pricing   The setting of a price based either on actual costs incurred after the service has been performed or the product produced or on the measured value the buyer realizes because of the service or product.

Contrast effect   See Assimilation–contrast effects.

Contribution   The amount of revenue remaining from the sale of a product or service after the direct and indirect costs related to that product or service have been subtracted.

Contribution per resource unit   The amount of revenue left from the sale of a product or service after the direct and indirect costs related to that product or service have been subtracted, divided by the number of resource units used to produce the product or service. Normally, the resource used to make the calculation is that resource that constrains the production and/or sale of the product or service.

Contribution pricing   A method of determining the price of a product or service through a relation between the direct or indirect traceable costs and the relevant costs of production and sale of the product or service.

Cost   Money expended to produce a product or service. See specific cost category definitions.

Cost-plus pricing   A method of determining the price of a product or service that uses direct, indirect, and fixed costs whether related to the production and sale of the product or service or not. These costs are converted to per unit costs for the product, and a predetermined percentage of these costs is then added to provide a profit margin. The resulting price is cost per unit plus the percentage markup.

Counter purchase   A form of countertrade in which the selling firm agrees to purchase, at a later time, goods from the buyer equal to the amount of the original sale.

Countertrade   The practice of requiring some of the payment for products or services to be in other products or services rather than money.

Coupon   A document that entitles the holder to a reduced price or to a stated amount off the actual purchase price of a product or service.

Credit   The transfer of a product or service in return for the promise of payment at a later time.

Cumulative quantity discount   A reduction in the price to be paid for purchases that exceed a given level of volume over a specified period of time. Also called a deferred discount or a patronage discount.

Customary pricing   The practice of establishing a price for a product or service and not changing it over a relatively long time. Prices are changed by varying the quantity or quality of the product rather than the monetary value.

Delivered pricing   The practice of quoting a price that includes both the list price and the transportation costs from a basing point to the buyer. In such cases, the prices are quoted as f.o.b. destination, meaning the manufacturer bears the responsibility of selecting and paying for the method of transporting the product.

Demand-oriented pricing   A method of pricing in which the seller attempts to set the price at the level that the intended buyers are willing to pay. Also called value-oriented or value-in-use (q.v.) pricing.

Depletion   An accounting charge that considers the use of a natural resource, such as gas, coal, or minerals, as a reduction in assets; used to reduce the income tax liability of the owner.

Depreciation   An accounting charge that writes down the cost of an asset, such as a factory or a machine tool, over its useful life. This charge is made for shareholder and tax reporting, but it does not require cash outlays.

Direct costs   Fixed or variable costs incurred by and solely for a particular product, department, program, sales territory, or customer account. Also called traceable or attributable costs.

Direct fixed costs   Costs that are incurred by and solely for a particular product or segment but which do not vary with an activity level.

Direct variable costs   Costs that vary directly with an activity level.

Discount   A reduction in price.

Dual-function discount system   Reduction in price granted distributors or dealers who perform different marketing functions for the manufacturer. For example, one channel of distribution may consist of wholesalers and retailers, while another channel used by the same manufacturer may consist only of retailers. In the latter channel, some of the functions performed by the retailers may be of a wholesaling nature, hence these retailers are performing a "dual function" for the manufacturer.

Economies of scale   The savings derived from producing a large number of units; e.g., in a situation where all inputs are doubled, output may be more than doubled.

Elasticity   The degree of change in one economic variable in response to a change in another economic variable.

End prices   The prices of the lowest and the highest priced products in a product line.

Even price   See Odd–even pricing.

Exchange   The act of relinquishing something for something else of equal value.

Experience curve   The reduction in costs per unit that occurs when production, marketing, and distribution increase cumulatively. Typically, these cost reductions occur because of learning effects, economies of scale, and improvements in technology.

Experience curve pricing   A method of pricing where the seller sets a price sufficiently low to encourage a large sales volume in anticipation that the large sales volume would lead to a reduction in average unit costs. Generally this method of pricing is used over time by periodically reducing price to induce additional sales volumes that lead to lower per unit costs.

Experimental demand curve   A price–volume relationship estimated by simulating actual market conditions in an experiment or other form of pricing research.

Federal Trade Commission Act (1914)   Placed a blanket prohibition against "unfair methods of competition" and created the FTC to enforce it.

Financial leverage   The use of debt to finance the operations of an organization. More formally, the degree to which operating profits before interest and taxes change relative to a change in operating profits before taxes.

Fixed capital   An investment by a firm of which only a portion will be recovered in the sale of a unit of the product.

F.O.B. origin pricing: A method of pricing where the seller quotes prices from the point of shipment. See Free on board.

F.O.B. with freight allowed   A form of delivered pricing where the buyer arranges and pays for the transportation but deducts these transportation costs from the invoice total and remits the net amount. See Free on board.

Free on board (f.o.b.)   Quoted price without delivery, i.e., it is the buyer's responsibility to select the mode of transporting the goods, choose the specific carrier, handle all claims, and pay all shipping charges.

Functional discount   See Trade discount.

Income effect   The increase or decrease in a consumer's real income as a result of the change in the price of a good or service.

Indirect traceable costs   Costs that are not incurred solely due to a particular activity but through reasonably objective means can be traced, in part, to the activity for which they are incurred.

Learning curve   See Experience curve.

Leverage   The degree to which a change in sales volume leads to a subsequent change in operating profits and financial performance of a company.

List price   The selling price for an item before any discounts or reductions in price.

Loss leader pricing   The featuring of items priced below cost or at relatively low prices to attract customers to the seller's place of business.

Margin   The difference between the selling price and total unit costs for an item.

Marginal cost   The net change in total cost that results from producing and marketing one additional unit.

Marginal income ratio   See Profit–volume ratio.

Marginal revenue   The net change in total revenue that results from producing and marketing one additional unit.

Markdown   The amount of a reduction from the selling price.

Marketing cost analysis   The attempt to determine the actual costs incurred for marketing
and distributing a product.

Markup   The amount of an increase in price over total unit costs.

Maximum acceptable price   The highest price a buyer is willing to pay for a product or
service. Also called reservation price.

Mixed bundling   The practice of offering for sale two or more products or services either at
individual prices or for one single price. The single price for the "bundle" is usually less
than the sum of the individual prices. See Price bundling.

Multiple basing-point pricing system   A method of pricing in which several locations are
designated as basing points and the price is determined by the point that yields the lowest
delivered cost to the buyer. See Basing-point pricing.

Multiple-unit pricing   The practice of pricing several items as a single unit. See Price bundling.

Multiple-zone pricing system   A pricing system in which prices are uniform within two or
more delivery zones. See Single-zone pricing.

Noncumulative quantity discount   A discount granted for volume purchase (measured either
in units or dollars) in a single point of time.

Odd–even pricing   A form of psychological pricing that suggests buyers are more sensitive
to certain final digits. In odd pricing, the price ends in an odd number (e.g., 1, 3, 5, 7, 9)
or just under a round number (e.g., 99, 98). In even pricing the price ends in a whole
number or in tenths (e.g., $5.00, 5.10, 5.90).

Odd price   See Odd–even pricing.

Operating leverage   The degree to which operating profits change in response to a change
in sales volume.

Opportunity costs   The amount of revenues forgone by not pursuing the next best alternative.

Overhead costs   See Common costs.

Overhead distribution   The practice of allocating (or spreading) overhead costs to the various business activities the overhead costs support.

Parallel pricing   Following the pricing practices of other organizations, particularly competitors.

Patronage discount   The offering of a price reduction based on previous customer relationship or preferred customer standing. Such a discount is usually offered because of an
established relationship between the seller and buyer.

Penetration pricing   The strategy of setting a product's price relatively low in order to
generate a high sales volume. This strategy is commonly associated with pricing new
products that do not have identifiable price market segments.

Perceived quality   The amount of quality buyers believe a product or service has. Perceived
quality is usually based on some information or cues about the product, e.g., its price or
brand name.

Perceived-value pricing   A method of pricing where the seller attempts to set price at the
level that the intended buyers value the product. Also called value-oriented or value-in-use
(q.v.) pricing. See Demand-oriented pricing.

Phantom freight   In basing-point pricing, when the seller quotes a delivered price that
includes a freight charge greater than the actual transportation costs.

Predatory pricing   The practice of selectively pricing a product below that of competition to eliminate competition while pricing the product higher in markets where competition does not exist or is relatively weaker.

Preemptive pricing   The practice of setting low prices to discourage competition from entering the market.

Price   The formal ratio that indicates the quantity of money or goods or services needed to acquire a given quantity of goods or services.

Price awareness   The degree to which buyers are knowledgeable of the prices of alternative products and services that they are interested in buying.

Price bundling   The practice of offering two or more products or services for sale at one price.

Price consciousness   The degree to which buyers are sensitive to differences in price between alternative choices. Generally, a price-conscious person seeks to minimize the price paid for an item.

Price cutting   The practice of reducing the prices of established products or services.

Price discounting   See Price cutting.

Price discrimination   The practice of charging different buyers different prices for the same quantity and quality of products or services.

Price elasticity of demand   A measure of the sensitivity of demand to changes in price. Formally, the percentage change in quantity demanded relative to a given percentage change in price.

Price fixing   The illegal practice of two or more sellers agreeing on the price to charge for similar products or services.

Price leader   In competitive situations, the seller who normally initiates price changes in the market. In some instances, the leader announces the price change after other competitors have made price changes. In this situation, the other competitors then adjust their prices to match those of the price leader.

Price lining   The offering of merchandise at a number of specific predetermined prices. Once set, the prices may be held constant over a period of time, and changes in market conditions are counteracted by changing the quality of the merchandise.

Price promotion   The advertising of a price for a product or service. Usually, the price being promoted is a reduction from a previously established price and may take the form of a lower price, a coupon to be redeemed, or a rebate to be received.

Price–quality relationship   The degree to which product or service quality covaries with price.

Price sensitivity meter   A research method for establishing the range of prices that buyers are willing to pay for a product or service.

Price structure   Some combination of the time and conditions of payment, the nature of discounts to be allowed the buyer, and where and when title is to be taken by the buyer.

Price thresholds   The lowest and highest prices that buyers are willing to pay for a particular good or service.

Proactive pricing   The managerial practice of deliberately analyzing the factors that influence prices before setting a price. Normally, a proactive pricer establishes specific objectives to be accomplished by the prices and then proceeds in the development of specific prices.

Product life cycle   The stages that a product is thought to go through from birth to death: introduction, growth, maturity, saturation, and decline.

Product line   A group of products sold by an organization to one general market. The products have some characteristics, customers, and/or uses in common and may also share technologies, distribution channels, prices, and services.

Product-line pricing   The setting of prices for all items in a product line.

Profit–volume (PV) ratio   The dollar contribution per unit divided by the per unit price. The profit–volume ratio indicates the rate at which fixed costs are recovered and, after the break-even point has been reached, the rate at which profits are earned as sales volume increases.

Promotional discounts   A reduction in price given to wholesalers and retailers in return for providing some promotion for the product.

Quantity discount   A reduction in price for volume purchases. See Cumulative quantity discount and Noncumulative quantity discount.

Rate-of-return pricing   A method of setting prices by adding a markup which will produce a predetermined return on investment.

Rebate   A return of a portion of the purchase price in the form of cash by the seller to the buyer.

Reference price   The price that buyers use to compare the offered price of a product or service. The reference price may be a price in a buyer's memory or the price of an alternative product.

Refund   A return of the amount paid for an item.

Reservation price   The highest price a buyer is willing to pay for a product or service. See Price thresholds.

Robinson–Patman Act (1936)   An amendment to the Clayton Act which prohibits price discrimination where the effect "may be substantially to lessen competition or create a monopoly"; prohibits payments of broker's commission where an independent broker is not employed; forbids sellers to provide allowances or services to buyers unless these are available to all buyers on "equally proportional terms"; and prohibits a buyer from inducing or receiving a prohibited discrimination in price.

Seller's costs   The costs that the seller incurs to provide the product or service to the buyer.

Seller's pricing discretion   The difference between the direct variable costs of producing, marketing, and distributing the product and the highest price that buyers are willing to pay for the product.

Semivariable costs   The costs that are incurred in a lump amount before any business activity can begin; they vary with volume once the activity is under way.

Sherman Anti-Trust Act (1890)   Prohibits contracts, combinations, and conspiracies which restrain interstate or foreign trade as well as monopolization, attempts to monopolize, and conspiracies to monopolize.

Single-zone pricing   Setting one price for all buyers regardless of their distance from the seller.

Target-return pricing   A pricing method that develops the markup over costs based on a percentage of the amount of money the company has invested in the operations. The target dollar return is divided by the expected sales volume to determine the per unit markup over unit costs.

Total revenue   Price per unit multiplied by sales volume and summed over all products and services.

Trade discount   The discount allowed to a class of customers (manufacturers, wholesalers, retailers) on a list price before consideration of credit terms; applies to any allowance granted without reference to the date of payment. Also called functional discount.

Transaction value   The subjectively weighted difference between the buyer's reference price and the actual price to be paid.

Transfer pricing   The pricing of goods and services which are sold to controlled entities of the same organization, e.g., movements of goods and services within a multinational or global corporation.

Value analysis   An analytical procedure to study the costs versus the benefits of a currently purchased material, component, or design in order to enhance the benefit–cost ratio as much as possible. Also called value engineering or, when performed by a seller, value-in-use (q.v.) analysis.

Value-in-exchange   The amount of money or goods actually paid for a product or service.

Value-in-use   The amount of money or goods that buyers would be willing to pay for a product or service. Value-in-use is always greater than value-in-exchange.

Value-oriented pricing   See Demand-oriented pricing.

Yield management   The practice of pricing to maximize the amount of revenue received per unit sold. Commonly associated with the pricing practices of airlines, hotels, and other sellers of "perishable" products.

NAME INDEX

SUBJECT INDEX